Verus Israel

THE LITTMAN LIBRARY OF
JEWISH CIVILIZATION

FOUNDER
L. T. S. Littman

EDITORS
David Goldstein
Louis Jacobs
Vivian D. Lipman

For the love of God
and in memory of
JOSEPH AARON LITTMAN

"Get wisdom, get understanding:
Forsake her not and she shall preserve thee".

Verus Israel

A study of the relations between Christians and Jews
in the Roman Empire (135–425)

Marcel Simon

Translated from the French

H. McKeating

Published for
THE LITTMAN LIBRARY
by
OXFORD UNIVERSITY PRESS
1986

Oxford University Press, Walton Street, Oxford OX2 6DP
London New York Toronto
Delhi Bombay Calcutta Madras Karachi
Kuala Lumpur Singapore Hong Kong Tokyo
Nairobi Dar es Salaam Cape Town
Melbourne Auckland
and associated companies in
Beirut Berlin Ibadan Mexico City Nicosia

Oxford is a trade mark of Oxford University Press

Published in the United States
by Oxford University Press, New York

Originally published in French by Editions E. de Boccard, Paris, 1964
English translation © Littman Library, 1986

British Library Cataloguing in Publication Data

Simon, Marcel
Verus Israel: a study of the ralations between
Christians and Jews in the Roman Empire (135-425).
—(The Littman Library of Jewish civilization)
1. Christianity and other religions—Judaism—History. 2. Judaism—
Relations—Christianity—History. 3. Rome—History—Empire, 30 B.C.–476 A.D.
I. Title. II. Series.
261.2'6'0937 BM535
ISBN 0-19-710035-X

Library of Congress Cataloging in Publication Data

Simon, Marcel, 1907–
Verus Israel.
(The Littman library of Jewish civilization)
Translation of: Verus Israel.
Bibliography: p. 419–32.
Includes index.
1. Christianity and other religions—Judaism. 2. Judaism—Relations—Christianity.
3. Church history—Primitive and early church, ca. 30-600. 4. Judaism—History—
Talmudic period,
10–425. I. Title. II. Series.
BM535.S51813 1985   261.2'6'09015   84-20681
ISBN 0-19-710035-X

Typeset by Burgess & Son (Abingdon) Ltd.
Printed in Great Britain
at the Alden Press, Oxford

Contents

Introduction   ix

Part 1: The Religious and Political Setting

1. The Aftermath: Palestinian Judaism   3
2. The Aftermath: The Diaspora   33
3. The Church and Israel   65
4. Rome, Judaism, and Christianity   98

Part 2: The Conflict of Orthodoxies

5. Anti-Jewish Polemic, its Characteristics and Methods   135
6. Anti-Jewish Polemic—The Arguments Employed   156
7. The Christians in the Talmud   179
8. Christian Anti-Semitism   202

Part 3: Contact and Assimilation

9. The Fate of Jewish Christianity   237
10. Jewish Proselytism   271
11. The Judaizers within the Church   306
12. Superstition and Magic   339
Conclusion   369
Postscript   385
Bibliography   419
Supplementary Bibliography   431
Notes   433
Translations from Greek, Latin, and German   508
Index   527

Editor's Note

This work, crucial for the study of the relationship between Church and Synagogue, was first published in Paris in 1948, and reprinted there with the author's *Post-Scriptum* in 1964, and again in 1983.

Despite the extensive academic progress in this field in the past twenty years we have thought it worthwhile to make *Verus Israel* available to the non-French reading public, without major alteration or revision. The author has concurred with this view.

We have added a translation by Hyam Maccoby of the Greek, Latin, and German citations in the text. We have also incorporated into the Bibliography titles of English translations of works cited.

D. G.

Introduction

Since the beginning of this century, and more particularly during the last twenty years, our knowledge of Judaism in the Roman period has very much increased./ Work done on the subject of Hellenistic Judaism, as well as on Talmudic and Midrashic literature, has produced a large variety of books, including the comprehensive works of Schürer, Bousset and Gressman, G. F. Moore and Father Bonsirven.[1] We have here a field in which recent generations of scholars have worked widely and well.

These ample labors have been enriched and stimulated by archaeological discoveries that have sometimes been sensational (e.g., the synagogues with images that were discovered in Palestine and elsewhere, especially the one at Dura), but they have been concerned exclusively either with Judaism, or with Judaism and its relations with the pagan world, i.e., with pagan culture and religion. The question of the relations between Judaism and Christianity, on the other hand, has been dealt with only rarely, and even then in piecemeal fashion. When it is raised at all, it is approached from rather narrow points of view. Ziegler confines himself to the first three centuries, Lucas, to the fourth, both of them in works of very modest dimensions; and both are far from exhausting the subject. The classic work of Hoennicke combines a history of Jewish Christianity (in the wider sense) and an account of what the Synagogue bequeathed to the Church. That of Parkes seeks in the conflict between the early Church and the Synagogue the origins of anti-Semitism. Though the book often gives us more than its title promises us, it deals perhaps more with social and even political history than with religious history in the strict sense. Finally, other works present themselves as no more than tools for the job; such are the collections by Strack and by Travers Herford of rabbinic texts, and the catalogue by Lukyn Williams of Christian anti-Jewish literature.

In sum, though the subject has been frequently touched upon, there is not, to my knowledge, any book that tackles it squarely and deals with it comprehensively. The large Church histories, when they do not ignore the subject altogether, confine discussion of it to a few pages, or even a few lines.[2] It is beyond dispute that there has been a gap here in the history of the two religions. I do not pretend to have

filled it completely. The attempt I have made has at least the merit of
novelty. May that excuse its imperfections.

This determined indifference that historians display to our question
proceeds from an unacknowledged assumption. Faced, on the one
hand, with the almost complete repulse of the Christian proclamation
in Israel and, on the other, with Judaism's ultimate answer, enshrined
in the Talmud, numerous worthy scholars have accepted that the two
religions, developing on radically divergent lines, very quickly ceased
to take any interest in each other.[3] They have, in consequence, refused
either tacitly or explicitly to admit that the problem really exists. For
in their view the Church directed her attention exclusively to the
gentiles, whilst Judaism became indifferent to everything outside
herself, so that there was not the least occasion for contact between the
two.

This completely negative view of the relations between Jews and
Christians appears, for example, in Harnack. At the same time as he
notes our almost total ignorance of the fortunes of Hellenistic Judaism
after the destruction of the temple, he takes this event as the turning
point: the diaspora itself would "from this moment at the latest" have
relaxed its ties with Greek culture, soon to break them altogether. As
for Palestinian Judaism, it would already before A.D. 70, in condemning Greek culture, have repudiated the universalistic idea.[4] Harnack
can in consequence affirm elsewhere that by the end of the first
century there was virtually no more contact between the gentile
Church and the Synagogue.[5] This is also the view of the majority of
critics and historians of his generation. For Duchesne the problem is
raised only in connection with Jewish Christianity, and even in this
restricted form it ceases to be a live issue, if not immediately on the
destruction of the temple, at least long before the triumph of the
Church.[6]

Jewish opinions are perhaps a little more varied. There is occasional
recognition, and sometimes even detailed discussion, of relations
between the two religions.[7] Nevertheless, with somewhat rare exceptions[8] it is reckoned that the missionary idea did not survive the crises
of the first and second centuries. Scholars who are Jews, either by
birth or religious conviction, tend all too often to read back into
history a state of mind that in fact developed only after the
universalistic experiment tried out by Alexandrian Judaism had been
abandoned. This state of mind still characterizes the present-day
Synagogue. For the present-day Synagogue, in both its orthodox and
liberal forms, is preoccupied with self-preservation. For Jewish
scholars too there is no real problem.

Against this dogma of the historians several voices have nonetheless been raised. Objections have mostly been expressed in the course of studies of special topics. E. Schwartz, in his work on Jewish calendars, formulates the hypothesis, though he does not develop it, that a Jewish proselytizing movement that was both strong and many-sided survived in the face of the victorious Church.[9] Bousset makes a study of the originally Jewish liturgy that appears in book 7 of the Apostolic Constitutions, and in his conclusions he insists strongly on the necessity for a more searching inquiry into the relations between early Christianity and the Jewish diaspora. Here, he thinks, the Hellenistic and universalistic spirit maintained itself much longer than is generally admitted.[10] Lastly there is Juster. His erudition is so extraordinary that there is no interesting question concerning ancient Judaism with which he is not conversant. And he has touched incidentally and on numerous occasions on that of Jewish-Christian relations. He has distributed through the notes to his book a multitude of observations, with references to facts and texts. These are often rather loosely connected with his subject. Better coordinated, they would give us a valuable basis for an answer to the question. His work remains fundamental to my own.

More recent researches and discoveries have revealed in the Judaism of the early centuries A.D. a hitherto unsuspected vitality. They have shown, in particular, that Talmudic Judaism was not imposed at a single stroke, to be henceforth the only standard of religious life and thought.[11] And they suggest, furthermore, that Talmudic Judaism was itself more flexible in some respects than was formerly believed. They have established, or at least suggested, that the effects of the destruction of Jerusalem on the development of Judaism were neither immediate nor violent, and that in particular the break with Greco-Latin culture came about progressively, and later than we have hitherto acknowledged. It seems, and Bousset has forcefully underlined this,[12] that if a Jewish document displays Hellenistic influences or reflects an interest in proselytizing, one can no longer refuse, in the absence of other indications of date, to allow it to be later than the destruction of the temple or the founding of Aelia Capitolina. This criterion is far from infallible. To apply it is to beg the question.

If the results already arrived at do not immediately shake traditional ideas concerning Jewish-Christian relations, they at least invite us to reconsider them. These traditional ideas demand revision, and manifestly require correction if they are to be brought into line with the evidence. For if Judaism did continue for some time to play a part, or to attempt to play a part, in the ancient world, Christianity must necessarily have come into collision with it. The problem therefore does exist, and the inquiry may be undertaken without fear that we are wasting our time. It remains only to define its method and its scope.

In studying the ties of relationship and dependence that connect Catholic Christianity with Judaism, it is not my intention to establish what the former owes to the latter. The Jewish contribution to the constitution of the Church, in the sphere of beliefs and organization as well as in that of liturgy and rites, has been explored many times.[13] Neither is it a question of retracing the history of the separation of the Church from Judaism, from the time of the ministry of Jesus to the establishment of the Church as a fully independent body. This is a very delicate chapter in the study of Christian origins. The texts that shed light on it are neither very numerous nor very reliable. At least this much can be said: the split came into being gradually, and at different rates in different places. Begun by St. Paul, it was effective from the start in communities that looked to him. Among Jewish Christians, on the other hand, it never was completely carried through. Between these two extremes there is room for many gradations. We catch a glimpse of much uncertainty in the early Church, of tensions that occasionally erupt into open conflict; tensions not only between Hellenistic and Jewish Christians, but, in spite of the compromise worked out at Jerusalem, between Judaizers and anti-legalists. The whole of the apostolic period is still dominated by this problem, colors all the New Testament writings. It is as well to state this at the point at which the aim and scope of this work are being defined.

I have made it my aim to examine the relationship entertained by the two religions, Christian and Jewish, which existed side by side in the Roman empire[14] as two distinct structures. I intend to trace this relationship from the moment when the Church became fully conscious of its own autonomy and universal mission, to the day when Judaism, no longer able to keep up the struggle, retreated into itself and showed no further interest in the gentiles. In other words, it is my object to do for the relations between Judaism and Christianity what others have done for the conflict between Christianity and paganism.

With regard to each of these subjects two closely connected questions arise. What attitude did the two rival cults adopt toward each other? And in what manner did the defeated party (paganism in the one case, Judaism in the other) withdraw, and how was it finally eliminated? It will be of interest to analyze, in contrast with the "pagan reaction" studied by de Labriolle, the reciprocal reactions of the Church and the Synagogue, and, cutting across these, the causes of the disengagement and transformation of Judaism.

For if the defeat of paganism led ultimately to its total elimination, Judaism, for its part, survived, though with a changed character. Judaism of the Alexandrian type, with its Hellenistic and universalistic leanings, disappears, and it is round the Talmud that the regrouping of the spiritual forces of Israel takes place. The question is, does this development spring, as is generally supposed, from internal causes, causes native to Judaism? More specifically, are the disasters in Palestine sufficient by themselves to account for it, and is it just by accident that the mission and victory of the Church happened at the same time? Or is it necessary, in order to explain this transformation of Judaism, to see the influence of Christianity operating as either a primary or a secondary cause?[15]

Furthermore, when paganism and Christianity confronted each other they did so, in spite of undeniable mutual influences and contamination, as two fundamentally incompatible bodies. Christianity and Judaism remained united, even in the midst of their mutual hostility, by the ties that a common origin had created. Christianity appeared at first to the pagans to be no more than a variety, a special shade of opinion within the *judaica superstitio*. And it was, indeed, soaked in Jewishness; its doctrines were impregnated with Jewish ideas and its practices with Jewish rites. The nature of its founder, and of its first members, being what it was, things could hardly have been otherwise. Moreover, the Church claimed as its own property and interpreted by means of its own theology (in the light of a symbolism that was itself of Jewish origin) the sacred book of Israel. It even refused the Jews, for having misunderstood their own Bible, all title to it henceforth. Having seceded from Judaism with the object of supplanting it made the Church no readier to renounce its origins. It boldly proclaimed itself to be the New Israel.

The nature of this situation, in which brothers were ranged in enmity against each other in battle over an inheritance, was bound to impart a very peculiar color to the relations between the two cults. It explains the sharpness of the conflict, the violence of the hatred. On the other hand, because Christianity, rooted in the Old Testament, was never completely stripped of its native Jewishness, some connections were established and preserved between particular elements among the Christians and particular elements among the Jews. The conflict between Church and Synagogue, however acute, represented only one aspect of Jewish-Christian relations, namely, that involving the orthodox members of each group. The sects maintained or renewed their ties, creating in this way new and original forms of religious life. Within the Catholic Church itself, to which we are confining our attention, the reactions toward Judaism were far from uniform. They varied from one place to another and from one kind of community to another. Above all, the reactions of the mass of the faithful corresponded only very imperfectly with those of the hierarchy and the scholars, and sometimes ran strongly counter to them.

It will be seen how this problem interacts with that of the separation of Judaism and Christianity. It is with reference to this separation that the chronological limits of my inquiry have been set. It is clearly impossible to assign to the split any precise date. It came about in such and such a period *or thereabouts*; at such and such a pace *more or less*; it was completed at different rates according to the local situation.[16] It is important, therefore, considering all the factors involved, not to fix the beginning of our period too early. The apostolic period must remain in the background of the investigation. The most useful procedure would be to choose as a point of departure a happening or date that had a definite significance for Christianity and for Judaism alike.

One thinks naturally of the crisis of A.D. 70. It represents, nevertheless, merely the first act in a drama that reached its climax sixty years later under Hadrian, with the Second Jewish War. From our present point of view it is difficult, and indeed somewhat arbitrary, to separate the two events. Without doubt, the former crisis is the major one. It wrecked Israel's cultic institutions, and it put an end to the last vestiges of Jewish self-government, as well as to the authority and even the very existence of the priesthood. To Jewish sensibilities it was the more distressing episode of the two. It is to this that one must refer if one wishes to appreciate the magnitude of the upheaval that took place, both in Jewish religion and in the Jews' state of mind. But a proper consideration of the matter shows not only the magnitude of the upheaval but its limits; shows, indeed, that to attribute to the events of A.D. 70 consequences either immediate or decisive is to simplify the issues to the point of falsification. The developments that were thus initiated proceeded to develop only slowly. The results became clearly perceptible only after, and in some cases a long time after, the final destruction of Jerusalem and the construction of Aelia Capitolina.

It must not be forgotten, for example, that the period between the wars was marked by a new, and final, explosion of intense Messianic and apocalyptic expectation. This is exemplified in literature by the Apocalypses of Baruch and Ezra, and in historical events by the bloody episodes in Egypt and Cyrenaica under Trajan. The Bar

Cochba rebellion was, on any showing, only the final result of this movement. The crushing of the revolt, and the consequent strengthening of the Roman hold on Palestine, put an end (if we may except some sporadic and small-scale eruptions) to this expression of the Jewish spirit, which combined in such a singular way both nationalistic and religious fervor. It is really A.D. 135 that from this point of view marks the end of a period. Only then did the eschatological and Messianic hope burn low. The stable authority of the Patriarch, recognized by Rome, replaced the ephemeral and rebel power of the Son of the Star, and in an Israel chastened and resigned was set up the exclusive rule of the Law.[17]

Similarly, the divorce of Judaism from the culture of the Greco-Roman world and the abandonment of the attempt to propagate the Jewish faith only became fully apparent after this date. The Hellenistic and proselytizing spirit in its pure form still found expression in the Jewish apologetic writing that is incorporated in the pseudo-Clementine literature. This cannot be earlier than the end of the first century A.D., for it presents as the champion of paganism the grammarian Apion and seems to presuppose the existence of the *Contra Apionem*, written between A.D. 93 and 96.[18] At what point did the decisive change take place? It is difficult to say. The lines of development are much more blurred than in the case of Messianism; the issues are less readily distinguishable; the documentary evidence is more sparse, and up to now less thoroughly exploited. We may say, at least, that the Second Jewish War furnishes us with a *terminus a quo*; not a very exact one, perhaps, but one beyond which it is not useful to go, except to convince oneself that the decisive moment in the disengagement of Israel did not coincide with the destruction of the temple.

Something similar could be said of the Christian side of the affair. The events of A.D. 70, though they were followed by important consequences for the development of Christianity, did not altogether clarify the position of the infant Church with regard to Judaism. If we leave aside the epistles of St. Paul, the New Testament writings, reflecting in their diversity all the complexity of the situation, are in the main later than the fall of Jerusalem. In the Fourth Gospel the designation "Jew" is used pejoratively. It is a term of abuse. Yet the book of Revelation is thoroughly Jewish in spirit, and, in common with Israel, expects the inauguration of the kingdom and the establishment of a New Jerusalem. The young Church in general was still not by any means at home in this present age, and still not at all freed from the grip of Messianism. And she did not necessarily see the destruction of the temple as evidence of the disqualification of Israel, regarding it rather as a forewarning of the parousia toward which she still strained. It cannot be concluded from this that the only autonomous Christian communities, even at this date, were those deriving from St. Paul.[19] But the issues do not yet appear to be absolutely clear cut. So far as we are able to judge, important elements in the Church, both in Palestine and elsewhere, maintained some contacts with Judaism.

The view clears at about the beginning of the second century. The positions of Catholic Christianity and orthodox Judaism with regard to each other were fixed at the time when the main lines of ecclesiastical organization were being laid down and made uniform throughout the Church. The Christians, gradually relaxing their hope for the imminent return of Christ, re-formed themselves to endure in an earthly society. By so doing, they underlined their independence of the Synagogue. Of this independence and the problems it raised for the empire, pagan opinion was well aware, as is proved by the famous rescript of Pliny to Trajan.

This consideration also adds its weight to my decision to commence my inquiry at about this date. But Hadrian's war, which the Christians saw as the breaking out on Israel of divine chastisement,[20] provides us, in this connection, with a point of departure all the more natural in that it coincides with the beginning in the Church of a literature that is specifically anti-Jewish. The dialogue between Jason and Papiscus, which is no longer extant, was without doubt a little later than A.D. 135. Justin's dialogue with Trypho, published at the end of the reign of Antoninus or the beginning of that of Marcus Aurelius, is supposed to have taken shape during the course of the war itself. In addition, it is to be remembered that the gnostic crisis took place more or less contemporaneously with these happenings, forcing the Church to define more exactly its position in relation to the Old Testament, and hence to Israel and Judaism. Moreover, Marcion arrived in Rome in 139, and separated himself from orthodoxy and began his preaching in 144. If these factors are borne in mind, it will be seen that there is here a crucial juncture in the development of Jewish-Christian relations.

The choice of a place at which to stop is easy enough. It is important, as with our starting point, not to fix it too early. Wherever one may be obliged to place its beginning, the process of disengagement, after which Judaism no longer counted as a rival to the Church, was not completed all at once. Between the moment when the first signs of the movement became evident, and the moment when it might be considered complete, there was a period of time, a transition period, which saw the passing of Hellenistic

Judaism and the establishment of Talmudic rabbinism. And it is desirable that this period should fall within the limits of the inquiry. Equally, in order that the enquiry might be of genuine interest and usefulness it is necessary to prolong it to include the triumph of the Church. It must encompass, at least, the fourth century. This is a period of prime importance in the life of Christianity, since this is when it emerges triumphant in its Catholic form. This triumph is important, too, for Jewish-Christian relations, since now that the Church is yoked with the state, the basic situation is seriously altered. As the imperial legislation reflects the changes that have taken place in the situation regarding the two religions, it is appropriate enough to stop where this was crystallized in the Theodosian Code. This event coincides, within a year or two, with the disappearance in 425 of the Jewish Patriarchate. It was about the same time, at the end of the fourth century, that the Jerusalem Talmud took its final shape, whilst the moving spirit of the Babylonian Talmud, R. Ashi, died at Sura circa 430. There was a shift in the center of gravity of Judaism. It was henceforth to be in Mesopotamia, outside the empire, and the Exilarch of Babylon took over from the Patriarch the headship of the dispersed people. We have here again, therefore, in the history of Judaism, and hence in the history of Jewish-Christian relations, an important turning point.

It is difficult to introduce within these limits any chronological subdivisions. The break made at the end of the fourth century by the triumph of the Church corresponds to a decisive change in the religious policies of the empire. It involved successive changes in the legal status of Jews that changed the whole appearance of Judaism and contributed to its final disengagement. Nevertheless, it did not affect in any immediately perceptible fashion the relations between the two cults and the strictly religious problem they posed. The Church's position via-à-vis its rival was considerably strengthened by the support the civil power henceforth gave it. The conflict meanwhile lost none of its sharpness. There are, on the contrary, indications that it was exacerbated, and that Judaism, far from capitulating immediately, made a supreme effort. Perhaps it was briefly stimulated by the anti-Christian and pro-Jewish policies of Julian. Some of the most interesting documents relating to Jewish proselytism come from the fourth century. It also happens that some evidence of Jewish-Christian contamination appears most clearly in this period, and the same period saw the rise within orthodox Christianity of ecclesiastical anti-Semitism. But theological controversy continued its course from one century to the next without notable change. And on the Jewish side, the dating of the Talmudic materials is, on the whole, too uncertain to allow us to trace a clear pattern of opposing views.

In sum, a profound transformation took place during this period, a transformation within Judaism itself, as well as in its relations with Christianity. There is no difficulty in registering the destination arrived at, and in thus assessing the distance traveled in three centuries. But if the general line of development is perfectly clear, it remains in itself too complex and too rapidly evolving for any clearly marked stages to be perceived. Two characteristics distinguish Jewish-Christian relations from one end of the period to the other: open hostility, on the one hand, contacts resulting in syncretism, on the other. It is around this that the study naturally organizes itself. The logical plan is here the natural one.

PART 1

The Religious and Political Setting

1

The Aftermath: Palestinian Judaism

"And we have nothing now save the Mighty One and his
law."

Syriac Apocalypse of Baruch, 85.3

We are not well informed about the psychological and religious
repercussions in Israel of the events of A.D. 135. The only material at
our disposal is that of the Talmud, and that is slight enough. This
material is, moreover, difficult to make use of, and when it speaks of
an open and general persecution in the last years of Hadrian, it lapses
into what is largely fantasy.[1] In order to make any accurate assessment
of the situation, we must begin from the crisis of A.D. 70. At least there
we have available some sources of information (Josephus, Apocalypses, Talmudic texts) that not only tell us about the background
situation against which the Bar Cochba revolt was to develop, but
help us to assess what were the consequences within Judaism of the
double disaster.[2]

I

The first reaction to the catastrophe was one of stunned grief. We hear
echoes of this not only in the words of contemporary witnesses but for
long afterwards, throughout the whole literary and religious tradition
of Judaism. Right up to the time of the Jewish-Arab conflict of 1947
Palestinian Jews would go to weep for the departed glory of their city
and sanctuary at the very place where the ruins were still visible. Since
that time, of course, Jews have no longer had access to the spot.[3]
Under the impact of the catastrophe Israel felt herself to have been
abandoned by Yahweh. For pious Jews, as Windisch so well expresses
it, "it was not just that a people, lately flourishing, had been trampled
under foot. What was at issue was faith itself in the power, faithfulness
and goodness of God. Over the smoking ruins of Jerusalem the
nagging and torturing question posed itself, the question of God. It
seemed more hopeless than ever to expect an answer."[4].

The unshakable certainty that they were the elect people had given
the people of Israel confidence in themselves as much as in God, and

they were quite ready to call God to account for what looked to them like a violation of the covenant. In the apocalyptic literature of the times we hear the poignant tones of a mutinous despair. "If Thou destroyest Thy city, and deliverest up Thy land to those that hate us, how shall the name of Israel be again remembered? Or how shall one speak of Thy praises? Or to whom shall that which is in Thy law be explained?"[5] Zion is desolate, Rome/Babylon triumphs. "And now I see that as for the world which was made on account of us, lo! it abides, but we, on account of whom it was made, depart."[6] And 4 Ezra is even more eloquently grief-stricken. "Out of all the peoples who have become so numerous thou hast gotten Thee one people: and the law which Thou didst approve out of all [laws] Thou hast bestowed upon the people whom Thou didst desire. And now, O Lord, why hast Thou delivered up the one unto the many, and dishonoured the one root above the rest, and scattered Thine only one among the multitude? And [why] have they who denied Thy promises been allowed to tread under foot those that have believed Thy covenants?"[7] And again: "If the world has indeed been created for our sakes why do we not enter into possession of our world?"[8].

Similarly, in the Talmud, for many generations the same sad question continues to be put: Why? And now and again someone is tempted, in almost sacrilegious anger, to rebel against that incomprehensible verdict. Three times during each night the Lord cries out, "Woe is me! for I have let my house be devastated, my temple be burnt, my children be led away into captivity among the nations." And when the Jews in their synagogues bless His name, the Lord shakes His head and says, "May the king live! May he be blest in his house! But woe to the father who banished his children, and woe to the children who are banished from their father's table!"[9]

But it is not in the temperament of the Jew to abandon himself forever to despair. Their capacity for optimism is unquestionably one of the most distinctive characteristics of this people that they have maintained throughout all the vicissitudes of their deeply tragic history. If in the aftermath of the destruction of Jerusalem they had momentarily doubted God, they lost no time in regaining possession of themselves. The feelings of rebellion passed. They began to reflect. Of course, the unavoidable question was still there to be answered. But when all things had been considered, it was not by any means necessary in answering it to throw doubt on the divine justice. Israel in the end recovered herself, strengthened by a twofold conviction: If God had thus cast off His people, then there must have been good reasons for His doing so; and if the righteous were being scoffed at, humiliated, and persecuted, then this could only be a temporary testing through which they had to pass. Israel sought refuge from the wretched present in that glorious prospect of a better future which the apocalyptists held out to the afflicted people.

The reason for the testing was, of course, the sins of the people. There had certainly been a breaking of the covenant, but the breaking was not done by God, but by the people. Once again they had wandered from the right way. Once the initial stage of shock and bewilderment is over, all the Jewish writers, Josephus, the rabbis and the apocalyptists, are found in agreement. Nevertheless, when it is a matter of specifying the exact nature of the fault, the same writers diverge, and their divergences shed a valuable light on the situation within Judaism after the downfall.

For Josephus responsibility for the catastrophe is to be laid at the door of the fanatical Zealots. They decided the city's fate when they strewed its streets with the corpses of their adversaries.[10] To their crimes were added transgressions of the ritual law: sacrificial worship had been discontinued, sacred vessels melted down, the oil and wine that belonged to the sanctuary had been distributed to the troops; the food laws had been violated, the temple defiled with dead bodies. For all these things the sanctuary had to be purified by fire.[11] Both the prophets beforehand[12] and omens that appeared during the course of the siege itself should have warned the Jews of the risk of these defilements and of the seriousness of the consequences. This only made their errors the less forgivable. Divine favor had therefore been transferred to the Romans, who were the rod of the Lord's anger. Since it was they who were carrying out His will, it was they who would reap the benefit of His support. The inheritor of universal empire was to be not the expected Messiah, but Vespasian, now under the guidance of God.[13]

There is no doubt whatever that Josephus was led to place this interpretation on events by political opportunism and in the interests of his own preferment. It would be unwise to think of him here as the spokesman for Judaism in general. In spite of this, he was not by any means alone in his opinions, for with the exception of the last in the above list they were shared by a number of his fellow Jews. The Talmudic rabbis, like Josephus, saw the chief cause of the disaster in the animosities that divided the Jews against each other, and in moral and ritual shortcomings.[14] Similarly, the apocalyptists agree in their assertion that God has dealt so severely with His people because of His single-minded pursuit of strict justice. The punishment exactly balances in its magnitude the magnitude of the sins committed. "Dost thou think that in these things the Most High rejoices, or that His name is glorified? But what will become of His righteous judgement [if He does not punish]?"[15]

The apocalyptists go on to say, and here they part company with Josephus, that if the Jews have forced God's hand in this way, compelling Him, almost in spite of Himself, to go to these extreme lengths in punishment, the gentiles too will be punished in their turn, and even more severely. Their ascendancy will be only for a time.

The book of Baruch is in all likelihood later than A.D. 70, at least in its final form. It combines in a very interesting way the points of view of both Josephus and the apocalyptists. It preaches obedience but announces vengeance. The introduction advises Jews to "Pray for the long life of Nebuchadnezzar king of Babylon, and of his son Belshazzar, and that their days on earth may endure as the heavens."[16] Israel will be rewarded for her loyalty. "We shall lead our lives under the protection of Nebuchadnezzar king of Babylon and of his son Belshazzar, and by our long service win their favour."[17] If, as there is reason to think, the passage is referring to Vespasian and Titus, we are here very close to the views of Josephus. Like him, Baruch ascribes the disaster to the sins of Israel. Among the sins mentioned is the sin of disobedience to the foreign overlords whom God has given His people.[18]

But this obedience to gentiles, though it is laid on Jews as a strict obligation, is only a temporary discipline, a testing of their patience imposed by the divine will. "My children, patiently bear the anger brought on you by God. Your enemy has persecuted you, but soon you will witness his destruction and set your foot on his neck."[19] And addressing Jerusalem, the prophet adds, "Trouble will come to all who have ill-treated you and gloated over your fall. Trouble will come to the cities where your children were slaves; trouble will come to the city which received your sons, for just as she rejoiced at your fall and was happy to see you ruined, so shall she grieve over her own desolation."[20]

Josephus, then, makes a solid front with the priestly party, though he never acknowledges this in so many words. Like them, he advocates collaboration with the Roman power. It is thus natural for him to throw all the blame on to the inflammatory nationalism of the Zealots, whom he sees as rebels against the divine plan. Baruch and the rabbis, for their part, assert the responsibility of the nation as a whole. Meanwhile, a quite different tendency manifests itself here and there in the apocalyptic writings, namely, an inclination to inculpate the priesthood itself. The author of the Syriac Apocalyse of Baruch, on receiving his commission to remain in the ruined city, is told to give orders to the priests to take the key of the sanctuary and throw it toward the sky, saying, "Guard Thy house Thyself, for lo! we are found false stewards."[21]

We have here an appearance of an antisacerdotal movement that is of great age. It went back at least as far as the prophets and it had never died out in Jewish thought. It maintained its existence on the fringes of official Jewish piety and organized religion. It made its presence felt in one strand, at least, of Pharisaism, and finds its clearest expression in the Psalms of Solomon. The author of these psalms, full of hatred for the illegitimate Hasmonaean dynasty, sees the intervention of Pompey and the consequent ending of Hasmonaean rule as an event full of significance. It heralds the coming of better times. The author awaits the Messiah, Son of David, and the true heir of Davidic sovereignty. He awaits the restoration of Israel and the subjugation of the gentiles.[22] In the feelings that this author expresses we observe something more than simply a hatred of extreme nationalism. We perceive too the animosity that certain sections within Judaism bore toward the temple party, the party that had supported these priest kings who had falsified the true religious message of Israel. The priesthood as a whole must bear the responsibility for what had happened, for they had "utterly polluted the holy things of the Lord."[23] The tone is very similar to that of pseudo-Baruch.[24]

For the author of the Psalms of Solomon, as for those apocalyptists who wrote after A.D. 70, the trials and temptations of the present time are the humiliating but necessary precursors of the glory to come. Against this kind of conviction no adversity could prevail. Disasters multiplied and intensified. The persecutions of Antiochus Epiphanes gave way, after the Hasmonaean interlude, to the tyranny of Herod. From the loss of political independence the Jews had proceeded to the loss even of the power to rule their own religious affairs. Pompey had desecrated the sanctuary, Titus destroyed it, Hadrian replaced it with a pagan sanctuary in a pagan Jerusalem. The blasphemers had triumphed. But they were nothing but tools of God, even now, and would be His victims hereafter. The more the heathen raged, the more certain it was that the time was near. As Adolphe Lods has emphasized: "It was precisely during the times of national disaster that men most confidently anticipated the breaking in of the new age."[25]

But further, faced with the ordeals of A.D. 70 and 135 the Jews looked to the more distant past and found a historical parallel that was perfectly clear. War and defeat, destruction of city and temple, foreign domination, exile; this was a series exactly reminiscent of 586 B.C. Whether Babylon or Rome, it was all the same, the foreign power was the servant of divine retribution. Now this former crisis, far from crushing Israel, had strengthened its hope and given a new impetus to prophecy. The people as a whole had refused to be resigned to the wretched state in which it found itself, and had turned instead toward the bright future Ezekiel and Deutero-Isaiah had visualized for it, with the dispersed Israel regathered into the restored Zion.[26] There is thus a perfect continuity between the exilic prophets and the apocalyptists of the first and second centuries A.D. This continuity appears most clearly in the ideas both subscribe to concerning the future Jerusalem.

It is widely recognized today that true Messianism, i.e., ideas about the actual figure of a Messiah, was much less fundamental to Jewish speculations about the future than used to be generally believed. As A. Causse says: "When we think of belief in the Messiah and the Son of Man as the central, pivotal belief of Judaism, we are looking at it from a peculiarly Christian point of view, for primitive Christianity was in essence a Messianic movement. In the Old Testament, for the most part, the role of the Messiah is secondary and incidental. There is a non-Messianic eschatology...but there is no eschatology at all without the great gathering at Jerusalem, centre of the world, city of the future, city of God."[27] This observation was made with reference to biblical theology, but it is entirely applicable to the Judaism of the Roman period. In some writings the Messiah has disappeared altogether. Even where he is given a part to play, it is frequently limited in scope. It is the city that is given the prominence.[28] Both the Apocalypse of Baruch and 4 Ezra allocate to the Messiah only a transitory role.[29] On the other hand, Jerusalem is to last for ever, like the kingdom itself, whose centre it is.[30]

The rabbis too had an interest in eschatology, though they indulged it only surreptitiously. When they spend their time collecting and codifying the minutiae of the defunct temple ritual, this reflects not so much an antiquarian preoccupation with the past as a dream of the future. For it was important to them that the sanctuary should be restored and the cult reestablished, according to the hallowed traditions. And the Synagogue never ceased to pray for that glorious day to arrive: "Have mercy, O Lord our God, according to the multitude of Thy tender mercies, on Israel Thy people, on Jerusalem Thy city, and on Zion the habitation of Thy glory; on Thy temple, where Thou dwellest, and on the kingdom of the house of David, Messiah of Thy righteousness. Blessed be Thou, O Lord God of David, who buildest Jerusalem."[31]

As the prayers of the Synagogue expressed this desire, the apocalyptists announced its glowing fulfilment. Again we may refer to

Baruch. In the first quotation the speaker is Jerusalem, exhorting and comforting her children: "Take courage, my children, call on God: He will deliver you from tyranny, from the hands of your enemies.... In sorrow and tears I watched you go away, but God will give you back to me in joy and gladness for ever."[32] Jerusalem in her turn is comforted: "Jerusalem, take off your dress of sorrow and distress, put on the beauty of the glory of God for ever, wrap the cloak of the integrity of God around you, put the diadem of the glory of the Eternal on your head: since God means to show your splendour to every nation under heaven, since the name God gives you for ever will be, 'Peace through integrity, and honour through devotedness.' "[33]

The new Jerusalem is not, however, to be a mere replica of the old. In this case destruction would have been pointless. If the holy city has disappeared, it is because she was not in her old form worthy of God. In pseudo-Baruch God says, speaking of the past, "Dost thou think that this is that city of which I said, 'On the palms of My hands have I graven thee'? This building now built in your midst is not that which is revealed with Me, that which was prepared beforehand here from the time when I took counsel to make paradise, and showed it to Adam...to Abraham...to Moses on Mount Sinai."[34] The same author adds later: "And afterwards [Jerusalem] must be renewed in glory, and perfected for evermore."[35] The reborn Jerusalem will be a perfect Jerusalem. To those who were convinced of this the city's destruction could be seen as something transitory, and ultimately for a good end. This splendid vision of the new Jerusalem was at the very center of the Jewish hope. From the time of the exile onwards the visionaries of Israel had been inviting the whole diaspora to join in an immense eschatological pilgrimage. Some, such as the writer of the Third Sibyl, even foresaw the gentiles joining it, having been converted to the true faith. And it was to the new Jerusalem that this pilgrimage should go. In the aftermath of the catastrophe it was the same confidence that still sustained Israel. "Arise, Jerusalem, stand on the heights and turn your eyes to the east: see your sons re-assembled from west and east at the command of the Holy One, jubilant that God has remembered them."[36]

It seems, then, that the disaster had only succeeded, in the end, in stimulating faith. The Jews were no more discouraged, in the ultimate analysis, by the destruction of Jerusalem than were the first disciples by the death of Christ. Just as the death of Christ was nothing but the prelude to a glorious resurrection and a glorious return, even so was the city dead, only to be raised to life. And the analogy may be pursued further. Among the Christians, as time passed, expectations of the parousia began to wane, and since the kingdom was slow in coming, the Church began to organize itself on a more lasting basis. At the very same time the Jews too, without ever explicitly renouncing their eschatological hopes, began to adapt themselves better to a situation they expected to continue, and to make themselves at home in "the present age."[37] For the rabbis this was where the interest really lay; their chief concern was with the here and now. And even the apocalyptists, in spite of their orientation toward the future, could not but reflect to some extent the shift of emphasis. And from the outset they proclaim the spiritual center round which the religious life of Israel was bound to organize itself for as long as it could expect to last. "But now the righteous have been gathered and the prophets have fallen asleep, and we also have gone forth from the land, and Zion has been taken from us, and we have nothing now save the Mighty One and His law."[38]

Judaism adapted itself all the more easily to the new conditions in that it was not obliged to make hasty improvisations. The events of the immediate past had already prepared the way for adaptation and removed some of the obstacles to it. It is an established fact that by the beginning of the Christian era the temple no longer occupied the place in Jewish religious life it had done several centuries previously. The prestige and influence of the priesthood had declined for a number of reasons. The rival authority of the scholars had grown. The priesthood had compromised itself and discredited itself by its weakness in the face of the political power, by its unedifying attitudes to religious issues, and by the pliability of the high priesthood itself in the hands, first of Herod, and then of the Romans. The genuinely pious in Israel had for all these reasons tended to turn away from the sanctuary.[39] Jewish religious life was organized not merely round the temple, but round the study of the law and the observance of its precepts. The living center of Judaism was the Synagogue. True, the temple was venerated, but what it stood for above all was the Jewish national tradition. It recalled Israel's past splendor, the glory of her kings, the ancient unity and independence of the land. When they came together for the solemn festivals, under the aegis of the High Priest, in the sacred enclosure where no Roman was allowed to enter, the Jews could for a moment enjoy the illusion that they were still free and were still masters in their own house. It was perhaps in this national sphere that the temple's destruction was felt most grievously. It marked, with the fall of the priesthood that accompanied it, the collapse of the last vestiges of autonomy.[40] When the Jews wept over the ruins, it was their glorious past they most of all bewailed, the glorious past of a nation now laid low. When they anticipated the future restoration of the temple, the real object of anticipation was their own resurrection as a sovereign people.[41]

These aspirations, crystalizing round the memory of the temple, gave it in retrospect a popularity it had not enjoyed during the latter years of its actual existence. After Israel's humiliation it was reinstated at the heart of its interests and attention, but we must not allow this fact to mislead us into thinking that it had always stood there. The destruction of the temple marked no radical change of direction in the development of Israel's religion. Rather, it brutally forced to its conclusion a development that was inevitable anyway.

It was not, as things turned out, an entirely ill wind that brought on the catastrophe. In certain respects it represented for Judaism, once the initial chaos had been overcome, more of a gain than a loss. Israel found new strength and unity as her people reasserted their belief in the two fundamentals, legalism and the eschatological hope. These two streams of thought, the legalist and the eschatological, existed after A.D. 70 side by side. They were not at all in opposition to each other. They intermingled, though without ever emerging into a single current. After 135 it was clear that apocalyptic had had its day. The day of the visionaries was over; their place was taken by the rabbis, who from now on were to fill the office of spiritual guide. The victory of the rabbis, gradually prepared for over several centuries, had become apparent by the time the first crisis, that of A.D. 70, was over. The second crisis, of A.D. 135, confirmed it. It will not be without value to consider briefly the significance of this change and the manner in which it took place.

II

Let us pause for a moment to consider the picture Josephus presents to us of the Judaism of his own time. The division he puts forward, into Pharisees, Sadducees, and Essenes (he also adds the Zealots), is too simple and artificial. But though the reality was infinitely more complex than Josephus's scheme suggests, the scheme does pick out the principal elements in the pattern. This was the pattern of Judaism on the eve of the catastrophe, one of whose consequences was to be a comprehensive redrafting of that very pattern.[42]

There can be no doubt that the Essenes were affected only indirectly by the events surrounding the fall of the city. They were a long way from Jerusalem, and very much on the fringe of official Judaism. We do not know very much either about their influence or their ultimate fate. One can, of course, speculate as some scholars have done about their having played an influential part in the genesis of Christianity, though any part they played is more likely to have been in the formation of Jewish-Christian sects. Our present purposes will not be served by following the subject further.

Of the other parties the one most directly involved in the events of A.D. 70 and 135 was that of the Zealots. It was they who began the conflict in A.D. 66, and they who were most seriously damaged by it. After 135 they are scarcely mentioned at all. For quite different reasons the struggle also led to the collapse of the Sadducees. The two wars marked the failure of their policy of cooperation with Rome. They did not know either how to counter effectively the powerful upsurge of militant Messianism, of which they disapproved so strongly, or how to stem the violence with which Rome suppressed it. They had no desire for the war, but being so closely bound up with the temple, they suffered from it most directly of all, and many of them lost their lives. Their religion was possible only in that unique sanctuary. They fell with it.[43]

The position of the Pharisees was markedly different. They certainly remained hostile to the foreign overlords, whose victory was in a sense their own defeat, but they managed to combine a firm hostility in principle with a considerable adaptability in practice. As Guignebert says: "What they held out for above all was recognition of their religious principles, and it seems to be no exaggeration to say that political independence appeared to them as no more than a means, albeit the best means, to realize their pietistic ideal."[44] "The best means," but not the only means. They came to terms with Roman occupation. As far as it was possible, and in any case to a much greater extent than any of the other parties, they came to terms too with the total destruction of the nation and the ancient cult. They could do this because they were far less closely attached to places and things. In contrast with the others they had, if one may so express it, a place of spiritual retreat, prepared long ago. They had the Torah. The religion to which they subscribed was already a religion of the book, and only secondarily a religion of the temple. It was a religion of the temple only to the extent that the temple rites represented one aspect of the law. In Pharisaic eyes the tradition of the wise had more authority than the succession of the priests.

If they did not in 135 formally discourage the movement for revolt, the majority of them did not actively support it. It is true that Rabbi Akiba was deeply committed, but he seems not to have involved with him the Pharisaic party as a whole.[45] Others, disinclined to make public examples of themselves, and having no inducement in the circumstances to do so, contracted out of the whole business. Trypho, in the dialogue with Justin Martyr, is generally recognized as having been modelled on an actual Pharisaic Jew and as fairly representing Pharisaic attitudes. Now Trypho is said to have fled from the war even before it could have been clear what the outcome was to be. He had spent most of the time in Greece and at Corinth.[46] This is significant. Trypho's behavior is unlikely to have been unique.

The attitude of the Pharisees during the course of the first war is equally characteristic. We are told that Johanan ben Zakkai, the most distinguished scholar of the time, managed to escape in a coffin from his besieged city. He then went to Vespasian and predicted that he would become emperor, and obtained from him authority to open a rabbinic school at Jabneh. This he did without making any great effort to intercede for Jerusalem and its temple.[47] The same Johanan, at the news of the destruction of the temple, tore his garments as a sign of grief. But he said to his distressed disciples, "As long as the temple was standing, the altar was intended to be the means of remission of sins; but now, it is the table" (i.e., the food given to the poor).[48]

Thus did the Pharisees make the best of a situation that they had certainly never desired, but that they were by no means unprepared for. The fall of the temple did not interfere in the least with the practice of religion as they understood it, and their grief over its destruction seems to have been comforted without too much loss of time. They carefully codified the temple ritual, against the day when it would be restored. At the same time they codified the religious obligations incumbent on a Jew, and placed them in a very clear order of priority. And of necessity, the traditional cultic duties no longer occupied the first place. For Johanan works of charity are as yet merely substitutes for the rites of the altar,[49] but for others they possessed from the beginning a superior value. Eleazar says: "Alms giving is better than all sacrifices." In another place he ascribes the superior value not to almsgiving but to prayer.[50] But both almsgiving and prayer must give pride of place to the study of the law.[51] He who thus sanctifies himself may dispense with every kind of temple sacrifice.[52] And perhaps the most striking axiom of all is the one that reads: "Teaching in school must not be interrupted, even for the rebuilding of the temple."[53] The saying implies a certain indifference both to eschatology and to the lost temple. It conveys something of the jealousy that the scholar felt toward the priest. And in its exaltation of study to the primary place it neatly sums up the Pharisaic ideal. It is attributed to Judah, the begetter of the Mishnah.

The ideal represented by this Pharisaic summary of the priorities of the religious life had, at the time of which we are speaking, not been fully realized; but it had been prepared for, and party realized, too.

The national catastrophe forced on at an explosive pace a development that had already begun, and showed up the Pharisaic ideal of religion as the one best adapted to the needs of the hour. The catastrophe ensured the victory of Pharisaism by putting all its rivals out of the running with a single, brutal blow. But the lines of development of Pharisaism itself were already laid down, and the disaster changed them hardly at all.

There is more to be said. It is generally admitted that the evangelists have passed down to us a portrait of the Pharisees that cannot be accepted without reservations.[54] At one period, that in which the gospels received their definitive form, the doctor of the law appeared to the Christians to be the enemy par excellence. He was the rock on which the gospel to the Jews finally perished. The unflattering picture of him in the gospels is thus a kind of left-handed compliment to him. It bears witness to the disappointment and frustration the Church felt in the face of Pharisaism. In its way, therefore, it bears witness to the vitality of the Pharisaic ideal.

No one will dispute that there were among the Pharisees some who were hypocrites, and even more who had a mania for sterile casuistry and pedantic formalism. The Talmud provides abundant evidence of this.[55] But what religion is without such eccentrics? That in common parlance in the Christian world the word "Pharisee" means "hypocrite," "casuist," "legalist," is perhaps one of the injustices of history. We may say without unfairness to the early Christians that in their picture of the Pharisees they have selected only those Pharisaic characteristics that were most useful for throwing discredit on their opponents and that they have magnified them grossly. Their witness, necessarily tendentious, must be used critically and carefully. It must not lead us to overlook either the positive virtues of the movement or its great variety and complexity. "When we have described a man as a Pharisee we have not really said very much about him, for there are Pharisees and Pharisees."[56] We know today that within this movement, which was to be so important in the future development of Judaism, we must distinguish different schools of thought and varieties of opinions. We know too that among the diverse elements of which Judaism was composed before A.D. 135 the Pharisees represented the forces of life and progress. Whether or not this is true of the ossified Pharisaism we find in the Talmud, it is certainly true of the movement's earlier period.

In the eyes of the conservative Sadducees, for whom the Torah constituted the last word of revelation and of truth, the Pharisees were innovators and revolutionaries. The Pharisees were accused of importing into the ancient biblical faith foreign elements such as angelology and the idea of resurrection. The appeal to tradition, which was one of the Pharisees' fundamental techniques, was a weapon with which they opposed the tyranny of the written text. The appeal to tradition was made in the interests of progress rather than of conservation. Its ultimate effect, whether intended or not, was to justify innovations, not to exclude them. When the scholars appeal to the past, they are generally seeking for precedents to justify their present attitudes. They are trying to show that the fathers had already gone beyond the letter of the scriptural revelation, and that their heirs are therefore entitled to continue to interpret scripture on the same lines. Pharisaic thinking takes the text as its starting point but does not rest there. The Pharisees see tradition as embodying a continuing revelation that accompanies and expands that of scripture.[57]

It is perhaps rash to look for the origin of Pharisaism, as does Isidore Levy, exclusively in foreign influences. Levy's research into this question has at least drawn attention to one fact that is too often overlooked, that there are distinct similarities between the spirit of Pharisaism and that of the Judaism of the diaspora. The doctrinal liberalism that sets the Pharisees apart from the conservative Sadducees, and that shows itself in their readiness to espouse new theological ideas, is derived in large measure from Hellenistic thought. If one cannot accept some of M. Levy's subsidiary conclusions, about the late date at which the movement appeared, for instance, or about the extent to which it drew on Pythagorean notions, one may nevertheless follow him here. "The Pharisees, becoming ever more numerous and active as we approach the Christian period, were the Palestinian disciples of the Hellenistic Jews of Alexandria."[58] It would be more exact to say that Pharisaism, with its capacity on the one hand for adaptability in doctrine, and on the other for rigorous orthodoxy in religious practice, effected a synthesis between elements that were specifically Palestinian and those derived from outside. It is perhaps going too far to say that this synthesis "reconciled Moses with Pythagoras, or if you like, with Plato." It did, however, appear in Judaism both inside and outside Palestine.

The case of the Essenes is in this connection very instructive. The question of the Essenes has given rise to many disputes among modern scholars, and no conclusions about the origin of the sect seem yet to command general assent.[59] Should we see in Essenism a native Palestinian growth, or ought we to recognize instead a foreign branch grafted on to the Jewish tree? It has been defined on occasion as "an extreme form of Pharisaism," yet at other times it has been represented as an aberration, a kind of pagan salient into Israelite religious life. Both opinions can be supported by convincing arguments. In favor of the former view may be cited the strict, legalistic piety of the Essenes, their cult of the Torah, their rigorous ideas about ritual purity and their extravagant pursuit of the same. In support of the latter view it is possible to appeal to the esoteric nature of their teaching, their secret books, the elements of the sun cult that are discernible in their devotional practice, and to some of their other habits. Amongst all this some have traced, and doubtless they have not imagined it, the influence of Pythagoreanism. Josephus himself lends support to this last contention.[60]

Is the dilemma insoluble? I think not. The two interpretations are not irreconcilable. Each throws into relief one aspect of the character of Pharisaic Judaism, or indeed, of Judaism in general, and together they give us a fuller and more accurate picture then either can give us by itself. It is beyond doubt that Essenism cannot be explained without recognizing that foreign influences have affected the movement quite profoundly. The fact remains that Essenism was never, during the period under discussion, repudiated by the Jews. In spite of the novelty of their organization and of many of their practices and beliefs, all of which placed them very much on the fringe of official Judaism, they were not on this account rejected by the Jewish religious authorities, whether priestly or scholarly. They were not by that time regarded as heretics, in the Christian sense of that term. Not only did the Jews refrain from execrating or persecuting them, they expressly recognized their right to exist, with all their peculiarities, and to worship God in their own fashion, repudiating bloody sacrifices. Josephus counted them as one of the great movements of which Judaism was made up. Philo gives them his ungrudging admiration.[61]

Not only in their rigorism but in the syncretizing tendencies that went alongside it the Essenes were like the Pharisees, but more so. In both these respects the Essenes represent the extreme, for both characteristics are found in normal Pharisaism, though in moderation. The rigorism succeeded in the end in suppressing the syncretism, and became itself the chief characteristic of Talmudic Judaism, which was the heir of Pharisaism. But in the beginning rigorism and syncretistic tendencies were complementary characteristics. If we subtract from Essenism what pertains to it specifically as a *community*, then what remains is very nearly identical with Pharisaism, and contains a number of ingredients foreign to Judaism as understood in earlier times, e.g., astrological speculations. Pharisaism is distinguished by its need to fill out and enrich the religious life. The Pharisees' interest always lay primarily in the realm of religious practice, and this practical interest in the end virtually ousted all others. It showed itself in the multiplicaton of religious duties and in an unparalleled development of the science of casuistry. However, the Pharisees did show some inclination to pursue doctrinal questions and theological speculations, and found that the stock of native Israelite ideas on such matters was small. This being so, they tended inevitably to favor notions imported from outside, though whether they were actually conscious of this tendency it is impossible to say. To look for foreign influences on Pharisaism only at the point where the movement originated is to limit the inquiry arbitrarily and intolerably. It is equally artificial to see the foreign influences as coming from only one or two particular directions, such as that of Mazdaean eschatology, or as influencing only one or two particular areas of Pharisaic thought, e.g., angelology. In reality the foreign influences came from all sides and made themselves felt over a very long period.

Even after the events of A.D. 70 and 135 it is still possible to speak of a Jewish liberalism. The phrase must not be understood as referring to the symbolic interpretation of dogma or to a strictly rationalizing concept of religion. It refers rather to a receptive attitude to ideas and influences from outside. "Liberalism" in this context denotes an attitude rather than a system. It enriched even the content of orthodox Judaism itself. Conversely, one could say that orthodoxy moulded and legitimized liberalism, by fixing the limits within which it was allowed to operate.

As Judaism became more and more preoccupied with questions of religious practice, there was a progressive reduction of contact with non-Jewish thinking in matters of doctrine and theological speculation, until in the end such contact disappeared entirely.[62] It is all the more interesting, therefore, to record how even in this field non-Jewish ideas continued to hold sway, making themselves felt through the medium of the diaspora in Palestinian Judaism itself.

III

One of the last and most unexpected results of rabbinic liberalism, appearing right in the middle of the Talmudic period, was a flowering of Jewish representative art. This art provides as clear evidence as one could wish, not only for the liberalism of the scholars, but for the existence of numerous connections between Palestinian Judaism and the Judaism of the diaspora. It also sheds light on the attitude of Jews in general to Greco-Roman civilization.

Few discoveries have been as genuinely revealing and at the same time as sensational as that of the synagogue of Dura Europos. It has given us an entirely new outlook on the history of Judaism, and has forced us to reconsider opinions that until now were accepted unquestioningly. It is no part of my present task to describe the remarkable decoration of this ruin, or to indulge in a detailed exposition of its significance. There is already an abundant literature available on the subject.[63] I would simply underline one or two facts and their implications.

Attempts to establish the existence of an old and authentically Jewish tradition of visual art have cited as examples the cherubim that guarded the ark, and other such isolated instances of the use of animal or human motifs. At Dura, by contrast, we find a whole sacred history in pictures, in which the artists have set out, sympathetically and with an altogether Hellenistic feeling for beauty, to demonstrate the glory of the human face. The art of Dura is no mere expansion or development of the artistic tradition of the old Jerusalemite cult. There is no continuity between them and one cannot judge them by the same standards.[64] If the antecedents of the Dura iconography must be sought, then it is in Hellenistic art that we must seek them.

The existence of an iconographic tradition in the Jewish diaspora is, to say the least, likely. It would be difficult to argue that the technical facility that produced the Dura frescoes had sprung to such perfection in an instant, on the bare soil of the Syrian desert.[65] But while we await fresh discoveries, which might improve our knowledge of this history of artistic development, we must make Dura our point of departure. The tradition whose existence we postulate may not have been very old. At Dura itself the introduction of this Jewish art did not take place before the building of this particular synagogue in 244. The synagogue immediately preceding it, portions of which remain, was also decorated, but exclusively with geometrical patterns. There are no representations in it of the human form. We can thus be very precise about the point at which the change took place in this particular community. It may well be that the agent of the change was "Samuel the priest," who is mentioned in some of the inscriptions.[66]

In the first century it appears that images were not yet allowed. Josephus makes the categorical statement: "Our lawgiver...has forbidden the making of images of any animal, and a fortiori he has forbidden the making of images of God."[67] By "animal" he evidently means "living being," man therefore being included. It is true that it is possible to interpret the prohibition as applying primarily to sculpture, to carved images. But the fact remains that the oldest monuments of the Jewish diaspora, particularly those of the Roman catacombs, are decorated only modestly, with a basic pattern composed of geometrical motifs or motifs derived from plant forms with the addition of a very few animal figures. The human form does not appear.[68] Similarly, the more recent mosaics of the Tunisian synagogue of Hammam-Lif, which make abundant use of animal forms, do not in their present state offer us any examples of human figures.[69] The biblical prohibition does seem to have been understood as applying to every form of art.

Shortly after the time of Josephus the Fourth Book of Maccabees, to which I shall have occasion to return, and which dates in all probability from the beginning of the second century, envisages decorating the sanctuary of the martyred brothers with a fresco depicting their sufferings. The discreet way in which the idea is introduced, "if it was lawful for us to paint, as might some artist, the tale of [their] piety,"[70] indicates that this idea might still be found shocking by some. This, at any rate, is the suggestion of the most recent commentator on the book.[71] If this interpretation is correct, then we have here, about a century before the building of the Dura synagogue, the beginning of a new attitude.

The new movement began in the diaspora and became widespread there. Eventually it reached Palestine, though only after an appreciable and significant interval. Palestinian synagogues most nearly contemporary with the one at Dura, the synagogue at Capernaum being the most noteworthy, still display sculptural decorations of a fairly restrained and inoffensive type. It is true that the traditional symbols of Jewish worship, that of the candlestick, for example, are mixed with motifs of pagan origin, wreaths, crowns, animal shapes, even pieces of Bacchic scenes. But these seem to be introduced purely for their ornamental value.[72] It is necessary to come down well into the Christian era before we encounter anything in the style of the Dura remains, and then we find the synagogues of Jerash, Beth Alpha, and Ain Duq (Noarah).

Not one of this last-mentioned group of synagogues is earlier than the fourth century. The gulf between them and the synagogue of Dura is thus considerable. And the gulf is not one of time only, but of technique and of style. We are dealing now no longer with mural paintings but with mosaics, whose clumsy execution contrasts sadly with the artistic perfection of the Dura frescoes. Even allowing for the incomplete and mutilated state of the remains, it is clear that the amount of decoration here has been much less. We have no epitome of Israelite history such as Dura offers us, but one or two scenes only. Nevertheless, the same inspiration lies behind both. We observe the same considered use of the human form. We have integrated and coherent scenes instead of the isolated and purely decorative motifs that are familiar from earlier Jewish art. We have the same concentration on a narrative and didactic purpose. The contrasts between the Dura frescoes and the mosaics of the Palestinian synagogues are manifest, and yet, when they are set together over against other examples of Jewish art of this period, it becomes equally clear what the group has in common. Referring to them, and only when referring to them, it is possible to speak of a true Jewish religious art.

The mosaic at Ain Duq[73] shows Daniel in the den of lions, that of Beth Alpha the sacrifice of Isaac.[74] At Jerash the picture is of the exit from the ark, and it features a triple procession of animals accompanied by human figures that are named in the inscription, though only the heads remain. They are Shem and Japhet.[75] The first two of these incidents are represented frequently in ancient Christian art, in paintings in the catacombs and in sculptures on tombs. They are generally interpreted, following Le Blant and in the light of the *Ordo Commendationis Animae*, as illustrating the divine mercy. The same interpretation is probably to be put upon them in the present case: Daniel saved from the lions and Isaac saved from death are symbolic of the chosen people, guided and protected by the hand of God.[76]

The scene pictured at Jerash is more unusual. Noah saved from the flood is also freely used in Christian symbolism as a type, a salvation figure.[77] But he is usually represented by himself, embarking alone in an ark of suitably reduced dimensions.[78] At Jerash, on the contrary, the figure of the patriarch, if it were represented at all on the mosaic, could not have taken up very much room. The animals overrun everything. The purely artistic concern of the originator largely explains this treatment of the theme. The artist has manifestly enjoyed himself in demonstrating his virtuosity, and his work is artistically far superior to the fragments from Ain Duq and Beth Alpha.

Does this mean that symbolism is entirely absent? I think not. It is not impossible that the selection of this episode, drawn from the pre-history of the chosen people, reflects an interest in universalism. The going out from the ark at the end of the flood, long before the covenant was made with Abraham, marks the reconciliation of God with humanity, or rather, with the whole creation. The view represented is not a narrowly Israelite one. The figure of Noah is connected with the Jewish mission. The observance of the so-called Noahic commandments was the minimum required of proselytes.[79] Of the three sons of Noah, one, namely Ham (in the person of Canaan), was cursed by his father.[80] It is perhaps just by chance that he has disappeared from this damaged mosaic, but it might also be that he never appeared in it. In any case, it is quite characteristic that Shem and Japhet should appear side by side. Shem was the ancestor of the chosen people, and Japhet, according to the rabbis, was the ancestor of the Greeks. Territory was promised to him, and he was to "dwell in the tents of Shem," which is to say, he would be called to the true faith.[81] It is unlikely to be accidental that out of all the possible biblical incidents that could have been illustrated, this one was chosen for the synagogue at Gerasa, in the heart of the Hellenistic Decapolis. The mosaic dates most probably from the beginning of the fifth century. It suggests that we ought not to be too dogmatic about the Jewish withdrawal into particularism having taken place even by this date.

The inscriptional material from these decorated synagogues suggests the same conclusions. Ain Duq provides only Hebrew or Aramaic inscriptions. At Dura, by contrast, the titles on the frescoes are in Hebrew, Greek, and Pahlavi. At Beth Alpha and Jerash, Greek takes as prominent a part as the Semitic languages. The same may be said of several other synagogues of the period, and particular the one at El Hammeh, the ancient Hamath, near Gadara.[82]

Thus, in spite of the anathema pronounced on the language of the gentiles by some rabbis of the early centuries A.D., it continued to be employed until well into the Christian era, and in Palestine itself at that. Furthermore, an examination of the proper names that appear in the inscriptions shows that only a part of them are properly Jewish. At Beth Alpha there is mention of a Marianos. At El Hammeh we find in a Hebrew inscription the names Hoples, Protone, Sallustius, and Photios, and the mention of a "comes" named Phoros.[83] Greek and Latin names and titles may be explained, perhaps, as Sukenik suggests, by the proximity of the Decapolis. They could belong either to converts or to those who were Jews by birth. Either way these names and titles attest the fact that right into the Talmudic period there persisted strong connections between Palestinian Judaism and Greco-Roman civilization. Their evidence thus supports that of the use of the Greek language and of the decoration of the synagogues.

Let us return to the subject of images. It is not merely that the use of images is in itself unexpected, the choice of themes and the manner of their execution also occasion surprise, and reveal a Judaism that is curiously open to outside influences. It has been noted before how at Dura Moses is shown as of superhuman proportions, far surpassing in size the figures that surround him. This is a device often used in pagan art in the portrayal of immortals or of semidivine heroes.[84] Perhaps we ought not to see here anything more than the rather mechanical application of a current technique, excused by the prominent part played by Moses in the history of Israel. But it is quite possible that the manner of depicting Moses does imply a particular interpretation of Moses' person and work. Goodenough has analyzed the picture of Moses to which Philo gives expression. He is the head of the hierarchy of the patriarchs. He is the most outstanding of the men of inspiration. He is at once the receiver of mystical illumination and the agent through whom it is bestowed. He is the veritable incarnation of divine power.[85] The same author suggests, and intends ultimately to prove, that the Dura frescoes are to be interpreted in the light of Philo's thought. If this is true, then this "heroization" of Moses is a striking piece of evidence for the potency of Hellenistic speculation within Judaism at a relatively late date.[86]

Without anticipating the proof that Goodenough has promised, it is not difficult to pick out from the synagogue imagery themes borrowed directly from the pagan artistic repertoire. At Dura, above the shrine for the Torah is pictured Orpheus enchanting the animals. The picture is integrated into the total decorative scheme of the alcove, if not visually, then at least in meaning. It is certain that Orpheus is here, as in some Christian art, a symbolic figure, a symbol perhaps of the divine wisdom communicating itself to the creatures.[87] The presence in a synagogue of this pagan hero, father, and patron of mystery religions is at least as surprising as that of a superhuman Moses. The Jewish community at Dura occupied a singular position, it is true. They were within the eastern boundaries of the Roman empire, and at a spot where Hellenistic and Persian influences met. At the same time, they were within the territory of the Semitic peoples and equidistant from Jerusalem and Babylon. They were within, therefore, what one might call the Talmudic sphere of influence. As far as the Jewish world was concerned they were a kind of halfway house between the pure Hellenistic Judaism of the diaspora and the Judaism of Palestine. Before drawing any further conclusions from these facts, a few cross-references must be made.

Corresponding to the Dura Orpheus, the synagogues of Beth Alpha and Ain Duq have the figure of the sun in his four-horse chariot, encircled by seven rays and surrounded by the twelve signs of the zodiac. The figures of the four seasons appear at the corners. Traces of the same artistic theme have been found at other synagogues, in particular the one at Esphia on Mount Carmel.[88] Though the example from Ain Duq is mutilated, the one at Beth Alpha displays all the features of classical pagan art that were popular in the iconography of the period of the empire. At both Ain Duq and Beth Alpha the sun figure makes an odd companion for the traditional Jewish symbols that accompany it, the shrine for the Torah, the candlestick, and other pieces of cultic apparatus. In some of the Jewish catacomb paintings and in the Capernaum sculptures it is possible to argue that pagan motifs such as centaurs, winged demons, grape-gathering cupids, etc., are purely decorative, but this interpretation here, as at Dura, is excluded by the central position of the image. This raises the whole subject of the orthodoxy of the synagogues in question.

As far we are able to tell, pre-Talmudic Judaism was radically opposed to the use of images. This is the attitude that, as we have seen, Josephus still maintains. It is based on a strictly literal interpretation of the biblical prohibition: "You shall not make yourself a carved image or any likeness of anything in heaven or on earth beneath or in the waters under the earth."[89] But it is quite clear that this prohibition is intended only to prevent idolatry. The verse of the decalogue in which it is set out is completed and explained by what follows: "You shall not bow down to them or serve them."[90] When the older Judaism therefore rigorously excluded *all* images, whatever their object, its rigor was due in part to an excessive caution and to a desire to withhold from its devotees all temptation, and in part to the need to distinguish its usage from that of the pagans, who made very free use of images. The prohibition was thus one of the means whereby Israel deliberately accentuated the difference between itself and the gentiles. Since the Jews did not cultivate the arts and techniques of image production, those images which did exist were generally executed by pagans, so that imagery was thought of as a sign of paganism. But as contacts with the non-Jewish world multiplied, especially in the diaspora, it became necessary to reconsider the question. For this problem was, after all, only one aspect of a general one, that of Israel's relations with the diverse forms of Greco-Roman culture.

So Judaism thought again about the prohibition of images and came round little by little to a more nicely stated view, a view we find in the Talmud. The Jews in some quarters had already taken over in their private lives, and doubtless without any sanction from authority, some non-Jewish attitudes and customs. When the Talmud makes some accommodation to these changes, the rabbis are thus, in a manner of speaking, cutting their losses. By legitimizing certain practices they aspired to forbid more rigorously certain others. Prohibition is in the majority of cases an indication that the prohibited behavior was in fact indulged in. "Halachic negation is a historical affirmation."[91] It is to be noted meanwhile (and it is important to get this clear) that the question initially under discussion did not concern the legitimacy of Jewish art and the limits within which it must work; it concerned the use which Jews were entitled to make of the products of gentile art. The precise discussions and scholastic distinctions that characterize the treatment of the subject in the tractate Abodah Zarah are related for the most part to objects and works of art produced by pagans. It is assumed throughout that though a Jew may, in certain cases, make use of images of living things, he does not make any such things himself.

The basic principle by which these art objects from pagan sources were judged was whether they were used for idolatrous purposes.[92] But how was idolatry to be defined? A good Jew would hardly be capable of indulging in it deliberately and on his own initiative. The determining factor was not the frame of mind of the user, but the nature of the object itself and the purpose for which it was intended. Some objects were regarded as possessing inherently a kind of idolatrous power, rather like a dangerous virus. This power was capable of infecting the faithful even against their will and without their knowledge. It was a maleficent demonic force, whose presence the rabbinic diagnosis was designed to detect.[93] Whether a Jew should reject a particular object with horror or, instead, might legitimately use it depended on whether it was or was not known to have been intended for idolatrous purposes, and on whether it was or was not devoted to idolatrous use, either regularly or occasionally. In the attempt to moderate the severity of the older interpretation the scholars argued with passion and with much display of casuistic skill. The types of cases presented for solution, and the answers given to them, were almost infinite in their variety. They varied from period to period as the argument went on, and in the same period they varied from rabbi to rabbi. It appears that each crisis or time of tension would be met with an upsurge of rigorism among the Jews,[94] and the shifts of opinion on the question under discussion reflect fairly accurately the changing relations between Israel and the gentile world.

Distinctions were drawn between the different forms of art, between the subjects represented, between the different uses for which an image might be intended, and between the secondary uses to which it might be put. Sculpture, "images carved and set up," was condemned more severely than painting, which is only done in two dimensions. Sculpture was felt to approximate more closely to the living form, and to lend itself more readily to cultic use. A similar attitude was taken to figures in relief. It was permissible to wear a ring that bore an inscribed human figure, but not to use it as a seal, since this would produce a figure in relief.[95] A very strict Jew would not even look at the statues the Romans erected, or at the figure on a coin, or at any other representation of the human form. It was asked concerning R. Nahum: "Why was he a man of such superior sanctity? Because he never in his life looked at the image on a coin." And when this same R. Nahum died, "they covered the pictures on the walls, saying, 'In life he was accustomed to see no images. Neither shall he see them in death.'"[96]

In general, animal figures were regarded as less objectionable than those of human beings. The exceptions were animals that were representations of divinities or associated with divinities. The dragon was forbidden, but not other serpents.[97] All representation of false gods or of angels was naturally prohibited. Images of heavenly bodies were in the main forbidden, but there were important exceptions. The Mishnah only disallows the sun and the moon, but allows the planets. And even sun and moon are forbidden only on vases.[98] R. Simon ben Gamaliel only condemns them if they are represented on precious vases, for "the greater or lesser value of the vase determines whether one worships it or not." R. Johanan is more liberal still. Any container, even if decorated with a "symbol venerated by Rome" is held to be inoffensive, because "once water has passed through such an object it is nothing more than a mere vessel."[99]

Thus, during the period with which we are concerned, a considerable relaxation took place in the rules regarding images, though it was a relaxation that depended on the making of a number of rather fine legal distinctions. I repeat that these discussions concerned themselves only with the use that Jews might make of objects whose origin was pagan. Nevertheless, they did prepare the rabbis for making the decisive leap and recognizing the legitimacy of a Jewish art.

Two Talmudic texts give us information about the matter. One informs us that in the time of the same R. Johanan whom I have just quoted, "they began to decorate the walls with pictures, and the rabbis did not forbid them."[100] The other says that "in the time of R. Abun they began to represent living forms in mosaics, and no one prevented them."[101] R. Johanan lived in the third century,[102] R. Abun at the beginning of the fourth. The former is virtually contemporary with the synagogue at Dura, the latter lived just shortly before the building of the Palestinian synagogues whose mosaics are known today. Thus the orthodoxy of the communities that built these synagogues is established. There are no grounds for classifying these examples of Jewish art among the manifestations of heresy or syncretism.

There is good reason to believe that the rabbinic authorization merely sanctioned already established usage. The diaspora, as we have seen, is unlikely to have waited until the Palestinian scholars made their pronouncements.[103] In Palestine itself private and secular custom prepared the way for communal and religious use.[104] The two texts quoted above are interesting for their very brevity. They relate only to paintings and mosaics, i.e., to images not in relief. Sculpture is tacitly forbidden.[105] On the other hand, once it was conceded in principle that Jewish art was legitimate, there was absolutely no need for lengthy discussions or the drawing of fine distinctions in order to clarify its application. An image, whatever its subject, was much less suspect if it was of Jewish origin that if it was of pagan manufacture. Its intended use was clear, and the need it met could be ascertained without difficulty. In such cases there could be no presumption of idolatrous intent, and the demonic power latent in objects made by pagans could not be supposed to exist in it.

In this way the presence of mythological motifs in synagogue decoration, such as the Dura Orpheus and the Helios of Beth Alpha and Ain Duq, can be explained. Such images when used by pagans were plainly idolatrous. Their appearance in Jewish decoration, and above all in the ornamentation of a place of worship, may at first sight be astonishing, but they are to be regarded as in some sense neutralized or exorcized by the context of Jewish iconography in which they are found. Their presence in a synagogue, devoted entirely to the public worship of the true God and to the study of the law, all undertaken under rabbinic supervision, was after all a guarantee that they would not give occasion for practices worthy of condemnation. The nature of their surroundings immunized such images against idolatry, as did the clearly ascertainable fact that they were produced specifically for Jewish purposes. This last still applied, even if they originated in pagan workshops. The demands of monotheism could thus be reconciled with the adoption of current fashion.

All the same, Orpheus is in all likelihood intended to be symbolic. As for Helios, he can scarcely be thought to represent the pagan divinity. Rather, he stands simply for the heavenly body, though the artist has rather slavishly followed pagan models in giving his portrait all the features characteristic of the sun god. And this heavenly body, even when depicted on objects of pagan provenance, was forbidden by the rabbis only in certain cases. In the synagogues the zodiacal signs make the meaning of the image plain: we are here in the realm of astrology.

Now an interest in astrology, far from being a sign of heretical inclinations, is quite characteristic of orthodox Judaism at this time. The importance of astrology is apparent both in Josephus and in Philo.[106] And a preoccupation with the subject is noted by Epiphanius as characteristic of the Pharisees. He accuses them of having learned from pagans in this matter and having translated the Greek names for the planets and the signs of the zodiac into Hebrew. Epiphanius gives a list of Hebrew and Greek equivalents.[107]

Epiphanius's evidence is fully confirmed. Astrology and angelology appear among the Pharisees, as among the Essenes, as two different aspects of the same speculative study. There is a connection of some kind between the astral powers, στοιχεῖα, and the heavenly powers that are personified as angels, though it is not always easy to say exactly what this connection is.[108] The influences that led to both kinds of speculation were foreign to the old Mosaic religion, but they became an integral part of later Judaism. Representations of the sun and of zodiacal signs in a synagogue cannot be interpreted, in the absence of supporting evidence, as signs of heresy, any more than human and animal figures can be interpreted in this way. Both phenomena are in the mainstream of orthodox Judaism.

This liberalism with regard to art ended by provoking opposition. At Ain Duq the Daniel mosaic has been deliberately mutilated, as have the sculptures at Capernaum. Those at Jerash and Beth Alpha, and the frescoes at Dura, may well owe their escape to the fact that these synagogues had already been abandoned when the iconoclastic reaction set in. In any case, this reaction did not manifest itself everywhere at exactly the same time. On the other hand, in view of the late date of some of the mosaics that escaped destruction, those of Beth Alpha in particular, it is by no means impossible that the iconoclastic movement, instead of representing a purely Jewish phenomenon, was influenced by the Christian iconoclasm that has left its mark on some eastern churches. Later still, it may have owed something to the attitude of Islam.[109] However that may be, iconoclasm is a late phenomenon in Judaism. It is contemporary with, one might almost say it is an aspect of, Judaism's final retrenchment and hardening.[110] The interesting thing to note is that images became naturalized in Judaism not during the flowering period of Hellenism, at the time of Philo, but in the time of the Amoraim, and within their direct sphere of influence. Now these Amoraim are of course the true heirs of the Pharisees. This is not too difficult to explain. Judaism, having been "immunized" by "several generations of Pharisaic discipline"[111] could allow itself some relaxation of the old and rigid rules. The appearance and development of Jewish art illustrates, apart from anything else, the adaptability and openness that were native to the Pharisaic genius. The events of A.D. 70 and 135 not only failed to shake the Pharisees' attachment to these principles but produced conditions they found in many respects congenial and stimulating.[112]

IV

It is the victory of Pharisaim, rather than the national collapse that led to it, which represents the decisive factor in the history of Judaism. Insofar as Palestine did adjust itself quickly to the new conditions, it is the Pharisees who deserve the credit, as Renan pointed out,[113] for they had already organized their religious life round a center other than the temple, namely, the synagogue. But it was also under the auspices of the Synagogue that work had been done during the preceding centuries toward the mission to and conversion of the gentiles. And again, the people who carried out this work had been the Pharisees, or at any rate Jews whose religious ideas and ideals corresponded very closely to theirs. The Sadducees, proud representatives of traditional orthodoxy and conformism, had made no attempt to proselytize. The Zealots, with their blind hatred of foreigners, were even less capable of such a move. The only proselytism they knew was the proselytism of violence; like that of the Sicarii, who, even after the defeat in A.D. 135, continued their fanatical practice of waylaying people on the road and giving their victims the choice of being circumcized or having their throats cut.[114] It was the scholars alone who took up the prophetic vision of an enlarged Israel and tried to bring about its realization. The gospel tells us this quite explicitly, in Jesus' condemnation of the Pharisees. We shall return to this later, when we deal at length with the question of proselytism and its survival after the destruction.[115]

It has been customary to see the Pharisees as the representatives of strict legalism and thus to conclude that they cannot have displayed any interest in apologetic, since this would accord badly with their contempt for foreigners. Such a conclusion goes a very long way beyond the evidence. It completly misunderstands the complexity of the Pharisaic movement and underestimates the extent to which it developed during the course of the centuries.

The Pharisees exerted themselves considerably to erect between Jew and gentile a barrier of rules and observances, but these did not by any means prevent them from trying to lead gentiles over that very barrier and turn them into Jews.[116] Opposed as they were to the kind of compromise with paganism the Sadducees allowed themselves, the Pharisees were far more concerned than their rivals to convert pagans from their idolatrous ways. The liberalism of the priestly caste was the liberalism of religious indifference and political opportunism. The religious "establishment" was concerned mainly to commend itself to the Romans and to make an accommodation with them. The Pharisees, by contrast, were inspired by a genuine and lively faith and felt the need to communicate it. Among the Pharisees the sectarian spirit did not exclude strong missionary tendencies.[117] In this respect they were by no means unique among religious sects. Those who knew themselves to be the chosen people reacted to outsiders in one or other of two ways: with contempt, or with active sympathy. Both reactions can be seen in Pharisaism. Some Pharisaic scholars display one attitude and some the other. But at the beginning of the Christian era the sympathetic reaction was certainly widespread. "Love thy fellow creatures, and draw them near to the Torah,"[118] is the watchword attributed to Hillel. Thus did the consciousness of his own superiority impress on the Pharisee a commanding obligation. It was Israel's duty to be the teacher of the nations.

It has been stated time and time again that after A.D. 70, and even more after A.D. 135, Israel turned away in disgust from the world outside and from its civilization. Renan writes: "Hated and despised by the world, Israel more than more turned inwards on herself. *Perishuth*, 'unsociability,' became a safety requirement."[119] We have here a rather too simple view which Renan himself was later to correct and to state more guardedly.[120] His second thoughts have not always been taken sufficiently to heart.

It is useful to distinguish at this point three different entities: Rome, the political power; the pagan inhabitants of the empire, and especially those of Palestine; and Greco-Roman culture.

For the Roman power that was the cause of their unhappy condition the Jews had very little affection. They did not bear their domination well, and they prayed daily to God to deliver them from it.[121] The bitterness increased after the destruction of the temple, and the suppressed hostility toward "Edom" broke out occasionally, as it did under both Trajan and Hadrian, in explosions of exasperated Messianism. But the events of 135 were the end. The ringleaders were not agreed among themselves, any more than they had been in A.D. 66, and the Jewish authorities occupied themselves throughout the events that followed in trying to maintain good relations with Rome. Whether their feelings inclined them in that direction or not, diplomacy dictated that they assume a conciliatory attitude. Johanan ben Zakkai obtained permission from the Romans to open the academy at Jabneh. R. Gamaliel II acknowledged their supreme authority over Israel.[122] We know for certain that after the end of the second century the Patriarch was installed officially.[123] And the friendship that existed between R. Judah I and "Antoninus" (which probably means Caracalla) is well known.[124]

Toward the pagans alongside whom they lived the attitude of the Jews varied from frank aversion to an open friendliness that sometimes issued in actively charitable behavior. On this matter too we have an illustration from a highly respected rabbi. It was said of R. Johanan ben Zakkai that no one could ever greet him first, not even a pagan in the market.[125] Similarly, the family of Gamaliel "maintained it as their principle, in their dealings with gentiles, to care for their poor, to greet them politely, even when they were engaged in idolatrous worship, and to pay their last respects to their dead."[126] Opportunism? In part, no doubt, it was. All the same, it is clear that the spirit of Hillel did survive the disaster and continued to inspire at least some in Israel.

The Jews did not confuse the Roman empire with the civilization whose carrier it had become. The Jews were far from unanimous in their rejection of the material and spiritual manifestations of Greco-Roman culture. The evidence of the synagogues with images is sufficiently telling in this regard. There is other evidence in plenty, which it would serve no useful purpose to relate.[127] Famous rabbis, such as R. Gamaliel, for example, frequented pagan baths, without taking offense at the statues of pagan gods with which such places were decorated.[128] R. Judah I, the compiler of the Mishnah, learned Greek, and had a fondness for the language.[129] The Patriarch Judah II not only moved the seat of the Sanhedrin from Sepphoris to Tiberias, which was a town with a large pagan population, but adopted for himself the style of living of a Roman dignitary.[130]

In fact there coexisted within Judasim after A.D. 70 and 135 the same two attitudes as had existed before. One was narrow, intolerant, and isolationist, the other open and broadminded. It was only by slow degrees that the former came to be dominant. It was not born of the disasters, but rather, it was this attitude itself which produced the disasters by encouraging the revolts that led to them.

The destruction of the temple and finally of the city not only made certain of the victory of the Pharisaic party within Judaism but brought another consequence in its train. To be a Jew had always meant, and still did mean, attachment to an essentially simple creed. It involved the affirmation of monotheism and the observance of the moral and ritual law. Now, some of the ritual laws could not be observed except in Jerusalem. They had been laid down in an age when there was scarcely any question of proselytism or of expansion of any kind, when the context of Judaism was purely national and Palestinian. Those of the diaspora, both proselytes and Jews by birth, had from the beginning regarded themselves as exempt from such laws by force of circumstances. In particular, all prescriptions that related directly or indirectly to the temple worship remained for the diaspora a dead letter.[131] In putting the emphasis on the application of the law to individual conduct rather than on the solemn ritual of the one sanctuary, the scholars had already provided the Jews outside Palestine with a religious ideal adapted to their situation, and offered to pagans favorably disposed toward Judaism a reasonable basis on which they might accept conversion. By making their religion in this way more personal, less closely bound up with geographical accidents and such external contingencies, they had weakened its national and particularist character.

When all this has been said, the temple still remained one of the foci of Jewish religious life. The more zealous Jews of the dispersion, including even proselytes, made it their ambition to make the pilgrimage to Jerusalem in order to participate at least once in their lifetime in the fullness of Jewish worship. At the great annual festivals Jews "went up" en masse to the Holy City from the four corners of the civilized world.[132] A Catholic living in Rome is not essentially in any better position than a Catholic living in any other province of the Church. Moslems living in Mecca have no real superiority over other Moslems, and this in spite of the value attached to the title of *Hajji*. For in the case of both Christians and Moslems the basic acts of worship are the same, whether performed in the holy city or in some other place. But among the Jews a real difference existed between those of Palestine and those outside. For the one, participation in the ceremonies of the temple was habitual, for the other exceptional or altogether impossible. Attendance at the temple was in fact only one element in the inequality, for residence in Palestine conferred, of itself, certain advantages.[133] In fact, if not in theory, those of the dispersion were second-class Jews and were often regarded by the Jerusalemites with a certain contempt. There can be little doubt that the contentions that in Christianity's early days beset the Hebrews and the Hellenists reflect antagonisms that were already deeply rooted in the parent Judaism.[134]

This inequality came to an end with the destruction of the temple and the abandonment of the cult, and with the upheaval in Palestine that accompanied it. All the Jews found themselves reduced to the same condition. Those of Palestine were at first, after Hadrian's war, forbidden to enter the capital on pain of death,[135] and even later the only privilege that remained to them was that of being able to weep occasionally at the ruins of the sanctuary.[136] Palestine was no longer their land. For the others, the non-Palestinians, the temple never had stood for anything of much positive value. Most of them not only lived but had been born among gentiles. They were separated from the land of their fathers, many of them by hundreds of miles, and had mostly had no opportunity to visit it. On the religious life of people such as this, the disappearance of the temple could have no radical effect, for that life had long been organized on lines that left the temple little place. But the destruction of the temple, by removing the differences between the Jews of Palestine and those of the dispersion, strengthened the unity that was given to Judaism by the Pharisees' triumph.[137] From this point of view it would scarcely be paradoxical to say that the disaster was a good thing. It represented a gain that was sufficiently great to be put in the balance against all the dire effects of the catastrophe, and that, if it did not outweigh them entirely, forbids us to emphasize those negative effects too much. Harnack says outspokenly: "The destruction of the temple did not, in reality, overthrow anything at all. It may be considered as a positive force shaping the course of the history of Jewish religion. And when pious Jews, contemplating this event, found the ways of God incomprehensible, they were mistaken."[138]

2

The Aftermath: The Diaspora

καὶ κατὰ πᾶν κλίμα τῆς οἰκουμένης τὸ διὰ προσευχῆς
καὶ λόγων ἀναπέμπεταί σοι θυμίαμα.
Apostolic Constitutions, 7, 33, 2

I

It is by no means certain that the Jews of the period were as
unanimous in their reactions to the events of A.D 70 and 135 as
Harnack assumes. Up to now we have looked only at Palestine. What
makes the reactions of the diaspora Jews all the more interesting to
analyze is that they were without doubt far more numerous than their
Palestinian brethren.

When the Third Sibyl makes her statement that not only the whole
earth but even the sea is full of Jews[1] she is making use of poetic
exaggeration. Philo must be recongized as speaking in the same
hyperbolic vein when he says that the Jews make up half of the
human species.[2] If it stood alone we should automatically ascribe to
the same national pride the witness of Josephus: "For there is no
people upon the habitable earth which have not some portion of Jews
among them."[3] However, when we find a similar statement supported
by a quotation from Strabo we are inclined to take the boast more
seriously: "Now these Jews are already gotten into all cities, and it is
hard to find a place in the habitable earth that hath not admitted this
tribe of men, and is not possessed by them."[4] The evidence of
literature, archaeology, and epigraphy provide the most telling
commentary on these claims.

Juster has been able to assemble an impressive list of Jewish
commuinities within the Roman empire.[5] Some are not of much
importance, but together the Jewish communities of Egypt alone
quite certainly add up to several hundred thousand.[6] The Jews of
Rome were numbered in tens of thousands. A figure for the world
population of Jews is difficult to arrive at, but at least there is some
agreement about the likely proportion of Jews in the population of the
Roman empire. Juster's estimate is about seven percent, or six to
seven million in a total population of eighty million.[7] Lietzmann, who

agrees with Beloch in suggesting a total figure of fifty-five million, nevertheless agrees with Juster's percentage.[8] Bonsirven suggests one-twelfth, i.e., about eight percent.[9] These figures mostly refer to the first century. At that time Palestinian Jews were a minority of the world Jewish population, and have been so ever since. There were about half a million of them, thinks Lietzmann.[10]

This imbalance between the numbers of Palestinian Jews and the Jews of the diaspora came about through the terrible wars of Titus and Hadrian, which significantly reduced the population of Palestine, while the diaspora not only maintained its old population but had added to it a new influx of Palestinian expatriates. It is true that between the wars the diaspora itself in some localities suffered considerable reduction in numbers. The war of extermination carried on by Trajan wrought frightful havoc among the Jews of Egypt, Cyprus, and Cyrene.[11] Nevertheless, it seems to me unlikely that this was enough to restore the balance in favor of Palestine when that balance had been so severely upset.[12] Some idea of the importance of the Jews, and of their cultural and religious influence in the Roman empire, can be gained by comparing their position in modern Europe. Modern Europe, including Russia, has a population of about 500 million, and of this total the Jews constituted, before this century's outbreak of anti-Semitism, no more than two percent, at most.[13]

Now, the large figures arrived at by most modern students of the subject do not only include those who were Jews by birth, and the dispersion did not owe its superior strength to them alone. In the total are to be reckoned a considerable number of proselytes, though in what proportion it is impossible to say. The figures certainly include those who had become thoroughgoing converts, who were proselytes in the fullest sense.[14] The comparison of the percentages of Jews in modern Europe and in the Roman empire would appear to confirm this analysis. The discrepancy between the two figures may be explained by the history of the Jewish people since those days, a history that has been tragic throughout. But in face of the amazing vitality of this prolific people, it is an explanation that is probably inadequate. If between the two periods the total number of Jews has increased so little, and if the proportion of Jews to non-Jews in the population has fallen to such an extent, it could be in part because of the change in the nature of Judaism which has taken place in the interval. In the earlier period Judaism was to a considerable extent made up of proselytes, but when she renounced her missionary efforts she ceased gradually to attract outsiders and no longer grew except from within.

We are probably justified in assuming that the diaspora as a whole did not, except in the most indirect and remote way, feel the repercussions of the Palestinian crises. With the exception of a few odd centers of unrest (such as, for example, Cyrene, which after A.D. 70 suffered some agitation by Zealot refugees from Palestine)[15] the Jews in most areas outside Palestine played absolutely no active part in the troubles. It is not even certain whether they were much involved emotionally in what happened.[16] In Palestine itself feelings were mixed, and even the Pharisaic leaders managed without much difficulty to adapt themselves to the new state of affairs. It is therefore hardly surprising that Jews of Rome and Carthage, Alexandria or Antioch should be still less moved by events that did not in the least affect them personally.

The status of Judaism in the diaspora did not change after A.D. 70, and even after A.D. 135 the only thing that affected the diaspora materially was the short-lived edict of Hadrian that prohibited circumcision.[17] Judaism remained, as it had been before, a legitimate and protected religion. The conditions of religious life for the Jews of the dispersion were no more affected than was their legal status. Insofar as the disappearance of the temple altered their situation at all, it altered it for the better.

The loss of the temple first of all removed the inequality we have already noted, between the Palestinian Jews, able to keep the whole law, and those outside Palestine, able to keep only part of it. Now that they were on an equal footing with their Palestinian co-religionists the Jews of the dispersion were much better placed in their relations with the gentiles. For Jewish universalism the temple was an obstacle and a hindrance. It was a forceful reminder of the connection between the Jewish religion and the territory of Palestine. It was a continuing witness to the national character not only of the cult, but of the whole religious tradition. In destroying Jerusalem the Romans forcibly dissociated the Jewish religion from the Jewish state, for manifestly the former continued to exist whereas the latter did not. In this the Romans in the long run did Judaism a service. Bouché-Leclerq says very rightly: "Far from overthrowing Judaism the destruction of the temple of Jerusalem relieved it of the embarrassment of the cult, giving it thereby a new vigour and making its apologetic task much easier."[18]

So then, while the Palestinians found their national pride seriously hurt and were deprived of their religious advantage over the diaspora, the Jews of the diaspora beheld the triumph of a kind of religion that was peculiarly their own. This was the religion that the Pharisees had nurtured in Palestine but that so well met the needs of Jews separated from their land.[19]

The Judaism of our period was composed of two elements that are in appearance, though only in appearance, contradictory, viz., rigorism and liberalism. It is against the background of diaspora Judaism that they can best be understood, for it is this situation that gives them their character. It is there more than anywhere that rigorism is defined by reference to its opposite. When the rigorists turned Judaism into a strict set of rules, they did so with the intention of protecting it from dilution by the surrounding syncretism. Rigorism was an attempt to safeguard Judaism's originality. But having taken this precaution, Judaism was then able to open its doors withoug fear to all kinds of outside influences and to allow in the realm of doctrine some very daring innovations. The characteristics of Pharisaism, unity and adaptability, were ones it already shared with Hellenistic Judaism. Thus, in this matter also, the differences between Palestine and the diaspora were smoothed out by events. The victory of the Pharisees was at the same time the victory of the Jews of the dispersion.

There is therefore some reason to believe that the Jews of the dispersion did not, on the whole, feel too deeply distressed at the destruction of the temple. Those of Jewish birth may have found their national pride hurt, as did the Jews of Palestine. They may also have felt irritated and insulted by the obligation that was put on them of paying the cult tax to Jupiter Capitolinus.[20] Their religious life, however, was not affected. This was, of course, even more true of the proselytes. For them no doubt the events of A.D. 70 and 135 were unhappy ones, but they did not amount to irremediable disaster.

It is not impossible that in certain Jewish circles these events were seen, indeed, in a more positive light, and were actually greeted as signs heralding new and better days. Already some thinkers in the diaspora had interpreted cultic observances allegorically. They had proclaimed the primacy of the spirit over the letter; of the moral law over the levitical legislation; of humility over sacrifice. Among them the message of the great prophets found a particularly receptive audience.[21] It is also possible to see here and there movements of thought and of piety that are clearly anti-Jerusalemite. The Essene community, as we know it from the Dead Sea scrolls and from the earlier-discovered Damascus Document, repudiated sacrifice and the temple cult as a whole, and this in spite of the fact that the priesthood was recognized by the Essenes and played a prominent part in the ordering of their community life.[22] The pseudo-Clementine writings, whose basically Jewish structure is clearly discernible under their

Christian varnish,[23] likewise reject sacrifice.[24] The diatribe against the temple that the book of Acts puts into the mouth of Stephen expresses, it would appear, not a new specifically Christian reaction, but the opinion of a party within Hellenistic Judaism.[25] But in comparison with normative Judaism, even the Judaism of the diaspora, all these movements appear to be somewhat unorthodox. It was a synagogue of Hellenists who took the initiative in the movement against Stephen.

It is true that the more daring allegorists went so far as to declare that the literal content of the ritual laws was of secondary importance. It is also true that there were those who regarded the cultic tradition as having distorted the true religion of their fathers. It is significant, however, that Philo, while he retains the allegorical method and approves of many of the results that are arrived at by its means, nevertheless takes good care to dissociate himself from extremists of both kinds. For himself, he stays faithful to the details of the actual observances, though this attachment may well be more sentimental than rational.[26] It was in any case difficult, as long as Judaism's firm connections with Jerusalem and its temple remained, to take up any other position without running the risk of putting oneself outside Judaism altogether. But once the temple had been removed by God's own will, it was easy for Alexandrian Judaism not only to make claims that would previously have been regarded as heterodox, but to see itself, in so doing, as representing the most authentic Jewish line of tradition. It could announce with confidence to all men of goodwill the advent at last of the religion of the spirit.

We are not, in out attempts to assess the mentality of the Jewish diaspora, reduced to mere speculation. Literary, epigraphical, and archaeological evidence exists that throws light on the thinking of the diaspora during the Christian era and shows us what were its basic characteristics.

The Fourth Sibylline Book is fundamentally a Jewish work, published after the eruption of Vesuvius in A.D. 79.[27] The attitude it takes toward the recent distresses of Israel is a very interesting one. It mentions them in a simulated prophecy, but very briefly, and almost in passing. Jerusalem, in fact, is only mentioned in a single long couplet, a very moving one, about the principal Greek cities that have been threatened with terrible dangers. It finds mention between "poor Corinth" and "poor Antioch," and is referred to in the same terms as they. "To Solyma [Jerusalem] too the evil blast of war shall come from Italy, and shall lay in ruins God's great temple."[28] Moreover, the responsibility for the disaster is laid not so much on the Romans as on the Jews themselves, for, "confident in their folly, they shall cast godliness to the winds, and commit hateful murders before the temple."[29]

The author's idea of the cult is too spiritualized for him to take his distress over the destruction of the temple to extremes. "For He [God] has not as His habitation a stone set up in a temple, dumb and helpless, a bugbear of many woes to mortals. But He is one whom none can see from the earth, nor measure with mortal eyes, seeing He was not fashioned by mortal hand. With all-embracing view He beholds all, yet Himself is seen by none."[30] We are reminded of Paul's discourse to the Athenians. Of course, what the author is attacking here is primarily the pagan temples. Yet the argument is well in accord with a polemical tradition that was developed by Jews against Jews. This tradition is easily exemplified in the prophets: "With heaven My throne and earth My footstool, what house could you build Me, what place could you make for My rest?"[31]

The conclusion can scarcely be resisted that this condemnation of idolatry implies a tacit criticism of the Jerusalem cult. In making this criticism, the author simply adds his assent to God's own condemnation, which could be read in the events themselves. And by making his criticism in this particular fashion, he avoids the risk of scandalizing even the most irascible of his fellow Jews. Once the Jews' own sanctuary was destroyed, he could without offense praise those who "disown all temples and altars, vain erections of senseless stones, befouled with constant blood of living things and sacrifices of four-footed beasts."[32] Only the pagans remained addicted to the use of temples and altars. The Jews, willy-nilly, no longer used theirs. It was all the easier to assert that to worship truly was "to look to the great glory of the one God," to abstain from murder, unjust and fraudulent gain, perverse desires and adultery, and from "the hateful and hideous abuse of males."[33] Here we have the true prophetic tradition, vindicated by events: οὐ θυσίην, ἔλεος δὲ θέλει θεὸς ἀντὶ θυσίης.[34]

Attitudes of this kind were perhaps less unusual in the aftermath of the crisis of A.D. 70 than the paucity of texts might lead us to imagine. As we have already seen, even among the Talmudic rabbis there appears here and there the idea that prayer, individual or corporate, was a superior form of worship to that provided for in the temple. And these were people who on the whole had something to lose by the disappearance of the official cult. Such opinions were bound to be even more common in the diaspora. Listen again to Justin, who was very well acquainted with the Jews of his time. In a controversy about the cult he says to Trypho: "And until now do you say in your love of controversy, that God did not accept the sacrifices in Jerusalem in the case of those who were called Israelites and dwelt there then, but that

He has said that the prayers of those persons of that race who in truth were then in the dispersion did please Him, and that He calls their prayers sacrifices."[35] This testimony is doubly curious. Trypho tacitly accepts the prophetic indictment of the sacrificial cult, which the Christians found so congenial. Yet he refuses to identify the sacrificial cult with Judaism and to accept the condemnation of the one as a condemnation of the other. Bloody sacrifice is in his eyes merely a degraded form of the true sacrifice, which is prayer. But, and this is the most interesting point, the order of merit in which he places the two forms of cult is extended to the two sorts of Jews, respectively, who practice them. And in so doing he audaciously reverses the order in which the two categories were traditionally placed. The diaspora, hitherto regarded as second-class Jews by comparison with those of Palestine, he treats as the religious élite of Judaism. It is no longer a privilege to live in Jerusalem, but on the contrary a dangerous servitude.

What we see in Trypho's words is therefore more than simply an answer to Christian arguments. The answer to the Christians is there, certainly. It consists in the assertion that Judaism not only could but must survive the destruction of the temple. But the words quoted also embody the proud response of the Jews of the diaspora to Jerusalemite pretensions. It is not difficult to imagine how the destruction of the temple must have reinforced this attitude; an attitude that without doubt was there already. The Jews of the diaspora were thus able to meet the Christians on the common ground of an optimistic interpretation of the disaster. They shared the view that it was part of God's deliberate purpose. But for the Christians the event could only be understood in connection with Christ. It was the result of Jewish blindness. Traditional Judaism was condemned by God because it had rejected the Messiah. The destruction of the temple was no more than an additional piece of evidence for that condemnation.[36] For the diaspora, on the contrary, the destruction of the sanctuary explained itself. It was the natural climax of a long development, of a process of refinement begun by the prophets. It marked the inauguration of spiritual worship.

I do not claim that these views were widely recognized among the non-Palestinian Jews. The mass of the faithful doubtless had arrived at no such clear and comforting estimate of divine providence. It is sufficient that these views were expressed by some, and that is beyond dispute. It is interesting to note that in pagan opinion, even informed opinion, there is little evidence of any knowledge of the Jerusalem cult. To gentiles, Judaism looked like a religion without images or sacrifices, a spiritual religion, whose external, cultic element was reduced to its simplest expression. They seem to have been entirely unconscious of the fact that in the recent past it had been quite otherwise.

Nil praeter nubes et caeli numen adorant, says Juvenal. Tacitus is more explicit. He emphasizes the Jewish belief in the uniqueness of God, but overlooks the traditional belief in the uniqueness of the sanctuary. *Judaei mente sola unumque numen intelligunt; profanos qui deum imagines mortalibus materiis in species hominum effingunt; summum illud et aeternum, neque imitabile, neque interiturum. Igitur nulla simulacra urbibus suis, nedum templis, sistunt.*[37] The temples mentioned here are evidently the synagogues. Of the one building that really deserved the name Tacitus makes no mention at all in this connection. He does mention it elsewhere on a number of occasions, and he gives a description of it, but he never considers it worthwhile to point to the fundamental distinction between the temple, properly so called, and the simple *proseuchai.*[38] Among the gentiles writing after A.D. 70 Julian is practically alone in emphasizing both the importance of the sacrificial cult in the ancient religion of Israel and the similarities between this worship and the pagan rites. He even attempted to revive it by restoring the temple.[39] But the accurate knowledge of Israel's religious past that Julian displays is of a very bookish kind. He owes it to his biblical education rather than to any familiarity with Jews or Judaism. Plainly, his emphasis on the cult has little in common with current opinion among the Jews of the diaspora. That opinion is reflected by Josephus when he writes (this at a time when the sanctuary was no longer standing): "There ought also to be but one temple for one God; for likeness is the constant foundation of agreement. This temple ought to be common to all men, because He is the common God of all men."[40] "Common to all men" the real temple never was, except in a very theoretical way. If the Jews of the dispersion did not exactly rejoice at its destruction, neither did they (taking them as a whole) make themselves too miserable about it.

The destruction does not seem to have affected significantly their relations with the world around them. It is quite certain that in Palestine the events of A.D. 70 and 135 prompted, at the time, anti-Roman and antipagan feelings. Yet one must not exaggerate the magnitude of the phenomenon, even among the Palestinians. It involved in the main those Jews who were already resentful of foreign domination and who repudiated any compromise with gentiles, with either their culture or their way of life. These were people such as the Zealots and their sympathizers, the very people who had fomented the insurrection and were, in A.D. 70 as in 135, largely responsible for the catastrophe.[41] Josephus condemns these elements among the Jews and unhesitatingly proclaims his support for the Romans. Not a few of his compatriots followed his lead. Now the Jews of the diaspora had even less reason than the majority of Palestinians for altering their basic feelings towards the gentiles. Their relations with them remained exactly as they were, good or bad according to the local situation. On the whole, if anything, relations improved.

The Roman authorities, for their part, never dreamed of implicating the whole of the diaspora in responsibility for what happened in Palestine.[42] Once Palestine, the center of chronic unrest, was pacified, the empire had no reason to persecute Judaism or the Jews in general, and had no desire to do so. With the final disappearance of national independence, the result the Romans desired seemed to have been achieved and the political problem resolved. Far from marking the inception of policies hostile to the Jews, the crises of A.D. 70 and 135 were quickly followed, as we shall see, by a return to the traditional benevolent policies from which the Jews, particularly in the diaspora, had always benefited. These benefits they had always earned by their loyalty. Very shortly after A.D. 70 Israel saw itself represented even in the court of the Flavian emperors in the persons of Berenice, Agrippa II, and Josephus.[43]

On the other hand, as far as pagan reaction to the Jews was concerned, a new factor had entered the situation, which made for rather more peaceful relations and which made the gentiles less disposed to outbursts of anti-Semitism. This new factor was the appearance of Christianity. As the new religion expanded, it focused ill-will and hostility on itself. Labriolle expresses it nicely when he says that the Jews benefited from the "transfer of animosity."[44] Labriolle, when he uses this phrase, is speaking of literary polemic, but it is just as apposite as a description of the reactions of the masses.

Among the sentiments the pagans express it is even possible to detect a new and more positive note. Little by little the old anti-Semitic spirit gives way, especially among the educated classes, to a distinct sympathy, nourished by a common hostility to the common enemy. When Celsus seeks in his controversy with Christians the assistance of a Jew, he is led to do so by purely tactical considerations. He does not really think much better of his temporary ally than he does of Christians, and the contempt he feels for Christianity rebounds against the Jews, of whom he is sharply critical.[45] He is prepared to credit Israel with the antiquity of its traditions, but not very much more.[46] This rather involved attitude is not characteristic of later authors, who have a much simpler approach. The notion of an appeal to ancient tradition begins to look like common ground, and there are hints (perhaps no more than hints) that it might be made the basis of a united front for the forces of conservatism against upstart, revolutionary Christianity. The clearest indications of advances made toward Judaism are among certain eastern writers, disciples of Plotinus. Porphyry, in particular, is very appreciative of Judaism.[47] He explicity includes Israel among wise and pious peoples, and he recognizes Israel's God as the Lord of creation. He approves of the Jewish food laws. Moses is for him an undisputed authority. Iamblichus has similar attitudes. Iamblichus attempts to produce a definitive system of pagan theology and among the oriental elements he inserts into his basic schemes are some Jewish ones. Accompanying these intellectual developments there are corresponding political ones. Particularly after the time of the Severi, imperial goodwill toward the Jews came to be more openly and clearly expressed.[48]

Pieces of evidence such as the Dura Orpheus allow us to conclude, in default of documentary proof, that the Jews did not always remain deaf to these calls. It is at any rate certain that the Jews of the diaspora did not respond in any churlish spirit. Even in the immediate aftermath of the Palestinian catastrophes it is very unlikely that the dominant feeling toward the gentiles was one of bitterness for the destruction of the temple and the city. As far as the Jews of the dispersion were concerned these were the same gentiles who left them in peace to carry on their normal business and to practice their religion as they chose.[49] When any hostility did show itself it was usually hostility toward Rome and her empire, not toward Greco-Roman civilization. The evidence of the Sibylline Oracles is relevant again here.

When the Jewish writer puts his discourse into the mouth of the Sibyl he is not merely obeying literary convention. He is motivated by Hellenistic ideals, the ideals we find so clearly expressed in Philo, and is attempting to create a synthesis between values derived from the Bible and those of Greek culture. He reacts to the crises of his time not only as a Jew, but also as a Greek. His attitudes are quite different from those expressed in the apocalyptic tradition of Palestine. The evils that have befallen Judaea are only one small part of a larger whole, one episode in a great drama. This larger drama involves all humanity, but in particular, it concerns all the Hellenistic east, of which the Jewish prophet feels himself to be firmly part. We have already seen how he is moved to pity by the fate of Greek towns and countries in just the same way as by the fate of Jerusalem and Palestine. The Fourth Sibyl weeps over poor Sicily, poor Corinth, and unhappy Laodicea; over Antioch, Cyprus, and beautiful Myra.[50] The Fifth likewise enumerates in its threnody the cities of the Hellespont and of Asia Minor, of the Archipelago and of Greece.[51] Certainly they are all of them victims of their own sins. It is idolatry and immorality that have called down on them the divine chastisements. But the Jews too have sinned and are engulfed in their punishment. This at least is how the Fourth Sibyl understands it. The Fifth is a little more nationalistic.

But the prophet's attitude to the Jews is not significantly different from his attitude toward the Greeks. In both cases it is pity that is the dominant emotion. Anger is reserved for the barbarians of the east, Assyrians or Thracians, who are destroyers of civilization, though they are instruments of divine wrath. There is anger also for Egypt, and for Rome, whose empire, dominating the world by force, is in the same succession as that of the Assyrians and Medes, the Persians, and the Macedonians.[52]

The prophet wastes not pity on Rome.[53] The woes he predicts for her he predicts with some relish. Rome is doubly guilty. Not only is she impious and sinful herself, but she has persecuted the righteous. In this respect she has emulated the cities of Egypt, which are citadels of idolatry and which initiated the practice of discriminating against Jews.[54] The Fifth Sibyl announces the same punishments on Rome as on the Egyptian cities, and gives the same reason for them. The chastisement of Rome is extended in scope to take in the whole of Italy, "on whose account many faithful saints of the Hebrews have perished, and the true people."[55] By Rome all abominable things are held in honor. The author ransacks his vocabulary for words with which to belabor this city, which is a "wicked city, most ill-starred of all...frenzied and poison-loving," with "a bloodthirsty heart and a godless mind."[56]

In the eyes of the Fourth Sibyl the eruption of Vesuvius, following so shortly after the fall of Jerusalem, is the forewarning of divine anger, "because they shall destroy the guiltless race of godly men."[57] The final catastrophes are about to unfold. Rome will, in a manner of speaking, perish by her own hand. Her own evil genius will make common cause with the barbaric hordes of the east when Nero, who is exiled but still alive, again crosses the Euphrates and ravages his own land. Rome will then remain alone in that once-splendid isolation in which she so gloried. In her pride and ignorance she has set herself up against the power of God. Her punishment will be frightful. "Didst thou not know what God can do and what are His designs? But thou hast said, I am unique, and none shall being ruin on me. But now God whose Being is for ever shall destroy thee and all of thine.... Remain, O lawless one, unique, and, wedded unto flaming fire, make thine house in the nether region of Hades where laws are not."[58]

The fundamentally Jewish inspiration of these predictions is obvious. They spring directly out of the events of A.D. 70 and they make sense only in the context of Israelite eschatology. But the literary form and literary techniques used are Greek. Even the themes are Greek in part. Jewish resentment of domineering Rome sometimes found a sympathetic ear among both Greeks and Orientals, and without doubt the animosity expressed in the Oracles of the Sibyl represents the feelings of at least a considerable part of the Hellenized east.[59] All the wisdom and liberalism of the imperial polity did not completely succeed in making the subject peoples forget that originally they were defeated peoples, and that the marvelous edifice of empire rested, in the last analysis, on brute force. The east knew perfectly well that it was the cradle of civilization which Rome had borrowed, and sometimes found it galling to be dominated by a pupil who, without this contribution from the east, would have remained half-barbarian. That this suppressed bitterness should have found its most articulate expression through a Jewish pen, mixed with the bitterness of the chosen people itself, is a convincing demonstration that the ties that bound the best of the diaspora Jews to the cultural heritage of Hellenism were not broken.

II

The universalistic idea was still alive and active. It is expressed in the Sibylline Oracles with an unequivocal clarity. If the immediate cause of the Jewish calamities was to be found in crimes committed against God and His people, $ἀθέσμων\ ἕνεκα\ ἔργων$,[60] their ultimate purpose was the conversion of sinful humanity, "that they may know the eternal immortal God who sits on the clouds."[61] God does not punish arbitrarily, not out of a desire for vengenance, nor even out of a concern for strict justice. The evils that befall men are meant to act as warnings, to turn them from sin. Only repentance can avert the final cataclysm. According to the Fifth Sibyl, "the godlike heavenly race of the blessed Jews"[62] will be spared these trials, because they have always put their confidence in God. They will be the first to benefit in the divine restoration that will follow the disasters. These disasters will in any case not overtake Palestine, whose glory the prophet celebrates in an enthusiastic couplet.[63] He is proud of his people, proud of the past magnificence of Zion; and he rejoices in its further glory. It is at Jerusalem that the kingdom will be inaugurated. The Messiah will remake the city, which will shine brighter than the stars. He will rebuild the temple, one tower of which he will raise so high that it will reach the clouds and be visible to all men, "so that all the faithful and all the righteous may see the glory of the invisible God."[64] For all men, as creatures of God, are called to the true faith.

It will be seen how Jewish national pride, far from leading to particularism, is here found consonant with universalism. The privileges that belong to the Jews carry with them a commanding duty, to be a light to the nations, to gather up on God's behalf all the righteous. And this will even include the righteous among the Egyptians, though the Sibyl has scarcely finished denouncing the offenses of which the Egyptians are guilty. A priest of Isis is to give the sign for their conversion. He is to build in Egypt itself a pure temple, where sacrifices will be offered to the one true God.[65] Whether or not we have here an allusion to the temple of Onias (the question is disputed),[66] the idea expressed at least portrays a Judaism liberal enough to renounce the dogma of the unique sanctuary. The primacy of Jerusalem is still upheld, and indeed insisted upon, yet it is admitted that God may be worshiped anywhere, by anybody, by the traditional rites of the Israelite cult.

The universalist inspiration is even more apparent in the fourth book. As we have already seen, there is here no question of any restoration of the temple or of the sacrificial cult. The book opens with a profession of faith in the spirituality of the invisible God, who is best honored by prayer and by doing good. The author has very little to say about the Jews. It is humanity as a whole that he is interested in. The revelation he offers is essentially a moving appeal for conversion, which is the only thing that can avert the divine wrath. "O ill-starred mortals, let not these things be. .... Wash your whole bodies in ever-running rivers, and stretching your hands to heaven, seek forgiveness for your former deeds, and with praises ask pardon for your bitter ungodliness."[67] Then God may change his mind and spare the righteous. The poem comes to its climax not with the vision of a restored Jerusalem but with a picture of the resurrection of the dead and the judgment of all men. The godless will then be cast into the infernal abyss, while the godly, *all* the godly, will live again on earth by divine grace under the gentle light of the sun. Happy is the man who shall live in that day![68]

It is not enough simply to assert that Jewish universalism did survive the events of A.D. 70. It is necessary to go on and describe more exactly what kind of universalism it was. For when Jews took their message to gentiles, they could adopt either of two distinct policies. They could ask the gentiles to accommodate themselves to the framework of traditional Judaism, which was asking of the gentiles a considerable effort; or they could choose to make the effort themselves and offer to the gentiles a broader, more adaptable kind of Judaism, one more suited to the gentiles' intellectual and religious needs, and more open to influences from outside. Traces may be found of universalism of the former type up to and including the period of the Talmud.[69] The latter type found its classical expression in Philo. The message of the Sibylline Oracles has most in common with the cosmopolitan spirit of Philo, but it is difficult to be more precise about their theology. This is due to the nature of these prophetic writings, for they allow little place for doctrinal discussion. But their theology is certainly distinctive. When the Fifth Sibyl calls on God (in a hymn whose liturgical affinities are manifest), it is not the God of Israel whom he invokes but the Lord of the universe and of all creatures, "The immortal God, the father Himself who is from everlasting, the chief of all, the true, the king, the father, sustainer of souls, the great eternal God."[70] But this is rather slight evidence on which to base a description of the writer's theology. If we wish to be properly enlightened on the thinking of diaspora Judaism, we must have recourse to other literature.

The Fourth Book of Maccabees, falsely attributed by tradition to Josephus, is a valuable help. It is also useful in that it takes us a little further into the Christain era. Whereas the Fourth and Fifth Sibylline Oracles are later, though probably not very much later, than A.D. 70, the Fourth Book of Maccabees comes in all likelihood from the second century A.D. The most recent commentator on the book, M. Dupont-Sommer, places it after Trajan's Jewish War, at the beginning of the reign of Hadrian. His arguments seem to me convincing.[71] He seems also to be on firm ground when he concludes that what we have in 4 Maccabees is in fact a sermon, delivered at Antioch at the tomb of the seven brothers. Antioch was the actual place of their martyrdom and M. Dupont-Sommer suggests that the local synagogue paid to them particular devotion.[72] I can do no better than follow his analysis of the work.

The Fourth Book of Maccabees is cast in a form dictated by the rhetorical conventions of the period. It presents itself as a philosophic treatise, φιλοσοφώτατον λόγον. It takes as its subject the sovereignty of reason over the passions, and illustrates its theme by the example of the Maccabaean brothers.[73] What it means by "philosophy" is the knowledge (γνῶσις) of things human and divine,[74] but this knowledge presupposes piety (εὐσέβεια) as its indispensable corollary. It works through pious reason (ὁ εὐσεβὴς λογισμός).[75] "Philosophy and religion are one and the same thing."[76] The true wisdom is thus equated, or perhaps confused, with Judaism. The author defines it as "instruction in the law" (ἡ τοῦ νόμου παιδεία).[77] All wisdom, all knowledge, and all understanding are to be found in the law. "The two ideas are so closely bound up together in the thought of pseudo-Josephus that sometimes, in his argument, where one expects 'philosophy' or 'reason' the word that actually appears is 'the law.' This is a substitution which comes so naturally to the author that he is probably not even aware of it." M. Dupont-Sommer goes on to describe the author as "a genuine philosopher and an authentic Jew,"[78] a judgement in which we may happily concur.

Even while the author is preoccupied with specifically moral problems he does not regard the law solely as a rule of conduct. He makes use of a concept elsewhere widely recognized in Judaism at this period and regards it as a revelation to the intellect.[79] It gives specific teaching about God: that He is the creator, a supremely wise and just Lawgiver; that He is also power (δύναμις) and above all, providence (πρόνοια). The revelation was given to Israel, a people dear to God, enshrined in the Torah, and was entrusted to Moses. But this Torah is nothing but a transcription of the natural law. Between Torah and natural law there is no discrepancy at all, for "the Creator of the world, as a lawgiver, feels for us according to our nature."[80] If God in this way feels for men it is because He is truly their Father and because "there is between them a genuine bond and a community of nature."[81]

In this writer's view, therefore, man carries about in himself a divine spark, that is to say, his soul, incorruptible and immortal. Of the doctrine of the resurrection of the body, favored by the Pharisees, he betrays no knowledge. One may in fact deduce that he rejects it, for though he keeps fairly close to 2 Maccabees, he pointedly deserts his model when it comes to any mention of resurrection.[82] The blessed immortality that is promised to the righteous is life in God. In this eternal life, which is the fruit of piety, the body can have no part.

We have here the clear influence of pagan philosophical speculation though pseudo-Josephus has combined into a strange amalgam the ideas of a number of competing schools. It is under Platonic influence that he has spiritualized the normal Jewish conception of the afterlife. But it is to Pythagoreanism that we must look for an explanation of another feature of his eschatology, his belief in an immortality amongst the stars. This belief is seen in the following passage, which is addressed to the mother of the seven martyrs. "Not so majestic stands the moon amid the stars of heaven as thou, having lit the path of thy seven starlike sons into righteousness, standest in honour with God; and thou art set in heaven (ἠστέρισαι) with them."[83] And when the author speaks of "the all-holy sevenfold companionship of brethren in harmony," who "as the seven days of the creation of the world do encircle religion,"[84] though there are some uncertainties in the text, it is apparent enough that he has the same sort of speculation in mind. In contrast with all this, the author's theory of the passions betrays a debt at once to Aristotle and to the Stoics. The high estimate of reason and understanding is one that is common to ancient philosophers generally, though as far as this aspect of the matter is concerned our author's closest afffinities are with the Stoics.

It is the business of the mind to control the passions. The mind is the "sacred guide." God has "set the mind on a throne" and to her has entrusted the law.[85] "The mind" or "reason," which is connected with wisdom, is designated by our author by the word λογισμός. The Stoics and Philo opt for the word λόγος in describing the same concept and it is not apparent why 4 Maccabees prefers a different term. The life of wisdom, which is the goal to which *logismos* is directed, is a life of victory over the passions. Reason achieves its end by supporting the virtues, the chief of which is prudence. Besides the four cardinal virtues, pseudo-Josephus recognizes several others, including the specifically stoic virtue of endurance (ὑπομονὴ). This is the virtue which so excellently sustained the Jewish martyrs. Their stand was exactly the kind of which the Stoics approved, and it was by virtue of endurance that reason carried them through. The Fourth Book of Maccabees is also familiar with the idea of the royal nature of virtue, a thoroughly Stoic idea. It is in fact the only kind of royalty he recognizes, for he has no time for Messianism. Equally attributable to Stoicism is the belief in universal brotherhood and the solidarity of the human race, of which there are distinct echoes in the book. It is this which gives the very noticeable universalistic slant to the writer's Judaism. Men are all equally susceptible to suffering, for they are all formed of the same elements. Reason forbids that they should bear ill-will to each other. "Reason through the law is able to overcome even hatred, so that a man refrains from cutting down the enemy's orchards, and protects the property of the enemy from the spoilers, and gathers up their goods that have been scattered."[86]

"Reason through the law..." This is where the author reveals himself to be not a philosopher only, but a genuine Jew. His achievement is that he manages to be just as much one as the other. The occasion for his works is the celebration of the heroism of men who were, above all, Jews. They incurred martyrdom precisely because they were determined at all costs to obey the dietary laws. In extolling the martyrs, 4 Maccabees extols ritual laws that are as peculiarly Jewish as anything could be. He defends these laws as grounded in reason, for God "has commanded us to eat the things that will be convenient for our souls, and he has forbidden us to eat meats that would be to the contrary."[87]

Here we see the nature of the bulwark which prevents a Judaism as Hellenized as this from being lost altogether in the paganism to which it manifestly owes so much. This bulwark is one of ritual observances. Protected by this barrier, Judaism kept safe its own originality. Because of this, it could with impunity lay itself open on the intellectual plane to influences of all kinds. The legalistic nature of this kind of Judaism, which was essentially an orthopraxy, explains the prominence given within it to moral problems, and its close links with ethics, for its connections with paganism are as much through pagan ethics as through purely metaphysical speculations.

On the other side of the events of A.D. 70 the Fourth Book of Maccabees carries on without interruption the intellectual and religious tradition of the diaspora. It most closely resembles the writings of Philo, though of course it has peculiarities of its own.[88] There is as yet no hint of retrenchment among the Jews, no trace of antigentile rancor. Neither does the book betray any interest in the future of the chosen people as a whole, or in their restoration to temporal dominion. It is manifest that the destiny of individuals and their survival in the hereafter matters far more to our author than any possible earthly kingdom of a Palestinian Messiah. There is reason to believe that 4 Maccabees is a communal document, i.e., the record of a discourse delivered in a synagogue. If this is so, we may take it that the document reflects the outlook of this synagogue. In such a case the value and significance of its testimony will be apparent.

Its testimony does not stand alone. This work of pseudo-Josephus, emanating from Antioch, finds echoes in the Jewish apologetic writing which is embedded in the pseudo-Clementine romance.[89] This is a work that is undoubtedly of Alexandrian origin.[90] Here again the Judaism that is reflected is of a singularly enlightened kind, and full of proselytizing enthusiasm.

The writing presents us with a discussion between Clement, here represented as a Jewish proselyte, and three opponents, Apion, Annubion, and Athenagoras. The discussion takes place in a garden setting and according to the other conventions dear to Greek dialogue. The author by this means delivers himself of a close-packed and often very pertinent criticism of pagan rites and beliefs, of mythology, and of philosophical fatalism. He shows himself to be possessed of a thorough knowledge of classical authors. Having been himself brought up on the thought of the Greek philosophers, notably Carneades, Poseidonius, Chrysippus, and Aristotle, he comes naturally to represent his own religion as a kind of philosophy. "Although I have examined many doctrines of philosophers, I have inclined to none of them, excepting only that of the Jews."[91]

Jewish philosophy consists in the doctrine of divine unity, "introducing One as the Father and creator of this world, by nature good and righteous; good, indeed, as pardoning the sins of those who repent; but righteous, as acting toward everyone after repentance according to the worthiness of his doings."[92] This doctrine has as its necessary accompaniment the keeping of the moral law. For to think rightly is not enough. It is necessary "to understand and do the things that are pleasing to God."[93] Paganism is not only false but fundamentally and inescapably immoral. This is abundantly demonstrated by the dubious adventures ascribed in mythology to the immortals. The author interprets the myths according to the principles of Euhemerus.[94] He contrasts these scandalous stories with the kind of literature that young people ought to be encouraged to read. He defends marital fidelity. He also defends very early marriage, as a safeguard against the running wild of adolescent passions.[95] This is the teaching of "the holy law of the Jews. It is by virtue of the righteous judgment of God that the law was given, and that the soul receives always, sooner or later, exact retribution for its deeds."[96] This author is no more interested than pseudo-Josephus in the resurrection of the body. He makes no reference to the ritual law. What he is putting forward is wisdom for pagans, and he puts it forward in an idiom they can understand and in a form acceptable to them.

In this work we have an especially remarkable example of Jewish-Hellenistic thought. It gives the impression of being fairly close in date to the work of pseudo-Josephus. Its mention of Apion forbids us to place it any earlier than the end of the first century A.D.[97] Its incorporation into a Christian work (which is the form in which it has come down to us) makes it hard to suggest a date later than the end of the second. Bousset has made the point that a work of this nature could scarcely be conceived after Judaism had abandoned its proselytizing efforts.[98] But the whole problem is to know exactly when this activity did come to an end. It certainly went on after A.D. 70. Why should A.D. 135 have put a stop to it? If in the last resort, and for lack of exact evidence on which to base a conclusion, we suggest a date for this writing a little before 135, as Schmidt and Cullmann do,[99] it is simply out of reluctance to bring its date too far beyond the lifetime of those whom it features as the principal protagonists in the dialogue. The memory of them is likely still to have been fresh at the time when the work was published. It is safer to argue thus than from any assumed knowledge of the development of ideas within ancient Judaism.[100]

We have so far examined literary remains emanating from Antioch and from Alexandria. Rome has left us no literary texts, but there are at least some textual remains of other kinds that help us to fill in the picture.

F. Cumont has drawn attention to a curious fragment of a sarcophagus that has been preserved in the Terme Museum at Rome.[101] It is of unknown origin. On this sarcophagus fragment we have a design of a type commonly found in Roman funerary sculpture. It represents the spirits of the seasons, and below a central medallion bears a picture of youths treading grapes in a winepress. The medallion itself is flanked by two winged figures of Victory and would in the ordinary way be expected to contain a bust of the deceased person. It does not. The place of the bust is occupied instead by a seven-branched candlestick. The whole Jewish-pagan assembly looks like a jumble of unrelated pictures. But in reality it is not so. It is susceptible of being interpreted as a coherent whole. Its different parts all illustrate aspects of immortality and the life to come. This theme unites at once the image of the wine, which according to Dionysiac ideas is the liquor of immortality, and the symbols of the seasons. The cycle of nature provides an image of human destiny. The candelabrum fits into the symbolic scheme, for according to Philo, it represents the eternal light of the stars and the seven planets, just as the twelve loaves of the shewbread in the temple cult represent the twelve signs of the zodiac.[102] Appearing as it does on a sarcophagus in the place normally reserved for a picture of the deceased, it signifies that the dead has been called to eternal life among the heavenly constellations. It corresponds closely to the pagan type of decoration in which the bust of the deceased appears within a circle of the signs of the zodiac. It bears witness therefore to the existence of a Judaism that has been curiously penetrated by pagan religious ideas.[103]

I do not think that it is necessary to read this interpretation into all the numerous instances in which the seven-branched candlestick appears on Jewish funerary monuments. F. Cumont, who originally made this suggestion, withdrew it in the revised edition of his article.[104] In most cases the candlestick indicates simply that the dead man was a Jew, just as Christianity is indicated nowadays by a cross, and in ancient times by the fish or the chi-rho monogram. It is true that there are instances in which the candlestick seems to take on a magical or apotropaic significance. This is a point we shall come back to.[105] But in the case which we are at present considering Cumont's explanation carries conviction, especially when we take into acount the archaeological context. It certainly illuminates the passage in pseudo-Josephus that speaks of the holy hebdomad of brothers being set in heaven.

The accuracy of this interpretation is confirmed by a second piece of evidence. In the catacomb at Monteverde was found a marble plaque on which the candelabrum is pictured. Over the candelabrum is written the word ACTHP.[106] This is evidently the name of the dead person, Esther. It is a name common enough among Jews of the period. But it is also evident that the name has purposely been written near the symbol in order to make clear what interpretation is to be placed upon it. The double meaning the word will bear has allowed this. We are not far from the ἠστέρισαι of pseudo-Josephus.

As Cumont has indicated, the catacomb of Monteverde has provided us with still more evidence of Jewish liberalism, i.e., liberalism both in doctrine and in iconography. A second set of representations of the spirits of the seasons has been found there, and, on the cover of a sarcophagus belonging to a child, the statue of the dead child, in repose. This last is of a type very common in pagan art but very unusual in a Jewish context.[107] Cumont has also noted another sarcophagus in the Terme Museum on which traditional Jewish emblems appear side be side with theatrical masks. Such masks are well known as part of the apparatus of the cult of Dionysus.[108] Do these different monuments belong to people who were Jews by birth, or to converts? It is impossible to say, and in any case it does not much matter. The interesting thing is their undeniably Jewish character and the fact that they appear in a necropolis that we have no reason at all to suspect was heterodox, and whose monuments presumably could not have been erected without the permission of religious authorities. The amount of evidence available from one part of the Roman empire or another, evidence both in the form of literary documents and of archaeological remains, demonstrates convincingly that we are not dealing with exceptional cases or aberrant examples.

The Monteverde catacomb is without doubt one of the oldest Jewish necropolises in Italy.[109] The monuments found there can hardly be later than the end of the first century. The sarcophagus fragment that bears the candlestick is reminiscent in the style of its decoration rather of the second century than the first, but its stylistic characteristics are not so clearly marked that we can be dogmatic on this point. Now the Fourth Book of Maccabees is almost certainly earlier than 135, and in all likelihood the same is true of the pseudo-Clementine literature. These different pieces of evidence therefore have a bearing on the period between the two wars, though not directly on the period with which we are at present concerned.[110] They do demonstrate that the events of A.D. 70 did not significantly affect the position of the diaspora with regard to Greeco-Roman thought and culture. This is an important point to have established.

It must be freely admitted that the disaster of A.D. 70 was more serious than the later one, and was felt more grievously by the Jews. The second catastrophe did little more than add the finishing touches to the disastrous effects of the earlier one. As far as the religious life of the Jews was concerned, the important happening was the destruction of the temple. The principal cause of the outbreak of the Bar Cochba revolt was Hadrian's proscription of circumcision. And since this was repealed almost immediately by his successor (at least as far as the circumcision of native Jews was concerned), this second crisis involved no permanent consequences for the Palestinians that were not already involved by the former one.[111] For the diaspora it is all the more certainly true that the events of A.D. 135 had no serious repercussions which had not already been felt as a result of A.D. 70.

III

In order to strengthen the argument we need positive evidence for the period after 135. That is to say, we need documents that can be dated without question after the Bar Cochba revolt. Such documents do exist.

At the end of book 7 of the Apostolic Constitutions, in chapters 33–37, appears a collection of five liturgical prayers.[112] Bousset, who first drew attention to them and has commented on them, has demonstrated irrefutably that in origin and character they are authentically Jewish.[113] Stripped of their superficial and rather clumsy Christian additions, which have ensured their preservation in the work in which they are now embedded, their Jewish character is clearly apparent. This discovery is of comparable importance to that of the Dura synagogue, though of course it is much less spectacular. Both these discoveries throw fresh light on the end of Hellenistic Judaism.

The prayer in chapter 35, which is the first one with which Bousset deals, faithfully follows the pattern of the *qedushah* as it has been preserved in the synagogue liturgy to this day (in the *yoser* and the *shemoneh ʿesreh*[114]). In the general arrangement of the petitions, in their content and style, and in the choice and groupings of the biblical quotations, the prayers in the Apostolic Constitutions are so very similar to those of the Jewish liturgy that there can be no possible doubt about their Jewish connections. Since it seems to be established that the *qedushah* goes back, in origin, to the second century, it is likely that this is the date of origin of our text.[115]

The prayer in chapter 36 is a Sabbath prayer. It begins with a eulogy of the Sabbath, which has been established for meditation on the laws of God and for the joy of souls, that they "might come into the remembrance of that Wisdom which was created by Thee."[116] A very clumsy Christian addition identifies this Wisdom with Christ. As Bousset points out, even by the standards of the author of the Apostolic Constitutions himself this has heretical implications, for he elsewhere describes Christ as γεννηθέντα οὐ κτισθέντα.[117] Another couplet, just as easy to identify as an addition, extols the festival of the resurrection, the Lord's day. After this the Jewish text resumes its eulogy of the Sabbath in a quite normal way and enumerates the other "sevens" that God has instituted. It does this in exactly the order that is followed by Philo in his *De Septenario*,[118] viz., the Feast of Weeks (seven weeks), the Seventh Month, which is specially sacred, and the seventh and fiftieth years.[119] The text ends with another tacked-on piece of Christology. It asserts the superiority of Sunday to all other festival days. In doing so, it breaks the unity of the passage and makes nonsense of it.

Chapter 37 is a prayer of supplication to God, who has taken pity on Zion and on Jerusalem by raising in the midst of her the throne of David His servant.[120]It cites the examples of just men of ancient times whose prayers were listened to. This list is similar in outline to that in the *Ordo Commendationis Animae*. It begins with Abel and goes down as far as the Maccabees, Mattathias and his sons. The original prayer makes no mention of any New Testament character, though Christian interpolators have attempted to rectify this. A similar list appears in chapter 38, and this too has been retouched by a very inexpert Christian hand.

The prayer in chapter 34 is one of the most important in the collection. It is a prayer of thanksgiving for the benefits of creation. For much of its length it exhibits connections with a passage in the so-called Clementine liturgy of chapter 8 of the Constitutions.[121] We are manifestly faced here with two different redactions of the same basic text. This basic text is a combination of the material given in the first chapter of Genesis with formulae borrowed from Hellenistic philosophy, principally from Stoic cosmology. The former of the two redactions we have before us in thoroughly Jewish, and we must therefore postulate a Jewish origin for the basic text.

Finally, chapter 33 presents us with another synagogue prayer. In it the deity is invoked at the same time as "the king of gods, who alone art Almighty, and the Lord, the God of all beings," and also "the God of our holy and blameless fathers, and of those before us; the God of Abraham, and of Isaac, and of Jacob."[122] The similarity to the *tephillah* is again perfectly clear. And besides, no one but a Jew could speak of the father of his race in these terms: ὑπέρμαχε γένους ᾿Αβραάμ, εὐλογητὸς εἰς τοὺς αἰῶνας.[123]

Pursuing his studies through the rest of the Apostolic Constitutions, Bousset was able to identify in another passage in the seventh book Jewish catechetical material for the instruction of proselytes. This material has been clumsily Christianized by the addition of a Trinitarian confession of faith.[124] On the basis of this identification, Bousset goes on to advance the hypothesis that the collection of prayers already analyzed was also intended primarily for proselyte instruction, to set before the proselytes the principal types of synagogue prayer. This theory is reasonable enough. Finally, by comparing the two texts, he demonstrates that the influence of this same collection has been decisive in determining the shape of the great liturgy that appears in the eighth book, the so-called Clementine liturgy. This is by no means the least interesting part of Bousset's exposition, but since it is relevant mainly to the history of Christianity itself and its liturgical usage, we need not stay to consider it. For our present purpose it is quite another point that demands our attention. Bousset, following a suggestion of Rahlfs, showed that some of the biblical quotations in the collection are based not on the Septuagint text but on that of Aquila.

We know that Aquila[125] was concerned above all to produce a literal translation of scripture. With this in mind, he sought an exact Greek equivalent for every Hebrew word. He replaced the words of the LXX, where necessary, with other Greek words which in his opinion more accurately reflected the sense of the original. But he was not always content with this. Where adequate Greek words did not exist he coined new ones specially for the occasion. Now in one passage of our prayers the writer is directly inspired by Gen. 15:1–18. In this passage, where the LXX has the word διαθήκη our text reads συνθήκη,[126] a word that is entirely characteristic of Aquila. It is found in the prayers in close conjuction with the word ὁραματισμός, which Rahlfs has recognized as one of Aquila's own creations. It corresponds to a verb ὁραματίζεσθαι, which Aquila coined to translate the Hebrew *hazah*, to distinguish it from the more common verb *ra'ah*, which regularly appears in Greek as ὁρᾶν.

There are one or two other indications in our text that the writer was using the version of Aquila. Nevertheless, most of the quotations are still from the LXX. This use of two different versions is only susceptible of two possible explanations. All the quotations were originally made from Aquila, but the Christian compiler corrected most of them, overlooking a minority. Alternatively, and this is the explanation that Bousset himself favors, the LXX quotations were mostly added by the Christian compiler and only the Aquila citations stood in the Jewish original. Whichever may be the correct explanation, the important fact remains that Aquila was used. This fact not only confirms the Jewish origin of the prayers but provides us at the same time with a *terminus post quem*. Aquila was a disciple of Akiba, a contemporary of Hadrian. His translation cannot have been imposed on the diaspora all at once, and immediately after its publication. The collection can hardly be earlier, therefore, than the middle of the second century. To be able to say this with such certainty makes the collection of imcomparable value for our estimate of the mood of the diaspora after A.D. 135.

The Judaism that this collection of prayers reveals to us is as open, as receptive, as broadly liberal and universalistic as ever it had been in the past. It is true that the pride of the chosen people finds quite open expression. The Christian redactor adds without any shame at all: Ἰσραὴλ ἡ ἐπίγειός σου ἐκκλησία—ἡ ἐξ ἐθνῶν.[127] Yet this reasonable pride contains no element whatever of contempt for the gentiles. The prayers celebrate God's goodness to Israel and the heroes of her past, but thanks are also rendered for the entire creation, and especially for the creation of mankind. This broader gratitude is expressed in a hymn which in its style is very reminiscent of Stoic hymns, and which is heavily impregnated with Hellenistic piety. All mankind, of which the Jews feel themselves to be firmly part, is called to share divine knowledge and divine life. "Man was disobedient, ... yet didst thou not destroy him for ever, but laidst him to sleep for a time, and thou didst by an oath call him to a resurrection."[128]

Man, having been made in the image of God and endowed with an immortal soul, is the crown and consummation of creation: he is the ornament of the world: κόσμον κόσμου. He is the thinking being, the citizen of the universe.[129] In this connection Bousset calls attention to a passage in Philo in which it is said that the Jewish High Priest makes his prayers of supplication and thanksgiving not only for all humanity, but also for the natural elements, earth, air, fire, and water, because the whole universe is regarded as his parish.[130] It is legitimate to doubt whether such formulae ever did appear in the ritual of the Jerusalem temple. Yet Philo has not invented this detail. He has in all likelihood derived it from the liturgical practice of the Hellenistic synagogue, whose usage our prayers faithfully reflect.

Alongside this "cosmopolitan" conception of humanity, this concern for the brotherhood of mankind and of the universe, goes a correspondingly liberal theology. The idea of the cult that is here subscribed to is a completely spiritual one. There is not a single reference to the temple sacrifices, or to the possibility of their future restoration. The glory of Jerusalem is spoken of in the past tense.[131] Henceforth the only sacrifices acceptable to God are sacrifices of prayer. These are the sacrifices to which Trypho attached importance, the sacrifices that are offered in every place by the diaspora and in which they take such pride. καὶ κατὰ πᾶν κλίμα τῆς οἰκουμένης τὸ διὰ προσευχῆς καὶ λόγων ἀναπεμπεταὶ σοι θυμίαμα.[132] This rational, spiritual worship is the only kind that befits the nature of man.

This is because man, like the rest of creation, was made through the agency of Wisdom, a hypostasis of the divine. It is to her that the well-known verse in Genesis refers when it says: "Let us make man in our own image." As the instrument of creation Wisdom is at the same time both the source and the object of that sacred knowledge which is the consummation of the religious life. The Sabbath was created so that men might have the opportunity to attain to the divine wisdom.[133] Like the practice of virtue, the exercise of the intellectual faculties is also an essential aspect of piety. The author indicates the nature of his ideals when he says that God has given to man "rational knowledge, the discerning of piety and impiety, and the observation of right and wrong."[134] Man is an intelligent being (the word λογικός is peculiarly characteristic) and in his intelligence he possesses by nature the means to distinguish righteousness from unrighteousness and to attain knowledge of the divine. By means of intelligence he apprehends the natural revelation inscribed in his heart, and also appreciates that innate natural law of which the written law can convey no more than the echo.[135]

It is in "knowledge," τὴν περὶ θεοῦ τοῦ ἀγεννήτου γνῶσιν,[136] that the religious life culminates. For just as God is the Father of Wisdom, ὁ σοφίας πατήρ,[137] so He is the Lord of knowledge, κύριος θεὸς γνώσεων,[138] and it is through knowledge that one may reach Him. Knowledge proceeds from faith (πίστις) and is an extension of faith. It was faith that led Abraham to the fullness of the divine revelation, afterwards enshrined in the Bible.[139] "Knowledge" (γνῶσις) is a basic term in these prayers, yet it is almost completely absent from the works of Philo, to which in other respects the prayers display numerous and close similarities.[140] It is in Christian literature that one must look for parallels. The use of the term, and the kind of thinking that lies behind it, connect our texts most closely with the epistles of St. Paul. In spite of this, there are differences between the two, for in the prayers knowledge is conceived as something more intellectual, less charismatic, and less mystical than in the Pauline letters.[141] But the similarity is there, and it is noteworthy that the same broadly universalistic spirit can be seen in both.

There is no need to stress any further the importance of these documents. It appears plainly enough from the outline of them that has already been set forward. The conclusions to be drawn from them concerning the history of Judaism are equally self-evident. The existence of this liturgy, Greek in its language and thoroughly Hellenistic in spirit, forbids us from now on "to believe that, shortly after A.D. 70 or at least after 135 Judaism drew itself apart from the surrounding world, renounced the use of Greek in the liturgy and relapsed into the Judaism of the Mishnah and Talmud."[142]

Once more it is necessary to be very clear about the nature of the relationship between the two kinds of Judaism, the very lively Hellenistic kind and the one that, at about the same time, was elaborated in Palestine and found definitive expression in the Talmudic literature. Ought we to treat both of them as representing authentic Judaism? Or should we take Talmudic Judaism as the norm, in which case its competitor must be classed as frankly heterodox or heretical? I have already emphasized that Pharisaism, from which the Talmud directly takes its rise, was always accommodating toward innovations, even quite bold ones. This very Pharisaism, having roots both inside and outside Palestine, was better able than any other movement to hold together the Palestinian Jews and those of the diaspora. It is against this background that we must see the religion that finds expression in the Apostolic Constitutions.

We have no grounds for suggesting that it arose outside the Jewish community. There is nothing in its doctrine that is incompatible with the teaching that came in course of time to be accepted as that of Jewish orthodoxy. If the role it assigns to Wisdom is sufficient to mark it out as heterodox, then by the same token we must refuse to regard Philo as a proper Jew and must similarly reject a large part of the Wisdom literature. And if we proceed in this fashion, what would there be left of Judaism at the beginning of the Christian era? Orthodoxy is not something given a priori. It is something that comes into being, that is progressively elaborated. At the point in history at which our inquiry has now arrived it has not yet found in Judaism its definitive form. The conception of Wisdom to which our texts give voice is so far from heretical that it does not even begin to erode the idea of the divine unity. Wisdom is created by God. If the scholars of the Talmud did eventually repudiate this kind of speculation, it was, as I hope to show later, in reaction against Christianity and Christology. They retained the ideas of the *shekhinah* and the *memra,* which are corresponding ideas, though they are somewhat pale reflections of the hypostatic conceptions favored in the diaspora.[143]

There are, moreover, quite definite affinities between traditional Judaism and the religion that lies behind our collection of prayers. The angelology of the prayers is in complete conformity with that approved by the Synagogue. The heavenly beings are creatures of the one God, whose task is essentially that of offering endless praise and adoration. There is no suspicion of any tendency to make them more than this. It is worth noting, in passing, that Palestinian Judaism itself did not entirely avoid the temptation, dangerous to pure monotheism, to expand the role of the angels, and scholars found it necessary to counteract this tendency.[144] Heresy was by no means peculiar to the diaspora. Furthermore, as we have seen, the prayers express firm convictions about Israel's primacy and attach great significance to the events and characters of biblical history. The legalistic interests of Jewish orthodoxy also find unequivocal expression. The Sabbath and other feasts are eulogized and the importance of the law is affirmed, though it is not so much νόμος, as νόμοι, i.e., both the natural and the written law. Both meditation on and practice of the law is the prime obligation of every Jew.[145] The correspondences between the prayers and the Synagogue liturgy (a liturgy still in use to this very day) are too close and too numerous to be explained otherwise than by a common origin.

Finally, and this is the decisive argument, the use of Aquila's version of the Greek Bible is enough in itself to force us to concede to the community (or communities) that produced these prayers the right to be reckoned orthodox. Aquila's translation was a Palestinian project. If it was not made on the rabbis' own initiative it was at least done with their approval.[146]

The Septuagint came into being in the diaspora, created by the diaspora Jews in order to meet their own religious needs, both liturgical and apologetic. Gradually, however, it became discredited as the Christians took it over and used it in their anti-Jewish polemic.[147] During the first century the diaspora Jews still venerated it as an inspired text, on the same level as the original Hebrew. Philo uses nothing else, and it is from him that we learn that the Jews of Alexandria held an annual festival "to thank God for the good gift so old yet ever young."[148] It is scarcely to be imagined that the Greek-speaking Jews would cheerfully abandon this venerable text without putting up some resistance. It was, after all, hallowed by ancient usage and closely bound up with the history of the Hellenistic Synagogue itself. Schürer compares the position of the LXX in the Hellenistic Synagogue to that of Luther's Bible in German protestantism.[149] That

a Jewish community close in its tradition to the Judaism of Philo
(which is what the community that produced these prayers appears to
be) should abandon the LXX in favor of Aquila is proof of its close
connections with Palestinian authority and its respectful acceptance
of the same.

But if the adoption of Aquila's translation by the Jews of the
dispersion points to the dispersion's increasing respect for the
Palestinian rabbis,[150] the fact that Aquila's translation was ever made
bears its own witness to the attitude of the rabbis to the Greek-
speaking Jews. It shows that for the rabbis these Jews of the dispersion
still counted as an important and legitimate branch of Judaism. The
two groups existed side by side and came to terms with each other,
just as at first Jewish Christianity and gentile Christianity did within
the infant Church. Within the Church it was Jewish Christianity that
little by little came to be rejected by the main body, whereas in the
Synagogue it was Hellenistic Judaism that was rejected. But the
processes of development are closely similar in the two cases. In
Judaism there was as yet no sign of a division. On the contrary,
Palestinian and extra-Palestinian Judaism influenced one another,
the influence being by no means all in one direction. If the diaspora
sometimes seemed to take orders from Palestine there were other
occasions when it also took the initiative. It is interesting to observe,
with Bousset, that when our liturgical collection develops its
speculations about $\gamma\nu\hat{\omega}\sigma\iota\varsigma$ and its relation to $\pi\acute{\iota}\sigma\tau\iota\varsigma$, the basis for the
discussion is a text indubitably taken from Aquila.[151] Thus, at least in
this instance, the new translation did not act as a brake on audacious
speculation, but on the contrary gave occasion for going further than
even Philo himself had done.

IV

The influence of the diaspora on Palestinian Judaism persisted much
longer than the written documents suggest. We come to a period from
which there are no known surviving texts of Hellenistic Jewish
literature,[152] and it is just from this period, as we have seen,[153] that we
have the series of synagogues with images, beginning with the one at
Dura. Once the movement had begun, it was taken up in Palestine,
with rabbinic approval. There was indeed little the rabbis could do in
the circumstances but sanction a development, the impetus for which
had come from outside.

We must be careful, therefore, of exaggerating the opposition
between the dispersion and the Palestinian Jews, or of taking for

granted the passivity of the former. To fall into either error would be to misrepresent the complex structure of Judaism during this period and to overlook its genuine cohesion. This cohesion appears clearly enough in the national and religious institutions of the Jews after A.D. 70.

Supreme authority belonged to the Patriarch.[154] The office existed officially from at least the end of the second century. It came into being as a direct result of the crisis of A.D. 135. The Patriarch was recognized by the Romans, and indeed invested with his authority by them. He was also styled "Ethnarch," and he replaced the lapsed High Priesthood as head of the Jewish people. But he was no High Priest, for the traditional cult had entirely come to an end. Neither was he a real head of state, for there was no longer any Jewish sovereignty in Palestine. He had no real political authority. The dynamic character of the office, hereditary in the family of Hillel, may have given the Patriarch some of the appearance of such authority, but it had no actual substance.[155] His powers, strictly defined and controlled by Rome, excluded anything that might encourage anyone to make him a rallying point for an attempt to restore the Jewish state. On the other hand, though the Patriarch lacked jurisdiction over the territory of Palestine, the authority he did possess extended not only over Palestinians, but over the Jews of the diaspora as well. "A sovereign without territorial power, he was in some sense the spiritual leader of all the Jews of the Empire."[156] So says Juster. This was an era in which, more than ever before, a Jew was defined by his religion, and the Patriarch was the head of Judaism, wherever it was practiced.

The authority of the Patriarch was no vague primacy. Besides the power to levy a tax, and to decide religious questions, the Patriarch, in his capacity as head of the hierarchy, had the right to nominate the religious functionaries of the Jewish communities and to prescribe what powers they were to possess. To the Roman authorities he represented the Jewish religion and the Jewish nation and was responsible for them. He was also, at least in theory, the protector of all the Jews of the empire. The Jews of the dispersion could not ignore him or refuse to obey him, if only for reasons of self-interest. For in the eyes of Rome it was recognition of the Patriarch's authority that defined Judaism. Neither communities nor individuals were allowed the privileges of Jewish status except insofar as they submitted to Judaism's recognized head, who was the only official intermediary between Israel and Rome.[157]

In the Jewish community everything was organized round the Patriarch, and this centralization created a strong bond between him

and the diaspora. The Sanhedrin, which had been reconstituted after
A.D. 70 as a purely religious academy, was made subordinate to him
and served as his council.[158] Patriarchs of provinces and heads of local
synagogues derived their powers from him. The Patriarch, for his
part, occasionally undertook pastoral tours abroad. Above all, he
appointed his "apostles." The tangible sign of the union between the
diaspora and the Patriarch was the payment of the Jewish tax, the
aurum coronarium which every Jew paid annually into the hands of these
"apostles." But the apostles were very far from being mere tax
collectors. They did act in a financial capacity, but also, and more
importantly, they were genuine *missi dominici,* the essential organ of
contol and coordination between the central authority and the
dispersed Jews. As the Patriarch's assessors, they supervised in his
name the leaders of the local communities and the teaching that was
given. They carried and explained his encyclical letters, and
transmitted his directives concerning the calendar and the dates of the
feasts. They organized the struggle against heresies, and in particular
against Christianity. They were the representatives of Jewish "ultra-
montanism" and were largely responsible for imposing on Judaism
the uniformity that Talmudic orthodoxy required.[159]

Ancient Judaism has occasionally been described as a Church, and
the use of the word has given rise to abundant controversy.[160] I do not
deny the validity of the objections to the application of this term to
Judaism, the chief of which is the national character that is inherent
in Judaism from the beginning and which persists throughout history.
It may nevertheless be said that if the description "Church" could
ever at any period be applied to Judaism, then this period with which
we are now concerned would be the chief candidate. For it was during
this period, after the definitive end of Jewish autonomy in Palestine
and of the Jerusalem cult, that the national aspects of the Jewish
religion were least in evidence.

For a time Judaism did possess the distinguishing marks of a
Church. It was a religious society, organized round a common faith
and common rites, under the auhority of a single head and a
hierarchy deriving from him. Looking at its Hellenistic branch, we
find it to be universalistic, both in its outlook and in its membership.
Something of this universalism was discernible even in Palestine, as
we shall shortly see.

The native Israelites seem to have been regarded, because of the
very fact of their having been born Jews, as a sort of aristocracy, whilst
the proselytes were ranked lower. And doubtless this continued to be
so, in spite of the leveling effect of the conditions that prevailed after
the fall of the second temple. But the differences between the two

ought not to be exaggerated. The difference was accentuated to the extent that the native Israelites stood for a strict and complete observance of the law and the proselytes for a reduced demand. Yet it is also true that just as an uncircumcised Jew who did not practice his religion was regarded as unworthy of the name, so a proselyte who was circumcised and carried out the religious obligations in full was accepted into the chosen people on an absolutely equal footing.[161]

If one was to belong to the community of Israel, blood was not everything. It would be more accurate to say that it was circumcision that made a Jew. Circumcision was the seal of the covenant, the sign of election. Its significance has frequently been misrepresented. "When speaking of Jewish nationalism people generally tend to see it as a kind of religious racialism, and to imagine that the rite of circumcision provides them with grounds for this view. Now the existence and importance of this rite prove precisely the opposite, that Jewish thought was not racialist ... Any man, of whatever race, may by submitting to this rite become a full member of the chosen people. In consequence, circumcision not only may but should be considered as a mark of the universalism of the Jewish religion."[162]

As we shall see, this seems to have been the opinion of at least some of the rabbis, even in Palestine. The texts we have already studied entitle us to conclude that in the diaspora it was the prevailing opinion. Apart from this, if it is allowable to contrast the two parties, Palestinian and diaspora Judaism, it must only be in a very general way. If we are to assert that universalism flourished especially in the diaspora and particularism especially in Palestine, we must go on to say that this contrast is complicated by all kinds of individual reactions and particular circumstances.

On each side of the dividing line there are particular communities or particular individuals who stand apart from their surroundings and who seem to belong more naturally in their attitudes and approaches to the opposite camp. As far as the diaspora was concerned, pagan observers were impressed sometimes by the proselytizing enthusiasm of the Jews and sometimes by their lack of dealings with their gentile fellows. Sometimes, indeed, they are impressed by both at once, for the sectarian spirit frequently managed to reconcile itself with proselytism.

Judaism never ceased to oscillate between the two poles of universalism and particularism throughout the whole length of its history. Once the Talmud had become for the Jews the sole recognized norm, particularism triumphed. From the second century this development, initiated in Palestine, was well established. It had behind it a tradition much older than had the mission to the gentiles.

We must not be in too much of a hurry to concede victory to it. Hellenistic Judaism maintained up to this point enough vitality to enable it to slow down the drift toward particularism, though it did not succeed in halting it. More was needed to cancel out the influence of Hellenistic Judaism than the double catastrophe could provide; more than the growth of Talmudic Judaism. In Palestine itself in the early Christian centuries other influences were at work besides the ones that led to Judaism's retreat into distrust.

In face of the new phenomenon of Christianity, Judaism was still strong, in spite of the national disaster. It was strong in resistance. In Palestine Christian preaching spent itself in vain. And within Judaism itself this Palestinian branch, with its extensions eastward, was the one that was to survive and inherit the future. It was still strong in attraction too. When Christianity came on the scene Judaism was prepared to take issue with it on its own ground, and meet it as another missionary faith. Its evangelistic activities covered the world. Its capacity for expansion was not lessened; in some respects it was actually increased. It seemed to be better equipped than ever for preaching its message to the world.

The battle that was joined was not simply one between two different movements within the one religion, though it had remained in this form for some time. We shall now analyze the evidence provided by Israel itself, and this evidence at least suggests that the conflict should be seen as one between two distinct religions.

3

The Church and Israel

Πάντας δὴ ἐκείνους ἐπὶ δικαιοσύνῃ μεμαρτυρημένους,
ἐξ αὐτοῦ Ἀβραὰμ ἐπὶ τὸν πρῶτον ἀνιοῦσιν ἄνθρωπον,
ἔργῳ Χριστιανοὺς εἰ καὶ μὴ ὀνόματι.

Eusebius, *Hist. Eccl.* 1, 4, 6

I

There is a curious passage in Sulpicius Severus (a passage that has sometimes been suspected of being inspired by Tacitus) according to which it was Titus's hope that his deliberate burning of the temple would extirpate at the same time both Judaism and Christianity: *Quippe has religiones, licet contrarias sibi, isdem tamen ab auctoribus profectas; Christianos ex Judaeis exstitisse; radice sublata, stirpem facile perituram.*[1] It may reasonably be doubted whether at that date the Roman authorities had quite such a clear grasp of the originality and importance of the Church as these words imply. It must also be stated that if Titus did hope to accomplish thus readily the elimination of the two religions he was very seriously mistaken.

For if Judaism survived the destruction of the temple and managed quite well to adapt itself to the new situation, Christianity for its part received a more positive bonus from the event. The originality that Titus is credited with perceiving so early was not fully apparent to the Church itself until after the catastrophe. The two crises of A.D. 70 and 135 were undeniably important to the Church in their ultimate effects. The former helped the Church to achieve autonomy and strengthened its feelings of independence.[2] The latter appeared to Christians as the confirmation of the divine verdict on Israel. From both events the Church's apologetic received a considerable impetus. In attempting to assess Christian reaction, it is as well, nevertheless, to distinguish between Christians of Jewish origin and Christian gentiles.

As far as Jewish Christians are concerned, we are hampered by the total lack of documentary evidence. We possess no document that may with certainty be ascribed to this party and gives us information about their reactions.[3] What we can at least do is to argue from the known characteristics and the basic attitudes of the Jewish Christians. This method enables us to guess with a high degree of probabiliy what their reactions were.

The dominant characteristic of Jewish Christianity was its unshakable attachment to the religious institutions of Israel. The Ebionites, for instance, felt such a strong sense of solidarity with Israel that even the Palestinian disasters could not impair it. Their flight from Jerusalem, a little before the outbreak of the first war,[4] did not damage this sentiment more than momentarily, and perhaps even then in a way that was more apparent than real. Once the crisis was over, many of them returned to the city, or what was left of it. During the time that followed they never ceased to hope for the restoration of the sanctuary, just as their non-Christian fellows did, and with this expectation in mind, they never ceased to observe zealously the traditional rites. Against this attitude curses and ill-treatment were unavailing. Even when Israel itself denied and rejected them, they could not cut themselves off from Israel.

Bearing all this in mind, we are surely right to affirm that, faced with the dramatic events of A.D. 70, their reactions were not fundamentally different from those of their countrymen. Like the rabbis and the apocalyptists, they saw these events as something brought about by God, as a just punishment. Thinking about the reasons for the punishment, they doubtless ascribed it to the sin of Israel, and above all to Israel's sinful rejection of Jesus the Messiah. But they did not therefore concur in the wholesale condemnation of the people. On the contrary, they felt all the more keenly their obligation to deliver the Christian message to their brethren and convert them to the Christian hope.[5]

In estimating the significance of the disaster, the Jewish Christians saw it not as a sign that God had abandoned His people, but rather as a sign that the final cataclysm was near, and with it an imminent change of fortune.[6] The destruction of the sanctuary and city was one of the disasters that would lead to the establishment of the kingdom. The synoptic apocalypse and its developments shed some light on this eschatological expectation, which at this early period was common to Christians of all origins and all shades of opinion. "When you see the disastrous abomination set up where it ought not to be . . . you will see the Son of Man coming in the clouds.[7]

The Jewish Christians knew who this Son of Man was, and this is what distinguished them from the generality of Jews, for whom the Son of Man remained a great anonymous figure. And because they awaited the return of Jesus a great gulf grew up, whether they desired it or not, between them and Israel. They were driven from Jerusalem on the eve of the first war, harassed from time to time by the religious authorities, anathematized in the Synagogue liturgy, and persecuted during the second war by Bar Cochba's troops.[8] This was only to be expected. One cannot serve two masters, or two Messiahs, at a time. In spite of the solidarity they felt, the reactions of the Jewish Christians did not with complete fidelity mirror those of the other Jews. They were regarded as dissidents, sectarians, by both Synagogue and Church. By professing Christianity, as the gentiles did, they had classed themselves as gentiles in the eyes of the Synagogue. The disaster of A.D. 135 seems to have accentuated this rupture.[9]

At this point in history there was not as yet any specifically anti-Christian legislation. The Ebionites therefore, insofar as they were Jews, i.e., because they were circumcized, fell under Hadrian's ban, which forbade any Jew on pain of death to enter Jerusalem-Aelia.[10] The Holy City was no longer their city. Only catholic Christians could return there, for after the war a community of gentile Christians was established in Jerusalem under bishop Marcus.[11] The establishment of such a community, at such a moment, had a certain symbolic importance. It marked the failure of Jewish Christianity, which had been rejected by both Christians and Jews, and it underlined the fundamental incompatibility of Christianity and Judaism. The gentile Christians made their entry into Zion as part of the trappings of Rome, and, taking advantage of the Jews' misfortune, they filled the place hitherto occupied by that rebellious people.

For the Christians the destruction of the sanctuary was a sign of divine anger and both the consequence and the proof of Jewish blindness. It was also a confirmation of Jesus's prophetic authority, for the events of A.D. 70 had been predicted by him. Moreover, it avenged the outrage the Jews had perpetrated against Jesus himself,[12] and by making impossible the observance of all but a fraction of the law, it demonstrated that the convenant was now void and that Israel's day was over. It further strengthened the position of the antilegalists in the face of the Judaizing party.[13]

Nevertheless, these were not the immediate reactions. It seems rather that at the very first the Church as a whole interpreted the disaster in a quite narrowly eschatological way, for all Christians were waiting intently for the parousia. In fact, Christians did not attribute any punitive significance to Israel's sufferings until after A.D. 135. This interpretation first appears in Hegesippus, but rather oddly, he sees the catastrophe of A.D. 70 as punishment, not for the crucifixion of Jesus but for the execution of James. Eusebius, who quotes him, asserts that this point of view is shared by "the more sensible even of the Jews,"[14] and supports his statement by appeal to the alleged testimony of Josephus. Eusebius himself looks at the matter on a broader canvas. He proposes in his history to recount, among other things, "the disasters...that fell upon the whole Jewish nation immediately after the plot against our Saviour."[15] The fate of Israel has been decided by that sacrilegious crime. It accounts for the events of A.D. 70 as well as those of 135; for the destruction, the slaughter, and the dispersion of the Jews. This is the way in which Tertullian[16] and Origen also understand the matter. Origen quotes Josephus, as Eusebius does, but considers it much more reasonable to see the destruction of Jerusalem as a consequence of the crucifixion.[17] Having stated that Jerusalem fell forty-two years after the passing of Christ, he adds: "And we say with confidence that they [the Jews] will never be restored to their former condition. For they committed a crime of the most unhallowed kind, in conspiring against the Saviour of the human race in that city where they offered up to God a worship containing the symbols of mighty mysteries. It accordingly behoved that city where Jesus underwent these sufferings to perish utterly, and the Jewish nation to be overthrown, and the invitation to happiness offered them by God to pass to others."[18] This was henceforth to be the unshakable opinion of the whole of the early Church.[19]

Thus, by the time Hadrian's war was over, entrenched positions had been taken up by both sides. We may guess without too much fear of error that it is around this period that we must look for the beginnings of anti-Jewish polemic among the Christians. This shows itself first in the epistle of Barnabas[20] and the lost dialogue of Ariston of Pella. The rupture between the two religions was then made final by the crystallization of dogma. There was also a significant shift in the balance between ex-Jews and ex-pagans in the Christian community. From the middle of the second century onwards the Christians of gentile derivation made up by far the greater part of the Church. Justin underlines this fact when he speaks of the multitude of gentile Christians and reports them to be more numerous and more faithful than those of Jewish or Samaritan origin.[21] Origen gives us more precise information. Commenting on Revelations 7:4, the passage that speaks of the 144,000 of the elect, he refuses to recognize this as the number of converted Jews, because the figure would be too high. "Those among Israel according to the flesh who have become believers are not very numerous, and one may safely say that they are not as many as 144,000."[22] We must understand this to apply not simply to the moment at which Origen was writing, but to the whole period since the Christian preaching first began. In Origen's time they must have been less numerous still.

From the point of view of Israel, the Church looked like a separate, autonomous body. Not only did it become increasingly gentile in its membership, but the spirit that animated it displayed more and more the marks of Hellenism, and betrayed it as *ecclesia ex gentibus*.

Nevertheless, the problem of the relations with Judaism continued to be raised.[23] The facts of the matter were that Israel still existed, and that she had not abdicated. The disasters in Palestine had not diminished either her vitality or her power to attract. The Church, which claimed to have succeeded her and to have supplanted her did no such thing, but simply existed side by side with her. Now there could not possibly be room for two societies, both of them claiming to be the Israel of God (Gal. 6:16). In the sphere of doctrine, the *Frühkatholismus,* whose main lines were being laid down during the reigns of Trajan and Hadrian, drew both its sacramental concepts and the kind of "pneumatic" mysticism that inspired it from its Hellenistic background. It owed its theology and Christology to Paul, but it was from Judaism that it derived its moralism and the substance of its liturgy.[24] It was again Judaism, the diaspora variety, that furnished it with a pagan clientele, prepared to listen to its message.[25] And from the same source it derived certain elements of its teaching, its method of interpreting the scriptures, and, in the form of the LXX, the text of the scriptures themselves.

This was the clearest sign of all of the connection between Judaism and the Church, the fact that the Church laid claim to the Jewish Bible and sought to apply all its teaching to itself.[26] The Church had done this from the beginning, and not only the Jewish Christian branch of it. St. Paul himself, in asserting Christian independence of Israel, had recourse to the Bible to prove his point. And from that time onwards it was by means of the Bible that Christian apologists refuted Jewish claims.

The importance of the scriptures was enhanced by the gnostic crisis, which occurred practically at the same time as the revolt of Bar Cochba. A fiercely critical approach and a radical dualism led Marcion and the gnostics to reject the Old Testament, which was already the basis of the ecclesiastical doctrinal structure. These heretics distinguished between the message of the Bible and the revelation of Christ and set them one against the other as irreconcilables. In opposition to this the Church affirmed the continuity between them and, indeed, their basic identity. At exactly the time when events were combining to put the two religions apart, the Church by its affirmation of the value of the Old Testament was acknowledging more plainly than ever before its debt to the Synagogue. The Church, then, made the Jewish canon its own, and clung steadfastly to the book that from the beginning had nourished the piety, faith, and thought of the Christian communities. By so doing it did not go so far as to make a united front with the Jews against the common enemy, but it did rehabilitate the Jews by recognizing them as the trustees of the revelation. The Church also came more and more to model its attitudes on those of Judaism. The LXX was accorded the status of an authorized version. Similarly, the priesthood, the system of Church discipline, the revived ritual obligations (which concerned fasting and the keeping holy of the Christian Sunday) showed signs of Jewish influence. They were a demonstration of the Church's claim to continue the true Israelite line and to inherit the promises.

Following this *via media* between the Synagogue on the one side and antinomian gnosticism on the other, and exposed to the criticisms of both, the Church had to defend itself on two fronts at once. Justin not only devoted a copious dialogue to the refutation of the Jews, he wrote another, now lost, against Marcion.[27] His example was followed by Tertullian. Both of them base their defense of this precarious position on arguments from scripture. Other authors were to imitate them in this respect.[28] The anti-gnostic controversy does not concern us here. Instead, what we must do is to discover on what principles the Church based its attitude to the past religious traditions of the Jews, and, passing on from there, what was its attitude to contemporary Judaism.

II

Toward Jewish traditions orthodox Christianity took an attitude of positive approval. The exigencies of the struggle against gnosticism and Marcionism placed close restrictions on its criticism of Israel's institutions. While Christians condemned the Jews for slowness and blindness they recognized that they had received the call of God, and they legitimized Jewish religious institutions retrospectively and in detail.[29] In agreement with Marcion, they believed that the ritual provisions of the Old Testament ought to be understood quite literally. They usually rejected the kind of purely symbolic interpretations that the epistle of Barnabas suggests. When the Lord demanded circumcision of the Jews it was a circumcision of the flesh he had in mind, and not a circumcision of the heart.[30] But in agreement with the Jews they asserted that all these prescriptions embodied the will of the one true God. They did not allow the distinctions suggested in Ptolemy's letter to Flora.[31] This work distinguishes (*a*) commandments that are of divine origin, though their author is not the supreme God, but the demiurge,[32] (*b*) commandments that derive from Moses, which are imperfect, if not downright bad, and (*c*) those which the Jews of ancient times invented for themselves. It is a scandal, and the Jews themselves thought likewise, "that God can even be falsely accused by them that have no sense, of not having always taught all men the same acts of righteousness," and that to these men, "such subjects of God's teaching seemed to be irrational and unworthy of Him."[33] The precepts of the law all have, in Justin's eyes, the same divine origin, and in former times they possessed imperative force. The Church recognizes no break at all in the continuity of the biblical tradition, and its claim as its own exclusive property the entire scripture in which that revelation is enshrined.

What this amounts to is that since the coming of Christ the Jews have forfeited all right to the scriptures. Pseudo-Barnabas writes: "Be not like those who add to sin, and say, 'that their covenant is ours also.' Nay, but it is ours only; for they have lost for ever that which Moses received."[34] St. Augustine relegates the Jews to a role no better than that of a porter. The sacred book was entrusted to them, not for their own use or salvation, but so that they might be its bearers for the service and benefit of the Christians, just as the slave in the library wears himself out by carrying volumes for his master. *Codicem portat Judaeus, unde credat Christianus. Librarii nostri facti sunt, quomodo solent servi post dominos condices ferre, ut illi portando deficiant, illi legendo proficiant.*[35] For having refused to recognize the Messiah whose coming was predicted in scripture by such unmistakable signs, they are condemned to understand scripture no longer.[36] Strictly speaking, it no longer has any meaning for them, for the old and the new covenant illuminate each other. *Novum Testamentum in Vetere latet, Vetus Testamentum in Novo patet* is an affirmation that has continued to be made by Christian theology.[37] To wish to dissociate the two, to refuse to recognize the indissoluble bond between them and the continuity that unites them, to retain only one-half of the diptych, is to beome blind oneself. This is what Marcion did. So, in the opposite way, do the Jews.

But having taken this stand, the Church found that formidable difficulties were involved in maintaining it. The Bible was not a mere repository of proof texts collected for the convenience of Christians. As well as the prophecies, there were the narrative books, which described how the chosen people were guided in their progress through history by the hand of God. And however the Church might deny that Israel's divine vocation was no longer valid, the Bible itself plainly assumed it to be everlasting. And the greatest difficulty of all was this: the tangible sign of the covenant that God had established between Himself and His people was the law, and the Bible codified that law, or rather, the Bible was the law.

Now the Christians were ready enough to recognize the value of the law, for times past. For the present and the future they rejected it as null and void. How could they claim the Bible as their own and yet at the same time empty it of so much of its content? Here we have the whole problem of the relations between the two religions in a nutshell, both the theory of it and some very patent practical implications. Judaism was not dead, and many Christians, including some of gentile background, continued to feel its pull.[38] Over some centuries Christian theology applied itself to find a satisfactory solution. I have no desire at this point to undertake a thoroughgoing history of these efforts, but it is necessary at least to offer a summary of the numerous, diverse, and sometimes contradictory assaults on the problem that were made by early Christian thinkers.[39] These attempts illuminate the positions the two religions took with regard to one another within the period I have marked out for this study.

The problem was not immediately raised for the new Church. The primitive Christian community conceived of no permanent distinction between the Church and Israel, for when the message had been accepted by all the Jews, which was initially the aim in proclaiming it, the two bodies would simply be one. Just as Jesus was identified with the Messiah spoken of in scripture, so the Church would be identified with Israel, an Israel renewed to meet the Messiah's glorious return. The prescriptions of the law thus kept all their validity.[40] Had not Jesus himself declared that not one iota would pass away from the law? The little group of apostolic Christians attempted through their piety to edify the other Jews, and those who were gathered to them from outside Judaism became Jews at the same time as they became Christians. Even when the body of Christians in Jerusalem was broken up by political forces at the time of the war, their thought and devotion continued on traditional lines. After the destruction of the temple, they persisted like the other Jews in observing the law as far as it was still practicable to do so.

The preaching of Stephen, with its attack on the temple, was not followed up.[41] The problem of the law, and the related problem of the connection between Christianity and Judaism, was first formulated clearly by St. Paul, and from him it received at the outset a radical answer. Paul conceives of the religious history of mankind as a vast drama in two acts. The decisive moment in this drama, its turning point, is marked by the death and resurrection of Christ. Paul allows to the Jewish law only a transistory and preparatory role. "The law was to be our tutor until the Christ came."[42] In this sense the law possesses a positive value, or rather, it did possess one. It has positive value for the children, but not for the mature man. The law was given to Israel, and the destinies of Israel and the law are bound up with each other. Both have had a part to play, but their part is now finished. Let the law make no attempt to hang on to life! For "now the law has come to an end with Christ."[43]

This idea, in one shape or another, had a notable career in the development of Christian theology. At the extreme end of the fourth century (taking care not to go outside our period) St. Chrysostom takes up the image of the paedogogos and develops it.[44] What he says, in substance, is this: the law was very well suited to human nature and its needs, but to persist in one's attachment to it even when it has served its turn (παρὰ καιρὸν) is to misunderstand its proper function and its true greatness. A paedogogos only achieves his real object when the young man entrusted to his charge grows to such a maturity of virtue that he passes out of his control altogether. Similarly, the law has so far achieved its ends that we no longer have need of its help. We owe it to the law that we are now capable of embracing a higher "philosophy." He who remains attached to the law forever does not owe it a great deal, but he who, when the moment comes, is able to detach himself from it and rise to comprehend the sublime teachings of Christ has every reason for praise and gratitude, for he has been allowed to pass beyond the pedestrian level of the letter of the law, τῶν ἐν αὐτῷ γεγραμμένων τὴν σμικρότητα.[45]

These two, the letter and the spirit, are already for St. Paul the two principles whose opposition represents the contrast between the new religion and Jewish legalism. "But now we are rid of the law, freed by death from our imprisonment, free to serve in the new spiritual way and not the old way of a written law."[46] The antithesis is expressed in an almost infinite variety of ways and on an almost infinite number of occasions. Sometimes, and this in St. Paul's own writings, the opposite to law is faith, which is presented as that which replaces law. "But now that that time has come [the time of faith] we are no longer under that guardian, and you are, all of you, sons of God through faith in Christ Jesus."[47] Sometimes it is not faith itself that is contrasted, but grace, the source of faith. "Indeed, from his fulness we have, all of us, received—yes, grace in return for grace, since, though the law was given through Moses, grace and truth have come through Jesus Christ."[48] Sometimes it is Christian hope. For "the law could not make anyone perfect; but this commandment is replaced by something better—the hope that brings us nearer to God."[49] Ignatius of Antioch uses the same antithesis, contrasting the old institutions (τὰ παλαιά) with "the newness of hope" (τὴν καινότητα ἐλπίδος).[50]

But these contrasts each represent only one aspect of the truth. Over and above them there is the great contrast between law and Christ. This is the real heart of Pauline thinking on the matter. At the same time as it prepares for Christ the law is in opposition to him. The law is in fact for St. Paul something far more than a mere collection of precepts. We do not misrepresent the thought of the apostle if we recognize it as one of the "powers" that are such a familiar feature of the religious speculations of the period, on a level with the "Wisdom" or the "Logos" of the Alexandrian thinkers. The law, according to Paul, emanates from God and is an expression of His will.[51] "The law is sacred, and what it commands is sacred, just and good."[52]

In spite of its incontestably divine character, the law is nonetheless bound up with sin. "Does it follow that the law itself is sin? Of course not. What I mean is that I should not have known what sin was except for the law. I should not for instance have known what it means to covet if the law had not said, 'You shall not covet.' "[53] The Christian is redeemed by Christ from both sin and law at the same time. He is dead to sin. He is also, by virtue of that very fact, dead to the law. It is not my aim to follow the difficult track of St. Paul's thinking as it is developed in the epistle to the Romans.[54] His arguments are well known, but sometimes appear to be contradictory. It may be said, however, without underestimating the magnitude of what he accomplished, that the apostle did not entirely succeed in rehabilitating for the past the law which he rejected for the present; rejected, that is to say, as good in principle but unfortunate in its practical effects.

If he had been more rigorously logical, more detached from the influence of Pharisaic atavism, he would perhaps have condemned it outright. He comes very near to doing so, as when, for example, he attempts to defend God from any compromising responsibility for the law by attributing its promulgation to angels, through the intervention of an intermediary. "Now there can only be an intermediary between two parties, yet God is one."[55] We are not really very far here from Marcion's radical solution. Marcion, who was very much a disciple of St. Paul, did no more than push the apostle's thought to its logical conclusion.

It is perhaps unnecessary to explain that the argument is a purely metaphysical one. The opposition between the two powers, Law and Christ, cannot properly be understood except in the categories of Pauline mysticism. There were doubtless few Christians who followed the apostle's thought in all its profundity. On this particular issue he found none to echo him, or at least none to echo him closely.

Yet in spite of all this, when he comes down to more mundane matters, that is to say, to the discussion of practical moral problems, even St. Paul puts the questions and frames the answers in terms very closely similar to those of Jewish legalism, or rather Jewish moralism. The only new principle, and it is admittedly a vital one, is that the conduct of a regenerate Christian, a truly "spiritual" man, is not governed by some external standard, but flows quite naturally from the life in Christ.[56] In actual fact there is not a great deal of difference between the Jew who applies himself to fulfil what the law prescribes and the apostle who spontaneously, without seeking to do so, lives in conformity with the law. There was even less difference between the ordinary Christian and the ordinary Jew. For the immense majority of Christians the commandments kept their old force, as they had always done. This was even more true after Christian theology had slipped into moralistic grooves very similar to those of Judaism, and made respectable again the ideas of merit and retribution that St. Paul had denied.

The antilegalism of St. Paul, therefore, so absolute in theory, had to be modified when it came to questions of actual conduct. This was done by making a vital distinction that the Church, in taking over Pauline theology, drew very carefully. The only prescriptions of the law that fell under the heading of "the dead letter" were those concerning ritual and ceremonial, namely, the laws of circumcision, Sabbath, fasting, and sacrifice. The moral precepts, on the contrary, retained all their force, as immutable expressions of the will of God.

Paul himself does not work out this distinction in any systematic way, but it is implicit in the practical instructions that occupy so much of his letters. Not to admit the distinction would be to make nonsense of the religious life. For the Jewish law (meaning in this context principally the decalogue) is in the apostle's eyes nothing other than the transcription of the natural law that is enshrined in the heart of every man and leads him on toward the truth.[57] It is nonetheless true that by pressing his indictment of the law with too much vehemence Paul left his own position in some doubt. His thought has sometimes been interpreted in a sense contrary to his real intention. The epistle of James, for example, indulges in polemic against him, though without ever naming him, and argues that "a body dies when it is separated from the spirit, and in the same way faith is dead if it is separated from good deeds."[58] By "good deeds" ("works," to use the traditional terminology) is meant moral praxis, the principles of which are laid down in the decalogue. This is the viewpoint of mainstream Christian thinking, at least as much as it is that of Jewish Christianity.[59]

III

St. Paul's ideas won the day, but from the time when they became normative in the early Church they were also modified, until the original anit-legalism became so blurred that it disappeared entirely. The coming of Christ, it is true, did mark the end of the law, but of the Jewish law only, understood in its narrowest sense. It was the end of *a* law, but not of all law. If Christianity retains its originality, it expresses it in terms quite different from those formulated by St. Paul. It is from now on very much a question of the new nomism.[60]

Was it not a fact that Jesus himself had announced that he came to fulfil and complete the law, not to abolish it? Had he not added to the old commandments certain new ones? It was true that these occasionally contradicted the earlier ones, but in most instances they sharpened and reinforced the old. To the old principle of the *lex talionis,* "eye for eye and tooth for tooth," he opposed the law of humility, of forgiveness and love. "If anyone hits you on the right cheek, offer him the other as well."[61] Other commands he made more rigorous. "You have learnt how it was said: 'You must not commit adultery.' But I say this to you: if a man looks at a woman lustfully, he has already committed adultery with her in his heart."[62]

Looked at as a whole, Jesus' message can be taken as one of extreme moral rigorism, of more radically exacting standards, of a more exalted ideal of perfection.[63] It is not so much a question of abolishing the law as of substituting one law for another. The vital contrast is no longer between Law and Christ, but between Christ's law and the law of Moses. And the law of Christ does not merely oppose the law of Moses, it replaces it. Christian art well illustrates this development in Christian thinking. On sarcophagus sculptures, as well as on wall paintings and mosaics, we frequently have St. Peter pictured as the new Moses. His prestige has completely eclipsed that of St. Paul. He is shown receiving from Christ the lawgiver the scroll of the new covenant: *Dominus legem dat.*[64]

The old covenant and the new are no longer conceived as antithetical. There is no longer any sharp break between the one and the other, but a natural progression from the incomplete to the perfect. If any contrast is seen between them, it is the contrast between a rough draft and the finished masterpiece. They represent two successive stages in the realization of the divine plan. And the unity of this plan is thus better safeguarded than in the more complex theology of St. Paul.

Though there is basically only revelation, the one revelation has been delivered piecemeal. For some writers the later instalments complete the earlier ones,[65] for others they supersede them,[66] but in either case the Mosaic law represents no more than a transitory phase in the progression. It marks neither the beginning nor the end of the process. Aphraates tells us that the earliest covenant had for its sign the prohibition against eating the forbidden fruit, which was imposed on Adam at the time when mankind was created. Next came God's convenant with Noah, and its sign was the rainbow. After that was the Abrahamic covenant, whose sign was first faith, and later circumcision. The Mosaic covenant has no more claim to eternal validity than any of its predecessors. For its sign it had the lamb sacrificed by the people. When it was broken in its turn, God abrogated it and promised in its place a new covenant that should not pass away.[67]

The same progression is seen in the giving of law. There is a law that contains in itself all the laws that preceded it, and at the same time surpasses them all. This is "the perfect law of freedom,"[68] "the new law of our Lord Jesus Christ, which is without the yoke of... necessity."[69] This is a curious adaptation of a familiar Pauline idea, and a paradoxical one, very boldly expressed. The heavy yoke of the law is thrown off, not by the liberating action of grace or of the Spirit, but by the law itself, in renewed, purified and spiritualized form.[70]

The Christian apologists had no great difficulty in showing that this replacement had been intended by God from all eternity. For the writer of the epistle to the Hebrews, the coming of a new law followed of necessity from the imperfection of the Jewish priesthood and other institutions. "Now if perfection had been reached through the levitical priesthood because the law given to the nation rests on it, why was it still necessary for a new priesthood to arise, one of the same order as Melchizedek, not counted as being of the same order as Aaron? But any change in the priesthood must mean a change in the law as well."[71]

Tertullian and others after him sought in the old covenant itself the affirmation of its own temporary character. *Ex hac domo Dei Jacob etiam legem novam processuram annuntiat Esaias.*[72] This new law is the law of love and peace, which replaces the *lex talionis. Nam vetus lex ultione gladii se vindicabat, et oculum pro oculo eruebat et vindictam injuriae retribuebat; nova autem lex clementiam designabat, et pristinam ferocitatem gladiorum et lancearum ad tranquillitatem convertebat.*[73]

Along with this notion of the new law, as a corollary of it, went that of the new people. The Mosaic law was intended for exclusively Jewish use. It lost all its value as soon as the Jews ceased to be the chosen people. The advent of a new community, whose members were drawn from outside the Jewish nation, was at once the sign, the cause, and the consequence of this change of law. Tertullian again explains:

Ideo nos, qui non populus Dei retro, facti sumus populus ejus, accipiendo novam legem supra dictam, et novam circumcisionem, ante praedictam.[74] This substitution, too, is announced in scripture itself. This is the real meaning of the two peoples who should come from the womb of Rebecca,[75] of whom the elder should serve the younger. *Utique Judaeorum, id est Israëlis, et gentium, id est noster.* The one who came first is certainly entitled to primacy. *Anterior tempore et major per gratiam primae dignationis in lege.*[76] It is manifest, nevertheless, that all his privileges have been transferred, by the divine will, to the new people who have come from without. *Procul dubio per edictum divinae elocutionis prior et major populus; id est Judaicus, serviat necesse est minori et minor populus, id est Christianus, superet majorem.*[77]

This new Israel, henceforth the only legitimate Israel, has completely replaced the Israel according to the flesh. The gentiles, having become regenerate by divine adoption, have entered into the heritage of which the Jews proved themselves unworthy. This analysis appears as early as the epistle of Barnabas and is repeated throughout the patristic literature. Such an outlook on the matter went along with the conviction that there was no longer any hope of Israel's conversion; a conviction that the evidence appeared to justify. Where hope of the conversion of Israel is still maintained, as in St. Paul,[78] it is projected into the far future and not expected until the last days. The supply of Jewish converts to Christianity dried up very quickly. Christian art, in this matter as in others, again faithfully reflects theological thinking. In the mosaics of St. Sabina, created at a time when the Church still found some Jewish converts, the *Ecclesia ex gentibus* and *Ecclesia ex circumcisione* are pictured in harmonious symmetry. On the doors of medieval cathedrals, by contrast, we have represented the figures of the victorious Church and the vanquished Synagogue, the latter pictured with her eyes blindfolded and lance broken.

Ideas of this kind, however well they represented the real facts, raised a number of difficulties in the realm of theory. Though less radical than St. Paul's thinking on the subject, they nevertheless left an awkward gap between the Jewish past and the Christian present. Thus to declare the Jewish people defunct was to condemn by implication the institutions of the Old Testament. Yet the Old Testament remained the basis of the faith, and indispensable to the Christian message.

A more serious difficulty was that this approach implicitly conceded that Judaism was the older, earlier faith. In the eyes of ancient Judaism, Christianity represented not merely an arbitrary break in the tradition but a revolutionary innovation. It was an upstart religion. It looked like this not only to Jews, but to its other opponents too. The political and religious conservatism of the pagans themselves was outraged by the novelty of Christianity, and on this ground they attacked the Church with vehemence.[79]

This theological problem was already complicated by the gnostic attitude to tradition, and as if this were not enough, it had a political aspect too. Christianity was suspected and persecuted precisely in its capacity as an innovation, as something distinct from legally recognized Judaism.[80] The apologists, who began by emphasizing with rash enthusiasm the novelty of their message, undoubtedly contributed unintentionally to the troubles of the Church. Christians were obliged to refute this dangerous suggestion not merely for polemical reasons but out of concern for their own safety.

Under these circumstances Christianity, which had begun by being so proud of its newness and originality, was led by degrees to represent itself as ancient. In a number of texts we find the idea appearing that the Church is not simply the legitimate heir of the promises, not simply the one who has succeeded to the title of Israel, whose failure has been so manifestly demonstrated by events, but that even in the past, and indeed from the very beginning, she was the only true Israel.[81]

The Old Testament, for those who have eyes to read it, relates the history, not of the Jewish people at all, but of the Church. The Church was preexistent, just as Christ its head was preexistent. Israel after the flesh was never more than a coarse outer shell for the spiritual reality within, which was the Church. The Church was already there in the Old Testment. She is Israel, for the moving power all along has been Christ, who from the beginning was the agent of the Father. In the theology of St. Paul and St. John Christ is responsible for creation.[82] Later authors apply this notion in detail to the biblical history. For Justin, it was Christ who appeared to Abraham at the oak of Mamre[83] and who revealed himself to Moses in the burning bush. Christ is eternally the agent of revelation, all revelation. And each time he appears in the Old Testament it is already the Church to whom he is speaking. The Didascalia puts into his mouth the words: "[I] in the law spake through Moses, but now myself speak unto you."[84] And again, in a solemn address: "Hear, thou Catholic Church of God, that wast delivered from the ten plagues, and didst receive the ten words, and didst learn the law, and hold the faith."[85] Wherever the head is, there are the members.[86]

Thus, Church and Israel are synonymous, Christianity and the true Judaism are indistinguishable.[87] Once the chronological distinctions have become thus blurred, there is no longer any question of contrasting the old covenant with the new, for they are fundamentally the same.[88]

They are *fundamentally* the same, but they are not the same in their actual historic forms. The difficulties involved in this approach are evident right from the beginning. It has the advantage of authenticating the moral prescriptions of the ancient law, albeit in the expanded and perfected form the new covenant gives them. But since the Church did in fact reject the ritual provisions of the law, it is also obliged to rationalize this rejection. The contrast is no longer basically a contrast between present and past but exists already within the past itself, between the enduring reality and ephemeral symbol. Israel's rites now have to be understood simply as a prefiguration of their Christian counterparts. One must look behind their valueless exterior to find the mysterious reality of Christian truth, as one must look behind the facade of the people of Israel in order to find the Christian Church.

To follow this line of argument is to find oneself back with the same chronological perspective it was desired to avoid. For this eternal Christian truth, immanent already in the biblical revelation, is not understood as such until after the coming of Christ in the flesh. And when he comes the old rites disappear and we are left with the new sacraments. The *Didascalia* makes the matter quite clear. "Instead of the sacrifices which then were, offer now prayers and petitions and thanksgivings. Then were first-fruits, and tithes, and part-offerings, and gifts; but today the oblations which are offered through the bishops to the Lord God. For they are your high priests; but the priests and Levites now are the presbyters and deacons."[89] The new institutions are closely in line with the old ones, but they are not on that account identical. To demonstrate the connection between the two it was almost inevitable that allegorical exegesis would be called in to help.

IV

In order to circumvent this difficulty another solution was suggested. Christianity, wishing to assert its originality, but not content to identify itself with Judaism, asserted instead its priority to Judaism. This was an audacious attempt to reverse the facts. Historic Christianity, it is true, is later than Judaism, for it springs from the preaching of Jesus, who was crucified under Tiberius.[90] But this Christianity is nothing more than a revived and more accurately stated form of primordial Christianity, whose essentials were given at the very beginning of the process of revelation. As such, it is far older than Judaism.

This was not simply a question of discovering prefigurations in the scriptures by means of allegorical exegesis. Such exegesis could always be readily contested. Rather, it was an attempt to use methods that had all the appearance of sane historical exegesis in order to distinguish the successive layers of a revelation that had not been made all at the same time. The method was based on the assumption that Christianity was to be sought not merely at the end of the process but at its beginning.

Careful examination of the diverse elements of which Judaism was made up revealed that Jewish ritualism represented a late and adventitious development. That which was characteristically Jewish, i.e., the elements in Judaism that specifically marked it off from Christianity, could not be of the essence of the biblical revelation. Correspondingly, what was given in the beginning, and possesses eternal and universal value (in particular the assertion of monotheism and the moral law) is not specifically Jewish. It is, from the beginning, Christianity.

Such is the principle. It was susceptible of being applied in a number of different ways. The differences do not only reflect differences in outlook among different individual thinkers. They reflect a degree of indecision on the part of the Church. The simplest application is of the kind already noted in St. Paul, who distinguishes between faith and the law. The latter, looked at against the background of the whole divine plan, is a late element, and consequently of secondary importance for salvation. Justification by faith is available not only after the coming of Christ, who is the end of the law for all who believe in him. But it was also a possibility in earlier times, before there was any law, for those who believed. "Take Abraham, for example: 'He put his faith in God, and this faith was considered as justifying him.'... Those therefore who rely on faith receive the same blessing as Abraham, the man of faith."[91]

This means that Christians, having been blessed for their faith, and having become, in one sense, a new people, may also, and more accurately be described as the primordial people. "By belonging to Christ you are the posterity of Abraham, the heirs he was promised."[92] It means also that Abraham, father of the nations, is mistakenly considered by the Jews as the progenitor of their race. One might even say that he only became a Jew by circumcision. "Think of Abraham again: 'his faith,' we say, 'was considered as justifying him,' but when was this done?... It was before he had been circumcised, not after."[93] The covenant existed before the rite of circumcision. And "once God

had expressed His will in due form, no law that came four hundred
and thirty years later could cancel that and make the promise
meaningless." The history that is specifically Israelite history does not
begin with the patriarch, but much later, on Sinai. Between that first
faith of Abraham and the last stage of religious development, which is
faith in Christ, the written law marks merely a transitory phase.
Similarly, between the Christianity of St. Paul and the "Christianity"
of Abraham the phenomenon of historic Judaism, born of Moses,
represents no more than a long parenthesis, if not an interlude that
actually breaks the continuity of the development.

From this point of view, then, Abraham and Moses are the
symbolic representatives of the rival cults. It is clear that St. Paul, to
be consistent, ought to have included in his repudiation of the law the
whole of the Mosaic legislation, not excepting the decalogue. Marcion
later did exactly this, and fell into heresy by doing so. But there is no
lack of orthodox thinkers who, though it is true they expressed
themselves more cautiously, said very much the same thing.

St. Paul's argument from the lateness of the law's delivery was
exploited to the full by the polemists of the early centuries. The
patriarchs, whom the Jews claim as their saintly ancestors, did not
observe the Sabbath, which proves that its observance cannot be
indispensable. Abraham pleased God before he was circumcised. Thus
circumcision too is *in signum temporis illius, non in praerogativam.*[95]
Examples and quotations could be multiplied.[96] It is Eusebius who
most clearly works out the idea, by means of an ingenious contrast
between Jews and Hebrews.

What he says, in substance, is this: the divine revelation was
manifested in Israel long before Moses, and long before there even was
a Jewish people.[97] The Jews in fact took their name from Judah, the
tribe that gave rise to the Jewish kingdom. This was at a very late
point in history. The Hebrews, on the contrary, owe their name to
Eber, the grandfather of Abraham. They are therefore earlier than the
Jews, whose first lawgiver was Moses. It was Moses who instituted the
Sabbath, the distinction between clean and unclean foods, the feasts,
the rites of purification, and all the detail of the ceremonial law.

This Mosaic law, promulgated at such a late stage, was never
intended for anyone except the Jewish people alone.[98] Even the Jews
themselves, if they live in the diaspora, cannot apply it.[99] Its
observance is only possible for Palestinian Jews, or more precisely, for
Jerusalemite Jews. Hence these are the only people of whom its
observance can be demanded.[100] Its validity is thus strictly limited
both in time and in space. Consequently it cannot possibly serve as a
rallying point for religious humanity. Now God is a God of all

mankind, and not only of one people. It is to all men that He offers the way of salvation, which has been embodied in Christianity. Is this then a novelty? By no means! The form of the religious life that the Church of Christ sets before the whole of humanity is none other than that which Abraham already practiced. For the Hebrews before Moses knew nothing at all of his laws, but practiced a free worship, ἐλεύθερον εὐσεβείας τρόπον.[101] They lived in accordance with natural law, without any need of written commandments. They possessed a sure knowledge of divine truths. Between them and the Christian Church there was the "Jewish" period of the history of Israel, which began with Moses and ended with Christ. Throughout this period the "Hebrew" prophets maintained the continuity of the same religious tradition.

These Hebrews who are thus contrasted with the Jews, and who existed before the Jews, we may recognize as Christians. Eusebius invites us explicitly to make this identification and takes back the Christian line even further than Abraham. "All these to whom righteous witness has been borne, going back to the first man, it would be no departure from the truth to style as Christians, in point of fact if not in name.[102]

The apologists present Christianity therefore as a concrete manifestation of the natural religion that was such a popular conception amongst the religious philosophers of the period. And this was a presentation of it that the anti-Jewish polemists found congenial and useful. In the prelegalist era of the patriarchs the divinely approved norm of conduct was the natural law. Christianity has now revealed this law explicitly to all men.[103] It was, in the interim, imperfectly embodied in the Mosaic legislation, but men were capable of responding to it, for there is something within every man's conscience that is aware of the natural law and recognizes it. Nevertheless, if we seek actually to identify among the men of former ages those who were, so to speak, "natural Christians," we find them more among the biblical patriarchs than among the best of the gentiles. This at least is Tertullian's opinion, when he uses the naturally Christian man as evidence against the pagans.[104]

The difficulty with this theory too is apparent from the outset. It is a long leap from the natural law and from spontaneous devotion to the acceptance in detail of Christian doctrines and practices. In order to show that primordial or original Christianity is identical in all respects with the Christianity of the Church, it is necessary to do considerable violence to the latter. It is necessary either to empty it of any content that is new or positive and to equate it simply with a naturally religious attitude to life and the conduct that accompanies it, or (and this was felt preferable) to trace back the teaching and practice of the Church into the most distant past.

If the apologists, for their part, sometimes presented to the pagans a Christianity whose dogmatic structure was so reduced that it would have satisfied Rousseau's Vicaire Savoyard,[105] others preferred the second solution. They claimed to find in the Old Testament, alongside the legal and ritual tradition of Judaism openly displayed there, another tradition parallel to it, equally ancient, equally precise. It was from this parallel tradition that Christianity took its rise and it may therefore be thought of as Christian from its very beginning.

The former group, laying their emphasis on the actual, manifest content of the Bible, make a contrast between priesthood and prophecy. They condemn priesthood, seeing it as representing the very essence of Jewish religion. In prophecy they recognize an early form of that Christianity which has existed throughout all ages. According to this scheme, the prophets were the true heirs of the patriarchs.[106] This contrast between priesthood and prophecy has appeared time and time again throughout Christian history. It lies at the heart of Stephen's speech. It reappears among modern thinkers in the tradition of liberal Christianity who contrast the religion of the spirit with the religion of authority. It is appealed to at all times by those who set a high value on prophetic inspiration and deplore ecclesiastical institutionalism.[107] Now in the period we are at the moment studying Christianity was already ossifying into a sacerdotalism very close in spirit to that of Judaism.[108] The meritorious nature of "good works" was once more established. There were good reasons, therefore, why the priestly/prophetic contrast should lose its appeal. More interesting, because more characteristic of the epoch, is the attempt to find for the Christian priesthood itself a prototype or model within Jewish institutions, or at least on the edge of them, which might help to provide it with a rationale.

The model selected is the priesthood of Melchizedek, a more ancient one than that of Aaron.[109] Melchizedek's priority in time was naturally interpreted as a priority of importance, as a primacy. And by emphasizing this priority Christian apologists managed, if the expression be permitted, to kill two birds with one stone. They moved back the origin of Christian institutions to the period of origin of the divine revelation itself, and at the same time they denied Israel the privilege of being the first to receive the divine call. Melchizedek, priest of the Most High, was not a Jew by race, yet the man whom the Jews claimed as their father paid homage to him. (In this instance the Christians chose to admit that Abraham was a Jew.) Melchizedek is the true father of the gentiles, and the claims of the gentiles are therefore older than those of Israel. In the person of Melchizedek the gentiles (that is to say, the Church) received the Jews' homage.[110]

By means of allegorical exegesis, prefigurations of Christian rites were discovered among the Jewish ones. Circumcision was the prototype of baptism, the Passover lamb prefigured the eucharist. This kind of interpretation revealed in the Old Testament the visible presence of Christian rites, and that at a period before the Jewish ones existed. Melchizedek offers to God, and presents to Abraham, not a bloody sacrifice but bread and wine.[111] Some eastern Christians were more daringly imaginative still. The Syrian author of the *Cave of Treasures*[112] claims as the father of Christian priesthood not Melchizedek but Adam himself. Did he not offer to the Lord, in a sacrifice curiously resembling the Christian Mass, first his own blood and then wheaten bread?[113] An unbroken line of priests existed alongside the Jewish priesthood and joins Adam to Christ. In this line Melchizedek occupies an important place, and this pious romance gives us a full account of his history.[114] In this way the origins of the Church are bound up with the origins of humanity itself.[115]

V

All these interpretations tend by different routes to the same end. Their object, in reversing the accepted order of events, is to prove that Christianity is a latecomer only in appearance. In reality it represents in the religious history of humanity the primary form of revelation. The innovations of the Christians, when looked at properly, are seen to be no more than a return to a tradition the Jews had culpably spurned. Properly speaking, it is the Jews who are the innovators: it is they who ought really to be called to account. It is quite in order, therefore, when they refuse to follow Christ, the restorer of the true tradition, to accuse them of apostasy. *Judaei veteres, sperando futurum Christum redemptorem, Christiani erant. Igitur apostatae habeantur necesse est, qui, dum Christum non recipiunt, rei sunt violatae legis... Quamvis graviter peccaverint Judaei reprobando domum Dei et digni sint morte, tamen... regressi ad fidem suscipientur cum laetitia.*[116]

The clearest evidence of the real nature of this long apostasy that we call the history of the Jews, is provided by the development of the ritual law. No one in Catholic Christianity doubted that the provisions of this law had been formulated by God, yet Christians were often ill at ease in expounding them. Could these commandments, so often either trivial or extraordinary, really be said to exhibit the marks of that divine origin which was so forcefully claimed for them? The variety of the interpretations Christians resort to is evidence enough of the embarrassment these prescriptions caused in ancient times.

For some the Jewish rites, as prefigurations of Christian ones, possessed a virtue that was at once symbolic and real. They possessed for the past, and only for the past, the value that a draft or plan possesses in relation to the finished work. "The law has no more than a *reflection* of these realities, and no finished picture of them."[117] For pseudo-Barnabas the law never did have, even apart from its relation to Christian rites, anything other than a symbolic value. His allegorical method refuses to allow the law to be anything but the image of spiritual realities. It was only by a gross misunderstanding that the Jews came to interpret and apply it literally.[118] For yet other interpreters, and this is the point of view that for our present purpose is the most interesting one, the ritual law takes its rise from the evil inclinations of the Jews.

This idea appears as early as Stephen's speech, when he denounces temple worship as unworthy of the true God and suggests that it was simply tolerated by Him; that it was a concession made to the Jews in order to avoid the possibility of a worse evil.[119] It appears still more clearly in some of the apologists. The epistle to Diognetus says: "But those who think that they are rendering due sacrifices to him by the blood and fat and whole burnt offerings, and that they are doing him reverence by these tributes, seem to me in no way better than those who show the same lavish honour to deaf images. For the one class seem to offer sacrifices to things unable to partake of the honour, the other to him who is in need of nothing. But in truth, I do not think that you need to learn from me that, after all, their qualms concerning food and their superstition about the Sabbath, and the vaunting of circumcision and the cant of fasting and New Moon, are utterly absurd and unworthy of any argument."[120] Similarly Aristides, though he recognizes that the Jews by virtue of their monotheism and the purity of their moral principles are superior to the pagans, denounces their ritualism as a corruption of true religion. "Meanwhile they too have gone astray from the truth, for they imagine themselves to be paying honour to God, whereas what they do is directed rather towards angels than towards God, when they observe Sabbath and New Moon, the Passover of Unleavened Bread and the great fast, circumcision and the food laws."[121]

Both these authors seem to assume that the ritual laws have been invented by the Jews themselves, and they seem to be inclined, as a result, to deny their divine origin. A commoner and more safely orthodox opinion was to assert that the Jews were unworthy to keep the moral laws of the decalogue as the one guide to living, and that the ritual laws had been imposed on them after the sin of the golden calf.

The ritual law on this view represents either a punishment imposed for the sin, or else a kind of homeopathic remedy. It channeled into the service of the true God a tendency that displayed itself in the first instance in the service of idols. Thus were explained the similarities, which were at first sight somewhat disturbing, between some of the rites described in the Old Testament and the rites of paganism. It explained, indeed, similarities between the very spirit of the ritual law and that of pagan ritualism. Interpreted in this way, there was nothing in the ritual law that could compromise the divine majesty and no reason to deny its divine origin. It represents the only specifically Jewish inheritance in the history of revelation, and it forbids the Jews to call themselves the chosen people. They ceased to be the chosen people at the very foot of Sinai. This is the clear implication of Moses' destruction of the tables of the law.[122]

In the interpretation of this episode two types of exegesis are employed. Pseudo-Barnabas emphasizes the symbolic meaning.

Let us, therefore, now inquire whether God has fulfilled the covenant, which he swore to our forefathers that he would give the people? Yes, verily, he gave it: but they were not worthy to receive it, by reason of their sins... [Moses] received of the Lord two tables, written with the finger of the Lord's hand in the spirit. And Moses when he had received them, brought them down that he might deliver them to the people. And the Lord said unto Moses, "Moses, Moses, get thee down quickly, for the people... have done wickedly." And Moses understood that they had again set up a molten image; and he cast the two tables out of his hands; and the tables of the covenant of the Lord were broken. Moses therefore received them, but the Jews were not worthy.[123].

The entire development of Israel's history from that point onwards is quite meaningless, except as an illustration of what the Sinai apostasy involved. It cannot be for a Christian in any sense sacred history. In fact, from the instant the destiny of Israel was reversed. Already, in the hearts of the righteous the Christian faith had taken the place of the Jewish law. "And Moses cast the two tables out of his hands,—and their covenant was broken, that the law of Jesus might be sealed into your hearts, unto the hope of his faith."[124] Thus Barnabas abandons to the Jews the whole of the revelation on Sinai, but asserts that it was marred by a sin committed at its very inception.

The law of Sinai was therefore void in its entirety before ever there was time for it to be applied.

This interpretation would be neither better nor worse than any of the others that allegorists put forward if it did not encounter one grave objection. Its author systematically ignores the incident that according to the biblical text itself is the complement to the destruction of the tablets. It ignores the making of the new tablets, according to the Lord's own command,[125] on which by the Lord's own hand were written the terms of the renewed covenant. It is not really admissible to treat the events thus separately. To do so falsifies the whole historical reconstruction of which they form part, for the second event marks a dramatic rehabilitation of the people. They are sinners still, but pardoned. There can be no doubt that this objection was made by the Jews, or anticipated by the Christians themselves, for we do have examples of an attempt to explain away the second lawgiving. The attempt finds its classic expression in the *Didascalia.*

Here an interesting distinction is made between the two codifications of the covenant. In the former case the code consists of the law, i.e., the decalogue, whose content is primarily moral, and of those precepts which were promulgated before the worship of the calf. This code is simple and easy to fulfil.[126] Insofar as it takes any account of ritual observances, of oblations or sacrifices, these are presented as discretionary observances and as prefigurations of things to come.[127] The second code, however, the *deuterosis,* is the one on which the author lays most emphasis. This is the primarily ritual code that Moses received during his second sojourn on the mountain. It is this code which the rest of the Old Testament, and especially the Deuteronomic and Levitical codes, is concerned to develop and fill out, and which was imposed on the Jews because of their idolatry.[128] It was meant for the Jews alone and was the instrument of divine punishment. The Lord himself promulgated it only with reluctance, in the heat of anger. It has been forever annulled by the redeeming death of Christ, because he put an end to the divine curse, even for the Jews. Nevertheless, the law, the first law, continues to exist as the way of salvation that is open to all men. This law was confirmed and made definite by Christ. It is the charter of Christianity, and, like Christianity itself, eternal.[129]

This idea of *deuterosis* is not peculiar to the *Didascalia* alone. The term itself reappears in other authors, but it undergoes a shift in meaning that sheds light on an interesting development in Christian thought.

The word occurs commonly in the patristic literature, where it appears sometimes in the singular and sometimes in the plural. The fourth-century writers apply it not to a part of scripture as the author of the *Didascalia* does, but to rabbinic exegesis, i.e., to the Jewish oral tradition. Δευτέρωσις appears most frequently, therefore, as the equivalent of παράδοσις. It is applied specifically to the Mishnah. It has indeed been correctly pointed out that the two terms, *Mishnah* and *deuterosis*, are etymologically exact equivalents.[130]

This new meaning of the word is defined precisely by St. Augustine. *Nescit autem habere praeter Scripturas legitimas et propheticas Judaeos quasdam traditiones suas, quas non scriptas habent, sed memoriter tenent, et alter in alterum loquendo transfudit, quas* deuterosin *vocant.*[131] Used in the plural, the word designates the *halakhah* and *haggadah*, the doctrines and precepts of the rabbis. *Pharisaei traditionum et observationum, quas illi* deuteroseis *vocant, justitiam praeferebant.*[132] The scholars themselves are frequently designated by the title δευτερωταί.[133] It is in this sense that the word *deuterosis* is used in the famous Novel 146 in the *Novellae constitutiones* of Justinian, which lays down rules for the worship and teaching of the Synagogue. The passage in which it occurs is similar in form to a proscription in Talmudic law: τὴν δὲ παρ' αὐτοῖς λεγομένην δευτέρωσιν ἀπαγορεύομεν παντελῶς.[134]

It is not absolutely clear how the transition from one meaning to the other took place in Christian usage. It seems certain, however, that both meanings reflect Jewish usage. The term *deuterosis* was in fact created for the benefit of Greek-speaking Jews around the time when the Mishnah was beginning to acquire the force of law, i.e., from the third century onwards.[135] It is from the Jews that the author of the *Didascalia* borrows the word, but when he applies it to the second revelation on Sinai, it is by wresting the original meaning of the word. This new meaning the fathers attribute to it gives the word a pejorative significance it did not have before. The problem is, how was the author of the *Didascalia* able to impose this peculiar meaning on the word?

The shift in meaning is in all likelihood connected with the rabbinic assertion that the Mishnah is an integral part of the divine revelation, and that it was made known to Moses on Sinai at the same time as the written law.[136] The *Didascalia*, as we shall see, was published in an environment where there were close contacts between Christians and Jews. Its author therefore doubtless knew this interpretation, whose object was to strengthen the authority of rabbinic law by thus conferring on it a divine origin. He naturally would not subscribe to such a theory. For him the Mishnah was of purely human origin. Yet in common with the Jewish scholars he sees the revelation on Sinai as the point where the Jewish oral tradition originated.

He thus identifies the point of departure with the second code delivered at the renewal of the covenant. It is this second code which the Mishnah explains and expands. He feels justified therefore in applying the term *deuterosis* both to the Mishnah and to this second code. It is useful to him as emphasizing the secondary nature of the revelation on which Jewish tradition is based. If it is secondary, why was it added at all? To punish the shortcomings of Israel. To seek the origins of the shift in meaning of the word *deuterosis* is thus to find ourselves in the domain of Jewish-Christian polemic.[137]

If the idea of *deuterosis* as the author of the *Didascalia* understands it had been wholeheartedly adopted by the Church, it ought logically to have entailed the rejection of part of the scriptures, which to the Christians had become a dead letter. The *Didascalia* effectively denied to the *deuterosis* any validity at all. Even when interpreted allegorically, it has absolutely nothing to say to the Christian concerning his spiritual life. It is of interest only as a curiosity. "Yet when thou readest the law beware of the Second Legislation, that thou do but read it merely; but the commandments and warnings that are therein much avoid, lest thou lead thyself astray and bind thyself with the bonds which may not be loosed of heavy burdens. For this cause therefore, if thou read the Second Legislation, consider this alone, that thou know and glorify God who delivered us from all these bonds."[138] All the same, the author does not go so far as to exclude the *deuterosis* categorically from the canon of scripture. The author of the Dialogue between Timothy and Aquila follows much the same line as the *Didascalia* but is bolder. He does exclude *deuterosis* from the canon. The book of Deuteronomy represents for him the very essence of *deuterosis* (his judgment is doubtless influenced by the similarity of the words). He thus denies to it all status as inspired scripture. "The fifth book is Deuteronomy, which was not dictated by the mouth of God but (adds one MS) 'deuteronomized' (δευτερονομισθέντα) by Moses. This is why it was not deposited in the 'aron, that is to say, the ark of the covenant.'"[139]

This is an interesting text, but it stands alone. The Church did not give assent to this idea, for it placed in question the unity of scripture, and this was regarded as dangerous. By reverting to the original sense of the word, the Jewish sense, the Church safeguarded the integrity of the biblical revelation, of which the Christians were the only legitimate trustees. The contrast between law and *deuterosis* is not on this showing a contrast between different deposits of Mosaic legislation, but between scripture, considered as inspired in all its parts, and the arbitrary expansions the rabbis superimposed on it. It thus contrasts God-given with man-given law.

Contemnentes legem Dei, et sequentes traditiones hominum, quas illi δευ-
τερώσεις *vocant.* Such is Jerome's estimate of the Jews.[140]

The history of the term *deuterosis* sheds a good deal of light on the
position the Church took up with regard to the Old Testament. The
struggle with gnosticism had made Christians lay claim to the Old
Testament *en bloc*, without attempting to distinguish between the
various elements of which it was composed. By means of subtle
reasoning and judiciously adaptable methods of interpretation the
Church managed to retain in its heritage both the moral and the
ritual law. It attributed to the former an eternal validity and claimed
it to have been confirmed by Christ. To the latter it allowed only
transitory force. Its main purpose was to prefigure things to come, and
it could only be properly understood in the light of the gospel. But in
different ways it claims them both. The Church could thus trace its
own antecedents not merely in the early stages of the revelation, where
it involved Noah, the patriarchs, or even Moses on Sinai, but in every
succeeding stage of the covenant. Christianity had the advantage not
only of age but of continuity. Judaism, on the contrary, had been
unfaithful to the divine call. It was deprived of every foothold in the
history of revelation and allowed no place except at the very end or on
the very edge. It was, like the Mishnah, which it had made into its
own charter, a creation of men, an unwanted by-product of the
processes of revelation.

VI

There is more in these speculations than mere theological virtuosity.
They have a real connection with the situation of the moment and a
very practical purpose. Though they approach it in different ways,
they have a single object, namely, to establish that the Church is the
only authentic Israel. And by establishing this it is hoped to solve the
problem of Jewish-Christian relations.

The arguments that are used have more than one audience in mind.
Before the triumph of the Church it was essential, in the first place, to
enlighten pagan opinion in general and the pagan authorities in
particular. It had pleased the first apologists to emphasize the novelty
of the Christian message in relation to Jewish tradition. They made
the Church appear as the new people, called to supplant the earlier
Israel as the object of God's choice. In relation to pagans and Jews,
Christians were the *tertium genus*, last to appear but lords of the future.
This was the natural attitude of youth. Nevertheless, it sprang also
from a more or less conscious opportunism. The Church might have

gained some advantage in the aftermath of the events of A.D. 70 and 135 by dissociating itself clearly from the Jews.

But the Church's spokesmen committed an error in insisting too outspokenly on the absolute newness of Christianity. They offended the sense of tradition that was so deeply rooted in the mentality of the age. It is this very sense of tradition that in the last analysis explains the peculiar status that was allowed to the Jews. This provides one reason that Christianity came so quickly to reverse its policy, though the change of direction is also partly accounted for, in its turn, by opportunism. By claiming the biblical tradition for itself alone, the Church was establishing its own credentials. By demonstrating its antiquity, it was safeguarding its right to exist in the present. Furthermore, by showing that the Christian people were the true, the authentic Israel, preexistent and eternal, it entertained a short-lived hope of displacing the Jews from the privileged position they had achieved.

The argument was aimed equally at the Jews themselves. It tried to refute the claim the Jews were still making, in spite of appearances, that they were the chosen people. The aim here was to confirm the rejection of the Jews. But the continued existence of both the Jewish nation and the Jewish cult posed another problem for Christian theology. If it was really true, as the Christians claimed, that the time of Judaism was over and that it must give place to the Church, i.e., to the redeemed gentile world, why had not Judaism been either absorbed by the Church or suppressed by other means? Since Judaism's past was discredited, why did it persist in the present? If it still existed, must this not mean that there was still a part for it to play, that it was not rejected irremediably?[141]

The Church's response to these objections was to assert that Israel finally would be redeemed. She remains in existence in order that, when the times changed, she might be saved.[142] But this was not an entirely satisfactory answer to the problem. It left unanswered the question: Why the delay? What is it that postpones Israel's redemption? What is there still to expect between the apostasy of Israel and its final conversion that justifies its continued existence?

The Christian answer to this is expressed most clearly by St. Augustine. The Jews are witnesses. This was their function in the past, when they were for a while the people with whom the revelation was deposited. And still today they are witnesses to the faith preached by their prophets, a faith locked up in the book that they claim as their own, but that they have in actuality rejected. They are witnesses also of the divine justice that weighs so heavily on them.[143] The Jews are marked like Cain, who was marked "to prevent whoever might come across him from striking him down."[144] The mark preserves them, for their preservation is essential. *Necessarii sunt credentibus gentibus.*[145] The Jewish nation continues in existence because it still has a mission to fulfil. It exists for the sake of the miseries it endures for not having believed in Christ. These miseries were predicted by the prophets and bear witness to the justice of God. If the Jews persist in keeping their law partly, and following the letter only, this also is in effect a sign, a piece of evidence, *ut sibi sumant judicium, nobis praebeant testimonium.*[146] Thus Christian apologetic not only reconciles itself to the continued existence of the Jews, but insists on the necessity of that existence.

The survival of Judaism, though it could be explained away in theory, was in reality fraught with danger. In showing how Israel had become disqualified, the fathers and the apologists are speaking to a Christian audience as well as to pagans and Jews. Perhaps it would be true to say that it is mainly for the benefit of the Christians that the demonstration is made. For the Church very quickly lost hope of gaining the ear of the pagan empire or of weaning the Jews from their delusion. On the other hand, the members of the Church continued to need aid in rebutting the arguments of the Jews, in defending themselves against the well-aimed shafts of Jewish apologetic, and in resisting Judaism's attractive power. The theological argumentation was directed to a practical end, to prevent the Church from succumbing to Jewish influence. The strenuous efforts that were made to deny Israel the right to be heard on questions of theology are explained by the seriousness of the Jewish danger. The objection St. Augustine puts into the mouth of a Jewish adversary was one that troubled not a few of the faithful. *Cur tenes Vetus Testamentum, cujus praecepta non servas?... Quid apud vos facit lectio Legis et Prophetarum, cujus praecepta servare non vultis?*[147] Underlying the debate was the question of religious observance. It was a question that was still raised in the fourth century, at least in certain circles, exactly as it had been at the beginning of the Christian mission. St. Paul had written to the Judaizers in Galatia: "If you allow yourselves to be circumcised, Christ will be of no benefit to you at all.... But if you do look to the law to make you justified, then you have separated yourselves from Christ, and have fallen from grace."[148] St. Jerome is of the same mind. Replying to St. Augustine, who would allow converted Jews at their own pleasure either to keep or refrain from keeping some of the Jewish laws, Jerome says: *Non illi Christiani fient, sed nos Judaeos facient.... Caeremonias Judaeorum et perniciosas esse mortiferas Christianis; et quicumque eas observaverit, sive ex Judaeis, sive ex gentibus, eum in barathrum diaboli devolutum. Finis enim legis Christus, ad justitiam omni credenti, Judaeo scilicet et gentili.*[149] And St. Augustine, trying to show him that he has misunderstood what he meant, replies: *Ego hanc vocem tuam omnino confirmo.*[150]

The discussion is a significant one. Jerome's reactions are those of a man who lived in daily contact with Jews, and in a situation where the temptation to give way to Judaizers was strong. The problem for him was a real and pressing one.[151] As a general rule we may say that those Christian writers who insist most strongly on the lapse of Israel's call are the very ones who are most occupied with combating Judaizing pressure. This is true, for example of the author of the *Didascalia*, of St. John Chrysostom, and of Aphraates. All of them are representative of eastern Christianity, and all write for a Christian public that is exposed to the influence of Judaism. Indeed, they themselves exhibit the signs of such influence. This is not only true of Chrysostom, whose anti-Jewish and antilegalistic bias is typical of Hellenistic Christianity as a whole, but of Aphraates, who is a Semite himself both by birth and in his ways of thinking, and also of the *Didascalia*, which stands (in common with Aphraates himself) for a somewhat attenuated kind of Jewish Christianity.[152]

The impact of Judaism is discernible here with especial clarity, but it appears also in Christianity as a whole. If Christianity reinstated by degrees, in an acceptably orthodox form, the ideas and practices it so strenuously opposed when they appeared in Jewish guise, it had a well-defined purpose in doing so. It was to guard itself against the danger of gnosticism. It also helped to neutralize the danger from Judaism, for the Church could thus fight Judaism on its own ground.

The situation was complicated by the fact that at the beginning of the Christian era there were within Judaism itself diverse tendencies. Some sections of the Jews had already subjected the prescriptions of the Old Testament to the same critical treatment as the Christians themselves employed. The details of this movement of Jewish criticism are now impossible to trace, for the written remains of it are few. Furthermore, when rabbinic orthodoxy achieved its ascendancy, some elements in the movement were neutralized or absorbed by orthodoxy, others were rejected, and if they survived at all, did so only among obscure or ephemeral sects. But though we can now only guess its influence, or reconstruct it from texts that have been adapted or worked over, such as the pseudo-Clementine literature, we have enough evidence to be certain that the movement did exist.

No one will now deny that one of the characteristics of Jewish gnosticism was exactly this, that it called in question the value and integrity of the scriptural revelation, and in particular of the scriptural law.[153] It treated the scriptures to a radical criticism and analyzed them into diverse elements it deemed to be of unequal authority. Scripture was indeed treated sometimes as a very hetero- geneous collection of materials. The very existence of the diaspora,[154] to say nothing of the disappearance of the temple and its sacrificial cult, which made it quite impossible to observe many important prescriptions, called in question their purpose and legitimacy. The Talmud settles the matter by roundly asserting their validity, but we hear at least an echo of other answers to the problem. These other answers, though they were rejected by the rabbis, were nevertheless proposed. It may well be that less orthodox Jews accepted them.[155] One result of the debate that went on around these suggestions was a fluctuation in ideas concerning the canon. We find first one part of the Bible and then another treated with suspicion. At one time it is the prophets, then some of the Hagiographa, and then certain parts of the Pentateuch. Only the authority of the law, in the rather narrow sense in which the *Didascalia* uses that word, is recognized by everyone.

The problem was posed in the same terms, if not exactly at the same time, in both Jewish and Christian circles. At the same time as one group of Christians maintained or tried to reinstate virtually the entire body of Jewish religious observances, there was a group of Jews who wished to abandon part of them. The apparently clear distinction between Judaism and Christianity turns out on closer examination to be rather more vague than appeared at first sight. At the two ends of the religious spectrum the two orthodoxies, the rabbinic and the catholic, were radically opposed to each other. (In spite of this, they had certain features in common, features that were derived from their common origin in the religion of Israel.) But the intermediate groups between these two extremes formed a continuous spectrum, shading imperceptibly from one to the other, and, quite frequently, having definite connections with each other. These intermediate bodies consisted of heterodox Christian groups and communities of dissident Jews, i.e., of the Jewish-Christian sects. It is often quite difficult to decide just where to draw the line between Christianity and Judaism, to determine where the one stops and the other begins. Those ancient writers who study the manifestations of heterodoxy are sometimes much exercised to know how to classify some of the aberrant religions of this period, whether to set them down as Jewish or Christian. The distinctions between the two are somewhat fluid. Indeed, to Christian minds at that time the whole concept of Judaism was a singularly imprecise one, or perhaps just a very complex one.

It is in fact curious to see just what the term *Jew* does imply, in the pejorative way in which Christians used it. Those who are accused of Judaism are, in the first place, all those who in the matter of religious observances assimilate themselves to Jewish practices, i.e., all those who may in the strict sense be called Judaizers. In fact, the terms *Jew* and *Judaizer* are often linked together and treated as synonyms. *Judaei et nostri judaizantes.* But also included in the charge of Judaism are all those who deviate from officially accepted teaching or profess erroneous opinions. Thus, those who are in error concerning the person of Christ, who deny his divinity or insist more strongly than is proper on his humanity are accused of being Jews. So are those who hold unorthodox views about grace and freewill.

The accusation takes in Arianism and related heresies, such as Adoptionism, Monarchianism, and the like. Paul of Samosata, for example, is known by his orthodox contemporaries as "the Jew."[156] Similarly St. Augustine denounces as Jews those who reject his doctrine of grace and rely on human will, and who seek to rehabilitate, this time in a general sense, "good works" and the idea of merit.[157] Doubtless to call people "Jew" in this fashion was to use the word figuratively, and those who so used it were not deceived by it. They would surely have known the difference between an Arian or a Pelagian and one who was a Jew in the proper sense. This manner of speaking is nonetheless significant. It bears witness to the interpenetration of the diverse forms of Judaism and Christianity. Above all, it illustrates the permanent preoccupation of the early Church with the need to define its own position in terms of its relation to and contrast with Judaism. It seems to me that this evidence, and the evidence we examined earlier, allows us to draw two conclusions.

First, Judaism continued throughout the early centuries of our era to be a real and important factor in religious life. None of the early Christian theological discussions makes sense if Israel had already withdrawn and ceased to be an effective force in the world at large. The speculations I have analyzed all have this in common, that they aim to exorcise this persistent influence of Judaism and to bring about that withdrawal that had not yet taken place. For, and this is the second conclusion, Judaism left its mark on the developing Christianity. The fact that Judaism is still powerful colors all aspects of the relations between the two religions. It may be read both in the scholarly polemic of the theologians and in the popular anti-Semitism of the Church at large. It is likewise presupposed by the existence of syncretizing movements. The claim of the Church to be the only true Israel represents a defensive reaction against Israel after the flesh. And in the ensuing argument the pace is set by Israel as it is. This argument introduces us at the outset to the very heart of the problem with which this book deals.

4

Rome, Judaism, and Christianity

Μάχεται Ἰουδαϊσμὸς Ἑλληνισμῷ καὶ ἀμφότεροι Χριστιανισμῷ.
St. Basil, *Homily Against the Sabellians*, 34:1

If we are to produce a satisfactory picture of the relations between Judaism and Christianity it is vital to see the two religions in their setting within the Roman Empire. The attitude of the Roman authorities to the two cults was not without influence on their attitudes to one another. Conversely, it is a priori unlikely that once Christianity had been recognized for what it was, a separate and distinct religion from Judaism, its rapid progress and widespread dissemination did not have some repercussions on Roman policy toward the Jews. And by the same token, if we wish to understand the anti-Christian measures taken by the imperial authorities, it is vital not to forget the Jewish factor. Even if we cannot unreservedly follow the early Christian apologists when they blame the Jews for initiating the persecutions, we must still ask to what extent the Jews were involved and what part they did play. The question of their responsibility, even if it was only indirect, must still be raised, and it seems to me it is capable of being answered. Finally, the conversion of Constantine constitutes a factor of the gravest importance, for under Constantine imperial policy changed radically, the empire becoming the protector of the Church. This policy was followed and developed by Constantine's successors.

I

I do not intend to undertake yet another full-scale enquiry into the legal status of the Jews.[1] It is enough to say that the privileges that were accorded to them at the beginning of the Christian era, in Palestine as well as the diaspora, were at once religious and political. They were allowed freedom to practice their religion, together with immunity from all requirements, obligations, and civil duties that were incompatible with their rigorous monotheism. In particular, they were given a dispensation that allowed them to refrain from taking part in the imperial cult. They were required instead to pray for the emperor.

The official status of the Jews was not changed at all in any fundamental way by the events of A.D. 70. At the same time as he demolished the temple, Vespasian deprived both the priesthood and the Sanhedrin of their authority. From that time Palestine was under the direct control of the Roman authorities. One imposition the Jews particularly resented was that they were from now on obliged to pay to the temple of Jupiter Capitolinus the didrachma they had previously sent to Jerusalem. But this was only, as Juster expresses it, "the price of Jehovah's continued existence. Provided it was paid, he could continue to be worshipped even by Jews who were Roman citizens."[2] In fact, there was no really significant change in conditions for the Jews, either under the Flavians or under the first Antonines. This was especially true for the diaspora. The Jews were even allowed to continue their proselytizing activities unhindered. The measures taken by Domitian mark no more than a brief interlude. The visitation he inflicted on the Jews and their adherents seems to have been primarily fiscal in its motives. Its object was to make sure that all those who were legally obliged to pay the tax actually did so. However, one of its results was to reveal how many proselytes there were, and this frightened the emperor.[3] The persecution that followed seems to be best explained as an outburst of despotic ill-temper. It seems to have been designed to suppress by every available means all opposition whatever, and appears to have made no clear distinction between Jewish proselytes and Christians. Thus, it does not reflect any considered policy. If it were otherwise, it would be difficult to understand how Nerva[4] could formally forbid the searching out of Jews and Trajan similarly that of Christians. In fact, it is necessary to come down as far as Hadrian, to the point at which I have chosen to begin my inquiry, to find any serious change in the Jews' status.

We know that Bar Cochba's revolt was a response to two decisions taken by Hadrian. The first was his decision to build a pagan temple in the reconstructed Jerusalem, the second was his prohibition of circumcision.[5] Both were adhered to in spite of the insurrection. The second would have had very serious consequences for the future of Judaism if it had been maintained by Hadrian's successors. To have put an end to circumcision would have made the practice of Judaism virtually impossible, for circumcision constituted as necessary a rite of initiation for Judaism as baptism does for Christianity. Talmudic texts tell us that after the war Hadrian took steps of a more general character designed to prohibit all Jewish cult practices. But these texts stand completely alone. They are not supported by any evidence whatever from pagan sources and can hardly therefore be given credence. It is worth noting that the prohibition of circumcision is in itself almost as comprehensive as the broader measures that the Talmudic texts allege were taken, since without circumcision there would eventually be no Jews. This at least is how it was understood by those who were affected by it, and this is sufficient to explain the violence of Jewish hatred for Hadrian, a hatred far greater than that shown to any other emperor, even Titus himself.[6] No doubt Hadrian hoped, by enacting such a drastic measure, to extirpate once and for all this turbulent people who were perpetually in revolt. If the edict had remained in force, Judaism could only have disappeared, unless it had adapted itself by means of some very radical reform.

The only obvious result was a further insurrection under Antoninus,[7] and Antoninus discreetly decided not to risk a repetition. He did not actually abrogate his predecessor's edict; instead, he made the formal stipulation that it did not apply to the Jews.[8] Thus the Jews alone escaped the edict's effect, though there is no doubt that it was originally made with them specifically in mind. To other categories of imperial subjects it continued to apply. The Jews thus saw themselves installed once more in that privileged position that they had previously enjoyed and that was not again to be contested. It was a return to the traditional benevolent policy that under Hadrian had been temporarily abandoned. The Roman power henceforth remained on normal terms with the Jews, friendly terms, even. Their privileges were not again seriously threatened before the victory of Christianity.

By comparison with the Jews, with their officially recognized status and all the advantages it conveyed, the position of the Christians seemed at first uncertain and precarious. Though it was virtually prohibited, Christianity enjoyed in practice a general toleration, punctuated by intermittent outbreaks of persecution. This situation continued until the edicts of the third century explicitly placed Christianity outside the law. Moreover, it seems certain that at the beginning the Christians received the benefit of a certain doubt about their standing. As long as the Roman state made no clear distinction between them and the Jews, they shared in the toleration that was extended to their rivals. Apart from the short Neronian persecution, which was confined to Rome itself, this state of affairs seems to have persisted up to the end of the first century. The measures taken by Domitian presuppose this. There is a stong presumption that his principal victims, Acilius Glabrio, Flavius Clemens, and Flavia Domitilla, were Christians. However, there is no conclusive proof of this. The possibility remains open that they were adherents of Judaism. The charge of atheism was equally appropriate to both religious groups.[9] At the beginning of the second century, on the contrary, the distinction is clearly made. The letters exchanged between Trajan and Pliny show that the state recognized the independent and autonomous nature of Christianity,[10] and there can be little doubt that Christians themselves hastened to enlighten those who directed the operations. The first Christian apology, that of Quadratus, falls neatly between the bloody outbreak in Cyrenaica under Trajan and Hadrian's Jewish War. Quadratus is scarcely more than a name to us, and we know nothing of his writings beyond a few lines that Eusebius preserves.[11] But the arguments did not vary much from one apologist to the next, (Tatian is the only exception here, and he was a "barbarian" and proud of it.) Certain themes make their inevitable appearance in every one of them. Bearing this in mind, and taking into account, too, the situation of the moment, we are bound to agree with Graetz[12] that the contrast between Jews and Christians is likely to have figured in Quadratus's apology as it did in those of his successors. Circumstances are likely to have impelled him to stress the distinction. The period was one that saw the development of tension between Romans and Jews, and the resurgence of Zealot influence, and it would have been politic to draw attention to the fact that Christians had severed their connections with the religion of Israel, and with the land of Palestine, and were blameless citizens of the empire. Thus were the authorities assisted, as Bouché-Leclerq puts it, "to distinguish cosmopolitan Christianity from Judaism and to show that it was separated from Roman society by a gulf less deep."[13] This distinction on which the apologists insisted was one the Christians in Palestine itself had made effective, for it was about this period that for the first time a bishop was appointed who was of gentile origin. This was Mark, the leader of the Christian community in Jerusalem.[14] Now, the significant thing is that up to this point the Jewish-Christian character of the Jerusalem community is attested on all hands. It was Jewish-Christian in its cult practices, its doctrinal position, and its membership.

Although for the Jews the reign of Hadrian was so difficult to endure, it brought no important changes of policy with regard to the Christians. In the course of the war any violence that they suffered was not at the hands of the Romans, but of Bar Cochba. The emperor's letter to Minucius Fundanus confirms the principles enunciated earlier by Trajan and refuses to make Christianity an offense in itself.[15] If then for want of explicit legislation concerning the Christians their undisturbed peace remained a rather precarious one,

Hadrian had at least done nothing to make their situation worse. They reaped the benefit of his scepticism; a contemptuous scepticism perhaps, but a tolerant one. It is not impossible, indeed, that for a little while the emperor was attracted to Christianity by a sympathetic curiosity. In any case, he reserved his severity for the Jews. Eusebius states with satisfaction that at the beginning of the second century "while everything connected with our Saviour's teaching and Church daily flourished and went forward more and more, the calamities of the Jews were at their height, and disaster followed upon disaster."[16]

During the hundred years that followed, that is to say, during the period of the later Antonines and of the Severi, there were no real developments in the empire's relations either with Christians or with Jews. As far as the Christians were concerned, there were some local persecutions, but, apart from the affair at Lyons in 177, there were no very striking happenings. On the Jewish side of affairs the storm of 135 was followed by a total calm. Under Antoninus both religions were treated with a similar benevolence. Marcus Aurelius, emperor and Stoic, was equally unsympathetic to both. He despised the Christians, who died out of sheer obstinacy and enjoyed the tragedy of their own demise.[17] The behavior of the Jews was even worse. Their turbulence reminded him of the barbarians of the Danube.[18] Yet neither Jews nor Christians were seriously disturbed during his reign or by his influence. If we are to believe Tertullian, he discouraged the activities of informers far more firmly than his predecessors had done.[19] Commodus was not interested in affairs of state or in his duties as emperor. For Jews and Christians therefore he was a tolerant ruler. The Severi were Africans whose Semitic sympathies were reinforced by their marriages. They were less firmly bound than their predecessors by the strictly Roman tradition, and were very open to the influence of the east in religious matters. They were avowed friends of the Jews, who were very appreciative of their beneficence. Jerome is reproducing rabbinic opinion when he says concerning Septimius Severus and Caracalla, *Judaeos plurimum dilexerunt.*[20] The Christians, for their part, had no more reason to complain of them than the Jews. At the same time as Caracalla[21] was behaving in such friendly fashion to the Jewish patriarch, Julia Mammaea was discussing theology with Origen.[22] If the emperors had been deliberately trying to distribute their favors equally between the two religions, they could not have achieved the result any better. Septimius Severus forbade the Jews to proselytize, but he forbade at the same time Christian evangelism. He does not seem to have been any more energetic or forceful in imposing the policy on one side rather than the other.[23] The two religions would both have been able, if they had been willing, to take part in the syncretistic faith that was the dream of Elagabalus and Alexander Severus. The former, being himself circumcised, could scarcely regard circumcision as a crime when it was practiced by others.[24] And in the biography of the latter we are told how he venerated in his private chapel, beside the images of Apollonius of Tyana, of Alexander, and of Orpheus, those of Abraham and Christ.[25]

But this century-long equilibrium between the two religions, which was the result of a general policy of toleration, was to be decisively upset in the Jews' favor. For the Christians the period of anarchy that followed the death of Alexander Severus, and the repeated attempts to restore order, marked the beginning of a policy of active intolerance. The era of the great persecutions was beginning. By contrast, the imperial goodwill toward the Jews did not waver. As we shall see shortly, even the Jews' attempts to spread their faith do not seem to have been seriously impeded at any time during the third century. Thus within a hundred years the situation of the two religions with regard to the Roman authorities had been completely reversed. The hopes that had been entertained by the Christian apologists at the beginning of the period, hopes encouraged by the difficulties of the Jews, had been disappointed. In Hadrian's time Judaism had been Rome's enemy, and the Church had been able for a while to believe that it could reap some advantage from the situation. After Decius it was the Christians with whom the empire was at war. During the interim the Jews had not been slow to climb back into favor. This had already happened under the Antonines, though the Christians were not yet explicitly put under an interdict.[26]

To summarize, there were two periods of intolerance. One, at the end of Hadrian's reign, was very short, and was characterized by anti-Jewish measures. The other, much longer one was the period of the great anti-Christian persecutions in the second half of the third century. In this latter period the hostilities were broken by not inconsiderable interludes of inactivity. Between the two was a period of transition during which, though the two religions appeared to be treated both alike, imperial hostility to Christianity gradually crystallized. At the same time the empire's attitude to Judaism remained in general a benevolent one, even if it did not actually improve. In this period, therefore, relations between the Roman state and the two religions were changing, but in the two cases they changed in completely opposite directions. The contrast is note-worthy; it was no accident. From the growth, first of anti-Christian attitudes, then of actual anti-Christian legislation, the Jews appear to have derived a positive advantage. The popular moods of anti-

Semitism, previously so frequent, no longer occurred. The popular hatred concentrated itself instead on Christianity. Among the Roman authorities the Jews met, at times, a positive goodwill, and at worst were treated with an easygoing indifference. And this was true throughout the period when Christians were being most seriously persecuted.

The contrast is all the more striking when we look at the attitude the Romans took toward Jewish proselytism. When Antoninus exempted the Jews, and them alone, from the prohibition his predecessor had enacted, he left in force the punishment laid down for the circumcision of individuals who were not of Jewish birth. Even Samaritans were still included in the ban. The practice of circumcision was under this law assimilated to the crime of castration, and carried the same punishment. *Circumcidere Judaeos filios suos tantum rescripto divi Pii permittitur: in non ejusdem religionis qui hoc fecerit castrantis poena irrogatur.*[27] This legislation seems to have had a double object. In the first place, it aimed at discouraging a practice that, quite apart from its religious significance, the Romans considered shameful and degrading. This is at least suggested by the assimilation of circumcision to castration. Both, in Roman eyes, consisted in *mutilare genitalia.*[28] Secondly, it was a blow at Jewish proselytism. Though the Jews were excepted from the general law, it seems as if the amendment was still intended to deprive them of the possibility of making proselytes. *Nascuntur, non fiunt Judaei,* one might say, to reverse a famous saying of Tertullian's.

That this was the intention of the edict is indicated by the other steps that were taken. These leave the imperial policies in less doubt. *Cives Romani, qui se judaico ritu vel servos suos circumcidi patiuntur, bonis ademptis in insulam perpetuo relegantur; medici capite puniuntur.*[29]

Thus interpreted, Antoninus's measures explain very well what was the Roman policy toward the Jews. Yahweh could be tolerated, but only on two conditions. He must not attempt again to set up in Palestine an independent kingdom, and He must not impose His worship on gentiles. Nationalism and proselytism were the two dangers inseparable from Israel. The former was no longer such a serious one after the suppression of the Jews in 135. It was the latter that Rome had set herself to neutralize.

But granted that proselytism was a genuine danger to the empire, Hadrian's measure was a singularly inappropriate means of combating it. In the last resort, Judaism and circumcision were not completely synonymous. Circumcision not only was, but still is practiced by people who have no attachment to Judaism. Conversely, there was no lack of proselytes, or at least semiproselytes, who were not circumcised.[30] Even during the Talmudic epoch there were rabbis who were willing to excuse proselytes the performance of this rite, which always proved a great stumbling block to them.[31] Furthermore, to limit the spread of Judaism by forbidding circumcision was to leave Judaism's very numerous feminine clientele entirely untouched.

Not only was the prohibition a roundabout method of combating Judaism, it was not even a really effective one. Furthermore, it was not very precise. In the term *Jew* itself there was an ambiguity. It had a geographical meaning, describing one who lived in or hailed from Judaea. It also had a religious sense, meaning "one who was attached to the Jewish faith." When the law allowed to Jews alone the right to practice circumcision from father to son, did it intend to reserve that right to those who could prove their Palestinian origin, at however far a remove, or did it include families of converts who for several generations had professed Judaism, and who were from the Jewish point of view counted among the chosen people? What was the legal position of Roman citizens who had already been circumcised? It does not appear that the law could have affected them retroactively. When it threatened with deprivation of citizenship those who were tempted to submit to circumcision, was it intended to make an exception in favor of those who, like St. Paul, were Jews by birth but possessed Roman citizenship, and of those who were the sons or remoter descendants of converted gentile citizens? How, above all, was it envisaged that the law should be applied after Caracalla's edict had abolished the distinction between citizens and *peregrini* and comprehended the entire Jewish people among the citizenry? Does not the lack of legislative texts to clarify these points justify the conclusion that the measure had already fallen into disuse?

The apparently straightforward nature of the texts is thus shown, on examination, to be quite illusory. The problem does not seem to have been squarely faced by the Roman authorities. One thing at least is certain, and to this Juster has drawn attention. If "by the penalties for circumcision Jewish proselytism was effectively halted," nevertheless "it was not punished as such by law."[32] But is it so certain that proselytism was effectively halted? We may reasonably suspect that the legislation was never strictly enforced. The only measures the emperors enacted against proselytism were indirect and lacking in clarity, and they never condemned proselytism as such. Moreover, Antoninus's successors displayed little enthusiasm for clarifying and applying these measures. From this it is often concluded that it would have been pointless for them to do so, since proselytism had declined.

This is a vital question, and we shall return to it in due course. I may say now that the explanation given does not seem to me to be acceptable. Proselytism did survive Antoninus's law. I shall not at this point go into all the arguments, for I intend to do so later, but for the time being I shall limit myself to the evidence of the imperial legislation. The biographer of Septimius Severus credits him with a radical measure against the Jews, a measure whose general import the biographer sufficiently indicates. *Judaeos fieri sub gravi poena vetuit.*[33] This time the situation is perfectly clear. What is in mind is proselytism itself, and at the same time Christian evangelism. *Idem etiam de Christianis sanxit.* This is proof that proselytism still went on, and proof, therefore, that the roundabout prohibition of Antoninus remained inoperative or ineffective.

The edict of Severus that reinforced it and enlarged its scope seems quickly to have joined it in oblivion. No trace of it remains in the legislative texts, which continue to recognize as punishable only circumcision itself. It has therefore been questioned whether Severus's edict ever existed, though this seems to me to be taking scepticism too far. I should be more inclined to regard the silence of the codes as evidence that it very rapidly ceased to be operative, if indeed it was ever operative at all. If, for the first and only time, it made the profession of Judaism an offense in itself, it cannot have been enforced for very long. It is not until we reach the Christian emperors that we find such an offense permanently on the statute book. This fact itself is a further proof, and may be supported by others that I shall adduce shortly, that until well into the fourth century Judaism was still a force to be reckoned with. The legislation of the Christian emperors is, in respect of its severity and effectiveness, in such marked contrast with the apparently indolent attitude to Judaism displayed by the pagan emperors that it is manifest that the pagan inertia cannot be explained by the disappearance of the proselytizing spirit from among the Jews.

Must we conclude that Christian evangelism was so much more insidious and effective than the proselytism of the Jews that the authorities were aware of nothing but the Christian threat and found the Jewish one by comparison negligible? Hardly so. Septimius Severus did prohibit both at once. It is also a fact that at the time of the great persecutions the Jews did not find themselves implicated in the attacks made on Christians. On the contrary, the Jews pressed their proselytizing attentions on the persecuted Christians themselves. A conversion to Judaism was as efficacious in avoiding punishment as a sacrifice to idols.

Eusebius tells us of a certain Domnus, at the beginning of the third century, who during a local persecution was converted from Christianity to Judasism. This apostasy provoked Serapion of Antioch into writing his Πρὸς Δόμνον.[34] The reason the incident was taken so seriously was doubtless that there was danger that Domnus's example might be followed by others. About the same time Tertullian set himself to demonstrate for the benefit of pagans the distinctiveness of Christianity, so that they should not say that "it sheltered somewhat of its own presumption under the shadow of a most famous, at least a licensed, religion."[35] We may, I think, legitimately suspect that in thus trying to clear up confusion the fiery polemist had in mind not only pagans, but also Christians, some of whom were tempted to exploit that very confusion by seeking refuge, when danger threatened, in the synagogue, *sub umbraculo insignissimae religionis, certe licitae.* Origen states, and deplores, the fact that the Jews often pressed believers to renounce their faith, presumably in favor of Judaism.[36] Finally, we have the evidence of the *Passio Pionii*, which recounts events that took place under Decius. The martyr before his death encourages his brethren to resist the pleas of the Jews, when, as he puts it, "they invite some of you to go to the synagogue," and not to avoid torment at that price.[37]

All this evidence compels us to the conclusion that under Severus the theoretical equality of the two religions before the empire, as Spartianus expresses it, had given way in practice to a distinct inequality. With regard to the Christians the prohibition was not rigorously enforced. With regard to the Jews it was not enforced at all. The inequality was accentuated by the developments that followed. The persecuting emperors forbade the practice and dissemination of Christianity, but they kept intact the traditional law regarding Jews. At the very time when the bloodiest persecution of all was going on Diocletian explicitly exempted the Jews from the necessity of offering sacrifice.[38] Even further, he closed his eyes to some of their religious activities that in theory were illegal.

II

If the empire was not impartial in its attitude and its policies toward the two religions, this is to be explained less by the overall circumstances than by the intrinsic character of the religions themselves. Above all, it is to be explained by Christianity's disquietingly novel features. In their anxiety to show the pagans that Christianity was no mere variant of Judaism, but something better, the apologists developed and made popular a threefold division of humanity into gentiles, Jews, and Christians. The intention was to establish the equality of Christians, as a group, with the other two already recognized categories.

In the beginning this division was regarded as a purely religious, or rather, purely cultic one. Thus, for example, the *Kerygma Petri* sets the new phenomenon of Christian worship against the two other, now outmoded ancient traditions, Judaism and paganism. "For what belonged to the Greeks and Jews is old. But we, who worship [God] in a new way, in the third form, are Christians."[39] Similarly, in the *Epistle of Diognetus* we read: "[The Christians] neither recognize the gods believed in by the Greeks nor practice the superstition of the Jews."[40] They are a distinct and independent group, in a category of their own. Nevertheless, their differences appear only in the sphere of religion, for "Christians are not distinguished from the rest of mankind by either country, speech or customs. The fact is, they nowhere settle in cities of their own; they use no peculiar language; they cultivate no eccentric mode of life."[41] But later, however, the division did take on a more distinctly social or national character. This is true, for example, for Aristides. "It is clear to us, O king, that the men of this world are of three kinds; those who worship what by you are called gods, the Jews, and the Christians. And those who worship many gods are again divided into three kinds; Chaldaeans, Greeks and Egyptians."[42] And in order to make it clear that he is speaking of actual societies, of peoples and not simply of cult groups, the author assigns to each an ancestor, who is the father of the *genos*. The Jewish race is derived from Abraham, the Christians reckon their origin from Christ: γενεαλογοῦνται ἀπὸ τοῦ κυρίου.[43] It is quite in accordance with this point of view that the author claims for the Christian *genos* the right to live in accordance with its own traditions, τὰ πάτρια.

This threefold division is only a transitory one. It must give way, and will in fact give way quite soon, to a twofold division. This twofold division is into Jews, who are excluded from the heritage, and gentiles, who are to be absorbed, renewed and rehabilitated by Christianity. The idea of a *tertium genus* cuts across that of the new people, to which I devoted some space above.[44] By virtue of a development closely bound up on one side with Christianity's progress and increasing Hellenization, and on the other with Judaism's repudiation of the gospel, the pride of the first generations of Christians in being strangers in the Greco-Roman world gave way gradually to a very different feeling, to a pride in their Hellenic heritage. From the time when the victorious Church extended its conquests to the limits of the civilized world it tended to confuse itself with that world and claim that heritage as its own. And when the fathers of the fourth century reply to the Jews, they do so not merely in their capacity as Christians, but in the name of the outsiders who have been called to replace Israel, *Ecclesia ex gentibus*. And this Jew/Christian dualism is to resolve itself finally, in its turn, into a unity. For in the last days the conversion of Jews, which has temporarily ceased, will begin again, and the Church will make up its quota of Jewish believers as the Synagogue, redeemed from its errors, is incorporated into the Church *en bloc*. Then at last "there will be neither Jew nor Greek," but only Christians.

According to this threefold division, the pagans constituted the *genus primum*, the Jews were the *genus alterum*, and the Christians the *genus tertium*. From the second century onwards these terms are found even in pagan writings. But if the pagans thus adopted the terminology, it was only in order to criticize it. The Christians' proud assertion that they were a species on the same level as the other two rebounded on their heads. They had put themselves outside the only categories that were officially recognized, and their enemies could therefore contest their very right to exist. In the arena they heard the crowds shout, *Usque quo genus tertium?*[45]

The officially accepted analysis of society conceived of it as consisting of two groups, and only two. Originally this twofold division was based on the antique distinction between Greeks, or Greco-Romans, and barbarians. In the period with which we are concerned this distinction has by no means been entirely abandoned. But as the barbarians themselves became Hellenized or Romanized under the aegis of the empire, and as the Greco-Roman world was influenced by them and acknowledged their influence, the contrast between Greek and barbarian came to possess a political rather than a cultural significance. It gave expression to the antagonism that existed between the empire and the countries beyond it. Though we cannot say that the word was used exclusively in this sense, yet it is in general true that *barbarian* referred primarily to those beyond the frontiers, especially Germans and Persians. But to ignore the barbarians and look only at the empire itself, the social and religious structure was again seen as twofold. On one side were the Hellenes, which is to say, all those, including Romans and ex-barbarians, who had accepted Greek culture. Now, since this was a time when a city without a cult was inconceivable, this cultural allegiance involved a religious one as well. Those who in cultural terms were described as Hellenes were in religious terms called pagans. The only exceptions to this cultural and religious unity were the Jews. Within the boundaries of the empire they were the sole representatives of the erstwhile barbarians. Though a minority, they nevertheless fell into a category of their own, incorrigible and unassimilable. And though this classification of humanity into two sorts had been invented by the Jews themselves, to correspond to their understanding of the divine purpose, the gentiles could not resist the logic of it. It was a simple expression of the facts, however much the gentiles might have wished them otherwise.[46]

Whatever complaints the Greco-Roman world made against the Jews, it did give them credit for the antiquity of their national and religious traditions. This was all that restrained the pagans from expressing their anti-Semitism in more extreme ways than they did. Josephus, having demonstrated in his history "that our Jewish nation is of very great antiquity, and had a distinct subsistence of its own originality," goes on in the *Contra Apionem* to pursue the same question. Indeed, the full title of the work is περὶ τῆς τῶν Ἰουδαίων ἀρχαιότητος. Its purpose is "to convict those that reproach us, of spite and voluntary falsehood, and to correct the ignorance of others, and withal to instruct all those who are desirous of knowing the truth of what great antiquity we really are."[47] The care with which Josephus goes about this question, and the size of the two works he devotes to it, are an indication of its importance. In pagan eyes Judaism and the Jewish people had a right to exist only insofar as they could establish that they had existed in the past. Tacitus, who can scarcely be suspected of sympathy toward the Jews, expressed not only his own opinion but that of the imperial authorities when he said, *Hi ritus, quoquo modo inducti, antiquitate defenduntur.*[48] Conversely, it was because it could make no claim to the past, but presented itself as a complete novelty, that Christianity incurred first distrust and then positive aversion and active opposition, both from public opinion and the authorities. Celsus expresses this point of view clearly when he accuses the Christians of having originated in Judaism but having abandoned the law of their fathers, τὸν πάτριον νόμον. They are Jews, he alleges, who have been misled by Christ into changing both their name and their manner of life. Origen finds it very awkward to reply to this accusation. What he says, in substance, is this: the Jewish Christians do continue to observe the law because they are not capable of going beyond it and wholeheartedly embracing the full truth.[49] This halfhearted vindication of the representatives of an outmoded and backward-looking kind of Christianity in reality admits the justice of the accusation when leveled against the Catholic Church.

Here we have the basic reason for the distinction the pagan authorities made between Christians and Jews. Christianity represented a threat to the established order, whereas Judaism by contrast was already tolerated and protected, and could, besides, be positively useful to that order. Strictly speaking, from the Roman point of view one did not become a Jew, one was born a Jew. It was in their capacity as a nation that Israel were guaranteed liberty to practice their religion.[50] But by comparison with Christianity and the insidious power of its evangelism, the Jews and Judaism appeared quite tame and tractable. A conversion to Judaism on the part of a pagan seemed a lesser evil than a conversion to Christianity. A conversion from Christianity to Judaism was at least a step in the right direction.

For a Christian to apostatize, whether he became a pagan again or turned into a Jew, was in either case to turn back to a legitimate tradition, to join himself again with a society the law allowed, and to be back within the fold of legality. Judaism's right to exist had always been recognized. All the evidence suggests that in the critical situation that was created by the intervention of Christianity the right of Judaism to expand had also been conceded, albeit tacitly. This right was recognized at least insofar as its expansion was at Christianity's expense. It is very difficult to believe that Jewish attempts to convert persecuted Christians were made without the cognizance of the Roman authorities. Even when the apostates did not go so far as to have themselves circumcised, they were nevertheless, if they claimed membership of the Synagogue, out of jeopardy and could not be accused under any law. The fact that they were thus lost to the old religion as surely as they were lost to Christianity does not appear to have disturbed the authorities at all. It looks as if the state, in its desire to eliminate Christianity by making apostates and not martyrs, accepted the two recognized religious categories, Jewish and pagan, as equivalents, and left to the defecting Christians themselves the choice whether to return to the religion of their ancestors by blood or to be converted to that of their ancestors in the spirit. We may be tempted to believe that the Roman authorities in some circumstances played the Jewish card against the Christians. And we can well see why an anti-Jewish polemical treatise should hold it as a grievance against the Jews that they had been *sceptro et legionibus fulta.*[51]

III

What we advance as a plausible hypothesis for the third century is certainly true in the reign of at least one emperor, Julian the Apostate. We have precise information in his case. We know not only how his Jewish policy worked out in practice but what the theory behind it was. No doubt Julian's case is a unique, and an extreme one. He was a fanatic. Furthermore, the period was one in which Christianity had already won a number of victories. It was no longer a question of arresting its progress, but of dislodging it from positions which it already held. Julian's policy is therefore dealing with the particular situation that Constantine bequeathed to him. Nevertheless, Julian's reactions to Judaism and Christianity, in spite of the particular slant that was given them by the circumstances of the moment and the peculiar temperament of the emperor himself, proceed from the same principles as had always guided the Roman government's religious policies. They thus shed an indirect light on the attitudes taken by Julian's predecessors.

The feelings to which Judaism gave rise in Julian were complex.[52] There was, first of all, the distrust of Julian the Hellene for a form of barbarism that was all the more disgusting and potent for having given birth to the sect of the Galileans. Many of the biting and sarcastic shafts he launches against Christianity find their mark just as readily in the religion from which Christianity sprang. This is particularly true when he criticizes the Jewish and Christian idea of revelation and attacks the content of the Old Testament. When he addresses the Jews themselves, he taunts them especially about their exclusivism, their claim to be the chosen people, and their mono-theism. Their cardinal error is that they have raised to the status of supreme and only God a divinity who was merely of local and national importance. Yahweh was simply an "ethnarch," and provided that he was willing to remain no more than that he could be allowed a place in the pantheon of restored Hellenism.[53]

Why is it that this god, if he is god not only of the Jews but of the gentiles also, gave so lavishly to the Jews the gifts of prophecy, of Moses, and the priesthood, the prophets and the law, and all the miracles of which their myths speak? ... Why did he not give any of these things to us gentiles? ... For tens of thousands of years, or at least for thousands, he has left peoples in the worst kind of ignorance, from east to west, from north to south, to serve idols—as you put it—the only exception being an insignificant race which, for a couple of thousand years at most were established in a corner of Palestine. Why, if he is in truth the god of all men, the creator of all things, has he so slighted us?[54]

But in spite of these weaknesses of Judaism, so obligingly pointed out by Julian, there were at least two things to be reckoned to its credit, and they were very important ones, viz., its legal prescriptions, principally those concerning its sacrificial cult, and its feeling for tradition. On both counts it had a good deal in common with paganism. Julian professed to find similarities between Jewish and pagan cults extending down to details of the rites. He was especially appreciative of circumcision. Was it not found, he argued, among the Egyptian priests? And was it not from this source, doubtless, that the Jews learned it? Abraham, again, as a Chaldaean by race, not only was careful to offer frequent sacrifices, but, like the pagans, he practiced divination by the stars and by birds, ἑλληνικὸν ἴσως καὶ τοῦτο.[55]

The Christians, by contrast, had not only abandoned the rites of paganism, but they had taken up Jewish ones only to throw them overboard in their turn. They thus made themselves guilty of a double crime of contempt for tradition, and this is what Julian most of all holds against them. "Why," cries Julian in indignation, "Why, when the Greeks are so superior in every respect, abandon them and run after the Jews?" But having done that, the Christians might at least have remained faithful to their adopted heritage! If they had only observed the law their God had given them! Then their situation would not have been so serious. They claim to follow Moses, who preached a rigorous monotheism. But they are not monotheists. And though it is true that the Jews do not any longer offer sacrifices, the Christians observe not one of the customs the Jews do still maintain. It is no good asserting that, though they are distinct from the Jews of the present day, they are in agreement with the message of the prophets. It simply is not true. In fact, they have thought up for themselves a new cult, καινὴν θυσίαν. This, in the eyes of Julian the unrepentant conservative, is the most serious of their offenses.[56] He adds: "The Galileans have rejected the good and noteworthy teachings to be found among us Hellenes, and also those of the Hebrews which go back to Moses. Instead they have kept notions from both peoples which accompany them like maleficent demons. Their atheism proceeds from the instability of the Jews, their careless and relaxed life from our own recklessness and unmannerliness."[57]

To those who object that the Jews themselves do not offer sacrifice any more Julian replies that they could not do otherwise, once the temple had been destroyed. If they have abandoned sacrifice, it is still out of respect for the law, which forbids it outside the one sanctuary. They do, by contrast, still carefully maintain the domestic cult, and observe the food laws scrupulously. But the Christians, who pride themselves on being innovators and have no need of Jerusalem, have no excuse for not offering sacrifices.[58] In short, there is a deeper gulf between these innovators, who abandon the heritage of their fathers (ἀπολιπόντες τὰ πάτρια)[59] and the Jews, than between Israel and the pagans. The real difference between the latter pair resolves itself into the one issue of monotheism. Everything else the two cults have in common, temples, altars, laws, and purifications.

On the basis of this agreement on the theoretical plane, an agreement reinforced by a common aversion to Christianity, it became possible to reach a mutual understanding. It is doubtful whether the Jews were aware of the similarities to which Julian had so ingeniously drawn attention. Julian himself was in their eyes an idolator, and there could be no other way of looking at him. This is the reason for the Talmud's silence concerning him, though this slience may at first sight be surprising.[60] Lacking any positive enthusiam for Julian, the Jews well understood the advantages of a diplomatic silence, and realized that their religious interests obliged them to go along with his views, for there was a possibility that they might have something to gain from him, namely, permission to rebuild the temple.

The Christians were disgusted with this eager opportunism. According to St. John Chrysostom, the initiative in the undertaking came not from the emperor but from the Jews themselves. When he wished to make them reinstitute sacrifices, they reminded him that they were not able to do so outside the confines of Jerusalem, and seized on this pretext to ask for the reestablishment of "the temple, the altar and the holy of holies," not at all ashamed to demand such a favor of an impious pagan. Julian was ready to accede to their requests, in the hope that the reestablishment of the sacrificial cult would lead the Jews in the direction of idol worship. He hoped too to falsify the prophecies of Christ, who had announced the lasting destruction of the sanctuary.[61]

Such testimony must be treated with caution. It is most unlikely that Julian agreed to any such suggestion of the Jews. He knew enough about them, as we are well aware, not to entertain any notions of converting them to paganism. We may nevertheless recognize as very likely motives for the undertaking Julian's well-attested fondness for sacrifical worship and the desire to give the lie to Christian prophecies. There may well have been yet other reasons. It has been suggested that he was moved by a wish to immortalize himself by leaving notable buildings behind him. Moreover, on the eve of his expedition against Shapur he might well have hoped to enlist the sympathies of the very numerous Jewish population of Persia. A modern analogy to this might be the policy adopted toward Islam by some contemporary statesmen.[62] None of these suggestions is implausible, any or all of the various motives suggested may have contributed to the decision. The primary reasons, however, appear to have been those which a reading of Julian's own works suggests, viz., a certain sympathy with a religion that seemed to Julian to be in many respects similar to his own; and, perhaps more important still, a desire to spite the Christians.[63]

Julian's Jewish policy, in fact, cannot be separated from his anti-Christian policy. They are opposite sides of the same coin, different aspects of a single aim, to unite the conservative forces of the empire in an endeavor to stem the overwhelming and disruptive flood of Christianity. There was a place for Judaism in this defensive coalition because it was as obstinately attached to its tradition as Julian was to his, and was as directly threatened by Christian preaching as was the old paganism. To give back to the Jews their temple, the focal point of their devotion and the unique center of their cult, would have put the Jews in Julian's debt and strengthened their loyalty to him. To restore the ancient ritual to its traditional form would restore at the same time Judaism's prestige, and might be expected (so at least Julian reckoned) to strengthen its appeal to Judaizing Christians and Christians of Jewish extraction, strengthening at the same time its resistance to Christians of other kinds. Finally, such a move would be a wounding demonstration of the falsity of a prophecy of Christ, and ought to shake the faith of the believers. Since he could not carry the Christians with him, as he wished, back into his own ancestral faith, Julian hoped at least to lead them toward Judaism, a Judaism to which he, Julian, would give new life, as he had given new life to Hellenism. By thus leading them back into the tradition in which they had originated but which they had renounced, he hoped to suppress the Christians and eliminate the *tertium genus*.

This carefully thought-out scheme was without precedent. On the basis of the analyses I have carried out above it is difficult to resist the conclusion that the third-century emperors, whose indulgent attitude to the Jews contrasts so sharply with their anti-Christian enactments, were guided by the same considerations as was Julian. Though their policies were not so explicitly formulated and were less consistently worked out, they tended, perhaps unreflectingly, in the same direction. Thus the imperial goodwill was bestowed on Judaism, and its acknowledged status as a *religio licita* interpreted as broadly as it could be. In this way it was allowed to bring to bear on Christianity not only the direct influence of its apologetic, but also the attraction of its immunity. The effect of such policies was to enlist Israel alongside the empire in the struggle against the common enemy.

IV

But the way was left open for the employment in this struggle of less peaceful methods of persuasion. If she could not make apostates, Rome would make martyrs. We are led thus to consider a further problem: what part did the Jews play in the persecution of Christians, and how much responsibility for them did the Jews bear? Some writers, making scarcely any examination of the matter, have taken it

for granted that the Jews were heavily implicated. Allard, among
Catholic scholars,[64] and Harnack among the Protestants have both
done so.[65] The question has been take up recently by Parkes in the
work already referred to, and he comes to a very different conclusion.
Perhaps he has given way too much to the pro-Semitism that
characterizes his whole book and has been a little too ready to
exculpate the Jews. Nevertheless, his analysis represents a definite
advance on the usually unsubstantiated assertions of his predecessors.
For the first time the problem has been genuinely discussed.[66]

There are two sorts of evidence we have to take account of, viz., the
testimony of ecclesiastical writers and the acts of martyrs. Both of
these may reasonably be suspected of a certain lack of objectivity. The
almost complete lack of either Jewish or pagan texts on the subject
makes the evaluation of the evidence particularly difficult.

The testimony of ecclesiastical writers is usually expressed in rather
vague terms, and really amounts to very little. The essence of it
consists of a few lines of Justin Martyr and Tertullian, which are
reproduced with varying fidelity by later writers. Justin, apostrophiz-
ing the Jews, declares: "You slew the Just One and his prophets before
him, and now you reject, and, as far as in you lies, dishonour those
that set their hope on him, and God Almighty and Maker of the
universe who sent him, cursing in your synagogues them that believe
on Christ. For you have not authority to raise your own hands against
us, because of them that are now supreme. But as often as ye could,
this also ye did."[67]

In all likelihood the reference is to the violent measures taken
against the Church in Jerusalem from the martyrdom of Stephen
onwards, which resulted in the death of a number of prominent
Christians. Included, no doubt, are the atrocities that accompanied
Bar Cochba's revolt. At the time when Justin wrote, i.e., some time
after the revolt of Bar Cochba, this violence suffered by Christians at
Jewish hands belonged to the past. And it seems that the Roman
authorities were not yet interested in exploiting Jewish hostility to the
Christians. The Jews therefore had to fall back on ineffectual
maledictions, or else cast themselves in the role of informers. This at
least is what we are given to understand in another passage of Justin's.
"For we, having been called of God by means of the mystery of the
cross, which is so despised and full of shame—and to our confession
and obedience and piety have punishments, even unto death, been
awarded by the demons and the host of the devil, through the service
rendered to them by you—[we, I say] endure all things."[68] "The host
of the devil" means, in a period when there was not yet any general
persecution, the pagan masses, and, on occasion, the local authorities.

As for "the service rendered to them" by the Jews, Justin is more explicit. "[You] chose selected men from Jerusalem and then sent them out into all the earth, saying that a godless sect, namely, of Christians had appeared, and recounting what all who know us not are wont to say against us. So that ye not only are the cause of iniquity for yourselves, but in fact for all others.... Against the only spotless and righteous Light therefore, sent to men from God, were ye zealous that these bitter and dark and unjust tales should be spread through all the earth."[69]

Thus the Jews were the first to denounce the *prava superstitio* and the *flagitia* of which the pagan authors speak. *Seminarium infamiae nostrae,* says Tertullian in similar vein.[70] They had, in doing this, raised the alarm, attracted the attention of the authorities to this new sect, and drawn upon it, in the first instance suspicion, and then active repression. This reconstruction of events makes good sense. We could well imagine how the steps that Jewish orthodoxy took to defend itself against the Christian preaching, and particularly the counter-measures taken among the Jewish communities by the Jewish "apostles," might sometimes have gone further than they were supposed to do and might have produced anti-Christian repercussions beyond the confines of the synagogues.[71] That some of the calumnies that circulated among the pagan masses had their origin among the Jews is entirely probable.[72] The Jews were anxious to dissociate themselves from the new sect and deprive it of the legal loophole with which the Synagogue might have provided it, and in their anxiety they were not always able to be scrupulous in their choice of methods. It is very probable that Jewish influences, working through Poppaea in the circles surrounding the emperor himself, account for the fact that, whereas under Nero the Roman government was sufficiently well informed to make a clear distrinction between Christians and Jews, yet thirty years later, in the time of Domitian, it appears unable or unwilling to make any distinction at all. The Jews therefore could have been, in a sense, at the bottom of the persecution in Rome in A.D. 64. Does this mean that we could, up to a point, convict them of responsibility, even though the main brunt of that responsibility must fall on Nero?

It should, moreover, be noted that what would have been possible in A.D. 64 would without doubt have been far harder in the middle of the second century. It would be difficult to sustain the view that the Jews, so soon after the events of 135, had enough influence to unleash any violence against their opponents. All the more reason, then, by skilful maneuvre, to shift on to the Christians as often as they could the hostility to which they themselves were exposed. It is surely not coincidence that the popular imagination accused both Jews and Christians of exactly the same vices. It is quite probable that the Christians were the victims, in the first instance, of a kind of anti-Semitism. Nevertheless, there is no reason to think that the efforts of the Jews ever took the form of a systematic undertaking, or achieved the universal success that Justin attributes to them.

There is more to be said than this. Let us not forget that Justin was not only an anti-Jewish polemist, but at the same time an apologist, addressing himself on Christianity's behalf to the Roman authorities and Roman public opinion. These two aspects of his activity shed light on each other. The main theme of Justin's defence of Christianity is that Rome's burgeoning hostility to the Church is due to a misunderstanding. The Romans lack accurate information about the new religion, and know of it only from the biased reports of those hostile to it. It is for this reason alone that the state treats the Church as an enemy. What Justin sets out to do is to show what Christianity is really like. The Roman people and their government err only through ignorance. The real responsibility for the wrong rests on other shoulders. Where else, if not on those of Israel? The tactics were not new. They go back to the very beginning of Christianity and are to be found in the gospels themselves. The authors of the gospels do their best to present the Romans in a good light, and they have manifestly gone out of their way to produce an account of the passion from which the Roman authorities, represented by Pilate, emerge almost blameless, whilst responsibility is not only loaded on to the Jews but readily accepted by them. "His blood be on us and on our children." The theological need to show the Jewish people as rebels against the divine message thus chimes in with the political need to exculpate the Roman power.

The parallel between Justin and the evangelists is perhaps closer still. The gospels and the apology of Justin were published in similar circumstances, the gospels just after A.D. 70 and Justin's work immediately following A.D. 135. In both cases it might reasonably have been expected that Rome, emerging from a bitter war with the Jews, would be ill-disposed toward them. And from this ill-will Christians hoped to reap some benefit. By showing their loyalty to Rome, and their "philanthropy," and by demonstrating the correspondence between the Christian "philosophy" and the natural religion to which the better pagans subscribed, they believed that they were preparing the way for an agreement. They hoped to give further impetus towards such an entente by showing that the Jews, incorrigible rebels against the Roman power, were also sworn enemies of Christianity, and that their schemes threatened at the same time the old-established state and the new Church. We know what became of that optimistic notion.[73]

It is doubtless no mere coincidence that the only real evidence that bears out that of Justin comes from another apologist who was also concerned with anti-Jewish polemic. Tertullian's lapidary formula remains in the memory of everyone: *Synagogas Judaeorum fontes persecutionum.*[74] Indeed, it is so epigrammatic that, to my mind at least, it invites suspicion. If Tertullian is speaking, as the context suggests, about the period when the Christian preaching began, we may unreservedly accept what he says. It was in fact in the synagogues that Christians first met with ill-treatment. The accounts of St. Paul's preaching and its results that are given in Acts afford enough examples of this. The same source shows equally well how the Jews, not content with acting as their own police force, sometimes tried to stir up the authorities against the Christians.[75] But to call these "persecutions" is a not entirely proper use of the word. If, on the other hand, the word *persecutions* is taken seriously, it suggests that Tertullian is thinking of more recent events, and even of contemporary ones, and asserting that the persecutions the Romans carry out habitually have their origin in the synagogues. If this is what he means, it is not easy to accept the allegation. Is is really necessary to appeal to Jewish influence in order to account for persecutions that were decided on and carried out by the Roman authorities? Are the reasons for the conflict between the Church and the state, as they are known to have existed around the beginning of the third century, not sufficient by themselves to account for the repressive measures that were taken? There is nothing that forbids us to believe that the Jews derived some satisfaction from the situation and did what they could to stir the fire, but that their influence was sufficient to set the blaze going in the first place is not easy to sustain.

It was normal among Christians to think of the martyrs as imitators of Christ, almost as reincarnations of Christ. Indeed, one African inscription describes the relics of martyrs as *Membra Christi.*[76] There is reason to think that Tertullian has been so far under the influence of this idea that he has been moved to accommodate the account of their sufferings to that of the sufferings of Christ himself, to the extent of imposing on it the accepted ascription of those sufferings to the Jews. This would come all the more naturally to him in view of his dislike of the Jews, though in his case the desire to shift the blame would not be reinforced by any considerations of political opportunism, for times had changed since the days of Justin. There is another saying of Tertullian's that probably represents the facts somewhat better than the rather too rhetorical phrase we have been examining. *Tot hostes ejus [of Christianity]* quot extranei, et quidem proprie *ex* aemulatione Judaei, *ex concussione milites, ex natura ipsi etiam domestici nostri.*[77]

Faced with the extravagant accusations made by ancient Christian writers, we must beware of leaning over too far backwards and absolving the Jews altogether. They did in fact persecute Christians when they were in a position to do so. They did so in their own country, Palestine, for as long as their own national and religious authorities preserved some freedom of action apart from the Roman power. They did so especially in the periods when they were in conflict with Rome, during which times they were temporarily in control of the country. Stephen, James, and those who suffered during the troubles of 135 were their victims.[78] In the diaspora they played a more modest part. By denouncing the Christian heresy, they helped the Romans to distinguish between the two religions and to recognize the dangers that lurked within the newer one. Yet a farsighted authority was well able to perceive these dangers for itself, without any aid from Jews. The Jews were able to assist in discrediting the Christians, by purveying scandalous stories about them. Yet they had no monopoly of such scandals, and the pagan masses did not wait for Jewish prompting before they took issue with the Christians. They had often enough taken issue in just the same way with the Jews themselves. It is probable that the more acute the conflict between Church and society became, the less became the Jewish part in it. For most of the time they no doubt did no more than associate themselves with the action taken by the pagans.[79] An objective examination of the evidence, such as we have just carried out, forbids us to accuse them of anything more than this. The evidence is at best rather sparse. A study of the *Acts of the Martyrs* confirms our conclusion. Parkes has made such a study, and done it very thoroughly. I can do not better than summarize the main points. His conclusions seem to me to be, in the majority of cases, the only ones possible.

V

It must be remarked at the outset that in all the vast literature of the *Acta Martyrum* (and the historical value of the genre as a whole is dubious) the number of documents that actually lay blame clearly on the Jews is not very great. It must also be noted that when several different versions of an account exist, though one version or more may mention the Jews, they do not all do so. In fact, those accounts in which a major part is attributed to the Jews nearly all relate to Palestine and to the first century.[80] For the period between Hadrian

and Constantine, which is not only the period in which we are
interested but the great flowering period for this kind of hagiographical literature, the evidence for Jewish involvement becomes very thin.
In most instances we are left in no doubt that for the authors the
responsibility for the persecutions was essentially that of the pagan
crowd and the Roman authorities. When the Jews appear, it is
generaly neither as the sole agents of persecution nor as actual
protagonists in the struggle, but usually as associates of the pagans.
Rather infrequently are they represented as denouncing the Christians, or as initiating action against them. For example, in the account
of the execution of Paul, Valentina, and Thea at Diocaesarea, the
Constantinople tradition and the Armenian tradition agree in
accusing the Jews of pressing the matter,[81] but Eusebius on the
contrary is content to indicate that Paul, in his last prayer, prays to
God for the Jews and for the pagans, which seems to imply that
responsibility is shared.[82]

According to some texts, the part played by Jews was most
frequently no more than that of giving assistance, often in a very
active and spiteful way, to the pagan persecutors. The classic example
is the martyrdom of Polycarp of Smyrna in 155. The initiative came
from the pagan crowd. Annoyed by the courage of the first group of
martyrs, they clamored for the execution of the bishop. The threats of
the magistrates were powerless to get him to sacrifice to the gods. It
was then the general public that, in a new outcry, demanded that he
be burned alive. "The whole multitude of gentiles and Jews who
dwelt in Smyrna cried out with ungovernable rage and in a loud
voice, 'This is the teacher of Asia, the father of the Christians, the
destroyer of our gods, that teacheth many not to sacrifice or
worship.' "[83]

Parkes has pointed out how unlikely such a cry would be in the
mouth of Jews. This is not sufficient reason to deny the Jews any part
at all in the affair. The documentary account emphasizes their part
insistently. "The mob straightway brought together timber and
faggots from the workshops and baths, the Jews giving themselves
zealously to the work, as they were like to do."[84] It was the Jews, again,
who persuaded the governor not to allow the Christians to have the
martyr's corpse but to reduce it to ashes.[85]

It has sometimes been objected that Jews would not have
frequented the theatre and would certainly not have carried wood on
"the great sabbath" which, according to the text, was the day of the
martyrdom. To this objection Parkes reasonably replies that we know
nothing at all about the Jewish community at Smyrna, and cannot
say how orthodox it was. And we certainly cannot say how orthodox

were the particular Jewish individuals who took part in the event. But the objection may at least be sustained thus far, that it is unlikely that the Jewish part in the affair was officially sanctioned and organized. What we have here are the proceedings of certain individual Jews. It is, of course, impossible to determine, even approximately, how many took part.

It is, nevertheless, just as well to keep in mind that the main preoccupation of the *Martyrium Polycarpi* is to demonstrate the perfect parallelism between the martyrdom of Polycarp and that of Christ. It asserts this in its opening words. Polycarp "by his sufferings put an end to the persecution; setting, as it were, his seal to it. For almost all things that went before were done that the Lord might show us, from above, a martyrdom such as truly became the gospel."[86] It is expressed with the same clarity at the conclusion of the work, where Polycarp is said to have been "not only an eminent teacher, but also a glorious martyr; whose death all desire to imitate, as having been in every way conformable to the gospel of Christ."[87]

It follows from all this that the Jews did play some part in the martyrdom. But if we are not entitled to deny this, we ought at least to entertain some reservations about how significant a part it was. If only one Jew had taken part in the affair, the Christian accounts of the matter would have made the most of it.

Perhaps it is also possible to trace in the details of the narrative the influence of the gospel accounts of the passion, just as in those accounts themselves we may trace the influence of Old Testament prophecy. As the gospels aim to show that in the sufferings of Christ the scriptures were fulfilled, so the *Martyrium Polycarpi* makes the sufferings of Polycarp conform to the divine pattern afforded by Christ. "For he expected to be delivered up, even as the Lord also did."[88] The officer who presided at the arrest and trial "bore by God's appointment the same name [as our Lord's judge] being called Herod."[89] As in the gospels, it is the crowd that forces the decision.[90] The *confector*, in order to finish Polycarp off, pierces his side, just as the centurion did to Christ.[91] Finally, the proceedings instigated by the Jews before the governor, to persuade him to refuse the Christians permission to take the body, recall the attempt made by the Jerusalem authorities before Pilate to prevent the faithful from getting hold of the body of Christ. The reason given is very curious. "Lest forsaking him that was crucified, they should begin to worship this Polycarp."[92] One is tempted to add, "by asserting that he is raised from the dead."

This same assimilation to the gospel account is seen very clearly in another document, whose veracity no one any longer dreams of defending, the *Acts of Pontius*. Pontius, having successfully resisted torture, is on the point of being freed, when a crowd of Jews intervenes. They cry, "Death!" and are granted their request. On this, Pontius thanks God for the similarity of his sufferings to those of Christ, and dies.[93] Another text recounts how, at Nicomedia in the time of Aurelian, a Jew, having revealed to the authorities the hiding place of the Christians, came by night with soldiers to arrest them. This is a manifest transposition of the story of Judas.[94]

Allard notes as a particularly important instance of Jewish participation the martyrdom of Pionius, who was a victim of the Decian persecution. His description of the Jews' activities takes on a warmly indignant tone. "The Jews assisted with a fierce curiosity, with a spiteful joy, at the trials imposed on the Christians. They besieged the entrances of the temples and feasted their eyes on the unholy sacrifices."[95] To speak in this fashion is to give perhaps too much credence to a text that does not lack signs of editorial revision. For example, it puts into the mouth of the martyr just before his death a very literary-sounding speech. The part it ascribes to the Jews could well be explained by reminiscences of the martyrdom of Polycarp. The likelihood of this is increased when we remember that both are set in Smyrna. But by the same token, Jewish participation is not to be excluded altogether. A sober assessment must take account of the local situation. The Jews were evidently numerous enough in Smyrna to influence pagan opinion, or at least to make themselves felt when they urged their point of view. Even so, they play no part here other than that of active spectators. Zeiller's judicious summary is perhaps as near as we shall get to a fair judgment on the matter. "The Jews seem to have been, then, at Smyrna if not elsewhere, especially incensed against the Christians,... [but] the *Passion of Pionius* does not say that it was they who instigated Pionius' arrest."[96]

To sum up, it does not appear that the few attested instances of active Jewish hostility to the Christians fell outside the category of individual and local enterprise. There is no question of any general conspiracy on the part of Judaism. Neither do the Jews in any of these cases play a decisive role. It is simply a matter of particular Jews who reinforce or stimulate popular hatred. "The statement of Jewish hostility in general terms is based on theological exegesis and not on historical memory."[97]

Apart from these few rather dubious texts, virtually all the acts of the martyrs are silent about any part played by Jews. The argument *ex silentio* has in this case considerable force.[98] We may be quite sure that if there had been any basis at all for the accusation, the Christians would have made it, for there was no love lost between the two. If Christian writers inculpate the Jews no oftener than is the case, it can only be because there was no occasion to do so. It is all the more significant that some writings not only fail to make any accusation against the Jews but assert that they showed goodwill to those who were persecuted. I am leaving out of account the texts that speak of tears wrung from the Jews by the sufferings of Christians, or of conversions proceeding from the same cause. They say the same just as frequently of pagans, and such statements in any case do not prove very much. They simply express one of the standard themes of hagiography.

It is interesting to see that Parkes records several instances of martyrs being buried in Jewish cemeteries.[99] This is a detail that Christian authors would scarcely have invented. If, as there is every reason to assume, these burials really did take place, they could hardly have done so without the agreement of the Jewish community concerned.[100] The fact can in any case be confirmed archaeologically. The excavations at Carthage in particular have shown that the first Christians were sometimes interred in the Jewish necropolis.[101]

We have here a salutary corrective to the assertions of Tertullian, whose evidence, as we have already discovered, it is wise not to take too literally. It may be objected that the evidence of Tertullian and that of the burials pertains to two different periods in Jewish-Christian relations in Africa. But even so, it ought to induce a certain caution and prevent us from imposing too great a degree of uniformity on the history of those relations. For even if it be argued that the burials in question are from the first half of the second century, and therefore antedate Tertullian, it must still be noted that the Jews and Christians in Africa remained on good terms even when relations between the two in Palestine were particularly bad.

Tertullian himself mentions that the Jews sometimes offered threatened Christians asylum in their synagogues, and if this is true, the Jews were perhaps not so unanimously detested as he pretends. The texts I have already quoted are enough, I think, to show that hatred was not always the only feeling of the Jews toward their adversaries. The fact that they were able to take advantage of the discomfiture of the persecuted Christians could certainly have given them a malicious pleasure. But who would dare deny that their proselytizing zeal could also have sprung from the best of motives, and that they preferred not the death of a sinner, but rather that he should be converted.

From all this one conclusion seems to emerge. If we are to arrive at an accurate assessment, we must take account of local conditions, of the circumstances of the moment, and especially of personal considerations, all of which affected the adherents of the two cults. We ought not to talk too much about Judaism and Christianity, but rather about Jews and Christians, for to rely on general appearances might lead us to make some very false reconstructions.

In order to be quite certain about the part played by the Jews in the persecutions it would be necessary to have information in each case about the degree of orthodoxy of the religious communities concerned, both Jewish and Christian. If we were so informed, we should without doubt be made aware of a considerable variety. Lacking such information, we must beware of dogmatic or sweeping assertions. Parkes has rightly pointed out that the influence of the leaders of the communities, Christian clergy and rabbis, seems to have been decisive.[102] Relations between the communities were openly hostile or reasonably cordial according to whether the rabbinic leaders saw the Christians either as fellow monotheists (even if the monotheism was of a rather attenuated sort) or as vile heretics. Israel felt no positive sympathy either for the persecuted Christians or for the persecuting empire. The latter it had to thank for troubles of its own. Jews were sometimes seized with hatred for the Christians, sometimes with pity. Some even, at times, felt a certain solidarity with them. Toward the empire the Jewish attitude was sometimes one of aversion, and sometimes it was dictated by opportunist considerations. These latter impelled the Jews to consolidate their privileged position and protect themselves from any repercussions by drawing the line of demarcation between them and the new sect very clearly, even to the extent of going along with popular reaction and official sanction. But it must in all honesty be added that Jewish hostility appears at the very beginning of the Christian period, when the Jews were still in a position to take action on their own initiative. After that, the Roman authorities were able to conceive of making use of the Synagogue in order to halt the triumphant progress of Christianity, but the Synagogue's active role became ever smaller, as it declined numerically and became less influential in the Empire's affairs.

VI

What we know of the policies of the empire toward the Jews after the conversion of Constantine confirms these conclusions. If the Jews really had taken a prominent part in the persecutions of the fourth century, the Christian emperors, who were very responsive to ecclesiastical suggestions, could hardly have failed to take some reprisals in the form of anti-Jewish legislation. They would have done it all the more willingly in that it would have provided a welcome opportunity to protect the good name of their pagan predecessors, with whom they felt themselves to be in continuity, by shifting the blame for the persecutions onto the shoulders of the Jews. Constantine did not lack the opportunity, if he had wished to avail himself of it, to shift the blame in this fashion. In fact, nothing of the kind happened. Though the traditional status of the Jews was indeed altered, it was only by degrees, and the change had nothing to do with the persecutions. At no point do the expositions of the laws concerned make any reference to the part played by Jews in the anti-Christian demonstrations of the preceding century.

The attitude of the Christian emperors toward Judaism is singularly complex, because the policies that served their political interests were in conflict with their religious inclinations. The emperors were the guardians of the law, and, as such, the heirs of the policies of pagan rulers. They were therefore, as far as the Jews were concerned, upholders of the traditional order. At the same time they were members and protectors of the Christian Church (whether orthodox or Arian matters little), which urged them to reduce ever further the acknowledged privileges of Israel. Their policies therefore varied according to whether they thought of themselves principally as emperors or as Christians. Within the period, and even within an individual reign, remarkable fluctuations are apparent in the relations between emperor and Church. Into the details of these fluctuations I shall not enter. Meanwhile, there was an overall drift in the direction of subordinating temporal interests to spiritual ones and the condition of the Jews became steadily worse. I shall return later to some aspects of this change of policy. For the time being I shall simply sketch its general lines.[103]

The Jews at first retained their old status, as it had been defined in earlier legislation. At least, it remained the same in principle. The Edict of Milan guarantees to everyone the liberty to practice his religion, and this liberty is extended to Jews as it is to Christians and pagans.[104] At the end of the century Theodosius can still remind certain clergy who are stirring up anti-Semitism that Judaism is an authorized religion. *Judaeorum sectam nulla lege prohibitam satis constat.*[105] This accounts not only for the maintenance of traditional privileges but for the granting of new ones in response to changing circumstances. Thus Honorius lays it down that when forced labor is exacted as fiscal dues, it is not to be exacted of Jews on the Sabbath.[106] It also explains the equivalences established between the grades of Jewish religious functionaries and those of the civil hierarchy (this is in connection with particular immunities that particular grades enjoy). The Patriarch has the rank of prefect and the title *Vir clarissimus et inlustris*.[107] He and the principal officers of the Synagogue are excused the onerous burden of the decurionate, as are the members of the pagan and Catholic priesthoods. This confirms the officially recognized equality of the three cults.[108] By the operation of the same principle, public offices were open to the Jews up to the beginning of the fifth century. Once paganism had ceased to be the state religion, these offices no longer involved idolatry.[109]

But as imperial policies became more and more favorable to Christianity this official neutrality quickly ceased to operate in practice. The equilibrium was upset. Pro-Christian enactments were paralleled by anti-Jewish ones, and thus the status of the Jews little by little was eroded. The first signs of this change appear immediately after the Church entered its period of peace.

The restrictions at first apply only to the outwardly directed activities of Judaism, to its relations with the Christian and pagan world. One of Constantine's first official acts after his victory over Maxentius concerns the suppression of proselytism.[110] This did not yet involve, strictly speaking, any substantial modification of the traditional position, because the Jews' right to proselytize had never been explicitly conceded. Proselytism was tolerated, not authorized. But it is clear that this formal enactment was prompted by religious and not political motives. It was designed to suppress dangerous competition with the Church. The context in which the prohibition appears is significant. It constitutes the second part of a law, of which the former part is aimed at protecting converted Jews from sanctions or reprisals inflicted by their former coreligionists.[111] Already the theoretical equality of the religions has given way to a flagrant inequality in practice, for Christians are guaranteed liberty to evangelize, and converts from Judaism are officially protected, while Judaism is absolutely forbidden to increase its membership.

This law of Constantine's was followed by a series of measures that continued until the promulgation of the Theodosian Code. The effect of these measures was progressively to reduce the opportunities for Jews to influence gentiles (either pagans or, more particularly, Christians) and at the same time to restrict them to the area they then occupied, on the fringes of society. On the other hand, since no hope remained of any massive or spontaneous conversion of Israel to Christianity, these laws aimed at further accentuating the peculiar position of the Jews, but in such a way that it no longer appeared as a privilege. Instead, the Jews' position was made to seem more and more like a burden placed on them; like a divine punishment falling on a class of people who are under condemnation.[112]

This development was intensified after the close of the period with which we are dealing. It was to lead finally to the ghetto. But during the fourth and fifth centuries restrictions began to be applied not merely to relations between Jews and the rest of society, but to the internal affairs of the Jews themselves. This pressure was applied for a double reason; first, because theology demanded that the Jews bear the penalty for their infamous conduct, and second, because their presence was a danger to the sometimes rather infirm faith of many Christians.

We shall return later to the subject of the measures relating to Christian slaves in the service of Jews, and those concerning mixed marriages. They had a double object; to suppress indirect forms of proselytism and to increase Jewish isolation. In a similar way, those regulations which progressively excluded Jews from one area of public service after another until, under Honorius, they were excluded from *omni militia*,[113] were intended to set the Jews apart from the rest of society, to reduce the number of opportunities they had for social contact, and to turn them into second-class citizens. The restrictions that were increasingly placed on the jurisdiction of the Patriarch began by denying his competence to judge cases in which Christians as well as Jews were involved. But these restrictions became more stringent. Purporting at first to accentuate the characteristic features of Judaism, and to safeguard its unique character and autonomy, they ended by interfering in the Jewish community's internal affairs in a way in which the pagan empire had always refrained from doing. After the prohibition of mixed marriages came into force,[114] a further edict extended to marriages between Jews the principles and prohibitions regarding consanguinity and family connections that were designed for marriages between Christians. These restrictions were applied instead of the normal rabbinic rules.[115] In A.D. 398 the jurisdiction of the Jewish courts was curtailed, so that they were entitled to do no more than arbitrate on matters of purely Jewish concern. By this means Jews were compelled to conduct virtually all their affairs through the civil courts, and at just about the same time Jews were prohibited from acting as judges.[116]

Similar steps were taken to limit the financial independence of the Synagogue. The Christian empire had at first recognized the Patriarchs' right to raise the temple tax from their own devotees, through their representatives the apostles.[117] This was a tangible sign of the Patriarchs' real authority within the Jewish communities. It was also, no doubt, the origin of the accusations of cupidity the Christians leveled at the Patriarchs. St. John Chrysostom, for example, calls them ἐμπόρους, "wholesalers".[118] Now in A.D. 399 an edict of Honorius stipulated that the money thus collected must go not into the patriarchal purse but into the state treasury.[119] This measure was repealed a few years later.[120] Perhaps it is to be accounted for by a temporary straining of the relations between Arcadius and Honorius. The latter was probably concerned to prevent the flow of gold from the western Jewish communities into the east.[121] In A.D. 429, when the patriarchate no longer existed, a new law forbade the local religious authorities to demand the temple tax. Though the raising of this tax was to be done through the heads of the communities, it was to be collected by imperial officials for the benefit of the imperial treasury.[122]

It is likely that this change was made largely for financial reasons, and especially with a view to avoiding fraud and other abuses that were, at least indirectly, prejudicial to the interests of the state. It was on the subject of finance and economics that the views of the empire and the Church, never identical on any subject, diverged most widely. Thus, for example, though the imperial law encouraged the conversion of Jews to Christianity and forbade conversion or reconversion to Judaism, it did envisage certain exceptions. Since baptism normally entailed remission of debts, there was a law that stipulated that Jewish debtors could not be received into the Church until their debts had been fully discharged.[123] Another law provided that those whose conversions from Judaism had been determined by pecuniary difficulties might return to Judaism without hindrance.[124]

Political considerations might also have played their part in some instances. Once the empire and the Church were so closely united, many Jews who were already hostile to Rome came to hate the Romans with an implacable hatred. There were several new attempts at insurrection in Palestine and the surrounding territories.[125] In addition, it seems certain that in the eastern half of the empire the Jews in some instances helped to undermine the authority of Rome and enlisted in the service of the Persians, under whose jurisdiction they were freely tolerated.[126] However, it is difficult to determine with certainty which was the cause and which the effect, i.e., whether the hostility followed the anti-Jewish legislation or was responsible for it. And quite apart from this, the attitude I have described was characteristic only of a section of the Jews. Those of the west were scarcely affected by it. The official position held by the Patriarchs shows clearly enough that they were not regarded as the leaders of a rebellious body. The Patriarchs seem to have done their best to keep relations with the civil power as cordial as possible, and by showing loyalty to the empire, to safeguard the Jews' traditional standing. When relations became strained and conflict did break out, it was for reasons that were essentially religious. On the whole, the restrictions placed on the Jews, and the changes for the worse that were brought about in their position, were inspired by the Church. They were part of Christianity's attempt at self-defense.

The most serious and significant struggle was the one in 415, between Theodosius II and the Patriarch Gamaliel VI. This was the culmination of an underground campaign against the patriarchate in which several parties had a hand, the ecclesiastical authorities, the imperial officials, and perhaps even certain elements among the Jews themselves, who were annoyed about the temple tax.[127] The motives asserted by those who mounted the campaign were diverse. The financial argument was advanced as an important one. Public hostility to the Jews was exacerbated by a number of incidents in different parts of the empire. At the feast of Purim the Jews customarily burned an effigy of Haman, and on this occasion they were accused of having turned this effigy into a representation of the crucified Christ. A law of A.D. 408 forbade such sacrilegious proceedings for the future.[128] This was the first occasion on which the civil power had interfered with Synagogue ritual. An upsurge of anti-Semitism followed, particularly in Alexandria, where the troubles continued for a number of years, often resulting in bloodshed.[129] An edict of 412 attempted to put an end to the hostilities, issuing a reminder that only the properly constituted courts were competent to punish the misdeeds of Jews, that the Jews ought not to be disturbed simply on account of their faith, and that the synagogues were under the protection of the law.[130] Then came the Imnestar affair. This happened again at the feast of Purim, when the Jews, no doubt drunk at the time, crucified on the gallows of Haman a Christian child. They could scarcely have done more to inflame the anti-Semitic passions of the populace of the eastern empire.[131]

It was against this background of violence (violence perpetrated by both sides) that the conflict between Theodosius and Gamaliel took place, on the anniversary of the Imnestar incident. The conflict was prompted by steps taken by the Patriarch. It was alleged that he had raised matters involving Christians before Jewish courts, that he had circumcised Christian slaves, and that he had built new synagogues.[132] Strictly speaking, it was true that, if the first two of these complaints were justified, then the Patriarch had exceeded his legal authority. But the building of new synagogues, though it did suggest that attempts at proselytizing were being made, was within the competence of the Patriarch as head of the Jewish Church. It was this issue that made the conflict such a serious one. It ended with the disgrace of the Patriarch. He and his successors were deprived of the dignity of prefect.[133] Deprived of its official standing and fallen from imperial favor, the patriarchate may fairly be said to have had its day. It finally disappeared, several years later, with the extinction of the patriarchal family.[134]

In the divided empire the legislation concerning the Jews became more and more restrictive and troublesome. In the west there was a little easing of the situation under the barbarian emperors, but in Byzantium there was no pause in the increasing stringency of the law. But from this time onwards the centre of gravity of Judaism was outside the empire. Once the Jerusalem Talmud was finished, it was "Babylon" that became the center of rabbinic activity. The emperors' pro-Christian policies had contributed in large measure to producing this shift within Judaism.

Thus a radical change came over the relations between Judaism and the empire, brought about by the victory of Christianity at the beginning of the fourth century and by its establishment, by the end of that century, as the religion of the state. Toleration and goodwill turned to hostility, and the hostility became, under the influence of the Church, more and more openly expressed. The common front between Judaism and paganism, which at times during the preceding centuries seemed to be on the verge of becoming a reality, gave way to an alliance between empire and Church. The restrictions that were progressively imposed on the civil and religious liberty of Jews ultimately had the effect of placing them on the same footing as heretics, with the sole difference that no one actually denied their right to exist, as dissident Christianity's right of existence was denied. It was not that, in the strict sense of the word, they were persecuted. Violence committed against individuals came from popular outbursts of anti-Semitism, which the imperial authorities reprimanded or winked at according to circumstances, but never actively encouraged.[135] The Jews were no longer recognized on account of the venerable antiquity of their nation and its institutions as an original and legitimate category of people. Sometimes their antiquity was interpreted by the Church as a sign of inferiority. Sometimes, when the Christians chose to regard themselves as the people of God from all eternity, it was roundly denied. What safeguarded the existence of the Jews were the demands of theology, which not only enforced their recognition but at the same time fixed the narrow limits of their legal status. As opposed to the heretics, it was necessary that they continue to exist—*maneat gens Judaeorum*—but in the reduced and depressed circumstances their sin had brought upon them. *Ecce Judaeus servus est Christiani*. This, at any rate, was the point of view of the Church, and it did its best to ensure that this state of affairs was realized in practice.

This new policy, at the same time as it accentuated Jewish particularism, ultimately denied the Jews all freedom of action and subjected them increasingly to arbitrary interference by the civil power; the civil power in this case acting virtually as the agent of the Church. Here we have a partial explanation of the retrenchment of Judaism, though this retrenchment has often been dated much earlier and set down as a result of the events of A.D. 70 and 135. It may be asserted at this point that it was not entirely spontaneous, since the legislation enacted by the Christian empire provoked, or at least hastened it. But whether this retrenchment was something that the Jews undertook willingly, or whether it was imposed on them, the political factors by themselves are insufficient to explain it. The goodwill of the pagan emperors toward them had not ultimately done the Jews any good, for the Christian Church, notwithstanding persecution, did prevail. The hostility of the Christian emperors was at first no more successful in gaining its end, for it did not neutralize the attraction of Judaism for Christian believers. It does not by itself account for Israel's final defeat. Between the crises in Palestine and the irritations of imperial legislation there took place the expansion of Christianity and the Jewish-Christian encounter. These were the decisive centuries for the development of Judaism. The empire provided no more than the framework within which this development took place. The real struggle was with the Church, and in its policies toward the Jews during the fourth century the empire was acting as no more than an extension of the Church. The question with which we are faced is not one concerning legislation or politics; it concerns primarily a clash of religions.

PART 2

The Conflict of Orthodoxies

5

Anti-Jewish Polemic, its Characteristics and Methods

Μὴ ἀρνούμενοι τὴν Μωϋσέως προφητέιαν, ἀλλὰ κἀκεῖθεν
ἀποδεικνύντες τὰ περὶ τοῦ Ἰησοῦ.

Origen, *Contra Celsum*, 1:45

From the Church's beginnings, and certainly from the time when St. Paul made it conscious of its own independence, it was in conflict with Judaism. The struggle from the outset is a struggle between two distinct religions, and the close ties that existed between them only made their mutual hostility the more implacable.[1] In the sphere of ideology the Church set out to show not only that Christianity was a religion in its own right and had a legitimate place, but that its rival had a legitimate place no longer. It was the Christians' aim to dislodge Israel from the position she held and to install the Church in her stead as the sole repository of revelation. For her part, Judaism was obliged to bend her energies to refute the polemical and doctrinal claims of the Church, and the Christian interpretation of scripture. She tried to prove that the covenant between God and His people was everlasting and that the innovations of the Christians were without validity. Each religion contested the other's right to exist at all. In Jewish eyes Christianity was an upstart; for Christians Judaism was a survival from an era that had come to an end. In the practical sphere the two religions fought over the pagan clientele that Judaism had built up for itself, and whose attention the Church tried to gain. It was to the synagogues of the diaspora and the fringe of pagan "Judaizers" that surrounded them that St. Paul took his message. If the rabbis did not give up the struggle to bring back to the fold the lost sheep of the house of Israel, neither did they give up the endeavor to bring in recruits from among the gentiles.

There can be no doubt that in the first century the fight was fierce. In what manner was it pursued during the period with which our study deals? I have already collected and referred in passing to the materials that provide us with an answer. What must now be done to make the answer clear is to study the evidence more closely.

I

For the Jewish side of the matter the task appears somewhat difficult. Hellenistic Jewish sources fail, as we have seen, after the end of the second century.[2] In Palestine the elaboration of the rabbinic writings seems to have absorbed practically all the intellectual energies available. Any original or independent work was swamped in that vast collective enterprise. Anyone who wishes to recover the remains of the struggle against Christianity is obliged to fish for them in "the Talmudic sea."[3] On the Christian side, by contrast, things are a little easier.

From the jumble of evidence bearing on Jewish-Christian relations one class of texts separates itself out quite readily and unmistakably. This is the anti-Jewish polemical literature. This literature was briefly catalogued by Juster[4] but has been dealt with more recently and in greater detail by Lukyn Williams. Lukyn Williams is a specialist in matters relating to the Talmud and to Jewish-Christian relations and his treatment of the polemical literature may reasonably be regarded as exhaustive. He traces the development of such literature from its beginnings (which coincide virtually with the beginnings of Christianity itself) up to the renaissance.[5] He gives a succinct analysis of each writing, outlining its essential characteristics and the arguments it uses. His work, as well as being an indispensable research tool, has the merit of drawing attention to a category of Christian literature that has hitherto received little study. It may nevertheless be regretted that he did not go on to examine the questions this collection of literature inevitably raises, for such examination is manifestly desirable.

Two problems in particular remain untouched. One concerns the history of the literary genre itself. What connections, if any, exist among the various works within this class? How far are they dependent on one another? Lukyn Williams deliberately sidesteps this question. He believes that each writing stands on its own feet. The similarities that may exist between particular ones are in his opinion superficial, and are explained by the persistence of similar methods of argument and by the use of the same scriptural texts. They hardly ever amount to evidence of direct dependence.[6] This categorical statement, which is sustained by no proof whatever, may well need to be reconsidered and to be expressed more carefully. I am not, however, concerned with this at the moment. I shall only touch on this problem to the extent to which it affects the second question, which is properly a historical one. The quantity of this polemical literature is impressive, and it was produced over a long period. Why was it produced at all? What is its purpose? Lukyn Williams pays no more attention to this question than to the former one. His belief that the writers did not copy from one another is based on the conviction that each writing was produced to meet the needs of its own time. He has no doubt that they were written "with the object either of winning Jews to Christ, or, at least, of enabling Christians both to understand and to withstand the attacks of Jews upon the Christian faith. For Jews have never been backward in attack."[7] In other words, these literary documents reflect real controversies. The question is thus assumed to be answered.

Such a conclusion had, in a sense, already been radically opposed by Harnack. Harnack published an attempt to identify the *Altercatio Simonis et Theophili* with the lost *Dialogue between Jason and Papiscus*, which tradition attributes to Ariston of Pella.[8] The attempt was an unhappy one, but while working on it, his attention was drawn to the whole question of anti-Jewish literature. He came to the conclusion that this literature could not be regarded as evidence for the nature of any real Jewish-Christian polemic. Harnack's conclusions may be open to criticism, but he has the merit of stating the problem in clear terms.

The anti-Jewish writings, he says,[9] do not contain any real answer to objections actually raised by Jews. The refutations of Judaism that they advance are too weak and theoretical. The figure of the Jew in these writings, whether he appears as an adversary in a dialogue or simply as the anonymous recipient of a treatise, is a purely conventional figure. The limitations of his outlook coincide exactly with those of his Christian opponent. He is not the real Jew of actual controversy but the straw Jew of Christian imagination. This ostensibly polemical writing is in fact apologetic, and apologetic produced by the Church for internal consumption only. The objections that are refuted are the objections that were produced by Christians themselves, or that could be prompted by the questionings of pagans who were attracted to Christianity but had not quite succumbed to it. Thus the Jew as we find him in these polemical writings is in reality a pagan under the skin, and this pagan stands in turn for the pagan that lurked under the skin of every Christian convert. The real object of the exercise is to demonstrate, by means of proofs drawn from scripture, the truth of Christianity, and this in a manner that would convince gentiles. The anti-Jewish coloring is simply windowdressing. The rabbi who appears as opponent in the dialogues is no more than a literary device. He is there as an *advocatus diaboli*, and the discussion in which he engages is entirely artificial. We may expect no light at all from these sources on the subject of Jewish Christian relations.

These arguments from internal evidence are based on a somewhat superficial analysis of the writings in question. Harnack adds to them an argument from external evidence that was perhaps in his eyes the most telling of all. These writings cannot represent any genuine discussion between Christians and Jews because no such discussions went on. From the time of Domitian any contact that was made between Hellenistic Christianity and the Synagogue was insignificant. It is a fact that the rabbinic literature speaks of controversies as late as the second century, but such controversy, outside Syria and Palestine, was very rare. In reality, Judaism did not disturb the Christians. It was not interested in them any more than they were interested in it. Not only were the two religions very far from confronting each other in actual controversy, they were content to remain in ignorance of one another.

Harnack's view of the polemical writings thus rests, in the last resort, on his negative estimate of Jewish Christian relations. It rests, that is to say, on an unproved assumption.[10] Instead of probing the literature to discover what these relations were, he denies at the outset that there were any. Just as Lukyn Williams takes for granted that Judaism was aggressive and evangelistic, Harnack assumes, without any evidence, that it was withdrawn and indifferent. This is the whole problem, and a very important one it is. It is a problem that is unlikely to be solved solely by a study of the anti-Jewish literature. Nevertheless, it is possible, if we put out of our minds preconceived ideas on the subject, that we may find in this literature the materials on which a solution might be based.

Harnack's theory encounters a number of difficulties right at the start, before any examination of the details is undertaken. The very existence of a body of ostensibly anti-Jewish literature is significant in itself. How could Christians even conceive the idea of directing these treatises against the Jews if they had not on some occasions had experience of attacks from that quarter? If indeed they had only pagan objectors in mind, why attempt to counter them in this curiously roundabout way? Why, when the argument takes dialogue form, is the opponent given the character of a Jew and not that of a pagan, especially since in this period Christianity was making converts almost exclusively from the gentiles? Why should Celsus introduce a Jew into a work concerned primarily with the duel between Christianity and paganism, unless he had seen around him Jews who were engaged in attacking Christianity?[11]

It is assuredly possible to assert that the convention of directing apologetic against the Jews is explained by the central part played in the debate by arguments from the Bible, and by the fact that both the

Christians and their adversaries were concerned to adduce from scripture proofs to confound their opponents. And it may well be that the importance ascribed to scriptural proofs explains why a number of Christian treatises attempt to slay Jews, heretics, and pagans all at the same time and by the same arguments. There is no need to suspect on this ground the authenticity, the integrity, or the practical utility of these works that are aimed at two or three different targets. This is why the *Adversus Judaeos* of Tertullian could be reused, whether by himself or by someone else we cannot be sure, against an entirely different opponent of Christianity, for it turns up almost word for word the same in the third part of his treatise *Against Marcion.*[12]

The use of the Old Testament as a repository of proof texts, a technique common to all the anti-Jewish polemical writings, is not in itself sufficient to show that they were genuinely directed against Jews. It must be conceded that Harnack is right when he says that the argument from prophecy, which purports to show that Christianity is the divinely given form of religion that has been intended by God from all eternity and announced beforehand by his spokesmen—that this argument would possess a certain force even for a pagan. To be convinced of this, one only needs to consult the apologies that are addressed frankly to the gentiles themselves. All the same, the primary purpose of such arguments in the evangelical literature is manifestly that of persuading Jews. Conversely, the idea of employing scripture against Christianity and thus to fight it with its own weapons could hardly have occurred to pagans unless they had first seen the same tactics effectively used by Jews. A controversy over scripture can only have started between Jews and Christians, where the opposing sides were agreed in recognizing the authority of scripture, and where both laid claim to it as their own. Arguments from scripture did lose some of their force when Christians addressed them to pagans, and when the pagans directed them back at the Christians, they were using no more than a tactical expedient. If Tertullian's *Adversus Judaeos* is compared with his *Apology*, or if Justin's *Dialogue with Trypho* is compard with his *Apology*, it will be seen that the number of scriptural references is significantly less in the works addressed to pagans than in those addressed to Jews. Indeed, in the latter the proofs from scripture form the basis of the arguments. Just to look at these few simple facts is sufficient to predispose one to take the anti-Jewish literature more seriously and to accept at face value its ostensible destination.

We must also take account of the very persistence of this literature. It is no doubt sensible to reckon with the force of habit and the tenacity of literary form. It is possible that the anti-Jewish polemical form gradually lost the real justification with which it began; that it became no more than an academic exercise, a conventional, but no longer really appropriate mould into which the traditional apologetic was poured. In spite of all this, even if a case were made out for such a point of view, if this progressive degradation of the literature were demonstrated, and if each treatise were shown to be dependent closely on its predecessors, so that the whole literary genre were seen to form a single closely linked chain of plagiaristic works; even so, nothing at all would have been proved concerning the origins of this literary form or bearing on the fundamental argument.[13] In any case, the points that Harnack makes apply principally to the dialogues, and these make up only a fraction of the total of anti-Jewish literature. It is true, of course, that the dialogues make up a literary genre of their own. But if a dialogue of this kind does not of necessity correspond to an actual discussion, neither is it of necessity completely remote from actual discussion. An artificial form may well conceal material drawn from life. The Jew in the dialogue often cuts a poor figure; but does Plato, in his dialogues, represent the interlocutors of Socrates in any better light? There is nothing to compel the conclusion that this Jew is merely a character of convention; it shows rather that the author responsible for his lines is not a very good playwright, and that he puts into his mouth such arguments as will allow the spokesman for Christianity an easy victory. Even allowing the maximum influence in the writing of these polemical works to convention and artifice, it still has to be explained why anti-Jewish writing of this kind was produced uninterruptedly to the end of the middle ages. Do men rage so persistently against a corpse? Or are they such slaves to habit that they will go on producing a type of literature that has lost, centuries earlier, its justification and purpose? It is surely not by chance that the tradition persisted most strongly in those countries which had a large Jewish population, and that it is peculiarly tenacious in mediaeval Spain, the land of crypto-Judaism and of the Marranos.[14]

Moreover, the monotonous and stereotyped nature of the anti-Jewish literature ought not to be exaggerated. It does in fact offer some variety, which is a sign of life. There is some variety in the acutal form the writings take. They include collections of biblical texts appropriate to the controversy, such as the *Testimonia* of St. Cyprian or pseudo-Gregory of Nyssa. There are treatises in epistolary form, like that of Barnabas, and expositions of doctrine, such as Tertullian's. We have the homilies of Aphraates, the poetical works of Ephraem, and the sermons of St. John Chrysostom. And lastly there are the dialogues, stretching from their prototype, that of Justin Martyr, to the dialogue between Timothy and Aquila and the one between Athanasius and Zacchaeus. Corresponding to this diversity of form is a certain diversity in the arguments used and in the methods of controversy. Lukyn Williams in his analyses of the literature has thrown these differences into relief. They might have given him some guidance in his attempt at classification.

He classifies the whole of the anti-Jewish literature under five headings: pre-Nicene works, Greek, Syriac, Spanish, and Latin. The classification is thus chronological, linguistic, and geographical all at the same time. Lukyn Williams is relying for his classification on a combination of external criteria, and takes no account of the content of the writings, of their style, of the way in which they are ordered, or of the kind of arguments they use. It is clear that the label *Adversus Judaeos* covers a multitude of different things. The principle I have just enunciated provides us with a basis for distinguishing and classifying the various works. It gives us a method that must be carefully applied but that is far more fruitful of results than Lukyn Williams's, and that leads us to modify both his conclusions and those of Harnack. We shall not be surprised if the truth turns out to lie somewhere between the two.

Lukyn Williams has in fact been aware of the method of procedure we advocate, and has made a beginning in applying it, for he has thought it worthwhile in his treatment of the Latin writings to include a special note on those by Spanish authors,[15] a group that begins with the treatise by Isidore of Seville. This is because he recognizes that these works by Spaniards mark themselves off from the rest of the Western literature of this type by the more accurate knowledge they display, not only of Judaism and its institutions but of the Hebrew language. These works, that is to say, bear witness to direct contacts between Christians and their Jewish opponents, and to the existence of actual controversy, at least between the scholars of the two sides. Several of these works are attributed, with some plausibility, to Christian converts from Judaism.

We might continue further down this road, along which Lukyn Williams travels all too short a distance. We might introduce similarly useful distinctions between other members of this abundant group of writings. We might draw attention to the fact that the sermons of St. John Chrysostom[16] have every reason to be considered as the products of real live controversy. Before being written down, they were actually delivered orally, and on an occasion that connects them closely with the actual religious life of Judaism, the great autumn festivals. Something similar could be said of the homilies of Aphraates. They betray a remarkably familiarity with rabbinic methods of argument, and in spite of the blast they deliver against Judaism, they are impregnated with the Judaic spirit and exhibit Jewish patterns of thought.[17] St. Ephraem falls into the same category. Lukyn Williams's classification might for this reason be improved in quite another respect. Its geographical grouping is not consistently carried through. For his Syriac group should be substituted a Syrian group, replacing the criterion of language with that of locality. This Syrian group should include both Greek and Semitic writings and would reflect, in different ways according to the particular character of each author, the virulence of the struggle that went on in the middle of the fourth century in the Christian east, both inside and outside the frontiers of the empire.

When we try to introduce distinctions among the more neutral works that make up the corpus of Greco-Latin polemical literature, we find ourselves in greater difficulties. An attempt has been made by A. B. Hulen, who suggested a logical classification in an article in the *Journal of Biblical Literature* in 1932. He has made an interesting contribution to the study of Jewish-Christian relations as they are seen in this literature, though it must be said that he has not taken us all the way to a successful solution of the problem.[18]

According to Hulen, some of the writings demonstrably possess the character of doctrinal or exegetical expositions and are intended to convert Jews by proving from the Old Testament that Christianity is true. These he calls *expository* writings, and includes as typical of the group Cyprian's *Testimonia* and the *Demonstratio Evangelica* of Eusebius. The second group he calls *argumentative*. The classical example of this type is Justin's *Dialogue*, and it includes all those works which are cast in the form of actual controversy. They are all in one way or other defensive, and are aimed at refuting Jewish objections. Third, and last, we have a group of writings that make no attempt at all to convert. They are diatribes. They consist of invective and condemnation and pronounce the Jews to be abandoned by God. The homilies of St. John Chrysostom are typical of this group. Hulen calls them *denunciatory*.

This classification calls for some comments. It seems to us a little too rigid, and is in some respects artificial. We rarely find the characteristics that Hulen takes as definitive appearing in quite such clear distinction from one another. The works in question generally present us with a more complex aspect than his scheme suggests, and a particular work may well lend itself to classification in one category just as readily as in another. The line between the first two classes is especially difficult to draw and the contrast Hulen professes to see between them is often an arbitrary one. For example, in Justin's *Dialogue* it seems to me that the exposition of the Christian point of view occupies just as prominent a position as the refutation of Jewish objections. In any case, to demonstrate the truth of Christianity by means of arguments from scripture is bound to involve, at the same time, the refutation of such criticisms as the attempt evokes. It is much better to take into consideration the general orientation of the work and the overall drift of the argument.»

This general tenor of the argument may be described either as positive, i.e., ordered primarily as an apology for Christianity and its doctrines, especially for its Christology, or it may be negative, i.e., it may be conceived essentially as a critique of Judaism, as an attack on its legalism and its religious rites. Even this distinction does not provide us with an infallible criterion for classification, for the two aspects, positive and negative, frequently appear in the same work.[19] But at least the proportions in which they appear give us something on which to base a judgment. When in a particular polemical work the emphasis is placed insistently not simply on a refutation of Jewish criticisms of Christianity but on a refutation of the beliefs of the Jews themselves, we may take it as certain that it is genuinely a work directed against Jews. This kind of argument would not be relevant to anyone but a Jew, or to a pagan who knew about Judaism and was attracted to it and influenced by it. When, on the other hand, its chief contents are apologetic arguments for Christianity, the diagnosis of its true nature is much harder. What Harnack thought was true of all such works may indeed be a correct judgement on some of them. That is, they may not really be polemical in intention, but may simply be tracts setting out the Christian faith and basing themselves on scriptural proofs. Such works may have been written with a number of different objects in view. This does not entitle us to reject the possibility that these writings were originally directed against Jews as if it were totally out of the question. For in the controversy that went on between Jews and Christians it is reasonable to suppose that the Jews attacked features of the Christian faith that they disliked at the same time as they defended their own position.[20] In fact, as may readily be shown, the arguments concerning Christology that are developed in the anti-Jewish treatises have their counterpart in the criticisms of Christology that are found in the rabbinic writings. Similarly, Christian attacks on Jewish legalism correspond to the rabbinic statements exalting the importance of observing the law.

Hulen takes care to emphasize the fact that his classification is not a strictly chronological one. In spite of this, his choice of examples seems to suggest that he believes he has detected a pattern of development. First, we have the defensive works, typified by Justin Martyr. Next come the writings that set out the Christian position. This sort is illustrated by the authors of the third century and the beginning of the fourth. Finally, with Chrysostom, we reach the era of the diatribe. This direction of the development is openly recognized by the author when he notes how as time goes on the original goal of the redemption of Israel drops out of sight, until it is displaced entirely by the object of strengthening the faith of the believers. To put it another way, as far as the later works of this type are concerned, Hulen tacitly lines up with Harnack. They point to a relaxation of Christianity's missionary endeavor among the Jews, and constitute, in reality, a form of apologetic that is simply for internal use.

Stated in this broad fashion such a view is correct, but one or two more reservations need to be made. It may be put more precisely. It leaves unanswered the important question: was the anti-Jewish literature intended to convert the Jews, or to prevent Christians being converted by them? The development of Jewish-Christian relations cannot be summed up simply as a gradual relaxation of Christian efforts to evangelize the Jews. It is also marked by a decrease in the sharpness of Jewish attacks on Christianity and a reduction in the power of Judaism to attract Christians. It was thus a double movement of recoil that led to the eventual loss of contact between the two faiths. But the pace of change was not the same on both sides. There are good reasons to believe, in spite of the suggestion implicit in Hulen's classification, that the Church gave up the attempt to convert Israel before Judaism had given up disturbing the Christians. The case of Chrysostom is here very significant. Chrysostom does denounce the Jews for their deep-rooted impiety and their irremediable blindness, and he despairs of their salvation. But in addition to this, he is careful to put his hearers on their guard against the temptation to follow them and become Judaizers. Now Chrysostom is a contemporary of Aphraates and his career coincides with the end of the period we are studying. The words of the Spanish school are all later in date. It is thus demonstrable that the principle of development that Hulen formulates is only partially confirmed within the chronological limits I have set myself. This means that the criterion of date is not by itself a sufficient one, but needs to be supplemented by the criterion of locality. The conflict between Christianity and Judaism remained a lively one in some areas whilst in others it had already died out. Where it remained alive it was the Jews who kept it so.

This is where we reach the crux of the problem. It is not necessary to decide whether the anti-Jewish polemical writings in every case have actual face-to-face discussions lying behind them. This is only one aspect of the matter, and not the most important aspect either, for the relations between Christians and Jews were not worked out exclusively in the sphere of scholarly disputes. Primarily, it is not even a matter of deciding whether these writings were actually addressed to Jews. Put in this way, the question is almost unanswerable. The real question to decide is whether or not the Judaism with which these works come to grips represents a real threat to the Church. Chrysostom's sermons enable us to see just what the danger was. They are not aimed at the Jews at all. It is the Judaizing Christians of Antioch who are addressed. Thus the arguments they offer really are for internal consumption, but not in the sense in which Harnack believed. If these arguments are intended to build up the faith of the believers, they do not do so by combating pagan criticisms, nor by rebutting objections that arise spontaneously in the Christians' own minds. It is the devices of the Jews and the drawing power of the Synagogue that they are designed to meet. Thus, though the people who produced these writings were not aiming directly at the Jews themselves, the title "anti-Jewish literature" is a proper and deserved one, for the Judaizing tendencies that appeared in the Church were a phenomenon that had not arisen spontaneously in Christian circles. They presuppose a stimulus from without. They did not spring from any reflection on scripture, but were prompted by living example. They developed through contact with strong and lively Jewish communities. There could be no Judaizers if there were no Jews.

It would be as well to show caution in estimating the significance of the monotony of the polemicists' arguments. Monotony is in any case a relative term. It is true enough that we have difficulty in distinguishing between the writings that represent genuine polemic and those which are merely literary or academic exercises. There is no infallible criterion here by which to judge. Aphraates, Chrysostom, and the Spaniards mark themselves off clearly at one end of the scale. There can be no doubt in these instances. But there is no certainty about the rest, i.e., about the vast majority of the literature in question. Insofar as the existence and persistence of this class of literature constitutes in itself an argument, it is an argument that can be made to cut both ways. If particular methods of argument and proof, particular themes and ideas remain constant throughout the series of writings, this lack of variation may either be a sign of the slavish dependence of each treatise on its forbears, or equally readily be explained by the simple persistence of the same objections and the same methods of attack on the part of the adversary. A minute comparison of the entire range of these works, though naturally I cannot undertake it here, may well demonstrate a falling off in their specifically anti-Jewish characteristics. I have in mind certain purely apologetic works that are quite broad in their aim and have no really well-marked anti-Jewish bias.[21] But there is every likelihood that such a study would reveal also that the great majority of the anti-Jewish polemical works genuinely deserve that title.

This analysis has shown us just what kind of problem it is that the anti-Jewish polemical literature presents us with. It is nothing other than the whole problem of Jewish Christian relations. It is, more narrowly, the problem of Jewish proselytism and Jewish influence. The anti-Jewish literature raises it for us at the outset, and the literature provides us with materials for a positive solution. Nevertheless, it must be firmly stated that the clue to the matter does not lie in these texts alone. Whether they are studied individually or compared as a group, they cannot provide us with all the evidence we need.

In this situation the method by which we should proceed is clear. We must first study this group of writings as a whole, with a view to elucidating the main themes of the discussion. In doing so, we must pay most attention to the major works, and not waste time in making minute distinctions. After that, we must bring together whatever information may be gleaned from elsewhere concerning Jewish life during our period, and in particular, concerning Jewish relations with Christianity. We must search for this information in both Christian and Jewish sources. This means, in the absence of any Hellenistic Jewish literature, that we must search the Talmudic texts. Only this kind of comparison and cross-checking, throwing the maximum available light on the content of the anti-Jewish writings, can clarify the main question of Jewish-Christian relations.

II

The common basis of the anti-Jewish writings lies in their method of argument, i.e., in their recourse to scripture, which is accepted by both parties to the discussion as a revelation of infallible authority.[22] In order to have any effect on Jews the proof must be grounded on the scriptural text. The apologists appeal to their opponents, not to be converted to an alien worship, but to come to a correct view of their own religion, of their own history and mission. They try to persuade them of the proper interpretation of the divine revelation, to see clearly for themselves. For this reason they must free themselves from the hold their own scholars have over them, for they "do not understand the scriptures."[23] They will thus be amenable to arguments $\dot{\alpha}\pi\grave{o}$ $\tau\hat{\omega}\nu$ $\gamma\rho\alpha\phi\hat{\omega}\nu$ $\kappa\alpha\grave{\iota}$ $\tau\hat{\omega}\nu$ $\pi\rho\alpha\gamma\mu\acute{\alpha}\tau\omega\nu$.[24] Thus a correct interpretation of the Bible should suffice to make them Christians, for all truth is contained in it, and all truth is Christian truth. The Bible, which they read without understanding, the Jews no longer have any right to claim as theirs. Justin speaks to Trypho of "your scriptures, or rather, not yours, but ours. For we believe in them; but you, though you read them, do not catch the spirit that is in them."[25]

The profound reason for the Jews' blindness to the revelation, a blindness God himself has willed, takes its rise from their carnal nature. They are slaves to the letter; the spirit escapes them. "You do not discern the reasons for a commandment.... But you have understood all things in a carnal sense."[26] It is a "pneumatic" interpretation which is the only legitimate one, which throughout controls the Christian proof. It rests on the postulate, without which the revelation makes no real sense at all, that Christ and Christianity are manifest in every line of the sacred text. In order to show this, the apologists had two methods open to them: the argument from prophecy, and the method of typological or allegorical exegesis.

The witness the Bible bears to Christ comes clothed in two different forms, prediction and symbol. The error of the Jews consists in the first instance in not realizing that the Messianic prophecies apply to the Messiah Jesus and can apply only to him. In the second instance, they have failed to perceive beneath the literal sense of the narrative, legislative, or prophetic text the Christian revelation. In fact, historic Christianity, in its ecclesiastical form, its Messiah, suffering at first and then exalted, its institutions and its teaching—all these are not only predicted in the Old Testament by the prophets but are also announced in prefigurations, which are prophecy's normal complement. Indeed, the prefigurations are sometimes included within prophecy, for the predictions themselves are not always formulated clearly. Quite often they must be interpreted in the light of allegorical exegesis. "What the prophets said and did ... they revealed in parables and in types, so that it is not easy for most of what they taught to be grasped by all."[27] In addition to this eternal, transcendent Christianity, Christianity in the shape of its fundamental affirmations and divorced from historical contingencies, is immanent in the Bible. It shows itself in the stream of thought and spiritual piety that from one end of the Old Testament to the other affirms the primacy of the spirit over the letter, of the moral command over the ritual, of purity of heart over respect for religious observances. In this ideal Christ explicitly proclaims his message beforehand, and it is present throughout the sacred text. It is presented by the prophets in both veiled and explicit terms. It underlies the very prescriptions of the ritual law itself, and one of the aims of exegesis is to pick it out.

To put it another way, the symbols of the sacred text must be interpreted sometimes in the light of the future, as premonitory signs, and sometimes *sub specie aeternitatis*, as the expression of a truth that is preexistent, a metaphysical and moral truth that lies at the very origins of the revelation, and that is from the outset the Christian truth. Christianity is not only the fulfilment of the prophecies and a development of the religious traditions of Israel, it is the form of religion that God has willed from eternity.

The sources of this exegetical method are indubitably Jewish.[28] Some at least of the Christian apologists interpret allegorically not only the rites and prescriptions of the Old Covenant, but also the episodes of Israel's history, and the words of the Lord and of His inspired spokesmen. They extend it to situations and acts, gestures and conversations, proper names and numerals. Now, in doing this, they were doing no more than apply the rabbinic principle that nothing in the sacred text is insignificant or accidental, but that every vocable, every number and sign has a value and a meaning, right down to the smallest letter.[29] But the rabbis, in their attempt to find out the reason for everything in scripture, in fact made quite restrained and moderate use of what is properly termed allegory.[30] In particular, they almost completely excluded it from halakhic exegesis of the Pentateuch. "As for the Torah and the commandments, thou mayest not interpret them by means of the *mashal* (parable)."[31] There was a tendency to restrict allegorization to those texts which invited it or whose literal interpretation seemed unsatisfactory, e.g., the Song of Songs. When it was applied to texts of other kinds, and this could even on occasion include the prescriptions of the law, it was well understood that the literal sense remained fundamental and that it was important to grasp it exactly and firmly as an expression of the divine will. In no single case could allegorical interpretation undermine it. Its business was simply to clarify and amplify the plain meaning.[32]

For example, the Jews content to abide by the text, see in Israel the blessed posterity of Sarah, the legitimate wife of Abraham, whereas the Ishmaelites, by which they understand the gentiles, are born of Hagar, the servant. On this interpretation they base their claim to primacy. Christian exegesis, by contrast, turns the whole thing upside down and draws a distinction between carnal sonship (which is the only kind the Jews recognize) and spiritual sonship. Spiritual sonship, which is the kind that really matters, is the natural possession of Christians. *Haec certe doctrina apostolica atque catholica satis evidenter indicat nobis secundum originem carnis ad Saram Judaeos, id est Israelitas, ad Agar vero Ishmaelitas pertinere; secundum autem mysterium spiritus, ad Saram Christianos, ad Agar Judaeos.*[33]

The same reasoning is applied to Jacob and Esau, and makes the former the true ancestor not of the Jews, which is what the sacred text plainly says, but of the Christians.[34] Yet again, when the covenant is renewed, following the apostasy of Israel, and the second set of commandments given, the Jews see the new code as a complement to the moral commands of the first decalogue and understand them according to the letter of the text. This is how the *Didascalia* understands them too, as we have already seen,[35] though it regards them as a divine sanction, to punish the Jews for their apostasy. Other polemists, however, are quite indifferent to the literal sense. They ignore the content not only of the second code but even of the first and put the emphasis on the fact of renewal, which they interpret as equivalent to abrogation. The tables of the law have been broken, and with them the covenant is broken too. The second tablets, which in appearance were meant to receive the ritual law, really symbolize the spiritual law of Christ and the new covenant.

From this point of view the decalogue itself, whose lasting validity the Church recognizes, stands for the old covenant, whose abrogation is signified by the destruction of the tablets of the law. This is already the interpretation of Barnabas. It is taken up again by Origen. Moses, he says, showed us, long before St. Paul, what a low estimate we ought to entertain of the letter of the law. Having received the tablets of the law, he thought so little of them that he threw them down and broke them, even though they were written by the finger of God Himself. Nor was he charged with any impiety for doing so. His gesture signifies clearly that the virtue of the law does not reside in the letter of the law, but in its spirit.[36]

Origen does not speak of the second code. Barnabas suggests, though not very explicitly, an allegorical interpretation when he contrasts the Jewish law and the broken tablets with "the covenant of the beloved Jesus," which from that time replaced it.[37] Some later authors express this line of thought more clearly, and anti-Jewish speculation comes to use the second of the episodes on Sinai in the same way as the first. Thus, for example, Commodian. The letter of the text, that is to say, the ritual prescriptions of the new legislation, counts for very little with him. The Jews, so zealous to observe the commands, are apparently amenable to the divine will. In reality they rebel against it, for it is only the allegorical sense that matters. This is the Christian law which symbolizes the renewal of the covenant.

> *Aspicis legem, quam Moyses allisit iratus*
> *Et idem Dominus dedit illi legem secundam.*
> *In illa spem posuit, quam vos subsannatis erecti*
> *Sic ideo digni non eritis regno caelesti.*[38]

Another work, inspired by Commodian, takes up the same idea but more forcefully. This is an anti-Jewish treatise falsely attributed to Maximus of Turin, but which in reality was written by another Maximus, the Arian bishop of Hippone, who was a contemporary and adversary of Augustine.[39] This author reviews all the instances in the Old Testament, from Abel to Joseph, of a younger brother's taking precedence over his elder, interpreting them all as representations of the Christian Church's being preferred before the Jews. Then he comes to the Sinai episode. Moses broke the first tablets because of the people's sin, but the second ones were preserved, and, he adds, they are called *Deuteronomy*, which means "the second law."[40]

This example demonstrates at what point allegorical exegesis parts company from what we may call positive exegesis, and how the two differ in both their methods and their results. The *Didascalia* rejected the renewal of the covenant, regarding it as a punishment imposed on the Jews for their idolatry. The Dialogue of Timothy and Aquila, remaining similarly close to the letter of the biblical text, goes so far as to refuse canonical status to Deuteronomy.[41] Yet here the notion of the second law is rehabilitated in order to serve Christian ends. For when Maximus speaks of Deuteronomy it is clear that he does not mean simply the biblical book of that name. Again like the Dialogue of Timothy and Aquila, he uses the word more generally to signify that *deuterosis* in which the *Didascalia* sees the essence of Judaism, and which now becomes, for the purposes of the cause, the symbol of Christianity itself.

It is this kind of exegetical virtuosity which inspires the rabbinic mistrust of allegorical interpretation. It is true that such mistrust chimes in very well with the rabbis' rather matter-of-fact juridical turn of mind, but the fact that this cautious attitude appears first among the Tannaim, and that later rabbis allowed more scope to the allegorical method[42] suggests that the caution was intensified at the outset by the Christian disposition to use allegory as a weapon. In fact, taking an overall view of the matter, the Christian-Jewish controversy over the use of scripture often looks simply like a clash between two different methods of interpretation, the allegorical and the literal. On the other hand, there are clear affinities between Christian exegesis and that of Hellenistic Judaism, especially that of Alexandria. With respect both to the principles and to some of the results a clear line of development is traceable from one to the other.[43]

Philo's use of allegory sprang from a desire to make acceptable to cultivated gentiles the details of scriptural institutions and commandments, as well as the biblical "mythology." It was essentially a philosophical method, and consisted in a search beneath the letter of scripture for an expression of transcendent truths, the same truths as those which gentile philosophy had arrived at by its own ways. Thus was demonstrated the agreement between Greek wisdom and the biblical revelation.[44] It is by a rather similar procedure that the Christian apologists are able to trace the more general, if not the more specific features of Christianity, throughout the entire Bible. The analogy between the methods of the Christians and those of the Jewish Hellenists is especially close where there is a question of interpreting in moral terms commandments that are actually concerned with ritual.

But as far as these commandments themselves are concerned, the attitude of Philo does not differ substantially from that of the rigorists, and his allegorical interpretations do not detract in the slightest from his respect for the literal sense. If he lays on the literal sense somewhat less emphasis than the rabbis do, he never goes so far in his halakhic discussions as to eliminate it altogether. On this point, as we have seen, the Christian apologists are by no means unanimous.[45] For some of them the religious institutions and religious prescriptions of Mosaism never did, even in the beginning, possess more than purely symbolic value. On this view the religious practice of Israel has always been based on a misunderstanding. Others, on the contrary, saw in these institutions and commands a validity that was real and normative, but temporary, limited to the past and done away with by the coming of Christ. In this case the sin of the Jews is their obstinacy in clinging to things that had served their turn and had now lapsed. But apologists of both sorts were agreed, and here is the essential difference that marks them off from Philo and the rabbis at once, that the Old Testament alone is insufficient and cannot by itself provide a satisfactory meaning. It can only be understood on the basis of a Christianity that, though it is at the outset included in the Old Testament, ultimately goes beyond it, and that in its developed historic form, crowns and illuminates it.

This exegetical method is found, with variations, in the majority of the Christian polemists. It was in full flower at the time when anti-Jewish literature began to be written. Pseudo-Barnabas is a master of this kind of argument, and Justin, whose dependence upon Barnabas is demonstrable, has recourse to it continually. Both writers provide us with curious and sometimes preposterous examples not only of prefigurative allegory but also of what might be called immanentist allegory,[46] that is to say, of the kind of allegory that finds in the institutions and prescriptions of the law not only premonitory images of Christianity, but the actual fundamental Christian teachings themselves.

For Barnabas as for Justin the scapegoat is a prefiguration of Christ. The scarlet wool attached to its horns prefigures the crimson garment of the crucified.[47] Barnabas goes on to recount the tradition that he who took the scapegoat into the wilderness removed the scarlet wool and placed it on a thornbush. This, too, prefigures Christ, and signifies that no one can come to him except at the cost of suffering and affliction. According to Justin, another prefiguration is the twelve bells (which, incidentally, Jewish writings never mention) that were hung on the high priest's robe. These symbolized "the twelve apostles, who were dependent upon the power of Christ the everlasting priest, by whose voice all the earth was filled with the glory and grace of God and his Christ."[48] Again, in order to show that circumcision is merely a figure, Barnabas says that Abraham succeeded because he was "looking forward in the Spirit to Jesus, circumcised, having received the mystery of the three letters. For the scripture says that Abraham circumcised 318 men of his house. But what, therefore, was the mystery that was made known unto him? Mark first the eighteen, and next the 300. For the numeral letters of ten and eight are *I H.* And these denote Jesus. And because the cross was that by which we were to find grace, therefore he adds 300, the note of which is *T.*" The author, who is manifestly proud of this interpretation, ends by calling Christ to witness that "I never taught to anyone a more certain truth."[49]

For Justin the unleavened bread signifies "that ye do not practise the old deeds of the bad leaven."[50] Barnabas interprets the food laws in similar fashion, giving them a moral meaning and denying to them any ritual significance. The prohibition of pork, for example, means, "Thou shalt not join thyself to such persons as are like unto swine; who whilst they live in pleasure, forget their God,—but when any want pinches them, then they know the Lord; as the sow when she is full, knows not her master; but when she is hungry, she makes a noise, and again being fed, is silent."[51] The prohibition against eating the flesh of the hare is understood as follows: "Thou shalt not be a corrupter of children; nor liken thyself to such persons. For the hare every year aquires an extra anus; and as many years as it lives, so many it has."[52]

We may well understand why the Jews were not quick to recognize the force of such arguments as these, even though Barnabas had learned his methods from Jews themselves. His technique of interpretation is simply that of the letter of Aristeas, pushed to ridiculous lengths.[53] It is equally natural that explanations of this kind were calculated to fill the rabbis with mistrust of allegorical exegesis as a method. It is natural too, in view of the limited success such arguments must have had with the Jews, that Christian authors should of their own accord go on to fill out their interpretations with the help of quite different exegetical and dialectical techniques. Otherwise, they were in danger of impressing no one except those who had already conceded the premises on which the proof was based, i.e., the necessity of faith in Christ as a foundation for the understanding of the Old Testament. When it was a question of dislodging Israel from its defensive positions, the polemists therefore laid alongside their allegorization a more down-to-earth kind of exegesis. This is where we may classify the arguments the *Didascalia* devotes to the ritual law. And in line with this development we may note the polemic of St. John Chrysostom, who, as a good Antiochene, allows a very limited place to allegory.[54] The efforts made in this direction are among the most interesting phenomena of the anti-Jewish controversy.

The problem of interpretive method was further exacerbated by differences in the actual biblical text. For the Christians, proper exegesis necessarily began from the text of the Septuagint, which was the only text accessible to non-Jews and which was regarded by them as completely authentic and fully inspired. The Jews, by contrast, though they had up till now unanimously recognized the Septuagint's authority, tended more and more to take exception to it from the time that Christians began to use it against them. Justin says boldly, "I do not believe your teachers when they do not agree with the interpretations by the seventy elders at the court of Ptolemy King of Egypt, but endeavour to give interpretations themselves."[55] The translations of Theodotion, Symmachus, and Aquila were prompted by this lack of confidence in the Septuagint and by the need to refute the interpretatons the Christians based upon it. These translations were in their turn attacked by the Christians. In the Dialogue of Timothy and Aquila it seems likely that the name Aquila is used advisedly. The work engages in vigorous polemic against Aquila's version and accuses its author of having deliberately falsified and multilated the sacred text.[56]

This part of the controversy is carried on by some authors with a quite remarkable display of scientific interest. Some of them were aware that the reservations and criticisms of the Jews concerning the Septuagint were at least partly justified, and they recognized the need to go back to the original text. St. Jerome, in the interests of the Latin translation he had undertaken, learned Hebrew, as Origen had done before him.[57] Origen, moreover, had compared the diverse translations of the Greek Bible and had brought them together in his parallel edition, the Hexapla. This care and accuracy nevertheless remained rather exceptional, as appears from the eulogy of Origen's work we find in Eusebius.[58] Most authors held fast to the Septuagint, and were so far from entertaining even the least suspicion of it that they happily accuse the Jews of having multilated the text by suppressing certain Messianic passages. Justin, in the sequel to the passage cited above, goes on: "And I would have you know that they have completely removed from the interpretations which were made by the elders at the court of Ptolemy many passages by which this very One who was crucified is plainly proved to have been proclaimed as God, and man, and crucified, and dying."[59] Almost immediately afterwards, on Trypho's demand, he supplies a list of passages that he says the Jews have suppressed in their Greek text. Some of these are mentioned in later Christian authors, though they no longer appear in our editions of the Septuagint. They do not appear in the original Hebrew either.

We are entitled to reckon such passages, therefore, not as ones that the Jews suppressed, but as Christian interpolations. They are quite possibly the glosses of commentators that inadvertently found their way into the text to which they were applied. It is not unlikely that some of them at least derive from the florilegia of biblical quotations with which Christian authors met the needs of controversy.[60]

It is not, in fact, directly from the text of the Bible itself that the apologists most often draw their arguments. The hypothesis that there were collections of scriptural texts specially chosen for purposes of preaching and controversy (particularly the latter) has proved a singularly fruitful one. This theory was first suggested by Hatch, taken up by Sanday and Headlam, and developed in a masterly way by Rendel Harris.[61] It was probably during the apostolic period that anonymous Christians extracted from the Old Testament the most convincing verses and arranged them into what amount to apologetic anthologies, their purpose being to convince Israel. Once again it is probable that they were doing no more than following the Jews' own example, for there is much to be said for Hatch's suggestion[62] that they too had compiled catenae of proof texts for the purposes of their mission among the pagans.

On the Christian side, the Testimonia of Cyprian give us an idea of the composition of these collections and of their general scope.[63] Cyprian's work represents neither an isolated attempt nor a new departure, but a link in a literary tradition that was already old. The same tradition is exemplified later in the work of pseudo-Gregory of Nyssa and of Isidore of Seville.[64] Rendel Harris postulated the existence of a single original collection of testimonies antedating the gospels and even the epistles of St. Paul. This he attributed to St. Matthew and held that its authority was accepted from the beginning by the primitive Church and was maintained through succeeding generations. Lukyn Williams has urged convincingly that there were, on the contrary, a number of different collections, which were subsequently reworked and made into integrated and systematic compositions.[65] It does not seem, however, that there were many differences between them in their choice of texts, which was fairly restricted. It is mostly in the grouping and presentation of the texts that they vary.

This is the explanation of the numerous correspondences between different anti-Jewish works in respect of the texts cited. These correspondences are too close to be fortuitous, but since they do not represent a firsthand use by each author of the vast repertoire of the Bible, there is no need to argue from them in favor of a direct dependence of one author on another. Furthermore, the hypothesis that the proof texts are drawn from earlier collections, whether one or many, accounts satisfactorily for the rather frequent errors of attribution we find in the anti-Jewish writings. Thus, when pseudo-Gregory of Nyssa credits to Isaiah a verse of Jeremiah, "For when I brought your ancestors out of the land of Egypt, I said nothing to them, gave them no orders, about holocaust and sacrifice," and immediately afterwards cites correctly a verse of Isaiah, "What are your endless sacrifices to me...?," the error is most likely to be explained by the fact that, in the collection the author was using, the two verses stood side by side under the same heading, "Sacrificial Cult." Under this heading would be grouped texts taken principally from Isaiah but accompanied by verses from other books that bore upon the same theme.[66] The hypothesis is further strengthened by the fact that the same two texts, this time quoted anonymously, already appear side by side in the Epistle of Barnabas. This correspondence, rather than arguing for any direct dependence of pseudo-Gregory on Barnabas, suggests that both used the same anthology of texts.[67]

The same may be said for the instances that appear in one author after another in which two verses from different sources figure in combination in a single quotation. Justin, for example, amalgamates Psalm 110:2 with Psalm 72:5 and 72:17. Pseudo-Gregory of Nyssa does exactly the same.[68] The combination of Psalm 110:1 and Isaiah 45:1 is common to Barnabas and pseudo-Gregory.[69] Even if, as is likely, the latter author both knew and used Barnabas and Justin, the simplest explanation is that the connection was already made in the manual with which each of these authors worked, and which, though like most collections of this kind it is no longer extant, was probably transmitted from generation to generation at least up to the end of the period of antiquity.

6

Anti-Jewish Polemic—The Arguments Employed

Fuit igitur altercatio legis.
Dialogue of Simon and Theophilus, 1:1

The anti-Jewish writers pursue a double aim, to demonstrate from scripture the truth of Christianity, and by the same means to refute the claims of Judaism. They take allegorical exegesis as their method and collections of "testimonies" for their tools. Looking at this body of literature as a whole, we may distinguish three principal lines of argument. These appear in all the works concerned, though the proportions of space devoted to the several arguments vary from one treatise to another. The three are Christological exposition; criticism of the Jewish law, especially the ritual law, which has been abrogated under the new covenant; and last, proof that Israel has been rejected and the gentiles called.

The same schema appears, with some variations, in the majority of the anti-Jewish works. Occasionally two of the three elements may be combined into one. Thus, for example, in Tertullian's treatise the first part shows at the same time the rejection of Israel and the abrogation of its law,[1] whilst the second is devoted to Christology.[2] The composition of the dialogues is in general less rigid, but even there these essential points of the argument invariably reappear, even if they are not always clearly distinguished from one another. They may be picked out among the repetitions and digressions of Justin's dialogue with Trypho. The Dialogue of Simon and Theophilus opens with a Christological controversy on which the author spends most of his time,[3] and ends with a discussion of religious observances.[4] In the works of Aphraates the same material is distributed among a number of different homilies. If we leave aside those whose anti-Jewish coloring is not strongly marked, there is left first of all a group[5] in which the various religious observances (circumcision, Passover, Sabbath, and food laws) are studied one by one, and one by one are shown to be invalid. In the next group the author proves that the gentiles have been called and the Jews irrevocably disqualified.[6] Along with this goes a demonstration that Christ is the Messiah.[7] There is thus a cyclic pattern to the series that shows it to be a coherent whole, a complete exposition of the Christian view of Judaism.

I

In the Christological expositions the person and message of the historical Jesus generally play a fairly restricted part. Jewish attacks at this point seem to have amounted to no more than some scandalous insinuations or assertions about Christ's legitimacy and accusations that his miracle-working powers were demon-inspired. Jesus, they said, was born of an adulterous union between Mary and a Roman legionary. He was an out-and-out charlatan and a magician. Yet hardly any hint of these slanders is perceptible in the anti-Jewish literature. We know them from a number of Talmudic texts,[8] and especially from some relatively late works of a popular nature, such as the *Toledoth Jeshu.* They appear in Celsus, put into the mouth of the Jew whom he introduces as one of his *dramatis personae*.[9] Perhaps they were as much pagan in origin as Jewish. On the other hand, attacks on Jesus' message seem to have come predominantly from the gentile direction. Judging by both the rabbinic literature and the Christian apologetic, few criticisms seem to have been made of this aspect of Christian preaching. It was manifestly not this which incensed the Jews against Christianity.

In any case, if we leave out of account the role in the economy of salvation he attributed to himself, or his disciples conferred upon him, the preaching of Jesus can hardly have been very shocking to Jewish opinion. The Jewish affinities of his gospel are today recognized.[10] These affinities only became apparent as a result of a movement of objective criticism that challenged the dogma of the thoroughly original nature of Christian teaching and of the rooted antagonism between it and the teaching of the Synagogue. In this movement Jewish critics have played a considerable part. Many of them today claim Jesus as one of the most authentic representatives of Jewish thought and spirituality.[11]

It is unlikely that the Jews of the early Christian epoch shared such benign opinions. For them, Jesus was the enemy, as were all who belonged to him. But this enmity was largely inspired by St. Paul, and by the exaltation of Christ as God. But the hostility that Jesus, in his capacity as head of the Church and as the object of Christian faith, inspired in the Jews did not necessarily make them deaf to the Jewish overtones of his preaching. Neither was the fidelity to his message that the first Palestinian Christians displayed regarded, in the first instance at least, as enough to exclude them from Judaism.[12] It seems to be the case at every period that Jesus' own gospel occupies hardly any place in the controversial literature. The only part of his earthly career that figures at all seriously in these writings is the end of it. The sufferings and death of Christ, the scandal of the cross,[13] the idea of a suffering Messiah, these are the subjects that regularly come up for consideraton. It is here that we recognize one of the basic causes of the Jews' rejection of Christianity. "You set your hopes on a man that was crucified," says Trypho in astonishment, although, as he says elsewhere, the scriptures "compel us to await One who is great and glorious, and takes over the everlasting kingdom from the Ancient of Days as Son of Man."[14] He makes no difficulty over seeing in Daniel's vision an announcement of the expected Messiah. He goes so far as to concede the idea of the sufferings of the Messiah. But having been so far convinced, he still rejects the notion of an ignominious crucifixion, and he denies that Justin's Christ possesses the true characteristics of the Messiah.[15]

In reply to these objections Christian apologists attempted to show that the Bible predicted not only the sufferings of the Messiah but the actual crucifixion. By thus demonstrating the correspondence between the sufferings of Christ and the prophecies, they established the identity of the Christian Messiah with the one expected by Israel. And in order to account for Jesus' lack of earthly success they stressed the idea of the two advents. The humiliations that were characteristic of the first coming of Christ were only the prelude to his coming on the clouds, as Daniel foretold.

A number of biblical texts that speak of the sufferings of the Righteous One were taken as Messianic and provided the apologists with proof that the sufferings of Christ were in conformity with the divine plan.[16] Prominent among these texts were Isaiah 53 and Psalm 22. But when they endeavored to go on to show that suffering specifically *on a cross* was to be the lot of the Messiah, the apologists did not find many really helpful texts. The only exception was the erroneous citation from Psalm 96:10, where the phrase "the Lord reigns" was expanded by Justin and others into "the Lord reigns from the wood." These writers then went on to accuse the Jews of having suppressed the addition.[17] Otherwise, the best they could do was to fall back on prefigurative allegory. The brazen serpent was one such figure.[18] So was the figure of Moses, praying with his arms extended as Joshua fought the battle against the Amalekites (Joshua himself, of course, being also a prefiguration of Christ). "Amalek was defeated, and Israel was conqueror, by the type of the stretching forth of the hands of Moses, and of the naming of the son of Nun by the name of

Jesus (Joshua)."[19] Similarly, when Moses, in the blessing on Joseph, declares, according to the LXX, "his horns are those of an unicorn,"[20] it is the cross of Jesus he is speaking of. For the cross is reminiscent in form of the horn of a unicorn. "For the one piece of wood stands upright, from which the upper part is raised up into a horn, when the other piece of wood is fitted on, and the ends seem like horns joined to that one horn."[21] An even more labored piece of exegesis allows Justin to recognize Noah's wooden ark, sailing over the waters, as a symbol of both cross and baptism at the same time.[22] He finds the same double significance in the rod that Elisha cast into the Jordan. He finds a hidden reference to the cross in every miraculous rod mentioned in the Bible.[23] The identification of Jesus with the biblical Messiah, first humiliated and then glorified, was demonstrated by the apologists by means of a number of other prefigurative symbols. They invoke, in addition, the prophecies of Daniel about the seventy weeks that were to separate the reconstruction of the temple as described in the book of Ezra from the Messianic times,[24] and they do their best to show that these figures can only refer to the Messiah Jesus who suffered under Tiberius.[25] They also draw into the argument a number of other texts that seem to them not to be explicable except as references to the person or work of Jesus. In this group we have, for example, Psalm 110,[26] which speaks of a "Lord" who is "priest for ever"; and Psalm 72,[27] which foretells the universal kingship of a preexistent sovereign, whose name will be blessed by his people.

It is interesting to note that the Jews, if Justin fairly represents their views, contested the fact that the texts at issue were Messianic at all. They understood Psalm 110 as referring to King Hezekiah,[28] and Psalm 72 as referring to Solomon.[29] There is no trace whatever of either of these interpretations in the Talmud.[30] We must not, however, on that account accuse Justin of having invented them. He is quite well informed concerning things Jewish. It is better to concede, on the strength of his testimony, that the Jews of the period abandoned for a time the Messianic interpretation of certain texts and contrived, in reaction against the Christians, to find other possible applications for them in Israel's past. Perhaps we have here only one symptom of a more general phenomenon, the temporary withdrawal of the Jews from Messianism, for the latter manifestations of Messianism, on the occasion of the Bar Cochba revolt, had only involved Israel in disappointment.

Trypho also applies to Hezekiah the celebrated verse of Isaiah, "Behold, a virgin shall conceive and bear a son," in which Justin sees a prophecy of the virgin birth of Christ. This time Trypho has the support of Talmudic interpretation. He corrects the LXX translation, as do Aquila, Symmachus, and Theodotion, substituting for *virgin* the phrase *young woman*, which is in better argeement with the Hebrew original.[31] We know how important this verse was for Christian apologetic. In the anti-Jewish controversy it is found at the very heart of the debate about Christology.

Jewish objections concerned themselves far more with the nature of Christ than with any aspect of his earthly career. "All of us Jews," says Trypho, "expect that Christ will be a man of merely human origin.... For your assertion that this Christ existed, and was God, before all ages, then that he was even born and became man and suffered, and that he is not man by origin, seems to me to be not only strange but even foolish."[32]

Accordingly, the main effort of the apologists, as far as Christology was concerned, was to prove from scripture the preexistence and divinity of the Christ-Messiah. The proofs vary from one author to another in accordance with the idiosyncrasies of each one's Christology. It may be firmly stated, from a detailed study of this aspect of the anti-Jewish literature, that it reflects faithfully the development of Christian doctrine, up to its crystallization in the Trinitarianism of Nicaea.

Yet chronology is not the only determining factor here. It is interesting to note in Aphraates, who lived outside the empire and who was bypassed by the great controversies of his century, a singularly archaic Christology. In order to demonstrate the divine sonship and nature of Christ, in reply to the objections of Jewish monotheism, he asserts that even from the point of view of Israelite tradition there is nothing exceptional here.[33] When Christians call Christ "God" and "Son of God," they can quote a number of precedents. God said of Israel that Israel was His son,[34] His firstborn. He used the same appellation of Solomon.[35] Adam, engendered by the thought of God, is His son, in the proper sense of the word. The name "God" itself was conferred on Moses,[36] with respect to his relations with Pharaoh and Aaron. There is thus nothing extraordinary in giving these names to Christ. This is to say that the bond that unites him to God is of no different kind from that which exists between God and humanity in general, or between God and the great inspired men of the Bible in particular.

The views expressed here are those of a man quite indifferent to the subtleties of theological speculation, a man for whom the problem is simply one of terminology. As far as religion and worship are concerned, Christ occupies for Aphraates the same position as he does for Christian orthodoxy as a whole; that is, he is the object of faith and adoration. But in the intellectual and doctrinal sphere "the Persian sage," though paying lip service to the Trinitarian formulae that had been worked out by Greek theologians, retains the simplicity of outlook of the first generations of Christians. There is a striking discrepancy between his devotion and his thinking. Living among Jews, and Jews, moreover, who had not succumbed any more than himself to the influence of Hellenism, he refutes them in language that comes naturally to him and is readily comprehensible to them. The same Semitic mentality finds expression both in their criticisms and in his replies.[37]

The arguments used by Western authors, whether Greek or Latin, are on a distinctly different level. It is not that they all interpret the preexistence and divinity of Christ in absolutely identical ways. Justin's Christology, for example, is clearly subordinationist. Christ, according to Justin, may properly be called "angel," "because he announces to men whatever the Maker of the universe, above whom there is no other God, desires to announce to them." He is also θεός, but not exactly on an equal footing with the Father, for the Father alone is entitled to be called ὁ θεός.[38] Post-Nicene authors, by contrast, profess the equality of the two persons. But for all of them the divine character of Christ represents an unparalleled and unique phenomenon.

In order to establish this fact, they collect from scripture all those texts which indicate the presence alongside the Father of "another God," another being who is associated with Him either in the creation or the government of the world. In addition, they endeavor to demonstrate that Christ is the power that was at work throughout biblical history.[39] For their evidence they rely largely on the numerous descriptions of theophanies that are to be found in scripture. These appearances can scarcely be identified with Him who "hath been seen of none, and hath never conversed personally with any, whom we know as creator of the universe and Father."[40] They can be ascribed to no other than the Christ-Logos.

This "other God" showed himself to the chief among the patriarchs. He appeared to Abraham at the oak of Mamre.[41] The three figures who are seen are not, as Philo takes them to be, God the Father accompanied by two hypostases, the Creative Power and the Royal Power.[42] Neither are they three angels, as Trypho (in agreement with the Talmud) believes.[43] They comprise the Logos, "who is also God and Lord, acting as servant to him who is in heaven," accompanied by two angels, who are subordinated to him.[44] It was with the same person that Jacob struggled at the crossing of the Jabbok,[45] and who also appeared to Jacob at Bethel.[46] The same again showed himself to Moses in the burning bush. For "no person whatever, even though he be of slight intelligence, will dare to say that the maker and Father of the universe left all that is above heaven, and appeared on a little section of earth."[47] According to the Dialogue of Simon and Theophilus it was the same one who, in the form of a pillar of smoke, guided Israel out of Egypt.[48]

Christ was thus the visible manifestation of God the Father, the mediator of His decisions to men and the agent through whom His will was carried out. He was also associated with Him in creation. We know that the lost Dialogue of Jason and Papiscus read at the beginning of Genesis, *In filio fecit Deus caelum et terram*.[49] The Dialogue of Timothy and Aquila gives the same interpretation, taking *In principio* as referring to the Logos.[50] It is quite regular and normal for the apologists to base their thesis on the verse that introduces the creation of man, "Let us make man in our own image."[51] Justin connects this verse with another, "See, the man has become like one of us, with his knowledge of good and evil," and he concludes from this that God "conversed with one different in number from himself and possessed of reason ($\lambda o \gamma \iota \kappa \grave{o} \nu \ \upsilon \pi \acute{a} \rho \chi o \nu \tau a$)."[52]

In some of the dialogues the Jewish interlocutor applies these verses to the angels, as, albeit somewhat rarely, do the rabbinic texts. In others the Jew is represented as following the custom of Alexandrian Judaism and understanding the verses in question to refer to Wisdom. For Wisdom herself said: "When He fixed the heavens firm, I was there." Justin himself recognizes in these texts the divine hypostasis, Wisdom, a "reasonable power... which is also called by the Holy Spirit the Glory of the Lord, and sometimes Son, and sometimes Wisdom, and sometimes Angel, and sometimes God, and sometimes Lord and Word." But he goes on to identify this hypostasis with Christ, which his Jewish opponent finds offensive.[53] In the Dialogue of Athanasius and Zacchaeus, the Jew Zacchaeus, like Trypho, cries, "Blasphemy," when his Christian opponent suggests this identification. According to Zacchaeus, Wisdom cannot become incarnate in a human body.[54]

Here we have the real stumbling block. Looked at purely as a matter of theology the difference between the Christians and the Jews was essentially this: the Jews, even those of Alexandrian background, absolutely refused to assimilate to each other these two great figures, the human Messiah and the divine Wisdom. Both were, to different degrees, familiar figures to them, but in their eyes they were essentially different.

The Jews had refused to recognize this fundamental identity. They had rejected the idea of a suffering Messiah. They had repudiated Christ, who was both Messiah and Logos. They were also blindly attached to laws and regulations that were now revoked. For all these reasons they had been excluded from the covenant and deprived of its benefits in favor of the pagans. The incarnation and death of Christ, in freeing men from sin, had put an end to the era in which they were subjected to the yoke of the law. These two themes, therefore, the abrogation of the law and the call of the gentiles, together with Christology, made up the essence of anti-Jewish polemic.

II

The criticism which the Christian writers made of the Jewish law, or at least of its ritual and ceremonial prescriptions, rested on a basis of allegorical interpretation, as I have noted already. In each commandment the Christian apologists saw either a prefiguration of the rites of the Church or a symbol of Christian truth. But though they used, and abused, the allegorical method, they did not usually restrict themselves to it exclusively. It was useful to them for proving their case concerning Christ and the Church. It was not, on the other hand, adequate to the task of demolishing the law. It was exposed especially to the objection that in the law itself all the regulations, even the ritual ones, have the same imperative character. Their observance is categorically stated in every line of the biblical legislation to be a strict duty. Would God have taken the trouble to stress this if the rites he was imposing on Israel were to be regarded as no more than symbols?

Most of the polemists, in consequence, allowed the precepts in question a real validity, but in an attempt to encourage the Jews to abandon them, and even more, to prevent Christian believers from falling in with them, they set themselves to demonstrate their purely relative nature. This meant, in the last resort, their irrelevance.[55] This demonstration takes on rather different forms in different polemical works. However, for all practical purposes it is organized on the following lines.

It sets out by making a fundamental distinction between the moral law, on the one hand, and the ritual and ceremonial law on the other. This distinction appears as early as Justin Martyr, when he invites Trypho to admit "that one commandment was appointed for piety and the practice of righteousness, and another command and action was in the same way spoken either as referring to the mystery of Christ or on account of the hardness of your people's heart."[56] Allegorical exegesis and positive exegesis are combined here in the interpretation

of the regulations. The ritual law was intended by God to be imposed
on Israel alone. The moral law, for its part, has an import that is both
universal and lasting. God wished to give everybody, Jew and gentile,
the opportunity of approaching Him. This is why the moral law is
inscribed in the heart of all men, so that it may guide them into the
way of salvation. It seems that this moral law is to be identified, as far
as its content is concerned, with the decalogue, but it antedated the
decalogue, as it antedated the covenant God made with Israel. "For
he exhibits among every race of men the things that are righteous at
all times and in all places, and every race is aware that adultery is evil,
and fornication, and murder, and all suchlike things.... For the law
given at Horeb is already antiquated and belongs to you alone, but
that other belongs to all men absolutely."[57] This is the natural law,
*naturalia legis per quae homo justificatur quae etiam ante legislationem
custodiebant qui fide justificabantur et placebant Deo.*[58]

Christ has simply confirmed and given precision to this natural law.
By contrast, he has abolished the ritual law, which was intended
strictly for the Jews alone: *leges particulares, praecepta servitutis,* is how
Irenaeus describes these regulations.[59] If the conscience of mankind
tells them nothing about these ritual obligations, it is because God
wished, in dispensing them to the Jews alone, to show that they were
not necessary for salvation.

It has been pointed out[60] that this distinction between moral
commands and ritual regulations was already familiar to the rabbis,
and indeed is derived, in the last analysis, from the biblical text itself,
with its distinction between *mishpatim* and *huqqoth.*[61] And even when
the Christian authors argue that, by laying the ritual precepts as an
obligation on Israel alone, God wished to show their futility, they are
doing no more than reframing an opinion the Jews themselves had, in
one form or another, tacitly allowed. For the Synagogue had imposed
on the "God fearers" as necessary but sufficient conditions nothing
more than respect for the so-called Noachic commandments, which
are primarily moral ones. They were advised, in order to become
proselytes, to add to these the keeping of the ritual prescriptions of the
Mosaic law, and in so doing, to become identified with the chosen
people.[62] But though the Jews agreed with their opponents in
recognizing the ritual laws as intended for themselves only, they went
on to see in them a special sign of the Lord's favor.

The Christians set themselves to refute this interpretation. The
anti-Jewish polemists commonly make a distinction, following from
the biblical chronology, between circumcision, which was enjoined on
Abraham, and the rest of the ritual provisions, which were dictated to
Moses and codified by him. They do not dispute the fact that

circumcision was a sign given to the Jews, and that it was intended to distinguish them from other peoples. Aphraates, insisting that it is a sign, is not convinced that it is therefore a privilege.[63] Justin thinks it better understood as a mark of infamy, which by the divine foreknowledge was inflicted because of the murder of Christ and of the prophets. But what end was it meant to serve? Justin, who writes in the aftermath of Hadrian's war, thinks that its function was to mark out the Jews, making it possible for the Romans to deny them access to the holy city, in order that "ye alone should suffer the things that ye are rightly suffering now...and none of you go up to Jerusalem. For by nothing else are ye to be known from other men, save by the circumcision that is in your flesh."[64] The same interpretation is found in Tertullian. Circumcision was imposed on the Israelites *in signum, non in salutem... signum unde Israël in novissimo tempore dinosci haberet quando secundum sua merita in sanctam civitatem ingredi prohiberetur.*[65]

The weakness of this argument is in its acceptance of circumcision as a purely Jewish phenomenon. In fact, it was practiced by a number of other peoples. Justin is not unaware of this, and he quotes Jeremiah, who speaks of "all who are circumcised only in the flesh: Egypt, Judah, Edom, the sons of Ammon, Moab," though he goes on to say that they are uncircumcised of heart.[66] Doubtless, the circumcision of these other peoples was not to be regarded as a sign. But the fact that circumcision was a rite the Jews shared with these several categories of pagans affords proof that it is not a privilege, and that neither, with even better reason, can it be the seal of the covenant. On the contrary, it follows that circumcision is entirely futile. "For it does not advantage either the Egyptians, or the sons of Moab, or the sons of Edom. But though a man be even a Scythian or a Persian, yet has the knowledge of God and of his Christ, and keeps the eternal acts of righteousness, he is circumcised with the fair and profitable circumcision, and he is dear to God."[67] The argument appears again in Barnabas, from whom, possibly, Justin borrowed it, and also in the Dialogue of Simon and Theophilus.[68]

This is not the only proof of the uselessness of circumcision. It follows also, for example, from the fact that women cannot be circumcised. "For God made even females able to keep all the acts of righteousness and virtue as well as men."[69] It follows even more cogently from the late delivery of the instruction regarding circumcision. This is something all Christian apologists make the most of. Abraham, when he received circumcision, was already justified by faith.[70] And the older patriarchs, from Adam to Enoch, and after them Melchizedek, lived and died uncircumcised.[71]

The same argument applies, a fortiori, against the rest of the ritual law, for it is even later. "It was all enjoined on you," says Justin, "because of your transgressions and your hardness of heart."[72] Unlike circumcision, which was designed to punish a crime that was still in the future, the rest of the ritual law follows immediately upon the worship of the golden calf and is part of the sanctions that that sin entailed.[73] The ritual law is thus at once punitive and preventive, "in order that by these many means you should always, and in every action, have God before your eyes, and not begin to commit injustice and impiety. For he also enjoined you to wear the scarlet fringe, in order that by its means forgetfulness of God should not come upon you; and he commanded you to gird yourselves with a phylactery of certain letters written on very thin parchments,—which we grant are holy in your eyes,—by these means pressing you ever to hold God in mind, and at the same time to have a sense of sin in your hearts."[74]

Similarly, each prescription of the ritual law is related to one particular sin, which it is intended both to punish and to forestall. The Sabbath is intended to keep always in the forgetful minds of the Jews the memory of the Lord.[75] The food laws are aimed at the suppression of gluttony and greediness, which distract men from God.[76]

All these regulations were made, not for the righteous, but only for the sake of the inveterate sinners among the Jews. For "God had granted to Noah, a righteous man, to eat every living thing, save flesh with blood."[77] Abraham, even after his circumcision, never observed the Sabbath at all.[78] Even after their promulgation, the regulations were on several occasions ignored by holy men without their being taken to task for the infringement. Thus Joshua had the ark carried round Jericho seven days in succession. This necessarily involved carrying it round on the Sabbath. He thus not only broke the command to rest but caused the priesthood and the army to break it. The Maccabees likewise fought on the Sabbath,[79] and they won a victory by doing so, whereas previously they had applied the law too strictly and suffered heavily. Following the example of these righteous men Christians not only may but ought to grant themselves a dispensation from such ordinances, because they are "laws that were not good, and observances by which one could never live."[80]

Interpreted in this manner, the law itself was seen to possess a transitory nature. There was a time when it was not yet in force. The time is now come when it is in force no longer. Since it was introduced as a consequence of sin, it will disappear as sin disappears, "and as an eternal and final law was Christ given to us, and this disposition is sure, after which there is no law, or ordinance, or command."[81] The law has been abolished for Christians, whatever their racial origins, by the redeeming grace of Christ, and even for the rebellious Jews themselves its essential provisions have been abolished, by force of circumstances.

For in condemning the law in the name of the new covenant, there was a risk of convincing none but the converted. This is why the polemists spend a good deal of their time in showing that the law is still invalid, even if the eruption of Christianity be ignored. The polemists attempt to do this by starting simply from the facts of Judaism's actual situation, and it is one of the most interesting aspects of their work. They treat the law as a whole, whose different parts belong indissolubly together, and they try to prove that since the conditions under which it was meant to operate no longer obtain, the observance of the law is ipso facto impossible. Every man who is circumcised, as St. Paul following rabbinic precept had already asserted, was bound to keep the whole law.[82] Correspondingly, the polemists reckon that if the law should become impracticable in part, then all its other prescriptions must automatically lapse.[83] The law stands or falls as a whole. Thus they are able to derive a condemnation of the entire legal structure of Judaism from the facts of the destruction of Jerusalem and the dispersion of the Jews.

These two historic facts, which are the Jews' punishment for their crime against Christ, have automatically involved as consequences the end of the sacrificial cult and the end of the priesthood. They ought logically also to put an end to the Passover rites. By continuing to hold the Passover the Jews commit a flagrant breach of the law, for since some of the essential elements in the Passover are now impossible to preserve, the entire ritual is a dead letter.

For some of the Christian authors sacrifice represents a degraded form of worship, not very different from idolatry and unworthy of the true God. This view is based on that tradition among the prophets that is hostile to bloody sacrifice. In particular, the upholders of this opinion base their case on two texts, which are brought together by Justin.[84] First, Jeremiah 7:22: "For when I brought your ancestors out of the land of Egypt, I said nothing to them, gave them no orders, about holocaust and sacrifice."[85] Second, Amos 5:25 ff.: "Did you bring me sacrifice and oblation in the wilderness for all those forty years, house of Israel? No, you carried the tent of Moloch on your shoulder and the star of the god Rephan, those idols that you had made to adore."[86] These two texts seem to the apologists to demand the conclusion that it was not the original intention of God to establish a sacrificial cult at all. The idea of a sacrificial cult was one that Israel herself had conceived, during the time when she had forgotten the Lord and was worshiping false gods. The Lord had done no more than tolerate this cult and lay down rules to govern it; this in an endeavor to contain the idolatrous tendencies of His people. The building of the temple was inspired by the same motive. "God accommodated himself to that people, and commanded them to bring sacrifices, as unto His name, in order that ye should not commit idolatry."[87]

This interpretation of the sacrificial cult was strengthened by the observation that God had confined the practice of it rigorously to the one city of Jerusalem and to the one temple. Tertullian contrasts this restrictive ordinance with Malachi's announcement of a pure sacrifice, to be offered to God throughout the universe. He resolves the contradiction between them by concluding that only spiritual sacrifices are acceptable, whereas the rites practiced by Israel are condemned for all eternity.[88] St. John Chrysostom takes up and develops the argument in his turn. Sacrifice, according to him, was a concession to Jewish weakness, a remedy for sin, and a stopgap. One might even allow cold water to a fever-stricken man if he threatened, for lack of it, to throw himself over a cliff or to hang himself. God, in the same way, seeing that the Jews were quite ready, such was the frenzy of their desire, to sacrifice to idols, authorized this form of worship, but only within closely regulated limits. Just as the physician might allow the sick man to drink, on condition that it was from one particular bottle, which he has secretly warmed, so God permitted sacrifice in only one place. Now this is the very place that today, of all places upon earth, Jews are forbidden to enter. For as the physician might end by breaking the bottle, thus God had destroyed the city. And it is clear that by breaking the keystone it is His intention to destroy the whole edifice.[89]

Without the sacrifices and the temple, which were its raison d'être, there is no longer any priesthood. It is Chrysostom again who, emphasizing the end of the priesthood, explains its disappearance not by the installation of a new priesthood, the Christian one, but simply by the fact that the ordinary conditions of its existence and functioning no longer obtain. God is thus indicating that it has lapsed. According to proper Jewish usage, it is incorrect to apply the title of priest to the patriarchs who in their time were leaders of the Jewish religious community, for there could not be any priests before there was an offering and an altar, and before there was a holy anointing, such as Moses administered to Aaron.[90] The true priesthood disappeared from Israel at the very point at which this ritual ceased to be observed. And with the priesthood there disappeared the entire ritual apparatus and life it was the priests' task to organize. Thus disappeared, for example the practice of presenting firstborn males to the Lord and the sacrifices of purification that Leviticus prescribes for various sorts of defilement.[91]

So Chrysostom, becoming, for the sake of the cause, more Jewish than the Jews, refutes their legalism in the name of the law. He makes use of the same quasijuridical criterion of legitimacy in order to condemn the Passover rite.[92] Just as in the case of sacrifice, God had explicitly limited its celebration to the one city, Jerusalem. For it is written: "You may not sacrifice the Passover in any of the towns that Yahweh your God gives you; but only in the place where Yahweh your God chooses to give his name a home, there you must sacrifice the Passover."[93] The Jews did in the past respect this commandment and all similar ones. Throughout the Babylonian exile they renounced sacrifices, songs, and feasting, turning low the flame of their cultic life.[94] Daniel abstained from food for twenty-one days at the time of the Passover itself, thus apparently infringing the law, which forbids fasting during the time of unleavened bread.[95] In fact, he was scrupulously observing the ritual laws. To refuse to apply them in a foreign land was actually to obey them. He would, on the contrary, have been breaking the laws if he had, as the Jews now do, complied with them outside Jerusalem. For the question of place is in this connection the principal one.[96] Having been dispossessed of Jerusalem, the dispersed Israel has only one course of action open to it, to renounce those practices which God has made it manifestly impossible to observe. For God's intention, in making their observance impossible, is to express His disapproval of them. It is not, as in the case of the Babylonian exile, a question of temporary suspension. God had comprehensively repudiated the cultic system, for he has smitten not only the law, but the people, who are so closely involved with it.

III

In this polemic, therefore, the rejection of Israel is the inevitable corollary of the abrogation of the law. The law was intended only for the Jews. The law alone, by restraining their evil propensities, was capable of keeping them in the right way. Once deprived of this safety barrier and left to themselves by the divine decree, the self-styled chosen people go straight to their own destruction.

This assertion, which stands alongside the claim that the gentiles have been called by God,[97] is buttressed by the polemists with two series of texts, which together shape their whole line of argument. The former series is of texts that refer to the apostasy of Israel, the latter of those which express universalist tendencies. In addition to these, they draw on the evidence of contemporary events.

If God had, by the mouth of the prophets, so clearly repudiated the traditional forms of the Israelite cult, it was not only because He found them uncongenial in themselves, but also because of the sinful dispositions of those who carried them out. When He rejects with horror "your new moons and your Sabbaths," the accent is as much on the possessive pronouns as on the substantives. God is thinking of the people as much as of the rites they practice. In the biblical past, nevertheless, Israel's sins and acts of apostasy were always followed, after a longer or shorter interval, by forgiveness. The covenant, so often violated by the people, remained in force until in the person of Christ is was brought to an end by the ultimate crime. The Christians used all their dialectical skill to demonstrate that Israel could no longer appeal against her present rejection. It was final, like the destruction of the people and the dispersion of the people, which symbolized it.

God, says Aphraates,[98] delivered Israel from exile only twice; from the captivity in Egypt by the hand of Moses, and from that in Babylon by Ezra. The Jews assert that they will again be gathered. They are wrong. For Isaiah, speaking of the Babylonian captivity, says: "The Lord will extend His hand yet a second time."[99] If there was to be another restoration, he would have said, "a third time." Chrysostom takes up the same idea and in similar terms.[100] The Jewish people have submitted three times to servitude. Each has been prophesied accurately. The Egyptian captivity lasted 400 years, as Gen. 15:13–16 said it would. Concerning the Babylonian captivity, Jeremiah said that it would last seventy years. The third trial was foretold in great detail by Daniel in his prophecy of the seventy weeks that would separate the rebuilding of the temple after the return from Babylon from yet another destruction. The period thus described ended with the Roman conquest of Palestine and the events of A.D. 70. This third trial differs from the other two in that no limit to it is indicated. It will last until the end of time. The sanctuary has been destroyed for good. The Jews have tried three times to rebuild it: under Hadrian, under Constantine, and under Julian the Apostate. Each time they met with total lack of success. This is because God has decided against it.[101]

In order to show that the gentiles have now been called by God, the polemists have recourse to several different lines of argument. They make free use of allegory, and search the history of the patriarchs for premonitory figures, such as Cain and Abel; the double issue of

Abraham (through Isaac, son of Sarah, and through Ishmael, son of Hagar), the two peoples born of Rebecca[102]; the abandonment by Esau of his birthright and blessing of Jacob by Isaac; the blessing of Ephraim by Jacob;[103] the history of Joseph, and a number of other features and episodes that, by illustrating the primacy given to younger sons over their elder brothers, all foretell the transfer of the covenant to the gentiles, the younger brother of Israel.[104]

More positive exegesis seeks in the biblical record not only such symbols (whose interpretation was always open to challenge) but concrete evidence of an election prior to the election of Israel. I have already drawn attention to the part played in Christian thinking by the uncircumcised priest Melchizedek. Melchizedek is the father of the gentiles and of the Christian priesthood at the same time. He is called to the service of the true God before Abraham himself, and Abraham pays homage to him, acting toward him in his paying of the tithe, as Chrysostom emphasizes, like a simple layman.[105]. In addition, Abraham himself, "father of a multitude," is as much the father of non-Jews as he is of Israel. And it is the gentiles, who in future were to be the Christians, who are blessed in his name.[106]

It is nevertheless from the prophetic texts that the controversialists draw the essentials of their arguments. They read there the threat, which was repeated several times by the Lord, to bestow on the gentiles the favor that His sinful and ungrateful people no longer deserve.[107] Above all, they find there the prediction of a new community of believers, coming from all the corners of the world, and gathered together in the spiritual worship of the true God. This prophetic vision has been made a reality in the Church. The biblical texts generally allocate a special place to Israel in the building of the city of God. The twelve tribes make up the nucleus round which the nations will come and gather under the law of the Lord. They will constitute thereby an enlarged Israel. This was not usually how the ecclesiastical writers saw it. For them the people of God ought not to be created by the addition of gentiles to a Hebrew nucleus, but rather by means of a substitution, a dispossession of the latter in favor of the former.[108] At best, the Jews might be able to give up their identity and be gathered into the Church. But it would be a Church that had been constituted apart from them, and they would be the humblest element within it. Even in the biblical period, says Aphraates, converted pagans always took precedence over the Israelites.[109]

The new Israel is therefore, as Justin emphasizes, a different Israel. Trypho reacts to this with surprise: "Are you Israel?"[110] And when he takes the texts Justin has seen as referring to gentile Christians and applies them instead to proselytes, Justin retorts that the proselytes, far from benefiting from the favor God has withdrawn from the Jews, are involved with them in the same condemnation. Proselytes have made themselves Jews and will be treated as Jews.[111] The Christian authors interpret in the same strain the failure of their Jewish mission. Its lack of success was part of the divine plan. And the facts as they saw them confirmed them in this opinion. The most convincing proof of the call of the gentiles was the initiation of a new covenant of which the gentiles were the beneficiaries. Along with this new covenant there had been transferred into gentile hands institutions and privileges that previously, i.e., up to the time of Christ's coming, had been peculiar to the Jews. These were the sign of election.[112]

At the same time, in fact, as the institutions of Judaism were crumbling, those of Christianity were being installed in their place. This coincidence of the two developments left no room for doubt about the decisive nature of Israel's rejection, and it forbade any thought of her restoration.[113] The spiritual temple had replaced the temple of Jerusalem. Instead of the bloody sacrifices of the old covenant, there was now celebrated the pure sacrifice that had been foretold by Malachi, namely, the Christian eucharist. The Christian priesthood, after the order of Melchizedek, had supplanted the priesthood of the Jews.[114] Later authors lay great emphasis on this point. Earlier ones, however, writing at a time when the hierarchy of the Church had not yet reached a fixed and definitive form, contrasted not the two priesthoods, but the spiritual gifts (charismata) of the two covenants. Prophecy came into being in Israel. It flourishes in the Church. "But after the appearance and death of Jesus our Christ in your race there has been no prophet anywhere [among the Jews]." However, "even until the present time gifts of prophecy exist among us, from which fact you yourselves ought to understand that what was of old in your nation has been transferred to us."[115] Thus does Justin find corroboration for his fundamental assertion: "We are the true and spiritual nation of Israel, and the race of Judah and of Jacob and Isaac and Abraham, who when he was still uncircumcised received witness from God for his faith, and was blessed, and was called father of many nations,—we, I say, are all this, who were brought nigh to God by him who was crucified, even Christ."[116]

Such, as far as its principal themes and main lines are concerned, is the argument of the anti-Jewish treatises.

The Christological developments would find a place in any apologetic work, whatever kind it might be. Nevertheless, among the majority of the authors who concern us, the Christological argument takes on a markedly anti-Jewish tone. The objections it meets are, as we have already noted in passing, of a specifically Jewish kind, and the scripture-based arguments that are used to refute them are of a variety specially designed for Jewish ears. Simply to acknowledge this creates a presumption in favour of the theory that the literature was genuinely aimed against the Jews.

There is even less doubt about the destination of the literature that is concerned specifically with criticism of Judaism itself. Its authors can only have had in mind either Jews, or, what amounts to the same thing, those gentiles, of either pagan or Christian origin, who were smitten with Judaism.[117] How could criticism of the old Jewish law interest a non-Jew at all, unless he was tempted to recognize the authority that Christian polemic was denying to it? The weakness of Harnack's theory springs entirely from his failure to see the force of this argument. Was controversial writing adapted to the object of its criticism or was it not? This is another problem over which I shall not pause. The answer varies according to the nature of the treatise. Their authors are not all equally able, and not all equally alive to the way in which their opponents were thinking. But at least there can be little doubt who these opponents were. Whether they were Jews or Judaizers matters little, for in either case it is Judaism which this literature is taking to task. Whether it is firsthand or secondhand Judaism is of no importance.

IV

We are, however, not restricted in this question to weighing the probabilities solely on the basis of the documents so far considered. Numerous witnesses attest the genuineness of learned controversies between Jews and Christians. These shed light on the real significance of the anti-Jewish literature.

Such testimony is particularly valuable when it comes from those who were themselves authors of polemical works, for it encourages us to think that the written works embody the substance of arguments used in verbal encounter. Tertullian says as much in quite explicit fashion when he declares at the beginning of his treatise that it is his object to present in writing a discussion in which he took part.[118] Origen is equally unambiguous. He refers to actual discussions with Jewish scholars.[119] The way in which Justin introduces his dialogue seems to indicate that he is taking as his point of departure some real conversations with a rabbi. Attempts have indeed been made, though without any very definite result, to identify this rabbi.[120]

Freimann has tried, by studying both the dialogue of Justin and the passages in *Contra Celsum* in which a Jew appears, to allot these Jewish protagonists in the anti-Christian controversy to their proper parties among the diverse elements that made up Judaism.[121] They are, he concludes, Jews of the Hellenistic type. Palestinian Pharisaism, on the contrary, was indifferent to external events, and quite absorbed in the study and practice of the law. It therefore remained a stranger to discussion with the rival religion. It was only in the diaspora that the Jews organized any resistance.

This kind of assertion is unacceptable. It springs from a too narrow conception of Pharisaism. It is in any case refuted by a whole series of patristic texts. It may be freely acknowledged that Trypho, and with even greater certainty Celsus's Jew, represent a strongly Hellenized version of Judaism.[122] Freimann has argued cleverly from Origen's reaction to the Jew of Celsus. Celsus's Jew quotes, as a Greek would, the pagan mythological stories, and Origen expresses surprise at this. It is not, he thinks, the way a real Jew would argue. Origen concludes that the Jew whom Celsus introduces into his discussion is merely a literary fiction, which corresponds to nothing in reality.[123] Freimann turns this argument round by asserting that Origen's surprise is explained by the difference in date between himself and Celsus. At the time when Justin and Celsus wrote the kind of rabbi they both present, thoroughly Hellenized, a spiritual descendant of Philo, actually did exist. In Origen's own period, owing to the progressive rupture between Judaism and Greek culture, he had ceased to exist, and had given way to the Pharisaic or Talmudic rabbi, withdrawn, legalistic, and regarding the outside world with a sullen hostility.

This explanation is ingenious, telling up to a point, but a little forced. It does not establish the author's general conclusions. Justin's *Dialogue* and the anti-Jewish parts of the *Contra Celsum* represent no more than a small part of the anti-Jewish literature, and no conclusions drawn from them alone could justify the assertion that only the Hellenistic Jews were interested in controversy with Christians. The opposition between Pharisaism and Hellenism was not, as we have already noted, so deep-rooted as has oftern been supposed. It is no longer possible to regard the Pharisees as concerned only with the contemplation of the law, and as uninterested in what was going on around them. The gospel recognizes their proselytizing zeal.[124] As guardians of legalist orthodoxy, and as men eager to make converts, how could they have done otherwise than react energetically against those whose sin consisted precisely in this, that in the name of the biblical revelation itself they rejected the law? Indeed, the first adversary of Christianity, going right back to the time when the Christian communities came into being, was the Pharisaic scholar, the doctor of the law. He it was who took issue relentlessly with Jesus himself. Did he then give up the struggle when faced with the disciples? The rabbis of the Mishnah and Talmud polemize assiduously against the heretics.[125] Freimann knows this, but he claims to recognize these *minim* as Jewish sectaries, having no connection with Christianity. I shall, at the proper time, examine this term, with a view to finding out exactly what it means and in what senses it is used. But even if Freimann's interpretation of the term turns out to be the right one, by what token does he assume that these rabbis, who so delight in argument with all and sundry, systematically excluded from their discussions all mention of Christians and Christianity?

Freimann's argument would only be acceptable if he could demonstrate that the stream of anti-Jewish literature dried up after the second century. This is the date he sets for the final elimination of Hellenistic and liberal Judaism. In fact, the production of this literature, far from falling off, actually increased. The works of Justin and Origen swelled the stream to a greater volume than before. And the series of witnesses to the reality of the discussions with the Jews continues right down to the end of our period. They come, for the most part, from the time when Judaism and Pharisaism were virtually the same thing. And the most interesting of them are connected with Palestine, where Freimann denies that any controversies between Jews and Christians took place. Harnack, conversely, alleges that the Judaism of the dispersion ceased to count for anything in the face of Christianity, which arose after the destruction of Jerusalem. He therefore will not have it that there were any polemical encounters *except* in Palestine, not after the first and second centuries at any rate.[126] In the light of the texts themselves, both opinions are untenable.

It is often difficult to decide from what geographical area a particular work comes, especially if it is anonymous or of doubtful authorship. It is in addition very difficult to assign the Jews who figure in the dialogues to any particular party, since their characteristics are generally too ill-defined. It is argued that the use of allegory implies that the Jews to whom it was addressed were Hellenists, for they would be in a better position to understand it than Palestinians. But this argument too will not hold water, for allegory was too widely used for that. There is, on the contrary, every reason to believe that the Judaism envisaged by the Christian polemists is not principally the Hellenistic kind at all.

The Hellenistic Jews were at first sight less well prepared to meet the Christian arguments than were the Palestinian rabbis, and more vulnerable to the Christian attack. If it is true that Judaism, taken as a whole, prepared the way for Christianity, this statement is true in the first instance of that particular variety of Judaism we call Alexandrian. The development of Hellenistic Christianity, which quickly became Christianity par excellence, cannot be accounted for if the prior existence of Alexandrian Judaism is forgotten.

The infant Church borrowed from the thinkers of diaspora Judaism, along with some of their apologetic themes, their allegorical method of interpreting scripture, the translation on which it was based, and the speculations about divine hypostases that were to prove so fruitful for its theology. This meant that the two sides were speaking the same language, and this proved fatal for the Jews, for they quickly found themselves the underdogs. For Christianity was rich with possibilities and was able to take over the weapons that Judaism had forged and use them against her far more effectively than she could use them herself.

If all trace of Hellenistic Jewish literature disappears after the end of the second century, this is partly because Talmudic rabbinism extended its authority over the diaspora and managed to regroup Israel's forces, and partly because, in the regions where Hellenistic Judaism was formerly a force, many of its adherents, both Jews and proselytes, may well have become Christian. In so doing, they were displaying a certain self-consistency. The allegorical methods of pseudo-Aristeas led perfectly naturally to those of the fathers. The logos of Philo prepared them to accept the Logos-Christ.

A study of the controversial literature confirms these impressions. The arguments developed there by Christian polemists seem on the whole to be conceived with a different type of Judaism in mind from the Alexandrian. Their allegorical interpretations are set not against other allegorical interpretations, but usually against a narrow insistence on the letter of the text, Their theme is: You do not understand what you are reading. It is rather rare to find the Jewish notion of divine hypostases raised at all. Christological proofs are framed not in terms of hypostatic ideas but in terms of strict monotheism. The arguments are designed to show, by recourse to scriptural proof, that the doctrine of the divine Wisdom (Wisdom naturally being identified with Christ) is a soundly based one. They do not attempt to demonstrate that Christ is to be identified with a figure of Wisdom that is already familiar to the adversary.[127]. The Messianic prophecies are relied on more heavily than the Wisdom literature.

In fact, the main effort is directed against the ritual law and against rigoristic legalism. And the exegesis on which this legalism is based is clearly of a literalistic kind far removed from that of the Alexandrians. This gives us every reason to believe that the chief adversary, and the most tenacious, was everywhere the strict literalistic rabbi. The evidence from the period after the disappearance of Hellenistic Judaism confirms this.

Eusebius, who had conversed with Jews at Caesarea, accuses them of gross errors in their interpretation of scripture, and asserts that it is necessary to foster controversy in order to convert them.[128] It is especially against them that he writes his *Demonstratio Evangelica*.[129] St. Jerome is still more definite. He freely admits that the arguments were often bitter, and that it was frequently the Jews who began them. He describes the aggressive enthusiasm of his opponents in the discussions that were staged, *solutis labiis et obtorta lingua et stridente saliva de rasa fauce gaudentium*.[130] Freimann asserts that the Jews avoided controversy and Justin says that some rabbis did advise this,[131] but according to Jerome, it was the Jews who sought opportunities for it.[132] Jerome accuses them of sidestepping Christian objections, and of extricating themselves from difficult positions by pursuing irrelevant side issues. There were certain arguments, he says, and certain interpretations of biblical texts, that they found especially difficult to stomach.[133] The Christians, for their part, who were often forced on the defensive, prepared in advance their answers to some questions they knew their opponents were bound to raise.[134] Jerome himself had taken an active part in this learned polemic. His exegetical work displays throughout the marks of his experience. It is nourished on Jewish traditions he has gleaned from the rabbis, who were his masters in exegesis as well as in the Hebrew tongue.[135] Jerome's exegesis is no more than a weapon of war. *Aliud Judaeis singula verba calumniantibus respondere* is the aim he sets himself in his commentaries on the Psalms.[136] Cyril of Jerusalem is even more emphatic about the passion for controversy that seized the Jews.[137] Further from Palestine, in a region in which Jewish influence was strong, Aphraates composes his homilies with the explicit object of providing ammunition for Christians who were daily engaged in doctrinal arguments with Jews or were exposed to their attacks.[138] Thus it is amply attested that real encounters did take place between Christians and Jews and that actual controversies did go on. We have therefore every reason to reaffirm our estimate of the anti-Jewish polemical literature. This is not to say that such literature is altogether an exact transcription of these controversies. A very careful dissection of it would doubtless reveal, I repeat, strands of very variable quality and interest. It would be very rash, for example, to suggest that if an anti-Jewish work takes the form of a dialogue, this is necessarily an indication that it is based on actual verbal discussion. Conversely, even works that cannot properly be classified under the heading *Adversus Judaeos* may display manifest traces of controversy.

This is especially true of commentaries on scripture, which often afford close points of contact with the anti-Jewish literature.[139] When this literature is looked at as a whole, its value as evidence on the subject of Jewish Christian relations is apparent. It proves that the scholars of the two faiths did on many occasions confront each other, either to goad each other or in response to goading. It proves, in a more general way, that Judaism and Christianity did not ignore each other, but rather were preoccupied with each other. All that remains is to seek some confirmation of these conclusions from Jewish literature itself. Now the Jews did not produce on their side any body of literature comparable to the polemical literature of the Christians, or at least, none with such a single and clearly defined object. We must look for our evidence therefore in the Talmudic and Midrashic materials.

7

The Christians in the Talmud

Ἐν ταῖς συναγωγαῖς ἐπαρῶνται αὐτοῖς καὶ ἀναθεματί-
ζουσι, τρὶς τῆς ἡμέρας φάσκοντες ὅτι Ἐπικαταράσαι ὁ
θεὸς τοὺς Ναζωραίους.

Epiphanius, *Panarion*, 29, 9, 2

If, as I have tried to show, the Christian polemists were engaged in a genuine struggle against a real enemy, the Jewish literature of the period ought to contain some traces of the battle. Do the Talmudic writers at any point have the Christian specifically in mind, and do they take issue with Christianity at all? This is the question that cries out to be answered. The word *Christian*, as is well known, does not appear in these writings, though whether it ever did appear or has been removed in later editing is another question, which we need not answer for the moment. But failing any specific mention of Christians, there are a number of texts that have polemical overtones and are directed against those called the *minim*. These call for our attention.

I

Jewish and Christian scholars, Talmudists and historians alike, have often paused over this word *minim*. It has already given rise to a considerable literature, and at a cursory glance one might well imagine that the problem had long ago been settled.[1] It is not so, and the question remains an open one. The reasons for this are many. There are considerable gaps in our knowledge. The texts themselves are fragmentary and obscure. And the difficulties of interpretation are all the greater in that there is always a suspicion, wherever there is a possible reference to Christianity, that the texts have been worked over or obscured by later editing. The seriousness of this difficulty must be faced right at the beginning. It is as important to avoid magnifying the extent and significance of these alterations as it is to recognize that they exist. And the undoubted fact that they do exist does not give us license to suspect them on every page and in every line, or to imagine that because Christianity is now mentioned nowhere in the Talmud it was once mentioned everywhere. Rather than attempt a hypothetical and hazardous reconstruction of the primitive text, it is better to rely on repeated and methodical examination of the text as it now stands. This is the likeliest way to gain assistance from it.

But whatever the deficiencies of the texts as they now are, there is one further point to be made. It may be said without presumption that if our question is still today so far from being decided, then this is due at least in part to the lack of a reasonable method of inquiry. It is not entirely the fault of the texts. Part of the blame must be laid at the door of their readers.

The problem appears to be a simple one: to find a meaning for, give a content to, the word *minim*. To what body of people was this obscure label applied? On surveying the mass of works that attempt to answer this question, it may be said that their authors, with very few exceptions have made two mistakes. First, they have put the question in the wrong way. The only solutions they have allowed themselves to consider have been ones that are too rigid, too absolute, and that give the impression of having been preconceived. Second, they have tried to derive the answer from the Talmudic texts alone, and the material here is so slight as to call for extreme caution. In limiting themselves to these texts, they have neglected to observe that there are scattered texts among the Christian writings that provide opportunities for cross-checking. Hardly ever are these two sources brought together. Yet such a procedure would appear to be indispensable. Without it, we are in an impasse.

It is necessary, in order to justify these strictures, to look briefly at the theories of two scholars who, as far as this question is concerned, are representative of many more, viz., Friedländer, in his *Der vorchristliche jüdische Gnostizismus*,[2] and Travers Herford in *Christianity in Talmud and Midrash*.[3] The one was a Jew, the other a liberal Christian, and both possessed a sound background knowledge of the Talmud. According to the former, the *minim* are the gnostics, and could not possibly be anything else.[4] The latter prefers to see them, generally speaking, as none other than the Jewish Christians. So here we have an open clash between the two current interpretations that command most support. To each of the protagonists the view of the other is completely out of the question, and Travers Herford, who is the later of the two writers, freely indulges in vigorous polemic against Friedländer.[5] A little less categorical in his judgments than Friedländer himself, and more inclined to caution in his statements, he does admit a number of exceptions to his main view, but in every doubtful instance he settles firmly for the Jewish-Christian interpretation. He has also done better than his opponent in that he has sketched out, or at least suggested, some links with Christian documents. But having thus made a beginning in the direction that seems to me the most promising one, he does not follow it through. His inquiry remains fragmentary, halfhearted, and not really searching enough. Of all the Christian literature available, Travers Herford has hardly gone any further than the Epistle to the Hebrews in his search for relevant material. The reasons for this curious choice are difficult to unravel, and they will not, in any case, bear scrutiny. He takes this epistle, seemingly on the basis of its title, which is manifestly not original, as representing in all its purity the theological thinking of the Jewish Christians. However interesting the epistle may be in some respects, it is difficult to see how this attitude to it can be justified. A much better case could be made out, surely, for taking it as the product of speculations in the Alexandrian style, for its points of contact with the exegesis of Philo have often been noted, and it is moreover not free from infiltration by gnostic ideas.[6] At this point it seems that Friedländer has the better of the argument. Nevertheless, having listened carefully to both protagonists in this debate, and being required to judge between them, our verdict must surely be that, though neither of them is completely wrong, yet we cannot accept that either is entirely right. The question must be taken further.

First of all, what conclusions can we draw from the word *minim* itself? There is almost complete agreement now about its etymology. The word *min*, in the singular, means "kind," "species." It is normally rendered in Greek, quite accurately, as γένος.[7] In the religious context it takes on a rather specialized meaning. It signifies a species or kind of people who mark themselves off. In this context it is often used pejoratively. It can be applied thus to all who forsake the right way, who secede from the main body and who place themselves, or are inclined to place themselves, on the fringes of orthodoxy as a self-contained body, a sect. It becomes progressively clearer that, having begun as a collective term, the word has followed the same pattern of development as the word *goy*, which originally meant "a foreign people," but came to mean "a foreigner"; i.e., it was used to designate individuals. Once the singular *min* had come to be used in the individual sense, it was reserved for this alone, and the plural *minim* was henceforth employed to designate a sectarian group, whilst the abstract noun *minuth* came into use to describe the heretical teaching such a group set up against that of orthodoxy. The term *goy* was never applied to any one pagan people rather than another, and similarly *min* and *minim* never meant any particular sect. *Minim* designated simply any dissident body, whatever its particular characteristics, which rejected in any respect the thought or practice of Jewish

orthodoxy. This is how we must interpret the statement in the
Talmud that at the time when the Jews went into exile, in A.D. 70,
there were in Israel eighty varieties of *minim*. Neither the Jewish
Christianity of that period nor Friedländer's Jewish gnosticism could
account for such an impressive catalogue. But nothing forbids us to
believe that both might have occupied a place in the list, along with
the γένος or *min* of the Sadducees.[8]

It is obvious from this how rash it is to talk of "Minism" as if it were
a system on its own, or even a well-defined movement, comparable to
Pharisaism or Essenism. Friedländer, who invented the term *Minism*,
has dangerously confused the issue. To speak of *Minism* in this context
is about as sensible as to use the word *Heresism* of a modern sect, or to
allow the word *Dissenters* to be used of no one but the Methodists.

It is true that Friedländer could appeal to a precedent, and one that
is not without force. St. Jerome himself, who was a considerable
expert on Jewish matters, speaks of the *haeresis Minaeorum* as if it meant
a single, distinguishable sect.[9] This argument, though it is at first sight
a strong one, nevertheless does not stand up to criticism. We must
note Jerome's own special standpoint. He is interested in Jewish-
Christian relations. He is not concerned with those Jewish heresies
which have nothing in common with Christianity, but only with those
which owe something to both religions and set up camp in the
territory between the two. He begins with a known fact, the existence
of Jewish heretics, and knowing that the Jews call them *minim*, he
assumes quite naturally that there is a heresy of that name. He equally
naturally makes a proper name out of what was really a general
description. This was all the more justifiable in that at the end of the
fourth century Jewish gnosticism was in decline and the reconstruction of Palestinian Judaism as a strict orthodoxy or orthopraxy was
already well under way. Under these circumstances the majority of
the Jewish dissidents in Palestine was made up of the various species
of Jewish Christians. The term *minim*, which was applied originally to
heretics in general might well have become restricted, until in practice
it became virtually synonymous with "Nazarenes," as Jerome
indicates.[10]

From this analysis of the word, and from the evidence, correctly
interpreted, of St. Jerome, we derive two conclusions. First, a
designation as elastic as the term *minim* could well cover, at different
times and in different places, very different things, and it is likely that
the precise meaning will never be beyond dispute. There are bound to
be many instances in which, for lack of precise information about the
milieu from which the text emanated, and in the absence of any sure
criteria for making a judgment on the matter, we must remain in

doubt. The second conclusion is that, at least during the fourth century, and in Palestine, the word *minim* primarily designated the Jewish Christians. To our original question, "Are the *minim* to be equated with gnostics or with Jewish Christians," we must reply: "They were sometimes the Jewish Christians."[11] But in any event we cannot accept the either/or form of the question. It reflects a misunderstanding both of the proper meaning of the word *minim* and of the complexity of religious life in the early centuries A.D. It represents certain things as being in watertight compartments that in reality were not so at all. Gnosticism and Jewish Christianity can only be seen as opposites as long as we fix our eyes on the extreme forms of both. But just as there was a Jewish gnosticism that antedated Christianity and remained out of touch with it, and a Christian Hellenistic gnosticism, whose chief preoccupation was to break all connection with the old covenant, so also, as we now know, there were currents of gnosticism within Jewish Christianity, running alongside the Ebionite form of it.[12] Further, if for St. Jerome the title *minim* applies only to Jewish Christians, a sect rejected by both the Synagogue and the Church, it is not in itself inconceivable that the Jews, for their part, continued to apply it to all Christians of whatever kind, even those who had broken with Judaism entirely, treating them all without distinction as heretical Jews. In short, for the Jews themselves the term *minim* may well have comprehended orthodox Christianity along with all the other dissidents.

The question thus cannot be dealt with in the simple terms in which it is often put. I shall not attempt to solve the whole problem, and I shall leave out of account those Talmudic texts in which, on the evidence available, the *minim* cannot be intended to mean "Christians." I shall limit myself to those texts which do lend themselves to this interpretation, and I shall look for materials that will verify, complement, or clarify what they have to tell us about Jewish Christian relations.

II

The texts in which the *minim* are explicitly connected with Christianity are in fact very few.[13] Here are two however that leave no room for doubt. Several Talmudic treatises relate, in more or less similar forms, the story of R. Eleazar ben Damah being bitten by a serpent. A certain Jacob of Kephar Sekanya wished to heal him in the name of Jeshua ben Pantera, but R. Ishmael, who happened to be present, prevented him, and R. Eleazar died.[14] Another version of this episode gives us to understand that the serpent had bitten the poor rabbi only in order to spare him from a more deadly infection, which a third version invites us to identify as *minuth*: "For one must have no fellowship with the *minim*, neither to let oneself be healed by them, nor to gain even one hour of life."[16] Jacob is here clearly called a *min*. Now, since he carries out his healings in the name of Jeshua ben Pantera, which means, according to Talmudic usage, in the name of Jesus, he is according to all the evidence a Christian. We know nothing whatever of this Jacob, but the two rabbis concerned with him in the story are Palestinian rabbis of the first half of the second century.

A similar sort of episode is recounted immediately after the one just mentioned, in T. Hull., 2:24.[17] R. Eliezer, having been arrested on a charge of *minuth*, was brought before the governor (Heb. *hegemon*, ἡγεμών), who, after an inquiry, released him. R. Eliezer then tortured himself with wondering how he could ever even have come under suspicion of *minuth*. His disciple R. Akiba suggested to him that perhaps a *min* had one day spoken to him a word of heresy. R. Eliezer than remembered having met, not long previously, on the street at Sepphoris, Jacob of Kephar Siknin. "He said to me a word of *minuth*, in the name of Jeshua ben Pantera, and it pleased me. And I was arrested for words of *minuth*, because I had transgressed the words of the law: 'Keep thy way far from her.'"[18] The authenticity of this episode is guaranteed by the fact that it involves, and in rather compromising fashion, a famous and respected rabbi. Since Rabbi Eliezer lived in Palestine at the end of the first and beginning of the second century A.D., Travers Herford has connected the incident with a local persecution of Christians that took place in Palestine under Trajan. This is the persecution Eusebius speaks of, on the authority of Hegesippus, and whose first victim was Simeon, the bishop of Jerusalem.[19] The hypothesis is ingenious and plausible. In any case, the *min* is here once more a Christian.

The same can be said about the next text, for, though it is less explicit than the two considered above, it is readily illuminated by evidence from Christian sources. R. Abbahu, we are told, commended R. Saphra to the *minim* as a learned man, and he was thus exempted by them from paying taxes for thirteen years. (We are to understand that they paid him a salary as a teacher.) One day they asked him to explain Amos 3:2: "You only have I known, from all the families of the earth; therefore I will visit upon you all your iniquities." "If one is in anger," they asked, "does one vent it on one's friend?" The rabbi did not know how to reply, and the *minim* mocked him. Along came R. Abbahu. When he was told of the failure of his protégé, he excused him by saying that he was learned in the oral tradition rather than in the scriptures. He added, "We who are frequently with you set ourselves the task of studying it [i.e., biblical exegesis] thoroughly. But others—the Babylonians—do not study it as carefully."[20] This episode took place at Caesarea at the beginning of the fourth century. R. Abbahu was a Palestinian rabbi. R. Saphra, a Babylonian, was a temporary resident in Palestine. The passage is interesting for a number of reasons.

First of all, it provides a rare confirmation of something we are told in Christian texts, that the Christian communities, until quite late in the early Church period, were in the habit of consulting the rabbis on questions of biblical exegesis, either in order to clarify, in the light of the Hebrew original, the exact meaning of a word, or because the thought of the biblical author raised difficulties of interpretation. This practice seems to have been quite widespread in those regions where there were sizable Jewish communities. We know how St. Jerome served his apprenticeship as an exegete with Rabbi Bar Hanina at Bethlehem, and then with a rabbi at Lydda, who charged him heavily for his lessons. *Memini me Lyddaeum quemdam non parvis redemisse nummis.*[21] We also know how, when a difficulty arose about the book of Jonah (the precise point at issue being whether the plant under which the prophet sat was a gourd or an ivy), the African community at Oea did not hesitate to appeal to the rabbis of the place to be arbiters in the dispute. The latter, having taken account of Jerome's translation, pronounced it to be at this point inaccurate, and the Christians, accepting their verdict, ceased to use Jerome's translation forthwith. This behavior earned them, from the irascible translator, the epithet of *cucurbitarii.*[22] The perfect agreement of this evidence, to which it would be easy to add more examples, with the evidence of the Talmud, is enough reason for recognizing the *minim* here as Christians. Simple common sense forbids us to identify them as gnostics, for the gnostics were in general disinclined to treat the Old Testament with such respect or to devote such scrupulous care to its interpretation. Neither is it likely that they were disposed to appeal for their interpretations to the authority of orthodox rabbis.[23]

We further learn from this text that though the Palestinian rabbis, exposed to daily encounters with Christians and to their questions and objections, were well versed in controversy, it was quite otherwise for their colleagues in Babylon. R. Abbahu implies, without saying so in so many words, that this was because the Babylonian rabbis did not live amongst the *minim*. Here again the Christian hypothesis is the one that best explains the facts. This is not to say that there were no Christians in Babylon. We know enough about the history of the Church outside the empire to be assured of the contrary. Yet there

were certainly fewer Christians in Mesopotamia up to the fourth
century than in the Greco-Roman east. This was due primarily to the
political conditions that existed at the time. And the Christians who
did live there were gathered in smaller and less tightly knit
communities than was usual in the Greco-Roman areas. It does seem
that Christianity had great difficult in establishing itself, even in the
north of Mesopotamia, outside the great centers of Edessa and Nisibis.
It is even more likely to have found itself rather thinly spread in
Babylonia proper. Babylonia was, on the other hand, a stronghold of
the Jews, whose rabbis were dispersed among the villages. The
opportunities for encounter would thus be very much reduced. All this
is in agreement with our text.[24]

Finally, the choice of the biblical verse that gives rise to the dispute
is not without significance. It raises the subject of Israel's divine call,
and of the special obligation it lays on her. Insofar as she has been
shown to be unfaithful, she had received punishment for her sins. This
is, as we have seen, a constant theme of Christian polemic. We may
reasonably assume that the *minim* in the story, in asking the rabbi
about this particular verse, were not motivated by disinterested
curiosity, but were laying a trap for him.

There is no need to think of them, as Travers Herford does, as in the
strict sense Jewish Christians. Real Jewish Christians would not
rejoice over God's severity to His own people. They are much more
likely to have been members of the catholic Church who took delight,
while being given a lesson in biblical exegesis, in being able to
embarrass their teacher.

III

This brings us to the most interesting group of Talmudic texts, viz.,
those which show signs of polemical purpose and allow some cross-
checking with Christian documents. If we find in the two series of
writings, Jewish and Christian, the same questions being raised about
the same scriptural texts, and if we find discussions exhibiting the
same pattern, we shall be justified in concluding that the questioners
are in both cases the same. There is a double interest in bringing the
two sets of texts into relation with each other. It will provide us with a
verification of the meaning of the word *minim*; it will also show that
the Christian anti-Jewish works are genuinely based on actual
encounters, i.e., that they are not merely academic dissertations, but
frequently bring us echoes of real controversies. Now, in fact, it is not
at all difficult to match the essential points of the Christian polemical

argument with a number of Talmudic passages that, according to all the signs, are intended to refute them. A few examples will suffice.

Throughout the anti-Jewish literature three fundamental problems keep appearing at the very center of the debate: that of the rejection of Israel and the corresponding call of the gentiles; that of the law and its observance; and that of monotheism and Christology. It is unnecessary to dwell long on the echoes of the first two of these in the Talmudic literature. The entire Talmud could be cited in evidence, since from beginning to end it both asserts and demonstrates the eternal and absolute authority of the old covenant, down to the last detail of its regulations. It enshrines, moreover, the unshakable faith of the rabbis in the providential destiny of the chosen people. However, at several points the Talmud is clearly refuting the Church's claim to have taken over the heritage. I shall restrict myself to examining one or two especially characteristic texts. Even though these make no explicit mention of the *minim*, they correspond so precisely with the objections that Christians made that it is impossible not to see them as examples of polemic against the rival cult.

The Christians' success in evangelizing the pagans appeared to the Jews not as a proof of their divinely ordained mission, but as one of the forewarning signs of the approach of the kingdom. "With the footprints of the Messiah," said R. Eliezer the Great, "presumption shall increase...and the Empire shall fall into heresy (*minuth*)."[25] R. Eliezer lived at the end of the first century. However, as Travers Herford has argued, it is doubtful whether the words are actually his. In parallel passages[26] they are attributed to R. Nehemiah, who is dated in the second half of the second century. In either case, the text in which the saying appears is embedded in an addition that is somewhat later, since it refers to the death of R. Judah haq-Qadosh, the editor of the Mishnah. Since the same saying is, in a different context, atrributed to R. Isaac, a contemporary of the Emperor Constantine, it is tempting to see him as the actual author, though it is not in fact certain that he lived to see the triumph of the Church. The saying is in any case not necessarily later than that event. A rabbi might well have spoken of the Christian takeover of the empire, i.e., the gentile world, as complete, even before the Church's formal victory. It is at all events clear that when the text speaks of a fusion of the empire with *minuth*, or at least of an association betwen the two, *minuth* can refer only to Christianity. Empire and *minuth* are, according to another text,[27] the two children of Gehenna.

 The same conclusion may be drawn from the following curious passage. R. Aha said, in the name of R. Huna: "Esau the wicked will put on his *tallith* and sit down with the righteous in Paradise in the time to come; and the Holy One, blessed be He, will drag him and cast him forth from thence."[28] "Esau the wicked" is, in the Talmud, a customary epithet for the Roman Empire. The *tallith*, or prayer shawl, is evidently a symbol of Judaism and its cult. We may therefore translate: the Christian empire, the church of the gentiles, makes itself out to be Israel. R. Aha, who lived at Lydda in the first half of the fourth century, did know of the triumph of Christianity. Travers Herford quotes, in connection with this passage, a text of St. Paul: "It is those who rely on faith who are the sons of Abraham."[29] It would be better to look for parallels in the numerous controversial texts, such as the epistle of Barnabas and the homilies of Chrysostom, which assert the claim of the gentile Christians to be the true Israel. It was a claim formulated with particular clarity by Tertullian. His argument rests specifically on the example of Jacob and Esau, and the prophecy about the two nations that were to come from the womb of Rebecca, the elder being destined to serve the younger.[30] *Prior et major populus, id est Judaicus, serviat necesse est minori, et minor populus, id est Christianus, superet majorem.*[31] The reasoning is not altogether unexceptionable. Tertullian has turned the passage upside down, and seems to have forgotten that Jacob, the younger, is the father of the chosen people, whose very name, Israel, is derived from him, and that according to scripture, it is rather the gentiles who are to be regarded as the descendants of Esau, *qui est Edom*,[32] the brother who was excluded from the heritage. It seems to be this very fact that the Talmud is attempting to recall, in terms that are discreet but unambiguous. To be sure, it is not Tertullian himself whom its authors have in mind, but his fellow Christians. It is difficult not to acknowledge here an echo of actual controversies with the Christians.

No room for doubt remains when we place alongside Tertullian's text one from St. Augustine. *Secundum originem carnis ad Esaü, qui dictus est etiam Edom, gentem Idumaeorum, ad Jacob autem, qui dictus est etiam Israël, gentem Judaeorum. Porro secundum mysterium spiritus, ad Esaü Judaeos, ad Israël pertinere Christianos. Ita quippe impletur quod scriptum est: major serviet minori, id est prior natus populus Judaeorum posteriori nato populo Christianorum.*[33] This manifestly presupposes knowledge of Tertullian's statement, which it explains and modifies. It equally presupposes a Jewish objection to which answer is being made. It proves that in Africa, no less than in Palestine, this question was being hotly disputed.[34] Between the two Christian texts R. Aha's statement fits perfectly naturally.

With respect to the alleged call of the gentiles, the rabbis stress with particular insistence the love the Lord has never ceased to exhibit toward Israel.[35] His forsaking of them, indicated by the destruction of the temple and the dispersion of the people, is only apparent, not real. It is in any case temporary. Israel, we are told, is like an olive tree. Just as the olive tree never loses its green leaves, so Israel will never come to an end, either in this world or in the world to come.[36] The Jews are less numerous than their rivals, and seem to have been abandoned by God, but they remain, nevertheless, His beloved children. "A certain *min* said to Beruria (the wife of R. Meir) 'It is written, "Sing, O barren, thou that didst not bear."'[37] ... She replied, 'You fool, look at the end of the verse, where it is written, "For the children of the desolate shall be more than the children of the married wife, saith the Lord." But what then is the meaning of "barren...didst not bear"? Sing, O community of Israel, who resemblest a barren woman, for not having borne children like you for Gehenna.'"[38] This text, which is so characteristic of those bearing on this controversy, also provides us with interesting information about the content of the word *minim*.[39] Here it is clearly applied to a category of persons fundamentally distinct from the Jews. Beruria's questioner may well be of Jewish origin, though we cannot be certain of that, but it is quite clear that he has broken off all connection with the Synagogue and its practices. Beruria does not recognize him as belonging in any sense to her party. He cannot therefore be a Jewish Christian in the usual sense of that term. The appellation *min*, as we shall have further occasion to insist, more probably comprehends a member of the catholic Church than an Ebionite.

To the Christian claim to be henceforth the chosen people and the true Israel it was natural to make further retort by quoting the numerous and lasting evidences of divine favor toward the Jews, and especially those which were contained in the oral tradition. Moses had wished to consign not only the scriptures but the Mishnah to writing. For not only the Mishnah but the Talmud itself, according to R. Simon ben Laqish, were revealed to him on Mount Sinai. But the Lord forbade it, because He knew that one day the nations would translate the Torah and would then say, "We are Israel. We are the children of God." This precaution allowed Israel the means to confound those who would usurp her position. The possession of the oral Mishnah would serve as a touchstone. They who held it were the true people of God.[40]

We are now back again with that other aspect of Jewish-Christian polemic, the one concerned with the law, its content, its raison d'être, and its permanence. For in attributing the Mishnah to Moses and regarding it as part of the Sinai revelation, the Jews were replying also to the Christian objection concerning the rabbinic regulations, that they were late, and therefore secondary. This criticism applied not only to the Mishnah, but to the entire ritual law, even that part which was attributed to Moses in the scripture itself. The Christian polemists went back before Moses, as we have seen,[41] and based their arguments on the fact that the patriarchs lived without knowledge of the ritual laws, and in particular that they knew nothing of circumcision. Their opponents replied that several of the righteous who lived before Moses were born circumcised, and that Abraham had had foreknowledge of the law, and had observed it, in anticipation, in all its details.[42] Better still, God Himself, having set an example over the Sabbath rest, continued to observe the regulations. In the course of a journey to Rome, R. Gamaliel II, assisted by R. Joshua, R. Eleazar ben Azariah and R. Akiba, developed in a sermon this idea that God, unlike men, never allows any discrepancy between His own conduct and the laws He promulgates. What He commands others to do, He does Himself. A *min* objects: "Why does He not observe the Sabbath?" "Is not a man allowed to move about in his own dwelling on the Sabbath?" demands the preacher. "The upper regions and the lower are the dwelling of God. As it is said, 'The whole earth is full of His glory,'" So then, in continuing to display on the Sabbath the unceasing activity by which He governs and maintains the universe, God does not infringe the commandments He has promulgated.[43]

We need not stop to say what we think of this as an argument, but if this passage be compared with those in which Christian authors, especially Aphraates, develop the same theme, it will be conceded that there is not much doubt that the *min* referred to was a Christian.[44] Gamaliel made his journey to Rome in A.D. 95. We therefore have every reason to believe, with Ziegler,[45] that this is one of the first recorded skirmishes in the controversy between Jews and gentile Christians.

There is likewise no doubt that R. Samuel ben Nahman was thinking of the Christians when he said, "According to the strict law one ought to recite the ten commandments every day. And why do we not recite them? Because of the claims of the *minim*; lest they should say, 'These alone were given to Moses on Sinai.'"[46] The intention of this saying is to emphasize the unity of the Sinai revelation and to meet the Christian objection that sought to dissociate the moral law, i.e., the decalogue, from the second covenantal code, mainly ritualistic, whose divine origin some went so far as to dispute.

The Christians further replied that between the two codes fell the episode of the golden calf, and that only in the light of this could the ceremonial laws be understood. They were imposed on the Jews as a curse and as a burden, in order to punish them for their sin.

In the discussions the rabbis devote to the ritual law we hear on numerous occasions the echo of replies made to these Christian interpretations. The golden calf incident is fully dealt with. It did, it is true, entail tiresome consequences, but they were quite different from the ones Christians alleged. It had prevented any more commandments and regulations from being promulgated, and had thus deprived Israel not only of additional means of salvation but of a source of happiness in the present world. The fact that the code of covenant renewal did follow immediately on Israel's apostasy is the best possible proof of divine forgiveness. According to R. Aha, Moses, having in a fit of anger broken the tablets of the law, was seized with remorse. But God consoled him with the words, "Do not distress yourself; on the first tablets there were the ten commandments alone. On the second tablets which I shall give you there are *halakhoth*, *midrashim* and *haggadoth*."[47] The prescriptions of the ritual law were not therefore, as the Christian polemists asserted, a punishment. They did not express the anger of God with His people, but on the contrary, His love for them.[48] The more explicit His solicitude for them became, the more the precepts were multiplied. The regulations and restrictions led Israel to God, and so were not a yoke but a joy. He who had tasted them was never *surfeited* with them.[49]

Another Christian objection was answered at the same stroke. There was no contradiction, and no break in continuity, between the divine law and the prescriptions of the rabbis. R. Simon ben Laqish tells us that from the moment the Sinaitic law was first spoken, the Mishnah was, in embryo, included in it, for all that the Mishnah does is to develop and make explicit the law of Sinai. R. Aha asserts this even more emphatically.

The Church in reply claimed that the Jewish law, and the old covenant, are alike rendered invalid by the fact of Christ. No, replied the rabbis, they are eternal, like God Himself, and they embody His immutable will. I have already analyzed the theory, as expounded by Aphraates, of successive covenants, each of which superseded its predecessors, until the final establishment of Christianity.[50] This is the theory the author of the following haggadic story seems to have in mind. Abraham, whose covenant had superseded the one God had made with Noah, was worried lest his own covenant should in turn be annulled one day for the sake of some men with more good deeds to his credit than he. He opened his mind to the Lord, who replied, "Be not afraid. I did not raise up among the descendants of Noah any pious intercessors. But I will raise some up among your descendants. Even when your children fall into sin, I will choose from among them a man who is able to set a limit to retributive justice and to say

'Enough!' He will redeem their errors, and will be a guarantor to me for them."[51] The anti-Christian reference is perfectly clear. At one stroke it affirms the immutable nature of the covenant and denies implicitly the Christian dogma of the redeeming death of Christ. Only the piety and good works of a faithful Jew have expiatory and redemptive power before God.

Moreover, if the temple has been destroyed and Israel scattered (and these are signs of God's abandonment of them only in appearance), this is not because of any crime committed against a self-styled Messiah, but it is a punishment for the sins of the people against their God. Jesus and Christianity are certainly involved, but not in the way in which the Christian polemists imagine. According to Ben Azzai,[52] Israel was only scattered after having renounced the One, the rite of circumcision, the ten commandments, and the five books of the Torah. It is tempting to see here, with Schoeps,[53] a reference to the Christians, spiritual offshoots of Israel, who deify Christ and repudiate the law; and especially to St. Paul, who was born a Hebrew according to the flesh, and whose career entirely antedates the destruction of the temple.

G. Hoennicke, in an appendix to his work on Jewish Christianity, sets himself to solve the problem of "minism," and professes surprise that the Talmudic texts concerned with disputes against the Christians never touch on questions of Christology, do not polemize against the person of Jesus, and further, never connect the name of Jesus with that of the *minim*. Yet, he says, in Christian treatises it is the person of Jesus and the subject of Christology that are the principal questions for discussion.[54] We are astonished in our turn, although we subscribe to the last statement, to find an expert in matters relating to Jewish Christianity expressing a judgment which is so uncompromisingly and so manifestly wrong.

It is true that there are some questions one might expect the rabbis to discuss in detail and on which they are almost completely silent. This is certainly surprising. But these questions are not exactly the ones Hoennicke picks out. The person of Jesus does feature in the discussions at several points. I have cited above two texts that mention simultaneously Jesus and the *minim*. We may at least agree with Hoennicke so far as to admit that these examples are not very numerous.[55] But as far as Christology is concerned, the facts are entirely otherwise. It occupies a large place, for those who care to recognize it, in the rabbinic controversies with the *minim*. I would go so far as to say that it forms the main substance of those controversies.

When the rabbis deny so emphatically that God had any son, there can be no doubt that this is an allusion to Christian dogma, even though the *minim* many not always be named in the context.[56] If they cannot go so far as to concede that God might have a son, they combat with equal vigor the idea that He could have allowed him to perish. How could He who refused to let Abraham sacrifice Isaac have allowed His own son to die?[57]

But far more often the question is not raised in this form. Throughout most of the Talmudic writings it is not the idea of the son of God that is discussed but that of the two powers the *minim* recognize in place of the divine unity. And the rabbis set themselves to the task, marshaling countless texts in their support, of waging warfare against this "other God." We should discount, with Travers Herford, the hypothesis that these disputes are concerned with dualistic gnosticism, for the two powers in question are always powers that are both good and that act in concord. The suggestion is sometimes made that the rabbis' opponents are a different kind of gnostics, who though they did not subscribe to radical dualism, did make a distinction between the supreme God and the demiurge. They thought of the former as having nothing to do with the work of creation and having no point of contact at all with the material world. But this suggestion too is to be dismissed, for as Travers Herford again notes,[58] whenever the Talmud raises the question of the two powers it is always in connection with creation, and its aim is always to show that creation is the work of the Lord, by Himself, and that He had no helpers. There remain two possibilities that do not rule out each other, taking account of the range of meaning the word *minim* at different periods and in different places could bear. The polemic we are discussing is directed either against Jewish speculations about the Logos and the Sophia, or else against Christian theology with its Logos-Christ. I do not wish to eliminate entirely the former possibility. I shall, however, try to show that the latter provides us with a completely satisfactory interpretation of several of the texts. What I have already said about the Christian characteristics of the *minim* supports this, as does a comparison with Christian sources. If scholars have not in general recognized this Talmudic distinction between the two gods as reflecting the Christian doctrine concerning the Father and the Son, this is possibly because they have unconsciously projected on to their material a Trinitarian scheme of which the first generations of Christians knew nothing.[59] But the comparison is convincing enough, as long as we remember that Christian theology during the first few centuries generally shows familiarity with only two divine persons, the Father and the Son ("Now the Lord is the Spirit"[60]) and that this pairing persists in the anti-Jewish literature long after Nicaea. There will be no need to multiply examples.

In B. Sanhedrin we have a story concerning R. Ishmael ben Jose of Sepphoris and his circle of disciples. R. Ishmael was himself a disciple of R. Judah haq-Qadosh, and lived at the beginning of the third century. A *min* challenging the orthodox view of the unity of God, quoted Genesis 19:24, "The Lord rained on Sodom and Gomorrah brimstone and fire from the Lord." "But," he said, *"from him* should have been written." One of the rabbi's adherents quoted in reply Genesis 4:23, " 'And Lamech said to his wives, Ada and Zillah, hear my voice, ye wives of Lamech.' But he should have said *my* wives."[61] The whole discussion is based on the principle of rabbinic exegesis that there is not a superfluous word in the Bible, but that all the pleonasms and apparent repetitions must cloak a profound meaning. But let us turn to the *Dialogue* of Justin. After a long discussion of Abraham's vision at the oaks of Mamre where the "other God" shows himself to Abraham, accompanied by two angels, Justin goes on: "One of the three, who is also God and Lord, acting as servant to Him who is in heaven, is Lord of the two angels. . . . When he had come [to Sodom] we have no longer two angels conversing with Lot, but him himself, as the word shows us plainly. And he is the Lord, receiving from the Lord who is in heaven namely the maker of the universe, the duty of bringing on Sodom and Gomorrah those punishments which the Word enumerates, saying thus: 'The Lord rained on Sodom and Gomorrah fire and brimstone from the Lord of heaven.' "[62] The same interpretation of the verse is found in other Christian authors. It was taught by the (non-orthodox) council of Sirmium, which went so far as to pronounce anathema those who denied it. *Si quis hoc dictum: pluit Dominus ignem a Domino non de Patre et Filio accipiat, sed ipsum a se ipso pluisse dicat, anathema est. Pluit enim Filius Dominus a Domino Patre.*[63] In the Dialogue of Athanasius and Zacchaeus[64] the same text of Genesis is the subject of a long discussion, and is interpreted by reference to Wisdom, which a Christian would automatically identify with Christ. Here we see how the "minism" of the gnosticizing Jews could link up, through the notion of divine hypostases, with that of the Christians.

Another verse the Christians made much use of in Christological controversy was Genesis 1:26, "Let us make man in our own image."[65] The rabbis also comment on it, noting the use that is made of the text by the *minim* and linking it with a quotation by which their views might be refuted. They are well enough aware of the difficulty. When Moses, writing the law, came to Genesis 1:26, he cried, " 'Lord of the world, what an opportunity thou hast presented to the *minim!*' And the Lord replied, 'Write; and he who will err, let him err.' "[66] Sometimes the rabbis cancel out the plural by appealing to the text in the next verse, where it says, in the singular, "God created man in his own image."[67] Similarly, R. Johanan points out that in every passage that the *minim* appeal to on this issue they are contradicted by the context.[68] Occasionally the rabbis invoke all the passages in which the unity of God is directly and emphatically asserted. Prominent here is Deuteronomy 6:4, "Hear, O Israel..."[69] Again, they sometimes explain the plural by saying that God is addressing Adam, before he was created, and through him the whole human race. This is the opinion of R. Simlai, a Babylonian who lived in Palestine about the middle of the third century. It may be that there is an echo of this explanation[70] in Justin's words: "You may not, by changing the words already quoted, say what your teachers say, either that God said to Himself 'Let us make'... or that God said 'Let us make' to the elements, namely the earth and such like, out of which we understand man has come into being."[71]

Lastly, if we are to believe the testimony of other Christian authors,[72] the rabbis sometimes applied the plural verb to the angels, who were associated with God in the creation. This fact could be connected with the accusation the Christians sometimes brought against the Jews, that they worshipped angels. We do not, as it happens, know of any example of this interpretaton in Talmudic literature,[73] but it is not inconceivable that some rabbis did subscribe to it. The rabbis did frequently bring in the angels to account for various incidents in history and they happily saw them at work in some biblical episodes that Philo has regarded as evidence for the existence of divine powers. And when the Christians claimed these same texts as evidence for the preexistence of Christ, the Logos, and the Wisdom of God, the rabbis refuted the claims in favor of the chief of the angels. For example, a *min* quoted Exodus 24:1: "It is written, 'And He said to Moses, "Come up to the Lord."' But surely it should have stated, 'Come up to Me'." R. Idi replied, "It was Metatron [who said this] whose name is similar to that of his Master. For it is written, 'For my name is in him.'"[74] "In that case," retorted the *min*, "we should worship him." It is to be understood that the name of beings or things expresses their very essence, and that a being who bears the name of God necessarily shares His divinity. To this R. Idi found no reply except an extremely forced interpretation of another verse.[75]

Friedländer gratuitously identified Metatron, the chief of the heavenly hierarchy, with the gnostic Horus.[76] This, as Travers Herford points out,[77] does violence to the text and unnecessarily obscures the meaning of a passage that is otherwise entirely clear. It is not in fact the *min* who introduces the figure of Metatron in order to embarrass his opponent. It is the orthodox rabbi who brings him into the picture in order to refute the *min* by denying the divine nature of the "Lord" mentioned in the text. The *min* clearly holds this interpretaton, which is contrary to Jewish monotheism. Despite Friedländer, the verse can be explained perfectly satisfactorily if we suppose that the *min* was a Christian, and that in claiming for the "Lord" the right to be worshiped he was thinking of Christ.

Nevertheless, we are not always limited to mere conjectures, however well founded they may be. Thus we have a text that reads: "If the son of the harlot shall say to thee, 'There be two Gods,' answer him, 'I am He of the [Red] Sea. I am He of Sinai.' " And again, "It is written, not *Gods*, but *'the Lord* hath spoken with you face to face,' "[78] The context does not indicate on what passage of scripture the heretics based their assertion. But the answer suggests that the passage in question was one in which the name of God was mentioned or invoked twice in succession. The rabbis give a similar explanation of Psalm 22:1: "My God, my God, why have you deserted me?"[79] The idea common to the exegesis of these texts is that we are to distinguish not between two Gods, but between two successive manifestations of the same Lord, as in the passage of the Sea, and on Sinai. Now, there were Christians, as we have seen,[80] who did not hesitate to recognize in the theophanies of the Old Testament not the intervention of the Father, but that of the preexistent Logos, the substitute for and agent of the Father. That the proof is intended to be anti-Christian is therefore very likely. This likelihood is transformed into certainty by the mention of "the son of the harlot." In the language of the Talmud this can only mean one thing, Christ, and by extension, Christians. And is it perhaps because it was primarily applied to Christianity, which was commonly referred to in such terms as "the son of the harlot," that the term *minuth* tends to become in rabbinic usage, as a result of a kind of play on words, synonymous with and equivalent to *zenuth?*[81]

IV

Since so many texts bear witness to the fact that the *minim* were Christians, we are entitled to conclude that the doctrinal controversies were real controversies. The Christian polemical works, in spite of their sometimes affected manner, genuinely echo these. To be sure, it would be gratifying to be able to complete the case with the help of texts emanating from the diaspora. We may at least safely assume that conditions in the diaspora were not very different from those in Palestine. Since the anti-Christian arguments of the Palestinian rabbis match up so well with the anti-Jewish polemic of non-

Palestinian Christian scholars, it is surely not too hazardous to suggest that both inside and outside Palestine Jews and Christians opposed each other in much the same terms. Although so little of the specifically anti-Jewish Christian literature can be shown to have originated in Palestine, other writings, notably those of Eusebius and St. Jerome, demonstrate how eager were both parties there to take issue with their opponents and to put them to rout. We may without presumption believe that the rabbis outside Palestine shared the same eagerness.

Judging by the evidence available to us, it does not appear that these theological duels were mere academic exercises. They cannot be divorced from the total life of the communities in which they took place. They must be taken as evidence that in this period both Jews and Christians were forced to take account of their rivals, and could not escape each other's influence and attentions. In both camps, therefore, the scholar's polemical task was to reduce the adversary's sway.

As far as the Palestinian conflict is concerned, it is possible to trace at least the major stages of its development. In the texts that speak of discussions with the *minim* the names of certain rabbis recur with particular insistence. Without going so far as to regard these particular rabbis as specialists (*Fachleute*) in polemics,[82] as Dubnow does, we may at least recognize that they provide us with the means to map out the territory.

The beginnings of anti-Christian polemic amongst the Jews are perceptible before the end of the first century, amongst the followers of R. Gamaliel II, with the perfecting of the benediction against the *minim*,[83] and the journey of the Patriarch to Rome. This anti-Christian polemic developed rapidly at the same time as an anti-Jewish literature was appearing on the Christian side. There is hardly a generation of the Tannaim and Palestinian Amoraim in which there does not appear some fierce adversary of the *minim*. Thus, to cite only a few of the names, in the first half of the second century Eliezer ben Hyrcanus, Joshua ben Hananiah, Eleazar of Modein, and Tarphon[84] are all credited with achievements of this sort. Ziegler[85] holds that the wars of Quietus and Hadrian brought about a definite interruption in the controversy, but this is by no means certain. These wars did not absorb all the energies of the rabbinic schools, or indeed command their unqualified support. In the second half of the century the movement continued, led among the Jews by Bar Kappara and his disciple Joshua ben Levi, among others. And when in the third century Christianity consolidated its position in Palestine the conflict intensified. Toward the end of the century Simlai at Lydda, Samuel bar Nahman at Tiberius, and Abbahu at Caesarea all figure as protagonists. All the places mentioned above were strongholds of Christianity.[86] Caesaraea in particular, being both the seat of a bishop and the site of a theological school, and at the same time an important theater of rabbinic learning, was a place of habitual contact between the scholars of the two cults. Origen was able to meet there several of the later Tannaim and early Amoraim.[87] He also met a certain Joullos (Hillel), whom he mistakenly entitles Patriarch. Hillel was simply a member of the patriarchal family, a son of Gamaliel III.[88] Finally, the evidence from Eusebius and Jerome, already cited, demonstrates that the controversy was kept up after the triumph of the Church.

The Talmudic passages concerning the *minim*, correctly interpreted, throw a useful light not only on the development of the controversy but on the nature of Jewish-Christian relations and on the way they evolved.

According to the oldest rabbinic evidence, insofar as the evidence allows us to classify it chronologically at all, the *minim* appear to be mixed among the orthodox Jewish communities. They continue to attend the Synagogue services and take an active part in the worship. They have not yet constituted themselves a separate sect but are merely a collection of individuals, the few black sheep among the flock of the elect. This picture corresponds with what we learn from elsewhere about the first Christians in Palestine, who before becoming Jewish Christians were Christian Jews. As a general conclusion it may be said that the impulse forcing them into schism came rather from the rabbis, who excommunicated the Christians. The celebrated insertion into the *Shemoneh 'Esre* of the formula condemning the *minim* was made at the suggestion of R. Gamaliel II some time after the fall of Jerusalem, in all probability somewhere around A.D. 80.[89] It reads: "Let there be no hope for the apostates, and the kingdom of pride mayest thou destroy quickly, in our days. And let the Nazarenes and the *minim* suddenly perish. Let them be extinguished from the book of life and not be written with the righteous. Blessed art thou, O Lord, who humblest the proud."[90] The Nazarenes appear alongside the *minim* only in the primitive Palestinian version. They later disappeared, for very good reasons. There is no reason that this explicit reference to the Christians (for that is what "Nazarenes" means) alongside the *minim* should forbid us to interpret the word *minim* itself in other contexts as including Christians. It is more likely that "Nazarenes" is a species included in the genus *minim*. And it may well be quite accurate to translate this phrase from the *Shemoneh 'Esre* as "the Nazarenes and other *minim*."

The object of including this formula is not merely, I imagine to curse the *minim* but to detect them.[91] When seen in its setting in Synagogue worship, it is obvious that the use of the formula amounts to the application of a real and serious test. Since the Synagogue had no clergy, in the proper sense of that term, all the members were liable to be called on from time to time to take part in leading public worship. Now a celebrant who was himself tainted with heresy would, of course, be reluctant to pronounce this benediction, and with it his own condemnation. The Talmud says quite explicitly: "If a reader made a mistake in any of the other benedictions they do not remove him, but if in the benediction of the *minim*, he is removed, because we suspect him of being a *min*."[92]

Other, later texts also preserve memories of the time when the *minim*, or some of them, belonged to the community itself and were distinguished by peculiarities in their ritual practices. when the Mishnah says, "if a man put [the *tephillin*] on his forehead or on the palm of his hand, this is the way of *minuth*," it is, I suppose, impossible to decide just what kind of heresy is being referred to. On the other hand, we can be fairly sure that we have a reference to Christianity when the rabbis accuse of *minuth* those who say, "The good ones bless thee," or, "We give thanks, we give thanks." For the plural in the former instance, and the repetition in the latter, are most readily interpreted as an oblique reference to the two powers.[93] The rule relating to benedictions is perfected and made more definite at the beginning of the fourth century by R. Simon, speaking in the name of R. Joshua ben Levi. It is permitted, he says, without serious offence, to omit two or three of the benedictions. The only omissions that are really grievous, and that entail the instant recall of the celebrant, are those of the three following phrases: "that makest the dead to live," "that bringest down the proud," "that buildest Jerusalem." Anyone who omits these is a *min*.[94] The denial of the resurrection was not, of course, made by Christians. Presumably the provision envisages late survivors of the Sadducees. However, those who threw doubt on the possibility of Jerusalem's being rebuilt most likely were Christians. As for the phrase about humbling the proud, it is simply the end of the formula devoted to the *minim*. We must concede, therefore, that even at this date there were still some Christians, no doubt isolated ones, who attended the Synagogue and who would not give up their claim to be Jews except under pressure.

Nevertheless, by the fourth century the Talmud often represents the *minim* as clearly separated from the Jewish community, in bodies that were fully independent and organized on their own lines. The *minim*, that is to say, comprise by this time a social and religious category as well defined as those of the Jews and the pagans. They have their own places of assembly, their bread, which is "the bread of the Samaritans"; their wine, which is "the wine of idolatry," and their books, which are books of magic. All these, apparently, are references to the Christians. They are much worse than pagans. Jews must not sell to them or buy from them; neither take from them nor give to them; neither teach their sons [trades] nor be healed by them. It is allowable to eat meat that has passed through the hands of a *goy*, but not if it comes from a *min*.[95] Although their books contain quotations from scripture, and even the divine name, they are to be burned without hesitation. This is already the opinion of R. Tarphon. A copy of the Torah, copied by a pagan, must be withdrawn from use. One copied by a *min* must be destroyed.[96] The same rabbi, if pursued by an enemy, would enter, of necessity, into a house of idolatry, but not into a house of the *minim*.[97] If a pagan falls into difficulty, one may leave him to struggle in it. One may similarly leave *minim* or apostates. But *minim* and apostates may not only be left in trouble but may legitimately be pushed into it.[98] Why this difference in the way the various adversaries may be treated? It is again R. Tarphon who gives us the answer. "The idolators do not acknowledge Him [God] and speak falsely concerning Him; but they [the *minim*] do acknowledge Him and speak falsely concerning Him."[99] Ignorance is less serious than error. If the Christians were not the only people envisaged when the anathemas were pronounced, they were at least included, and may well have been the offenders principally in mind. To be assured of this it is necessary only to compare the text of the *Shemoneh 'Esre* with Justin Martyr's statements about the curses the Synagogue heaps upon his brethren.[100]

By the second century, and all the more so by the fourth, Christianity represented for Judaism the archenemy. Our study of the persecutions has already shown us that the Jews often preferred pagans over Christians. And this was only to be expected. "The Jews willingly joined forces with the pagans, because the pagans possessed the power, and they detested them less, being less afraid of the influence of their religious ideas."[101] But we are left in no doubt that gentile Christians are included in the term *minim*. In order to qualify for the title *min*, one did not need to have any ethnic connection with Israel. Its significance was essentially religious. The term was therefore applied at an early date not only to apostate Jews, but also to Christians of all kinds, lumping them together as one vast apostasy from Judaism.

But there are equally weighty reasons for believing that the anathemas came quite quickly to be applied especially to the non-Jewish Christians. Between the gentile Church and Judaism the opposition was implacable. For the Church claimed to have deprived the Synagogue of all its rights, and this meant that there was a deep-rooted antagonism, even though in practice relations were sometimes at least bearable. But as far as the Jewish Christians were concerned, whether individually or as a body, the attitude of the rabbis always remained, as we shall shortly see, less rigid. Attitudes varied. Sometimes the rabbis thought of the Jewish Christians primarily as Christians, and at others they felt that they were basically Jews, and their sentiments fluctuated accordingly between outright aversion and quite strong sympathy. The gentile Church, on the contrary, was composed of people who were *goyim* and *minim* at the same time, and they were treated, as a result, to a double dose of hatred.[102] Antipathy was, of course, mutual, and the rabbinic maledictions are perfectly balanced by the imprecations of Christian anti-Semitism.

8

Christian Anti-Semitism

... κοινὴν λύμην καὶ νόσον τῆς οἰκουμένης ἁπάσης
Chrysostom, *First Homily against the Jews*, 6

I

The phenomenon of anti-Semitism was a familiar one to the ancient world long before the advent of Christianity. It was a product of friction between Jewish colonies and the surrounding pagan communities, and we may suppose therefore that it is practically as old as the Hellenistic diaspora itself.[1] In this respect there is no discontinuity between the pagan and Christian periods. Christian anti-Semitism, nevertheless, took on characteristics that were quite new and peculiar to itself. It can be detected even before the Church's triumph under Constantine, and took more definite shape during the fourth century. In order to appreciate the distinctive marks of Christian anti-Semitism, it is necessary first to set out the characteristics of the pagan anti-Semitism it replaced. If the two sorts of anti-Semitism have anything in common, in respect, for example, of their motivation, of the kinds of complaints that are made about their victims, or of their methods, it is only to the extent that anti-Semitism anywhere, in any age, displays the same features. These common features may be found just as readily in the resurgent anti-Semitism of certain modern ideologies.

The basic cause of Greco-Roman anti-Semitism[2] lay in Jewish separatism. This means, in the last analysis, that it lay in their religion, since the religion produced the separatism. Any racist element was entirely lacking.

In any case, the notion of "race," in the modern, pseudoscientific popular understanding of the word (I am thinking especially here of the distinction between Jews and "Aryans") is quite foreign to the ancient way of thinking. Naturally the Western peoples, the Romans in particular, were conscious of differences between themselves and the Jews. But as far as the differences were, either on the physical or psychological level, innate and not acquired—i.e., insofar as they were not ones deliberately adopted, like the religious differences—the Romans seem to have attached little significance to them. Or at least, they were no more aware of differences between themselves and the Jews than of those between themselves and other Semites or other Eastern peoples in general. In the eyes of the ancient authors the Jews were, ethnically speaking, simply a variety of Syrians, just as, geographically, Palestine was merely a subdivision or prolongation of Syria. In current usage the term "Syrian" often included the Jews. They were then not primarily thought of as a religious body, i.e., as sectarians who devoted themselves to the worship of Yahweh, but rather as a cultural one, as agents of the many-faceted Eastern culture. Ovid, for example, speaks of the "Syrians of Palestine."[3] The Jews, like their neighbors, were Levantines. They were distinguished only by their religion.

Even in Egypt, where, in view of the proximity of Palestine and the large Jewish colonies within its borders, we might expect common opinion to be better informed, the finer distinctions are not always clearly appreciated. According to the biographer of Alexander Severus, the Alexandrian crowd greeted him as a young emperor with the sarcastic title of "the Syrian archisynagogos." They thus showed that they knew both of his Syrian antecedents and his active sympathy for the Jews.[4] Similarly, Apion, who informs us not only about anti-Semitism but about Alexandrian nationalism and the ancient rivalry between Egypt and Syria, taunts the Jews with having come originally from Syria.[5] In this form the objection expresses a general xenophobia rather than specifically anti-Jewish sentiments.

Thus, ancient anti-Semitism had no racist background. Nor had it an economic basis. There is never any imputation of a Jewish stranglehold on commercial or industrial activity. Jews are not generally accused of an immoderate lust for money, of any special eagerness for gain, of passion or genius for business, of a lack of commercial morality or of any of the oddities of this kind that figure invariably in the mythology of modern anti-Semitism.

Such complaints are not completely absent from ancient literature, but they are aimed at people other than the Jews. They are the common coin of international jealousy. The Romans launched such accusations against the Carthaginians and the Greeks, who had a firmly established reputation throughout the West as traffickers in dubious merchandise and as commercial parasites.[6] The same reputation extended to all Easterners, without distinction of country or race.[7] There is only one pagan text in which the Jews are clearly accused of being overfond of money. This is in a letter from Hadrian to Servianus. It is preserved by Vopiscus and its authenticity is suspect. The letter contains a diatribe against various national and religious groups, of whom Israel is one. Egypt is "light, inconstant, changing at the slightest sound"; in the cosmopolitan society of Alexandria charlatans and astrologers flourish amongst all social classes: "their only god is money; the one who is worshipped by Christians, Jews and everybody else."[8]

Neither does it seem that the Jews were specially noted as preferring particular vocations. They did not all gravitate to the same social class; far from it.[9] It seems that they were not often very prominent in society. Some of them appear in Egypt, taking out leases of tax rights, or of royal domains. In Alexandria there were Jewish shipowners, bankers, and millionaires.[10] But looking at the empire as a whole, the Jewish population were mostly not high up the social scale. Jewish slaves are fairly numerous. At Rome, none of the Jewish quarters, Trastevere, Porta Capena, or Suburra, possessed much distinction. The remark most often made about the Jews was not that they were rolling in money but that they were ragged and filthy. If we are to believe Martial and Juvenal, the Jewish beggar, "trained to beg by his mother," "whose entire property was a basket and some hay,"[11] was a characteristic sight in the lower quarters of the capital. We may presume that the Jews were not altogether strangers to commerce, but for the most part they were concerned in it in fairly humble capacities. They were peddlers or door-to-door salesmen, offering oriental knickknacks for sale. Here again, there was nothing to differentiate them from the mass of "Syrians"; nothing to encourage any specifically anti-Jewish feelings.[12]

All that distinguished the Jews, therefore, was their religion, and, up to a point, the peculiarities of their political situation. The two are so closely related that it is difficult to distinguish one from the other. It was in their capacity as a religious community that the Jews had been repeatedly involved in political difficulties with Rome, and they continued to give trouble in this way until the destruction of the holy city, when they were finally deprived of their national independence. In Palestine the virulent anti-Roman Messianism of the masses certainly increased the animosity of the gentiles toward the Jews. And even in the diaspora there were some elements among the Jews which from time to time were infected by the same unrest and gained the Jews a reputation as a turbulent people, difficult to live with. Nevertheless, the importance of these Messianic outbursts ought not to be exaggerated. They were occasional, and usually of local significance. They never had more than a limited effect on the diaspora.[13] After A.D. 70, and all the more after A.D. 135, the political problem ceased to be a pressing one. It is very doubtful whether Jewish Messianism and Jewish political aspirations ever impressed themselves much on Roman opinion, apart from that of the Roman leaders. For the pagan authors the Jews are the people who worship without images, the people of the law. They are not primarily the people of the Messiah. The same is true for the generality of Romans, who knew little of Palestinian history and were badly informed about the details of Jewish belief.[14] It was these features which bound the Jews throughtout the Mediterranean lands into a unity, and which aroused the amazement, the distrust, and the hatred of their neighbors. A Jew who apostatized no longer aroused these feelings, and a proselyte exposed himself to them unavoidably.

When the pagan polemists characterize Jewish monotheistic beliefs as "atheism," the charge is hardly more than an academic one. What really excited public distaste was not Jewish beliefs, however odd they might appear, but Jewish behavior. What was objectionable was the law and its power to isolate its devotees. The law, by enclosing the Jews' daily life in a web of rules and regulations, placed them beyond the bounds of society, outside the ordinary rules and the ordinary pattern of life. It turned them into a tightly knit group, in spite of the fact that they were individually scattered; a group that was unassimilable, exclusive, and therefore an enemy of the human race.[15]

This was the really basic complaint, and from it sprang others. Because they kept themselves apart and had no relations, except at a superficial level, with the pagans among whom they lived, and because they were united by the observance of rules and rites whose meaning was often difficult for outsiders to comprehend, they left themselves exposed to all the accusations that the malice of the mob could invent, and that it delights to invent about closed societies. The Freemasons in our own day, and the early Christian communities in the Roman Empire, have both been the object of just the same kind of suspicions and slanders. We may note in particular the similarity of the ancient reactions to Judaism on the one hand and to the nascent Christianity on the other. In both cases the accusations of a sinister exclusiveness lead to those of "misanthropy," and then to accusations of immoral practices, of perversion, and of ritual murder.[16] These accusations were worse in the case of the Christians because they maintained a closer silence about some of their ritual practices. In its beginnings Christianity was often attacked as a variety of Judaism. The anti-Christian attitudes of the pagan world were at first merely a form of anti-Semitism.

Basically, this anti-Semitism was a spontaneous reaction, an elementary and instinctive social reflex rather than a considered attempt to defend pagan religious convictions. Jews were suspected and slandered and occasionally persecuted, just as Christians were, because they were members of a foreign group who would not assimilate. Religion was not an issue except insofar as it was the agent that isolated and marked out the members of the group, and pointed the contrast between them and the surrounding world. The examples that have come down to us of pagan polemical literature against the Jews are in general hardly more than learned and systematized transcriptions of popular opinion.[17] Real anti-Semitism was popular in its roots. It reflected the general animosity against those who did not live as the rest of the world. It reflected feeling, not thought. To recognize its basic character is to be aware immediately of its limitations.

Anti-Semitism, as we might expect, flourished only in those regions or cities were there was a large Jewish population. It flourished in Rome, Antioch, and Alexandria especially. Its intensity was always proportionate to the numerical strength of the Jewish community. Two factors tended to restrain it, though without anywhere limiting it entirely. First, there was Judaism's legal standing. Judaism was officially recognized by imperial authority and everywhere given a measure of protection as a *religio licita*. Second, there was the lively influence of the synagogues of the diaspora. The beliefs, the precepts, and even the ritual practices of Judaism exercised a considerable attraction for much of the pagan populace.

Balancing the anti-Semites among the pagan population were the proselytes, the *metuentes*, and those who, though not proselytes, were nevertheless impressed by the antiquity of the biblical tradition, by Judaism's high ethic, and by the purity of its teaching. There was thus, at one extreme, virulent hatred, and at the other, sympathy and admiration. These were the two extremes between which pagan opinion concerning Judaism oscillated.

From the moment when Christianity appeared on the scene it attracted more and more attention. Sometimes it was sympathetic attention, productive of converts; sometimes it was outright hostility.[18] Up till then, and for some time afterwards, Judaism's attractions had to some extent acted as counterweight to anti-Semitic feeling. The accommodating Judaism of a Philo was able, in presenting Judaism as a philosophy, to dampen some of the misgivings that intellectuals might feel regarding Mosaic practice and teaching. By becoming receptive to influences from outside and by increasing its apologetic effort, such Judaism had rid itself of some of its strangeness. The gentiles who associated themselves with Israel doubtless exposed themselves, in many instances, to the same mistrust and hostility as Israel had to endure, but sometimes their example helped to repel, in their own immediate circle at least, gentile malevolence. Around the synagogues, therefore, there grew up an atmosphere in which a better understanding was possible. This is a fact that ought to be considered, along with Juvenal's sarcastic comments and the diatribes of Apion.[19]

None of this was sufficient to wipe out the hatred completely. Even while they continued in their liberalism and universalism the Jews intransigently maintained their firm monotheistic convictions and their staunch belief in their own prerogatives. In any case, strict legal observance in practice was the indispensable counterpart of liberalism in doctrine. Now, it was this very legal observance, whose rigor was relaxed only by one or two dissident Jewish bodies, which was the essential precondition of anti-Semitism. And anti-Semitism was able to vary in its extent and intensity from period to period and from region to region. It must neither be exaggerated nor minimized. The anti-Semitic attitudes of the pagan world were, on any showing, the foundation on which Christian anti-Semitism was built. And even though many of the characteristics of Christian anti-Semitism were native to itself, some of them were not, but were inherited from the pagan past.

II

When did this hostile attitude to the Jews first appear in the history of the growing Church? To find out the answer to this question it is necessary to go back to quite an early period. It dates, it would appear, from the time when Christianity turned away from Israel, where its mission had had more setbacks than successes, and found among the gentiles the compensation for its initial disappointments. Anti-Semitism became more widespread when the later expansion of Christianity was accomplished by preachers born in paganism. By this time Judaism's initial repulse of Christianity had hardened into a permanent rejection, and the Church was no longer simply a small sectarian body on its edge, but embodied in herself the redeemed gentile world. There is no shadow of anti-Semitism in St. Paul. He was disappointed in his countrymen but incapable of hating them.[20] Anti-Jewish feeling is manifest in the Fourth Gospel, where the word *Jew* takes on a pejorative sense.[21] Christian anti-Semitism is in the first instance an expression of the resentment aroused by Israel's resistance to the gospel. It is a concomitant of the new church's claim to have taken over the privilege of election. In addition, it arises from the need to explain the outright rejection with which the Jews greeted the message meant for them.

This is to say that the basis of Christian anti-Semitism was neither social nor in the proper sense religious. At least, it was not religiously based in the sense in which this could be said of the pagan variety. The Christians could not accuse the Jews of an exclusivism they themselves also practiced. They approved of Jewish beliefs and customs, as they were codified in the Old Testament, since they were equally the foundation of the Christian faith. By the same token, they even approved of the Jewish attitude to the gentiles. But Christians approved all these things, as it were, retrospectively. The religious institutions they considered legitimate for the past they repudiated for the present. And whereas they displayed the same intransigence to the pagan world as the Jews did, they condemned that intransigence when it opposed their own message.[22]

Though Christian anti-Semitism, thus described, existed, at least in rudimentary form, at the very beginning of Christianity, it only unfolded fully in the fourth century. At that point it appears in all its complexity. On the one hand, in spite of the conversion of Constantine, it may be regarded as the continuation of the pagan world's hostility toward the Jews. The pagan world had been Christianized. It retained, nevertheless, the pagan attitude to the Jews. It took over the arguments and the complaints that public opinion had always advanced against Jewish religious and social nonconformity. On the other hand, and this is Christianity's essential contribution, the new anti-Semitism expressed the opposition that the Church felt toward the Jews as obdurate dissidents. It expressed the condemnation uttered by Christian teaching of those who crucified Christ and rebuffed his call. Although clearly different, these two aspects of the phenomenon were intimately mingled. One was secular and popular, the other was ecclesiastical and learned, and was nourished by the Bible itself. From the Bible it drew the material to support its assertions and its condemnations. This was where the genuinely Christian element was rooted. And this true Christian anti-Semitism was theological through and through.

The chief complaint, which formed the theoretical foundation for the whole case, finds expression as early as the Gospels, especially in the fourth. The Jews are worthy of hatred because they killed Christ, persecuted his disciples, and rejected his teaching. "Pilate was anxious to set him free, but the Jews shouted... 'Take him away, take him away! Crucify him!'"[23] The responsibility for the crime therefore falls on the whole people, and it is a crime that the Christian authors characterize as deicide.[24]

For some of these authors the death of Christ is the cause of Israel's rejection. For others it is not a cause but an indication. Many signs have demonstrated that the people have long been unworthy of their ancient election. But his sign shows more clearly than all the others how deep-rooted their perversion had become.[25] The Jews had therefore killed their savior, not by the exercise of their own free will, but because God, seeing their incurable wickedness, had condemned them to perdition, as the prophets had foretold.

Such is already the Johannine interpretation of Jesus' trial and passion. "Though he had done so many signs before them, yet they did not believe in him; it was that the word spoken by the prophet Isaiah might be fulfilled: 'Lord, who has believed our report, and to whom has the arm of the Lord been revealed?' Therefore they could not believe. For Isaiah again said, 'He has blinded their eyes and hardened their heart, lest they should see with their eyes and perceive with their heart, and turn for me to heal them.' "[26]

The murder of Christ is thus explained by the whole of the past history of the Jewish people. It is the natural consequence and culmination of an uninterrupted series of transgressions, of grave offenses and crimes that demonstrate the people's unworthiness. This proof is repeated ad nauseam throughout patristic literature.[27] It is already there in outline in Stephen's tirade before the Sanhedrin: "You stubborn people, with your pagan hearts and pagan ears. You are always resisting the Holy Spirit, just as your ancestors used to do. Can you name a single prophet your ancestors never persecuted? In the past they killed those who foretold the coming of the Just One, and now you have become his betrayers, his murderers."[28]

To a people whom their own history, written by divinely inspired men, portrayed as criminals and sinners one may legitimately attribute, in the present, any crime and any deficiency. The old accusations, which sprang originally from pagan malevolence, gain a new lease of life under the pens of Christians. They also gain a new virulence. They thus continue, in a revived form, the traditional animosity of the Greco-Roman world, lately Christianized. Juster has prepared a catalogue of the principal taunts thrown at the Jews during ancient times.[29] It is interesting to note, as Juster does, that almost every one the pagans manufactured is reused by the Christians. Both pagans and Christians charge the Jews with turbulence and a tendency to revolt. Apion and Celsus tax them with having committed sedition.[30] St. John Chrysostom calls them ἔθνος πολεμοποιόν.[31] The Latin Church writers echo this with *rebellantes Judaei*.[32] Pagans and Christians alike declare them to be bitterly envious, headstrong, and mean-spirited. As far as invective is concerned, the continuity between pagans and Christians is as close as it could well be.

There are, however, some charges the Christians are reluctant to take up, perhaps because the same charges had too often been made against themselves. If they are made at all, it is with circumspection, and generally in a sense that differs significantly from the spirit in which they were originally intended. There is, for example, the accusation of misanthropy. Tacitus denounces Jews and Christians on this score in identical terms. It is curious to see Origen defending the Jews against the charge and declaring that, far from detesting pagans, they reserve their hatred for the Christians, who have forsaken idols for the worship of the true God.[33] In later writers the complaint reappears, but always in this new form. The Jews hate Christianity, not the human race. Under the Christian empire these two views tended to become confused. This second reworking of the idea is no less characteristic.

Again, Christian polemists make interesting distinctions between the charges the pagans formulated against the Jews. For instance, the accusation that the Jews worship angels appears from both sides,[34] but the Jewish distaste for images, which had so impressed the pagans,[35] does not appear in the Christian list of charges, even in an age in which the use of icons had already been initiated in the Church. Neither is the Sabbath idleness condemned by Christians, because as an image of the Sunday rest it contained nothing that a Christian would find scandalous. The fundamental institutions of Judaism, such as circumcision and the dietary regulations, which roused the sarcasm of the pagans, are not in themselves denounced by the fathers. They are denounced because the advent of Christianity has rendered them void, and in maintaining their attachment to them, the Jews are once more displaying their spirit of disobedience. It is true that Tertullian says, *Haec et nos risimus aliquando*, but this is in an attempt to emphasize the fact that Christians are not Jews, but are gentiles by birth. He adds shortly afterwards, *De vestris sumus*.[36] He is in any case speaking of biblical truths and not of the rites themselves. And what he says about them applies to the pagan period in the lives of the converts. These truths the Church has made its own. As for the Jewish rites, however odd they may seem to a Christian who has come from a pagan background, their divine origin forbids him to laugh at them.[37]

The accusation that the Jews worship the ass, which is a commonly reiterated theme of pagan polemic,[38] is absent altogether from that of the Christians. The reasons are perfectly clear. The Church recognized the sancitity of the Jerusalem Temple, and any suggestion that a grotesque and idolatrous worship went on there would have been blasphemous. Besides, it would be understandable if the Christians, who had had the same slander thrown up at themselves, had been reluctant to throw it back at the Jews, even though the Jews had sometimes joined in the calumny when the pagans gave the lead. The Jews might have hoped, by turning this stupid accusation off on to the rival cult, to have been rid of it themselves for the future. The Christians, by contrast, had nothing to gain. All the world was aware of the connection between Christianity and Judaism, and mud of this kind, if thrown at the Jews, was likely to come off on themselves. It was better policy to join the Jews in demonstrating the accusation's inanity. Tertullian tells how a certain Jew of Carthage walked down the street one day carrying a caricature of Christ, decorated with an ass's ears, and bearing this inscription, "Onocoetes, the God of the Christians."[39] But he elsewhere recounts, following Tacitus, the legend of Jewish ass worship, and takes the trouble to refute it, adding, *Atque ita inde praesumptus opinor, nos quoque, ut judaicae religionis propinquos, eidem simulacro initiari.*[40]

The same explanation may be given for the fact that the accusation of ritual murder, which the pagans brought against both Jews and Christians, was not made by Christians against Jews until a relatively late date. It did not really flourish until the Middle Ages.[41] Prudence and, it may be supposed, simple honesty moved the Christians thus to pick and choose a little among the weapons the pagan world bequeathed to them.

But though the Christians sometimes modified the traditional complaints, they did not neglect to augment their list of charges by drawing on the ancient catalogues of accusations and calumnies. These may have originated for the most part in Alexandria, but they had been peddled across the empire and had become common coin. When the much-discussed epithet that Claudius applied to the Jews, "the plague of the world," turns up word for word in the same form in an anti-Jewish homily by St. John Chrysostom it is not a mere coincidence.[42] Having started life in some pamphlet or other, it very likely became part, both in Antioch and Alexandria, of the popular repertoire of anti-Semitic slogans. The fact that it reappears after more than three centuries in the second document demonstrates how tenacious the old prejudices and hatreds were, in spite of the religious revolution that had intervened, and how fixed were the formulae in which they were expressed. Christians too, in the early years of the Church, had heard themselves described in the same sort of terms. That they did not turn these slanders against the Jews until the very end of the fourth century, when there was no longer any risk of exposing themselves to the same vilifications, is not fortuitous. By that time they could speak in the name of the whole gentile world, which had been called and adopted in place of the Jews.

III

There is, however, more to Christian anti-Semitism than a simple plagiarizing, or even adaptation, of pagan themes. Both in its spirit and its methods it displays considerable originality.

One of the most striking characteristics of Christian anti-Semitism is its subordination of social accusations to moral and religious ones. It is not the supercilious insularity of the Jews that chiefly annoys the Christians, nor even the narrowness and jealousy of their self-sufficient community. Their primary accusation is that the Jews are addicted to all the vices, and that under cover of their scrupulous observance of the law they are really immoral and irreligious.

Here again the Christian polemists are not entirely independent of their pagan predecessors. The charge of impiety is a repetition, in suitably revised form, of the old accusation of atheism. This latter charge could hardly be reused at it stood. It would have come oddly from a people who themselves fell under the same condemnation. Those who professed belief in the God of Abraham, Isaac, and Jacob could scarcely associate themselves with the criticisms that the gentiles made. However, they could and did see in the beliefs and practices of post-Christian Judaism an aberration, a caricature of true religion, and in the last analysis a form of worship not far removed from idolatry.[43] In the eyes of the pagans Jewish atheism was repaid by the hatred of the gods. Poseidonius of Apamea calls them μισουμένους ὑπὸ τῶν θεῶν.[44] Similarly, for the Christians Israel's rejection is evidence of her impiety.[45] This is one of the basic themes not only of popular anti-Semitism but of learned polemic.

Not that accusations of immorality and, in particular, of debauchery, are lacking from the old pagan repertoire of anti-Jewish slanders. Tacitus, for example, insists that the Jews are libertines: *projectissima ad libidinem gens*.[46] However, it is not among the commonest accusations. Among the Christians, on the contrary, it appears with special frequency, and for the fourth-century Christian authors immorality is a characteristic Jewish failing.[47]

This assertion too had earlier been thrown up at the Christians. When turned against the Jews, it can be explained otherwise than by pure malice. It is an exaggerated expression of the conflict between Jewish and Christian conceptions of sexual morality. The period was one in which the ascetic ideal, an ideal that set a high value on virginity, was gaining ground in the Church. Now, this ideal was quite foreign to the religious tradition of Israel, and remained incomprehensible, not to say quite disgusting, to the Jews. In opposition to it, they exalted the ideal of family life, as illustrated by the patriarchs. And they quoted the ancient biblical command, "Be fruitful and multiply." For them procreation was a duty, and an abundant offspring the sign of divine favor. Tacitus again expresses it for us: *generandi amor.*[48] Whereas Christians, or at least Christians of a certain kind, sought a remedy against the temptations of the flesh in absolute chastity, the Jews were content with the obligation of conjugal fidelity. What the decalogue and the rabbis condemned was not sexual activity, but simply adultery.

It is understandable that the ascetic party, seeing the Jews exalt the ideal of the conjugal life, should regard them as advocates of debauchery. It is equally conceivable that their views, thus expressed, might have provided material for popular malice to work on, popular malice needing little encouragement in this particular direction. We have evidence from a number of sources that in the Eastern countries, where there was a large Jewish population, and where there was still close contact between the adherents of the rival cults, this very question was the subject of keen debate. Aphraates, for example, devotes one of his homilies, which are such a rich source of instruction on the subject of Jewish-Christian relations, to the subject of virginity. His object is to arm the faithful against Jewish attacks, for the Jews, he says, "because of their sensuality and their carnal desire," rebel against this virtue and by cunning insinuations turn the simple away from it. They laugh at those who practice it and say to them, "You are unclean, because you do not take a wife. We are holy, because we have assured our posterity.[49]

We know also that the monks, who became a weighty influence in the history of the Eastern Church after the fourth century, made themselves foremost in the struggle against the Jews. They were the militant anti-Semites. And it was they who were largely responsible for the reputation for debauchery the Jews acquired. And part of the reason, we may imagine, that so many of the fathers take up the accusation, is that they were in close touch with monastic circles.[50]

It is against the same background that we must evaluate the accusation, rarely made by the pagans, of Jewish greed. Christians, by contrast, were loud in their complaints that the Jews were fond of money, of luxury, of the pleasures of the table, and of every form of wealth.[51] This was a feature of the Jewish mentality the pagans had not noticed, for if they had noticed it, they would not have been slow to include it in their criticisms. It is very difficult to believe that in a relatively short interval of time, at a period when the Christian authorities had not confined the Jews to activities such as moneylending, which Christians were forbidden to take part in, this love of

money and its equivalents should suddenly have become so characteristic of the Jews. It is not that this accusation was leveled against the
Jews alone. When Jerome reproaches one of the Jews who taught him
Hebrew, a famous rabbi, for having charged too much for his lessons,[52]
and goes on to denounce the Jews in general for being fond of money
and good living, these accusations must be set against the same
author's concession, elsewhere, that they were generous to the poor,
even the Christian poor.[53] Besides this, he condemns the Romans as
well as the Jews for cupidity,[54] and says that the Syrians are worse
than either of them.[55] It is wise not to accept these generalizations
without reserve. And as Parkes has pointed out,[56] none of the sermons
against usury that have come down to us from this period makes any
mention of the Jews.

But in any case, St. Jerome and, in differing degrees, the others who
pass such strictures on the Jews are all ascetics, who affect to despise
the good things of this world. For men such as these, at what point did
a taste for money or for gluttony begin? Coming from them, the
accusation carries the same weight as the claim that the Jews were
libertines. But quite apart from thoroughgoing asceticism, there was a
real difference between Christian and Jewish ideals at this point.[57]
The former rested upon a pessimistic view of the world and of life in it,
regarding them as part of the empire of evil. Contempt for the flesh
was only one aspect, though the most important aspect, of this
fundamental attitude of renunciation. For the Jews, on the contrary,
the creation was good, and it was legitimate for men to enjoy the good
things God had placed at their disposal. Success in worldly affairs was,
like a large progeny, a sign of God's blessing. The Jews expected a
reward for the righteous in this world. The Christians did not
anticipate it until the next.

Nevertheless, this was only one aspect of Judaism, just as asceticism
was only one aspect of Christianity. Christianity, in coming to terms
with "the world," arrived at a mode of life that was noticeably similar
to that of contemporary Judaism.[58] Conversely, Judaism by no means
ignored the idea of righteous suffering. It had discovered the hard
way, throughout its history, that God's chosen ones were never far
removed from tears and persecution. Job is just as typical of Judaism
as are the patriarchs, full of years, of satisfaction, and of wealth.
Jewish morality was no more inclined than that of the Christians to
make material felicity the infallible criterion of virtue. When the
Christian polemists emphasized with such satisfaction the vices of the
Jews, they were far from taking a detached and objective view. They
spoke under the influence of hatred and were looking through the
distorting glass of asceticism.

But the really characteristic contribution of Christianity to anti-Semitism lay in its methods of argument and its techniques of combat. Whereas the accusations of the pagans were generally reproduced gratuitously and without proof, the Christian writers proceeded to back them up with texts of scripture. The Old Testament was an arsenal of which they made free use. Their accusations are supported by invective drawn from holy writ.

This anti-Semitic exegesis of the Bible had two different objects. It endeavored to show that the criticisms the Church had made of the Jews since the murder of Christ were in conformity with the Jewish character. Their own recorded history and the writings of their own prophets bore witness that the self-styled chosen people had never been anything other than a pack of villains. Conversely, by projecting into the present the most conspicuous features of the prophetic indictment of Israel, and by picking out the most questionable episodes from Israelite history and dwelling on them alone, it lent weight to the accusations that were made against contemporary Judaism and justified the malice with which the Jews of its own day were met.[59]

Thus the Jew, as the animosity of his enemies painted him, was no longer the Jew as he appeared in front of them but the Jew against whom the Lord had declaimed in the past, and whose shortcomings and vices the prophets, the instruments of God's anger, had denounced. The portrait of the Jew was built up by pasting together verses of the Bible. The complaints the inspired writers had made were torn from their contexts of time and place and, combined into a single portrait, provided all the evidence that could be wished for of the utter depravity of the people of God. Thus was created the picture of the eternal Jew, a conventional figure, a literary fiction. And, as a Jewish critic comments bitterly,[60] it was the prophets, the flower of Israel, who involuntarily were responsible for the hatred the early Church stirred up against their brethren.

The Bible provided the Christians with a repertoire of offensive and damaging epithets with which they invariably accompanied every mention of the Jews. Though the "perfidy" of the Jews, which the Good Friday liturgy had immortalized, reflects the memory of the death of Christ,[61] the majority of the other descriptions applied to the Jews are drawn from the Old Testament. A few pagans had explored this source already, but their attempts had been no more than isolated exercises. In the Church, however, daily familarity with the sacred books made the harvest particularly easy to gather.

One of the commonest epithets is "the stiff-necked people," which occurs a number of times in the sacred text.[62] In ancient Christian literature, from Stephen's speech onwards, the phrase had a note-worthy career. It was meant to express the headstrong determination in pursuit of sin that led the Jews to reject the Messiah. Augustine and Ambrose use it, as does Julian the Apostate, whose use of its bears witness to his thorough knowledge of the Bible.[63] It appears in Commodian.[64] Its popularity among their enemies is attested by the Jews themselves. R. Abun claims in the fourth century that "the gentiles reproach us as the stiff-necked people."[65] The description becomes in its repetitiveness an almost Homeric epithet.

Jewish stubbornness, persisted in, has resulted in blindness. This theme naturally recalled the words of the Psalmist: "They have eyes, but see not; they have ears, but do not hear." The Psalmist, of course, was speaking of the idols, but the Christians readily overlooked this and used the words as if they described the Jews. Thus St. Ambrose, drawing attention at the same time to the traditional "perfidy" of the Jews, says: *Sciebat durae cervicis populum Judaeorum, lapsu mobilem, humilem, perfidia promptiorem, qui aure audiret et non audiret, oculis videret et non videret, lubrico quodam infantiae levem et immemorem praeceptorum.*[66] This stubborn adherence to error and evil, and this blindness, are signs of a more deep-seated failing. The Jews are carnal creatures, insensitive to the life of the spirit. This is demonstrated by their conception of religion. They have interpreted in an absolutely literal way precepts whose value is entirely symbolic. And they repudiated Christ and Christianity when they arrived because they had failed to recognize their prefigurations in scripture. Their whole religion is based on a gross misconception. The epistle of Barnabas develops this argument at length. Most later writers, without exactly taking over his point of view, reuse different components of his argument. The theme is one of the most hackneyed in ancient apologetic.

Stubborn, carnal, and murderous, the Jews were assuredly both the prey and the instruments of the evil one. Everything they did, whether in the profane or the religious sphere, was a standing offense to God. Their prayers and psalms were like the inarticulate cries of animals, *grunnitus suis et clamor asinorum*, according to Jerome's gracious description.[67] No adjectives are too strong, no comparisons too odious to be applied to the Jews. Gregory of Nyssa provides us with a notable enough specimen of these vitriolic tirades: "Murderers of the Lord, murderers of prophets, rebels and full of hatred against God, they commit outrage against the law, resist God's grace, repudiate the faith of their fathers. They are confederates of the devil, offspring of vipers, scandal-mongers, slanderers, darkened in mind, leaven of the Pharisees, Sanhedrin of demons, accursed, utterly vile, quick to abuse, enemies of all that is good."[68]

IV

But the master of anti-Jewish invective is without question St. John Chrysostom. In him all the complaints and all the insults are gathered together. It is here that we see most plainly the fusion of the several elements that went to make up the Christian polemic; the themes of popular anti-Semitism, the specifically theological grievances, the use of biblical texts. And all these are presented with such violence and at times such a coarseness of language as to be without parallel. This anti-Semitism pervades the whole of Chrysostom's work, but it inspires especially his eight *Homilies against the Jews.*[69]

The first of these homilies is perhaps the most characteristic. It opens with the traditional accusations. The Jews, says Chrysostom, who had been overwhelmed with benefits by God, rejected them all. They had been sons of God, by adoption, and they became like dogs. No people could be more mean than this, for they managed to exasperate God not only by breaking the law but even by observing it. When they ought to have kept it, they broke it. Now that it has been abrogated, they obstinately insist on maintaining it. They have always resisted the Holy Spirit. They are stiff-necked. They have broken the yoke of Christ, though it was a light one. They have made themselves no better than senseless beasts.[70]

This comparison is one the author keeps on invoking. Like beasts, the Jews are voracious, gluttonous.[71] All their vices are derived from this. And now we have a text supporting the accusation: "Israel ate and was filled and became fat, and the beloved kicked."[72] The Jews, being dominated by gluttony and drunkenness, have fallen into the worst evils. Like well-fed cattle incapable of work, they are no longer fit for anything but slaughter.[73]

The catalogue of criticisms is extended further. The Jews are gluttons, drunkards, and carnal-minded even while they are fasting. Their fasts are in any case an insult to God. Their Day of Atonement is an opportunity for indecent festivities. They dance barefoot in the marketplaces. They gather choirs of effeminate young men and motley collections of women of doubtful reputation. They collect in the synagogue people from the stage and theater, for synagogue and theater are on much the same level.[74]

At this point we may imagine there were signs of protest among the audience. Chrysostom is aware of having momentarily gone too far and begins to defend himself in advance against objections. Let no one accuse him of impertinence. He has done no more than quote prophecy: "You maintained a prostitute's bold front, never thinking to blush."[75] For those carried away by their polemical enthusiasm, the

Bible's metaphor became a literal statement of fact. The orator seizes on it, warms to his theme, and insists: "The place where you find a harlot is called a brothel; or rather, the synagogue is not only a brothel and a theatre but a brigands' cave and a wild beasts' den."[76] The prophet once more provides support: "Do you take this temple that bears my name for a robbers' den?" And again, "I have abandoned my house, left my heritage.... For me my heritage has become a lion in the forest."[77] God has abandoned the Jews. They have disowned the Father, crucified the Son, and refused the help of the Holy Spirit. Cave of brigands? No! Worse than that. Their synagogues henceforth are the seat of demons and the place of idolatry: and not only their synagogues, but their souls. And here Chrysostom, reminded that some Christians think of the rites of the Jews as solemn rituals, and that they visit their assemblies and treat them as holy places, launches into an astonishing diatribe in which the comparison between Jews and animals is further worked out. "They live only for their belly, their mouths always gaping; they behave no better than pigs or goats in their gross lasciviousness and excessive gluttony. They only know one thing, namely, how to gorge themselves and fill themselves up with drink."[78]

Chrysostom turns next to the Judaizers, whom he tries to convince of the horrifying nature of their behavior. But he soon leaves them to make a fresh onslaught on the Jews, the cause of all the trouble. How can anyone have anything to do with these miserable, demon-possessed creatures, brought up on crime and murder? One had much better fly from them. And here we have reiterated, though in a more brutal and naked form, the famous formula from Claudius's letter to the Alexandrians: shun them "like filth and like a universal plague."[79] What transgressions have they not committed? The Psalmist tells us that they burned their sons and daughters to satisfy the demons.[80] The author's indignation builds up and his wrath rises, and again the Jews are compared with beasts. They are wilder than any beast,[81] for beasts sometimes give their lives to save their young, but the Jews have massacred theirs with their own hands in order to honor demons. Which ought to anger us more, their impiety or their cruelty? But even apart from this, their every action expresses their bestial nature: "Sex-crazed stallions, each neighing for his neighbour's wife."[82] "Have they not, in their lasciviousness, surpassed even the most lustful of senseless animals?"[83]

What more can be said of them? They are guilty of "expropriation, covetousness, abandoning the poor in their need, and profiteering."[84] A whole day would not be long enough to deliver a catalogue of their vices. They were completely consumed by them even before the murder of Christ, but his murder has set the seal on their abominable behavior. And even after this, Christian people will go and associate with the criminals, will deliver themselves, soul and body, to the demons! The sermon culminates in a moving appeal to the Judaizers. Let them cease this behavior, which can lead only to their own loss! Let everyone apply himself to bring them back into the right way by persuasion, or if necessary by force.

The homilies that follow are devoted to theological discussion of particular points, and their tone is more restrained. It is only in the sixth homily that the polemic again takes an aggressive turn. Chrysostom proposes to expatiate on the present misery of the Jews. Ezekiel is witness that they have always been sinners. They worshiped the calf, tried to kill Moses, blasphemed against God, and sacrificed their children to demons. In spite of all this, God showered upon them signs of His favor. If now they have ceased to practice idolatry and no longer put to death their prophets or their own children, why are they in permanent exile? It is because they killed Christ. This was the supreme act of wickedness, which has left them no hope either of forgiveness or of amendment of life. Their lot henceforward is to be shame and misery. The Christians, by contrast, the followers of him whom they killed, are exalted. Once Christ was dead, prophecy came to an end in Israel, the temple was destroyed, sacrifices ceased, the priesthood vanished. Let not the present Jewish Patriarchs contradict this! They are not priests, but pirates, "traffickers, profiteers, sated with every sort of fraud."[85]

Jewish worship is genuinely divine in origin, and was once worthy of respect, but it is now no more than a caricature of what worship ought to be. "Everything the Jews now do is a grotesque joke, at once laughable and disgusting."[86] The presence of the holy books is not enough to make the Synagogue holy. Christ himself said of the temple that the Jews had made it into a brigands' cave, and that in spite of the fact that it contained the ark and the divine spirit. What shall we say then of the Synagogue of our own day, where nothing goes on except impiety? It is "now a brothel, place of all evil-doing, resort of demons, devil's citadel, ruin of souls, precipice and abyss of perdition. Everything that can be said of it falls short of what it deserves."[87]

The methods by which Chrysostom blackens the Jews are apparent enough. When he is not simply retailing gross and gratuitous slanders, he is taking prophetic condemnations, isolating them completely from the context in which they are recorded and the circumstances in which they were uttered and from which they derive their meaning, and applying them to the present. The texts that speak appreciatively of Israel, in which the Bible abounds, are never called in evidence.

This one-sided exegesis, used by the author's undoubted oratorical skill, turns the Jew into an eternal figure, a type; and it is a monstrous, villainous figure, calculated to inspire in all who look at it a proper horror.[88]

Chrysostom's use of metaphor is especially noteworthy. One example will be sufficient. The author emphasizes the intemperance of the Jews at the beginning of the first homily, and he returns to the theme more than once. Everything suggests that we are meant to take the accusation in its simple, ordinary sense. But the accusation of gluttony is in fact based on the text of Deuteronomy I quoted above. As for the charge of drunkenness, its basis is even more infirm. Chrysostom himself, having lightly asserted that the Jews are given to drunkenness, explains in passing, at the end of the cycle of homilies, that it should be understood metaphorically. "So passes the Jews' fast, or rather the Jews' drunkenness. For," he goes on, "it is possible to get drunk even without wine."[89] For these things too may be classified as drunkenness: anger, sensuality, avarice, love of honor. And with even better justice may we call "drunkard" the impious man who blasphemes against God and resists the law, which is to say, the Jew. "For drunkenness means nothing other than departure from the path of reason, derangement of mind, loss of the soul's health."[90] And the basis of this entire accusation is, as far as can be discovered, a single text, originally intended in its true sense: "They are drunken, but not with wine."[91]

We should be justified in speaking of bad faith if it were not perfectly obvious that Chrysostom, carried away by the intensity of his anger, has not himself made any clear distinction between real drunkenness and the metaphorical kind of which he is speaking. The two ideas are muddled in his own mind, just as the two vices, in his eyes, are combined in the twisted personality of the Jew.

The same may be said of the accusation of debauchery and the slanderous complaints made against the Synagogue. The prophet had said to his people, "You maintained a prostitute's bold front." There is a tacit syllogism connecting this text with the treatment of the Synagogue as a place of ill-repute. The Jews, who are compared to a prostitute, frequent the Synagogue. Now, the place where prostitutes live is called a brothel. Hence, the Synagogue is a brothel.[92]

Once the fire of his anger has been damped, Chrysostom is perhaps not taken in by his own arguments. But by the time he cools down he has already done quite enough to confirm the reputation for debauchery and vice with which popular imagination had credited the Jews.

The procedures Chrysostom employed had a not unremarkable career in the history of the anti-Jewish controversies. Some of their results were very serious. It is these methods which explain, for example, the recrudescence of the accusation of ritual murder, which reappeared in the Middle Ages, and which has contributed so much to the misfortunes of the Jews. Pagan anti-Semitism was already familiar with this charge, and extended it, quite naturally, to take in the Christians too.[93] The same accusation has been made in our own time against the Freemasons. It is the sort of slander that popular hatred produces spontaneously. But the insistence with which mediaeval Christianity employed it against the Jews, usually, be it noted, in connection with the Feast of Unleavened Bread, suggests that there was a special reason for it in this case. There seems to be no connection between this particular rite and ritual murder except for one very, very tenuous one provided by a biblical text. Oort has recently shown[94] that the origin of the accusation is to be sought, in all likelihood, in the *Altercatio Simonis Judaei et Theophili Christiani*, which is dated at the beginning of the fifth century.[95] This dialogue ends, in accordance with the usual plan of such works, with the conversion of the Jew. The occasion of the conversion is a discussion about unleavened bread. "Prove to me," says Theophilus to Simon, "that scripture forbids you to drink the wine of the Christians, and I shall show you how it forbids to us the wine of the Jews and their unleavened bread."[96] The Jew is unable to quote any text in his support. The Christian, however, produces several. Concerning the unleavened bread, he quotes: "Your hands are covered with blood"; concerning the wine: "Their stock springs from the vinestock of Sodom and from the groves of Gomorrah: their grapes are poisonous grapes." And again, "Their feet run to do evil, are quick to shed innocent blood."[97] The Jew, finding the argument conclusive, is baptized.

Once having recognized this as its point of departure, it is easy to see how the allegation of ritual murder developed. Hands covered with blood are, of course, the hands of criminals. This is how Theophilus understands the matter. "See with what feet and what hands you prepare the wine and the unleavened bread," he cries, commenting on his quotations. From this it is only a short step to saying that the hands became thus soiled in the preparation of the rite itself. Oort rightly notes that in areas where there was a large Jewish element, popular superstition had always credited the rites of unleavened bread with magical properties. The non-Jews were readily impressed by the rituals, to them very mysterious indeed, that accompanied both the preparation and the consumption of the bread.[98] At the same time they had always ascribed great potency to human blood, especially to the blood of children, in the preparation of sorcerers' spells and potions. It was therefore very natural for the pagan populace to assume that children's blood was a component of the *mazzoth*. The accusation of ritual murder grew up, beginning with a text of scripture as its point of departure, by the application of this method of exegesis, whose most notable exponent is St. John Chrysostom.

Chrysostom represents, in respect of his anti-Semitism, an extreme case in the early Church. His passion in the cause, and the violence of his invective, are without parallel in the literature of the first few centuries. This is explained partly by the individual temperament of the author and partly, as we shall later have occasion to see, by the local situation. It is a specifically Antiochene phenomenon. But if the case is an extreme one, it is not a unique one. Every time the subject of the Jews crops up in the Christian writings of the period Chrysostom's attitude and methods reappear.

The anti-Jewish state of mind was not confined to the principal officers and scholars of the Church, and did not find expression only through them. We not only have the diatribes of Chrysostom and the more or less veiled insinuations of other ecclesiastical writers. We have the liturgy itself. This is a matter to which Juster has drawn attention,[99] though in such a way that he scarcely presents us with a fair picture of the facts. One gets the impression from reading his work that there are anti-Jewish elements to be found throughout the liturgy. He asserts: "Anti-Jewish polemic in the Church was repeated almost as often as the divine service itself. It was thus driven into the minds of the believers and shaped their entire way of thinking. Being thus reinforced day by day, anti-Jewish sentiments hardened in their minds."[100]

A close study of the liturgical texts themselves does not support this conclusion. In fact, not only are diatribes against the Jews, and even wounding epithets applied to Israel, rare, but allusions of any sort to the Jews are fairly thinly spread. They do, however, collect quite thickly around certain points in the liturgical year, and especially around the celebrations of holy week.

For this reason, Juster's conclusions concerning the difference between pagan anti-Jewish polemic and the Christian variety need some modification. The pagan polemic, he says, consists of "the mere publication of literary works" of an "abstract and aristocratic" kind. He contrasts this with the Christian polemic against the Jews, which he describes as "propagandist, and retailed daily among the populace." For the Christians introduced it "into divine worship, in which solemn and almost dramatic context its impact would be reinforced by all the means which liturgy has at its disposal to move the mind and the emotions."[101] This analysis, it seems to me, divorces the anti-Jewish writings from the popular sentiment in which they were rooted. The roots of pagan anti-Semitism went very deep, and Juster does not recognize this. It is hardly to be supposed that in areas where there existed a large Jewish population anti-Semitism was the exclusive prerogative of intellectuals. The masses shared it, in full measure. At the same time Juster errs, when he speaks of the part played by the liturgy, in exaggerating the importance of anti-Semitism in the Church.[102]

Nevertheless, there was a fundamental difference between the anti-Semitism of pagans and that of Christians. We must give Juster credit for perceiving this, even if he has not noted very accurately what the difference was. Christian anti-Semitism, insofar as it was officially espoused by the Church, did have a sanction as well as a coherence that the pagan sort always lacked. It was used to serve theological ends and it was given theological backing and encouragement. It did not base its arguments on ascertainable facts, not even, for that matter, on the hearsay evidence of popular gossip, but on a particular kind of exegesis of the biblical writings, an exegesis that interpreted them in the light of the death of Christ as a long indictment of the chosen people. Where pagan anti-Semitism was, for the most part, spontaneous and unorganized, that of the Christians was devoted to a well-conceived end. Its aim was to make the Jews abhorrent to all, to sustain the dislike of those in whom the Jews already aroused dislike, and to turn the affections of those who were well disposed.

Let us recall Chrysostom. The Christian, he says, must shun them "as a plague which has afflicted the world." He must follow the example of the martyrs who, because they loved Christ, hated the Jews, for it is not possible to love the victim without hating his murderers. Whereas pagan sentiment accused the Jews of misanthropy, the Church actually practiced it on them. It strengthened the barriers that Jewish religious observances had already erected between Israel and the outside world, its intention being to safeguard believers from contact with these dangerous creatures. The mediaeval ghetto was to be the result, not simply of Jewish particularism, but of the Christians' systematic exclusion of the Jews from Christian society. There was no ghetto in antiquity. But Christian anti-Semitism, as I have just described it, entailed some of the same consequences, which I must now draw attention to.

V

In the first place, anti-Jewish feelings stimulated by Christian polemic issued quite naturally from time to time in outbursts of violence against the Jews either against their persons or against their property.

In this context we must not forget that there were occasions on which the Jews themselves stirred up trouble. There were times when the measures the Christians took might fairly be represented as reprisals. But this judgment applies mainly, and perhaps only, to those geographical areas in which Jews felt numerically strong enough to take the initiative, and these areas naturally became fewer and fewer as Christianity extended its grip upon the empire. By the fourth century the most that the Jews could generally do was to seize the occasion of the Christians' doctrinal dissensions and intervene in their quarrels, quarrels that were often enough attended with actual violence. At Alexandria, for example, they took the part of the Arians against the orthodox.[103] And when the orthodox party emerged triumphant the Jews suffered the same ill-treatment as the vanquished Christians. But their intervention in Christian quarrels is not an adequate explanation of the large number of cases in which violence was directed against the Jews alone. There can be no doubt that the imprecations hurled at them from the pulpit by ministers of the Church, if they were not deliberately designed to incite violence, certainly worked to that end, acting as a dangerous leaven in the minds of the masses.

The fairly frequent pogroms that took place in the cities of the East during the pagan period continued after Constantine. It cannot be said, however, that they became any commoner. On the other hand, the general harassing of Jews did tend to become more widespread and more frequent from century to century, though whether this was a result of the decisions of imperial authority or whether it sprang from popular feeling and the initiative of local authorities we do not know.

Within the chronological limits of the present inquiry the clearest instance of the persecution of Jews is their expulsion from Alexandria in A.D. 414. This took place at the instigation of the Patriarch Cyril, against, it appears, the wishes of the prefect. This expulsion was accompanied by the confiscation of both the private and the communal property of the Jews, in particular by the confiscation of synagogues.[104]

This hostility to the synagogues is characteristic of Christian anti-Semitism. During the pagan era the destruction of synagogues was uncommon. Indeed, the only such case that is firmly attested is the destruction of the synagogues of Alexandria under Caligula, and it appears in a series of violent measures enacted against the Jewish community of Alexandria as a whole.[105] During the Christian period, on the contrary, such actions became significantly more frequent. It was Judaism in its capacity as a religion that aroused the hostility, and this is demonstrated by the choice of the places of worship as the principal objects of attack. In exactly the same way, Christians attacked the temples of the dying paganism. Pagan sanctuaries and Jewish synagogues were both alike temples of error. It was therefore not only legitimate but meritorious to destroy them or appropriate them for the true worship.

Numerous instances of confiscation or destruction, generally destruction by fire, are attested throughout the fourth and fifth centuries, both in the West and in the East. The local Church authorities usually gave such proceedings tacit condonation or open approval. Sometimes they even went so far as to instigate the action. At Tipasa in Africa the synagogue became at the beginning of the fourth century the Christian Church of Saint Salsa.[106] At about the same period the bishop of Dertona in Spain led his people in an attack on the synagogue, which he then turned into a church.[107] It was most likely by a similar act of violence that the synagogue at Antioch, which marked the tomb of the seven Maccabaean brothers, passed into Christian hands along with its relics in the second half of the same century.[108] At the beginning of the fifth century, at Edessa, Bishop Rabbula turned the synagogue into the Church of Saint Peter.[109]

Instances of destruction are equally numerous. At Rome in A.D. 388 the usurper Maximinus attempted to force the Christians to rebuild a synagogue they had set fire to. By so doing, he lost both their sympathy and the favor of their God.[110] At Magona in Minorca in A.D. 418 the transfer of the relics of a Saint Stephen, a victim of Jewish persecution, resulted in a violent outburst of anti-Semitism, stimulated by the bishop and clergy. An attempt to take over the synagogue was foiled by the Jews' determined stand, but by a subterfuge they were drawn away from the building and it was sacked and burned.[111] In the East incidents of this kind, particularly numerous during the fifth century, were most often due to the fanaticism and aggressiveness of the monks. In Palestine at the beginning of the century a certain Barsauma, assisted by forty *illuminati*, a species of brigand monks, seems to have made a speciality of exploits of this type. He carried on his activities without disturbance for forty years, finishing off his destructive work, when opportunity presented itself, by massacring Jews.[112] When during the same period, Theodosius II tried to restore to the Jews of Antioch the synagogues taken from them by the Christians, he was severely reprimanded by St. Symeon Stylites and forced to abandon the project.[113]

The most famous and the most characteristic episode is that of the synagogue at Callinicum, which was a small town in Mesopotamia. The incident took place in A.D. 388 and was in itself quite trivial. The Christian population of the town, prompted by the bishop, set fire to the synagogue. The civil authorities informed Theodosius, who sent a rescript laying on the bishop the obligation to indemnify the Jewish community and to rebuild the synagogue at his own expense. He further ordered that those who had set fire to the building should be bastinadoed. St. Ambrose, on becoming acquainted with the imperial decision, immediately intervened.[114] Full of indignation, he condemned the stand the emperor had taken as sacrilegious. A Christian prince has no right thus to show favor to the Jewish error. It is legitimate to set fire to synagogues. If the laws forbid it, it is because they are bad laws. This being so, it is a duty to disobey them, and Ambrose, if he had known earlier of such a prohibition, would have felt compelled to set fire to the synagogue of Milan. God himself has already approved the destruction of these edifices. Let Theodosius therefore revoke his decision! Let him abrogate his rescript! It will redound to his eternal salvation and that of his sons.

As is well known, the matter did not stop there. Theodosius at first persisted in his policy and Ambrose took him to task publicly, in church, during divine worship. He threatened him, if he did not relent, with exclusion from the communion.[115] An argument ensued. The emperor attempted to justify himself, but finally submitted. A second rescript moderated the severity of the former one, and then a third followed, which abrogated both, and annulled the award of reparations that had originally been made to the Jews in Callinicum.

The episode is a significant one. It is only one incident, but it throws light on the whole problem of the latent opposition between Church and State and the encroachment of the ecclesiastical authorities on government and administration. Theodosius behaved at the beginning as a pagan emperor would have done, anxious to maintain order and justice and treating his subjects with equality. His action was based on respect for the accepted rights of the Jews to practice their own religion freely and was aimed at protecting their places of worship. For Ambrose, on the contrary, to show goodwill toward the Jews, or even simple equity, was inconsistent with the profession of Christianity. A Christian emperor had no business to be holding an equal balance between truth and error. It was his job to use the power

God had given him in the service of his faith.[116] If he was prevented from doing this by the law, or by the principles of justice on which it was based, then he must change the law or annul it. The law had in any case been handed down from pagan times.

In any event, it was the Church that had the last word. The episode of the synagogue of Callinicum enables us thus to put our finger on another consequence of ecclesiastical anti-Semitism, namely, its effect on imperial legislation concerning the Jews. Both Juster and Parkes in turn have dealt fully with this aspect of the matter. All that I need to do is to emphasize the essential points.

That the ecclesiastical authorities did influence legislation concerning the Jews is not open to doubt. Just as in matters relating to the various heresies the imperial code is more often than not simply an echo of the conciliary canons, so in matters relating to Judaism each amendment to the legislation is made in response to the intervention of one ecclesiastical dignitary or another. St. Ambrose brought about a modification of the law concerning the protection of synagogues.[117] St. John Chrysostom was the moving spirit behind several anti-Jewish laws promulgated by Arcadius, and Arcadius reverted to a more liberal policy as soon as the patriarch had been expelled from Constantinople.[118] To look at the legislation affecting Jews as it develops through the successive texts of the Theodosian Code is to be immediately aware of the increasing hold religion exercised over politics.

The influence of religion appears in the very expressions that the law uses to denote Judaism. It uses offensive terms that are not compatible with the objective neutrality which one expects in legal documents. The tone it uses is that of the anti-Jewish pamphlets.[119] It is manifest that for the man who drew up these laws the Jews are no longer merely one element in the population of the empire, but have become that detestable brood who murdered Christ. That is to say, they have become for him what they are for the ecclesiastical polemists. At every point, as Juster remarks, the legal texts betray a theological motivation for their anti-Jewish dispositions.[120]

And it is not only the tone of the texts that betrays the increasing influence of the Church. Their very spirit and intent is seen to be progressively modified in a direction that is more and more unfavorable to the Jews. Christian apologetic demanded that the Jews and Judaism should continue to exist. They were witnesses. But it demanded that they should exist in misery, that they should enjoy a precarious status, a diminished existence that would mark them out as the people who were once chosen, but now condemned.

The protection the pagan empire had granted to the persons and property of the Jews was thus relaxed. The law became more indulgent toward those who did them injury or violence, but more severe toward their own shortcomings.[121] And already there appears the desire to harass the Jews in their cult activities, and without altogether withdrawing the protection the Synagogue had previously enjoyed, to make things difficult for it. From this point of view, the affair at Callinicum marks a major new departure.

Up to this time the destruction of synagogues had fallen under the censure of the law.[122] It had at least entailed as reparations the rebuilding of the edifice by the guilty parties and, where appropriate, corporal punishment. This is the law Theodosius applied initially at Callinicum.[123] Although in this instance he capitulated to Ambrose, the law nevertheless continued for a time unchanged. Legally, the destruction of synagogues remained a crime. In fact, the law was violated constantly and with impunity, for the ecclesiastical authorities encouraged people to break it and hindered any attempt to enforce it. The fact that the texts prohibiting the destruction of synagogues continued to be republished is evidence that the legislators were unable to enforce obedience to them.

From one edition to the next, moreover, the severity of the laws is moderated. In A.D., 393 some years after Callinicum, Theodosius published a reminder that Judaism was not forbidden by law and that therefore the destruction of synagogues ought to be punished.[124] But he modified the procedure so that what had been a crime that must be remitted to the imperial tribunal now became a matter for the jurisdiction of local authorities. The laws of 397, 412, and 418 again recall in general terms the protection the synagogues enjoy. The second forbids their confiscation, the third forbids incendiarism.[125] Contemporary events, which I have referred to above, show that these texts often remained a dead letter.

The next step is that the imperial authorities make a fresh concession to the Church, in accepting the seizure or destruction of synagogues as a fait accompli, about which nothing could be done. In three laws published during the space of a few months, all of them in the year 423, there is no longer any question of restitution, or of rebuilding at the expense of those responsible.[126] Those responsible, which is to say the Christian communities or their leaders, are required to restore merely the cult objects, or, in cases where these have already been appropriated to Christian use, to pay the value of them. They are obliged, in addition, to provide ground where the Jews may, at their own expense, build a new synagogue.[127] These legal texts, with their astonishing indulgence toward the guilty, and their undisguised discrimination against the Jews, surely acted as a tacit encouragement to repeat the violent actions they were ostensibly desiged to punish.

Already by this date another law was in force, and had probably been so for several years, for the laws of 423 cite it. It forbade the Jews to build any new synagogues (except in the instances provided above) and even to repair or improve the old ones.[128] Repair was only allowed on the grounds that the building was in danger of collapse, and special authorization had to be given for it. If a synagogue was illegally built or repaired, the authorities were to see that it was pulled down.[129] A later *novella* of Theodosius II allows the transformation of such an illicit synagogue into a church, and lays a heavy fine on its constructors.[130] It was for an infringement of this law, amongst other misdemeanors, that the Patriarch Gamaliel was deprived of his honorary prefecture.

It was, however, only by slow degrees that the Christian emperors, having inherited from their pagan predecessors the duty of protecting the Jews, turned to bullying and harassing them. Constantine seems scarcely to have departed at all from the traditional policy. The important changes occur in the second half of the fourth century, for the most part after the reign of Julian. They are partly to be explained as a reaction against Julian's pro-Jewish policies. Even then resistance is not lacking. It is possible that Chrysostom's frantic anti-Semitism had offended the court of Arcadius and contributed to his disgrace.[131] Theodosius only capitulated in the Callinicum affair under threat of ecclesiastical discipline and eternal punishment. Furthermore, what he had lost on the roundabouts he attempted to regain on the swings, by suppressing the political activities of the monks who were the chief instigators of anti-Jewish violence: *Monachi multa scelera faciunt*,[132] as he puts it. Later legislation reflects similar hesitation, and sheds abundant light on the suppressed conflict between civil and religious authority. Measures that tend to protect the Jews alternate with those which shelter Christians from their missionary activity. The result of all this was a confusion about their standing; from which confusion, we may imagine, they derived no benefit whatever. It is nevertheless true that the imperial authority, though it was vacillating, and from the outset less dependable than in the pagan era, did manage sometimes to exercise a certain restraint upon the violence of Christian anti-Semitism.

Theology, for its part, set its own limits to anti-Semitism. Even after the coming of the Christ whom they rejected, the Jews had a place to fill and a part to play. They were, as we have seen, witnesses, *testes iniquitatis suae et veritatis nostrae*.[133] So then, at the same time as it encouraged both official and popular anti-Jewish attitudes, the

Church did have an eye to the survival of Judaism and the Jews. Hatred must not be pushed to the point at which the Jews were exterminated.

The law takes account of this theological necessity. In the legal texts the preamble commonly justifies the privileges accorded to the Jews either in the name of toleration or on the grounds of their antiquity. But as Juster points out,[134] these motives could just as readily have been appealed to to protect pagans, but the Church was not slow to persecute them. The decisions of the councils freely associate Jews with heretics, and the imperial legislation speaks of both in the same breath. But this juxtaposition does not quite amount to an assimilation of the one category to the other. The Jews are accorded the right to exist, a right that was denied to heretics, and, after Theodosius, denied to pagans also. In practice the leading party in the Church, whether it happened to be Arian or orthodox, always maintained the protected status of the Jews, albeit in a precarious and doubtful condition. And it did this, even though at the same time it might behave quite pitilessly toward its Christian opponents.

Furthermore, it was not only the cold reason of the theologians that placed some restraint on the wilder excesses of anti-Semitism. It must in fairness be acknowledged that the imprecations and hatred did leave room for more benevolent sentiments, more in keeping with the gospel. When an author fulminates against the Jews, allowance must always be made for the exaggeration of rhetoric and oratory. The word is often more violent than the thought.

St. Jerome, for whom Judas is the image of Judaism,[135] overwhelms the Jews with sarcastic remarks and offensive epithets,[136] but the animosity these reprobates (*Judaici serpentes*) inspire in him is not carried over into his personal relations with Jewish individuals. Just as well-known bishops were able to be on sympathetic, even friendly terms, with pagans, so Jerome was in constant touch with rabbis. He asked them for lessons in Hebrew (though he did swear about the price they charged),[137] which implies a certain confidence not only in their competence but in their intellectual probity. And his daily meeting with them for the lessons presupposes at least a minimum of human politeness and amity. It is possible to represent this as an accommodation that the exigencies of life demanded, as a utilitarian adaptation of behavior. All the same, one cannot help noticing here and there among the patristic writings evidence of a sympathy that, though qualified, is real enough, even when it takes the form of pity. Christian charity is on occasion displayed toward the despised Jews, who, it must be remembered, cherished the same feelings for the "Nazarenes" as the Christians, for the most part, did about them.

The Church held it to be a duty to pray for the Jews, and the fathers frequently recall the fact. Israel had prepared the way for the Church and the Church owed its existence to her. St. Paul had stressed this. Speaking of the Church as a wild olive shoot, grafted on to the Jewish stock, he had asked the Christians not to boast over Israel.[138] His thought, and the image in which it was expressed, was often taken up, as was his assertion of Israel's eventual redemption, in the mercy of God. Thus St. Jerome says: *Nos in radicem ipsam inserti sumus; nos rami sumus, illi radix. Non debere maledicere radicibus, sed debemus orare pro radicibus nostris.*[139] And St. Augustine similarly: *Nec superbe gloriemur adversus ramos fractos. Sed potius cogitemus cujus gratia et quanta misericordia et in qua radice inserti sumus.*[140]

Amongst the fragmentary knowledge of God that the Jews possessed there existed yet a portion of truth. Christian opinion readily assented to the qualified praise that the apostle accorded them: "I bear them witness that they have a zeal for God, but not according to knowledge."[141] St. Augustine likewise gives them credit for their fidelity to what they believe. When all other peoples adopted paganism, they alone remained unshakably attached to their law, and no power on earth can prevent them from being Jews.[142] They are recognized as possessing other qualities too. St. Ambrose, for example, declares: *Judaei habent castimoniam*,[143] and his testimony provides us with an additional reason for treating with reserve the allegations of sensuality and carnal excesses that are brought against the Jews. We have already noted that St. Jerome mentions in passing the Jews' generosity in giving alms. It is true that these praises are scattered and grudgingly given. Such as they are, however, they provide a welcome counterweight to the virulent diatribes of Chrysostom.

Some of the fathers,[144] even though they are sparing of actual praise, betray a relative sympathy by the moderate tone in which they speak of the Jews, and by the absence of complaints that others make so freely. If this falls short of sympathy, it speaks at least a laudable desire to be just and moderate, and conveys a genuinely human feeling.[145]

The differences of outlook that appear in the writings of the fathers and show that the picture was not uniformly dark are also reflected in popular Christian opinion during the period. It is going too far to say, as Parkes does, that anti-Semitism in the period was not a popular phenomenon, but something artifically worked up by the ecclesiastical hierarchy.[146] If the Christian populace so many times threw itself into the attack on synagogue after synagogue, it was not because it passively accepted orders given from above. The mass of believers, who were of gentile birth, had not on conversion shed their pagan feelings of dislike toward the Jews. If the anti-Jewish polemic was so successful, it was because it awakened latent hatreds and appealed to feelings that were already there.

This, however, is only one aspect of the matter. We learn from Chrysostom that among the people "many stand in awe of the Jews and even today treat their religious institutions with reverence."[147] We cannot know how these two tendencies, toward hatred and toward sympathy, were balanced. But having weighed the information we have at our disposal, it seems safe to say that the anti-Jewish bias of official ecclesiastical circles was counterbalanced by equally well-marked pro-Jewish sentiments among the laity and among some of the clergy too. Or rather, it is the existence of the pro-Jewish sentiments among the laity that is the real explanation of Christian anti-Semitism. Anti-Semitism was the defensive reflex of the orthodox hierarchy to the Jewish danger, the Jewish disease.

Whatever the Emperor Claudius thought, and his opinion was shared by the pagan world at large, this disease did not consist simply of unsociability and turbulence, issuing in civil disorder and seditious conspiracy. The symptoms of the disease were analyzed with minute care by Chrysostom, and he finds it to be essentially a moral and religious malady. With Israel it is congenital, but it is transmitted also to Judaizing Christians.[148] When the Jewish sickness is regarded in this light, as a contagious thing, anti-Semitism takes on the character of therapy.

We are here very close to the real roots of the phenomenon. The vices of the Jews, whether real or imagined with the help of biblical texts, the murder of Christ—these are not the real grounds for hatred. They are merely the arguments that are used to stimulate or to reinforce hatred. If the Jews are painted so black, it is because to too many of the faithful they appeared at first sight not sufficiently unattractive. The most compelling reason for anti-Semitism was the religious vitality of Judaism.

This vitality showed itself in a negative way in the doggedness with which the Jews opposed the Christian gospel. It was shown more positively in the lasting power of Jewish beliefs, and especially of Jewish rites, to draw an important minority of Christians from the very bosom of the Church. It was shown in the attraction the Synagogue and its message still managed to exercise over the believers. This was the first and great complaint, rooted neither in the biblical past nor in the bygone days when the gospel was first preached, but in the present situation. The Synagogue was an ever-present reality. The caricature the gospels offer us in place of a portrait of the Pharisees expresses the disappointment and distress of the newborn Christianity, and was produced in an epoch when the doctor of the law had been responsible for the failure of the mission to Israel. Similarly, the anti-Semitism of the Church, or at least those elements in it which are original and specifically Christian, expresses the Church's annoyance at Israel. For Israel, far from either abdicating or being converted, continued to make her influence felt within the Church's own confines, and she did so, sometimes by making a serious effort, and sometimes without even trying.

Religious competition seems to have played the same sort of part in the rise and development of Christian anti-Semitism as has been ascribed to economic competition in the rise of modern anti-Semitism. The extreme form it took can only be explained in terms of a still active proselytizing movement and of the survival of numerous forms of syncretism between the two religions.

PART 3

Conflict and Assimilation

9
The Fate of Jewish Christianity

Dum volunt et Judaei esse et Christiani nec Judaei sunt, nec Christiani.

St. Jerome, *Epistola 89 ad Augustinum*

I

The term *Jewish Christian* may be understood in two completely different senses, one ethnic, the other strictly religious. It may designate, on the one hand, Jews who had been converted to the Christian faith, i.e, Christians who were of Jewish birth. On the other, it may be applied to those Christians who continued to mix their religion with elements drawn from Judaism, and in particular, who went out of their way to observe all or part of the ritual law.

These two distinct meanings have at times been confused, and an inclusive definition has been advanced, describing Jewish Christians as "the Christians of Jewish origin who held to the regulations of Mosaic religion as well as the beliefs and practices of Christianity."[1] Such a definition, though it does correspond to a fairly common use of the term, seems to me valueless. It is too narrow. For there were Jews such as St. Paul, who, on being converted to Christianity, broke all their ties with their ancestral religion. At the same time there were some among the ranks of the Judaizers who did not belong to the chosen people by birth. The two meanings of the term *Jewish Christian* do not entirely coincide. The true facts are much too complex to allow us the luxury of an over-rigid definition.[2]

Even if we retain only the religious definition of a Jewish Christian, not allowing the name to Christians who happened to be Jews by birth but only to Judaizing Christians, it is still not easy to be precise about whom exactly it ought to apply to. If we say simply that Jewish Christianity is a combination of elements drawn from Judaism with those derived from Christianity, we shall find different interpreters, applying different criteria, affixing the label to very different articles. How are we to decide, in the context of early Christianity, what is originally and specifically Christian and what is drawn secondarily from Judaism? In the first Palestinian community Jewish Christianity and normative Christianity were hardly to be distinguished, for until the preaching of St. Stephen and St. Paul, Jewish Christianity was the only kind of Christianity in existence. For the scholars of the Catholic

Church, from the second century onwards, Jewish Christianity was no more than a heretical body outside the pale of orthodoxy. By contrast, in Marcion's view the whole Catholic Church was Jewish-Christian, since it retained the Bible as the norm of its faith and recognized the New Testament as continuous with the Old, persistently identifying the biblical demiurge with the good God whom Christ had preached.[3] Some of our present-day racist ideologies, venturing into the field of theology or religious history, similarly repudiate all existing forms of Christianity, Catholic and Protestant, as tainted with Judaism. They espouse instead either a Teutonic neopaganism or a fictitious, purely "Aryan" Christianity, with an "Aryanized" gospel and an "Aryanized" founder. The Marcionite concept of Jewish Christianity has thus enjoyed in our time a renewal of favor.

In this form, however, it is of interest only as a curiosity. Students of the history of religion, whatever their confessional background, have generally defined Jewish Christianity with reference to the Catholic Church and with deference to the Catholic point of view. They have seen it, that is to say, as an aberrant manifestation of early Christianity, linked at once to normative Christianity and to Judaism. As a body midway between Church and Synagogue, it was distinguishable from both. It was Christian as regards faith in Jesus, it was Jewish as regards the scrupulousness with which it observed the law. It is true that the Catholic Church itself became equally legalist, but its regulations concerning, for example, the keeping of Sunday and the observance of fasts, and concerning "good works" of all kinds, regulations that by slow degrees it created and imposed on its members, were substitutes for the Jewish originals that inspired them and superseded the models on which they were based.[4] The legalism of the Jewish Christians, on the contrary, devoted itself to the observance of those very forms which Jewish usage had hallowed and which were still venerated by the Synagogue. What was characteristic of the Jewish Christians was just this combination of Christian belief and Jewish practice.

In saying all this, Jewish Christianity has still not been exhaustively defined. The combination was capable of assuming diverse forms, according to the proportions in which the constituents were mixed. If the closeness of the Jewish-Christian communities to the Synagogue depended on the varying number of regulations to which they demanded obedience, so their closeness to normative Christianity was governed by the content of their faith. Elements of orthodox dogma are found among their teachings, but in an incomplete and, as it were, stunted form. If they were heretics, then they were heretics in a negative way, heretics, so to speak, by omission. This is what their opponents meant when they called them "Ebionites," though originally they may well have given the name to themselves.[5] The "poverty" in which they gloried was that which, according to the teaching of Christ, is a condition of entry into the kingdom of God.[6] But when applied to their doctrinal position, the name "Ebionite" expressed contempt. It denoted their inability to embrace the wealth of speculation in which the orthodox delighted. It indicated, in particular, the rudimentary nature of their Christology, which, knowing nothing of the developments and excesses of orthodoxy, remained in a backward stage of doctrinal development.[7]

But here again the picture needs some correction. The definition we have accepted is a description of Jewish Christianity in what might be called its classical form. It is a description of Palestinian Jewish Christianity, the successor in Palestine of the primitive Christian community.[8] But it leaves out of account other manifestations of Christian life and thought that did not stem so directly from the original apostolic form of Christianity but that just as surely deserve the name of Jewish Christianity.

Within the early Catholic Church itself there were a number of believers who, though they were not in the strict sense of the word heretical and did not form themselves into independent bodies, nevertheless took it upon themselves to keep some of the Mosaic rules. The importance and size of this minority varied from one area to another. As far as our information goes, such Christians were distinguished by no doctrinal peculiarities whatever. And orthodox writers, though they express annoyance with them, never challenge their right to belong to the body of the Church.[9] The conciliary canons and the writings of the fathers call such people "Judaizers," and condemn them. This is surely a second form of Jewish Christianity, more difficult by nature to pin down and define than the preceding form. The fact that it was not an organized and coherent body has insured that the majority of the manuals of Church history and of the history of doctrine pass over it in silence.[10] It nevertheless represents an important manifestation of the impact of Judaism on early Christianity. Indeed, when we consider how widespread it was, we ought perhaps to judge it the most important manifestation of all. The historian has no right to ignore it.

A third type of Jewish Christianity is made up of the syncretizing sects described by the Church's heresiologists. Such sects were not content to assimilate themselves to Judaism in matters of practice, but in addition advanced distinctive doctrines that were not only radically at variance with those of orthodoxy but at the same time far removed from the doctrinal poverty of the Ebionites. This type is a specially complex group and is made up of a motley assembly of

bodies that flourished both within Palestine and without. I can do no
more at this point than note their existence.

We may say, in brief, that there existed not a single phenomenon
called Jewish Christianity, but several Jewish Christianities. These
were doubtless interconnected but were nonetheless clearly differen-
tiated from each other. The description "Jewish Christianity,"
which at first sight appears so straightforward, turns out on
examination to cover quite a number of different phenomena.
Jewish Christianity did not remain the same either from place to
place or from period to period. If the simplicity of the phenomenon
has often been taken for granted hitherto, that is only because
we have allowed ourselves to be misled by our own terminology.
The word *Ebionism* is doubtless at the bottom of much of the
confusion. The confusion also springs from an erroneous understanding of the Judaism of the period, an understanding that has
long gone unchallenged. It was assumed that the structure of
Judaism was, in contrast with the complex nature of Christianity,
comparatively simple. Recent study has shown that in fact Judaism
contained numerous different strands, differing not only in their
thought but in their piety. It has in particular brought into
prominence the phenomenon of Jewish gnosticism. All this has
allowed us to correct the false idea of Jewish Christianity to which
our false idea of Judaism had given rise.[11] Jewish Christianity was
as varied and diverse in its forms as non-Christian Judaism for, as
Harnack has already noted,[12] Jewish Christianity reproduced the
main features of all the different kinds of Judaism. Any kind of
Judaism could be taken over and have a Christian stamp superimposed on it.

This diversity was generally not recognized by the ancient writers
from whom we derive our information about Jewish Christianity. It is
partly at their door, perhaps even primarily at their door, that we
must lay the blame for the misunderstandings that abound concerning Jewish Christianity. Especially are they responsible for the
confusion concerning Jewish Christianity in Palestine. It is the
Palestinian Jewish Christians whom most authors call Ebionites. The
exceptions are Epiphanius, who calls them Nazarenes, and Jerome,
who uses both descriptions.

II

Our principal sources of information may be divided into two
categories: first, the catalogues of heresies, beginning with that of

Irenaeus and proceeding through Hippolytus, pseudo-Tertullian, and Philaster to Epiphanius. Second, we have a series of authors who give us information of a less systematized, more occasional nature, in particular, Justin Martyr, Origen, Eusebius, and Jerome. The difference between the two groups corresponds broadly to a geographical one. The former group, except for Epiphanius, are Westerners either by birth or residence, and for this reason could only possess an indirect knowledge of Jewish Christianity. The latter group, however, consists of Eastern writers. Their testimony has the great advantage of being firsthand and independent. The facts we glean from them are therefore of real value. The catalogues of heresies, by contrast, borrow from and reproduce each other quite freely, and in addition the classification and systematization that writers of this sort of work are obliged to indulge in have placed certain limitations upon them.

These heresiological works are preoccupied with doctrine. They deal essentially with the intellectual aspects of the heresies, treating them as theological systems, schools of thought, and only secondarily as religious bodies, as churches. The actual religious life of the communities concerned is thus left in the background. Now, as far as the Jewish Christians, properly so called, are concerned, it is the doctrinal aspect that is secondary, since, if they are at all distinguishable from normative Christianity in point of doctrine, it is only by their lack of theological speculation. Their chief characteristic, i.e., their maintenance of Jewish ritual practices, was doubtless not unknown to the heresiologists, but it is not on this aspect of the matter that they choose to place the emphasis. The picture they give is thus a curiously distorted one.

But even granted the limitations of their method, and considering Jewish Christianity only from the doctrinal standpoint, the heresiologists' presentation is marred by the imposition of a quite arbitrary scheme of classification. They were very anxious to classify the various dissident bodies in families, according to their common features. But in doing so they often seized on superficial resemblances, resemblances connected with matters important to themselves, such as theodicy or Christology, but which were sometimes of secondary importance to the sects concerned, or not even fundamental to their views.

The Ebionites are usually dealt with in company with the systems of Cerinthus and Carpocrates.[13] The regularity of this feature of the lists demonstrates the artificiality of the classification criteria employed. It rests on the alleged fact that all three rejected the miraculous birth of Jesus, making him the son of Joseph. Their agreement on this point is of very little importance. To make it a principle of classification is to ignore at once the profound differences among the three sects and the genuinely distinctive features of Jewish Christianity. Jewish Christianity's theodicy was the same as that of orthodoxy, and its Christology was radically different from that of the two docetic gnostic systems to which it is claimed to be related. Irenaeus, for example, makes Jewish Christianity merely a doctrinal variant of the heresy of Cerinthus, declaring that on the subject of the person of Christ they shared the same opinion.[14] He goes on immediately afterwards to give a fairly exact summary of Jewish Christian attitudes to scripture and the law. This is the crux of the matter, but Irenaeus manifestly does not recognize it as such. Because he has based his classification on a defective principle, the real point has escaped him. For "in their case it was not a question of any real heresy, such as those of Cerinthus or Carpocrates, but merely of a late survival of an undeveloped primitive Judaic-Christianity."[15]

The danger inherent in this kind of presentation of the subject matter, though its results are still not fully apparent in Irenaeus, looms larger in the works of his successors. The system takes control of the facts in a quite disturbing way. Several writers, treating Ebionism as a doctrinal system, and assuming, no doubt, that every doctrinal system necessarily originates in someone's brain, provide it with a mythical father called Ebion. Anxious to express the affinities and connections of their families of doctrines in a concrete way, they made Ebion a disciple of Cerinthus, himself a disciple of Carpocrates. This blatant misrepresentation of the chronological relationships turned the direct heirs of primitive Palestinian Christianity into latter-day sectarians of the third remove.[16]

They carried out this inversion of chronology on the principle that Christian truth, as it was expressed in the eternal and immutable affirmations of orthodoxy, necessarily antedates all the corruptions of it that have appeared. Hegesippus said, according to Eusebius, that the primitive Church "was called 'virgin,' for it has not yet been corrupted by vain teachings."[17] Ebionism was therefore a late development, like all the heresies. It was reckoned as having been outside the Church from the beginning, a sectarian movement from its very origins.

As a result of plagiarism, the picture becomes more and more distorted as we pass from one author to another. At the end of the series comes Philaster. He makes no mention at all of the Judaizing character of the Ebionites. He passes over them quite rapidly, reporting only that "Ebion, a disciple of Cerinthus, shared many of his errors." He does not stop to tell us which errors these were. Later, however, he does expand a little, telling us that the characteristic error of these people was that "they made the Saviour into a man, the son of Joseph according to the flesh, and with nothing divine in him."[18] After this, he passes on to consider Valentinus, regarding him as chronologically the successor to Ebion. In this curious presentation the essentials are blurred, the incidentals are exaggerated ridiculously out of proportion, and furthermore, as we shall soon see, the actual statements of fact are wrong.

In order to obtain a more accurate idea of the origin and character of the Jewish-Christian movement, it is necessary to go back to that evidence which has come down to us in less systematic form. The witness of Justin Martyr is especially valuable.

The subject of Jewish Christianity crops up in his dialogue only once, in connection with a discussion of ritual observance. Justin asserts that Judaism's ritual rules have become in part impracticable since the destruction of the temple and that they are therefore of no importance. But he adds that, in his opinion, a Jew who is converted to Christianity may, if he wishes, continue to obey these rules without danger to his soul, provided always that he does not attempt to impose them on gentile Christians by making them out to be necessary to salvation.[19] He goes so far as to admit that a convert from paganism who at the instigation of a converted Jew submits to the Mosaic law may also, nevertheless, be saved.[20] Legalism only constitutes a mortal danger if it leads on to apostasy. When a Christian passes from Jewish Christianity to Judaism and renounces Christ, he is lost for certain, just as the unconverted Jews are. He can only be saved if, before his death, he repents of his error.[21]

Justin's opinion is interesting in a number of respects. On the question under dispute it may be summarized thus: ritual observance is in itself a thing indifferent and inoffensive. It should neither be forbidden nor imposed. To submit to ritual rules is the sign of a timorous mind, but it is not by any means a sin.[22]

This liberal attitude is expressed in an age when Jewish Christianity does not yet constitute a body separate from the Church as a whole, but merely a tendency within the Church. This situation, arrived at by means of a compromise worked out by the primitive community, was an unstable one. At the council of Jerusalem the Hellenists had had some difficulty in getting their point of view accepted. But shortly afterwards, by a sudden reversal of fortunes, it was Jewish Christianity that was struggling for survival. Justin tolerated it, but around him voices were raised challenging the legitimacy of the whole idea of Christian adherence to the Jewish law. The more the gentile element predominated, the louder were the voices raised in protest. Justin does in fact inform us, in a reply to a question of Trypho's, that his view of the matter is not universally acknowledged and that some Christians, less tolerant than he, refuse to have any dealings with Judaizers and deny that they have any hope of salvation. On his own submission, his attitude is a conservative and dated one.[23] At this juncture, therefore, Jewish Christianity is in process of being rejected by the Church and ranked as a sect. Only a little later, in the time of Irenaeus, this rejection was an accomplished fact.

The excommunication of the Jewish Christians was carried out not because their doctrines diverged so much from orthodoxy, but because their practice did so. This, too, we learn from Justin. Neither in the passage already referred to nor in the one concerning the virgin birth is the doctrine of the Jewish Christians called in question.[24] If differences of doctrine did exist, Justin apparently considered them to be of negligible importance. This fact by itself is enough to show how unwarranted is the description of Ebionism provided by later heresiologists.

Their cardinal error is that they looked at the situation of their own time, noted the divergences between Jewish Christianity and orthodoxy that doubtless existed, and projected them back into the period of the sect's origins. In fact, these divergences had arisen only over the years, and they had arisen, in large measure, not because the Ebionites drifted further and further from orthodoxy, but because orthodoxy itself was continually developing toward greater precision of doctrine. The Jewish Christians, left out of the mainstream of this development, represented what was really a static or, one might even say, fossilized form of Christianity. The "system" of Jewish Christianity is a mere abstraction, produced by the elaboration of ecclesiastical dogma itself. Jewish Christianity's adversaries assumed that the matters that at that time absorbed them in debate were the fundamentals of the faith, and had always been so. The distinctive marks of Jewish Christianity were, I suppose, not exactly accidental, since they represented the survival of a position that Catholicism had abandoned, but the only important ones among them were concerned with ritual observance. Its opponents failed to appreciate this and misrepresented it entirely by ascribing to it an intellectual content that was not only too rigidly defined, but that did not accurately represent the beliefs the Jewish Christians held.

It looks, in fact, as if the heresiologists in their descriptions of Ebionite Jewish Christianity have ascribed to it characteristics borrowed from Judaizing gnostic sects. These sects, in contrast with Jewish Christianity, differed from orthodoxy not by virtue of possessing an undeveloped and primitive theology, but by having developed their theological speculations along a different line from that followed by the Church at large. They shared with the Church the characteristic of having emerged from the primitive stage of doctrinal poverty. But the speculations peculiar to them led in a quite different direction from those of the Church, and these gnostic bodies did exhibit a connection with early Ebionism since, in common with the Ebionites, they were attached to all or part of the Jewish ritual law. The heresiologists did not always recognize that they were faced here with two distinct, though not entirely unconnected phenomena.[25]

There are, however, some exceptions to this general ignorance of the true nature of Jewish Christianity. The most clear-sighted of the Christian authors is, without a doubt, Origen. He, at least, clearly perceived and distinguished the features of Ebionism that connected on the one side with Judaism and on the other with the primitive Church. When Celsus criticizes Jewish converts to Christianity for having changed their name and mode of life, Origen says in reply that Celsus does not realize "that those of the Jews who believe in Jesus have not abandoned the law of their fathers; they live in accordance with it and their name is derived from the poverty of that law. For among the Jews a poor man is called *ebion*, and those of the Jews who recognize Jesus as the Christ call themselves 'Εβιωναῖοι." He adds, "Peter himself seems to have observed for a long time the Jewish customs in accordance with the law of Moses, as if he had not learnt that Jesus had exalted the spiritual law above the literal law."[26] Origen then gives an accurate exposition of the dissensions between Palestinians and Hellenists in the first Christian community, following the account in Acts. This is to put Jewish Christianity into its proper historical perspective, something the majority of the heresiologists completely fail to do.

Origen is nevertheless not entirely alone. Others, without reaching such a correct assessment, did look in the right direction. This is especially true of Epiphanius. He perceived the real origin of the Jewish-Christian movement. His work is marred by the addition of new factual material that is of doubtful accuracy, and by an insufficiently critical method.

Epiphanius gives us accounts of Jewish Christianity under two different headings, Nazarenes and Ebionites. He applies the word *Nazarenes* to ordinary Jewish Christians, the sort that the majority of authors call Ebionites. He keeps the term *Ebionites* for a body of Jewish-Christian gnostics.[27]

This use of the two terms seems to be erroneous. The two titles do not properly refer to two different sects but are in reality interchangeable and virtually synonymous. Jerome proves this quite cate-

gorically: *Quid dicam de Hebionitis? ... Quos vulgo Nazaraeos noncupant.*[28]
All the same, St. Jerome, making his observations and doing his
writing in Palestine, apparently has in mind only the classical type of
Jewish Christianity, the Palestinian one. His Ebionites/Nazarenes are
equivalent simply to the "Nazarenes" of Epiphanius.

There is thus, in the clumsy and inadequate use Epiphanius makes
of his terminology, the echo of a historical fact that Jerome neglects,
viz., the complexity of what may be called Jewish Christianity in the
wider sense. The actual phenomenon was a varied one, and
Epiphanius was faced with two terms by which it might be described,
both hallowed by usage. The one was perhaps more popular—*quos
vulgo noncupant*—the other less commonly used. In his love of
classification Epiphanius cannot bring himself to admit that the two
mean the same thing.[29] The rigid way in which Epiphanius deploys
his terminology is artificial, or forced, but there really was a
difference, nevertheless, between the rude Jewish Christianity of the
people at Pella and the burgeoning Jewish-Christian sects in Palestine
and elsewhere that were of more or less gnostic character.

I shall leave out of account Epiphanius's Ebionites and deal only
with those whom he describes as Nazarenes. Epiphanius knows that
the word *Nazarenes* was the first title applied to Christians. "Thus all
Christians were at that time called Nazarenes." "Everyone called the
Christians by this name because of the town of Nazareth."[30] He also
knows that in his own time the Nazarenes were "Jews by race" and
were a Judaizing sect. He is the only one among the heresiologists who
emphasizes this peculiarity. His definition of Jewish Christianity is an
entirely accurate one. "Only one thing distinguishes them from Jews,
as only one thing distinguishes them from Christians. They disagree
with the Jews in that they have made an act of faith in Christ. They
distinguish themselves from Christians in that they are still bound by
the law, including the law of circumcision, sabbath observance, and
the rest."[31]

In essentials, that is the same view of the matter as we find in
Origen. Nevertheless, having recognized clearly both the primitive
meaning of the name *Nazarenes* and the really distinctive features of
the Nazarene sect Epiphanius does not go on to connect his two
insights and see the sectarians of his day as the late but authentic
legatees of the first Christian community. Although he did realize that
what he was faced with was a phenomenon with a history behind it,
he could not admit that a heresy might be derived in direct line from
Jesus and his immediate disciples. In accounting for the origin of his
Nazarenes, he has therefore to fall back on a somewhat embarrassing
explanation. The sect began, he says, in Pella, when all the Jerusalem

Christians, warned by a divine vision, had fled from the city during the siege.[32] The fact that they bore a name that had previously been applied to the whole Christian community is pure coincidence. The identity of the name is nevertheless awkward, and Epiphanius goes to some trouble to explain it.

As applied to the first Christians, there is no difficulty with the term. It had at the time no other connotations, and Jesus himself is called a Nazarene by the scriptures. And this would still be a legitimate name for Christians if the sectarians had not monopolized it and brought it into disrepute. But it is a name to which they are not entitled. They were called it in error, just as all kinds of sectarians, Manichaeans, Marcionites, gnostics and others are often called Christians, though they are not so in reality.[33] Each of these heresies is pleased to add the name *Christian* to the one it properly bears, because for them it is an honorable name, in spite of the fact that they have usurped it.

Thus Epiphanius not only denies that the Nazarenes, from the time of their origins, were ever part of the Catholic Church, but challenges their right to be called Christians. "They are Jews, and nothing more."[34] The information he conveys, added to that given by other authors, provides us with a fairly accurate picture of the sect.

III

The basic characteristic of Ebionism was its respect for ritual observance, especially the rite of circumcision.[35] Although they do not always lay emphasis on this feature, the witnesses are unanimous in mentioning it. Irenaeus adds the interesting footnote that they worshiped Jerusalem as though it were the dwelling place of God, from which we deduce that they turned towards the holy city when they prayed.[36] As late as the fourth century the liturgical language of the Ebionites appears to have been Hebrew.[37]

The significance of this attachment to the ancient Jewish law differed according to whether the Jewish Christians were content to impose it on themselves alone or endeavored to inflict it upon gentile converts too. In the former case all that adherence to the law achieved, perhaps all it was meant to achieve, was the creation of differences of status among the believers. Those who observed the rules, and in particular the rite of circumcision, constituted themselves a kind of privileged minority. Their adherence to the law drew attention to the fact that their acceptance of Christianity had not deprived them of the dignity and eminence of being Israelites. This made non-Jewish

Christians into a lower order of believers. The distinction corresponds to the one that existed in the Synagogue between semiproselytes and Jews who observed the whole law. It is in this way that the pseudo-Clementine literature draws a distinction between circumcised Christians and the rest. It does not deny that the latter may be saved; it merely refuses to admit that they have been fully initiated into the faith.[38]

When, on the other hand, Jewish Christians attempt to submit all believers, whatever their racial origin, to the law, the implication is that the keeping of the law is indispensable to salvation, and that no one can be a Christian without remaining or becoming a Jew. The former attitude runs counter to the egalitarian and universalistic spirit of Christianity; the latter destroys the fundamental basis of Christianity itself, as St. Paul laid it down. In either case, the Jewish Christians were in head-on conflict with Pauline teaching, and it is another characteristic of theirs that they displayed a strong aversion to the apostle.

Apostolum Paulum recusant, apostatam eum legis dicentes.[39] In consequence of this, the Ebionites excluded the epistles of St. Paul from their canon of scripture. Their canon was simply the Old Testament, and therefore coincided exactly with that of the Jews, except insofar as they had their own special way of interpreting the prophets, which is what Irenaeus tells us.[40] Irenaeus gives us no further details about this. Anti-Paulinism seems to have been a feature of Ebionite Christianity throughout its history and in all its forms. Origen distinguishes two categories of Ebionites, those who accepted the virgin birth and those who did not, but he credits both of them with antipathy to St. Paul.[41] The Jewish-Christian sects as a whole shared this hostility.

We are also told that the Ebionites used only one gospel, but our informants do not agree as to what was its name or its distinguishing characteristics. According to Irenaeus, followed by Epiphanius, they used St. Matthew.[42] Eusebius, on the contrary, calls their gospel the Gospel of the Hebrews.[43] This is a thorny problem, which has been much discussed by modern critics, but the few facts at our disposal make its solution impossible with any degree of certainty.[44]

The use by certain Christians in Egypt of a gospel called the Gospel of the Hebrews is attested by Clement of Alexandria and by Origen.[45] But this composition, which existed in Greek, has evidently nothing to do with the one the Jewish Christians made use of in Palestine.[46] Epiphanius says explicitly that the Jewish Christians in Palestine read not only the Bible but the gospel too in Hebrew.[47] This is probably not therefore the original title of their gospel. Perhaps it was normally indicated by the title Hebrew Gospel (τὸ Ἑβραϊκόν) and became later, by confusion and by comparison with the Gospel of the Egyptians, the Gospel according to the Hebrews, καθ' Ἑβραίους.[48]

If we accept what Papias tells us (or rather, what Eusebius says Papias tells us) about the *Logia* of Matthew, and if we relate what he says to the Gospel according to St. Matthew, we may be tempted to identify this *Ur-Matthäus* with the text of which Epiphanius speaks. This hypothesis has, however, been widely abandoned at the present time. St. Jerome also calls the gospel the Nazarenes used the Gospel of the Hebrews, and he too connects it with St. Matthew, but he says that the language was not Hebrew but Aramaic.[49] The connection of the Nazarenes' gospel with a canonical or precanonical Matthew seems assured, though whether this was Matthew's gospel in its original form, in the form of a Semitic translation, or, as is more likely, in an adapted version, we cannot say. It is not possible, in my opinion, to be more exact about what the connection was.

The peculiarities of Jewish-Christian usage, and even those of the Jewish-Christian canon, are relatively easy to determine. It is much more difficult, however, to throw any light on the peculiarities of their teaching. The difficulty lies, as I have already made clear, in the manner in which the heresiologists present their picture; in the frequently artificial correspondences they see between Jewish Christianity and other sects, and in the divergences and contradictions among their various accounts. We must simply give up the attempt to produce an exact or complete analysis of Jewish-Christian teaching, even if we restrict ourselves to that of the classical Nazarenes. With even better reason must we renounce any endeavor to reduce the diverse manifestations of Jewish Christianity to a single or coherent doctrinal system. There are distinct differences of view even within the dogmatic poverty of Jewish Christianity, just as there are differences within the wealth of Hellenistic speculation. This is the impression gained from an examination of the texts.

As far as theodicy is concerned, there does not seem to be any point of contention at all between the Ebionites and the orthodox. The differences bear essentially on Christology. *Qui autem dicuntur Ebionaei consentiunt quidem mundum a Deo factum; ea autem quae sunt erga Dominum similiter ut Cerinthes et Carpocrates opinantur.*[50] In contrast with the numerous gnostic systems that drew a distinction between the supreme God and the demiurge, and in contrast with the systems of Cerinthus and Carpocrates themselves,[51] the Jewish Christians maintained the same strictly biblical view of creation as orthodox Christianity. In both cases, of course, it was derived through Judaism. On the subject of the person of Christ, on the contrary, they held opinions at variance with those of the Church, without there being any complete uniformity of opinion among themselves.

These differences of opinion relate not only to the nature of Christ but at the same time to the circumstances of his birth. The first heresiologists, in relating the Christology of the Ebionites to that of Cerinthus, allege that they rejected the divinity of Christ. But the interpretations they ascribe to the Ebionites do not all accord with one another. Later authors, when the question arises of defining the Ebionites' doctrinal position in relation to that of orthodoxy, show more discretion.

If we could accept unreservedly the claim that the Ebionites held similar views to Cerinthus, we should be obliged to regard them as Adoptionists and Docetists. Irenaeus, followed closely by Hippolytus, tells us that according to Cerinthus the man Jesus, the son of Joseph and Mary, surpassed all other men in righteousness and wisdom, and was endowed with a Power called Christ, who made him "the herald of the unknown Father." But when the end came, "Christ departed from Jesus.... Jesus suffered and rose again, while Christ remained impassible, inasmuch as he was a spiritual being."[52]

Presented in this form, such a definition of Jewish-Christian belief is almost certainly false. The notion of an "unknown Father" smacks disquietingly of Marcionism. It is not compatible with the perfectly orthodox theodicy with which the same authors credit the Ebionites. If the world was the work of the true God, who is abundantly shown forth in His creation, He could hardly be "the unknown Father." Here we put our finger on a specially striking example of the failings of this method of classification. It sees a connection between two sects, a connection based on a single common feature. The similarity, though real enough, may be entirely fortuitous, but on the basis of it the two systems as a whole are arbitrarily assumed to be related. Furthermore, on the basis of a common appellation—in this case the name Ebionites—a number of fundamentally different phenomena may be treated together. It is very likely that the syncretistic sects, which combined a Judaizing practice with a gnostic analysis of the biblical revelation, proposed a Docetic dichotomy of the person of Jesus Christ. But it is safe to assert that a system of this sort can hardly have sprung from the Palestinian Ebionites as that term is usually understood.

I am equally sceptical when Hippolytus goes on to describe the alleged reasons that Jesus was chosen as the fleshly vehicle for Christ. According to the Ebionites, he says, "Jesus was justified by fulfilling the law. And therefore it was that he was named the Christ of God."[53] Up to this point there is nothing unlikely in the statement. Jesus was a model of legalism who on that account, and on his own merits, was elected to the position of Messiah. This idea seems to be in tune with the cast of mind of strict Jewish Christianity, which was not very receptive to metaphysical speculations, but ever ready, by contrast, to emphasize the importance of good works. But what follows is more alarming.

It was because of his exceptional fidelity to the law that Jesus was given such a distinction by God, for "not one of the rest [of the Jews] had observed completely the law. For if even any other had fulfilled the commandments of the law, he would have been Christ. And [the Ebionites allege] that they themselves also, when in like manner they fulfil the law, are able to become Christs; for they assert that our Lord himself was a man like any other." Leaving aside the last phrase, it is no longer Marcion that we are reminded of, but of his master, St. Paul. The idea that the law could not be observed in all its fullness is entirely Pauline, and so is the idea of the Christian's identification with Christ. But for Paul the impossibility of fulfilling the law provides the motive for rejecting it, and the believer becomes identified with Christ by a mystical process in which he is made a participant in grace, which raises him above his fleshly ($\psi v\chi\iota\kappa\acute{o}s$) condition and absorbs him into the spirit ($\pi v\epsilon\hat{v}\mu\alpha$) of the Lord. We have here a kind of upside-down Paulinism. It is by keeping the law as faithfully as Christ himself that the Christian becomes identified with him.

It is certainly not impossible that in some Jewish-Christian circles Pauline ideas were used in this topsy-turvy manner. But it may be confidently asserted that the mystical notion of "Christification," even in this curious form, with legal observance taking the place of grace, was not the invention of the people of Pella, the spiritual heirs of James the Nazirite.

No doubt it is not really a question of absorption into Christ, and of being identified with him in that intimate way. It is rather a matter of becoming equal to him by imitation. This idea of a multiplicity of Christs is no less surprising.[54] Even when it is remembered that they refused to acknowledge Christ as anything more than a man chosen by God, it may nevertheless be doubted whether the Ebionites conceived the ambition to "become Christs themselves." I can scarcely believe that any Jew, whatever ideas he held about the Messiah, ever thought of becoming equal to him. Besides, if up to the time of Jesus the Jews were held to be incapable of keeping the whole law, how were the Jewish Christians to do any better, if they had only human means at their disposal? The ability of Christ's disciples to keep the whole law presupposes the help of a new and supernatural element, which we might well call grace. Jesus was the first to benefit from this, and the fact that he was the first gives him a primacy for all time. Once identified with Christ, he becomes the one who dispenses grace. It is not therefore simply "by following the example of Jesus" that one may hope to achieve that fullness of observance of the law which makes the believers into Christs, but by participation in some mystical way in the Christ-Jesus.[55] We thus find ourselves back with Paulinism. Transplanted into strictly Jewish-Christian soil, this notion of assimilation to Christ becomes hardly meaningful, and quite impossibly obscure.

It is within the tradition of Jewish monotheism that we must seek the explication of Nazarene Christology.

As we have seen, Hippolytus's Ebionites saw Jesus as "a man like any other."[56] Identical or closely similar formulae are found in the works of other heresiologists. If Jesus was superior to ordinary mankind, it was by virtue of an election of the same kind as that of the prophets. *Sicut omnes prophetas, sic et eum gratiam Dei habuisse adserebat*, says Philaster concerning Ebion.[57] According to Tertullian, the Ebionites ascribed to Jesus an eminence above that of the prophets, and though they did not, like the Docetists, distinguish between Jesus, an ordinary man, and Christ, the preexistent divine power, they did believe that an angel dwelt in him.[58]

All the heresiologists are agreed on the Ebionites' rejection of the virgin birth. *Neque intelligere volentes quoniam Spiritus Sanctus advenit in Mariam, et virtus Altissimi obumbravit eam.*[59] Jesus is therefore the son of Joseph. Irenaeus says that, in order to support their opinion, the Ebionites followed Theodotion and Aquila in their translation of Isaiah 7:14, Ἰδοὺ ἡ νεᾶνις ἐν γαστρὶ ᾽έξει καὶ τέξεται υἱόν, rejecting the παρθένος of the Septuagint, which was the official translation of orthodox Christianity.[60]

These assertions cannot be accepted without hesitation. They need to be set beside the testimony of other authors. According to Origen, the question of the virgin birth split the Ebionites into two distinct camps, Ἐβιωναῖοι ἀμφότεροι, who nevertheless agreed in their repudiation of St. Paul and his epistles.[61] The one group preferred orthodox views of the virgin birth, the other taught that Jesus was born like other men.[62]

Eusebius, too, notes the existence of two parties. For the one "held him [Jesus] to be a plain and ordinary man who had achieved righteousness merely by the progress of his character, and who had been born naturally from Mary and her husband." The others, who were also called Ebionites, "do not deny that the Lord was born of a virgin and the Holy Spirit, but, like the former group, they refuse to acknowledge his pre-existence."[63] Epiphanius maintains a discreet reserve on this question. He says he does not know for certain whether the Nazarenes share Cerinthus's errors regarding the person of Christ, or whether they acknowledge his birth from Mary through the operation of the Holy Spirit.[64]

St. Jerome, however, is quite categorical on the matter, and asserts as clearly as one could wish the complete conformity of Ebionite Christology with that of orthodoxy. *Credunt in Christum filium Dei, natum de virgine Maria, et eum dicunt esse qui sub Pontio Pilato passus et resurrexit, in quem et nos credimus.*[65] Thus, according to Jerome, there was complete agreement between the Ebionites and the orthodox with respect to Jesus' divine sonship and virgin birth, and the reality of his passion and resurrection. There was agreement, that is to say, at all the points at which the heresiologists report fundamental divergences. All the doctrinal peculiarities ascribed to the Jewish Christians, Monarchism, Adoptionism, Docetism, and all the rest, are blown away by Jerome as a cloud of mythology.

It is difficult to reconcile all the different statements. It is also difficult to dismiss out of hand the evidence of Origen, Eusebius, and Jerome, who knew the Jewish Christians far more intimately than any of the other writers. Faced with these contradictory assertions, two explanations are possible. We may postulate that Ebionite Christology underwent a development that brought it closer and closer to orthodoxy until the two positions were identical. The varying statements about it would, if plotted chronologically, lend themselves to this explanation. The oldest authors, namely, Irenaeus and those dependent on him, describe the divergences of Jewish Christianity from orthodoxy. The later ones, Jerome and Epiphanius, throw doubt on them or deny them. In the interim, first Origen and then Eusebius speak of two tendencies. It is possible that one at first predominated and was at the beginning of Ebionite history the only one or the controlling one, but that gradually it gave way to the other, under the influence of orthodox thinking, until it disappeared entirely by the end of the fourth century.

However, we are still faced with the fact that Justin knew nothing of any discrepancy between Jewish Christian teaching and that of orthodoxy, and that his conception of Jewish Christianity, as a movement in favor of Judaizing practices, agrees with that of Jerome. Another explanation therefore commends itself. It is that even Jewish Christianity in the narrow sense of the term was not, as far as its teaching was concerned, a homogeneous body. Leaving aside the fact that the heresiologists found it possible to attribute to the Ebionites the peculiarities of other Judaizing sects, Jerome on the one side and Irenaeus and his imitators on the other have neither been able to see more than one aspect of the truth.

After all, the two explanations are not irreconcilable. Both for Jewish Christianity in the broad sense (i.e., including the syncretistic sects) and for Palestinian Ebionism the same is true. They varied from time to time and from place to place. If some Jewish Christians found themselves able to adopt doctrinal positions indistinguishable from those of orthodoxy, yet without letting themselves be absorbed by orthodoxy, that is no reason to suppose that all were in the same condition. The internal divisions that Origen speaks of, and which there is no reason whatever to doubt, might well have lasted until the time of Jerome without his observing them.

A double conclusion emerges from this analysis. First, the poverty of Ebionism, if it is understood as simplicity and homogeneity, cannot be accepted without question. Second, the essence of the movement, the feature it displays in all its forms and is noted by all who offer descriptions of it, lies in its attitude toward observance of the law. As far as Justin is concerned, this is the only point at issue; and for Jerome the Jewish Christians' stand on this matter is sufficient, even when divergences of doctrine are all smoothed away, to induce him to deny their right to be called Christian.[66]

IV

The Jewish Christians' regard for the law was not enough, however, to gain them recognition as proper Jews. It was at any rate not enough for St. Jerome. *Nec Judaei sunt, nec Christiani.* Epiphanius, by contrast, regards them as nothing else but Jews. But these are simply the personal judgments of individual Christian writers. The real point of interest is what the Synagogue thought of them.

According to Epiphanius, there was implacable hostility between the Jewish Christians and the Jews. Three times a day, he tells us, in the course of their liturgy, the Jews call down the divine curse on the Nazarenes.[67] We have in fact already noted the existence of this formula of anathematization in the Synagogue liturgy. The real problem is to know who are the *nozrim* at whom it is aimed.

It is not at all certain that they are to be identified with those whom Epiphanius calls the Nazarenes. It is true that when St. Jerome, in his turn, draws attention to the maledictions the Pharisees, i.e., the orthodox Synagogue, call down upon the heretics, he identifies these *minim* with his "Nazarenes" (Jewish Christians). But other writings of St. Jerome prove that the Synagogue's anathema envisaged a far wider group than merely the Jewish Christians. It took in the whole Church. *Ter per singulos dies in synagogis sub nomine Nazarenorum anathematizant vocabulum Christianum.*[68]

It seems to me that the clear implication of these words is that for the Jews the word *Nazarene* had kept its original significance and was synonymous with *Christian*. The term survived from a bygone age when the membership of the Church was drawn predominantly from Judaism and when Christianity could still, because of this, reasonably be thought of as a Jewish heresy. The meaning of the term in Jewish use does not correspond to the meaning it bore in Christian circles. Both sides applied it to a dissident body; the Church used it of the Jewish Christians, and the Synagogue of the Church.

This interpretation is confirmed by the still firmer assertion of Justin. Addressing Trypho, he accuses the Jews of "cursing in your synagogues those that believe in Christ." The context leaves hardly any doubt about the identity of the accursed, for Justin straightaway goes on: "You have no power to lay hands on us, thanks to those who now govern us; but each time you have had the power, you have made use of it."[69] On this evidence the gentile Christians are involved in the anathema just as the Jewish Christians are.

If such was the case in the second century, at a period when the ex-pagan part of the Church's membership was already gaining ground, there is no reason to believe that things had changed by the end of the fourth century, and that the malediction had by then become restricted and took account only of the Jewish Christians. The hatred for the Catholic Church can only have increased with its increasing success and with its triumph under Constantine.[70] We still have no evidence of the Jewish reactions to the Ebionites strictly so called. In acknowledging that they were swept up in an all-embracing hostility to every form of Christianity, we may imagine that the hostility in their case took on a special color of its own. It remains to be discovered whether the fact that they were Jews as well as Christians, and that they maintained their attachment to a large part of the law, made them more acceptable to the rabbis then ordinary Christians or less so. Were they brothers at war with each other, all the more bitterly at war because they were brothers? Or were they "separated brethren," with the regretful sympathy that phrase implies, brothers who, it was hoped, would some day be gathered in?

The answer to this question can only come from Jewish sources. St. Jerome makes the word *Nazarenes* synonymous with *minim*. I have already expressed my opinion about this identification, which seems to me too rigid to be altogether acceptable.[71] It arbitrarily limits the term *minim* to only one of the categories it properly includes. It actually means nothing more precise than "heretics." It undoubtedly includes Christians, and even tended, in practice, to be limited to them alone as the other forms of Jewish heterodoxy receded in importance. But originally it was not applied exclusively to them. There is at least no doubt that, if it did become synonymous with *Nazarenes*, it was in the broad sense in which the Jews understood that term; it included gentile Christians on the same footing as the others.

There are even good reasons, as we have seen, for supposing that it came to be used with the gentile Christians primarily in mind. If my interpretation is correct, there were two ways of becoming involved in *minuth*, either by gross dereliction with regard to the moral or ritual law, or by the expression of openly heterodox views on doctrine. The latter really envisages a challenge to the doctrine of God's unity, which was the only one on which rabbinic Judaism proved completely immovable, and it is this aspect of *minuth* which seems to me to be the vital one. This was the one thing that marked off orthodox Judaism equally from the Jewish gnostic dualists and from the orthodox Christians. Hence, the Jewish Christians, since they were faithful to the law, could only be strictly guilty of *minuth* if they accepted the creed of the Catholic Church. Now they did not all do so.

St. Jerome's Ebionites, who held to an orthodox Christology, were of course, as he himself says, *minim*. But by contrast, those who denied the supernatural birth and divinity of Christ could not be called *minim* without an abuse of terminology. Since the Jewish populace at large was doubtless neither well informed about nor particularly interested in the niceties of Christian theology, such an abuse of terminology meant nothing to them. We may, on the other hand, be more confident about the discrimination of their scholars. It is hard to believe that these specialists in casuistry and masters of the fine distinction had not grasped the difference between Catholic dogma and the rudimentary Christology of the first disciples and their spiritual heirs. We are therefore justified in searching the Talmudic literature for a name that applies specifically to the Jewish Christians. A recent work[72] has drawn attention, in this connection, to the term *posh'e yisrael*.

In itself the term is no more self-explanatory than *minim*. Used alone, without any determinant, the active participle *posh'im* means "rebels." In a religious context it indicated those who rebel against and transgress the divine law, sinners, in other words. It is with this meaning that it is found frequently in the Bible.[73] In post-biblical literature, which is what interests us at the moment, the word appears generally in the construct, in the phrase *posh'e yisrael*.[74]

The evidence suggests, then, that it refers to Jewish sinners, to those who are in rebellion against the law of Israel, which is the law of God. In a period in which the people of Israel was in essence simply a religious community, the phrase must necessarily have a religious content. Some texts contrast the *posh'e yisrael*, the black sheep of the chosen flock, with the *posh'e ummoth ha-'olam* ("sinners of the nations of the world") i.e., the gentile world, for whom the state of sin is in some sense congenital and normal.[75] The peculiarity of the *posh'e yisrael* is that they remain, even in their disgrace, recognized members of the Synagogue. This, it seems, is the whole difference between a *poshea'* and a *min*. The latter is of a different and evil "kind." Whether the *min* himself wishes it to be so or not, there is between him and the Jew an absolute distinction. The *poshea'*, on the contrary, remains a *poshea' yisrael*, in rebellion against the people's law but still within the people. The most satisfactory translation in this case seems to be "wicked Jew" or "bad Jew."[76] The word preserves that meaning, in fact, to this day in the Yiddish spoken by the Jewish communities of central Europe. It will be familiar to readers of *L'Ami Fritz*, who will recall that the old *rebbe* uses it on a number of occasions.

Although the term *posh'e yisrael* is more restricted in its application than the word *minim*, and necessarily so, since it is applied only within the Synagogue, it does not at first sight allow us to be more exact about its content. Just what kind of rebellion does it envisage? What categories of sinners does it include? Are their sins infractions of the law or aberrations of doctrine? Such questions are very difficult to settle. Again we must refrain from demanding too much precision of the word. It is susceptible of being used in a number of different senses. And before attempting to solve the problem facing us, it is necessary to state it properly. We ought not to be asking whether all the *posh'im* were Jewish Christians but whether the term was ever applied to Christians at all.[77]

It is certain that these sinners were members of the Synagogue. What is more surprising is that the rabbis readily recognized this membership and acknowledged that the *posh'im* were entitled to it. R. Simon the Pious asserts this forcefully when he says that a fast day that the *posh'im* do not observe is not a regular fast.[78] During the period when the temple was still standing, it was legitimate to accept their offerings.[79] What then was held against them? Rab is obliged to give an explanation to his Babylonian disciples, who were unfamiliar with the term *posh'e yisrael* (we know that the *minim* remained for a long while unknown in Babylon).[80] The *posh'im*, he says, are "those who do not wear the phylacteries." It is obvious that this cannot be an exhaustive definition. It is an entirely empirical one and simply points to the one matter that, in that particular community, a third-century Jewish scholar took to be the principal complaint against the dissidents.

More generally, and in spite of their preserving the rite of circumcision and their keeping of the festivals, the *posh'im* are accused of following the ways of the gentiles, of being too much inclined to assimilate themselves to their non-Jewish surroundings, of being guilty of a lack of interest in the fate of their people, and of discouraging Israel from the fulfilment of the law.[81] Some rabbis predict for them the torments of Gehenna. But this verdict on them is energetically contested by R. Simon ben Laqish, who says: "The fire of Gehenna has no power over the *posh'e yisrael.*" This is because they "are full of good deeds".[82] What may we conclude from these contradictory assessments? First, that there were *posh'im* and *posh'im*, not all being on the same footing. Second, that these bad Jews, taken together, rejected some of the ritual rules but continued scrupulously to respect others.

As far as doctrine is concerned, it does not look as if they could be charged with any serious heresies. With regard to the essentials, they remained within the mainstream of orthodoxy. No one accuses them either of impairing the divine unity by professing belief in "another God," or of preaching that the people of Israel are irrevocably cast off. Quite the contrary. They had a firm expectation of the redemption of Israel and the rebuilding of Jerusalem. They also conformed to orthodoxy in their faith in the resurrection. "The *posh'im* say 'Amen' with all their might to the resurrection, and they pray, 'Blessed be thou who givest life to the dead.'" Their merits are such that the text of Psalm 31:24 is quoted with reference to them: "The Lord preserves the faithful."[83] The same midrash nevertheless distinguishes them from good Israelites. They and the good Israelites are at one in this threefold hope, but with some qualifications. The orthodox await the resurrection, "though it has not yet happened," and the Savior of Israel, "though he is not yet come." We are surely justified in deducing from this contrast, so discreetly formulated, that for some of the *posh'im* envisaged here the savior had already come, once, though they continued to await him, and that at least the "first fruits" of the resurrection, as the apostle calls them,[84] were in the past. How can we help thinking here of the Christians?

An individual who rejected the law, even if it was only in one particular, had done enough to be classed among the *posh'e yisrael.* But the Jewish Christians seem to have been thus classified not as individuals but as a body. The combination of characteristics noted in our texts describes them perfectly. This position midway between the strict rabbinic adherence to the law and the attitude of the Church is just the one that Christian witnesses ascribe to them.[85]

Let us go back to the word *minim*, which we studied earlier, and let us compare it with the term *posh'im*. It seems that, though they did both exist in the Jewish vocabulary before the advent of Christianity, they were both used, by the time our period is reached, to designate Palestinian Christians. It also appears that the two terms are not interchangeable. The designation *minim* is applied especially to the autonomous Christian communities, to those which belong to Catholic Christianity, whether their membership is principally Jewish or otherwise.[86] Between the *minim* and Jewish orthodoxy stands the whole bulk of orthodox Christian theology. The *minim* challenge the fundamental dogmas of Judaism and its whole ritual life. The *posh'im* differ from Jews in ways that are much less clearly defined, in the realm both of doctrine and of ritual practice. This is the first difference between the two.

Once their striking peculiarities had been recognized, Judaism expelled the *minim* as a foreign intrusion, no better than the pagans. And the *minim* for their part seem to have had no urgent desire to keep in touch with the parent body. The *posh'im*, by contrast, even when they capitulated on some issues to outside influences, remained devoted to Jewish practices, and they were never forced to make a final choice. And this is the second difference. The *posh'im* still felt themselves to be Jews, and the Synagogue, with few exceptions, did not at the outset reject them. Even when they set themselves up as a distinct sect, outside orthodoxy, the Synagogue laid claim to them on occasion, as sheep who had temporarily strayed but who would come back to the fold. The rabbis at first sustained a firm hope of bringing them back some day into Judaism, and this no doubt is the reason for their indulgent attitude. This hope, as we know, was not altogether a vain one. At least a section of the Jewish Christians, left to vegetate midway between the two religions, finally made the return to the Synagogue. Thus the two terms we are considering, properly understood, well convey the two essential aspects of the relations between Jews and Christians; on the one hand, implacable opposition, and on the other, the tenacious persistence of ethnic and religious ties.

Once we have recognized that some of the *posh'im* are to be identified as Ebionites, we see how the rabbinic texts fill out the picture of these sectarians we have derived from Christian documents. As far as the observance of the law is concerned, it appears that they obeyed the basic laws to the letter but repudiated the elaborations of Pharisaic rigorism. Thus we may explain the contradictory judgments the scholars pass on them. Two features in particular mark them off from orthodox Judaism, their faith in Christ and their indifference, or relative indifference, to the Jewish people and its destiny.

These two complaints did not always weigh equally heavily on the relations between Jewish orthodoxy and the sect. Faith in Jesus as Messiah did not immediately render suspect in Israel all those who subscribed to it, any more than adherence to the ritual rules was at first enough reason in the eyes of Christians to excommunicate the Judaizers. The book of Acts emphasizes how enthusiastic the first disciples were in their support of the temple cult, and how high they stood in Jewish estimation.[87] It was only gradually that Christianity on the one side and Judaism on the other became more intolerant. The former became intolerant of Mosaic ritual practices, the latter of belief in Christ, in each case ultimately deciding that a matter that they first regarded as of no vital consequence was incompatible with their respective faiths.

The development of Christian attitudes is explained by the principle that the Church applied to the question of the ritual law, and by the fact that more and more of its members were drawn from outside Israel. The condemnation of the Jewish Christians was a defensive measure by the gentile Christians, anxious to preserve the autonomy of a cult they had made their own. The stiffening attitude of Jewish orthodoxy was partly prompted by the development of Catholic theology, which exalted Jesus more and more above the merely human condition. It was the thought and the influence of St. Paul that brought the Jewish Christians, on both sides of the wall of partition, under suspicion and anathema. Without him Judaism might well not have taken the initiative in breaking with the Ebionites, who began by benefiting from Judaism's broad toleration of differences in doctrine.

The Synagogue never to our knowledge repudiated those who maintained that Bar Cochba was the Messiah, not even after the failure of his attempt had proved that God was not with him. Akiba, who was one of his followers, has remained one of the most respected scholars in Israel's memory.[88] Besides, the Messianic hope was not the touchstone of Jewish orthodoxy. Support of a false Messiah did not entail certain excommunication unless this allegiance was accompanied by deviations in doctrine or religious practice. These conditions were not fulfilled either in the case of the insurgents of A.D. 135 or of the Palestinian Nazarenes. It is probable that the Synagogue would not have treated the latter any differently from the former if the name of Jesus had not enjoyed such a large following outside Palestine, and if it had not ranged a Church of gentiles against the

Synagogue.[89] If in the long run their faith in Christ was held against the Jewish Christians, it was chiefly because this faith lent itself to development in a Trinitarian direction, and more generally, because it created a solidarity between them and the Catholic Church, a solidarity that was recognizable in spite of divergences and was nontheless real, if unwished-for.

This is already the explanation of the execution of James, the brother of Jesus, who was the head of the Jewish-Christian community and a respected *nazir* in Israel. He was put to death by the Jews, Eusebius tells us, because "with a loud voice and more courage than they had expected, [he] confessed before all the people that our Lord and Saviour Jesus Christ is the Son of God." And "they could no longer endure his testimony, since he was by all believed to be most righteous because of the height which he had reached in a life of philosophy and religion."[90]

It is not certain that the confession of faith ascribed to James was as rigorously orthodox as Eusebius would have wished. By contrast, the circumstances that provoked the violence of the Jews against him are very significant. "When Paul appealed to Caesar and was sent over to Rome by Festus the Jews were disappointed of the hope in which they had laid their plot against him and turned against James...and demanded a denial of the faith in Christ before all the people."[91] Whatever we may think of the content of James's testimony, it emerges from Eusebius's account that he would never have been called upon to give it if the subversive preaching of Paul had not rudely turned Jewish opinion against all things Christian. Thus, by an irony of fate, the brother of Jesus, the notorious opponent of the apostle to the gentiles, seems to have perished in his place, the victim of a solidarity about which he, doubtless, had reservations. The solidarity was perhaps less marked than Eusebius would like to think, but it was there. And it is probable that the Jews were conscious of it too.

When the Jews accused the Nazarene *posh'im* of not being wholeheartedly involved with their own people, we see the essential difference between them and the disciples of Bar Cochba. The independent nature of the Jewish-Christian movement was emphasized unintentionally by the way in which the Palestinian Christians, when Jerusalem was besieged, voluntarily left the city.[92] This act, committed in such serious circumstances, took on a symbolic significance. It immediately placed them outside the community of Israel and exposed them to the rancor and hatred of the nationalists.[93] This hatred was violently demonstrated during the second Palestinian crisis, when Bar Cochba persecuted the Jewish Christians who refused to accept his lead.[94] Presumably the Messianic nature of Bar Cochba's claim is enough to explain why those who believed in Jesus refused to follow him. No man can serve two masters. But the precedent of A.D. 66, which was simply a national insurrection with no question of a Messiah, prompts the thought that even if the uprising in A.D. 132 had not possessed this character, the Nazarenes would still have refused to join it, simply on the grounds that they disapproved of nationalistic violence.

But here again we must beware of exaggerating the tension and its significance. Neither in A.D. 66 nor 132 were the Nazarenes the only people who disapproved of the rebellion. In both cases the troubles were stirred up by extremist elements. And these extremists, though they succeeded in rallying a fair proportion of the population around them, never commanded unanimous support. Rabbinic opinion was divided even within Palestine, to say nothing of the diaspora. In A.D. 66 Josephus, himself a Pharisee in his sympathies, was enlisted against his will by the rebels. His capture by the Romans was a welcome relief to him. Furthermore, as I have already recalled, it was during an actual siege that Johanan ben Zakkai fled from his city and founded the academy at Jabneh that was to assure Judaism's future. Only the "politicians," to use Bertholet's phrase, persisted in revolt. In the time of Hadrian, Akiba gave himself wholeheartedly to the cause of Bar Cochba, whilst other rabbis chaffed him for his support.[95]

Besides, once the crises were over, the Jewish Christians devoted themselves to living in hope and desire for the restoration of Israel, that is, to the restoration of its traditional religious institutions and its independence, to the rebuilding of temple and city. If they did draw any distinction between religious and political expectations, it was not a very rigid one. Between their hope and that of the Jews there was no substantial difference in principle.[96] Both groups gradually became used to the idea that, however desirable the restoration might be, it had been remitted to the end of the age and that it would herald the coming of the kingdom of God, a coming that was perhaps still in the remote future. The restoration would be carried out, for the Jews, at the instigation of a Messiah who was as yet unknown. For the Jewish Christians, its author was to be the returning Messiah Jesus. It does not appear that the rabbis felt this difference to be a reason for discord.

In summary, it does not seem that Judaism was very quick to assume an attitude of complete intolerance toward the Jewish Christians. At first it regarded their views as deviating to some extent from traditional Judaism but still permissible. Their religious peculiarities made them suspect in the eyes of some, but others were prepared on the whole to accept them. In the time that followed, the reactions they evoked varied according to circumstances. They varied from rabbi to rabbi according to the rabbi's own standpoint. They varied with the type of Jewish Christianity concerned. To be more exact, the deciding fact was whether a rabbi was impressed most by the strength of their fundamentally Jewish characteristics or by their affinities with the catholic Church. According to his impressions, he would classify them either as inoffensive *posh'im* or dastardly *minim*. This is the explanation of the oscillation between intolerance and indulgence that characterizes the Synagogue's relations with the Nazarenes/Ebionites.

If these relations could be plotted on a graph, they would not produce a regular curve. It would in any case be difficult to trace their development chronologically since the materials of the Talmud are so difficult to put in any chronological order. Certain phases may, however, be clearly distinguished, partly with the help of Christian texts. The toleration the Jerusalem community enjoyed was marred for the first time by the martyrdom of James.[97] The Jewish War, breaking in on these developments, temporarily aggravated the tension. A few years after the catastrophe came the introduction of the blessing of the *minim*, which at the time was aimed just as much at the Ebionites as at other Christians. But it affected them more directly than the others, for they were at the time still inside the Synagogue, which is where they desired to be. The return to Jerusalem of the people from Pella softened the antipathy, but it hardened again with the rebellion under Hadrian. After that, better relations were established, which were at least bearable, and this state of affairs probably lasted until the end of the third century. This change for the better took place at the same time as, and indeed because of, the Church's rejection of the Ebionites from the Christian community.

Once the Church had allied itself with the empire, it endeavored to promote an intolerant and aggressive imperial policy toward the Jews. This was bound to damage severely the relations between Jews and Jewish Christians. We may agree with Marmorstein that all the appreciative judgments given by the rabbis on the Jewish Christian *posh'im* come from the period preceding the conversion of Constantine. But from this point onwards the distinction hitherto drawn between Jewish Christians and Christians of other sorts disappears. The Nazarene *posh'im* are now redefined as *minim*, and this classification was doubtless final.[98] At the same time the Church, having fixed the boundaries of Nicene orthodoxy and laid down the rules of Catholic ritual practice, rejected once for all those who thought or behaved otherwise. Now that both sides put the pressure on them and forced them to choose, the Jewish Christians were obliged to renounce their peculiarities and adopt one of the two normative religions.[99] Just how they did this, and how many of them passed into Judaism, how many into Christianity, and how many to other syncretistic sects we do not know. But the nucleus of dyed-in-the-wool Jewish Christians became smaller and smaller and ceased from this time to count for anything amongst the religions of the East.

V

However, the story of Jewish Christianity is by no means limited to the confines of Palestine and of the chosen people. There was an extra-Palestinian Jewish Christianity, scattered throughout Oriental Christianity.

The center of gravity of the movement was in the area of the Trans-Jordan. Its principal strongholds were Pella in Peraea, and Kokhaba in Batanaea.[100] In Palestine itself the Jerusalem community, reconstituted after the siege, remained Jewish Christian and until Hadrian's war was under the jurisdiction of bishops "of the circumcision."[101] Other communities existed in Galilee and Judaea.[102] In addition, the movement spread throughout the Near East, to the point of constituting a kind of Jewish-Christian diaspora. Epiphanius cites as one of its centers, besides those mentioned above, the town of Beroea in northern Syria.[103] It was in these same areas of the Trans-Jordan that there grew up the particular type of Jewish Christianity for which Epiphanius reserves the name *Ebionite*.[104] This latter, he informs us, was widespread all round the environs of Palestine, from Moab as far as Paneas. Cyprus was swarming with its devotees, and it had even reached Rome.[105] The two gospels used by Egyptian Christians, the Gospel of the Egyptians and the Gospel of the Hebrews, may well be an indication that there, too, Jewish Christian communities existed side by side with those of the Hellenistic kind.[106] The circumstances in which this expansion took place remain somewhat obscure, but the fact that it did take place faces us with the question, whence did Jewish Christianity derive its members?

When some authors take it as self-evident that a Jewish Christian was bound to be a Christian of Jewish origin, they are basing their assumption on a definition of "Jewish Christian" that is ambiguous, and that is, in the last resort, so narrow as to be misleading.

What, indeed, can the phrase *Jewish origins* mean in a period when the ranks of the chosen people had been so much swollen by proselytes? If none but native Israelites are entitled to be described as "of Jewish origin," then we can apply it strictly to Palestinian Christianity, which was a direct extension of the original Christianity. But as for the more marginal Jewish-Christian groups and those of the diaspora, can we say with confidence that none of their adherents was of gentile origin?

To restrict the appellation *Jewish Christian* to those of Hebrew ancestry makes no more sense at this period than to allow the title *Jew* only to authentic members of the twelve tribes.[107] By the rabbis' own standards the criterion of Jewishness was religious practice, and not merely birth. Similarly, Jewish Christianity, understood in religious terms, can only be related rather imprecisely either to Israel conceived as a political or ethnic reality, or to ordinary Christianity, thought of as a gentile phenomenon. It is at least sensible to refrain, on general grounds, from restricting the term *Jewish Christian* to those who were descendants of Abraham according to the flesh.

The conversion of a pagan to Christianity could be brought about in a number of different ways. It could happen quite directly and all at once. This quickly came to be the normal sort of conversion. But it could also happen with the Hellenistic Synagogue as intermediary. For the pagan clientele of the Hellenistic Synagogue provided the Church with numerous recruits, especially when the gentile mission first began.[108] In such a case the respect for Jewish observance might be transitory and come to an end with baptism. But it might also survive baptism. A man might become a Christian without ceasing to be a Jew.[109] Two other possible courses are conceivable. A new convert might, by attaching himself to a Jewish-Christian group, become a Jew and a Christian at the same time. Alternatively, he might begin by becoming a Christian of the ordinary sort and then be seduced by the appeal of the Mosaic law, and at a second stage integrate the observance of that law into his practice of Christianity.[110]

It will be seen from this how hazardous it is to introduce into the definition of Jewish Christianity the criterion of birth. The whole problem is to see to what extent, if at all, the various theoretical possibilities correspond to the facts. The problem is to understand the processes by which the Jews made proselytes and the Christians made converts of native Jews.

The missionary endeavor of the first Jewish Christians, i.e., of the Palestinian disciples, represents basically an extension of Jewish proselytism. If non-Christian Jews felt the need to propagate their religion, it is not at all surprising that the Jews who claimed Jesus as their leader should have done the same, and that they should have preached the law and their faith in Christ at the same time. For the law, after all, was such an indispensable means of salvation that the Master himself could not wish to see it abolished. In fact, the argument between the disciples of Paul and the Jerusalem community did not turn on the legitimacy of the mission beyond Israel. It was about the conditions on which gentiles might be allowed access to the Christian faith; about whether or not they were required to observe the law. The compromise that was worked out at Jerusalem, as reported in Acts,[111] absolves the Christians of pagan origin from obedience to the bulk of the observances. But though they made this concession to the Pauline point of view, and made it, it would appear, with not very good grace, the "pillars of the Church" were not prevented from organizing another mission on their own account, based on other principles, and they seem to have looked outside Palestine for recruits who, if they were not Jews already, would on conversion to Christianity become Jews and accept both circumcision and the obligation to observe the law.

Besides this, the letters of St. Paul, especially the epistle to the Galatians, plainly show that the Jewish Christians were not satisfied to proselytize merely in the places where St. Paul had not been, but that they were busy in his wake, and even prosecuted their cause alongside his, endeavoring to bring the communities he founded round to the same way of thinking as the Jerusalemites.

In recent years there has been much discussion of the part played by Peter in this counteroffensive, which was aimed at neutralizing the Pauline infection and reestablishing the unity of the infant Church on a Jewish-Christian basis. Some scholars, recalling the ideas of the Tübingen school, have stressed the opposition between the two apostles. They have represented this opposition as total, and have ascribed to Peter personally a missionary activity that was deliberately anti-Pauline. This view has been propounded by Lietzmann with authority and skill.[112] For him Peter's journeys are an indisputable fact. He was active in his rival's tracks, at Ancyra and Corinth, for example. At Rome he was there first, and the epistle to the Romans, written while Peter was still in the city, was aimed at putting the local community, comprised of Christians of pagan origin, on their guard. The situation would on this view be quite close to that which gave rise to the epistle to the Galatians. There was one difference only, and this accounts for the difference in tone between the two letters: in the Roman case the Church was not one that Paul himself had founded. Consequently, since his own self-respect is not threatened, Paul denounces the danger of Judaizing with less vehemence than in the case of his "dear Galatians."

These views have prompted criticisms and objections.[113] They encounter a number of difficulties, the details of which are unimportant for my present work. It is possible to disagree about the identity of the instigators of the counterevangelistic work. Peter may have been one. Others regard James as Paul's most obstinate and militant adversary. More likely, we should recognize as leaders of the enterprise men who, whether in good faith or not, made use of Peter's and James's names.[114] But whatever may be said on this score, there is almost complete agreement that the anti-Pauline countermission did go on. Just how effective it was is almost impossible to discover. St. Paul's indignation gives us cause to think that at least in the case of the Galatians his adversaries achieved considerable success. For the majority of instances we are reduced to conjecture.

If we ask how long this counteroffensive persisted, we receive the same reply. We have definite evidence of it only during the apostolic period. After that period Christianity of Jewish-Christian type was still being preached in Arabia and, if we are to believe Eusebius, as far afield as India. By this is probably meant the southern part of the Arabian peninsula. Tradition ascribes the preaching of the gospel in these parts to the apostle Bartholemew. It would have been he who left in the district the Hebrew text of St. Matthew, which was recovered at the end of the second century by Pantaenus, the Christian philosopher from Alexandria.[115]

Jewish-Christian evangelism was still going on in the second century, as is proved by the text of Justin quoted above. The epistles of Ignatius of Antioch show the same. The Judaizing movement against which they are directed exercises its influence within the Christian communities themselves. It works for the reinstitution of the observance of the old law,[116] the replacement of Sunday by the Sabbath,[117] and the readoption of the Jewish name.[118] The Judaizers go so far as to celebrate their Eucharist separately from the brethren. This, doubtless, is in compliance with the dietary laws.[119] The movement is supported by people who are not Jews by birth,[120] and who, if they are not circumcised, are nevertheless in favor of keeping the whole ritual law.

Symmachus's translation of the Bible affords us further proof of the preoccupation of Jewish Christianity with missionary endeavor. Symmachus, who lived at the end of the second century, was a Jewish Christian.[121] His version was later than Aquila's and was doubtless intended to eliminate from the usage of his sect at one blow the Septuagint, which had become the Bible of the Catholic Church, and the version of Aquila, which had supplanted the Septuagint among the Jews of the dispersion. It shows that the Jewish Christians were not all Hebrew or Aramaic-speaking; not all living in Palestine; and not all of Jewish birth. It also bears witness to their conviction of their own independence both in beliefs and organization.

Ancient tradition makes the Ebionite translator a member of the sect of the Symmachians. This sect is not mentioned by anyone except the Latin authors of the fourth and fifth centuries.[122] According to Ambrosiaster, they were connected with the Pharisees. They observed the whole law and rejected the divinity of Christ. For them Christ was only a man.[123] These are exactly the characteristics of the Nazarenes of Palestine. St. Augustine, for his part, gives the two terms, *Nazarenes* and *Symmachians*, as synonyms. *Quidam haeretici, qui se Nazarenos vocant, a nonnullis autem Symmachiani appellantur.*[124] What he says about them reinforces the evidence of Ambrosiaster. They practiced the rituals of both baptism and circumcision,[125] and for their fidelity to the Jewish law they claimed the support of Christ's own example, *quod Jesu dixerit se non venisse solvere legem.*[126] St. Augustine adds here the interesting detail that, though themselves of Israelite origin, their policy was to impose the observance of the law even on gentiles.[127]

This combined testimony allows us to recognize the Symmachians as a non-Palestinian offshoot of classical Jewish Christianity. There appears to be nothing that distinguishes them from the Palestinian Ebionites except their language. The name Symmachians is perhaps derived simply from the fact that they used Symmachus's translation. It is hardly necessary to attribute to Symmachus any decisive part in the birth of the sect, since there is so little about it which is distinctive. It is possible that in the west they retained the Greek language, just as the Jews sometimes did.[128]

Augustine speaks as if he had had direct contact with the sect.[129] There existed therefore an African Jewish Christianity. There was doubtless also an Italian one, for Ambrosiaster too seems to have known the group at firsthand. The career of Jewish Christianity, therefore, is confined neither to the country of Palestine nor to the period of the early centuries A.D. It may be supposed that, having suffered a setback because of the events of A.D. 70 and 135, its capacity for expansion was not very great, except perhaps that Palestinian Ebionism might have had some appeal in its Semitic hinterland. At the time when St. Augustine mentions it, the sect of the Symmachians was a mere remnant, but he says that it was a singularly tenacious one. *Usque ad nostra tempora jam quidem in exigua, sed adhuc tamen vel in ipsa paucitate perdurant.*[130] This statement should discourage us from dismissing too contemptuously this interesting manifestation of early Christian religious life.

The history of Jewish Christianity sheds light on only one aspect of Jewish influence in the Church, and not the most important aspect at that. In its efforts to expand Jewish Christianity was hampered by its own hybrid character. Lacking a clearly defined and universally recognized religious authority, such as Judaism possessed in the Patriarch and his entourage of rabbis, or like the episcopate the Church acknowledged, Jewish Christianity was at the mercy of erosive forces. It was not only torn between the Synagogue and the Church but was exposed besides to the attractions of the sects. If it was to satisfy the souls for whom its simple doctrines were not enough, it had no alternative but to open its doors to syncretistic gnostic speculations. There must have been a number of its communities that, beginning with the original Ebionism, slipped into the gnosticism of the "Ebionites" whom Epiphanius describes.[131]

We may add that outside Palestine Jewish Christianity must, in view of its original Jewish membership, have been a short-lived phenomenon without very much influence. In Palestine itself the Ebionites were a small minority in comparison with the body of the Church. Their decline was uninterrupted, and their position made it certain that they would sooner or later disappear. Judaism, on the contrary, was everywhere present. It was firmly based, and the misfortunes that befell Israel only strengthened it further. It was Judaism itself that continued to exercise upon the early Church an influence strong enough and widespread enough to disturb the ecclesiastical authorities. The real and lasting danger that the early Church had to meet came not from little groups of Jewish Christians in the Trans-Jordan or elsewhere, but from Judaism itself, which was widely distributed across the empire.

In order to understand these Judaizing tendencies, it is necessary to reckon with the fact that in antiquity large sections of the gentile populace were imbued with Jewish ideas and especially with Jewish practices. If the pagans were affected by Judaism to such an extent, there was all the more reason for its influence to be felt by the adherents of a cult whose very roots were in Judaism. The radical division between Judaism and Christianity that St. Paul carried through in the sphere of doctrine could not be put into effect in the practical realm without some difficulty. One might speak in this connection of a kind of Judaizing atavism, which Christianity continued to suffer from long after the apostle had set up Christ and the law as the two great incompatibles. Judaizing continued because of its own aquired momentum.

There were thus certain innate Judaizing tendencies within the Church, derived from its commerce with the holy book, and from its own idea of itself as the new Israel. To these were added the persistent attraction the Synagogue possessed for certain categories of believers.

This resulted in a Judaizing pressure that operated from without, and this was much more persistent and of much greater weight than any influence the Jewish Christians brought to bear from inside, either in their early days or in the persons of their successors. This outside Judaizing pressure could not have been brought to bear against the will of the Jews, or even without their cooperation. It is only fully comprehensible if they actively participated in it. In most cases, the existence of this Judaizing influence implies the survival in Israel of the missionary, proselytizing spirit.

10
Jewish Proselytism

'Ερρίφημεν ἵνα καὶ διδάσκαλοι γενώμεθα τῆς οἰκουμένης.
St. John Chrysostom, *In Psalm.*, 8:34

In the history of Judaism around the beginning of the Christian era there is no more controversial question than that of proselytism.[1] For our present study it is of prime importance. If Judaism had withdrawn into itself, then it no longer really confronted the Church but restricted itself to a conflict in the realm of theory, to a bookish, sterile controversy around the sacred texts. If it was still a proselytizing movement, then it was a real and dangerous rival. If we were to throw light on this question, we should possess a clear picture of the state of Jewish-Christian relations. We should also, speaking more generally, have a much fuller understanding of the nature of Judaism during this period. We should be able to decide whether it was a universalistic religion, or whether it was rather the cult pertaining to a closed religious society, or even a strictly ethnic religion, in the sense that the old Yahweh cult of ancient Israel was an ethnic religion. We shall decide this question one way or the other as we establish whether the missionary spirit survived among the Jews, even in an attentuated form, or whether it disappeared completely.

Not long ago it used to be accepted (and there are some who accept it still) that the catastrophes in Palestine put an end to Jewish expansion. Says Duchesne, "The religious life now became very narrow. The day of liberal Jews, who coquetted with hellenism and with the government, was past and gone for good. There is no longer any desire to stand well with other nations, nor to make proselytes. That field is left to the Nazarenes. The Jews retired within themselves, absorbed in the contemplation of the law."[2]

Doubts have been expressed about this opinion. E. Schwartz, for example, has postulated that proselytism survived for a long time, and he has gathered some of the materials required for a proof, though without, so far, having explored the matter really thoroughly.[3] I have taken up his postulate as a working hypothesis, as it seems to be the only hypothesis that satisfactorily explains certain facts, and I have attempted in one place or another to bolster it with new evidence. It is appropriate now that in making a frontal attack on the problem I should set out the arguments afresh and fill out the evidence. It will also be useful to determine at the same time, if possible, in what manner and at which time and under what influences Judaism at last turned its attention away from the *goyim* and devoted itself wholly to the flock of the house of Israel.

I

Holders of the traditional view, which sees the crises of A.D. 70 and 135 as marking the end of Jewish expansion, can support it with two principal arguments. First, from the time of these crises the imperial authority placed impediments in the way of Jewish proselytism. These were an expression of the discredit into which Judaism had fallen, in Roman eyes, through the political events in Palestine. Second, and more important, the rancor and hatred the Jews themselves felt toward the gentiles would have driven them into isolation and sullen particularism. These primary causes of the withdrawal lay, therefore, in the attitudes and policies of the pagans toward the Jews, and in those of Israel toward the outside world. Christianity is not a factor in this situation except of the most subsidiary kind. The connection between Christianity's appearance and the recoil of Jewish missionary activity was coincidental, not causal. The appearance of Christianity at the same time did, of course, hasten the recoil, but it was not responsible for it. Christianity derived benefit from the Jewish withdrawal, but did not bring it to pass, and the development of Judaism and its relations with the gentile world would not have taken an appreciably different course if Jesus and St. Paul had never existed.[4]

I have already indicated what, in my opinion, we ought to make of the emperors' attitudes to Judaism. Even if it were established that legislation unambiguously prohibiting proselytism was enacted, and that it was enforced, this would not be enough in the absence of other indications to prove that Jewish missionary activity was effectively curtailed. The measures taken against the Christians did not arrest the victorious progress of the Church, because Christians were able to defy the law. Were not the Jews capable of doing the same? In actual fact the activities of the Jews were not curtailed. For we can take it as established that their position in the empire was not affected by the events concerned. If the right to practice their religion openly and fully, and to be circumcised, was in principle confined to those who were Israelites by birth, it was not in practice easy to distinguish between these and the rest, and the state did not show much enthusiasm for doing so.

There was one rather unexpected consequence of the Christians' much more assertive style of preaching. In engaging the attention of the authorities, it turned that attention away from Judaism, which from now on was regarded as a lesser danger and a lesser evil. Proselytism, which was theoretically, indirectly and incompletely prevented by the prohibition of circumcision, could in fact still go on. The emperors, for the most part, closed their eyes to it.

We have also noted that neither the standing of the Jews in pagan eyes, nor their influence on pagan opinion, seem to have suffered because of the Palestinian crises. The state of Roman relations with Persia did not impede the remarkable progress within the the empire of the Mithraic cult, and some reputable citizens, having been initiated into its mysteries, were admitted to the grade of "Persian." Then why should the spread of Judaism have been damaged by similar circumstances, especially after Hadrian's war had definitively settled the political problem?[5] On the purely religious level the destruction of the temple marked a step toward universalism, for it broke the attachment between the Jewish cult and Palestinian soil. From now on it was no longer only in Jerusalem that worship might go on, but in every place. The spiritual religion of which the Johannine Christ speaks to the woman of Samaria could be understood in purely Jewish terms. The suppression of the sacrificial cult made the diaspora Jews, proselytes included, the equals of the native Palestinians. An enlightened Jew could justifiably say, adapting the words of St. Paul, "There is no longer either Hebrew or Hellenist, Palestinian Jew or Jew of the diaspora."

We have here indisputably a set of circumstances favorable to missionary activity. This at least is how it looks from our point of view. It remains to be seen whether the Jews, or any among them, saw the situation in the same way, and whether they were able to take advantage of it. The question of proselytism is merely one particular aspect of the problem Judaism faced, the problem of adapting itself to new conditions. This is the question I was studying when this work began.

Theoretically, neither the Roman legislation nor the new features of Jewish religious life should have prevented the continuance of proselytism. The latter, indeed, were more in favor of Jewish expansion than against it. We are not entitled thereby to conclude that proselytism did not in fact continue. And if the first argument in favor of the theory under discussion cannot be maintained, it is still

expedient to examine the second. What was the basic attitude of
Judaism itself in this period toward the question?

We have already noted that there existed in the Hellenistic diaspora
a type of Judaism that was in principle universalistic and continued to
address its message to the gentiles. We have found echoes of such a
Judaism in the Sybilline Oracles and in the pseudo-Clementine
apologetic literature.[6] It was also in the diaspora that the proselytizing
spirit was most at home. The Jews of the diaspora, having been less
directly affected by the two crises than were the Palestinians, were
better able to make use of those features of the situation that were to
the chosen people's positive advantage. It is now necessary to
interrogate the Talmudic sources. These not only give us some
information about the state of mind of the Jews in the East, who were
the ones most inclined toward retrenchment, but also provide us with
supplementary evidence concerning the theoretical attitudes and
practical activities of Jews outside Palestine. For if the rabbis of
Palestine or Babylon approved in principle of proselytism, there is all
the more reason to believe that the diaspora of the mediterranean
lands would have remained faithful to what it saw as its vocation and
would have continued its missionary activities.

We seek in vain in the Talmud for any uniformity of attitude
toward proselytism, or any consistent teaching concerning it. What we
do find there represents no more than a collection of individual
opinions. These opinions are varied and often contradictory. They
vary from scholar to scholar according to the individual's temperament, and they vary from time to time and place to place according to
the circumstances. All the same, we may hope to detect a dominant
trend and to be able to plot a graph of opinions. In the very
discrepancies themselves we have a witness to the complexity of that
phenomenon whose entirety we designate "rabbinic Judaism."

The saying of the celebrated Rabbi Helbo, a Babylonian who was
living in Palestine during the third century, has often been cited as
expressing the balance of opinion. "Proselytes are as injurious to Israel
as a scab."[7] We may associate with this unkind view a number of other
expressions of opinion that, though less bluntly put, are substantially
the same.[8] These indubitably reflect the animosity that, from this
period onwards, some of the Jews harbored toward the gentiles. It was
the same animosity that was to contribute very largely to the final
retrenchment. But other sentiments are perceptible behind these
formulae. In particular, they are expressions of the distrust that was
roused in the rabbis by uncertain converts. Such converts, in times of
crisis and danger, often renounced their temporary church, or they
were soon seduced by the evangelism of the Jews' rivals, who

were more broadly universalistic than the Jews could ever be, and thus passed over into Christianity.[9] Perhaps also, since thoroughgoing conversions, sealed by circumcision, were forbidden in any case, such sayings as those quoted bring us hints of difficulties that Judaism had had, on occasion, with the Roman state. It is perfectly understandable that such unfortunate experiences may have led Israel's scholars to scrutinize with a jaundiced eye, or at least with a very circumspect eye, every application for admission.[10] But it would probably be going too far to interpret even R. Helbo's statement as a formal condemnation of proselytism. It is in any case far from representing the dominant opinion of the period. In order to be convinced of this, one only needs to consider a series of other texts, which are explicit enough to leave no room for doubt.

To make proselytes was a meritorious work. "Whoever leads a pagan into a knowledge of God, it is as if he had created a life".[11] R. Simeon ben Johai, a contemporary of R. Judah II, makes the point forcefully. "Lord of the world, Rahab saved two lives, and thou didst recompense her by saving many lives. How much more may I hope for salvation, whose fathers have led so many foreigners to thee?"[12] Proselytes enjoy an eminent dignity. According to R. Hanina, who lived at the beginning of the fourth century, "the evil peoples are saved by the merits of one proselyte who each year is raised in the midst of them."[13] Proselytes become by conversions the equals of Jews. From the point at which Ruth thinks of being converted scripture puts her on the same footing as Naomi.[14] "Their names, says the Holy One, blessed be He, are as dear to Me as libations made upon the altar."[15] A pagan who fulfils the law, we are told in another place, is the equal of the High Priest.[16]

Some scholars even reckon that the merits of proselytes are superior to those of Israel, for without the miracle of the revelation Israel would not have accepted the covenant, whereas the proselyte, without having seen even the least "sign," spontaneously gives himself to God.[17] Let us listen again to R. Simeon ben Johai: "Of the righteous it is said that they love God [Judg. 5:21]. Of the proselytes it is said that God loves them [Deut. 10:18]. Who then is the greater, he of whom it is said that he loves the king, or he whom the king loves?"[18] There is moreover an exacting obligation upon Israel to be active in proselytizing. "The stranger must not remain without. When proselytes are gathered one repels them with the left hand but draws them with the right. Not so did Elisha with Gehazi, for he repulsed him with both hands."[19]

For R. Eleazar ben Pedath, who lived at the end of the third century, the afflictions of Israel are intended to make it easier for her to accomplish her task. "[God] did not exile Israel among the nations save in order that proselytes might join them, for it is said: 'I will sow her unto me in the land' [Hos. 2:25]. Surely a man sows a *se'ah* in order to harvest many *kor!*"[20] If conversions are becoming less numerous, it is a sign that God is withdrawing Himself from His people because of their sins. "A king had a garden, which he gave to his son. As long as the son did what he wished, the king looked around for good cuttings and transplanted them into his son's garden. But when the son stopped being amenable, the king deprived him of the cultivation of the garden. Similarly, as long as Israel did His will, God, when He found a righteous person among the nations, Jethro, Rahab, Ruth, Antoninus, led them to Israel and gathered them to her number. But now that Israel has become recalcitrant He removes the righteous from her midst."[21] But this falling off in conversions is no more final than God's abandonment of Israel. "In the time to come," says R. Jose ben Halafta, a disciple of R. Akiba, "idol worshippers will come and offer themselves as proselytes."[22]

What clearly emerges from this evidence, and particularly from the latter examples, which bear the marks of the situation in which they were uttered, is that Judaism's basic position with regard to proselytism did not change from one period to another. Rabbinic opinion remains divided, but a majority persist, it appears, in their devotion to the missionary ideal. Israel, once having surmounted the upheavals that followed the catastrophe and the distrust of the surrounding world it engendered, is seen not to have renounced its universal mission. The differences of opinion are concerned less with the principle than with the way in which it should be put into practice, and their roots go back far beyond the disaster of A.D. 70. There was conflict already between the schools of Hillel and Shammai. This conflict, which goes to the heart of Judaism itself, was a conflict of different temperaments and different approaches as much as a doctrinal one.[23]

One section of rabbinic opinion that seems to have gathered more and more support laid down very strict rules with regard to proselytism. Circumstances appear to have strengthened the case for this. Their cautious approach is clearly exemplified in the very significant ritual of admission practiced in Palestine after Hadrian's war. The question is asked, "What reason have you for so desiring to become a proselyte? Do you not know that Israel at the present time is persecuted and oppressed, despised, harassed and overcome by afflictions?" There follows a precise and detailed list of duties that reminds the candidate of the obligations, observances and rites that will fall upon him when he becomes a disciple of the Torah. He is made aware of the penalties for breaking them, but also of the rewards that accompany the keeping of the law. "Be it known to you that the world to come was made only for the righteous."[24]

In a similar way some rabbis at the end of the second century insist strongly on the necessity for the proselyte to accept the whole law and the whole tradition, as if the object were to discourage dubious converts. If the candidate refuses even a single word of the Torah, he must be rejected. He should also comply with the smallest details of the prescriptions of the scholars.[25]

But these stern affirmations are not insisted on merely in order to avoid unpleasant surprises for the proselyte. There is a better reason for them than that. To say that the proselyte must accept every obligation that falls upon an Israelite is implicitly to allow his conversion to make him equal with Israelites, a Jew in the full sense.[26] By making the conversion to Judaism more difficult, by making a rigorous selection of the candidates, the tendency was to do away with the intermediate categories by which previously a pagan had been able to come into Judaism. These categories made up a hierarchy of grades between those who had been born Jews and those who had become Jews. Such stringent demands naturally reduced the numbers of proselytes, but they made certain of their quality. And it may be understood that the scholars did not stint their admiration for those who took the plunge, especially in times that were difficult for Jews. This admiration shines clearly through the hyperbolic language that describes the convert as equal to the High Priest, or that gives him preference in the eyes of the Lord over native Jews.

But these intransigents, who demanded that converts should keep the whole law on equal terms with born Jews, who rejected the semiproselytes and who in fact brought about a steady reduction in the rate of Jewish recruitment from outside, these were not the only body of opinion. The more lax party continued to make it easy for pagans to gain access to the truth. For some particularly broad-minded rabbis any conversion was valid, whatever the motives that prompted it.[27] The same leniency made them ready to accept converts even from peoples whom the Bible regards as accursed, such as Ammonites and Moabites. To R. Gamaliel, who wished to forbid such conversions, R. Joshua replies that the biblical prohibition is no longer to be taken at its face value, for the Ammonites as such no longer exist, because of the invasions that have mixed up the former peoples of Asia.[28] Toleration was even extended to proselytes from Palmyra, who had a bad reputation among some of the Jews.[29] It is still more remarkable that well into the second century R. Joshua and R. Judah ben Ilai, representatives of the most orthodox Jewish

opinion, could express the view that the baptism of proselytes, even
without circumcision, could be sufficient to make them equal to
Israelites.[30]

The practical repercussions of such toleration are manifest. To
exempt proselytes from a rite that many of them, doubtless, were
reluctant to submit to was naturally to still their misgivings and to
remove one of the principal obstacles to the spread of Judaism. On the
other hand, in a period when it was not strictly an offense to be a Jew,
but when the law simply forbade the circumcision of non-Jews, such a
rule meant that Judaism could make converts with impunity.
Perhaps, indeed, it was designed to weaken the inhibiting effect that
ritual observance had on Jewish missionary activity, to its disadvantage compared with its rival Christianity. Christianity was much less
demanding in this matter.[31]

To summarize: Israel's position with regard to proselytism seems
scarcely to have been affected by the events in Palestine. The two
schools of thought, conciliatory, and rigorist, existed side by side as in
the past.[32] Jewish status, and the privileges that went with it, were
reserved exclusively for full proselytes, that is to say, circumcised or at
least baptized ones. But the situation was no different before A.D. 70.
Those whom we call, as a body, semiproselytes, the *metuentes*, never
had been thought of as members of the holy community, as *bene berith*.
They remained in the outer court as permanent catechumens.
However highly they may have been regarded, from the Jewish point
of view they remained impure.[33] It is nonetheless significant that this
category of adherents should still be known in the third century and
should be looked on with a benevolent eye, even in Palestine itself.[34]
According to a rabbinical master, the rejection of idolatry is such that
whoever undertakes it, it is as if he had acknowledged every detail of
the Torah.[35]

II

In these judgments about proselytism and the rules relating to it there
is more than a mere manifestation of the rabbis' characteristic love of
disputation and codification. Unlike the discussions about the ritual
of the defunct temple, these arguments have a more than theoretical
purpose. If they are not enough to establish that real missionary
activity did go on, they at least create a presumption that it did so,
and this presumption may, when supported by other testimony, turn
into a certainty.

It is true that there is some difficulty in discovering direct evidence for the results of this proselytizing activity, or in making a reliable estimate of its scope. Our ignorance of Jewish missionary activity in this period has frequently been remarked on and regretted.[36] Information is scarce and not very exact. There is no indication at all of the numbers of people involved. But this state of affairs is hardly surprising, and the unhelpfulness of the documentary sources does not entitle us to deny that which every other consideration leads us to assume. On the Jewish side, we lack any Hellenistic writings, for all trace of them disappears after the second century. The Talmudic literature, for all its discussions and controversies, offers us little useful information, even in its haggadic sections. The help it does offer is incidental and indirect.

The pagan authors, insofar as the religious situation of their day interests them, are struck most by the missionary activity of the Christians, which was doubtless not only livelier but infinitely more efficacious than that of the Jews. Of Jewish missionary work they hardly ever speak. This is not sufficient evidence for asserting that Jewish missionary activity had by then ceased to exist. There are, in addition, some well-known exceptions. The Christians, finally, though producing abundant polemic against the Jews, are naturally disinclined to mention their rivals' successes. Faced with the magnitude of the Judaizing movement against which he struggled at Antioch, St. John Chrysostom can do no more than advise his faithful flock to keep silent, ὥστε μὴ γενέσθαι δήλην τὴν φήμην .[37] The silence in this instance, and perhaps in others, was tactical. There is a significant contrast between this and the insistence with which the fathers warn Christians against the Jews. It contrasts also with the explicit and repeated legislative measures the Christians took during the fourth century to protect themselves against Jewish expansion. We may conclude then that the evidence from Jewish, pagan, and Christian sources, scattered as it may be, is yet not totally lacking. Some pieces of that evidence are quite decisive.

In the Talmud, besides the theoretical rules we have just looked at, there are certain regulations of a practical kind. It is said, for example, that proselytes are obliged to set aside money to be kept for the consecratory sacrifice, against the day when the temple will be restored. Graetz is doubtless correct in supposing that this prescription implies the existence of proselytes.[38] On the other hand, though they may be rare, and their rarity in writings of this nature ought not to surprise us, a few contemporary instances of conversion are noted.[39] Rabbinic tradition also reckons as proselytes, or as sons of proselytes, several scholars, some of whom are by no means insignificant. There are Shemaiah and Abtalyon before the destruction of the temple.[40]

And from the period that at the moment concerns us we have Aquila, the translator of the Bible,[41] Meir, and Akiba himself, who was one of the most nationalistic of the Palestinian rabbis.[42] Two of Akiba's disciples are themselves also explicitly designated as proselytes, an Egyptian, Menyamin, and an Ammonite, Judas.[43] We have here, *mutatis mutandis*, an illustration of the saying we noted above: "The proselytes are destined to become priests exercising their office in the temple."[44] The scholar has replaced the priest, and he is in a more genuine sense the spiritual head of the chosen people.

We are likewise informed that R. Joshua ben Levi, at the beginning of the third century, assisted the Patriarch Judah II in a ceremony for the reception of proselytes at Laodicaea. On the other hand, the rabbis sometimes complain that the pagans are so hardened that they never allow the truth to touch them. R. Joseph of Pumbeditha, explaining Isaiah 46:12, "Hearken to me, you stubborn of heart, you who are far from righteousness," takes the verse as referring to the Gobaeans, for never yet has a proselyte emerged from them. R. Ashi, for his part, applies the verse to the inhabitants of Mata-Mechasya, another Babylonian city, because, in spite of the fact that twice a year they witness public conferences at which the Torah is magnified, they have never yielded a single proselyte.[45]

This last piece of evidence is particularly interesting. R. Ashi was not only head of the school at Sura, but the first compiler of the Babylonian Talmud, and at the end of the fourth century and beginning of the fifth he was one of Judaism's foremost authorities. The public conferences of which he speaks, and which were probably arranged on his initiative, were certainly inspired by propagandist motives, like the publicity the Jews in various places, and especially in Antioch, gave to the ceremonies of Synagogue worship.

The information derived from non-Jewish sources is more extensive and equally convincing. On the pagan side there is no break in the chain of testimonies after A.D. 70. Some of the most eloquent witness is of later date than A.D. 70. The sarcasms of Horace[46] are echoed in the first third of the second century, between the two Jewish wars, by those of Juvenal.[47] To judge by the vehemence he brings to his denuciations, it does not appear that the danger had lessened during the interval. It would seem rather that in the circles the satirist is concerned with, the commitment to Judaism had become stricter and more absolute from one generation to the next. For the intensification that is evident is more than simply an effect of style. Where the father has been satisfied with the monotheistic faith and some of the essential practices, such as Sabbath observance and abstention from pork, the son has accepted total conversion and become circumcised.

> *Quidam sortiti metuentem sabbata patrem*
> *Nil praeter nubes et caeli numen adorant*
> *Nec distare putant humana carne suillam,*
> *Qua pater abstinuit; mox et praeputia ponunt.*

From being a simple "God-fearer" the proselyte has become a full Jew, submitting to every particular of the Mosaic law, in contempt of the Roman traditions.

> *Romanas autem soliti contemnere leges*
> *Judaicum ediscunt et servant ac metuunt jus,*
> *Tradidit arcano quodcumque volumine Moyses:*
> *Non monstrare vias eadem nisi sacra colenti,*
> *Quaesitum ad fontem solos deducere verpos.*

This text is of prime importance. It is enough to establish with indisputable certainty the survival, even the increease, of proselytism, this being at a period in which some believe it to have been already on the wane. The text also gives us a valuable indication of the family setting in which conversions often took place. Without any new intervention of missionary activity from outside being necessary, conversion could be effected solely by the power of example, by the combination of paternal authority with the prestige of the rites themselves, and by the urge that leads the younger members of a family, in any field of activity, not only to emulate but to surpass their elders.

It is true that the facts pointed to by Juvenal antedate the law forbidding circumcision, and, strictly speaking, his evidence bears only on that transitory period that separated the two Jewish wars. It at least proves that the former of these did not entail the consequences that have sometimes been ascribed to it. It neither diminished the prestige of Judaism in gentile eyes, nor discouraged the Jews from missionary endeavor. It shows too that Hadrian's prohibition, which Antoninus maintained insofar as it applied to non-Jews, was combating a very prevalent practice. Since in later times the enactment seems to have become a dead letter, there is every reason to believe that the proselytizing movement went on after A.D. 135 just as it had done after A.D. 70.

Ought we to say that these thoroughgoing conversions were only the exception? If they had been, would they have engaged Juvenal's attention as they did? At all events they show that the stringent demands of the strict rabbis did not discourage the most determined converts, and that they can only be interpreted as a hurdle placed in the proselyte's way. Making due allowances for Juvenal's spitefulness we may deduce this much from his testimony, that Judaism, perhaps more so than in the preceding centuries, was making its mark in the world, and that even in the diaspora it continued to make converts from its implacably hostile rival. The accusation Juvenal hurls against Judaism is very similar, and cast in very similar terms, to that *odium humani generis* of which people accused the Christians, and of which Tacitus too accuses the Jews and their proselytes.[48] To be converted to Judaism was to break with the world. This at least is the impression which these contemporary writers had of the matter. They would doubtless not have felt this to the same degree in the milieu of a Philo, under whom Judaism itself made the effort of adaptation that otherwise it demanded of its proselytes. A stricter particularism was certainly one of the characteristics of Judaism after A.D. 70, but it was a particularism exactly comparable to that of the Christians. Far from excluding missionary activity, it was nourished by such endeavor, to the extent that those who were Jews by adoption came to react in precisely the same way as did the Jews by birth. The example of R. Akiba is sufficiently instructive here.

It seems to be completely established that the distinction between Jews and proselytes was thus gradually blurred, and that, at least in orthodox Judaism, semiconversions were discouraged until they disappeared altogether. Juvenal deplores the fact with vehemence. Dio Cassius, a century later, says with a historian's detachment: "The land [Palestine] is also called Judaea, and its inhabitants Jews. Whence is the name derived? I do not know; but it is applied also to those amongst other men, who, although of different race, observe zealously their laws. Such people are met even among the Romans."[49] This means that there was still an effective proselytism in this period, and that common opinion, even enlightened opinion, tended to confuse converts and native Jews as the Romans did.

The evidence from Christian authors is equally explicit and confirms the same conclusions. Justin Martyr expressly asserts that by circumcision a proselyte is assimilated to the Jewish people and becomes the equal of those born Jews.[50] The same author notes that the Jews in their struggle with Christianity have employed what amount to counterevangelistic missions, designed not merely to put the diaspora communities on their guard against this αἵρεσις ἄθεος καὶ ἄνομος, but also to dispute with the rival religion the possession of gentile converts.[51]

The anti-Jewish writings will freely introduce one or more converts as characters in their dialogues, and even apart from this device such writings clearly presuppose the existence of proselytism. Justin, in his dialogue, addresses himself to "Trypho... and to those who wish to become proselytes".[52] Like all good neophytes, these newly fledged Jews seem to have been particularly zealous to defend and propagate their faith. In the struggle against Christianity they played a major part. It is Justin, again, who emphasizes the particular keenness with which they carried on the conflict, i.e., as compared with the enthusiasm of the born Jews.[53] Tertullian likewise, at the beginning of his *Adversus Judaeos,* states that his treatise is intended to summarize and record an actual discussion in which a Christian and a proselyte engaged for an entire day. He ironically draws attention to the fact that the self-constituted champion of Judaism was a gentile. *Proxime accidit: Disputatio habita est Christiano et proselyto Judaeo.... Nam occasio quidem defendendi etiam gentibus divinam gratiam habuit hinc praerogativam quod sibi vindicare Dei legem instituerit homo ex gentibus nec de prosapia Israelitum Judaeus.*[54] Origen likewise notes that proselytism was still very much alive in his time.[55]

It is relevant to cite the celebrated verse of St. Matthew: "Alas for you, scribes and Pharisees, you hypocrites! You who travel over sea and land to make a single proselyte, and when you have him you make him twice as fit for hell as you are."[56] Friedländer, who denies that there was any proselytizing spirit among the Pharisees, has proposed a curious interpretation of this. The mention of the single proselyte who so engages the Pharisees' zealous endeavors indicates, he says, that they were opposed to mass conversions. It was only in exceptional circumstances that they would share their faith, and then only with rare individuals who had been properly tested and were reckoned worthy to be associated with the spiritual aristocracy, the Pharisees.[57] Besides, he argues, how could the Christians have complained when the Pharisees put into practice one of the essential commands of Jesus himself, the command to be apostles to the unbelievers?[58]

This is a complete misunderstanding. All the evidence points to the fact that it is not the principle of missionary activity that is at issue. The complaint is that the missionary work is done by those who are not fit to do it, and the results, for those converted by their efforts, are disastrous. For instead of leading to salvation, as a conversion to Christianity would do, Pharisaic conversion only leads to destruction. It is also evident that the mention, in the singular, of one proselyte and one only, is not meant restrictively. On the contrary, the uniqueness of this convert, like the difficult missionary journeys across the breadth of the earth, expresses the doggedness with which the

Pharisees exploit every opportunity, even the smallest, for preaching their faith.[59] Perhaps it is also meant to suggest that the results are not at all in proportion to the effort expended. It is in any case eloquent testimony to the proselytizing spirit of the rabbis, and also, let us note yet again, an unequivocal indication of Christian annoyance at the competition of a hated rival.[60] What was true at the time when the gospel took shape (by which time, since the temple had been destroyed, Pharisaism and Judaism were practically synonymous) was still true in the centuries that followed. The testimony of Origen, for whom the gospel's invective is always alive and relevant, entitles us to believe this.

It would be gratifying to be able to arrive at some conclusions about the extent of the Jewish missionary movement and its results. But precise information on this count is lacking. The texts give us no figures of any kind. One might at first sight expect help from Jewish epigraphy, as recently catalogued by Frey, but this source of information gives us nothing bearing on our question except some rather deceptive indications. Volume 1, the only one that has so far appeared, of the *Corpus Inscriptionum Judaicarum*, which contains more than 700 European Jewish inscriptions, records only nine relating to proselytes. Only four others mention *metuentes*.[61] It is not many. But as Frey himself notes, quoting Cumont, the *argumentum ex silentio*, when applied to epigraphical materials, is not a very strong one.[62] Everything depends on what happens to have been found, and new discoveries are liable to alter the state of our knowledge quite radically.

Furthermore, practically all the inscriptions in this collection are of Roman origin. The Roman capital was always a great center of Jewish life. Now most of the inscriptions seem to be later than A.D. 70,[63] and it may legitimately be argued that, if after that date the government kept an eye on proselytizing, it would be in Rome, above all, that its precautions would be effective. It is possible that in these circumstances the converts, especially if they were men, might sometimes have gone to some trouble not to divulge the fact that they were proselytes, and that in order to avoid making difficulties for their relatives and friends they might not have indicated it on their epitaphs.[64] To have mentioned these things might well have caused trouble. Besides, it would ordinarily be hopeless to try to trace a proselyte burial when the person in question was a second- or third-generation convert. Such people were not regarded as proselytes but as real Jews. The distinction between proselytes and native Israelites is all the more difficult to draw in that frequently a Jewish name was given on conversion, which was added to or substituted for the

Roman name, and conversely, genuine Jews often bore Greek or Latin names.[65] Juvenal's evidence attests the frequency with which Judaism was passed on from father to son, and this prompts us to interpret the epigraphical evidence with caution. The paucity of proselytes explicitly mentioned in the inscriptions does not entitle us to conclude that there was a shortage of proselytizing activity.

We may go further. Nearly all the inscriptions available to us come, so far as we can judge, from a somewhat strict orthodox community. It was strict enough, if not to reject semiproselytes altogether, at least to exclude them from the community. The epitaphs of *metuentes* are to be found outside the great Jewish cemeteries.[66] Now, there is every reason to believe that, although straightforward conversions did take place, most gentiles who were smitten with the religious disease favored partial conversion. The consequences of this were less serious. Even the Palestinian rabbis, or at least some of them, continued to accept such partial converts. They filled the outer courts of the synagogues of the diaspora. Not only that, but they provided the population for the complex world of the sects, the Jewish-Christian, the Jewish-pagan, and the Jewish-pagan-Christian.

In either case, it is to be expected that they would leave little evidence behind them in the way of inscriptions. Neither is it surprising that inscriptions relating to *metuentes* should be even rarer than those of proselytes. The "God-fearers" represented a fairly well-defined category. Yet alongside them are visible (sometimes very plainly visible) a host of Judaizers, pagan and Christian, some of them stuck halfway toward strict orthodox observance, some attached to one or other of the syncretizing sects. These did not amount to positive acquisitions for Judaism, but they do indicate nonetheless that Judaism at this period retained not only its power to attract but also its will to conquer. For although the Jews preferred wholehearted conversions (and there is no doubt at all that this is so), and though they devoted their energies to producing such conversions, they were nevertheless willing to accommodate the scruples and hesitations of the wider circle of their hangers-on. The Judaizing movement itself was far from being a spontaneous phenomenon. Its existence must be put to the credit of the Jewish missionary movement. Similarly, the swarm of Judaizing sects, even though they were disregarded or despised by the orthodox rabbis, are firm witness to the vitality and adaptability of a Judaism that the rigid framework of Talmudic legalism simply failed to contain.

In addition to all this, Jewish missionary activity took on a multitude of forms and used a multitude of different methods, and these are so various that they frequently escape proper investigation.

Their results, however, are clearly perceptible. Jewish proselytism is based on a threefold appeal. The three components do not always bear the same relationship to one another. Sometimes one is the more important, sometimes another, and the proportions in which they are combined vary considerably. The three factors are the monotheistic idea, the moral law, and the attraction of Jewish rites. The first two of these brought Judaism a number of discerning recruits, whereas the last helped to diffuse its influence more widely, though it was not always, and perhaps not often, the deciding factor in total conversions.[67]

It is Tertullian who, among early authors, bears particular witness to the hold Jewish rites had over the pagan masses. *Vos certe estis, qui etiam in laterculum septem dierum solem recepistis, et ex diebus ipso priorem praelegistis, quo die lavacrum subtrahatis aut in vesperam differatis, aut otium et prandium curetis. Quod quidem facitis exorbitantes et ipsi a vestris ad alienas religiones. Judaei enim festi sabbata et cena pura et Judaici ritus lucernarum et jejuna cum azymis et orationes litorales, quae utique aliena sunt a diis vestris.*[68]

This diffuse influence, which acted upon Christians as much as on pagans, cannot properly be called a form of proselytism. But it is a side effect of proselytism, and presupposes its existence. Proselytizing and Judaizing declined in step with one another. The falling off of the one entailed the gradual disappearance of the other. Conversely, as long as the Judaizing movement continued we may legitimately infer that proselytizing continued also. The spread of what St. John Chrysostom called the Jewish sickness demands as its primary agent a Judaism that has not yet withdrawn into itself.

The allusions Christian authors make to Jewish "baptism" provide us with a definite piece of evidence concerning the popularity of Jewish rites and the persistence of proselytism.

The word translated "baptism" (*tevilah*) has two meanings in rabbinic usage. It designates the repeated ablutions practiced by the Jews whenever they found themselves in a state of ritual impurity, and it also denotes the act that was ordinarily associated with circumcision, in which converts were made members of Judaism.[69]

The baptism of proselytes was surrounded, it seems, with special solemnity, rather as Christian baptism was.[70] As a rite accompanying circumcision, it was peculiar to proselytes, being without equivalent for those who were Jews by birth. Its importance increased in the second century when the circumcision of non-Jews was forbidden by imperial law. In some communities it was thus able to be treated as a substitute for circumcision, as the only initiatory rite. Certain rabbis, as we have seen, regarded it as sufficient in itself.[71] But both in its form, as a rite of immersion, and in its effects, it was identical with the

Levitical ablutions, for it eliminated ritual impurity. The impurity in the case of the Jew was accidental and in the gentile's case congenital. The purity it conferred on proselytes was acquired by them once and for all. It did not, however, absolve them from the use of the regular purificatory rituals afterwards.

The close similarity between the two rites explains why the Christian authors, when they speak of Jewish baptism, apply to it the name of the Christian sacrament and speak of it as if it were familiar to their readers, without always clearly distinguishing the rites from one another. Sometime when they use the word *baptism* they are thinking of the regular ablutions, which is why these authors sometimes emphasize, as a contrast between Jewish baptism and Christian, the fact that the Jewish rite is repeated.[72] Most frequently they are thinking of proselyte baptism and purificatory baths at the same time.[73] But they always put the Jewish rite and Christian baptism side by side, and set themselves to demonstrate the conspicuous superiority of the latter. The former can have no effect except on the body. Only Christian baptism is capable of purifying the soul.[74] St. John Chrysostom does allow to Jewish baptism a religious value, which distinguishes it from the ordinary bath taken for hygienic reasons.[75] Pope Damasus is manifestly thinking of the initiatory rite when he contrasts not only the profound reality and efficaciouness of the two sacraments, but their formulae. *In Patre et Filio et Spiritu Sancto solum baptizamur et non in Archangelorum nominibus, aut Angelorum quomodo haeretici aut Judaei aut etiam Gentiles dementes faciunt.*[76]

It is at first sight astonishing to find heretics, pagans, and Jews all thrown together in this way, and it might be tempting to dismiss the combination as fantastic if we did not know from elsewhere that angelology played an important part in some Jewish circles at this period, and that in this respect Judaism powerfully influenced the degraded forms of syncretizing gnosticism, both pagan and Christian.[77] A baptism in the name of the angels, unlikely as it would be in orthodox Judaism, would be quite compatible with what we know of common syncretism. And in the development of such syncretism the Jews of the diaspora played a large part.

All this evidence bears witness to the Christian authors' determination to discourage believers from engaging in practices with which they were all too familiar. We see this even more clearly with Isaac of Antioch, when in a sermon in which he takes the Jews vigorously to task, he denounces those who, though they are baptized Christians, go on to receive "the ablutions of demons."[78] This means those who avail themselves of proselyte baptism, or at least of the Levitical purifications, and who in general indulge in Judaizing activities.

We are well informed about the spread of the "Jewish sickness." We are not sure, however, about the numbers of true proselytes or how they compared with the numbers of the various sorts of Judaizers. One fact at least stands out clearly: Judaism continued to make itself felt during the first centuries of the Christian era, and in many and varied ways it affected considerable numbers of both pagans and Christians.

III

How long did the effort to proselytize remain potent enough to disturb the Church, and for how long were its successes sufficient to be an embarrassment? We cannot hope to obtain a precise answer to this question. It is obvious that no actual date can be given. There was no sudden break between the period of active missionary effort and that of retrenchment. The transition from one to the other was made imperceptibly. Ancient Judaism was moved by two essential preoccupations, expansion and conservation, to increase itself by conversions and to preserve its cohesion and its peculiar character. It was only by slow degrees that these two objectives came to be seen as incompatible. The equilibrium that had earlier been attained was progressively upset, though we are unable to trace in detail the stages by which this happened. We only know that the development ended by Israel's relinquishing completely her missionary function. Some groups seem to have remained faithful to the proselytizing ideal until well into the Middle Ages.[79] Amongst others the retrenchment was already under way by the beginning of the Christian era.

It was under way, but not achieved. It must be conceded, regarding Judaism as a whole, that at the end of the period we are dealing with proselytism was still going on. The Jewish, pagan, and Christian sources of the second and third centuries we have already cited are echoed by the fathers of the fourth.

There are perceptible variations between one region of the empire and another. In Italy missionary activity, or at least the tally of its successes, seems to have been reduced, perhaps because the imperial authorities were vigilant and close at hand. Ambrosiaster notes that, though it does happen that pagans are converted to Judaism, it is nevertheless somewhat rare.[80] In other provinces, on the contrary, there are indications suggesting a revival of missionary activity.

It looks as if the triumph of the Church had, here and there, galvanized the Jews into a final effort. A number of pointers may have led them to believe that the game might not yet be irrevocably lost.

Among these were the internal divisions of Christianity, and in particular the spread of Arianism, in which the Jews perhaps saw a hint of a return to strict monotheism.[81] There was also Julian's benevolent policy toward Israel.[82] As late as the beginning of the fifth century a legislative text notes a renewed audacity among the Jews of Africa. This doubtless means a renewed proselytizing zeal.[83]

In the east the phenomenon is even more in evidence. It was at the beginning of the fourth century that there broke over the Christian community in Antioch the Judaizing wave that Chrysostom took it upon himself to stem. Doubtless this was a chronic problem in the Syrian capital; Josephus had already noted that a large part of the population there were Judaizers.[84] But at this particular point in time it became especially acute. The very distress it arouses in Chrysostom himself indicates the exceptional nature of the threat. It presupposes something quite other than the populace's atavistic tendency to succumb to the lure of Judaism.

It was a genuine missionary campaign, deploying all available resources. The campaign was buttressed by the very wide publicity given to the Jewish cult, both inside and outside the synagogues, especially at the time of the great autumn feasts, New Year, Yom Kippur, and Tabernacles, and by very careful staging.[85] It not only made use of the prestige of these rites and ceremonies but appealed to the innate love of the populace for spectacle of any kind.[86] There was not only the ceremony of trumpet blowing at the New Year, but singing by choirs and, it seems, sacred dances[87] performed in the open air. Believers were often drawn to take part in Jewish ceremonies by motives that had nothing to do with religion, and even by idle curiosity, ἐπὶ τὴν θέαν. But mere spectators quickly found themselves participants; συνεορτάζουσι.[88] And this is just what the Jews were aiming at in their attempt at communal evangelism. Chrysostom is quite explicit about this. The Jews, more wicked than any wolf, make preparations as their feasts approach to attack the flock. We must therefore, says Chrysostom, get ready our weapons beforehand.[89] The same image is used by St. Jerome in drawing attention to the same danger. *Atque utinam sanctorum orationibus non nos inquietarent judaici serpentes... quorum turba in similitudinem luporum gregem Christi circuientes non parvas nobis excubias et laborem incutiunt, dum volumus oves Domini custodire, ne ab his dilacerentur.*[90] Jerome, it appears, is thinking of direct, individual endeavor, completing the evangelistic work of the Synagogue. It will be better not to insist too strongly, as Strack and Billerbeck do, on the passivity of the rabbis, ready to collect proselytes but not much inclined to prompt conversions.[91]

It may perhaps be objected that these facts relate only to certain localities—localities, moreover, in which there were important Jewish communities. Non-Jews in such places would thus, by virtue of their cultural situation, be more exposed than Jews elsewhere to Jewish influence. And it is true that the Syrian and Semitic East and, for rather similar reasons, North Africa were easy territory for Jewish missionary work.[92] But other pieces of evidence suggest that we ought to see the persistence of proselytism as a much more general phenomenon. This evidence consists chiefly of the conciliar canons against Judaizers, of which I shall speak again shortly, and the repeated statements of the Christian legislation that aimed to suppress Jewish missionary activity.

Legislators, whether ecclesiastical or lay, are scarcely the people to make a habit of combating phantom threats. Of all the anti-Semitic measures that have been enacted in our own time by racist or fascist governments, none that I know of takes account of Jewish religious missionary endeavor, for the very simple reason that it is an extremely long time since the Jews have indulged in such activity. The Christian empire, on the contrary, made the issue a strictly religious one. Its legislation reflects the preoccupations of the Church. The Jews were in some respects outside the common law. The Christian emperors continued to recognize, as their pagan predecessors had done, the Jews' special status. All this must be regarded, at least at the outset, as being in the Jews' favor rather than as a vexation to them. Of the privileges thus sanctioned, privileges that were of both a religious and a social nature, only one was explicitly and immediately withdrawn from the Jews, and this was the very one concerning which modern laws are silent, the right to propagate their faith. The contrast here is not simply a contrast between the mentalities of the two eras concerned. The emperors condemned Jewish missionary activity because the Jews continued to indulge in it throughout the empire.

Whereas the pagan emperors restricted themselves, in respect of proselytism, to a few rather random attempts at suppression, and did not in the event do anything effective or lasting to put a stop to it, in the fourth century precise legislation on the subject was laid down. This is a vital aspect of a change of attitude whose other manifestations we have already noticed. It is a change that demonstrates the increasing grip the ecclesiastical authorities exercised over the public authorities.

The measures restricting proselytism were among the first of many that, little by little, altered the status of the Jews. And it was natural that, before withdrawing the rights that had been expressly accorded to the Jews, the Christian legislators should suppress an activity that under the pagan empire had never been more than tolerated. It was theologically necessary that the Jews should continue to exist, but only the genuine people of Israel, the descendants of those who crucified the Christ. They alone were of any use as witnesses. It was not permissible that they should, in addition, recruit new members from outside.

It is clear, however, that theology was not the only matter, or even the primary one, at issue. There was also the immediate interests of the Church to be considered. In a world remodeled on Christian lines there was no occasion for error to exist freely, side by side with truth. The spread of Judaism would have been a scandal of the same order as the offensive return or too audacious survival of paganism. Doubtless, God was able to insure the triumph of His own cause. It was nevertheless a good thing for Christians, including Christian princes, to give a helping hand. They gave it energetically. The struggle was unquestionably a fierce one.

Judaizing Christians were susceptible to ecclesiastical discipline. Against the proselytizing Jews and their converts the Church could do nothing. It was the job of the secular arm, placing itself at the disposal of the faith, to prevent the latter from overstepping their legal rights, and to hold the former to their duty toward Christian society. And if either should transgress the prohibitions laid down, it was the job of the secular arm to mete out punishment.

The laws suppressing proselytism form a series stretching from the peace of the Church under Constantine to the redaction of the Theodosian Code. The very fact that they are repeated, and the severity of the penalties laid down, are proof both of their ineffectiveness and of the seriousness of the danger. Some of the enactments strike directly and explicitly at proselytism. Others achieve the same end obliquely, being aimed at suppressing particular forms of proselytism or removing particular opportunities for it.

From A.D. 315 onwards Constantine prosecuted the new policy energetically, forbidding conversions to Judaism on pain of death.[93] The prohibition was several times renewed by his successors. Constantius provided for the confiscation of the goods of apostates,[94] Gratian forbade them to leave their property in a will.[95] The softening of the penalty doubtless reflects the personal inclinations of the legislator rather than a relaxation of the danger. For the law of Valentinian on the same subject attaches guilt not only to the convert but to him who prompted the conversion. It does not lay down a fixed penalty for the latter but leaves it to the discretion of the tribunal. The nature of the relaxation here reveals itself very clearly. What it is really doing is shifting the penalty from one party to another, and changing the law's approach to the problem. The Christian convert to

Judaism is now made to look more like a victim than a guilty party, and the absence of precision about the punishment to be inflicted on the proselytizing Jew is a thinly disguised invitation to severity. In fact, in 409 Jewish missionary activity is assimilated by a new law to the crime of lèse-majesté.[96] And in 438 the death penalty is reintroduced, but this time not only for the Christian convert to Judaism but also for the proselytizer.[97]

Alongside the antiproselytizing legislation, and complementary to it, measures were elaborated that envisaged the reduction of possible opportunities for proselytism. The question of marriage was thus dealt with. Constantius, in a law whose harshness contrasts with the relative mildness of his law on conversions, forbids Jewish men to take Christian wives and lays down the death penalty for the Jewish husband.[98] There is no mention of the marriage of a Jewish woman with a Christian husband, doubtless because it is tacitly assumed that the woman in either case would ordinarily be expected to adopt her husband's religion, or at least be under pressure to do so.

In this matter too the law becomes more stringent toward the end of the century, in accordance with the increasing hold the Church gained over the civil power. A law of Theodosius, taking over the view of the Church councils, treats all mixed marriages of Jews and Christians, even those in which the woman is the Jewish partner, as cases of adultery, and punishes them as such.[99] The desire to prevent conversions is combined here with the desire to keep Judaism in its isolation. It may be concluded from these measures that the mass of believers did not share the aversion for the Jews that was felt by the ecclesiastical authorities, and that the Jews were not always so spontaneously inclined to withdraw into themselves as has often been claimed. Either the old prohibition did not extend to all gentiles, or, especially in the diaspora, it was not entirely respected.[100]

The enactments relating to marriage were paralleled by the legislation concerning slaves. This attention to slavery had begun as early as the reign of Constantine. Early in his reign he had forbidden conversions to Judaism, and in a fresh enactment toward the end of it he included within this prohibition all conversions of slaves, whether enforced ones or willing. He forbade Jews to circumcise their Christian slaves and decreed that circumcision carried out in defiance of the law should be followed by the manumission of the slave concerned, though as yet no penalty was laid down for the slave owner.[101] This legislation was tightened up in later enactments, and modified in the direction of greater severity. The prohibition went so far as to include the very acquisition of non-Jewish slaves, whether pagan or Christian, though the punishment was different in the two cases. A law of Constantius threatens with the death penalty the master who circumcises non-Jewish slaves. He who buys pagan slaves must give them up again, the value of them going into the public treasury. He who buys Christian slaves suffers in addition the confiscation of his goods.[102] During the period that followed there were nevertheless some fluctuations in the law relating to slaves. Honorius restored to the Jews the right to possess Christian slaves, on the condition that they were allowed to practice their religion freely.[103] Theodosius II finally reimposed the prohibition on the Jews' acquiring such slaves, but allowed slave owners to keep those which they already possessed. Besides this, he renewed the provision of the death penalty with confiscation of goods for those who imposed circumcision. This is the main burden of his enactment.[104]

This collection of measures helps us to understand the legislation concerning the synagogues that we were considering above,[105] for this legislation about synagogues springs partly from the same preoccupations. For in the ancient world the proselytizing efforts of Israel were always organized around the synagogue, which was open to all *goyim* who were in search of truth. Chrysostom's appeals to the faithful, adjuring them not to go near these places of perdition, illuminates this aspect of the code. In order to counteract proselytism, it was not enough to forbid Jews to practice it in open and aggressive form. It was also necessary to reduce the permanent possibilities for proselytism that the public worship of the Synagogue provided. This was, as we have seen, a potent influence. Civil legislation could hardly forbid non-Jews access to the synagogues; that was a matter for preachers and for the councils of the Church. But by limiting the Jews' liberty of action in the matter of buildings for worship the emperor gave useful assistance to the clergy.

It is noteworthy that when Patriarch Gamaliel VI[106] was found guilty of proselytizing and deprived of his honorary prefecture, he was charged at the same time with having circumcised Christian slaves and having illegally built new synagogues.[107] Such building is a sign of religious vitality. A religion that by governmental decision is restricted to an altogether static role is obliged to exist on what it already possesses in respect both of members and of places of worship. The legislation concerning synagogues is a logical complement to the enactments suppressing proselytism.

The question of synagogues was all the more important for proselytism since worship seems to have been carried on most frequently in the vernacular, and the commentary on the law, which constituted catechetical instruction, was done through the same

medium. We have here another extremely useful criterion for
determining the duration of proselytism, the persistence of Greek and
perhaps Latin in Jewish religious usage.

Greek was employed in the synagogues not only of the diaspora but
of Palestine. In the diaspora it was used almost exclusively, but in
Palestine it was employed alongside Aramaic or Hebrew. And as long
as this state of affairs continued the opportunities for Israel's
missionary work remained open. Linguistic differentiation from the
gentiles may be taken not only as the clearest sign of retrenchment,
but also as a cause and a consequence of retrenchment. On the day
when it became necessary, in order to understand the synagogue
liturgy or participate in its worship, to have a prior knowledge of
Hebrew, the enthusiasm of the Judaizers would be very likely to wane.
And it might well be said that the fate of Greek in the Synagogue and
the fate of Jewish proselytism were bound up together. It is
noteworthy that on these two questions the Talmud reflects the same
hesitations, the same divergences of opinion, and the same contradictions.

At the end of the second century Greek language and culture were
still held in honor among the family and entourage of Rabban
Gamaliel II, because, as the scholars explain in their attempts to
excuse him, he was by virtue of his position in close contact with the
Roman authorities.[108] It is significant that the crisis of A.D. 70 did not
bring in its wake any immediate reactions on this score. At all events,
hatred of the Romans did not seem to be obliged to express itself in
hostility toward the Greek language. The Jews, like all the Eastern
subject peoples of the Roman Empire, knew when to make a
distinction between the political authority of Rome and the culture
that the Romans had appropriated and spread, but that originally
was not theirs at all. The example of the Sibylline oracles is from this
point of view very significant. The Jewish author's animosity against
Rome does not prevent him from reacting as certain Greeks
themselves doubtless did with regard to the ruling power. We have
here an expression of the curious solidarity of sentiment and culture
that existed throughout those Eastern lands which Rome had
annexed but never assimilated.[109]

It is at the beginning of the second century that the rabbis are seen
to anathematize the language of the pagans and those who use it.
Rabbi Joshua and Rabbi Ishmael (the latter was to be one of the
victims of Hadrian's War) say ironically that the study of Greek is to
be undertaken only at an hour that is neither day nor night. All the
rest is to be devoted to the study of the Torah, for it is written: "You
shall meditate on it day and night."[110] Whoever teaches Greek wisdom

to his children is accursed.[111] And Rabbi Elisha ben Abuya's apostasy
is put down by the rabbis to his busying himself with Greek books.[112]

A number of critics, including Bossuet in particular, have rightly
seen in these hostile attitudes a basic factor in the move toward
retrenchment, and their appearance as the first evidence of the
change.[113] But many years, centuries even, were needed before the
prohibition was accepted and applied throughout the whole Jewish
world. The condemnations I have just quoted come from Palestinian
rabbis, for whom Greek was a foreign language. To do without it was
no trouble to them. For the Jews of the diaspora, and this means, let
us not forget, the majority of Jews, who conversed as well as prayed in
Greek, to renounce the language would have been to renounce their
mother tongue and to upset completely their whole way of life.

The epigraphical evidence is here especially valuable. The part
played by Hebrew is reduced almost to nothing.[114] All that remains is
a few brief formulae, one or two stereotyped phrases, which were in
any case not always understood by those who used them. They are
precisely similar to the appearance in our own days of the words *De
Profundis* or *R.I.P.* at the end of an epitaph or a notice of death. The
commonest Jewish formula of this sort is the ritual *shalom*.[115] The
earliest-occurring Hebrew inscriptions are later in date than the
period that interest us, and even then they are usually accompanied
by Greek or Latin translations.[116] Not only was Hebrew not used in
normal life, but it is not certain that it was used, at any part of the
period, even in worship, with the possible exception of certain
liturgical readings. Lacking direct evidence,[117] we can by no means
confirm this, but the likelihood is that the language of public worship
was Greek.

This was the situation at the beginning of the Christian era, and so
it seems to have remained for several centuries among the major part
of the diaspora communities.[118] For if much practical use had been
made of Hebrew, the pagan and Christian writers who give us our
information about Judaism would doubtless not have omitted to let
us know, for it would have been an additional mark of the
particularism to which they took such exception. The *argumentum ex
silentio* would seem to have some force in this instance.

There are other, more positive indications. The fact that the Jews,
in their anxiety to attract pagans and Christians, gave such publicity
to their worship, leads us to imagine that the Synagogue services must
have been largely in the vernacular. It must, in particular, have been
used in the sermon, whose importance in Jewish worship is known.[119]
Even in Palestine Greek was freely employed as a liturgical
language.[120] There is all the more reason that such should have been

the case in the diaspora. The experience of Rabbi Meir is noteworthy. While making a tour of Asia Minor he did not find anywhere among his Hellenized fellow Jews a single copy in Hebrew of the book of Esther. When he wished, on the feast of Purim, to follow the custom with which he was familiar and to make a liturgical reading from the book of Esther, he was reduced to writing one out from memory.[121]

Even in those regions where Greek was a foreign language, and where one would not therefore expect it to be preeminent, it nevertheless shows an astonishing liveliness in Jewish usage. It is especially surprising to discover that in Spain in the fifth century, and perhaps even in the sixth, a time when Spain was under the control of the Visigoths, the inscriptions of the synagogue at Elche are in Greek.[122] In the trilingual epitaph from Tortosa, which should in all probability be dated in the sixth century, Greek appears alongside Latin, the common tongue, and Hebrew, which was perhaps already the liturgical language.[123] From the same period, in the catacomb of Venosa in Apulia, Greek and Latin are also used conjointly with Hebrew.[124] One cannot help but be struck by the similarity between this use of Greek and that of the first Christians of the west.[125] Both Jews and Christians must sometimes have appeared, in the eyes of the Westerners, to be behaving like foreigners. While the children of Israel remained faithful to the East as their spiritual home, they demonstrated this fact by their attachment not to biblical Hebrew, but to Greek.

From the examples referred to, it would seem that the Jews were more tenaciously devoted to Greek than the Christians were, for the Christians fairly quickly became latinized.[126] Albertini, commenting on the Elche inscriptions, points out that the use of Greek in Spain, where it was a rarity, can only be properly explained by the supposition that this was a period in which knowledge of Greek, however scanty, was something to be displayed with pride.[127] It was thus a means of defense against barbarism, triumphant under its Latin veneer. By clinging to Greek with such remarkable tenacity the Spanish Jews were behaving like good citizens of the empire and of the civilized world. Their fate under the rule of the Visigoths does not interest us here. But to restrict our attention to the end of the Roman period only, we do not lack indications that connect the apparently cosmopolitian character of Spanish Judaism with the persistent uneasiness its religious practices aroused in the Church authorities. This uneasiness is attested by the decisions of the council of Elvira concerning Judaizing practices.[128]

It is even more significant that Greek maintained its position alongside Hebrew or Aramaic, and maintained it with great tenacity, in Palestine itself and in the areas that could be regarded as within the Palestinian sphere of influence. Recent archaeological discoveries have confirmed the evidence of the texts.[129] The case of Dura may pass almost without comment. Everything at Dura bears witness to a cultural and religious liberalism that implies that the synagogue membership was drawn from a wide circle. The trilingual inscriptions in the frescoes are only one sign among many. The decoration of the Galilean and Trans-Jordanian synagogues is less striking in both its nature and its quality. These synagogues are, on the other hand, richer in inscriptions. This fact, together with their later date and their geographical situation, makes them all the more interesting from our point of view. The synagogue at Ain Duq, which may be dated at the beginning of the fifth century, has inscriptions in Hebrew and Aramaic only. By contrast, Greek occupies a very important place in the inscriptions of Beth Alpha, Jerash, and El Hammeh, which are from the same period, or even a little later. The same is true of the inscriptions brought to light in 1938 by the excavations at Sheik Abrek, near Haifa, and which should in all likelihood be dated in the third century.[130] The interest of these last materials is increased by the fact that, once Galilee had become the centre of rabbinic Judaism, Sheik Abrek became one of the residences of the Patriarch. Greek could not have been used there without his permission.

Besides all this, the Mishnah expressly recognizes the right to recite the essential prayers of the liturgy, in particular the *Shema*, the *Tephillah*, and the blessings over meals, in any language whatever. Only certain formulae, such as, for example, the priestly benediction, or certain texts, must of necessity be pronounced in Hebrew.[131] And it is not, even so, quite certain that the diaspora held rigorously to the latter prescription. The scholars comfort themselves by saying that it is better to pray in Greek than not to pray at all.[132]

Thus they were quickly obliged to moderate their intransigent attitude, even with respect to cult usage. In rehabilitating Greek, all that they had done was to ratify a usage that was too deeply rooted to be got rid of by anathemas. They did this, moreover, with a good grace, or so it appears. Let us beware, therefore, even when speaking of the most orthodox Talmudic rabbinism, of emphasizing retrenchment too strongly, and above all, of dating it too early.

From the testimony of St. Jerome it emerges that at the end of the fourth century rabbinic teaching itself was still given at least partly in Greek. *Si quando certis diebus traditiones suas exponunt, discipulis suis solent dicere*: οἱ σοφοὶ δευτεροῦσιν.[133]

The prohibition formulated at the beginning of the second century is exactly contemporaneous with the troubles that marked the reign of

Trajan. These troubles affected both Palestine and certain parts of the Eastern diaspora.[134] The prohibition, like the troubles themselves, seems to be connected with the passing wave of nationalism, or, more exactly, of Jewish political Messianism. It was an ephemeral manifestation of Zealot fanaticism. There is nothing to suggest that, even at the time, the majority of rabbinic opinion favored it. In any case, this negative attitude toward Greek did not last. As early as the end of the second century Rabbi Judah han-Nasi, grandson of Gamaliel II, withdrew the earlier formula of prohibition. In keeping with the tradition of his family, he was himself imbued with Greco-Latin culture. He was on excellent terms not only with Rome, whose civilizing work he recognized and appreciated, but with the emperor himself.[135] It is not surprising that he explicitly authorized and encouraged among his entourage the study and use of Greek, and that in this way he gained the favor of the ruling classes.[136] It is, moreover, very significant that this skillful and enlightened diplomat at the same time actively promoted the compilation of the Mishnah and gave his official blessing to it, as Bacher and Watzinger have rightly stressed.[137]

The same rabbis would have liked to eliminate from Palestine "vulgar Aramaic," and wished to see spoken there only two languages, the sacred tongue and Greek.[138] Certain rabbis drew a distinction between Greek wisdom and the Greek language, repudiating the former and consequently only accepting the latter as a mere means of communication it was useful to be adept in.[139] This was not the point of view of the patriarchal family. On the contrary, followed by a number of scholars, they applied themselves to assimilating Hellenism's cultural values. In the household of Rabbi Gamaliel, says the Talmudic tradition, 500 young men used to study the Torah and 500 others the wisdom of the Greeks.[140] Was this not the attitude of the enlightened diaspora, which took pleasure in emphasizing the agreement between the biblical revelation and the teaching of Greek thinkers, whom it regarded as unconscious disciples of Moses? Similarly, Rabbi Abbahu, in the name of Rabbi Johanan, allows girls to learn Greek, because it is an ornament to their minds.[141]

There is more to these liberal attitudes than mere opportunism or snobbery. They doubtless reflect a concern for proselytism. In order to make an impact on the pagan world, it was necessary to know and understand it. The rabbis were conscious of their immunity to the bad influence of pagan thought. The reading of Homer was no more harmful than the reading of a simple letter.[142] But it did leave its impression on their minds and they were thus all the better armed for their mission. This preoccupation was kept up for a long time, at least by certain individuals. The rabbi who initiated Jerome into Semitic languages knew, besides Hebrew and Aramaic, not only Greek but Latin. He quotes Virgil.[143] It may be imagined what a help the knowledge of these things would be to him in the controversies that, according to Jerome, the Jews were always so anxious to engage in with the Christians.

The fuel for these controversies was biblical texts. Until Christianity appeared on the scene, the Septuagint had been the version officially approved and the one that in practice the synagogues of the diaspora used. But from the moment when the Christians began to draw their arguments from it, and appropriate it in order to confound the Jews, the latter are seen gradually to turn away from it. From the third century onwards the Jews as a community seem to have abandoned it and substituted for it new translations, in particular that of Aquila.[144]

By comparison with the Septuagint, this translation reflects a manifest recoil from Hellenism. It displays a slavish literalism that does violence to the genius of the Greek language. The fact remains, nevertheless, that it answered a need. It was addressed, within Judaism, to a public incapable of reading the sacred text in its original tongue. These people had to be armed with weapons adapted to the situation and forewarned against the scripturally based objections that Christians raised. The prohibition of Greek, coming a little earlier than the Bible of Aquila, was contemporaneous with the Christian takeover of the Septuagint. It may therefore have been aimed not so much at Greek culture itself but at the Septuagint, which in the eyes of most Jews was Greek culture's representative, and which for many of them provided the only opportunity they had for effective contact with Hellenistic thought. Was not the condemnation of the Greek language essentially an instruction not to read the Septuagint?[145] Looked at in this way, the measure takes on a relative and transitory character. It is anti-Christian as much as anti-Greek. It condemns Greek insofar as it has become the instrument of the rival proclamation. It is a temporary expedient while Judaism makes ready a new translation.

This new translation bears witness not only to the survival of an important Greek-speaking section of Judaism and the desire to protect it from the Christian blight. It demonstrates also the will to make some impact yet on the world outside. There was still the will to confound and convert Christians, and to dispute with Christianity over pagan souls.

It is not insignificant that, according to a quite firm tradition, Aquila was a proselyte. In translating the sacred text, he must have had in mind the missionary activity of which he himself was a product and which now, because of the intervention of the Christians, was in need of new methods.[146] This is not mere speculation. The most illustrious rabbis of the time, Eliezer, Jehoshua, and Akiba himself, patronized Aquila's translation, apparently expecting beneficial effects on Judaism's expansion. They say in praise of the translator, "You are the fairest of the sons of men,"[147] a biblical quotation, but also a play on words. The beauty of which he partakes (*yaphyaphitha*) is that of Japheth (*yapheth*) whose descendants are the Greeks. The beauty, more exactly, is that of the Greek language. When the rabbis comment upon the benediction of Japheth,[148] which itself contains a play on words, they are again thinking of Aquila when they apply it, quite explicitly this time, to the Greek language. "May God give room to Japheth, may he live in the tents of Shem." The "room" becomes, in their interpretation, beauty.[149] The most beautiful thing Japheth possesses, namely, the Greek language, lives in the tents of Shem. It was introduced there by Aquila.[150]

Japheth means the Greek language. It also means the Hellenistic gentile world by which it is spoken. "The tents of Shem" stand for Judaism. We may translate: the new Bible, for its non-Jewish readers, is the means whereby they may come to belong to Israel. In this way the parabolic language of the rabbis lays down the program for the world mission it is the job of Aquila's translation to serve. And we can see here, at the same time, to what extent the Jews' reactions to the profane tongue can provide us with information about the fate of their missionary activities. We have here a sure touchstone. To remain faithful to Greek was to remain faithful to their proselytizing message. The repudiation of the Septuagint was not a repudiation of all missionary activity. In spite of its weaknesses, Aquila's translation, so favorably received, remained popular among the Greek-speaking Jews. It was still in use in Justinian's time among the communities of the diaspora. The point at which it appeared was one at which a decisive change was taking place in the linguistic and religious history of Israel, a change that closed one period and opened another. It is illustrated by the imperial *Novella 146*.[151]

This official enactment attempted, among other things, to settle the conflict that had arisen in the Synagogue concerning the language of the liturgy. The Hebraist party wished to use only the sacred tongue, even for the reading of the Bible. Their opponents wished to sanction the simultaneous, if not exclusive, use of Greek. It was at the request of the latter that the emperor intervened, and he laid it down that they should have their way.

If, in order to gain their ends, they were obliged to appeal to the civil authority, it is evident that the supporters of Greek were in a minority and that the dominant tendency of the age was in favor of conducting worship solely in Hebrew. In arguing in favor of Greek, they were trying to maintain a practice that for a long time had been the norm in the diaspora.[152] Thus was Hellenism still a live issue, live enough to divide Jewish communities four and a half centuries after the decision that condemned it in principle. It was a decision that was not followed up, and that therefore did no more than herald from afar the coming retrenchment. Hellenism was no longer strong enough, however, to win the day without support. It could only gain its ends by means of assistance from outside.[153]

The victory was an ephemeral one. From now on, the concern for conservation became progressively more dominant over the concern for expansion. Judaism became more rigidly devoted to meditation exclusively on the law, and to the practice of its ancestral rituals. This was the point at which the divorce from Greco-Roman civilization became absolute.[154] The day of active and effective proselytism was over. For Judaism to repudiate the Greek language, to refuse access to the revelation to those who knew no Hebrew, was in effect to renounce all efforts to gain recruits, or, alternatively, to make an indirect admission that she was powerless to do so. In reenacting the measures against proselytism that his predecessors had laid down, it looks at if Justinian was doing no more than finish off the dying.

IV

On the basis of the evidence presented, it may be concluded that proselytizing activity received hardly any setback from the events of A.D. 70 and 135, though it was very perceptibly impaired toward the end of the fourth century. The tide did not turn decisively against it until after the period that concerns us. The facts concerning the linguistic use of the Jewish communities provide us with a useful criterion. It remains only to demonstrate more exactly the significance of this.

The statement that the fortunes of proselytism and those of the Greek language among the Jews were closely bound up together is true of the Mediterranean diaspora only. This observation, and to speak more generally, all the results so far derived from this study, are valid only for a part of the world of antiquity, that part with which we are most familiar, the classical world. These were the lands that came within the sphere of influence of Greece and Rome. But this leaves out an important part of the ancient world, the Semitic part, whose peculiar character remained intact under the veneer of Greco-Roman civilization. In the Semitic world conditions obtained that were quite different from those in the Hellenized provinces, and here the Jews were provided with a striking opportunity.

I cannot here tackle the problem in all its depth. That would take us well outside the scope of the present study, for the Semitic world extended far beyond the frontiers of the Roman Empire. And I am relieved of the need to raise the entire question afresh by a study I have made of one particular instance, that of Berber Africa,[155] in which Judaism came into contact with Semitic or Semitized peoples. The situation as I reconstructed it and the conclusions to which I came could doubtless be repeated in the case of Palestine, Syria, and Arabia, to say nothing of less typical areas, firmly outside the empire, such as Ethiopia and Mesopotamia. All I can do here is to offer a brief résumé, and refer the reader to my previous work.

As it turned away, gradually, from the Greco-Roman world and its culture, Judaism was not at first condemned to passive immobility. Its retrenchment did not involve, at least at the outset, the end of all proselytizing. The grip that was lost or weakened in one quarter was reasserted, or rather tightened, in another, i.e., in the lands around the eastern Mediterranean. Israel's cultural and religious influence seems to have made itself felt in the environs of Palestine well before the Christian era. This is illustrated in the first century by the conversion of the royal family of Adiabene,[156] which was probably accompanied by that of an important part of the country. The appearance of Islam six centuries later cannot be explained apart from Jewish influence. It is beyond doubt that the Judaism that was presented to these peoples was not like the Judaism of the Mediterranean diaspora, and that the success of the two movements is to be explained in two quite different ways.

Here again we must insist on the importance of the linguistic factor. In the Greco-Roman world Hebrew (and to a greater extent Aramaic) was an indication of the separateness of the Jews and a factor encouraging particularism. But in those areas whose populations were Semitic by race, language or culture, the Jewish languages provided a very effective point of contact. Hebrew created a real link between the Jews and the North African Berbers, for example, for the latter were largely Semitized through the influence of Carthage, and very many of them spoke Punic, a language closely related to that of Israel.[157] The return to Hebrew was facilitated in North Africa by the presence of Punic and therefore took place there quite early, and in that region it served the cause of proselytism rather than hindering it. It attracted to Judaism a new clientele, different from the cosmopolitan public that it had gained for itself in the towns and from the seaboard. This new public came from inland, from the rural areas, and was derived from those elements of the population who who were least assimilated to the Greco-Roman culture, whose sentiments and linguistic affinities (with all that these entailed in the way of mental affinities too) predisposed them to accept the message of the Jews. The legend about the Canaanite origin of the Berbers, which was so strongly held at the end of the period of antiquity and in the Middle Ages, was probably originated by the Jews. It is found in the Talmud, where it is accompanied by a rehabilitation of the Canaanites; this doubtless being connected with the success of Jewish missionary activity in Berber lands.[158]

Thus is explained the existence of Berber Judaism, which according to Ibn Khaldun was found by the Arabs on their arrival to be practiced by a quite important section of the indigenous population.[159] The two groups, Jews and Berbers, met on common ground, provided by their use of related dialects; by the Semitic ideas and aspirations they shared, which went back to a common root; and by their common distrust of the foreigner, the Roman and the Westerner. And it is from the very time when the gulf between Judaism and Greco-Roman civilization begins to widen that Judaism begins to make contact with those elements which were obstinately opposed to foreign influences.

The origins of Jewish missionary work in Berber Maghreb go back, in all probability, to the events of A.D. 70 and their African counterpart. The exodus from Palestine that followed the crisis brought to Africa, principally to Egypt and Cyrenaica, some of the most active representatives of Palestinian religious and nationalist fanaticism. These were fiercely hostile to Rome and its culture in any form. This explains the violent upsurges of Zealot feeling and of political Messianism that shook in particular the Jewish community at Cyrene, first under Vespasian and then under Trajan.[160] They were suppressed with severity but were followed by Jewish penetration of the surrounding territory, which may have extended eventually as far as the Niger.[161]

According to E. F. Gautier, this penetration of Palestinian Jews must have coincided, in Tripolitania and Maghreb, with the arrival of the great tribes of camel nomads, and the two movements may have joined.[162] We should therefore picture the Jewish missionary effort as unfolding in an atmosphere clearly hostile to Rome and to the Roman world, and see its successes as those of Semitic particularism. The movement was assisted by the pro-Semitic policies of the Severides, which unintentionally contributed to the weakening in these regions of the Roman idea,[163] and it discovered a new impetus once the empire had officially become Christian.

Judaism took its place, therefore, alongside Donatism and the Circumcellion movement, and such local heresies, if not in actual league with them, as part of Africa's defensive reaction against official orthodoxy; as part of the religious, social, and political opposition to the religion of the townsmen and the romanized bourgoisie, the opposition, that is, to imperial Christianity.[164] Judaism persisted among certain tribes right up to the Arab conquest, and by helping to keep alive African Semitism, assisted as it was in this by the cultural and linguistic legacy of Carthage, it perhaps made easier the establishment of Islam.

It was about the same time, in similar circumstances and in exactly the same way, that Judaism began to spread in those regions of the East which were Semitic or which had Semitic affinities, i.e., the eastern end of the Mediterranean, the environs of Palestine, and in particular the area on both sides of the Red Sea.[165] The spread of Judaism in these directions was a new phenomenon, and its importance, which is considerable, cannot be gauged by the bulk of the remains it has left behind, for the evidence is very incomplete.

When we take account of this, we are obliged to emend the accepted reconstruction of Jewish history at the beginning of the Christian era. Even if we consider only the diaspora of the Mediterranean lands, there is no sudden transition from a period of missionary work to one of retrenchment. There is a slow and gradual change. When we look at the entire sphere of Jewish activity, we see that there was an intermediate stage, one in which Judaism, already in process of turning away from the West and from the traditional forms of its preaching to the gentiles, drew nearer to other peoples who were closer in their culture and their ways of thinking to the outlook of ancient Israel. These peoples were more easily accessible to Jewish missionaries and made fewer demands on their adaptability.[166]

After its attempt to turn itself into a religion acceptable to the Greco-Roman world, but before becoming again merely the religion of the scattered Israelites alone, Judaism made an effort to become the religion of the Semites. And by "Semites" is not meant here simply those peoples that the book of Genesis catalogues as such, and that Israel had always recognized as brothers, albeit sometimes enemies. But it now includes some of those classed by the Bible as descendants of the accursed Ham, such as Canaan, but which modern scholarship classifies by virtue of their language and culture as true Semites. The ancient hatreds toward such as these were overborne when it was realized what there was to gain. They were rehabiliated that they might be the more readily won over.[167]

Judaism was thwarted in its aims by the Eastern churches. They too expressed the opposition of the subject nations to Byzantine orthodoxy, but by means of unorthodox theology. Judaism was finally put to an end by Islam. Judaism had prepared the way for it, only to see Islam supplant it as the major religion of the Near East. At this point, if we disregard some very sporadic and localized outbreaks,[168] the period of proselytism seems definitively to have ended.

Within the chronological framework I have set myself for this study, and within the Roman Empire, pagan and Christian, the religious activity of Judaism went on to the very end. Is this to say that it was notably successful? We can hardly say so. Indeed, it seems that, taken as a whole, the results were rather slight. This is true, at any rate, if we reckon only wholehearted and total conversions. The reasons for this failure are diverse and complex. The time has not yet arrived to try to sort them out.

But the extent of Judaism's influence on the ancient world that was now drawing to its close is not to be reckoned simply by the number of *goyim* who took on themselves the whole yoke of the law. In a similar way it could be said that the impact of Christianity on modern civilization is not to be estimated by the size of the Church's membership or the number of "practicing Christians." The proselytes who observed the whole law, a species that became steadily more and more rare, indicate only one aspect of Jewish influence in society. The Synagogue's efforts and the attraction of Jewish rites succeeded most frequently in doing no more than producing Judaizers. There were large numbers who thus succumbed to the varied and subtle forms of "the Jewish sickness." They were not, it is true, a positive gain for Israel, but for the Church they were a matter for grave concern.

The Judaizers within the Church

Non quidem nomine, sed tamen errore judaizant.
Augustine, *Epistola 196 Ad Asellicum*

I

Even within the sphere of orthodoxy itself Judaism's influence on the life of the early Church appears in several guises. I am not speaking now of the very general influence that was in some sense part of the Church's own makeup, and that affected not only its entire system of belief and morals, but also its liturgy and organizational structure. In this sense the Church, however much it owed to the foreign elements that came to be built into it, was the direct heir of both the Synagogue and the Bible. I have in mind only the more specific and more readily defined effects of the Jewish impact, which produced a kind of enlarged Jewish-Christian movement. This movement was characterized by a combination of orthodox Christian elements with features drawn from Judaism, or with Judaizing tendencies. Two principal forms of the movement may be distinguished.

In the first instance there was a number of groups whose orthodoxy could not be suspected on any other grounds, but who deliberately and persistently organized their Christian observances, the cycle of their festivals and some of their ritual practices in conformity with Jewish models and with the norms of the Synagogue. Secondly, there were certain believers who, in defiance of their pastors, with no regard for logic and without any attempt at actual synthesis, simply added to the usual manifestations of Christian piety the practice of Jewish rites. Along with the Church fasts they observed the Mosaic dietary laws; they not only attended Church, they frequented the Synagogue.

It is strictly speaking only the second of these two forms of syncretism that can properly be called Jewish Christianity. The former movement is related to it rather as an attenuated form, reflecting the same tendencies and following the same line of development. Both forms grew up in the same regions of the East, close to Judaism's important centers. They grew up in contact with each other and, to a large extent, in reaction against each other. For the former movement was partly the result of attempts to remedy the latter, by keeping it within limits compatible with the demands of orthodoxy. Both groups of Christians were agreed in allowing to the

Jews and to the usage of the Synagogue an authority that the Church as a whole had categorically repudiated.

This phenomenon is a much more varied and complex one than ordinary Jewish Christianity. It is a more diffuse, less well-defined phenomenon, for it represents not a sect beyond the boundaries of the Church, but merely a tendency within the Church, a direction in which Catholic Christianity in some areas felt itself drawn. Its geographical distribution is sufficient to establish that its essential cause was direct contact with the Synagogue. The Semitic affinities of at least some of the Christian bodies it affected, and their real linguistic and cultural connections with Israel, doubtless helped.

I

When dealing with the details of Judaizing practices or with rites borrowed from the Jews, it is often difficult to make a rigorous distinction between what has become, through the medium of superstition, the current usage of both pagans and Christians, and what betrays a positive and deliberate attachment by certain sections of the Church to Judaism's religious forms. Certain rites and customs in particular give rise to hesitation on this score. In this category comes the use of *tephillin*, for example, and the use of certain very brief liturgical formulae of which we have a number of examples in inscriptions.[1] Popular belief doubtless attributed efficacy to these as exorcism formulae. Nevertheless it is sometimes possible to draw more definite conclusions concerning the contact between Christians and Jews.

Recent studies by Peterson have drawn attention to an epigraphical formula that is very widespread in the East, particularly in Syria where, up to the time of writing, it has been attested ninety-three times. The formula in question is εἶς θεός. It is sometimes completed by the Christological addition, καὶ ὁ χριστὸς αὐτοῦ, and less frequently by a Trinitarian addition.[2] Thanks to a hagiographical text, the Passion of St. Romanos,[3] dating in all likelihood from the fourth or fifth century, and probably of Antiochene origin, Peterson has been able to establish the liturgical character of the formula and the way in which it was employed. The Christians of Syria recited it in their morning prayer, and we are justified in regarding it as the equivalent of the Jewish *Shema*, which was similarly used. The proof is provided by a bilingual inscription from Amwas, in which the Greek εἶς θεός is completed in Hebrew by the words "Blessed be his name for ever and ever." We may consequently take the words εἶς θεός as a Greek transcription of the ineffable tetragrammaton. And we are justified therefore, since the rabbis allowed the use of Greek in reciting the *Shema*, in regarding the Christian formula as a direct borrowing from the daily liturgy of the Synagogue.

In addition to this, the formula appears in a number of instances in funerary inscriptions with the addition of the word μόνος. Peterson[4] has suggested an ingenious explanation of this second usage. We should recognize here, he says, an echo of the Jewish funeral liturgy, which is being imitated by the Christians. The hypothesis is based on a detail not, to be sure, of the Synagogue funeral rite, which in its present state preserves no trace of this usage, but on that of the Samaritans, who washed the corpse three times with water, reciting as they did so the *Shema* in the following form: "There is but one God; the Lord is our God; the Lord is One."[5] If it be conceded that the Samaritan liturgy has here preserved a detail that has today disappeared from the Jewish rite but at one time figured there, then it may also be allowed that Christian ritual usage here depends directly on that of the Synagogue. The Samaritan text further provides us with an explanation of the word μόνος, which was sometimes added to the formula. It represents the emphatic affirmation of the divine unity.

It is scarcely likely that the Christians imitated Jewish ritual in only this one instance. It is to be expected that Peterson's projected study of the Syrian Christian liturgies will reveal other connections. But in the meantime we have at our disposal a number of texts that provide ample confirmation of his interpretation. There is hardly any doubt of the Jewish origin of the so-called Prayer of Manasseh, which appears in the *Didascalia*,[6] and whose presence in this work is explained by the use that was doubtless made of it in the third century by Syrian Christianity.[7] The same applies to the seventh century liturgy contained in the Apostolic Constitutions, of which I spoke earlier.[8] One point of interest, it will be recalled, is that it provides us with information about the date of the borrowing, or at least offers us a *terminus post quem*. The use it makes of Aquila's translation excludes the idea that it could have been taken over by the Christians before the middle of the second century. This matter of dating is of the greatest importance.

In fact, the entire Christian liturgy, even in its present day forms, exhibits the influence of Jewish models both in its general arrangement and in respect of its constitutive elements.[9] The first Christian communities, whose members had been born Jews, quite naturally organized their corporate prayers according to the patterns and the models with which they were familiar. Their liturgical life therefore followed that of Judaism closely, both as to the form of worship and the cycle of the festivals. The Jewish patterns were taken over and Christians were satisfied at first simply to add certain specific rites, such as baptism and the Eucharist.[10] The affinities between Christian and Jewish ritual were thus merely one aspect of that general dependence that made early Christianity a product of Judaism.

Later, however, the liturgical organization of the Church became progressively distinguished from that of the Synagogue, as the Christians stressed their autonomy more and more. This happened quite early in the Pauline communities, and perhaps even before St. Paul's time among the first Hellenistic groups. The progressive liberation from Jewish forms proceeded at very different rates in different circles. At the very end of the first century the Didache bears witness that in the circles it represents, the liberation was still incomplete.[11] Nevertheless, taking early Christianity as a whole, the development seems to have been completed, for all practical purposes, by the beginning of the period with which we are concerned. The Church is by then fully autonomous in its ritual as well as in its organizational practices and in its beliefs. We must henceforth speak, not of a simple taking over of Jewish rites, but rather of a transposition of the Synagogue's liturgical patterns.

By contrast, in the epigraphical literary texts I have just cited, it is not a matter simply of resemblances, but of a basic identity, which is poorly concealed by a few superficial alterations. The elements of Jewish ritual have not been reworked, as is usual, to bring them into line with the Christian community's own needs. Instead, they have been incorporated as they stand into the liturgy. These documents are interesting on two counts. They reveal quite specific and deliberate borrowings, made by Christian groups we have no reason to think were composed entirely of converted Jews. Moreover, these borrowings took place not by virtue of that basic connection which existed between Christianity and Judaism, but, if I may so put it, laterally. And this was at a period (this is certain at least as far as the liturgy of the Constitutions is concerned) when Church and Synagogue already existed side by side as two entirely distinct bodies, bodies that were, in most of the regions of the empire, frankly hostile to each other.

It is consequently necessary to concede that in certain provinces of the Church some sections of early Christianity, perhaps important ones at that, did not entirely follow the general direction of development. They may not have stood aside from it altogether, but they followed some considerable way behind the rest, and remained in more or less permanent and close contact with Judaism, and therefore with Jews. And it is necessary to emphasize that there is no question here of actual dissident elements. Everything combines to convince us that they were members of the Catholic Church. The εἷς θεός formula is too widespread to be put down simply to sectarian use. Furthermore, the Passion of St. Romanos bears witness to the orthodoxy of those who employed it. Both the *Didascalia* and the Apostolic Constitutions, which use it too, are Church documents in the fullest sense of the term. The liturgical usages they enshrine were, at that period, approved by the local hierarchy. They disappeared gradually, as the rites of Eastern Christianity became more uniform and distrust of things Jewish became more pronounced. But they were not eliminated without strong resistance. They can be traced right through the period, alongside other manifestations of this muted Jewish Christianity.

The liturgical borrowings, in fact, were only the reflection of a deeper debt. There were some types of Christians in these Eastern circles, and especially among the Syrians, who were profoundly attached to the basic institutions of Jewish worship, i.e., both its rites and its festivals.

II

This is not the place to go over once again the origins of the Christian Sunday, or the history of the Christian festival of Easter and the paschal controversy. Much has been written about these questions[12] and we are well informed about the main lines of development of both institutions. Sabbath and Sunday at first existed side by side, the one a solemn, the other a joyful occasion. But quite quickly the latter displaced the former, and Sabbath-keeping was condemned as being tainted with Judaism.[13] By the beginning of the second century Sunday had become the only weekly festival among the Hellenistic communities. This fact emerges from Pliny's letter to Trajan and is confirmed later by Justin Martyr.[14] As far as Easter is concerned, the Christians at first only differed from the Jews in the new significance they attached to the old Passover rites, which they now connected with the Last Supper and the passion of Christ, and, perceptibly later, with his resurrection. The Churches then felt the need to adopt a different date from the Jews for the celebration of their festival. The reckoning of this date gave rise to much controversy. For a long time several different systems were in use and their reduction to a common usage was accomplished only with difficulty. The decisions of the council of Nicaea mark an essential step in this process, but unanimity was not reached until the end of the eighth century.

But whether it was a question of Sunday or of Easter (the latter being itself celebrated on a Sunday), the object of the operation was the same; to put an end to the synchronism of the two institutions, Jewish and Christian, and thus to guard against any Judaizing.[15] The Church in this way emphasized its independence of the Synagogue, challenging at this point, as at all others, the humiliating suggestion that she should bow to the Synagogue's authority. The Church declared null and void the Jewish rules for fixing the liturgical calendar, and she substituted, though at the cost of considerable difficulties, new principles. Once she was sure of her method she would go so far as to accuse the Jews of having wrongly calculated the date of their own festival.

The paschal controversy took the form of a conflict between different regional groups of Christians. The bitterness of the conflict and the tenacity with which the opposing points of view were supported is explained by local pride and by the attachment each province felt for its own usage. But in the Eastern provinces it reveals yet another feature, the weight that the practices and standards of the Synagogue still carried with some Christians. Whether we look at the question of the date of Easter[17] or at the significance attributed to the festival, we are made sharply aware of the influence of the Jewish prototype. The *Didascalia* is again the most revealing document.

The ostensible authors of the work, the apostles, recalled the events of Holy Week, which they witnessed, in a day-by-day account.[18] They then insist on the necessity of commemorating these events by a fast. This is not because of Christ's death, or to associate the worshipers in any way with his passion. It is because of the Jews, the agents responsible for his death. It is intended to be an act of penitence undertaken in their stead, with the intention of procuring forgiveness for them.[19] This prescription is aimed particularly at those Christians who are of gentile extraction. Having been called to fill Israel's place, they ought to bear a part in her redemption, "For because the people was not obedient [says Jesus] I delivered them [the gentiles] from blindness and from the error of idols and received them: that through ... your service during those days, when you pray and intercede for the error and destruction of the people, your prayer and intercession may be accepted before my Father who is in heaven."[20]

The spirit of the Jewish Passover thus undergoes a fundamental transformation. From being a joyful festival, celebrating the flight from Egypt, it becomes in its Christian guide a solemn occasion, a day of vicarious penitence for the sins of the blind Israelites.[21] Looked at in this way, all the importance and seriousness of the feast are concentrated on Holy Week. Easter, properly so called, scarcely enters into consideration. Just at the point where the Jews rejoice, solemnity is demanded. It is the existence of the Jews that has prompted the demand, for it is manifestly intended to counteract their influence.

The same preoccupation manifests itself when it comes to the fixing of fast days. It is prescribed as early as the Didache that the weekly fast days should be Wednesday and Friday. This is in order to distinguish Christian usage from that of the "hypocrites" (i.e., the Jews) who fast on Mondays and Thursdays.[22] The *Didascalia* repeats both this prescription and the motive for it:"[Fast] according to the new testament which I have appointed you: that you may be fasting for them on the fourth day of the week [Wednesday] because on the fourth of the week they began to destroy their souls, and apprehended me. . . . But fast for them also on the Friday, because thereon they crucified me, in the midst of their festival of unleavened bread."[23] This is the rule throughout the weeks of the year. For the week preceding Easter the command concerning fasts was at first moderated. Later, however, the Friday, the day of the passion, was made more emphatically a day of fasting; and then the Saturday; and finally the fast was extended to the whole week, excepting only the Sunday, the day of resurrection.[24]

The Saturday paschal fast took on a special importance, not only because it was "the sleep of the Lord,"[25] but because Moses himself, by instituting the Sabbath, had wished it so. It was by a gross misunderstanding, in fact, that the eternally blind Jews had interpreted it as a day of joy. According to the intention of their lawgiver, the Sabbath was actually designed so that they should make an anticipatory expiation for the murder of Christ by sorrow and mourning. "He bound them beforehand with mourning perpetually . . . mourning for their own destruction." The true Sabbath is therefore a solemn festival, as is shown by the close similarity between mourning customs and the prescriptions for the Sabbath idleness.[26] It is curious to find this line of argument confirming the pagans' impression, which several of their authors remark, of the *morositas* of the holy day.[27]

We perceive here, as we do in the similar reversal of mood the Christians imposed on the Jewish Passover, the wish to transform the spirit of the Jewish festivals when the festivals themselves could not be done away with. It is not impossible that the joyful nature of the Jewish Passover, and the consequent Christian reaction against it, retarded the development of the Christian festival of the resurrection, especially in the Semitic East. Conversely, once this festival was established, the Church did its best to prevent assimilation of the Jewish and Christian rites by denying that the Jewish prototype should have had a joyful character at all. That is to say, they did to the Passover what they had done to the Sabbath. They recalled that the unleavened bread, which had to be eaten with bitter herbs, was "the bread of affliction."[28] The result was that Jews and Christians in the celebration of the festivals each did, almost automatically, the reverse of what was done by the other. There is a text that Epiphanius borrows from an apostolic *Diataxis*. It was in use among the Audians and is closely allied to, if not identical with, the usage of the *Didascalia*. It is quite explicit on this score. "When they hold festival, fast, and mourn on their behalf, because they crucified Christ on the feast day. And when they mourn and eat their unleavened bread with bitter herbs, for your part, hold festival."[29]

All these developments have the same aim, to counteract the Jewish infection that lurked in some of the rituals that Christians observed, and to alter the character of the rites and festivals in such a manner that they took on a new character of their own, distinct from that of the corresponding Jewish institutions. In addition to changing the character and meaning of a festival, the Church more often that not also changed the date.[30] Of this additional precaution, which was not only more radical but also, doubtless, more certain in its effects, no trace at all appears in the *Didascalia*. And this is the chief interest of the document. Far from having recourse to this device, it envisages exactly the opposite procedure. It assumes that in fixing the date of Easter the Church will simply comply with the synagogal custom. It is understood that, in contrast with Jewish usage, the Christian celebration of Holy Week will be very sorrowful and will be marked by a rigid fast, but this apart, it will coincide exactly with the Jewish Passover. For the dating of the festival the *Didascalia* appeals not to the past usage of Christians but to the present usage of the Jews. Its direction in this matter is absolutely plain: "And do you make a beginning when your brethren who are of the people keep the Passover."[31] The beginning of the Christian paschal ceremonies is therefore the traditional date of the fourteenth Nisan, calculated according to the Jewish reckoning.

The position is a curious and singularly complex one. The document is eradicating the contaminating influence of Jewish ritual, at the same time as it sets up the Jewish calendar as a standard for Christian practice. In order to offset the attractiveness of the Jewish paschal ceremonies, which culminate in a meal, it substitutes a fast. Yet the fast itself is a Jewish rite, though the Jews observe it in a different context. In order to counteract the allure of the Sabbath, the *Didascalia* makes it a day of penitence. In support of this, it invokes the intentions of Moses himself, and actually claims to be going back to the most authentic Israelite tradition, a tradition the Jews have falsified, but whose true significance the Church has reestablished.

Are we to conclude, then, that the anonymous authorities whose views the *Didascalia* represents were subject to such pressure from the multitude of Judaizers that they hesitated to make a frontal attack upon them and to thrust them out of the Church, but, instead, attempted, by making concessions, to channel them in an orthodox direction, being obliged to sacrifice something to their opponents in order to carry the day? Yes; up to a point this is a fair judgment. It must, however, be more precisely stated.

There can be no doubt at all that there existed, within the circles with which the *Didascalia* is connected, groups of more radical Judaizers. This is apparent from the insistence with which the book puts its readers on their guard against the observance of the *deuterosis*.[32] However, we must not, in the circumstances, exaggerate the opposition between the teaching Church and the rank and file of the membership.

We have no reason to proceed on the assumption that the principles laid down by the *Didascalia* are reluctant concessions. In fact, the hierarchy was susceptible to the impact of Judaism, and sensitive to the prestige attaching to Jewish rites by reason of their antiquity and the antiquity of the Jewish people, just as was the mass of believers, though to a different degree. The respect with which the book's compiler treats Jewish standards seems to be a sincere, not an opportunistic one. He exhibits a genuine feeling for "the people." And in this title itself, given as it is in an entirely direct and unqualified way, there is something of respect. The intercessory fast that is enjoined on the Jews' behalf bears witness to the same feeling, and so does the moderate tone in which the Jews are spoken of, full of sad compassion. The way the Jews are referred to as "brethren" is as significant as it is unusual. "Know, therefore, our brethren, that [as regards] the fast which we fast in the Pasch, it is on account of the disobedience of our brethren that you are to fast. For even though they hate you, yet ought we to call them brethren; for we have it written in Isaiah thus,[33] 'Call them brethren that hate and reject you.'"[34] We are here a long way from the hate-filled diatribes of Chrysostom. We are also far from the usual tone of ecclesiastical literature, or even from that of the common liturgy, in which prayers for the Jews are invariably accompanied by offensive epithets.

This fact is all the more remarkable since, as the evidence indicates well enough, the religious community whose views the *Didascalia* represents is neither exclusively nor even essentially Jewish Christian, in the ethnic sense of that term.[35] The mixed nature of its membership is emphasized by the injunction given to "those who are of the gentiles" to take part in the intercessory fast for the people. It is quite possible that the leaders of the community themselves, the authors of the document, or at least some among them, were of gentile birth. When they speak of those who are of the gentiles as if they were a category distinct from themselves, this is explained by the literary fiction that places the instructions in the mouth of the apostles. There are a number of indications that they are in fact outsiders as far as Israel is concerned: the way in which they speak of "the people," of their present fall from grace, and of the election of the pagans; the way in which they address themselves, on the subject of the Sabbath, to "the brethren among the people who have come to believe," adjuring them to renounce "these bonds"[36]; and the position they assume with regard to the ritual law, all reinforce this conclusion.

But they do live in close contact with Israel. There are Jews within the community. There are certainly Jews in the surrounding territory. It is inconceivable that such a work could have been written except in a region with strong Jewish communities, where the whole population, men of all faiths, were impregnated with Jewish ways of thinking. The problems raised by this close proximity to Jews are a constant preoccupation of the writers of the *Didascalia*. They are reflected clearly in the interpretation given to the paschal fast. Jewish influence is consciously acknowledged and accepted, but care is taken to confine it within limits compatible with catholicity. When the *Didascalia* accepts, in connection with Easter, the Jewish calendar as normative, when it rehabilitates the ritual fast as part of Christian practice, it attempts to counteract the dangers inherent in these suggestions by finding new explanations for them. The imitation of the Jews is paralleled by a defensive reaction against them. The evil carries its remedy with it. No anathema is formulated against those believers who might be tempted to go further. They are simply adjured to avoid "the old bonds." The courteously argumentative tone adopted toward those who continue to be attached to the keeping of Sabbaths demonstrates that such behavior is not regarded as outright sin, but rather as proceeding from an erroneous interpretation of the divine will. And the object of the argument is merely to prove that Sunday ought to take precedence over the Sabbath.[37] Thus is orthodoxy safeguarded, without there being any need to resort to more radical methods, which were manifestly as repugnant to some of the leaders as to the rank and file of Church members.

We may say with certainty that this was not the opinion of the Church in general. At the very time when the *Didascalia* was proclaiming the obligation to bow to Jewish usage in the matter of Easter, it represented an outmoded view, already rejected by the greater part of Christianity. Pseudo-Cyprian, who appears to be practically contemporary with the *Didascalia*, codifies the usage of the Western churches, and indignantly repudiates Jewish authority in the matter. His whole treatment of the Jews (i.e., of the Jewish nation and the Jewish religious authorities alike) is extremely scornful. *Nunquam posse Christianos a via veritatis errare et tanquam ignorantes, quae sit dies Paschae, post Judaeos caecos et hebetes ambulare.*[38] The council of Nicaea pronounced upon the question of the date of Easter, and the imperial authority sanctioned its decisions. It was henceforth forbidden to celebrate Easter, even with specifically Christian rituals, at the same time as the Jewish Passover. And the practice laid down by the *Didascalia* thus became heretical.

The *Diataxis*, which I quoted above, is doubtless nothing more, as E. Schwartz has shown, than a variant of the *Didascalia*, or at least a variant of the same basic work. Now the *Didascalia*, because it was compiled during the third century in circles that were at the time orthodox, was used by the authors of the Apostolic Constitutions and thus made part of the traditions of the Catholic Church. The *Diataxis*, by contrast, was no longer regarded as acceptable in the fourth century except among the dissident sect of the Audians, whose heresy, according to Epiphanius, consisted precisely in this, amongst other things, that they celebrated Easter in agreement with Jewish usage.[39] This example illustrates how far the Church had moved between one century and the next. The *Diataxis* gives express instructions: "Keep [the Pasch] when your brethren of the circumcision do so. Keep it together with them." And the apostles, who are supposed to be speaking, add, "Even if they are in error, that is no concern of yours."[40]

The addition is significant. It is a clear contradiction of the affirmations of orthodoxy, according to which the Jewish calculations for fixing the paschal cycle were erroneous. The *Diataxis* does not strictly exclude the possibility of such error, but regards it as unimportant, doubtless on the grounds that the antiquity of the Jewish tradition on this point was sufficient reason for complying with it. To this the orthodox replied that though the Jewish computation had been perfectly accurate in the past, the present usage of the Synagogue, since the destruction of the temple, was in error. It was consequently impossible to appeal to a tradition that had notoriously been falsified.[41]

Meanwhile, the decision of Nicaea ran into strong opposition, even within the Church itself. Polemizing on the subject of Easter went on until the end of the fourth century. One of St. John Chrysostom's cycle of anti-Jewish homilies is devoted to those Christians who celebrate Easter principally by fasting and according to the Jewish reckoning. His entire argument, which is a defense of the Nicene position, is completely at variance with the prescriptions of the *Didascalia*. We may summarize it as follows:

If the Church, which formerly fixed the time of the paschal feast in the same manner as the Jews, has now renounced this practice, it is because she prefers internal consistency in the system of fixing the liturgical year.[42] Since the 300 fathers of Nicaea have decided the question, there is in any case no further room for discussion. It needs a remarkable presumption to place more weight upon the authority of the Jews than on that of a council of the Church catholic. The Jews of today have broken with their own tradition. According to the scriptural law, the Passover ought not to be celebrated except in one place, Jerusalem. Now that the city has been destroyed, the rite is no longer valid, and God, by authorizing the destruction, intended to detach the Jews, in spite of themselves, from their ancestral usage.[43] To persist in maintaining it is to violate the law. Though it is true that Christ celebrated the Passover together with the Jews, he did so as a symbol of things to come. And in doing so, he instituted the new Passover, the Passover of his body and his blood, for which reason the apostle can speak of "Christ, our Passover."[44]

The Christian Pasch, Chrysostom goes on to say, is therefore not by any means to be regarded as a fast, but as an oblation. This is celebrated not merely once a year, like Lent, but several times a week, and always in the same way, at every synaxis.[45] As for the Lenten fast, the fathers decreed this in order that believers might approach the holy mysteries in a state of purity on the anniversary of their institution. Christians do not fast because of Easter, or because of the passion, but in sorrow for their own sins.[46] Easter, in fact, is an occasion neither for sorrow nor fasting, but for joy and cheerfulness. He who receives the communion with a pure conscience, though he has not fasted, has celebrated the Pasch, whatever day of the year it may be. It is, in addition, not only paradoxical but offensive to establish the date of Christ's death by referring the question to his executioners.[47]

Furthermore, to follow the Jewish usage is to accept an erroneous calculation. It is also to make it impossible for oneself to fix the date of the Christian festival. Jesus in fact celebrated the Passover and was crucified on the first day of Unleavened Bread, which fell that year on the eve of the Sabbath. But the two days do not always coincide. In the year when Chrysostom was actually writing, the first day of Unleavened Bread fell on a Sunday, so that in order to follow the

Jewish reckoning, Christians would be obliged to fast on the day of resurrection![48] Faced with such absurdities, what further room is there for argument? Only one thing matters: the concord and peace of the Church. It would be best, in these circumstances, to sacrifice the older custom.

This bare account is enough to show what a gulf there is between Chrysostom and the *Didascalia*. While the *Didascalia* wishes to eliminate Judaizing tendencies, it has no desire to renounce the synchronism of the Jewish and Christian feasts. It accordingly puts the emphasis on the paschal fast, with the intention of purging the Christian festival of the more cheerful elements derived from its Jewish counterpart. Chrysostom, however, dislikes Jewish things so much that he goes so far as to treat with suspicion the rite of fasting that has been reestablished in the usage of the Church. He regards it as a poor substitute for a thoroughgoing separation of the Christian from the Jewish rites. But to adopt a Christian reckoning for fixing the date of Easter seems to him not enough to offset the danger. He is clearly embarrassed at the prospect of allowing the Christian festival a position of importance in the liturgical year, even without any coincidence between its date or other features and those of the Jewish Passover; for when everything has been said, the Christian Easter was no more than a transposition of a Jewish celebration. He thus refuses to regard Easter Sunday as being any different from other Sundays, or indeed, from any other day on which the Eucharistic synaxis is celebrated. The Christian Pasch is nothing other than the sacrifice of Christ, which is commemorated and reenacted in every celebration of the Eucharistic rite.

Aphraates falls somewhere between these two points of view. It is interesting to take account of an author who lived in the same century as Chrysostom, but whose position, in comparison either with Chrysostom's own or with that of the council of Nicaea, is so clearly archaic and in many respects so close to that of the *Didascalia*. This archaic quality, which is characteristic of the whole of Aphraates' theology,[49] reflects the situation of his Church. It was beyond the frontiers of the empire, and because of its geographical isolation, the great controversies of the fourth century and the doctrinal developments that took place in the Greco-Latin churches quite passed it by. But if the Church of Mesopotamia thus lived on the fringes of the great movement of Mediterranean Christianity, it lived in permanent contact with large and active Jewish communities, whose influence makes itself felt in every line of Aphraates' homilies. The paschal question exhibits particularly clearly the impact of Jewish forms on Semitic Christianity.

It appears that Aphraates is still not familiar with the festival of the resurrection.[50] Easter is for him a sorrowful occasion that commemorates the passion. Like the *Didascalia*, he places the emphasis on the paschal fast, which constitutes one of the festival's principal elements.[51] But like Chrysostom, he also stresses the place of the Eucharistic rite, and gives it the same central position in the Christian celebrations as the Passover meal occupies in those of the Jews. The Holy Communion is the true Passover, and the Passover lamb is merely a symbolic prefiguration of this.[52]

This idea controls the ordering of the entire feast, as Aphraates conceives it. The Eucharist commemorates the Last Supper, at which it was instituted. But it takes its proper significance from the death of Christ, who was offered up as the true paschal lamb, the Passover lamb being the prefiguration of his death.[53] Consequently Aphraates fixes the beginning of the Christian festival, which was inaugurated by the Eucharistic synaxis, not on the day of the Last Supper, but on that of the crucifixion. Or more exactly, since the Eucharistic meal takes place, according to him, on the evening of Thursday, the thirteenth of Nisan, after nightfall, it is actually on the same day as the crucifixion, viz., the fourteenth of Nisan, because according to Jewish usage Friday begins with Thursday's sunset, and the Thursday evening is thus part of Friday.[54]

However, while Aphraates declares that the Friday is the most solemn day in the paschal celebrations, he prefers the Jewish custom of celebrating the festival according to a fixed day of the month, rather than the Nicene method of celebrating it on a fixed day of the week.[55] This date is the evening of the fourteenth, which is thus the beginning of the fifteenth. It is at this point, the time of Christ's death, not the evening of the thirteenth, when Jesus ate the Last Supper with his disciples, that Aphraates places the Eucharistic synaxis that opens Holy Week.

Since the seven-day structure of the week is given, Aphraates insists that there is a strict obligation to celebrate Easter not merely for a day, but for an entire week.[56] But instead of culminating on the Sunday, which was otherwise the normal day for it to end, this week would always run from the fifteenth to the twenty-first Nisan, and correspond therefore with the Jewish days of Unleavened Bread. The main Easter celebration will therefore follow the principal day of the Jewish festival, instead of preceding it and being a preparation for it. There is only one exception to all this. When the fifteenth Nisan falls on a Sunday, the Easter week should not be inaugurated until the following day, since it would be inappropriate to begin a fast with the joy of the Lord.[57] At all events, the Easter week should be from beginning to end, Sunday excepted, a week of fasting, and the Christian fast should take the place of the Jews' days of Unleavened Bread.

Aphraates therefore borrows his weekly schema directly from the Jews.[58] Speaking more generally, the whole ordering of the paschal celebrations is modeled closely on those of the Jewish feast. Far from eliminating similarities Aphraates emphasizes them, for the close analogy between the Christian rites, which are the only real and efficacious ones, and their Jewish models is in accordance with the divine plan. Just as the Passover delivered Israel from service to Pharaoh, so the cross of Christ delivers Christians from bondage to Satan.[59] It is laid down that the Jews should eat the lamb with their loins girded; Christians go to the Eucharistic meal with their loins girded with the true faith. The bones of Christ were not broken, just as it is decreed that the bones of the lamb should not be broken. Israel was baptized in the sea on Passover night. On the same night Christ, in a ceremony that prefigured baptism, washed the feet of his disciples.[60] The parallels are freely elaborated, down to the last detail, according to the methods of allegorical exegesis. The object of this is to demonstrate that the Jewish rites, which were no more than a crude prototype, have been comprehensively replaced by the real thing, which is the Christian rite. This has made all the rites of the old Passover redundant. Furthermore, Aphraates, like Chrysostom, draws attention to the fact that the celebration of the Passover is not allowed outside Jerusalem. It is no longer possible for the Jews of the dispersion. God has thus clearly demonstrated its abolition.[61] When the Jews still ostensibly celebrate the Passover, they do so in defiance of the regulations. On this aspect of the matter we find in Aphraates the same arguments as in Chrysostom.

But these few points of contact are insufficient to offset the basic contradiction between the two viewpoints. When Aphraates takes issue with the Jews, he fights, as it were, with their own weapons, and on ground they themselves have chosen. Chrysostom, though with due deference to the decisions of the councils, seems ready to conclude that there is futility and danger in all ritual, for it is not altogether compatible with the true worship, which is "in spirit and in truth." Now Aphraates, for his part, codifies Christian observances, distinguishing them from those of Israel, but modeling his work at the same time closely on them. In so doing Aphraates shows himself to be deeply imbued with the Jewish spirit. He concluded characteristically: "Let us not seek difficulties and quarrels about words. They will not profit us. What is important is a pure heart, which observes the commandments and keeps the feasts, the seasons of worship and the daily offices."[62] "Feasts," "seasons," "offices": Israel's own lawgiver spoke in no different terms. Between one religion and the other the terms of the regulations vary. The Christian rites are not those of the Jews, but they are laid down on the basis of what is written in the Old Testament, and as far as dating is concerned, Jewish usage provides the norm.[63]

The method Chrysostom envisages for counteracting the Judaizing tendencies is to abolish the synchronism between the Jewish and Christian festivals and to minimize the celebrations. Aphraates, on the contrary, accepts as self-evident the need for synchronizing with the Jewish feasts. He asserts the lasting value of the observances and regards them as being changed only in form. For the former there is nothing in common between Christianity and Judaism, and the arrival of the one marks the abolition of the other. For the latter, Christianity is an extension of Judaism that substitutes the new and perfect law for the old and imperfect one. But both bear witness to the extent to which Eastern Christians, both within and without the empire, were sensible of the prestige and attraction of Jewish rites. Chrysostom demonstrates this by his anti-Jewish radicalism, Aphraates by the concessions he makes to Jewish ways of thinking and to the liturgical usage of the Synagogue.

III

The discussions Chrysostom and Aphraates devote to the subject of the Pasch can only be properly understood if we take into account the contexts in which they are set. In each case the discussions of the Pasch are part of a wider and well-ordered polemic that takes issue with the whole structure of Jewish institutions and beliefs. Chrysostom and Aphraates are each writing a series of anti-Jewish homilies, dealing with the subjects of circumcision, the Sabbath, the dietary laws, the call of the gentiles, and the Jewish hope. In each case we have a coherent cycle, aimed expressly at the Jews, but at the same time taking account of Judaizing Christians.

For if the spirit of Jewish observance continued to exist, though in a modified form in Aphraates and the *Didascalia*, it also survived elsewhere, and in clearer form. It survived, that is to say, not only in certain sects, but in the Church too, and in this instance against the will of the Church authorities. This was true at any rate in the East. As I have already asserted, in this connection we may rightly speak of Jewish Christianity. Audians and Novatians, amongst others, continued long after Nicaea to celebrate Easter at the same time as the Passover, and perhaps, according to a ritual that in certain respects followed the Jewish pattern.[64] Within the orthodox Church the prohibitions and diatribes of the scholars and the condemnations of the councils did not entirely succeed in suppressing Judaizing tendencies. The fact that they needed to be repeated so often is a witness to their ineffectiveness.

There was at least one result. All official approval of Judaizing practices was withdrawn. Once the Jewish rites had been banned from Church use, those who still wished to submit to them but who had received orthodox baptism and were members of the Catholic Church had only one course open to them; they were obliged to practice clandestinely the rites of the Jewish domestic cult, and for their public worship they had to resort to the Synagogue in order to obtain what the Church refused to give them. They did not on this account become open converts to Judaism, and they did not break with the common observance of the Church. They continued to think of themselves as belonging to the Church, and the Church for its part still claimed them as its own and exercised discipline over them as its members.[65] They were commonly described as *nostri judaizantes*, and the possessive pronoun is a clear indication that the Church authorities were not willing to count them, without more ado, as ordinary heretics.[66]

Here we have indicated the essential characteristics of this form of Jewish Christianity. It is not, like Ebionism, a genuine synthesis of diverse elements. It merely lays the elements it takes from Judaism and from Christianity side by side, in no ordered or integrated way. It is in essence a spontaneous and popular movement. It does not embody any tradition going back to the origins of Christianity and it cannot be accounted for in this way as an ancient survival. It is produced by the appeal of an alien tradition, that of Judaism, which some Christians blindly followed.

The synchronism of the Christian and Jewish festivals was, for those sections of the Church most exposed to Jewish influence, practically an invitation to syncretism. Duchesne, writing about the question of Easter, says: "At the time when the festival was celebrated on the fourteenth, there was a good deal of temptation to celebrate it in the Jewish manner, keeping to the Jewish rite as well as to the Jewish date."[67] The same remark could be made concerning all the other feasts that were originally Jewish ones. But in order to avert the danger, it was not enough simply to change the dates. The Judaizers' response to that was to celebrate two festivals instead of one.

This phenomenon is especially striking with regard to the Sabbath. For a long time after Sunday had become the holy day there were circles in which Saturday continued to be regarded as holy too. It is curious to find the Apostolic Constitutions still sanctioning this usage. "Let slaves work for five days, and on Saturday and Sunday let them rest."[68] On the other hand, the council of Laodicaea, meeting at a date that was probably quite close to that of the Apostolic Constitutions, explicitly condemns this practice. "Christians must not Judaize by resting on the Sabbath, but work on that day. They should accord special sanctity to Sunday, by resting on it as far as is possible. If they Judaize in this way, may they be anathema in the name of Christ."[69] This is the same conflict, though on a different question, as we have between Chrysostom on the one hand and Aphraates and the *Didascalia* on the other.

Chrysostom characteristically declines to make a frontal attack on a custom that was doubtless too firmly entrenched. Besides, his conception of biblical revelation forbade him to deliver an unqualified condemnation of it.[70] He merely tries to show that the Sabbath is not really what the Jews have made it, and that, though it is legitimate to observe it, one ought at least to refrain from observing it in the Jewish manner. While certain authors deplore the Sabbath idleness, Aphraates for his part asserts that the Sabbath was not given for the justification of men, but so that they might rest.[71] To observe it was beneficial to health, though it made no difference to salvation. If it had been otherwise, Sabbath observance would have been prescribed from the foundation of the world, and for all creatures animate and inanimate. Now, the patriarchs did not observe it, though they were chosen of God.[72] Neither is the Sabbath kept by any of God's creatures except those who do work. The Sabbath was brought into being only for the sake of those creatures which are constrained to do regular and laborious work. Thus domestic animals observe the Sabbath rest along with men, even though for them there are no commandments and no divine reward.[73] Therefore the Sabbath rest is a matter of physical need, not of religious duty. For this reason it is legitimate, and always has been, for a man to set it aside when he thought it was in his interests to do so. Thus he may set aside Sabbath observance during a war, as Joshua did, and the Maccabees (after insistence on the Sabbath rest on one occasion had proved disastrous).[74] Let the Jews, therefore, not boast about their devotion to it. They gain no credit from it at all. It is a good institution, and one approved by God, but the benefit it provides is merely that of needful recreation.

It may be concluded from this that in Aphraates' community the Sabbath was observed alongside Sunday, as is laid down in the

Apostolic Constitutions, and that by certain Christians it was kept in the Jewish manner. Aphraates does not dare to abolish it completely, and does not wish to do so. He would merely like to deprive it of its Jewish taint by conferring on it the character of a simple rest day. He wants to secularize it. It is with the same idea in mind that the *Didascalia*, attempting to turn Christians away from the Sabbath rites rather than from the Sabbath itself, shows how similar they are to mourning customs and represents their observance as a punishment laid upon the Jews alone.

What is said of the Sabbath is equally true of the Pasch. Up to the fourth century there were Christians who, while they did not refuse to celebrate Easter, continued to keep festival also on the fourteenth Nisan and the days of Unleavened Bread, and this in accordance with the ancient rites of Israel. The discussions the fathers devote to the subject of the paschal lamb are too numerous and too urgent for us to imagine that they were inspired by anything other than a persistent practice among the ranks of the Christians themselves. The line of argument varies from one author to another. Some authors demonstrate that the sacrifice of the Passover lamb, which ought not to be carried out except at Jerusalem,[75] represents, even from the Jews' own point of view, a transgression of the law when it is carried out by those of the diaspora.[76] Others repeat that the sacrifice of the lamb is no more than an image of the true sacrifice, that of Christ. Even in the beginning its value was symbolic only, and now it possesses none at all.[77] And to those who cited the instance of Christ himself, who at the Last Supper set an example of fidelity to the ancestral rite, it was asserted that the Lord did not eat the Passover of the law. He himself was the true Passover, announced beforehand, and made actual at the appointed time.[78]

All these arguments would be enough in themselves to convince us that there were Christians who persisted in eating the paschal lamb. But we have clearer proof of this custom in the protests that ancient writers make against those who comply with it.[79] The same is true of the eating of unleavened bread. St. Ephraem's hymn on the unleavened bread, whose every line blazes with hostility to the Jewish people, piles up its warnings to the faithful: "My brethren, keep far from the unleavened bread in which is symbolized the sacrament of Judas. Flee, my brethren, from the unleavened bread of Israel, for beneath its whiteness there is hidden shame. Do not accept, my brethren, the unleavened bread of this people whose hands are stained with blood."[80]

This is not mere rhetoric. The council of Laodicaea explicitly forbids "receiving the unleavened bread of Jews and taking part in their impieties."[81] And if Aphraates and the *Didascalia* alike attach such importance to the strict observance of the paschal fast, we may conclude that this was done partly in order to discourage Christians from eating the lamb and the unleavened bread. The conciliary canons forbid, on numerous occasions, eating with Jews. This doubtless means not merely that Christians should not share festival meals with them, but also that they ought not to comply with the Mosaic dietary laws.[82]

It is in fact curious to note that even the more troublesome obligations of Jewish observance found a large public willing to comply with them. Judaizing was far from being merely a superficial craze, and Judaizers did not keep up only those rites which were easiest, and hesitate over the ones that called for effort.

St. Jerome gives us to understand that converted Jews continued happily to circumcise their sons, to observe the Sabbath and the dietary laws, and also to sacrifice a lamb on the fourteenth Nisan.[83] There is every reason to believe that Eastern Christians who were not of Jewish extraction sometimes did the same, and were prompted to do this by the example of Jews, baptized or otherwise, and by a certain Semitic atavism as far as circumcision was concerned. The practice of circumcision is not only attested among certain sects,[84] it infiltrated in one or two places into the orthodox Church. However, the texts are not as explicit on this point as we might wish.[85] It is the imperial legislation, not that of the councils, which forbids the circumcision of non-Jews.

On the other hand, we do know that among the various sorts of Oriental Christianity there existed convinced advocates of the view that Christians should abide by the laws of ritual purity. The way in which the *Didascalia* develops the notion of *deuterosis* is clear evidence of this.[86] The distinction the *Didascalia* draws between the first and second redactions of the Sinaitic covenant code has a purpose that is not merely theoretical. Its aim is to distract the faithful, both those of Jewish origin and others, from observing the *deuterosis*.[87]

The coming of Christ has effected a distinction between two classes of precepts that are contained in the old covenant: those which have saving value, and which ought to continue, and those which are no longer of any use, and which ought to be abrogated. In doubtful cases the touchstone is provided by the gospel: that which is in perfect agreement with the message of Jesus, and that alone, is legitimate. To comply with the prescriptions regarding bodily cleanness and sexual functions is thus to contravene the spirit of the gospel and blot out the grace of baptism. "For she also who had the issue of blood was not chidden when she touched the skirt of our Saviour's cloak, but was even vouchsafed the forgiveness of all her sins."[88] And so there is no purity except moral purity. As for Christians, male or female, whether they are in a state of ritual impurity is of no consequence. "Let them assemble without restraint, without bathing, for they are clean. But if a man should corrupt and defile another's wife after baptism, or be polluted with a harlot, and rising up from her should bathe in all the seas and oceans and be baptized in all the rivers, he cannot be made clean."[89] "For in the Second Legislation, if one touch a dead man or a tomb, he must bathe; but do you...come together even in the cemeteries...and offer an acceptable Eucharist....For they who have believed in God, according to the gospel, even though they should sleep, they are not dead."[90]

These instructions imply that some people did observe the precepts referred to. We also learn, this time from Aphraates, that "the minds of ignorant and simple people are anxious about that which enters the mouth, and which cannot make a man impure. And those who torment themselves about such things speak thus: 'God gave instructions and commandments to His servant Moses concerning clean and unclean foods.'" And Aphraates sets himself to prove that the dietary laws[91] were imposed upon the Jews not for their salvation, but as a punishment for their errors, and that they are included among those "commandments which were not good," of which God spoke through the prophets. Chrysostom gives us similar information about the attraction the Jewish ritual fasts had for the members of the Church at Antioch. The Judaizers did not scruple to observe the total fast of Kippurim, and where Aphraates, for his part, replaces the eating of the lamb with a Christian fast, Chrysostom, correspondingly, suggests that the believer should force the Judaizers to eat on the great Day of Atonement.[92]

From this point of view Chrysostom's homilies are of prime value as evidence. They show that the Judaizers' enthusiasm was not for any one rite in particular, but for the entire religious life of the Jews. The occasion for the preaching of the homilies is that of the great autumn festivals of the Jews, Tabernacles, New Year, and Yom Kippur. Their celebration had been followed by a fresh outbreak among the Christian community of the Jewish sickness.[93] On this occasion a great crowd of Christians had gone along to the synagogue. Chrysostom admits at the beginning of his first homily that "many even of those who are reckoned to belong to us and who say that they think as we do, go along, some for the sake of the spectacle and others even to take part in the celebration and associate themselves with the fast. It is of this pernicious practice that I intend now to rid the Church."[94]

According to Chrysostom, women were especially ready to succumb to Judaism's charm.[95] This is something Josephus had noted earlier, in connection with Damascus and its pagan population.[96] But the women were far from being alone in this. In his eighth homily, recapitulating his arguments and drawing up a balance sheet of the situation, Chrysostom shows alarm at the scale of the mischief. It demands, he says, to be taken with the utmost seriousness. He advises his hearers not to ask, either to right or left, how many took part in the Jewish fast. Even if they were many, do not let it be known. Do not let us advertise what an evil situation the Church is in, but rather let us cure it. If anyone says, "Many took part in the fast," silence him. The news must not be spread or the scandal break out.[97] These adjurations provide an eloquent acknowledgement of the facts.

Though it was especially virulent at the festival periods, the Jewish sickness persisted throughout the year. It affected the whole life of those who were smitten with it. In every situation of their lives they automatically resorted to Jewish practices. If they were ill, they would ask the rabbis for healing, or seek it in the Synagogue by the method of incubation. If the occasion arose for them to take a specially solemn oath, they would take it not on the Church and the gospel but on the Jewish Bible and the Synagogue.[98]

Properly understood, some of these practices must be seen as vulgar superstitions. But this does not explain everything. We must recognize that the Judaizers of Antioch and elsewhere were inspired at least partly by more elevated motives, and by convictions that, though not well considered, were genuinely religious. The struggle in which Chrysostom is engaged is not simply a struggle between Christianity on the one hand and a degraded form of religious behavior on the other. It is a struggle between two cults that still fought over the same members, even when those members were not connected with Israel by birth at all.

It does not appear that the Jewish impact generally extended to the matter of beliefs, or that it involved those who submitted to it in any characteristic errors in the sphere of dogma. The authors who denounce it are quick enough, on occasion, to pick out heresies of this sort or that which are connected with Judaism. But they do not accuse the Judaizers within the Church of being contaminated with heresy, or of disputing, for example, the divinity of Christ. It is manifest that doctrinal speculation is in general quite foreign to these supporters of the Synagogue. If it is possible, notwithstanding, to pick out evidence here and there of contamination with Jewish ideas, such contamination is confined to the realm of Messianism and eschatology.

The first generation of Christians had lived in expectation of the Parousia. But the hope of an early return of Christ to earth in judgment and in triumph gradually dwindled. For Greco-Latin Christianity the power that the idea of the Messianic kingdom still retained attached itself to the notion of the Christian empire, in which, under the law of God and by means of a close union between the Church and the civil power, the ideal society of believers was to be brought into being. If we leave out of account the Eastern provinces, such as Syria and Palestine, eschatology had its last fling with Montanism and some similar but more isolated phenomena. But in Eastern Christianity the eschatological outlook largely survived the triumph of the Church, and it was the proximity of the Jews and their example that was partly responsible for keeping it in being.

The Eastern Judaizers' idea of the coming kingdom was an entirely materialistic one. If it did have its roots in Jewish conceptions, it had even more definite connections with the Islamic notion of paradise. If we are to believe St. Jerome, who is here our principal witness, they believed that the body was to be raised, and was to enjoy for a thousand years the pleasures of the flesh and of the table, while it awaited the final judgment.[99] These blessings were to be accompanied by the comprehensive restoration of Jewish observances.

The part allotted to the Messiah seems to be rather a vague one. Hope is centered less on the Messiah than on Jerusalem, the seat of the kingdom. *Judaei et nostri judaizantes putant auream atque gemmatum Jerusalem de caelestibus ponendam.*[100] This characteristic is typical of what we know of the Jewish eschatology of this period. Moreover, as we have seen, the Synagogue acknowledged that the *posh'im* awaited, with all the faith they possessed, the glorious restoration of the city, and they counted this to the dissidents' credit. This attachment to Jerusalem and to Jewish rites went along with a deferential regard for the Jews themselves. In these circles the authority of Jews, even unbaptized Jews, in matters of biblical exegesis, was readily acknowledged. Even quite eminent Christians suffered from this defect: St. Jerome, when he denounces the aberration, refuses to give their names for fear of causing offense.[101] But Jerome is consistent in saying that it was among the masses that the Jewish sickness really raged.[102] The same impression is given by Chrysostom's homilies. Josephus had noted earlier the spread of Judaizing tendencies among the populace of Antioch.[103] Such tendencies were of long standing. In this respect the intervention of Christianity did not change things very much.

IV

Even if it had been restricted to Palestine with its Syrian hinterland, and to Mesopotamia, i.e., to the Semitic East, the Judaizing movement would have been important. But it was not confined to these areas altogether. It appeared, generally speaking, wherever there were considerable communities of Jews. This statement by itself is enough to show that did not arise from contemplation of the Bible or from any special interpretation of the sacred text. It was prompted by living example.

In the East, apart from the areas already studied, which were specially favorable ground for Judaizers as well as for Judaism, Egypt provides some evidence of the phenomenon. It was an area where, for example, Sabbath observance was strongly entrenched. But this evidence is much less than we should expect, taking into consideration the size and age of the Jewish colony there. This exceptional situation doubtless arises from the deep and ancient antipathy that existed between Alexandrian Jewry and the Greek or Hellenized population. Relations between the two communities, whether before or after the advent of Christianity, were for the most part openly hostile and did not encourage syncretism. In the surrounding territory, by contrast, it may be suspected that there was interpenetration, favored, as in Berber Africa, by cultural affinities. The traces of this interpenetration are still to be seen in Coptic and Ethiopian Christianity. This question, however, falls outside the confines of my study.

Leaving aside Palestine and Syria, it was in the heart of Asia Minor, in Phrygia and Galatia, that Judaizing Christianity most made its influence felt. The canons of the council of Laodicaea are amongst the most pointedly anti-Jewish in all the conciliary literature.[104] Those which relate to the Sabbath are especially interesting.

Although the Sabbath rest is condemned, services of worship are envisaged, at which "the gospels and other portions of scripture" are read.[105] The apparent contradiction between these two rules may be resolved if it is conceded that the Church authorities were powerless to deprive the Sabbath of all its standing, and were doing their best to give it purely Christian content. The obligation to read the gospel does not amount to an obligation to make the day a sacred one. The authors of the canons are thinking of those Christians who, in conforming to the Synagogue pattern, read nothing on that day but the Old Testament, and perhaps did their reading together with Jews. To add the gospel to the other scriptural texts was to diminish the danger. The Saturday became in this way a kind of anticipation of the Sunday, and the same council is thus able to lay it down that during Lent the Eucharistic synaxis ought not to be celebrated "except on Saturdays and Sundays."[106]

But it is clear that this treatment of the Saturday is merely a concession to Judaizing tendencies. It antedated the decisions of the council. We find ourselves again in company with the *Didascalia* and with Aphraates. Without searching for evidence from other areas, we need to look no further than the divergent canons of this one council in order to give the lie to Hefele-Leclerq's assertion that "about the middle of the fourth century, and even more noticeably in the second half of that century, we meet hardly any trace of the Judaizing movement."[107] On the contrary, there is every reason to think that what we are faced with is an uninterrupted tradition of Judaizing, reaching down from the time when the epistles to the Galatians and the Colossians were written. This tradition was a persistent one, and defied all the anathemas of the Church authorities, so that those authorities were obliged, in order to avoid a worse evil, to accommodate themselves to it in some measure.

In the West the density of the Jewish population was, on balance, perceptibly less than in the East. The West therefore provides us with less evidence of Judaizing movements. It will be noted, however, that Christian literature written in Latin contains not only a certain number of anti-Jewish polemical works, but what is more revealing, several treatises devoted to particular aspects of Jewish ritualism, such as the dietary prohibitions, circumcision, and Sabbath observance.[108] These correspond exactly to the practical preoccupations of the Church. Novatian's *De cibis judaicis*, like other lost treatises by the same author, was a pastoral letter. The Bible remains today, as it was in the days of the early Church, the norm of faith. But what bishop would any longer dream of dealing with such a subject? No one would, because there are no longer any Judaizers.

Rome and northern Italy possessed important Jewish communities. The curious personality of Isaac the Jew bears witness to the intellectual vitality and the high degree of culture of this Western Jewry. Isaac was converted to Christianity under Pope Damasus, and is probably to be identified with the mysterious Ambrosiaster, author not only of a commentary on the epistles of St. Paul, but also, in all likelihood, of the *Quaestiones Veteris et Novi Testamenti*. He later returned to the Synagogue. His career shows that Judaism was well capable of giving the Church serious cause for concern.[109]

But all the while, it is outside Italy that Judaizing tendencies are best perceived, and most clearly of all in Spain. The literary tradition of anti-Jewish polemic, maintained in Spain right through until the Middle Ages, is bound up with the persistence of propagandizing tendencies among the Jews of that country.[110] To stay within the chronological limits of my period, the canons of the council of Elvira themselves betray the presence of important Judaizing elements within early Spanish catholicism. At a number of points they echo the decisions of the Eastern councils. They forbid marriage with Jews of either sex. They forbid the making of the Sabbath into a festival. They prohibit eating with Jews and the blessing of harvests by them.[111]

Africa is in no way behind Spain. And here we must call on Commodian as a witness. It is true that his personality, and the place and date at which he lived and wrote are, for the critic, sore problems, not dissimiliar to the problems raised by Ambrosiaster. It is nevertheless extremely likely, though not absolutely certain, that he is to be placed in Africa, and very probably before the triumph of the Church.[112]

His entire work is animated by a violent hatred of the Jews. Monceaux calls it "turncoat's spite,"[113] for Commodian, who was born a pagan, seems to have entered Christianity by way of the Synagogue. He doubtless owes to this contact with Judaism not only his apocalyptic attitudes and millenarian hopes,[114] but likewise his high opinion of the law, which reminds us of the *Didascalia*.[115] His knowledge of the Judaizers is thus the knowledge of personal experience. He attacks them by showing up the contradictions in their attitude. They run from pagan temple to Synagogue only to go back to pagan temple. They celebrate in turn, and with the same enthusiam, the rites of idolatry and those of Israel.[116] These are precisely the attitudes that Chrysostom describes and condemns: τί μιγνύεις τὰ ἄμικτα;[117] he asks the Judaizers of Antioch. And Commodian similarly: *Quid? Medius Judaeus, medius vis esse profanus?*[118]

Between the two cases there is nevertheless a difference. The Judaizers of Antioch are inside the Church; those whom Commodian is slaying with his pen are almost exclusively, it seems, pagans or syncretizing heretics. This fact is in agreement with what we know from elsewhere about the religious situation in north Africa and it strengthens the presumption of Commodian's North African origin. His evidence reinforces that of Tertullian concerning the penetration of Jewish rites and practices among the pagan masses of the country.[119] I have elsewhere drawn attention to the fact that the Christian Judaizers of the Maghreb seem to have been recruited almost entirely from the sects,[120] such as Caelicoles or others, and I have tried to give an explanation of this fact. The very definitely latinized and Romanized nature of African orthodoxy to some extent protected it against a Judaism that had once more become heavily semitized in language and in outlook. Judaism's appeal was therefore exercised principally upon the least Romanized strata of the indigenous population. These were the same strata from which the Christian sects, the representatives of social, cultural, political, and religious dissent all at the same time, also drew their adherents. When we compare this situation with that of Eastern Christianity, in which the impact of Judaism was felt equally in the Greek environment of Chrysostom and the un-Hellenized circles in which Aphraates moved, we perceive a fundamental difference.

African catholicism was nevertheless not completely free of Judaizing infiltration. The contrast with the situation in the East is not so radical as all that. On this topic we must consult St. Augustine. His treatise against the Jews gives a prominent place to the question of ritual observances.[121] It is nevertheless conceived in very general terms, and it gives a very brief résumé of the whole Christian argument against Israel. Other indications are distributed throughout the rest of his homiletical and exegetical work.[122] But the most interesting information we have concerning the Judaizing movement in the African Church is provided by Augustine's letter to Bishop Asellicus,[123] in which he expresses his views not simply on the question of the old covenant, but more precisely on the practical problem of the observance or nonobservance by Christians of the ritual law.

The basic principle is forcefully asserted in the opening lines: *Christianos maxime ex gentibus venientes judaizare non oportere Paulus apostolus docet.*[124] There follows an appreciation of the moral law, in the Pauline manner, and a sketch of a theory of grace, which includes a condemnation of Pelagianism. After this, the author demonstrates that the Christians are the true Israel. He bases this on the traditional contrast between letter and spirit and calls on allegorical exegesis for help. *Si itaque sumus Judaei non carnaliter sed spiritualiter, quemadmodum sumus semen Abrahae, non secundum carnem . . . sed secundum spiritum fidei.*[125]

Well then, it might be asked, is the Christian entitled to call himself "Jew" or "Israelite"?[126] No, replies the author, for the terms lend themselves to ambiguity. They would need in this case to be understood in their spiritual sense. Now, in view of the sense in which they are normally used, they would not be thus understood. They could only cause confusion.[127]

Certain Christians did make use of the titles *Jew* and *Israelite*, but these were precisely the people whom we are talking about, the Judaizers. A certain Aptus, whom Augustine does not know personally, but who has been mentioned by Asellicus, is forcing Judaizing practices on the faithful. He enthusiastically enforces the dietary prohibitions and the whole apparatus of ritual observances. Not only so, but he adopts for himself and his disciples the names *Jew* and *Israelite*.[128]

It does not appear that this movement, whose existence provides the occasion for Augustine's letter, was of very serious proportions. It was large enough, nevertheless, to disturb the Church authorities.

Asellicus, who was the first to be informed, referred the matter to Donatian, Primate of Byzacena, who passed the letter to Augustine, asking him to reply to it. Asellicus is known to us from other documents as Bishop of Tozeur, in southern Tunisia.[129] As for the obscure Aptus (*Aptus iste nescio quis*) whom St. Augustine treats with such disdain, he could be the Donatist bishop of the same place,[130] who took part along with his Catholic colleague in the conference of the African episcopate at Carthage in 412. Consequently therefore, in spite of everything, the affair has a certain importance. And if Asellicus raised the alarm, this was doubtless because Judaizing tendencies, originating in the Donatist community, had affected his own flock.

The movement is interesting in many respects. The Syrtes coast was one of the areas in which at the end of the period of antiquity Punic culture remained most lively.[131] In all likelihood it was by joining with these influences that Judaism was able to exercise such appeal to Christians. The fact illustrates therefore what I have said elsewhere about Jewish missionary activities and Jewish expansion in North Africa.

But it is clear that the usual explanations of the phenomenon, the influence of the Synagogue, the presence of a sizable Jewish community, or even the atavism of the Judaizers, are not the only ones operating in this instance. The official theology is itself partly responsible for the malady. By asserting in too unqualified a way the Church's claim to be regarded as the true Israel the apologists had sown confusion in the minds of some who were deaf to theological subtleties, unprepared for allegory, and unable to perceive the distinction between the carnal, superficial sense of words and things and their symbolic, spiritual sense. Anyone who belonged to the true Israel surely qualified to be called an Israelite. Such seemed to be the plain logic of the situation. And *Israelite* is synonymous with *Jew*. Why not, therefore, adopt the title? It is easy to take the word *Jew* again in its literal sense and with that short step to become a Judaizer, for the Jew is characterized by a particular religious attitude. This was a step the Christians of Tozeur had taken, and it has to be admitted that the somewhat embarrassed arguments that Augustine advances against them are not specially convincing.

V

African Christianity provides several other sidelights on the character and genesis of Judaizing movements. Tertullian, in his *Apologeticum*, refutes the accusation that Christians indulge in ritual murder by saying: "Let your sin blush before us Christians, who do not reckon the blood even of animals among meats to be eaten, who for this cause also abstain from things strangled and such as die of themselves, that we may not be defiled by any blood even buried within their entrails." And he adds that pagans know of this prohibition and put Christians to the test by leading them into sin, offering them black puddings to eat.[132]

This text does not stand alone. The same argument, replying to the same accusations, reappears in Minucius Felix, who may have borrowed it from Tertullian.[133] Finally, according to the letter the Church at Lyon wrote to the communities of Asia concerning the persecution of 177, the executioners attempted to extract from the martyr Biblis, under torture, a confession that the accusations brought against the Christians were justified. He replied in similar terms: "How would such men eat children, when they are not allowed to eat the blood even of irrational animals?"[134]

It emerges clearly from this evidence that at the end of the second century and the beginning of the third the Christians of Gaul, like those of Africa, complied with the prescriptions laid down by the apostolic group at Jerusalem.[135] They are the regulations found in Leviticus.[136] Those who observed them were in effect making themselves into semi-Jews, for the prohibition of blood and of things strangled, joined with the prohibition of idolatry and the practice of the moral law, represent in Jewish eyes, and according to the expression used in Acts itself, the "necessary things" (ἐπάναγκες). They are the Noahic precepts, imposed by the Synagogue on the Jewish-pagan *metuentes*.[137]

It is known that St. Paul refused to impose the smallest ritual obligation on his gentile disciples, and that he claimed to have the agreement of the "pillars of the Church" themselves.[138] He therefore did not put the Jerusalem compromise into effect in the communities he founded. Even on the question of things sacrificed to idols, which were also forbidden by the apostolic conference, he remained intransigent. His sole concern was to avoid scandal: "If an unbeliever invites you to his house, go if you want to, and eat whatever is put in front of you, without asking questions just to satisfy conscience. But if someone says to you, 'This food was offered in sacrifice,' then, out of consideration for the man who told you, you should not eat it."[139] As for the prohibition of blood, Paul puts it on the same level as the rest of the ritual law. To eat meat that has been sacrificed to idols is not to behave like a pagan, as long as one knows and believes that "no idol is anything in the world."[140] But to observe the rules relating to blood would be to behave like a Jew. It would be a rejection of grace.

The texts just quoted prove that this point of view was not universally accepted, and that many communities, who were not either in a direct or indirect sense Pauline communities, considered themselves bound by the apostolic decree, whether they were applying the directions laid down in Acts itself, or whether, having been drawn originally from circles already influenced by Jewish propaganda, they took the prohibition in question to be self-evidently valid.[141]

Once this minimum of ritual observance was conceded, and given the help of Jewish missionary activities, it is not surprising that some Christians, just like the pagan *metuentes*, should have been tempted to go further. They had been given what looked like an invitation to Judaizing, issued by the Church authorities themselves. The Church's efforts were henceforth devoted to demonstrating that this minimum of ritual observance was in fact a maximum.

It was a maximum, at least, as far as ritualism was concerned. For there were some who, in a desire to Christianize the prohibition, expanded it. Just as in the matter of the ritual fast the aspect of mortificaion had been accentuated, so the prohibition of things strangled and of blood was expanded to include every sort of meat. Thus Christian asceticism appears not only as an attempt to go beyond the regulations, but at the same time as a means of depriving the observance of its Jewish character. Already in the Didache there are hints of this development. "And as regards food, what thou art able, bear."[142] What the author has in mind, evidently, is the distinction between clean and unclean foods, and he is giving us to understand that respect for the corpus of dietary laws is desirable to say the least, and is in any case meritorious. But the wording of the phrase allows also a more general interpretation: he is saying, "Practice abstinence, with all the powers which you possess."

This ascetic ideal is not imposed on everybody. It quickly came to be understood that one cannot demand from the generality of believers an effort that is beyond the ordinary powers of man. Therefore another way had to be found to counteract the risk of Judaizing that was inherent in the prohibition of blood. In the Latin Church this prohibition gradually fell into disuse. By the end of the fourth century it was outmoded. This at least is the picture St. Augustine presents.

Augustine explains the apostolic precept in two ways: as a question of hygiene, and as a matter of expediency. He tends to do with it what Aphraates had done with the Sabbath rest, i.e., to deprive it of any genuinely religious significance. The meat of fattened animals is, he says, harmful. It is for this reason that it ought not to be eaten.[143] As for the rule concerning blood and things strangled, the main reason for its inclusion by the apostles was to create between Jews and gentiles in the Church a bond of common observance, and by this means to strengthen the cohesion of that structure whose two walls were Jews and gentiles and whose chief cornerstone was Christ.[144] It was chosen for the very reason that it was easy for the faithful to bear. But once the numbers of ex-Jews in the Church began to fall off and the Church came to be composed of gentiles only, there was no longer any reason for the observance. Moreover, the few old-fashioned Christians who continue to observe this rule, and who refuse so much as to eat a hare that has been clubbed to death without bleeding, are a laughing stock among their brethren,[145] for everyone knows that "what goes into the mouth does not make a man unclean; it is what comes out of the mouth that makes him unclean."[146]

What looks to St. Augustine like a defunct and anachronistic rule retained the force of law in the Church of the East.[147] The decisions of the councils are explicit. It is particularly curious to note that the council of Gangra, about the middle of the fourth century, not only makes a clear distinction between the total abstinence from meat, as practiced by the ascetics, and the normal Christian abstinence from meat offered to idols and from things strangled, but it goes on to condemn the one and to confirm the obligatory nature of the other.[148] At a much later date (A.D. 692) the so-called Trullan Synod even more explicitly renews the prohibition of blood, on pain of deprivation of office for those who are ordained, and for laymen on pain of excommunication.[149]

Now the same council takes issue with the Judaizers. It forbids the celebration of the new moon by lighting fires in front of houses and workshops, and by dancing around.[150] The dance is evidently not simply a rite connected with the new moon. It is perhaps no more than a popular custom. But the habit of lighting fires is mentioned in the Mishnah[151] and among the Christians it probably represented a borrowing from local synagogue usage. The council further forbids believers to eat unleavened bread, to consort habitually with Jews, to accept medicines from them, or to take baths with them.[152]

It is quite in character that the council should not only recall the prohibition of blood, and thus authenticate one aspect of ritual observance, but that it should authenticate it in the name of scripture, which is to say, by reference to Genesis and Leviticus, not to the decrees of Acts, which merely reassert the Old Testament position. At the same time, it lays down the limits beyond which Christians must not go if they are to avoid the charge of Judaizing.

We should like to know what the Jews' reactions were to those Christians who complied with their rites. But on this point we are particularly short of documentary evidence and are reduced to hypotheses. Even when we have clarified the meaning of the Talmudic terms *minim* and *posh'e yisrael* and their application to the Christians, it is difficult to make out a case for saying that they properly refer to the Judaizers, for the Judaizers do not come precisely into either of the two Talmudic categories. Their nominal attachment to orthodox Christianity would classify them among the *minim*; but they had voluntarily reestablished a connection with the Synagogue. Yet they are not on that account to be reckoned among the *posh'im*, if, as I believe, this term as applied to Christians was restricted to one who had been born a Jew, or at least been a full proselyte, before being eventually won over to Christianity.

It is, however, impossible that a category as important and obvious as that of the Judaizers should have failed to attract a certain amount of attention from the Jews. It emerges from the homilies of Chrysostom that the Judaizers did benefit from a certain sympathy on the Jews' part. The Jews were pleased to see them resorting to the Synagogue and received them with enthusiasm, encouraging them to persevere, hoping perhaps that they would go as far as total conversion. We are justified, consequently, in asserting that the Jews viewed the gentile Judaizers as semiproselytes.[153]

Lacking Jewish documentary material, we may say that the practices we have just analyzed themselves bear out this interpretation. The apostolic decree, laying down as conditions for the admission of gentiles the so-called Noahic precepts, is in line with the attitude of the Jewish missionaries. In Jewish eyes, the gentile who complies with these observances is a "God-fearer," and is entitled to the Lord's goodwill and that of His people. But in the case of Christians, there were always other considerations, and other reactions to take into account. When an orthodox Christian observed the Noahic commandments, he did so because the Church had so instructed him, not for the sake of drawing closer to the Synagogue. But the Church was the great enemy. If, on the other hand, the believer went further than this, if he indulged in what could fairly be called Judaizing and went against what the Church authorities commanded, in spite of their fulminations, then he would come within the traditional category of the *metuentes*.

From this point of view, then, there was no break in continuity between the pagan and the Christian epoch. Already, before the intervention of Christianity, semiproselytes had sometimes been designated by the term ἰουδαΐζοντες, the same that the Church applied to its own members who were smitten with the Jewish "sickness."[154] Both classes hovered on Judaism's threshold, without committing themselves in any definite way. Like their pagan predecessors, the Christian Judaizers accepted the essentials of Jewish observance and added to the Noahic commandments, which alone constituted the strict requirement, the principal obligations of the Mosaic law.

It may be objected that the Trinitarian belief imposed on these Judaizers by their baptism must have been an obstacle to a monotheistic faith such as the Synagogue preached, and such as it demanded of those of its sympathizers who became full converts. But it is not certain that Judaism was always very particular about the quality of the monotheism exhibited by its pagan *sebomenoi*; and without these it would have been totally cut off from secular society.[155] Furthermore, compared with pagan idolatry and polytheism, Christianity might well have appeared to be a lesser evil, and the Christian Judaizers' dogmatic shortcomings might in addition have been offset in the Jews' eyes by their strict adherence to ritual observance.

Faced with Christianity, two reactions were possible for a Jew of this period. If he thought principally of its doctrines and its rites, he could consider it to be essentially a branch of Judaism, detached, and fallen from truth into error. It was then a species of the execrated *minuth*. But if he thought of its membership, he could instead see it as a movement leading the *goyim* toward the true faith. He could view Christianity as a step on the way to conversion. Though the former is clearly the predominant view (though not the only one) as far as normal Christianity is concerned, it could very well be imagined that the latter attitude was the prevalent one with regard to Judaizers.

But Christianity and Judaism were not alone concerned. Their conflict was played out in a world shaped by paganism. Judaizing tendencies did not always manifest themselves in a pure form. They were often entangled in the minds of the faithful with survivals of pagan usages, in combinations in which logic played little part. I am not speaking here of the sects, but of what went on in the Church at large. A Christian, properly baptized, might celebrate the new moon, observe the Sabbath scrupulously, and refuse on that day, once the sun had gone down, to render a light to his neighbour. But he might celebrate also the emperor's birthday, according to the traditional rites, and practice ornithomancy.[156] Here we have another manifestation of Jewish influence, that which, in the form of popular superstition, worked on the masses as part of the universal syncretism.

12
Superstition and Magic

φησὶ δὲ ὁ Κέλσος αὐτοὺς σέβειν ἀγγέλους καὶ γοητείᾳ
προσκεῖσθαι, ἧς ὁ Μωϋσῆς αὐτοῖς γεγονεν ἐξηγητής.
Origen, *Contra Celsum* 1:26

I

Superstition and magic are without doubt fundamental to ancient man's way of thinking. They were especially characteristic of the ancient world in its decline.[1] There is abundant evidence for the vitality of these beliefs from top to bottom of the social scale. Even among the best and most enlightened Romans astrology was taken very seriously. Those who laughed at the traditional myths and the old rites nevertheless continued to be afraid of the evil eye, and were convinced of the influence of the stars on human life, both beneficent and baleful. Even the most outlandish miracle workers, such as Alexander of Abonoteichos, could always be sure of an enthusiastic following among the masses, whereas the sages, for their part, felt obliged to cover their superstition with a veneer of philosophy, and had recourse to the theory of demons and genii. Everyone believed in marvels. The well-known miracle of the rain that fell for the benefit of one of the legions during Marcus Aurelius's Danube wars is not only given credence by pagans on all hands, but by Christians too.[2] The philosopher emperor himself, though he ordered that "he who by superstitious practices puts to fright the moving soul of man should be banished to an island,"[3] did not fail, when important matters were afoot, to consult the oracles.[4]

Even now, when much more research has been done on the subject, the judgment of J. Réville remains a valid one: "All Roman society, from the humblest inhabitant of Rome, consulting for a few pence the astrologer at the circus, to the philosopher conjuring up his demon; from the poor peasant asking the Syrian goddess, as she passes through his village, about the prospects for next year's harvest, to those with a lust for empire, inquiring from the Chaldaean or from this or that renowned sanctuary on what day and at what hour their ambition might be satisfied—all Roman society was enwrapped in a vast web of superstitions which east and west had combined to manufacture."[5]

It was a web whose knots the Jews had largely helped to tie. To their pagan entourage they appeared as magicians and sorcerers. This attribute of theirs was universally recognized. It enhanced their reputation among the credulous masses, while the anti-Semitism of the better educated seized on it as a stick to beat them with. The accusation is found again and again in the writings of pagan authors. For Juvenal, the Jews are the lowest sort of charlatans, who sell their oracles for profit:

> *...aere minuto*
> *Qualiacumque voles Judaei somnia vendunt.*[6]

One of Lucian of Samosata's characters suffers from gout, and mocks at all the cures suggested for his condition. Lucian puts into his mouth the words: "Another idiot allowed a Jew to say incantations over him."[7] If we are rightly informed, Alexander of Abonoteichos himself was using Jewish methods of trickery when he pronounced the obscure words, οἷαι γένοιντ' ἂν Ἑβραίων ἢ Φοινίκων.[8]

In the opinion of the ancients, magic was, as it were, congenital in Israel. They agreed, indeed, to attribute its origin to Moses, who occupies an important place among the great magicians. According to Celsus, the Jews "are addicted to sorcery, which Moses first expounded to them."[9] Moses, or occasionally his predecessor, Joseph, is sometimes presented as the disciple of the wise Egyptians. "In Egypt Joseph, thanks to the acuteness of his mind, learnt the secrets of magic and soon became the king's favourite. He was indeed adept at explaining marvels and was the first to interpret dreams... His son was Moses, who was equally remarkable for the skill which he inherited from his father and for his beauty."[10] Sometimes, on the other hand, Moses is presented as the enemy, and his spells are counteracted by the defensive magic of the Egyptians. According to Numenius of Apamea, Jannes and Jambres, Egyptian temple scribes, were considered to be second to none in the art of magic. At the time when the Jews were expelled from Egypt they were chosen by the Egyptian people to deal with Mousaios, the chief of the Jews, whose prayers were very powerful with the divinity. They proved themselves capable of turning from Egypt the worst calamities Mousaios unleashed upon it.[11] Not one of these authors dreams of throwing doubt either on the talent of the Jewish magicians or on the efficacy of magic in general. They are in both respects typical of their times.

The Jews shared this secure reputation with the East in general and it was a well-established one. It is amply attested by the numerous magical texts and illustrations, and by the inscriptions, talismans, gems, and amulets that bear the mark of Judaism.[12] If these bear

witness to Jewish influence in the pagan world, it is to the lowest and
crudest forms of that influence. But it must be remembered that they
were also its most widespread and effective forms, because they were
in harmony with the spirit of the age, and that historians have found
traces of them in every corner of the ancient world. E. Schwartz has
made this point specifically: "It must not be overlooked that Judaism
derived publicity not only from its apologetic, properly so called, but
also a more debased sort of publicity through the practitioners of
magic and sorcery. It is curiously common to neglect the Jewish
elements in the syncretism which underlies magic. They are really the
most important and interesting elements in it."[13]

Though it is true that Judaism, by means of its theodicy and its
morality, was able to seduce the noblest of the pagans, it also exercised
a more murky influence on the masses by its reputed ability to ward
off the Powers. This aspect of Jewish influence, which was older than
Christianity, continued to make itself felt even within the Christian
ranks. The Church was subjected to this in spite of itself and suffered
it a long time. Even when the flowering period of proselytism was
over, although the competition weakened, Judaism thus continued to
manifest its presence, in indirect and very humble ways, and to
exercise a dangerous influence on the Church from inside.

Christian authors themselves denounce, on occasion, the magical
practices of the Jews.[14] But instead of regarding it as a fundamental
characteristic of their nation or of their religion, or attributing its
origin to Joseph or Moses, they readily interpret it as one sign among
other of Israel's decadence, and as a consequence of her fall from
grace. It is because they rejected and killed Christ that the Jews have
been delivered up to demons and have become addicted to their
deadly errors.[15]

In order to exonerate themselves from these accusations, the Jews
are sometimes content simply to return them, accusing their pagan or
Christian adversaries of resorting to magic too. According to the
rabbis, and also according to Celsus, who was doubtless inspired by
the Jews at this point, Jesus was a magician whose miracles, which are
not in doubt, are explained by the connections he had with demons.[17]
This back-handed acknowledgment of Jesus' powers is accompanied
by explicit condemnations of magic, which is repudiated by the rabbis
as an activity incompatible with true religion and as a pagan
contamination of Judaism.[18] Yet they do draw a distinction between
black magic and healing magic. The former is entirely to be
condemned, although, even so, it is useful to be well-enough informed
about it to be capable of defending oneself against it. The latter is in
certain instances legitimate.[19] As for the populace at large, it is certain

that the Jewish masses, like the pagan or Christian ones, not only believed, as the rabbis did, that magic was efficacious, but practiced magical rites with considerable enthusiasm. The insistence with which the Talmudic writings keep coming back to the subject proves that this was a burning contemporary issue.[20]

If Judaism is to be defined with reference to its monotheism and its moral law, then magic is compatible only with its debased forms. The same is true of Christianity. But the point of view of history is not that of theology. It is not always easy to draw a clear dividing line between religion and magic, even when the religion in question is one as developed as Judaism or Christianity. For the historian, a religion is what its adherents make it, and to reduce it to its most spiritual elements is an arbitrary proceeding. To do so in the present case would be to neglect an aspect of religious activity that, though doubtless it was neither approved nor encouraged by the orthodox authorities, nevertheless constitutes a curious phenomenon and one that existed on such a large scale as to be an important and characteristic feature of the age.

We may recognize, with Blau,[21] that in this matter paganism exercised a more powerful influence on Judaism than Judaism did on paganism. It is easy to pick out the foreign elements in Jewish magic, Egyptian, Babylonian, and Iranian ones. The Jews were not alone in enjoying a reputation as magicians, for this was common to the East as a whole.[22] Their magic was in some respects no more than a facet of the activities of the undivided East, though from the point of view of Jewish monotheism it represents a form of syncretism. The fact of the matter is that Judaism, because of its unique cohesion and its remarkable geographical distribution in the diaspora, had an important part to play in the diffusion of this syncretistic magic. It was largely by the agency of Judaism that the ancient world was impregnated with it. So prominent were the Jews in this process that pagan opinion assumed magic to be an integral and characteristic element of Israel's religion. "The Jews, who were initated into the secrets of the teachings and practices of the Irano-Chaldaeans, were indirectly responsible for making certain formulae known wherever the dispersion was spread."[23]

For the rest, despite some incontestably foreign contributions, Jewish magic reflects an authentically Israelite tradition, which fuses these borrowings into a single whole, impressing its peculiar and special character on them. In making Joseph, Moses, or Solomon the patron of magicians, the ancient authors, whether admirers of Judaism or its critics, had an obscure intimation of the truth. The roots of this Jewish magic which at the beginning of the Christian era manifested itself with such astonishing vitality throughout the empire, are to be sought in the Bible, in the beginnings of Mosaic religion, and even further back, in the old pre-Mosaic Semitism. It is no part of my present purpose to trace the development of this tradition through the Old Testament.[24] I merely wish to point to the principal strands of which Jewish magic in our period was composed, and to make clear what the factors were to which it owed its success, for success it certainly had, not only in the pagan world but among the Christians.

II

First of all, there was the language of the Hebrew scriptures. This was of unquestionable importance. Though Hebrew is almost completely absent from Jewish epigraphy in the diaspora, it is, by contrast, commonly used in magical inscriptions, whether on papyrus, gems, or amulets. It is true that in these instances it is often a matter of a few words only, as in the funerary inscriptions. But the very presence of these words, which appear sometimes alone and sometimes in a Greek or Latin context, is evidence that great importance was attached to them. It is evident that these mysterious characters, undecipherable by the vulgar mind, assumed greater power the less they were understood.[25] This is a characteristic of sorcery in any age.

It did not matter that, in accordance with the usual custom, the Hebrew words were transliterated into the common character, for though this made it possible to pronounce them, they nevertheless remained incomprehensible. The following formula appears in a long incantation found on a magical tablet from Adrametum, dating probably from the third century: Ιαω Αωθ Αβαωθ θεον τον Ισραμα.[26] The last word ought surely to be corrected to 'Ισραηλ, and there is no difficulty in recognizing the corrupt transcription as a piece of Hebrew whose original is found in the Bible: *Yahweh Sebaoth Elohe yisrael.*[27] But if this equivalence is clear to a modern scholar, however unfamiliar he may be with the Bible, it is certain that it escaped the man who used the incantation or, if not, that he was utterly indifferent to it. What mattered to him, for his purposes, was not the meaning, but simply the physical pattern of the letters. The formula would be mechanically reproduced and each character would be regarded as possessing its own inherent efficacy.[28]

Here we touch on another aspect of Jewish magic, the power of the name. There is doubtless nothing specifically Jewish in this. It is rather a characteristic of all primitive ways of thinking. To know the name, and to pronounce it correctly, is, according to the primitive mind, to have power over the object or being it designates, or rather, whose nature it expresses and sums up. But at the period with which we are dealing, Judaism provided the clearest example of this belief, which was based on an old biblical tradition.

The mystery which surrounded the divine name, ὄνομα κρυπτὸν καὶ ἄρρητον, the prohibition against pronouncing it, the dreadful potency with which the ineffable tetragrammaton was charged, all contributed an invitation to both Jews and gentiles who were smitten with sorcery to make use of it in their incantations. For according to the rabbis, Moses' miracles were accomplished thanks to the divine name engraved on his staff.[29] The exact pronunciation of this name was something the Jewish scholars flattered themselves that they knew. But they were forbidden to divulge it, the reason being precisely to prevent magical or blasphemous use of it.[30] The secret, however, was learned, and the entire ancient world made use of the divine name, either in its Hebrew form or in Greek transliteration.[31]

The order of the Greek vowels, ιαωουε, which is so common in the magical texts and is a departure from the normal order, evidently owes something to this transliteration.

The tetragrammaton, which represents the most perfect, efficacious, and potent form of the divine name, is not the only one to be employed by Jewish and syncretistic magic. All the appellations applied in the Bible to the God of Israel appear there, mixed with formulae from the Synagogue liturgy or reminiscences of them, in combinations almost infinite in number.[32] To use the greatest possible number of these in conjunction with one another was to maximize one's chances of putting one's finger on the true name, and in any case, it increased the effectiveness of the formula. At the same time, in order to ensure the greatest possible effect, it was a good thing also to add the names of pagan deities, which were generally Oriental ones, most frequently Egyptian. Thoth occupies a prominent place alongside Yahweh, whose diverse titles are sometimes fused into barbaric words. Thus we have such a curious Jewish-pagan amalgam as βαρβαραδωναι κενταβαωθ ιαβεζεβυθ, or even a Jewish-Christian formula such as this one: Ωρ Ωρ φωρ Ελωει Αδωναι Αδωναι Ιαω Σαβαωθ Μιχαηλ Ιησου χριστε.[33]

Furthermore, the divine names were not the only ones to which this prestige was attached. Everything directly or indirectly connected with the Bible shared in it. We know from Celsus that pagans freely used the names of the patriarchs for magical purposes.[34] Celsus' evidence shows that in the formula that is so commonly used in the magical documents, "God of Abraham, Isaac, and Jacob," it is not only to the divine name that mysterious power attaches, but that each of the patriarchal names possesses its own potency. But in the operation of magic, assistance was asked not only from the persons of the Old Testament,[35] but from the heavenly powers. This is the third of the basic elements of Jewish magic, angelology.

Angelology represents a late and adventitious element in Israelite religion, and there is general agreement that its origins are to be sought outside Palestine, principally in Zoroastrianism. But in the period with which we are concerned it was an essential part of Judaism, or at least, one of the essentials of Pharisaism, and Pharisaism tended at the beginning of the Christian era to become more and more identified with Judaism.

Angelology was prominent both in the speculations of the scholars and in the preoccupations of the mass of Jews, and was something, therefore, that even superficial observers were aware of. It is by reference to angelology that Celsus defines Judaism. The Jews "worship heaven and the angels which live there."[36] And he connects Jewish worship: "They worship angels and are addicted to sorcery, which Moses first expounded to them."[37] If this is meant as a definition of orthodox Judaism, it is manifestly unacceptable, for the angels remained subordinate to God, as the agents by which His will was executed.[38] It is, however, probable that in certain syncretizing Jewish circles, which were more important, perhaps, than our surviving Jewish texts would lead us to imagine, Judaism's fundamental monotheism was seriously compromised by angelological speculation, and that in such circles these beliefs genuinely did influence the cult. Evidence from pagan and Christian sources agrees too well for this conclusion to be avoided.

The epistle to the Colossians already has to combat a syncretizing and Judaizing sect in which the worship of angels played a large part.[39] According to Aristides, the Jews' intercessions were directed "rather towards angels than towards God."[40] The same opinion is expressed in the *Kerygma Petri*: "The Jews...thinking that they only know God, do not know Him, adoring as they do angels and archangels, the month and the moon."[41] Other quotations reinforcing this could be gleaned from ancient Christian literature. But the still more eloquent magical texts make it superfluous to cite more.

Jewish tradition knows the names of the chiefs of the celestial cohorts, the archangels. There are three, four, six, seven, or sometimes more of them, according to which book we consult.[42] And all the names figure alongside the divine names in the regular repertoire of incantations and exorcisms. We have just noted a formula in which the name of Michael appears. Those of Raphael, Gabriel, and others also occur frequently, either alone or in combination with others, especially when the object is to exorcise a demon.[43]

Angelology and demonology are inseparable. In Judaism they developed simultaneously, and the principal role assigned to angels in popular belief was to combat and counteract the unclean and malevolent demons in the struggle between the forces of light and the forces of darkness.[44]

The power of the angels derives from several factors. It derives from their names, which conceal that of the divinity, El, and share its power.[45] As far as Michael is concerned, and by extension all the others too, the power is derived from the role assigned to him in Jewish and Christian tradition, the power to cleave the dragon, the genius of evil.[46] It also derives from the correspondence that exists between the angelic and the astral powers. Sometimes the latter, the στοιχεῖα τοῦ κόσμου of which the apostle speaks, are confused with demons. Celsus ascribes this identification to the Jews, and is astonished that the Jews "worship heaven and the angels which live there, whereas the most august and powerful heavenly beings, the sun, the moon, the fixed and moving stars, they dismiss as of no account."[47] Sometimes, however, the heavenly bodies are more or less explicitly identified with the angels. The number of the seven archangels, which appears in some strands of Jewish tradition, is clearly connected with the number of the planets.[48]

But in any case, the distinction between angels and demons is not always clearly made. The distinction is simply between spirits that are positively good and those which are plainly evil. Now if there are fallen angels, which are as dangerous and as wicked as demons, there exist also demons that are amiable and accommodating. Some of these latter were on speaking terms with the rabbis.[49] Firm logic and strict classification do not exist in such material, and I shall be in no hurry to introduce them. In any case, one point is beyond dispute: it is that a close connection exists between angelology and astrology.

This explains the idea, which was widespread in the early Church, that the Jewish festivals, the date of whose celebration was determined in accordance with astronomical considerations, were manifestations of angel worship and were mixed up with magic. It explains also, or helps to explain, the presence among the decorations of some ancient synagogues of the signs of the zodiac, and even of the figure of Helios with his radiating crown.[50] Finally, it explains how the Jewish worship of angels could be denounced by the Christians as worship of demons. To use magic in order to enlist the aid of angelic powers was either to invoke or to counteract the astral powers, according to circumstances. And this is doubtless one of the basic reasons for the proliferation and success, in a world devoted to astrology,[51] of angelology and the Jewish magic that went with it.

The Christians, faithful to the biblical revelation of the God of Israel and His whole heavenly court, were exposed more directly than the pagans to the impact of these Jewish ideas, and were more profoundly influenced by them. And, again owing to the affinities that existed between Judaism and Christianity, the danger to Christians from Jewish magic was far more insidious than that from pagan superstition. The danger from pagan magic did nevertheless remain, for since there were no watertight divisions between the varieties of magic, it could enter Christianity through the medium of Judaism, as it were by subterfuge.

The Jewish-syncretistic influence appears especially clearly in magical texts and on amulets of all kinds. These are too often classified, by an abuse of terminology that Perdrizet has recently denounced,[52] as gnostic. It is certain that gnosticism is in some respects a product of a superstitious attitude of mind that was widespread during the early centuries of our era—its most significant product, since it was given systematic form. The analysis of its component elements reveals that syncretizing Judaism played a large part in it, and that this Judaism was at least as influential in the rise of gnosticism as were the pagan mystery religions or the pagan systems of religious philosophy. At least we may say that syncretizing Judaism and gnosticism were connected.[53] But let us suppose that we are faced with a document that reflects a preoccupation with magic, that in it there figure the biblical names of God, used apotropaically, and that these names are in more or less distorted form and are mixed with pagan words and names. We cannot on these grounds alone, and in the absence of more positive indications, classify it as gnostic. There was no such rigid barrier between orthodoxy and the gnostic sects as one might imagine from reading the assertions of the fathers. This was a barrier they took it upon themselves to erect and strengthen. But certain ideas, certain ways of thinking and modes of expression, certain practices of a gnostic kind, became widely diffused outside the circles of the initiated who made up these sects. They fell, if one may so express it, within the public domain and became common coin.

All the efforts of the ecclesiastical authorities could not prevent them from entering the Church, at the humblest levels. They left their mark on popular devotion and in particular they characterized what Guignebert calls the "demi-Christians."[54] To judge by the ceaselessly reiterated efforts of the hierarchy and the scholars to recall these doubtful elements to the right way, there were times and situations in which the "demi-Christians" made up a large proportion of the Church.

But if there were "demi-Christian" paganizers who, having been baptized, reverted to their atavistic ways, there were also Judaizers. The number of converts from Judaism among them was a tiny minority, so if they were swayed by the appeal of Judaism, it was not at all because of any tendencies inherited from their past. It was because the entire mass of the populace in the ancient world was, as it were, impregnated with this debased Judaism, and because a conversion to Christianity, far from eradicating the infection, exposed the convert to a further dose of it, owing to the connection that existed between the two cults.[55]

III

Although the magical formulae current in early Christianity almost without exception bear the stamp of Judaism, there are significant variations among them. These variations sometimes allow us to assign a particular document to the precise type of Judaism from which it emanated. Some magical texts presuppose a strict monotheism and therefore derive from a Judaism that is still in a pure state and exhibits no trace of syncretism. The most characteristic example is the formula in the tablet from Adrametum already cited. It was published by Maspero, and commented on first by Deissmann[56] and then by Blau.[57] The formula was used for very profane ends, appearing in an incantation to secure love, yet this document is, in the well-chosen words of Deissmann, "an epigraphic memorial" of the Old Testament.

The text contains no mention of any pagan divinity, only of the God of Abraham, Isaac, and Jacob, of Yahweh Sebaoth, God of Israel, and of "the sacred name which is not uttered." Verses of the Bible, accurately quoted, are combined with formulae from the Synagogue liturgy. Or, more exactly, these scriptural texts are alluded to rather than quoted directly. This is in accordance with a practice very characteristic of the Synagogue.

It is simple reminiscence of the Sabbath liturgy that explains the allusion to the beginning of Genesis and to the different activities of God, "who divided the light from the darkness...who set the luminaries and stars in the heavens...that they might lighten all men."[58] The mention of men at this point, although the biblical text speaks only of the earth,[59] is peculiar to our formula and the liturgy, and clearly attests the dependence of one upon the other. Similarly, when the incantation summons the demon it is exorcising to hear τοῦ ὀνόματος ἐντίμου καὶ φοβεροῦ καὶ μεγάλου, it is simply taking up and applying to the Name the epithets applied by the *Shemoneh 'Esre* to the Lord himself, "the great, almighty and fearful God."[60] It is explained, therefore, not by simple reminiscence of scripture, but by the direct influence of postbiblical Judaism. It would even appear that the biblical references, which in general seem to reflect the text of the Septuagint, sometimes presuppose the version of Aquila, which, from the time when the Christians took over the Septuagint, gradually replaced it in Synagogue use. This is supported, for example, by the occasional use of κτίσαντα instead of ποιήσαντα, and by the use of the phrase φωστῆρα καὶ ἄστρα to describe the "luminaries" of Genesis 1:16. The number of Hebraisms also points in the same direction.[61]

What we are faced with here, therefore, is a Jewish magical document, which, it may be freely concluded, reflects orthodox Judaism. As far as its general import is concerned, it would doubtless not be disowned by the rabbis, for they always recognized not only the existence of demons but also the right to combat them by legitimate means. The use of the singularly efficacious name was a legitimate means, as was the use of biblical texts, whose every verse, and even every letter, was charged with prophylactic and apotropaic power. It is clear that this document emanates from the Synagogue. But the copy that has come down to us was in all probability copied by a non-Jewish hand, by a pagan or a Christian. For it would be difficult to imagine that a Jew, even if he were not well educated or very expert at dealing with Greek, would in the formula τον θεον του Αβρααμ και του Ιαω και του Ιακου, Ιαω Αωθ Αβαωθ θεον του Ισραμα, write Ιαω for Ισακου, Ιακου instead of Ιακωβ, Αωθ Αβαωθ for Σαβαωθ, and Ισραμα for Ισραηλ.[62] This illustrates what happened to the formulae worked out by the Synagogue when they left the Synagogue and descended to popular use.

In other instances, magical texts reflect a background of Jewish-pagan syncretism. This is the case with the great exorcism formula published and commented on by Dietrich.[63] Here again the principal events in the creation of the world are recalled, as are the events of Israel's early history; flight from Egypt and crossing of the Red Sea, the annihilation of Pharaoh's troops, and the march through the desert following the pillar of fire. The basis of the document is made up not only of texts from Genesis and Exodus, but also portions of Psalms and numerous excerpts from the prophets, all combined with reminiscences of the liturgy. The "great God Sebaoth" is invoked, "he who is praised by all the powers of heaven, angels and archangels."[64] The demons are given the names of nations who are enemies of Israel:

Jebusites, Gergashites, and Perizzites.[65] To conjure them up, the document appeals to Solomon and to his seal, which "placed upon Jeremiah's tongue, cured him of dumbness."[66] The fire that burns in the temple of Jerusalem is alluded to,[67] and so is the prohibition of pork.[68]

But though the Jewish origin of the document is thus firmly established, it is equally certain that the Judaism it reflects is not orthodox. As Dietrich has shown, the syncretistic character of the fragment appears in the reference to $\tau\hat{\omega}\nu$ $\dot{\iota}\epsilon\rho\hat{\omega}\nu$ $\alpha\dot{\iota}\acute{\omega}\nu\omega\nu$,[69] and especially in the allusion to the giants whom God incinerated with lightning.[70] This brief reference is to an episode we know in more developed form in extracts from Eupolemus that Eusebius preserves.[71] One of these texts tells us that the survivors of the flood, the giants, founded Babylon and lived there in the tower they built. God destroyed the tower and scattered the giants throughout the earth. According to another text, which doubtless represents the primitive form of the legend, the giants, who were inhabitants of Babylon, were destroyed by the gods because of their impiety, and Belos, the sole survivor, built the tower.[72] The legend is evidently pagan in origin, and the religious circles that took it over were on the edge of orthodox Judaism, within the orbit of two religions, or even three, if the curious mention of "Jesus, God of the Hebrews" is taken into account.[73]

This last fact proves that, in any case, this text was not intended for Jewish use, any more than the one previously considered. For even a syncretizing Jew would scarcely have dreamed up such a phrase. It is aimed at those outside the Synagogue, as is proved by the closing formula, $\dot{o}$ $\gamma\grave{\alpha}\rho$ $\lambda\acute{o}\gamma\sigma s$ $\dot{\epsilon}\sigma\tau\grave{\iota}\nu$ $\dot{\epsilon}\beta\rho\alpha\ddot{\iota}\kappa\acute{o}s$.[74] Jews would naturally have recognized it as such, as far as its basic elements were concerned. It is to authenticate the quality of the product and to emphasize its efficacy that the peddler of the talisman thus draws attention to its trademark. This shows that the use of Hebrew was at this period designed to impress.

As for the $\kappa\alpha\theta\alpha\rho o\grave{\iota}$ $\mathring{\alpha}\nu\delta\rho\epsilon s$ with whom the formula is supposed to be deposited, Dietrich has suggested, with sound arguments,[75] that these should be identified with the Essenes or the Therapeutae, whose interests in magic and whose contacts with pagan religious thought are well attested. It is not impossible that our incantation was originally, in Jewish circles of an esoteric sort, a prayer of intercession, modified later in various ways to make it suitable for use in exorcism. It comes to be addressed to demons, and no longer to God, and God's miracles, which were originally referred to as benefits for which He is to be thanked, are now mentioned as proofs of His power, which the evil spirits will be unable to resist. The hypothesis is a likely one, and so is the suggestion that those responsible for the elaboration of the document into its present form were the Orphic Jews. However this may be, this curious text shows that Judaism was sometimes capable of compromises that doubtless increased its prestige and its appeal with the vulgar masses.[76]

Finally, we also possess evidence of a Jewish-Christian syncretistic magic, which from our point of view is the most interesting of all. For if the two types of texts we have already examined could have been, and certainly were, made use of by Christians, those of the third type were intended specifically for Christian use. Indeed, they actually emanate from Christian circles, and attest better than do the other types the lasting impression that Jewish ideas and practices made upon Christian believers.

One of the most typical examples is provided by a formula engraved on a leaden lamella, found at Amorgos and published by Hololle.[77] The object of the formula is to cure a tumor, which is to say, according to ancient popular ideas on the subject of medicine, to exorcise the demon that is the tumor's cause. The adjuration resorts to the classical procedures of Jewish magic, but these are combined, on this occasion, with specifically Christian elements, proving conclusively that the formula was composed by Christians and for Christians.[78] Christ is alluded to, though never actually named. Sometimes he appears as the direct and active agent of the operation: "I adjure you by him who descended into the lower kingdom and who on the third day was raised from the dead."[79] The descent into hell and the resurrection illustrate his triumph over the evil powers of darkness. Sometimes, and this is more characteristic, Christ is brought in only, if one may so describe it, at one remove, as an instrument in the Father's hands. He is thus on the same footing with regard to the almighty divine power as the angels. "I adjure you, malign tumour, by the name of him...who through his Son enlightened Jerusalem with a torch, of him who killed the twelve-headed dragon by the hand of Michael and Gabriel, the holy archangels[80]...by the creator of the holy archangels, Michael, Gabriel, Uriel and Raphael; by the author of the insubstantial powers." The real, effective agent here is the divine name. The powers,[81] Christ, and the angels enter only as intermediaries. "I adjure you, malign tumour, by the truly sovereign name.... Great is the name of God. Come out, and do no more evil."[82]

The idea that Christ is the light of Jerusalem is itself sufficiently unusual to be recognized as sure evidence of a judaizing ideology.[83] And the Christian elements in the text do not succeed in disguising its undoubtedly Jewish inspiration. The Jewish coloring appears both in the mention of angels (and especially in the appearance of some names, such as Uriel, which Christian angelology did not take over) and in the clearly theocentric nature of the formula.[84] And when God the creator is described as, "he who measured the heavens with the span of his hand and the earth with his fingers, who has sustained the universe like an arch," we are again conscious of the fact that the exorcism has derived its text of the Bible by way of the Synagogue liturgy.

In addition to these more extensive documents, there survive also simple formulae of a few words or a few letters, or even of inscribed signs, whose diffusion throughout the length and breadth of the empire attests the extent of Jewish influence. We may be especially sure that the formula εἷς θεός, which is so frequently used by Eastern Christians,[85] and which is a Greek form of the abbreviated Hebrew *Shema*, was credited, in at least some of the spheres in which it was used, with magical potency. We have particularly clear evidence of this in the case of an amulet to which Perdrizet has drawn attention.[86] The amulet bears in exergue a picture of Solomon, with a halo, mounted on horseback and transfixing with his lance a female devil. Beside it is the legend, εἷς θεὸς ὁ νικῶν τὰ κακά. On the reverse side several animals are mentioned that are resistant to the evil eye. The same virtue is ascribed to the *pentalpha*, often called the seal of Solomon, for its picture was supposed to have been engraved on the ring the Lord gave to the royal magician.[87]

Still more interesting is the famous magic square, *sator arepo*, which has been much discussed over a number of years.[88] The hypothesis that it is of Christian origin is based on the fact that the rebus conceals the twice-repeated words, *pater noster*. But this hypothesis has been called in question recently by the discovery of a copy of the formula at Pompeii. Following this new discovery, Jerphanion, who had previously defended the Christian interpretation, demonstrated how many difficulties the theory had to meet, and how hard it is to maintain. His arguments seem to be decisive.[89] He has shown instead that in the present state of our knowledge the hypothesis of a Jewish origin is the most satisfactory.

The credit for being the first to suggest this should go to Cumont.[90] He pointed out that the solution to this little problem of epigraphy seems to lie in the text of Ezekiel. Ezekiel[91] in fact provides two of the essential ingredients of the rebus: the streets, *rotas*,[92] and the *T*, the Hebrew *tav*, sign of salvation, which is repeated four times at the center of each face of the magic square.[93] Perhaps we could go further. Alone of the letters that make up the square, the central *N* figures only once. I am tempted to see in it the initial of the word *nomen*, the Latin equivalent of the Hebrew *shem*, which appears frequently in magical documents. It is the divine name, unique, and hence the symbol, or rather the repository, of all divine power. It is the center and origin of all things. The four *T*'s, arranged in the form of a cross around the *N*, would then indicate the saving power, understood in the vulgar sense as the power that triumphs over demons, radiating and emanating from the ineffable name.[94] In order to explain the *pater noster* included in the rebus, it is not necessary to suppose either that the authors and users of the formula were unaware of it, which seems unlikely, or that it must be ascribed to Christians. The idea and its expression are as much Jewish as Christian.[95] As for the *A* and *O*, which, once the double *pater noster* has been extracted, remain as a kind of twice-repeated leftover, they are bound to remind us of the Apocalypse: "I am the Alpha and the Omega, the beginning and the end."[96] But here again, apart from the reminiscence of the Apocalypse, which is in any case a composite writing, influenced by Jewish thought and especially by Ezekiel, there is nothing specifically Christian. The mystique of the letters puts us again at the heart of Jewish speculation, a speculation that, through the influence of the diaspora, had become common property. *Aleph* and *tav*, the first and last letters of the Hebrew alphabet, are in rabbinic literature symbols of the *Shekhinah*.[97] Even before the publication of the Apocalypse the Jews of the dispersion could have attributed the same significance to the initial and final letters of the Greek alphabet. And in these magical papyri, which so clearly exhibit the marks of Judaism, the series $\alpha \, \varepsilon \, \eta \, \iota \, o \, \upsilon \, \omega$, which could, it may be supposed, be summed up on occasion by referring to the first and last vowels, signifies the universality of the world and of the divinity.[98] It is amongst Jews familiar with both these languages, as well as with Latin, that we most naturally look for the origin of a rebus that can be read in the Greek or Latin manner, from left to right, or equally well from right to left, like Hebrew.

The puzzle seems to me capable of a triple solution. First, there is a literal meaning, which can be grasped at first reading, except for the word *arepo*, whose significance remains obscure. Dornseif and Jerphanion disagree about the meaning of this term. For the former it is a common noun, and for the latter a proper name,[99] but they agree in the interpretation of the rest. "The sower [of fire] takes in his hand the enflamed streets and their work." The reference, according to this interpretation, is to the angel in the Book of Ezekiel who receives the order, "Go to the crossways of the streets, your hands full of burning coals taken from between the cherubim, and scatter them on the city."[100] The words thus take on an eschatological significance. They are an announcement of judgment, of the day of the Lord.[101]

Under the literal meaning there is a hidden meaning, which can be extracted from the magic square by breaking up the order of the letters and regrouping them into *pater noster, A O*. This signifies God the Father and creator. Finally, it is perhaps possible to see in the square, in addition, a kind of figurative schematization of Ezekiel's vision,[102] of the divine chariot with the four wheels that are before the four faces of the four heavenly beings, "all four of them alike, and each as it were a wheel within another wheel." This doubtless means that they were set at right angles to each other. At the center of this device, and represented by its initial letter, is the ineffable name, the source of salvation and power. Whether one accepts this exegesis or not, it seems to me that the Jewish origin of the rebus is beyond dispute.

Magical formulae, papyri, and tablets are all objects of Jewish origin that have passed into common use. It is even more interesting to observe that the early Christians, successors in this respect of the pagans, ascribed magical powers to Jewish religious symbols and to the Jewish religious rites themselves.

The superstitious use of phylacteries is attested by a number of witnesses, particularly in the East. According to St. Jerome, ignorant women in their piety made much use of them. The *mulierculae* of the Palestinian communities made for themselves phylacteries containing pocket gospels, or fragments of the true cross or other relics, thinking they were pleasing to God.[103] St. Jerome connects their use directly with the use of phylacteries by the Pharisees, and in addition he makes it clear that, under Jewish influence, amulets with Hebrew writing on them were used in the same way.[104] The Church authorities were, as we shall see, sometimes affected by this practice.

There is every reason to believe that the candlestick, the emblem of Judaism, which the Jews themselves regarded as a symbol of the planets, was also endowed in popular belief with apotropaic virtue. The significance of the number seven in the realm of magic is well known. In a milieu with such a taste for "signs" as the ancient world, the seven-branched candelabrum was bound to figure prominently in the symbolism of syncretizing cults. Ecclesiastical writers saw it as a symbol of Christ[105] or of the Church.[106] But there is no evidence for the assertion that is sometimes made[107] that for that reason it was taken over into Christian iconography. Its Jewish character was too well-marked for orthodox Christianity to be able to use it.[108] When it appears in the decoration of Christian catacombs, it is correctly attributed to Judaizing influences.[109] The famous lamp from Carthage in which Christ is represented treading the candelabrum under foot[110] may stand not merely for the ideological victory of the true faith over the Jewish error, but for the triumph of the Christian cult over the demoniac, maleficent, and seductive rites of the Synagogue. It is not impossible to see the lamp itself as a talisman intended to exorcise the evil influences of Judaism.[111]

The same superstitious respect is given to the unleavened bread of the Passover, since the preparation and eating of this bread were accompanied by mysterious rites, which included, among other things, a form of prayer in Chaldaean, designed to delude and repel the evil spirits. This was as good as an invitation to interpret both the rites and the food itself in magical terms, and we can understand why they were so concerned not to give any excuse, in the carrying out of the rite, for accusations of magic.[112] In fact, popular Jewish devotion did see the unleavened bread as a precious talisman, and Jews would keep it from one Passover to another, selling it on occasion to credulous gentiles.[113] Oort has shown that the accusation of ritual murder could have originated in a tendentious interpretation of some biblical verses relating to the preparation of the unleavened bread.[114]

The ritual fasts, the dietary laws, and the observance of the Sabbath all possessed a similar magical power in the eyes of the Christian masses.[115] St. John Chrysostom is the most eloquent witness to this superstition, which he combats energetically in his homilies against the Jews. The Judaizing Christians of Antioch resorted to the Jews to obtain healing for their diseases. Some of them practiced incubation in the synagogue at Daphne, which is no better, asserts the preacher, than the temple of Apollo, because both alike are only self-styled sanctuaries that are really the abode of demons.[116] Others, when they wish to take an oath, go to the synagogue to do so, and this forces others Christians to follow their example, because the oaths that are pronounced in the synagogue are the most dreadful of all.[117] The serious nature of oaths taken in synagogues arises no doubt from the use made of Jewish liturgical formulae, and especially of the divine names that played such a large part in exorcisms.

Finally, the very persons of Jews shared in the magical prestige that attached to their religion. They possessed a secure reputation, collectively, as healers. This means not simply as doctors, but also, since at this period the two were often connected, as sorcerers.[118] They had acquired this reputation, not because they passed through any particular initiation into medical skills, but by virtue of their rites and their sacred books. That is to say, simply by virtue of the fact that they were Jews they were treated by pagans and Christians alike as physicians and miracle workers.[119] They did not practice their healing at all by the methods of secular science, but rather by means of incantatory formulae of a ritual kind, i.e., of the very kind we have just briefly examined. The miracle-working type of rabbi is not peculiar to the ghettoes of eastern Europe, mediaeval or modern. He is well represented in the ancient world.[120] To have recourse to the Jews was to recognize tacitly, and perhaps unconsciously, the inherent virtue of their religion. It was, in consequence, to Judaize. When the fathers of the Church condemn such practices, it is not because of anti-Semitism in the sense in which we understand the word. The condemnation is a defensive reflex of a genuinely religious kind, an attempt to forestall the contamination of Christianity by the rival and execrated cult.

IV

Just as the Jewish infection took a variety of forms, so did the Christian defense against it. First of all, there was persuasion. The writings of the fathers abound in warnings intended to put the faithful on their guard against the danger. These warnings are particularly urgent among the scholars of the Eastern Church, and especially those of Syria, where, as we have shown, the Jewish element was strong and the terrain was, in addition, of a kind that was congenial to their influence. Two sources of evidence, among the rest, merit closer examination, viz., Isaac of Antioch and St. John Chrysostom.

From Isaac of Antioch we have a very important sermon on magic.[121] The author begins by asserting that the time is at hand, and that yet, in spite of this, men turn aside from justice and piety and devote themselves to sin, avarice, and luxury. The world, he says, belongs to Christ in name, but in fact it is the devil's. He goes on to analyze the evil that is at the very root of all this: superstition and magic. The Church and the heavenly physician are ignored, and men resort instead to the house of magic. Instead of holy benedictions, they substitute the curses of the sorcerers. Today a man will receive the baptism of the Holy Spirit, tomorrow he will accept the ablutions of demons. When he comes to church he will be accompanied by Satan, who is on his head or around his neck. Even children, who are innocent, are made to carry demons' names on their bodies. That is what they really are, demons, though they are falsely invoked as angels. The Bible gives us the names of two angels only, Gabriel and Michael, but despicable priests make use of the names of demons. Ruphael and Raphuphael, the devil's ministers, appear even in the books of the Church. May they be accursed![122] Priests, turning aside from God and the holy gospel, peddle books of magic. From love of money they prescribe divinatory spells and incantations and impose ablutions and purifications they derive from scripture.

Throughout these accusations it is possible to perceive not only the Judaizing but the syncretizing character of the superstition that is being pilloried. It appears in the use made of books that allow an important place to angelology and are connected with a genuinely Israelite tradition. It appears also in some of the practices the preacher condemns: "Whoever writes a *yodh*" (it is the smallest letter, but the initial consonant of the divine name) "with his own blood puts himself in the place of the notorious magicians Jannes and Mambres."[123] Similarly, the "bonds" that the author several times denounces, and that evil Christians take upon themselves, are, it is impossible to doubt, the bonds of the observance of the Jewish law, the *deuterosis*, against which the *Didascalia* also warns the faithful.[124] For the rest, the Jews are taken to task directly. "He who eats with magicians, let him not eat the body of the Lord. He who drinks with soothsayers, let him not drink the blood of Christ. He who eats with Jews, may he have no part whatever in the world to come. For these three classes of people will be cast into the fire. Whoever has dealings with them shall, like them, have Gehenna for his portion."[125] And these are the source of all the evil that afflicts the Church: "The Jews and the magicians, and Satan their chief."

And the cure? The cure, for Isaac, is a salutary fear of chastisement to come. He describes it in the second part of his sermon with a precision almost worthy of Dante. The end of the world is near, and with it comes judgment, fearsome even to the righteous. Everyone, both the living and the dead, will be summoned before the judge, and, beginning with Adam, will be put to the test. Each will be rewarded according to his deserts. The outcome for magicians and their followers will be dreadful. They will be stripped naked, with no one to hide them. The angels and the righteous will pronounce a curse upon them for having by their execrable deeds corrupted the order of nature. Then a curtain of light will be stretched before the judge, to hide from his view the demons and their terrified followers. Everyone will be obliged to leap over a sea of fire, and this is where the division will take place. The righteous will cross it safely; the wicked, encumbered by the weight of their evil deeds, will be cast down, and will thus go to their eternal abode in fire or filth, in the endless darkness and the unfathomable depth. For comparison, the author describes the joys of heaven. They too will be graduated according to each man's sanctity. May the divine mercy be willing to grant the preacher a very little place, the humblest of all. It will be sufficient for him.

The arguments are tolerably close to those with which Chrysostom opposes the Judaizers of Antioch, though they are developed here at greater length. For many, the appeal of magic was part of the appeal Judaism had for them. It was in their capacity as healers and physicians that the rabbis were consulted. And Chrysostom warns his hearers throughout the eight homilies against the illusory healings that give health to the body by casting the soul into perdition. To visit the synagogue is to frequent an evil place.[126] To appeal to the rabbis is to resort to Christ's executioners.[127] To fast with Jews is to sit at table with demons.[128] To seek from them a cure for physical afflictions is to ask of the devil. One may as well resort to pagan deities, for they too boast of healings, which they bring about by the same means. What folly, to gain a little relief at the cost of falling into eternal fire! Far better to die directly than to be healed at this price. Let the sick, rather than seek an illusory relief, follow the example of Job. In spite of all his miseries, which Chrysostom catalogues in detail, he resorted neither to diviners nor to magicians; neither did he make use of amulets. It was from God alone that he looked for salvation.[129] Lazarus likewise "did not resort to sorcerers; fastened no magical tablets to his body; indulged in no charlatanry and called in no enchanters."[130] He preferred to die rather than to deviate, by however little, from the right way. What forgiveness, therefore, can they expect, who for the slightest fever or most trivial injury rush to the synagogues or call in magicians or charlatans for consultation? Their destruction is assured. It is necessary to prevent them at all costs, to save them, even in spite of themselves. To this public work of salvation Chrysostom invites all believers, for each is responsible for his brother's soul and must, when the day comes, be called to account for it.

Did this eloquent appeal do any good? We do not know, but the insistence with which Chrysostom reverts to the question leads us to doubt it. It is not certain that his arguments, impressive as they are, were enough to put a stop to the evil. However, Christian society did on occasion use more forceful methods. Since threats and persuasion failed to work, they were accompanied by more positive sanctions, carried out either by the "secular arm" or by the Church authorities.

The Christian emperors legislated on a number of occasions against both Judaizers and the exponents of magic. But they do not ever seem to have identified or even connected the two offenses. The Theodosian Code always groups under two quite distinct headings legislation relating to Judaism and measures enacted against magic. This should not surprise us. Magic was in fact thought of by Constantine and his successors as essentially a corruption of paganism. It was forbidden during the period, which covered most of the fourth century,[131] when the official rites of the old religion could still be freely practiced even by the highest dignitaries in the imperial hierarchy. And if the condemnation of magic was in fact the first step in the application of antipagan measures, the emperors who enacted it could nevertheless represent it as being in the higher interests of a religion whose supreme pontiff they still remained. They could thus present themselves as purging that religion of abuses that disfigured it. The prohibition of magic was therefore seen as a reform of paganism rather than an intolerant act, and could be explained more easily by fidelity to Roman traditions and to the religious policy inherited from Augustus than by Christian zeal.[132]

Does this mean that the importance of the Jewish elements in syncretizing practices had escaped the legislator's attention? I think not. It is true that there is no mention of Judaism in the enactments concerned with pagan religion. But we should not expect it. Yet these laws nonetheless affect Jewish magic, to the extent to which it was mixed up with the pagan sort, and in this field there were no clear dividing lines. In addition, Jewish magic fell within the scope of the laws concerned with Jewish missionary activity and with Judaizing movements. There was no need at all to mention it again explicitly among the diverse forms of the νόσος ιουδαϊκός, all of which were punishable.

Furthermore, whether it was a question of magic or of Judaizing practices, the offense was the same either way: it was the offense of *superstitio*. The label eventually came to apply to paganism too, and as *superstitio* it was forbidden and punished.[133] The term begins by designating any religious practice that was regarded as contrary to the norm or that was beyond the bounds of traditional religion.[134] As long as a state of equilibrium was maintained between the two cults by the Christian emperors (albeit a very unstable equilibrium), *superstitio* was the label attached on the pagan side to the aberrant forms of the old religion, and in Christian circles to all the heretical sects and movements, including the Judaizing heresies.[135] Looked at from this angle, Judaism, which was a recognized and legitimate cult when it was practiced by Israel, ought logically only to be called *superstitio* insofar as it attempted to take members from its two rivals, i.e., when it was practiced by non-Jews. In fact, however, the title *judaica superstitio*, which doubtless was originally intended to be offensive, becomes the normal term for designating the Jewish religion, even in contexts in which the Jews are being accorded privileges. From the point of view of the objective legislator, Judaism was a *religio licita*. In the eyes of the Christian emperor, it was a *superstitio*.[136] All the more reason, then, that the same label should be applied to a syncretizing

Judaism with leanings toward magic, and should in this case mark out
such a religion as an offense: for magic was *superstitio* par excellence, in
whatever form it appeared. And it was *superstitio* by whatever subjects
of the empire it was practiced, and whatever might be their religion.

It is to be noted, however, that though the offenses of Judaism and
superstitio were essentially the same, the penalties envisaged for the two
were significantly different. The Judaizer was not punished by death
unless he had had himself circumcised. In all other instances
punishment was much less severe, consisting of confiscation of goods
and deprivation of the right to make a will.[137] It was for the
proselytizing Jew, not for his converts, that the law reserved its full
rigor, a rigor that increased during the course of the fourth century.
This increase was due to the persistence, even the recrudescence of
proselytism. By contrast, as far as magic was concerned the sanctions
were terrible from the start. The crime of divination or magic was
placed in the same category as murder. The guilty were punished by
death, and torture could be applied to the witness in order to make
him talk.[138] When Valentinian I declared his paschal amnesties, the
crime of magic, *maleficiorum scelus*, with several others, was excluded.
The reasons for this were not purely theoretical. We know how
prosecutions for magic increased in number, and how dreadful they
were, under Constantius II, Valentinian, and Valens. Maurice has
drawn attention to the essentially political character of these
prosecutions. The emperors saw in the practice of magic an especially
dangerous method of conspiracy.[139] This "terror of magic" did not,
however, survive the end of paganism. Once the latter was banished
from the empire, magic was classed with it under the heading of
superstitio, a word that henceforth was more broadly defined. Then, by
a process of development the very reverse of that which the anti-
Jewish measures had undergone, the legislation regarding it became
progressively less severe. The death penalty disappeared, and so did
the use of torture. They gave way to milder punishments: deportation,
confiscation, deprivation of the right to make a will.[140]

Magic was still practiced, however, within the very bosom of the
Church. It continued to flourish, supported by people who were
neither pagans nor heretical sectarians, but merely bad Catholic
Christians. Now that it had become a malady internal to the Church,
and a diffused one, affecting for the most part the ostensibly orthodox
masses rather than being characteristic of a determined dissident
party, the civil power ceased to show much interest in it. The job of
suppressing it fell to the authorities of the Church. Although in the
eyes of the imperial legislation Judaizers and magicians had always,
in spite of everything, represented two distinct categories, in the

Church's eyes, by contrast, they were invariably associated, if not altogether confused. The Church, with more perspicacity and energy than the State, denounced and hunted down the Jewish influence, even in its subtlest forms, wherever it showed itself.

On a number of occasions the conciliary canons strike at Judaizers and practitioners of magic simultaneously. In this manner the council of Laodicaea prohibits Judaizing, ἰουδαΐζειν, in general, on pain of anathema, and then goes on to enumerate its various forms. Thus it condemns successively and explicitly the observance of the Sabbath, the invocation of angels, participation in the feasts of Jews or heretics, or the giving of presents to each other on these occasions, and the eating of unleavened bread.[141]

The connection the council makes between Judaism and magic appears especially clearly in the prohibition of phylacteries. "It is forbidden to priests and clerics to use magic, incantations or astrology, or to make the objects which are called phylacteries, and which are shackles for their souls."[142] There is hardly any doubt about the Jewish character of these phylacteries. It is true that, etymologically speaking, the term could designate any kind of amulet or talisman, and there are examples of this in secular usage.[143] But in religious usage, and ever since the famous diatribe Matthew's gospel places in the mouth of Jesus,[144] it refers primarily, if not exclusively, to the *tephillin* of the Pharisees. There is every reason to believe that the council borrowed the term from St. Matthew and that in the gospel and in the canons it refers to the same objects.

Apart from this, the apotropaic character ascribed to the *tephillin* in popular Jewish thinking is well attested. The rabbis were sometimes concerned about this and forbade their followers to pray or sleep with the *tephillin* in their hands, which was tantamount to forbidding their use as amulets.[145] The term *phylacteries* puts the emphasis on what these objects stood for, especially in the minds of the mass of Jews and Judaizers. And when the council, making a play on words, asserts that the phylacteries shackle the soul, we are left in no doubt at all about the precise nature of these amulets, which Jewish ritual prescribes should be attached to the forehead and the arm. The word *bonds*, which is used freely in Christian polemic to designate, metaphorically, all Jewish observances,[146] here takes on its strict meaning.

The anathemas of Laodicaea do not stand alone. The collection of canons attributed to St. Caesarius of Arles, sometimes mistakenly said to be the canons of the fourth council of Carthage, command that those who give themselves up to the use of divination and incantations, and who observe Judaic superstitions.[147] are to be expelled from the assembly of believers. Similarly, the council of

Elvira, particularly explicit on this point, forbids Christians on the one hand to eat with Jews and on the other to have the harvests blessed by them.[148] The former of these errors only involves for the delinquent a provisional excommunication, *ut debeat emendari*. The latter, by contrast, is punished by a comprehensive excommunication. The wording of the prohibition explains the special gravity of the penalty: the Jewish blessing acts against the Christian blessing, and so seriously as to render it inoperative. It is thus capable of destroying the prestige of the Church's rites and discouraging belief in their efficacy. Energetic suppression was therefore called for. This is an especially good example of what Juster calls "a competition over the quality and efficacy of rites."[149]

We touch here on another aspect of Christian defense. Belief in magic was too firmly rooted in ancient opinion for there to be any hope that it could be completely eradicated. Persuasion, threats, and sanctions were often in vain. The very people who condemned them never cast serious doubt on the effectiveness of the practices they condemned. Their estimate of this did not differ from that of the people who indulged in them. At the beginning of the fourth century the State started off by taking a point of view that was religiously neutral. Its condemnation of magic was tempered by utilitarian considerations. As far as magical operations were concerned, it drew distinctions in accordance with their use and their effects. Constantine, in an edict of 319, allows the working of magic when it is inoffensive or useful, as when it is designed to protect the harvest or restore the sick to health. But he forbids the immoral or criminal use of it. *Eorum est scientia punienda et severissimis merito legibus vindicanda, qui magicis adcincti artibus aut contra hominum moliti salutem aut pudicos ad libidinem deflexisse animos detegentur. Nullis vero criminationibus implicanda sunt remedia humanis quaesita corporibus aut in agrestibus locis, ne maturis vendemiis metuerentur imbres aut ruentis grandinis lapidatione quaterentur, innocenter adhibita suffragia, quibus non cujusque salus aut existimatio laederetur, sed quorum proficerent actus, ne divina munera et labores hominum sternerentur.*[150] The distinction is clear. Only back magic is condemned; white magic, on the other hand, is tolerated. The efficacy of both is assumed.

The Church's view of the matter was appreciably different. In its estimation of magical practices it took account not only of their object but of their methods. Sure enough, those which served bad ends were condemned, but the Church also condemned those which were devoted to praiseworthy or indifferent purposes, such as promoting the fertility of fields or the health of men, if they employed processes or formulae of which orthodoxy disapproved. All use of magic was abominable, to the extent that it appealed to evil powers, to demons. This was the case with pagan or with paganizing magic. It was the same with regard to Jewish or Judaizing magic, in all its forms.

Everything, in fact, that had to do with Jewish practices, even the apparently ancient rites of synagogue worship, was to different degrees demon-inspired. St. John Chrysostom reminds those who seek healing at Jewish hands that to do so is folly, criminal folly, for Israel, since her rejection of Christ, μετὰ τὴν θεοκτονίαν,[151] is given up to dealings with demons. To ask help from Jews is to appeal to demons. Now, demons are capable of doing harm, but not of healing. Or at least, if their power sometimes does accomplish healings, it is only because God allows it in order to put the faith of Christians to the test. When all is said and done, it is better to be ill than godless and damned. The cures of demons "are profitable to the body, which in any case is destined shortly to die and to decay, but they do harm to the immortal soul."[152]

But believers are not restricted to the choice between sickness or damnation, between the fires of fever and the fires of hell.[153] The early Church not only recognized that magic actually worked, it opposed unorthodox magic, which it condemned even when its effects were beneficial, with a strictly orthodox ministry of healing. This orthodox therapy was not called magic, but it possessed all the marks of magic, nevertheless.

The early Christians readily interpreted physical ills as manifestations of moral ills, just as the pagans and the Jews did. Sickness was a sign that an evil power, a demon, had taken possession of an individual, both body and soul. Sickness and demon possession were closely associated terms, sometimes treated as synonyms. Jesus healed the sick by expelling their demons. When human remedies were found powerless, it was still possible to resort to the supernatural ones of which the Church was the guardian. Exorcism formulae continue to be used in Catholic rituals. Their medical use has disappeared. Their religious use is restricted to as few cases as possible.[154] In antiquity, by contrast, they enjoyed a singular success. At that time the Church, although it forbade its members to make use of the demons, was quite ready to deliver them from any demons to which they were a prey. It expelled the demons in the name of Christ and of the Trinity.

Socrates tells an instructive story about a Jewish paralytic. The prayers of his fellow Jews had failed to give him any relief, but he was healed by baptism, which doubtless means by the baptismal exorcism.[155] Sin and sickness are here the double manifestation, i.e., spiritual and bodily, of demon possession. The two ills disappear together, with the unclean spirit that is responsible for them, under the influence of a rite that confers at the same time holiness and health. The word *salus* in the ancient world bore both meanings, and the early Christians did not despise the second. It might be conceded, without doing them any injustice, that the health was sometimes of more immediate concern to them than the holiness. The idea of Christ the healer is not peculiar to the gospels. It is to be found everywhere in the Christian tradition.[156] It is illustrated epigraphically by the famous inscription of Timgad, which is an invocation of Christ the physician: *Solus medicus, sanctis et paenitentibus amare, manibus et pedibus Dei.*[157] What is in mind here is, in all likelihood, the medicine of the soul. But on the level of corporeal medicine, too, Christ is the only truly effective physician, contrasted both with popular therapy and with the curative magic of the charlatans, which too often battened on the faithful.[158] Rites were opposed with rites. The most effective and comprehensive way to counteract Judaizing magic was the homœopathic way.

Origen makes a clear distinction between Church exorcism, which goes back in origin to the miracle-working power of Christ, and the very widespread practice of Judaizing magic. *Qui autem aspicit Jesum imperantem daemonibus, sed etiam potestatem dantem discipulis suis super omnia daemonia, et ut infirmitates sanarent, dicet, quonian non est secundum potestatem datam a Salvatore adjurare daemonia: Judaicum est enim. Hoc etsi aliquando a nostris tale aliquid fiat, simile fit ei, quod a Salomone scriptis adjurationibus solent daemones adjurari. Sed ipsi, qui utuntur adjurationibus illis, aliquoties nec idoneis constitutis libris utuntur: quibusdam autem et de Hebraeo acceptis adjurant daemonia.*[159]

This Christian exorcism was able to combat the use of magical incantations. It was not, however, the only means of doing so. To such formulae were added certain equally efficacious ritual gestures, and in particular the sign of the cross.[160] Chrysostom suggests this to the Christians of Antioch as an infallible remedy against the maleficent influence of Judaism.[161] Moreover, Christianity had its phylacteries too, which the Church authorities at different times and places, or in accordance with their differing inclinations, approved or condemned in turn.[162] These talismans, with the image of the cross inscribed upon them, or liturgical formulae, or the names of God, of Christ, or of the saints, enjoyed special popularity. And the Jewish *tephillin* found their exact parallel in the verses of the gospels that were used as amulets.[163]

To these different kinds of amulets we may add the increasingly popular use of relics. I use the word *relics* here in its most general sense, i.e., to refer not merely to the bones of holy persons, but to any objects that, by contact with them, had become impregnated with their miraculous powers. The adoration of the saints runs parallel to the preoccupation with medicine, and not only in the piety of the masses, but throughout the whole Church in this early period. When a saint was invoked, the prayers were directed to him usually in his capacity as miracle worker or healer, rather than as confessor or apostle. In spite of everything, the idea of Christ as physician retained something of an abstract quality. Christ did not come alive as a real and active figure as in the time of the gospels. In fact, first in popular preference as healers were the saints, who were tangible realities, accessible at their tombs or in their ashes. For the theologians it was still Christ who worked through them. An African inscription describes their relics as *membra Christi*.[164] But it is doubtful whether this distinction was clearly appreciated by the Christian populace at large. What we have in this development of the cult of the saints is doubtless a spontaneous manifestation of Christian piety, which in this matter was the heir of pagan devotion. However, we have every reason to believe that, if the Church authorities not only tolerated but encouraged it, this was, among other reasons, because they saw in it a means of combating the popular and dangerous practice of magic, notably of Judaizing magic. A few examples will be sufficient to confirm this.

There are innumerable instances of miraculous healings effected by the intervention of saints, i.e., by contact with their relics. These figure not only in the hagiographical writings but throughout patristic literature.[165] St. Augustine notes no fewer than twenty-five cases whose genuineness can be vouched for, being duly attested in writing.[166] Nearly all of them were brought about in Africa, by the relics of St. Stephen. The identity of the particular saint concerned is not perhaps irrelevant. When we learn from another source that the relics of the same saint had, in Minorca, converted 540 Jews in eight hours,[167] we are tempted to conclude that the first martyr, who was not only the most violently anti-Jewish of all the confessors of the primitive Church but, like his master, the direct victim of the *perfidia judaica*, had specialized after his death in the struggle against Judaism.

This posthumous victory over the Jews of Minorca was not his only revenge.[168] If he could thus, on occasion, convert his executioners, he could also confound them in argument. Our witness is again St. Augustine. He tells the curious story of Petronia.[169] Petronia, who was a noble lady of Carthage, sought healing at Uzalis near Utica from the relics of St. Stephen. But at the same time, in order to increase her chances, she took care to bring with her, on Jewish advice, an amulet. She was effectively healed before the relics of the holy deacon. But already, before she got there, another miracle had taken place. The ring she carried had been on a string, knotted at its ends. Now the ring had become detached, without either string or ring being broken. Augustine sees in this marvel a forewarning and guarantee of the healing, and ascribes it to the saint, although it appeared to be due to the magic power of the Jewish amulet. Petronia kept this amulet carefully until the day when she was healed. It was only afterwards that she threw it away, and that, in all probability, as Harnack observes in his comments on the episode,[170] was because the malady was now loaded on to the object, rather than because she was renouncing her Judaizing errors. The healing was thus, for Stephen and the Christians, only a partial victory.

St. Stephen was not, however, alone in the struggle against Jewish influence. His special field of activity was in the West.[171] In the Eastern world, which was even more exposed to the Jewish infection, the local martyrs played the same part. Particularly active, as I have tried to show, were the seven Maccabaean brothers. Their tomb at Antioch was venerated by the Christians, who had deprived the Jews of it.[172] Like Stephen, though for different reasons, they were well adapted to the part. When they confessed the Jewish faith before pagans, it was Christ whom they confessed in anticipation, since both before and after Christ's coming there can be not martyrs but Christians.

St. Stephen, first martyr of the new covenant, was accompanied in the ranks of the one and indivisible Church triumphant by Eleazar, the teacher and model of the seven brothers, ὁ τῆς παλαιᾶς πρωτόμαρτυς.[173] These Jews, who were Christians before Christ, ought, as the fathers regarded the matter, to be an example to their people. St. Augustine is astonished that Judaism can lay claim to them and dispute possession of them with the Church.[174] It was their special task to incite conversions and to forestall among the faithful the detestable influence of Judaism. Miracles were worked at their tomb. It is, I imagine, of them that St. John Chrysostom is primarily thinking when he lays down the methods by which Jewish superstition and magic were to be counteracted, and calls in aid the concept of Christian therapy.

He does so, it is true, with some hesitation and almost with regret. The ideal, he thinks, is to accept every illness as a trial sent by God, even if it proves fatal. To do this is, like Job and Lazarus, to make certain of salvation, for it is a form of Christian martyrdom.[175] But since all such exalted views, which run counter to the demonological explanation of illness, are in great danger of being lost on ordinary Christians and on Judaizing sinners, Chrysostom moderates his ideas. One is certainly not *entitled* to healing. God, in putting the faithful to the test, does it for their own good. But in any circumstances, to resist the temptation to seek healing at Jewish hands is to increase one's chances of reaching heaven. For the Christian who closes his door against the Jewish magician will be an example to others. If anyone copies him it will redound to his credit. And the saints will be so pleased that they will obtain healing for him from God who has been thus rendered beneficent. For those who regard such intervention of heaven as too uncertain or too slow, there is a sure resort, a positive remedy, of which Chrysostom reminds them: "If God put you to the test, do not go to his enemies the Jews... but to his friends the holy martyrs... who have a great influence with him."[176]

To go to the martyrs meant perhaps to send up prayers to them. It also meant, more specifically, to visit their tombs and to touch their relics. The bones of the saints had in fact a much greater power than the emperor, who could arbitrarily give liberty to his subjects or deprive them of it. For "they overcome and torment the demons, and deliver from their cruel chains those who are bound by them."[177] Thus Chrysostom, since he cannot get rid also of this very popular form of devotion, seeks to put it to good use. Although he seems to countenance it only with a bad grace, it nevertheless appears to him as a lesser evil, since it can be a means of restraining Judaizing practices.

There is hardly any need to emphasize the success of this orthodox therapy, which in saving the body also saved souls. In their attempt to defend themselves against the Jews, the Church authorities un-doubtedly obtained definite results by promoting it. One of the most important of these results was the decline of angelolatry. Lucius, drawing attention to this, rightly attributes it in part to the theological opposition, and partly also to the martyrs, who success-fully competed with the angels. The latter was perhaps the principal cause, but the two reinforced each other.[178] The worship of angels, which was taken over from contemporary Judaism, lent itself readily to heterodox development. This explains why the Church regarded it with a suspicious eye and tried so hard to keep it within limits compatible with orthodoxy.[179]

The council of Laodicaea, as we have seen, forbade the invocation of angels. We need not be surprised at this, especially since the pronouncement itself is made on Phrygian soil. Phrygia was a favorite ground for syncretizing and Judaizing cults. St. Paul had already denounced such errors at Colossae.[180] Although the cult of angels had undergone a somewhat exceptional development in this area, and in some others to the East, manifestly aberrant forms of it were represented throughout the Mediterranean world, as is shown by the magical papyri and incantations. In the Church itself the angels were largely ousted from their role as healers, this being taken over by the martyrs. The latter were endowed with the same virtues, but were closer at hand, more immediately accessible and effective. The only celestial spirits who were given the explicit right to be cited by name in Christian worship were the three archangels, Michael, Gabriel, and Raphael, and of these three only the chief, the illustrious Michael, remained genuinely popular.

But he too was invoked in the early Church chiefly for purposes of healing. Lucius is surprised at this metamorphosis of warrior into healer.[181] But there is nothing surprising in it, if it be remembered how fluid is the distinction between moral and physical evil. Michael, the conqueror of demons, was well equipped to conquer sickness, which was a demonic manifestation. It was again in Phrygia, as far as we can judge, that the Christian cult of Michael originated. At Chaeretopa, between Colossae and Hierapolis, there was a miraculous spring, activated by Michael, which healed all who called upon the three members of the Trinity in the name of the archangel. It is possible, and even likely, that Lucius is right in suggesting[182] that Michael had replaced here some pagan deity of the hot springs. Perhaps it was Apollo himself, who, like Michael, was a *numen* of beneficent light. But the substitution was in all likelihood pre-Christian, and had been engineered by those syncretizing Jews whose influence can be glimpsed through the polemical arguments of the Epistle to the Colossians.

The insertion of the Trinitarian formula in the local ritual is characteristic. Its purpose was to remind the believers using the spring that the archangel was only a servant of God, an agent of the only source of all good, his sovereign will. It was to remind them too that God is one, though in three persons. At the cost of this precaution, Michael's Christianized cult could be practiced by all early Christians, though it did not, however, manage to rival that of the most illustrious martyrs. It was these who appeared as the best and most effective safeguard against the *superstitio judaica*.[183]

Conclusion

I

Having finished this inquiry, I am perhaps entitled to assert that the problem of Jewish-Christian relations in the ancient world is a real one. The two religions did confront each other, in a conflict whose principal aspects I have attempted to delineate. From beginning to end of the period we have been considering, Judaism did not cease to trouble the Church.

The reasons for the attraction Judaism held for Christians are diverse. There was the persistence of proselytism. There was the widespread influence of Jewish ritual, with which, through the agency of the diaspora, the mass of the ancient world's populace was thoroughly familiar. There was also the position of Christianity itself, which made it necessary for the Church, as the new Israel, to establish its rights as against those of the people whom it claimed to dispossess. It had to explain why, in taking over the heritage, it rejected part of it, accepting the name and the book, but refusing to be subjected to the observances that authenticated the name and that the book laid down.

The first of these three causes is the determining factor. For the spread of Jewish practices was a product of the missionary activity, representing, as it were, a halo effect around it. The observance of Jewish ritual by gentiles implies as its precondition an effort on the part of the dispersed Jews to make themselves felt in the gentile world. It is a reflection of that effort and it waxes and wanes in keeping with it. And the doctrine of the new Israel was only a problem to the believers to the extent that Israel after the flesh was there to highlight its weaknesses. It was because the militant and missionary vitality of the Synagogue gradually weakened that the attractive power of Judaism declined.

This movement is already perceptible within the compass of our chosen period. It is necessary to repeat that its progress was neither absolutely regular nor brought to a conclusion within our period. Right up to the end there were counterattacks, principally in the East. As late as A.D. 691 the Trullan Synod reenacted some of the most characteristic prohibitions against Judaizers. It condemned those who eat unleavened bread in the company of Jews, who have too much to do with Jews, who resort to them in sickness, accept their remedies, and who attend Jewish baths to submit to their ritual ablutions.[1] It is like listening to the voices of the fathers and the councils of the fourth century. The symptoms of the "Jewish sickness" had not become less marked during the period since Chrysostom's denunciations. This means, as I emphasized at the beginning, that though the different aspects of the conflict, competition on the one hand and contamination on the other, can be readily distinguished, it is very difficult to pick out clearly marked phases. What is at least manifest is the many-sided and enduring influence of Judaism on early Christianity and the methods the Church used to counteract it.

It is much harder to be precise about the contrary phenomenon, Christianity's influence on Judaism. If one takes the view that Christian evangelism did not make any impression on the monolithic Israel, except to an insignificant extent, and that those among the Jews who were converted to Christ preferred in general to remain Jews even when they became Christians, then one will perhaps be inclined to deny that Christianity had any influence on Judaism at all. But it is a priori unlikely that the influence between the two was exerted in one direction only. Though Christianity does not seem to have possessed any positive attraction for the majority of Jews, it did not remain without effect on the eventual development of their religion.

The question that is posed is thus the whole question of the retrenchment of Judaism. Why was there a withdrawal of Hellenistic Judaism during the first centuries of the Christian era, and parallel with it, though not proceeding at the same rate, a slackening of missionary effort? Are we obliged to explain it, asks Harnack, solely by the national collapse and the consequent "rigidification"? Or did other factors play their part, such as, for example, the increasing competition of Christianity?[2] The illustrious historian does not dare to venture an answer, though he is elsewhere very much inclined to anticipate the rupture between Israel and Greek culture, and consequently to minimize the problem of Jewish-Christian relations, even to the point of denying that it exists. It seems to me that it is now possible for an answer to be given.

The explanation that it was all due to the Palestinian disaster is inadequate. Its shortcomings are illustrated by the survival, not only afer A.D. 70 but even after 135, of a Hellenistic Judaism that was very open and very receptive. They are demonstrated especially by the conflict between Church and Synagogue itself, whose reality Harnack disputes. Such a conflict is inconceivable once the final retrenchment of the Synagogue had taken place.

Neither the destruction of the first temple, nor the exile, nor foreign domination, nor the profanation of the Holy Land and sanctuary by the gentiles, had either prevented the universalistic idea from springing up or impeded its development. Why then should it have been otherwise with the crisis of A.D. 70? Only a small section of the Jews, those of Palestine, were at all closely affected by it. It only appears to us to have been decisive for the history of Judaism and to have been so much more serious than the previous catastrophes in the light of Jewish withdrawal, and because it is the last of the series of disasters, and its visible results, the destruction of the temple and of the Jewish state, have continued in being up to our own day. The Jews of the period were unable to judge the event as we do, for they looked back on their people's past and refused, such was their confidence in the future, to believe the disaster irremediable.

If, against all probability, the events of A.D. 70 had, nevertheless, brought retrenchment in their wake, they must have done so with brutal suddenness, in the bitter feeling and disarray of the moment. Now, careful study reveals the retrenchment to have been, on the contrary, slow and gradual. Only a few years after the catastrophe the Sibylline Oracles proclaim a message that doubtless represents the culmination of the universalistic movement in Judaism. If such a message could be expressed in the aftermath of the disaster, how much more readily could it have been expressed later, when the disarray had been overcome and the bitterness softened? And if in fact it was not repeated with the same clarity in the years that followed, and if the echoes it aroused became ever weaker until they died away altogether, the principal cause must be sought elsewhere than in the disaster. It is not conceivable that the catastrophe should at first have stimulated the missionary movement and then, some time later, have extinguished it. Only one explanation is possible, the one that Harnack perceives but does not stop to consider. The deciding factor in Judaism's gradual development toward total retrenchment was Christian competition.

This truth would doubtless be generally recognized if if were not for the fact that the crisis of A.D. 70 coincided with the beginning of Christian preaching. This simultaneity, and the optical illusion to which it has given rise, explains how it is that the results have been attributed to one of these events for which the other is primarily responsible.

II

At the time when the Christian threat appeared, Judaism had a number of possible lines of development open to it. These possibilities became ever fewer as the success of the rival cult increased. Judaism was obliged to make a choice among the different ways before it. It was forced to renounce the course that Christianity was following with a success it could not emulate, and to adhere to the one that the Church, for its part, avoided and condemned. This is the explanation of the rapid disappearance of Hellenistic Judaism and the triumph of Talmudic rabbinism.

In the first century Hellenistic Judaism was at the peak of its strength. Having behind it a rich and already ancient tradition, it went on to find, in the person of Philo, its most noteworthy representative. The adaptability of its allegorical exegesis enabled it to put forward for the benefit of gentiles who rejected the thoroughgoing Jewish observance a less onerous practical rule, and a more liberal interpretation of scripture for those who disliked the literal one. It was not taken aback by the national catastrophes. It was able to give a hopeful explanation for the destruction of the temple and the end of the sacrificial cult, an explanation worthy of a spiritual religion. We have seen how this view is still very much alive in the Sibylline Oracles, the Fourth Book of Maccabees, the apologetic writings of the pseudo-Clementine literature, and the Synagogue liturgy from the Apostolic Constitutions. But, however well armed Hellenistic Judaism may have been against these events, it found itself weaponless before the Christians, as its Palestinian counterpart did not.

For Christian theology took precisely the same stand as Hellenistic Judaism. It took as its point of departure the same premises from which Hellenistic Judaism began. It borrowed the same methods and made use of the same concepts. But handled by Christian thinkers, the methods became even more fruitful and the concepts still more rich. The Alexandrian Jews used allegory to make the oddities of the law acceptable: Christianity used it to throw the oddities overboard. To Philo's lifeless hypostases it opposed the incarnate Logos, who possessed a human personality and an earthly life. It identified, in a way that had never occurred to Jewish thinkers, Wisdom and the Messiah. On this battlefield the struggle clearly could not last very long.

The newborn Christianity quickly robbed Hellenistic Judaism of its pagan following and doubtless rapidly absorbed it. The stream of Alexandrian Jewish literature dries up at about the end of the second century. The latest examples of this literature, which I have listed above, have been preserved for us by the Church, having been taken up into the Christian heritage. The Church saw the possibilities in them, not the Synagogue.

It is customary to mention, in connection with this subject, the changing fortunes within Judaism of the Septuagint, and of the figure of Wisdom. The Alexandrian Jews commemorated the anniversary of the translation of the Septuagint with a joyful festival.[3] For the Talmudic rabbis it was a day of mourning and cursing, like the day when the golden calf was made.[4] Wisdom, which was regarded as a divine hypostasis by Hellenistic Judaism, is identified in the Talmud, as it is in the work of Ben Sira, with the Torah, but "so pale of face and so indistinct in outline that it can no longer be called a hypostasis."[5] This was a twofold reaction against Christianity, which monopolized the Septuagint and worshiped Jesus as Wisdom incarnate. More generally, from this point onwards the Synagogue repudiated allegory since its adversary had used it and abused it against it. It likewise repudiated hypostatic speculation, because Christianity enthroned such speculation at the center of its doctrinal system. It strengthened the regard for legal observance because the Church scoffed at it.

The insertion of the Synagogue liturgy into book seven of the Apostolic Constitutions gives the illusion that the entire community that used it (and it was doubtless a community consisting partly of proselytes) passed over into Christianity. The Christianizing alterations to the text, clumsy as they are, tell us something of the mechanics of this conversion. The type of theological thought familiar to these people led them straight toward Christianity. It is significant that Alexandria, the classic stronghold of Hellenistic Judaism, took a rather modest part in the polemizing, and, as far as we can judge from the places of origin of the documents, was not much concerned in the history of Jewish-Christian relations in general. There is nothing comparable at Alexandria to the great waves of Judaizing activity to which Antioch and its Syrian hinterland were subjected, and against which Chrysostom and Aphraates were obliged to take action, Christianity does not seem to have had to fight long on this battlefield. It was, on the contrary, assured of victory.

As Hellenistic Judaism was collapsing, resistance to Christianity seems to have been taking shape on other lines. I am speaking now of the Jewish-pagan front to which I drew attention earlier. We can see this being worked out, on the common basis of the idea of tradition, with at least tacit approval from the imperial authorities, from the end of the second century. The initiative came from paganism. The idea appears already in Celsus, and Numenius, Porphyry, and Iamblicus bear even clearer witness to it. Eastern Semitic circles, especially the Syrian variety, constituted a connecting link between pagans and Jews.

We do not know what kind of welcome the Jews gave to the advances made to them. Usually, one would suspect, it was not a very warm one. Even the liberal and enlightened Jews must have been aware of the dangers inherent in such an alliance. Some common ground doubtless existed; the monotheistic tendencies of pagan philosophy, the continuance of Alexandrian Jewish speculation, and a common respect for tradition, for example. But to have met the pagans halfway would have been at fatal cost to Judaism. As things turned out, the Jewish-pagan rapprochement never acquired any substance, any more than did the regrouping of pagan forces around Julian's solar theology. And those Jews who were able to fall in with the venture, such survivors of Hellenistic Judaism as had not yet been captured by the Church, managed to do no more, in the event, than to swell the ranks of the syncretizing sects, where all that was characteristic about their Judaism was irrevocably diluted.

If Israel was not to be absorbed either by Christianity or by syncretism, she had only one remedy, the law. Already, in the course of the preceding centuries, the law had been the safeguard of Judaism's spiritual autonomy. The only new thing was that it now appeared as the only means of salvation. What Judaism had previously had recourse to spontaneously now became for her an ineluctable necessity. The rabbinic writ ran ever wider; from Palestine, where it began, its authority, enshrined in the Mishnah, spread throughout the Jewish world, the Mediterranean West as well as the Babylonian East.

Why, asked Harnack, was it the law that Judaism seized on to keep it firm against the Church's onslaught? It was by a sure instinct of self-preservation. It was the law that bore the brunt of the Christian attack. By proclaiming and demonstrating that the law was defunct, the Christians expected to prevent Judaism's survival. To destroy the one was to bring down the other. The solidarity between Israel and the law was thus reinforced. In order to safeguard its own existence, to protect its members from the infection that had begun in its own ranks, Judaism could not do other than cling to the very thing that was at issue, to strengthen the meshes of its protecting barrier. Christianity was soon to be defined as the assertion of faith in the divine Christ and as adherence to the Church's creed. The criterion of Judaism would be the scrupulous practice of the law. Judaism was essentially an orthopraxy. The opposition between the two religions was focused principally on two issues: Christology (the other God of which the rabbis spoke) and the law. For the fathers as well as for the Talmud these are at the center of the controversy.

III

Cemented in such a way, Israel's internal cohesion was proof against everything. But though her survival was thus assured for centuries ahead, it was at the price of her expansion.

It was not that she renounced missionary activity. Legalism pushed to its limits is not, in principle, incompatible with proselytism. As we have seen, there is much evidence that proselytism did in fact continue. But legalism does make proselytism extremely difficult. It compromises its effectiveness in advance.

Judaism was most successful, according to the description given in Juvenal, within the setting of the family. It was there, in fact, that the climate most favorable to conversion was created. The process worked, if I may so put it, by acquired impetus, the son being happy to go a little further along the track marked out by his father. On the other hand, it is almost certain that the number of individuals entering Judaism directly, i.e., without any previous acquaintance with it within the family, continued to diminish as the pressure of persecution increased.

If they were to pursue their missionary work in the face of Christianity, the Jews had two equally dangerous courses open to them. They could continue to admit semiproselytes, as certain rabbis did. This was to open the door to religious eclecticism and in particular to Christian contamination. The risk here was of producing a Judaism robbed of all that should be characteristic of it. Alternatively, they could admit only total converts. This in fact tended to become the rule. Such converts would then be on an absolutely equal footing with true Israelites. To take this course meant the progressive reduction of recruitment from outside, in spite of the fact that this was not the intention. In this dilemma proselytism eventually came to an end, and at the root of the dilemma was Christian competition.

No mistake should be made, however, about the extent of the revulsion against legal observance. It was not rejected in principle, but only in its tyrannical and extremist forms. The attractions of the Jewish rites had always been a useful tool in the service of the missionary effort. We have several times had occasion to assert that it was through its rites that Judaism managed to prolong its influence far beyond the confines of our period. The Judaizers were not usually people whose doctrinal scruples led them to reject the Trinity: they were not Unitarians before their time. They were those who succumbed to the fascination of the Synagogue liturgy, the cycle of the solemn festivals, the call of the shofar, the mysterious power ascribed to the unleavened bread, and the majesty of the Name. But to appreciate the sources of this attraction is to be aware also of its limits.

To the intellectual aspirations of the religiously inclined in the ancient world Judaism no longer had very much to offer. Its religious thinking, refusing from now on to draw anything from the springs of Greco-Oriental wisdom, simply hardened. After the intervention of Christianity, and as a direct result of that intervention, anyone who departed from the strictest monotheism was very quickly charged with *minuth*. Judaism became nothing more than a set of practices that were not counterbalanced as previously by an open-minded liberalism of doctrine. When strict observance had been accompanied by liberal thinking, its dangers had been neutralized. This impoverishment turned the ancient world's intelligentsia away from Judaism. The intelligentsia was to be found henceforth among the Christians, orthodox or dissident, or among the gnostic groups that abounded and of whose teachings Judaism provided no more than a single component. In these they found what the dry old biblical credo could not give them.

From now on, though Jewish influence continued to make itself felt, it was at a much humbler level, and by degraded means. The attraction it exercised was of a somewhat equivocal kind. According to fourth-century Christian authors, the circles it appealed to were the masses of the populace. Their testimony may be confidently accepted, for this is exactly what we should expect. Isolated from the religious tradition of which they formed a proper part and from which all their meaning was derived, Jewish rites became charged with a murky potency. They degenerated almost inevitably into an instrument of superstition.

The charm they thus acquired was no more than moderately effective, if its practical results are considered. However strongly people came under the spell of Judaizing, they did no more than dabble in it. From the doubtless large numbers of Judaizers few thoroughgoing converts seem to have emerged. Those who took the decisive step, who, for example, went to the trouble of having themselves circumcised, were quite rare. The limitation, under the Christian empire, of the privileges of the Jews and the restrictions imposed at that time on Jewish missionary activity certainly encouraged this falling off. But the conditions the Jews themselves laid on gentile seekers after truth were doubtless still more effective.

Hellenistic Judaism, in its missionary endeavors, went out to meet the pagans. Conversions were the result of a mutual effort of adaptation. But from now on Israel was to demand of its recruits total commitment, and expected from them an effort it made no move to reciprocate. The result, by an apparent paradox, was that semi-proselytes multiplied at the very time when the Synagogue was accepting none but thoroughgoing conversions.

The appeal of Jewish observance nevertheless did produce one positive result, such as it was. It helped to crystallize the ritual institutions of Christianity and the observances of the Church. Their development doubtless represents a natural phenomenon in the growth of religion. The Church, in order to stay alive and make progress, was bound to give its faith not only a doctrinal content but material support. The crystallization of Christian observances is not explained merely by the need to offer the Judaizers an equivalent to or substitute for what they derived from the Synagogue. It is nevertheless not possible to understand it, to my mind, if the Jewish factor is altogether disregarded. It was to be expected that Christianity, being itself derived from Judaism, should seek there its inspiration and the models for its activities. But this spontaneous development was accompanied by a systematic dissimulation, the mechanics of which are illustrated by the practices of the Eastern churches, which we studied earlier.

Jewish contamination obliged Christianity to align its position with that of the Synagogue. The initial anti-legalism and the charismatic Christianity of the first pagan-Christian communities was succeeded by a moralism and a neoritualism very close in spirit, and sometimes in manifestation, to the Synagogue's. In order to put a stop to the Jewish "sickness," the Church itself was forced to become a Judaizer in its own fashion. This could be seen, from some points of view, as Judaism's revenge. But it was also, and more important, one of the reasons for its final disappearance.

Ritual observance, then, was reinstituted in the Church and widened in its scope, though without ever taking on the tyrannical proportions the rabbis allowed it. And to the extent that this took place, the temptation to drift to the Synagogue was lessened; for why seek elsewhere what one can find at home? To the cycle of liturgical festivals and the corpus of Church practices were added the humbler manifestations of popular devotion. They certainly did not always conform to the ideal of a worship "in spirit and in truth." The Church, however, left them alone, for it saw in the talismans and amulets with which popular credulity surrounded itself a sure antidote, once it has put its own mark upon them, against the pagan virus and the Jewish infection alike.

IV

We here reach the deepest causes of the Jewish defeat. Judaism had in the beginning accepted the struggle. It faced the attack, at the outset, with a good deal in its favor. Faced with a rival whose activities were illegal, it possessed the valuable asset of a legally defined and advantageous status. Once the political crises were over, the imperial goodwill, appreciating the threat of Christianity, quickly came to interpret Judaism's legal status in the most favorable light possible. Pagan opinion, for its part, was amenable. And meanwhile, in spite of the vitality it possessed and in spite of these external advantages, Judaism was ultimately vanquished. Why?

A national religion, says Harnack,[6] can turn itself into a universalistic one in two ways: it can either reduce itself to its basic elements, acceptable to everyone, or it can assimilate a host of new elements, borrowed from the people it wishes to win over. For Judaism, the former of these methods entailed cutting observances to the minimum and preaching to the gentiles the doctrine of divine unity and the moral law. The second involved padding out the poverty of its own sources of teaching by borrowing from pagan mythologies and theologies.

Leaving aside the Palestinian Pharisees, whose teaching was amplified by means of imported elements, Judaism in the diaspora employed both methods concurrently. But the opportunities this afforded it vanished when Christianity appeared on the scene. Christianity in fact provided the most outstanding example of a universalistic religion of the second type. Although it kept itself aloof from syncretism, just as Judaism did, it nevertheless enriched its theology and its ritual practice with contributions brought in from the entire ancient world. In this sphere Judaism could not rival it. It was unable, in particular, to meet the demands of the salvation mystique that was a characteristic feature of the age. This mystique was catered to by the mystery religions, but interest in it was by no means limited to the coteries in which these religions were practiced. Christianity, by contrast, with its incarnate savior who died and was raised to life again, was the very model of such a religion of salvation. There was, as it were, a preestablished harmony between it and the religious thinking of the ancient world. The drama of Calvary provided a historical anchorage point for all the diffuse aspirations of the pagan spirit.

Having rejected the subtleties and vagaries of Alexandria, the only course left for Judaism was to revert to the traditional positions of biblical monotheism. It did not, however, on that account find the other road to universalism. For the doctrine of monotheism was handicapped by the rigorous interpretation that had already been put upon it, and it still suffered from this handicap even when God was preached as the creator of the world rather than as the Lord of Israel. It did not answer to the gentiles' major aspirations, as the success of Christology and Christolatry had revealed them, and as that of the cult of saints was soon to do. The situation was made worse for Judaism in that as theological speculation declined, ritual observance increased out of all proportion. This meant that most emphasis was laid on that very element in Israel's religion which most clearly expressed a rigorous particularism. For the ritual code was meant above all, as far as its main intentions were concerned, to convey in concrete form the privileged nature of the chosen people, and to isolate the holy flock from the impure *goyim*. It is ironical that this contraction took place at the very time when the end of the sacrificial cult and of the Jewish state could have created a climate most favorable to universalism, by raising Judaism above the contingencies of things Palestinian.

This, probably, is the crux of the matter. The poverty of its doctrine, the absence of the mystical element, the burden of ritual observances, all these go a long way to explain why Judaism was not long able to sustain its appeal to the gentiles in competition with the Christians. It suffered from the further disadvantage, perhaps the most important one, that its character was inherently that of a national religion, and that it never entirely succeeded in divesting itself of this.

On the contrary, this national character was accentuated in the struggle. In order to reply to the Church's assertions that she was defunct, and to cope with the disarray that followed the Palestinian disasters, Israel emphasized with increasing force the enduring and renewed benefits that she received in her capacity as the chosen people. The effects of Christian competition and of the national catastrophes here reinforced each other. The legalistic ossification of Judaism was bound up with these attitudes, since the Torah, which God had originally offered to all the peoples of the earth, and which none had wanted except Israel,[7] had become the national charter of the Jews. The more intensely she concentrated on the practice of the law, the more acute became her conviction of divine favor. Gathered together round the Torah, united in ritual observance, the scattered people remained a nation, even when it had lost its political and territorial independence. In gentile eyes Judaism was no longer a universalistic monotheism, even when it invited them to enter into the covenant. It had tended to become this in Alexandrian circles, but now it was first and foremost the religion of Israel.

Nation and religion were a single thing. In the biblical past the great inspired men were the same as the national heroes. As preached by the rabbis, "Palestinian universalism was really no more than an expression of particularism, of the chosen people's desire to absorb the world of the *goyim*."[8] Ought concessions to be made to converts? That would be to establish a hierarchy among the children of truth, to create first- and second-class Jews. Categories did exist among the Christians also; laity was contrasted with clergy. But the Christian priesthood was not a caste. No one was born a priest. But Israel after the flesh, the upholders of wholehearted adherence to the law, represented a spiritual aristocracy that could be entered only by birth. If, however, the proselyte should take on himself all the practices the children of Israel observed, he would then become their equal. He might aspire to the rabbinate, lay claim to priesthood. A small shade of distinction nevertheless remained: when in the liturgy the God of the patriarchs was invoked, only Jews by birth said "*our* fathers." The proselytes said "*your* fathers."[9]

After some generations doubtless the distinction faded and disappeared. But a proselyte purchased his equality at a high price. He must accept the whole Torah, and all the prescriptions of rabbinic law. He must make himself, in addition, a spiritual expatriate, *exuere patriam*, as Tacitus forcefully puts it.[10] Conversion was also a naturalization. Before the intervention of Christianity, those whose religious needs drove them in this direction were resigned to the price they must pay. But after that, there was more hesitation, and more frequent refusals.

Judaism struggled toward universalism. Christianity attained it without effort. Christianity was free from the beginning of any ethnic ties. It was rejected by Israel. It could thus proclaim that now there was neither Jew nor Greek. And soon came to identify itself with the gentile world; and indeed more and more it genuinely was so identified, both in its membership, in the substance of its doctrine, and in its spirit.

True, it began by breaking with the Greco-Roman tradition. It drew its devotees, at least as long as it was a minority, out of pagan society. But it did this only to integrate them into a group that was self-constituted, or that had its origins in that same society, not into an already existing foreign people.

De vestris sumus, asserts Tertullian. And though he goes on to add, *Fiunt, non nascuntur Christiani*,[11] it is only in order to emphasize more strongly that Christianity is not, like Judaism (which he identifies for the purposes of his argument with the people of Israel) an already existent fact but something in the process of formation, within the womb of the gentile peoples. The reasoning is not unobjectionable. For Judaism too, even though the main part of its membership was there by the accident of birth, did make up its numbers by conversion. Besides, and in spite of Tertullian's efforts, his pagan contemporaries had always had the feeling that Christianity was something foreign. Whatever they did, the Christians remained the *tertium genus*. But what was true in the second and third centuries was no longer true in the fourth.

As Christianity extended its conquests, until the emperor himself was officially Christian and there developed a Christian culture, built upon the classical culture, the old break between Christianity and the rest of the world disappeared. A man could become, or, as often happened now, be born a Christian, without ceasing to be a "Hellene." Alexandrian Judaism, in order to demonstrate its deep affinities with the gentiles, had to resort to a fiction. Plato, it was said, was a disciple of Moses. Christianity repeated the same fiction, but the demonstration was for the Church a less strained one because it had learned from Plato more effectively and wholeheartedly than the Synagogue ever did. It did this quite spontaneously. Its theologians, reared in paganism, or at least educated in Greek ways of thought, worked these into their teaching.

Faced with the barbarians, the fathers of the fourth century took pride in their Greek culture and their Roman citizenship.[12] *Nos qui non populus Dei retro*, says Tertullian, speaking for Jewish ears, *facti sumus populus ejus*.[13] And St. John Chrysostom tells us that "they who were the sons called for adoption have become like dogs; and we, the dogs, are raised to the dignity of sons."[14] "We," as opposed to Israel, means the pagans of yesterday, the redeemed gentile world.

The traditional division of humanity into three parts, "Greeks," Jews and Christians, disappeared after the triumph of the Church, and with it disappeared the idea of the *tertium genus*. There remained only two groups, Jews and "Greeks." The Greeks were hitherto idolators, now Christians. The idea that they were a new people continued, but with a difference. When Christians described themselves in this way, it was no longer in order to dissociate themselves from the Greco-Roman tradition, but solely to contrast themselves with the old Palestinian nation, who were still attached to error and were now repudiated. Their rival remained now as a broken reminder of those national attachments that had had a certain usefulness at the beginning of the Christian expansion, a usefulness they had now outlived.

V

The frescoes of the Dura synagogue have been analyzed suggestively by Grabar, who has compared them with those of a Christian baptistery of about the same period. Both sets of frescoes work out a kind of catechism in pictures. They set out the essential characteristics, respectively, of Judaism and of the Christian hope.

The central idea that inspires the synagogue decoration is the sovereignty of the Lord, the fundamental dogma of Judaism. But there is to be found here no trace at all of the cycle of creation stories, and no reference to original sin or the flood,[15] no cosmogony. This divine sovereignty is not something that God exercises over the world and humanity. It "shows itself within a national framework, and is expressed in the Lord's acts of sovereign government over His people."[16] What is portrayed is not by any means "the history of divine activity," but the history of Israel, and shining through it the Lord's solicitude for the Jews. The episodes from the biblical past that illustrate this guarantee its continuance into the future.

It is true that a way of thinking that is at once more universalistic and more individualistic appears here and there in this collection. In particular, the idea of the salvation of the righteous and the condemnation of the wicked is everywhere present. But who are the just, if not the Jews who are faithful to the law, or the converts who have made themselves members of Israel? Israel stands at the center of the demonstration, certain of its glorious restoration, which will manifest the invincible power of the Lord. Theology here takes on the form of a national epic.

We ought not, doubtless, to judge too hastily by one example. Hellenistic Jewish literature provides us with others that allow us to modify the picture that emerges from Dura. But this evidence is all of it earlier than the Dura frescoes. The idea of the call of the chosen people is never completely absent, even in the most enlightened Jewish circles. The transformation it undergoes during this period reestablishes it in its primary position. The Dura example is all the more revealing in that it comes from the very middle of this development and that it emanates from a Judaism that was liberal enough to have acquired a religious art and yet at the same time conformed strictly to rabbinic orthodoxy. There is a striking contrast between the frankness and boldness of the imagery and its doctrinal content.

A comparison with the frescoes of the baptistery throws this even more into relief. These frescoes, the product of modest resources, and the expression of a still unsophisticated way of thinking, "represent, nevertheless, an essay in theology, and are well able, in their own fashion, to convey transcendent truths." Just like those of the catacombs, "they give an important place to the pattern of saving events in the past, for these are the prefigurations and guarantees of the ultimate salvation of those who believe in Christ."[17] On the one hand, then, we have Israelite Messianism, on the other, universalistic and individualistic soteriology. This example shows up the flagrant imbalance of forces between the two cults, both of which doubtless put religious art at the service of their apologetic. It was not an equal struggle.

This, it seems, was the situation that finally led Judaism to renounce its attempts at conquest, at least in the Greco-Roman world. It did not do so gladly. Some liberal Jews of our own day see Christianity as the advance guard of monotheism, with the task of preaching the true faith in a form acceptable to the world, while to Israel is apportioned the static work of conserving in its original purity the sacred deposit of the revelation. This is a view completely foreign to the rabbis of our period. Christianity for them was the enemy, with whom the ground had to be disputed foot by foot. Even the triumph of the Church seems to have sparked off at first a final burst of Jewish missionary activity. But for the future such activity was to be exercised outside the borders of the civilized world, close to the barbarian regions, principally Semitic ones.

In the Mediterranean diaspora there was lively missionary activity as long as Hellenistic Judaism lasted. It even seems to have survived the disappearance of Hellenistic Judaism to a large extent. It was a feature of the situation in Palestine too. But in both spheres of operation it soon came to experience little but setbacks, or no better than partial successes, and in the long run there was only discouragement in store for it. Without ever actually abandoning the missionary principle, the Jews progressively cloistered themselves in a more passive and occasionally suspicious attitude, to which they had always been prone. The Jews became used to thinking that it was up to the gentiles to come and be gathered in, without there being any need on Israel's part to go and seek them. Israel would then receive them willingly, if not enthusiastically, provided that their vocation was authenticated by a readiness to observe the whole law.

It is important to get the order of events clear. It was because, in the face of Christian preaching, successes became rare that the intensity of missionary activity fell off. It was not because such activity had already been reduced that successes diminished in number. It could be said that the national catastrophes, by helping to intensify interest in observances, created the conditions for withdrawal and determined the direction that withdrawal would take. They were not its direct or primary cause. The restriction of Jewish missionary effort proceeded not so much from the gentiles' indifference to it or their active hatred. The gentiles were not, in this way, responsible for the Jews' troubles. Judaism's withdrawal stemmed from the acknowledgment of its own powerlessness. But the structure of Christianity, which was progressively taking shape, would doubtless have been different if there had been no struggle. By defending itself so fiercely, Judaism had helped to make her rival, in Justin Martyr's phrase, into "another Israel."[18]

Postscript

Fifteen years have passed since the first edition of this book was published. A second edition, entirely reset, would have needed time on my part that is not yet at my disposal. It would also have entailed costs that were out of the question. But in any case, the problems dealt with have not been, up to now, so completely reshaped that I feel obliged to take up the matter again from the beginning. I have therefore opted for a system of additional notes, or, to use the terminology of one of my predecessors in the business, a *retractatio*. The following pages take account of particular remarks or criticisms that my book has called forth on the part of reviewers. They attempt, furthermore, to make use of material that has appeared on the subject, or on connected subjects, during the interval, to the extent to which it has come to my notice. Heavy administrative work has long delayed this task. It is far from being complete. But I cannot delay it any longer. It was necessary at this point to accomplish it quickly, in order that a work whose stocks had been exhausted so short a time after publication should be put back into print.

I

The welcome given to *Verus Israel* by scholarly critics has been, on the whole, favorable and kindly. In particular, almost no one, as far as I know, has contested the validity of my central thesis, that Judaism, very far as yet from having completed its withdrawal, was throughout the period I have dealt with a real, active, and often successful competitor with Christianity. Some have expressed regret that I did not include within my terms of reference the period of Christian origins. But those who have made this complaint have usually conceded that if the inquiry had been thus enlarged its results could not have been encompassed within a single volume. L. Goppelt's recent work, *Christentum und Judentum im ersten und zweiten Jahrhundert* (1954), encroaches on the beginnings of my period in his Part Four, which deals with Marcion, Valentinus, and Justin Martyr. But Goppelt is mainly concerned with the preceding period and could perhaps be said in most respects to meet the requirements I laid down in my critique. Those who are interested in my own views on relations between Judaism and the Church in the apostolic period may be referred to the brief sketch I devoted to the subject in *Les Premiers Chrétiens* (Paris, 1952; 2nd ed., 1960), and to the analysis I attempted in *Saint Stephen and the Hellenists in the Primitive Church* (London, 1958) of one particular aspect of these relations.

On the same theme, surprise has sometimes been expressed that I chose as my point of departure the date A.D. 135 rather than A.D. 70. S. G. F. Brandon, in *The Fall of Jerusalem and the Christian Church* (London, 1951, 2nd ed., 1957) shows forcefully how considerable were the repercussions on the Church of the A.D. 70 catastrophe, and he has taken me gently to task in his introduction. The objection was foreseen. I thought I had replied to it in advance (see pp. xiv ff.) when I explained my reasons for the choice of 135. I do not in the least underestimate the importance of the destruction of the temple for Judaism and Christianity, or, in consequence, for the relations between the two. I have already stated how it appears to me. But the period between the two wars in Judaea was a very complex one, and it raises problems I could not broach without expanding my work inordinately. These problems are the ones Brandon applies himself to in the last chapter of his book, and the most outstanding of them are those concerning the elaboration of the various gospels and their *Sitz im Leben*. And after all, as Maurice Goguel recognizes (*Revue d'Histoire et de Philosophie Religieuses*, 1949, p. 239), if one is trying to shed light on the origins of the rivalry between the two religions, "A.D. 70 is no more valid a starting point than A.D. 135, since the attitudes of Hellenic Christianity towards Judaism (Hellenic Christianity being the only sort of Christianity which mattered from henceforth) were fixed before that date, as were the attitudes of Judaism towards Hellenic Christianity." It seems to me as it does to Goguel (for Goguel in the last analysis proves me right) that relations between Jews and Christians have been fully dealt with by those who have written on Christian origins, "although beyond this point infinitely less has been done and it is an important and interesting task to attempt to do it." As far as Jewish-Christian relations are concerned, the gnostic crisis was at least an important as the disaster of A.D. 70. It occurred almost contemporaneously with Hadrian's war, and apart from anything else, it marks the end of an epoch in Jewish literature and religion, the epoch of violent Messianism. It seems to me that we have here both numerous and varied reasons for selecting the starting point I did.

If I were rewriting my book now, I should modify or even rework at certain points the picture of Judaism I presented. In this connection

the discovery of the Dead Sea Scrolls has been of prime importance. The possible influence on primitive Christianity of the
group from which the scrolls emanated—a body that all the evidence
suggests should be identified with the Essenes—has been much
discussed, at first with some violence, and latterly with more restraint.
The fact that there was some Essene influence on the primitive
Church is hardly disputed any longer. The differences of opinion
concern its extent and seriousness. I am happy to do no more than
refer to the vast literature on the subject. The Qumran texts have been
translated by A. Dupont-Sommer, *Les Ecrits esséniens decouverts près de la
Mer Morte*, (Paris, 1959) (English translation, *The Essene Writings from
Qumran*, trans G. Vermes, Blackwell, Oxford, 1961). This work, which
is a veritable Qumran compendium, crowns a whole series of earlier
investigations and publications by the author. It explores the various
questions these documents raise and suggests a solution. The final
chapter, "Essénisme et Christianisme," is especially noteworthy.
There is a succinct bibliography, which can be filled out (for works
prior to 1957) from the exhaustive one collected by Burchard,
Bibliographie zu den Handschriften vom Toten Meer (Berlin, 1957). I have
given a review of the problems raised, in connection with both
Judaism and Christianity, in my little volume, *Les Sectes juives au temps
de Jésus* (Paris, 1960). It seems to me difficult to dispute the
importance of both the Qumran community and the Qumran texts
for the history of Christian origins. But everything suggests that the
Essenes, as an organized body, disappeared from sight as a result of
the disaster of A.D. 70. Essenism therefore made its influence felt
particularly in the apostolic period, and, to the extent that it was at
least partly amalgamated with the primitive Church, during the years
immediately following. It appears to have stopped exercising any
influence, at least within the Catholic Church, during the period I
studied. If in fact the Qumran community is to be recognized as
Essene, as I believe, what I said about the connections of the Essenes
with official Judaism (p. 16) needs to be rectified. It is impossible to
trace with precision or in detail the development of this relationship.
But the history of the sect, as we glimpse it through the Dead Sea
Scrolls, shows the Essenes to have been fundamentally opposed to the
Jerusalem priesthood, and to have sometimes been persecuted by
them. By the same token, they kept their distance from the Temple,
not because they were against it in principle, but because they
reckoned that in the present state of affairs it was contaminated by an
unworthy priesthood. Though it is true that the Essenes, or some
among them, were sufficiently tainted with the Zealot spirit to
support the revolt of A.D. 66–70 against the Roman oppressor,

we are surely justified in our submission that the destruction of the sanctuary, which they had already ceased attending, neither caught them at a disadvantage nor caused them excessive grief. It is difficult to weigh the influence the Essenes had outside their closed communities on the people at large, but it was probably considerable. But insofar as they did exercise such an influence, it contributed, along with the synagogue system that owed so much to the Pharisees, to the surmounting of the disaster of A.D. 70.

The picture I presented of Judaism at the beginning of the Christian era has been fairly widely accepted. Maurice Liber, however, shows some surprise at certain aspects of it. He criticizes the use I made of recent archaeological discoveries. I have not proved, in his view, that the frescoes and mosaics of the synagogues in Galilee and Dura Europos "are faithful to traditional Judaism" (*L'Amandier Fleuri, Cahiers de Pensée et de Vie Juives, 1,* October–November, 1949, p. 70). A watertight proof is perhaps difficult to produce. But it is equally difficult to demonstrate the heterodox character of the synagogues with images. In fact, archaeologists are generally agreed in regarding these synagogues as belonging to "traditional" Judaism, though they do diverge as to the period and locality in which this Jewish figurative art originated. I might be allowed to refer back to my "Remarques sur les synagogues à images de Doura et de Palestine," a note republished in *Recherches d'Histoire Judéo-Chrétienne* (Paris–La Haye, 1962, pp. 188 ff.). The problems relating to Jewish figurative art have been studied deeply, methodically and exhaustively by E. Goodenough in his *Jewish Symbols in the Greco-Roman Period,* of which eight volumes have already appeared between 1952 and 1958. The volume that deals with the Dura synagogue is awaited eagerly. However, the author believes he can find a symbolic significance in the smallest details of this art. His interpretations cannot be accepted without discussion. C. H. Kraeling (*The Excavations at Dura-Europos, Final Report,* VIII, Part I, *The Synagogue,* New Haven, Conn., 1956) is inclined to look for the origins of this iconography in the illustrations that were added to manuscripts of the Bible. These began in the Hellenistic diaspora and were intended for gentiles rather than Jews. The oldest of them would go back, thinks Kraeling, to the third century B.C. It was only at the beginning of the Christian era that this decoration, which had become normal in the manuscripts, passed over into the synagogues. The author admits that this interpretation is hypothetical. A. Grabar has recently published work on the possible connection between Jewish and Palaeo-Christian art (*Recherches sur les sources juives de l'art paléochrétien,* in *Cahiers Archéologiques*

11, [1960]: 41 ff, and 12 [1962]: 115 ff). See also H. Stern, *Quelques problèmes d'iconographie paléochrétienne et juive* ibid., pp. 99 ff. The problem is raised afresh by the recent discovery of a catacomb in Rome near the Via Latina. An exceptionally high proportion of its abundant and beautiful decoration is drawn from the Old Testament, and it contains a number of scenes that up to now have been unknown in paleo-Christian funerary art. The account of it is published by A. Ferrua, *Le Pitture della nuova Catacomba di Via Latina* (*Monumenti di Antichità Cristiana*, second series, 8, Vatican City, 1960). Ferrua comes to no conclusions about the possible Jewish origin of the imagery. The question of chronology seems to me to be the decisive one here, though it is not always easy to clarify the chronological relationships. It appears that, as far as our information goes at present, there is no example of synagogue painting that can be dated with certainty to a period earlier than the origins of Christian art. The oldest collection of Jewish pictorial work, that from Dura, is some years later than the frescoes in the Christian chapel from the same town. It would doubtless be sensible to make allowances for chance. A new discovery could eventually put a completely different complexion on the whole affair. But for the time being the negative and positive evidence (see above, pp. 18 ff.) suggests no reason for thinking that Jewish figurative art could have appeared much earlier than Christian art. It is difficult therefore to assert the clear dependence of the latter upon the former. It seems rather that they came into existence almost simultaneously and underwent a parallel development. It is to be understood that influence of one upon the other is not ruled out. As far as the relatively late paintings are concerned, such as the fourth-century ones of the Via Latina, the theory of direct Jewish influence seems superfluous. Christian iconography was well established by that date, and the novel features exhibited by the pictures in the Via Latina catacomb (novel, that is to say, by comparison with paleo-Christian funerary art as it was known to us before those discoveries) are sufficiently explained by the influence of Church decoration. As for the clear preponderance of Old Testament scenes, as opposed to episodes from the gospels, it is perhaps sufficient explanation to say that concern for symbols tended at this period to take second place to an interest purely in narrative. And the Old Testament provided suitable material more abundantly and in greater variety than the New Testament. However this may be, two conclusions appear to be justified: first, that Jewish art took its rise in the diaspora; second, as Kraeling believes, in its initial form it effectively met not only catechetical needs but the needs of the proselytizing movement.

II

On the question of Jewish proselytism my thesis has not only received assent in a good many quarters but has also excited surprise, and even scepticism, in others. Liber, to whom I have already referred, merely asserts his astonishment at the discovery of "a missionary side to the Pharisees, who have been thought, by virtue of their very name, to have been unsympathetic to proselytism." To say this is to forget that the "separated ones" very quickly left their isolation and became spiritual guides to their people and, at least in certain instances, made efforts to bring the truth to the gentiles. What only evokes surprise in Liber evokes denial from Munck, who, in connection with my book, refers back to ideas he had already developed in *Paulus und die Heilsgeschichte* (Copenhagen, 1954, pp. 259–65), "Jewish Christianity in Post-apostolic Times" (*NTS* 6, no.2 [1960]:103–16). His line of argument, presented in the form of polemic against Schürer, rests in essence on the following points:

It was always possible for non-Jews to get themselves accepted into the Jewish community, and about the beginning of the Christian era the influx of converts became considerable, Judaism benefiting from the interest that was aroused in all the Eastern religions. But this was not a result of any missionary effort. Judaism had no theory of mission and no consciousness of any call to gather in the pagans to the ranks of the elect. There is no evidence to show that the Jews of the diaspora were any more active in this respect than the Palestinians. The idea of a mission to the pagans originated in Christianity, which preached a universalistic message. The saying about the proselytizing zeal of the Pharisees (Matthew 23:15) probably describes a state of affairs subsequent to the beginning of the Christian mission. It could also, perhaps, be a reference to the proselytizing efforts made as part of the attempt to marry off the family of Herod, when pagan princes were converted to Judaism and circumcised as a preliminary to marriage. If one wished to retain the saying as a genuinely dominical one, it would be necessary to say that it refers to Pharisaic proselytes, i.e., to recruits to the Pharisaic movement within Israel. The substantial amount of Jewish-Hellenistic literature, which tries to show the absurdity of idolatry and which preaches monotheism and encourages conduct in accordance with the moral law, is not evidence for the existence of a missionary spirit in the diaspora. It is for internal use, like the greater part of the corresponding Christian literature. Its intention is to forearm the faithful against the infection of paganism. Munck then turns to the texts which Schürer had appealed to in support of the existence of Jewish proselytism, and tries to show that their significance is less than Schürer supposes. He does admit that at the beginning of the Christian era there was a considerable number of proselytes, but again asserts that this presupposes not the least missionary effort on the part of the Jews. He cites evidence of the vogue for Oriental religions, which impelled the pagans to seek salvation now in the mystery cults and now in the Synagogue. It was an entirely spontaneous phenomenon, he alleges. Finally, following Fridrichsen and Aalen, he draws a distinction between *Proselytenwerbung* and true missionary activity, and claims that at no time was Judaism preoccupied with either.

The arguments used in support of this paradoxical position boil down to a series of assertions, repeated several times but still, in my opinion, very debatable. I do not suppose anyone would accept Matthew 23:15 as a reference to the matrimonial politics of the Herodian family. This verse, which Munck finds so obscure, still seems clear enough to me. To be frank, I can see only two possible interpretations: first, it may be contrasting the intensity of the Pharisees' missionary efforts with the insignificance of the results obtained. This does not exclude the possibility that there may be in the author's mind, as Munck suggests, a tacit contrast between the already remarkable success of the Christian mission and the lack of success of that of the Jews. Second, the emphasis is solely on the extraordinary missionary zeal of the Pharisees, who, even when there is a prospect of making only one convert, do not hesitate to devote their all to the task. This would make the saying into a kind of afterthought to the parable of the lost sheep. "If a man has a hundred sheep, and one of them has gone astray, does he not leave the ninety-nine on the hills and go in search of the one that went astray?" (Matthew 18:12; see also Luke 15:4–7, where it appears in a more natural and satisfying context). The difference is that the sheep lost and found is a symbol of the saved sinner, whereas the proselyte gained by the Pharisees can only be hastening to his own destruction in the eyes of a Christian of the period. In whichever way it be interpreted, and whether the verse records a genuine saying of Jesus or merely reflects the reactions of second-generation Christians, it attests the existence of a Jewish mission that was worldwide in its scope.

It is a purely arbitrary procedure to postulate that Alexandrian Jewish literature is of necessity intended for a single category of readers, Jews or pagans, and then to opt, without further argument, for a Jewish destination. This is all the more odd in that Munck concedes that the Christian apologetic literature is also addressed, at least in part, to a pagan audience. See P. Dalbert, *Die Theologie der hellenistisch-jüdischen Missionliteratur*, Hamburg, 1954.) It is quite widely

accepted that the translation of the Septuagint was already designed
not only to meet the needs of the Greek-speaking Alexandrian Jews,
but to serve the ends of proselytism. The work of Philo, too, is in
principle universalist. On the last point see, alternatively, A. Jaubert,
La Notion d'Alliance dans le Judaïsme aux abords de l'ère chrétienne (Paris
1963, pp. 389 ff.) and especially H. A. Wolfson, *Philo, II* (Cambridge,
Mass., 1947, pp. 355–73). After all, though the initiative for the Jewish
mission came from the Hellenized circles of the diaspora, it
nevertheless remains true that the roots of the missionary tradition go
back to the Bible itself (A. Jaubert, *La Notion,* pp. 302 ff.). It is in any
case unwise, as the text of Matthew 23:15 reminds us, to contrast in
too absolute a fashion the diaspora with Palestine. On the question of
proselytism and its survival into the Talmudic era there could be
added to the works cited B. Bamberger, *Proselytism in the Talmudic
Period* (New York, 1939); W. A. Braude, *Jewish Proselytism in the First
Five Centuries of the Common Era* (Providence, R.I., 1940); and G. Kittel,
"Die Ausbreitung des Judentums bis zum Beginn des Mittelalters" in
Forschungen zur Judenfrage 5 [1941]: 290 ff. See also J. Jeremias, *Jesu
Verheissung für die Völker* (Stuttgart, 1956, pp. 2–16).

The contrast between true mission and *Proselytenwerbung* cannot be
sustained, or at least, it is difficult to draw a firm line of distinction
between the two. What Aalen, quoted by Munck, says about Judaism
and Israel could just as readily be said about Christianity and the
Church. Referring to the δόξα, which is connected with Israel and
Jerusalem, he writes, "Niemand kann ihrer teilhaftig werden ohne
'herzukommen,' Proselyt zu werden, d.h. ohne Jude zu werden." Did
early Christians ever imagine that a pagan could work out his
salvation without "drawing near," i.e., without being converted to
Christianity and being gathered into the Church?

It seems to me, nevertheless, that two points may be conceded to
Professor Munck. In the first place, Judaism, being an established
body, national and religious at the same time, indissolubly bound up
with Israel and founded on the concept of the chosen people, was less
spontaneously and less unanimously inclined than post-Pauline
Christianity ever was to gather in the nations to hear its gospel. For
early Christianity was not an existing body, but one that was still
growing and coming into being. Doubtless Judaism as a whole
possessed no *Missionstheorie.* And secondly, for want of the will, or
sometimes the power, to make its converts accept the observance of
the whole law, Judaism did allow the rise of a class of semiproselytes,
whose charter was represented by the so-called Noahic commandments. These had no Christian equivalent.

Rabbinic tradition teaches that for the general run of mankind the keeping of the moral law and a minimum of ritual observance is sufficient for salvation. This teaching may be interpreted as the symptom of a supercilious condescension, which by creating a category of second-class believers preserves the preeminence and privileges of Israel intact, or it may be interpreted as evidence of a remarkable breadth of vision. This latter is perhaps a less likely interpretation, or perhaps it is an implication that the rabbinic view less frequently conveys. But could these semiproselytes or God-fearers, whose existence and importance Munck does not dispute, have collected in such numbers around the Synagogue without any effort at all being made by the Jews to attract them? It is difficult to believe. It is even harder to conceive that the instances of thorough-going conversion, which are well attested, even though it is not easy to guess their numbers, could be brought about, without encouragement, by the efforts of the proselytes themselves. For these conversions were sealed by circumcision, which was physically painful and, for a pagan of that period, morally humiliating. There is, it seems to me, a contradiction in denying to Judaism all missionary activity worthy of the name and yet speaking in the same connection (as Fridrichsen does, cited by Munck, *Paulus*, p. 265, n. 37) of a "Jewish expansionist thrust" and of "synagogal imperialism." To contrast this movement, inspired by impure motives, with "the true mission in the light of the kingdom of God" is probably to give way, unconsciously, both to a preoccupation with Christian apologetic and a subtle form of anti-Semitism. For how, in the end, could the Synagogue have so directed its missionary preaching as not to incur the charge of imperialism? And what right have we to suppose that the Jews, when they recruited proselytes, did it only to further their own glory and were interested only in personal success? Why not for the glory of the Name and the salvation of their converts? Doubtless it is going too far simply to equate with one another the Jewish and the Christian mission. There were differences between them, which I shall refer to shortly. But there is no evidence leading us to deny either the continuity between the two or the very existence of the former. E. Lerle's recent work, *Proselytenwerbung und Urchristentum*, (Berlin, 1961), endeavoring to show that the Christian mission was prepared for by the missionary urge of Judaism, has usefully brought this question into focus.

On the opposite side from J. Munck, who reproaches me for believing in a missionary Judaism, B. Blumenkranz complains that I do not believe in it strongly enough or, more exactly, that I place its disappearance too early (*Theologische Zeitschrift*, 1949, 4). Not only did it continue to the end of the period of antiquity, around the beginning of the fifth century, the Jewish mission will have survived until the

opening of the crusades. Blumenkranz makes this claim when dealing
with the subject of my book, and tries to prove it in his work, *Juifs et
Chrétiens dans le Monde Occidental, 430–1096* (Paris–La Haye, 1960). I
have already intimated in a review of that excellent work (*Revue des
Etudes Juives*, January–June 1961, pp. 167 ff.) the modifications which
seem to me to be called for in the author's views. It seems a priori
unlikely that proselytism could be carried on freely and effectively in
mediaeval society, organized as it was on a Christian basis and hostile
to the spread of any heretical doctrine or teaching foreign to
Christianity. If there really was, here or there, any missionary activity
during the period envisaged, it seems to have been done on an
individual basis rather than by the Synagogue. The few instances of
conversions the author refers to (Bode, Vécelin, etc.) probably do no
more than illustrate the attraction that Judaism held for certain
minds, and do not necessarily presuppose any positive missionary
effort on Judaism's part. Munck's views, though they are incorrect to
my mind when applied to the period of antiquity, do, on the other
hand, fit the mediaeval situation very well. The recent examples of
Aimé Pallière and the Italian peasants of San Nicandro, who came
into Judaism without any missionary intervention and practically in
defiance of the rabbinic authorities, show that proselytes can be
genuinely made even in the absence of proselytism. (On this
interesting sociological and religious phenomenon, see E. Cassin, *San
Nicandro* [Paris, 1957]). These remain, nonetheless, exceptional instances. There is nothing to suggest that in the Middle Ages
conversions to Judaism were any commoner, and in particular, we
have no reason to believe that the few proselytes whose names we
know, since they were persons of high station, were accompanied by
any anonymous crowd of lesser men who passed with them from
Church to Synagogue.

Blumenkranz emphasizes the case of slaves, and sees there the only
instance in which missionary activity became institutionalized in the
Synagogue. Doubtless, in putting pressure on his slaves to accept
circumcision, the Jewish owner was merely obeying a precept of the
Mosaic law (Genesis 17:12 ff.). But this precept itself reflected a
particular and very definite preoccupation. In the circumstances in
which it is delivered, it is not so much a question of disseminating the
faith of Israel as of preserving the members of the same household in
the state of ritual purity necessary for their life together. Blumenkranz
himself notes this: "It was after he had become a Jew that the slave
could appropriately be given any work that came to hand. Only then,
especially, could he be employed in cooking and in the manufacture
and handling of wine" (p. 184). In such circumstances it is difficult to

speak of "mission" without a misuse of terminology. I have tried to show that Jewish missionary activity came to a stop only by degrees. I am ready to concede to Blumenkranz that in some places it continued beyond the chronological bounds I set for my study, though the extent to which it did so is difficult to determine. It remains true that by the end of the period of antiquity the life had already gone out of it, even if it was not completely finished, and that the very establishment of a Christian state, which was much more concerned than the pagan emperors had ever been to prevent any expansion of Judaism, contributed largely to its disappearance. In support of the *terminus ad quem* that I chose, Andreotti very appropriately recalls (in the long review of my work in *Rivista di Filologia et di Istruzione Classica*, 1949, p. 172) that it was during the troubles of A.D. 415 that the Jewish community disappeared from Alexandria, a community that was "the oldest, the most assertive, and the most illustrious in the diaspora." He quotes in this connection H. I. Bell, "Anti-Semitism in Alexandria", *Journal of Roman Studies*, 1941, pp. 1 ff.

III

The problem of Jewish expansion and of the spread of its influence is bound up with that of anti-Semitism, as I have tried to show. Dom Botte—who, it may be said in passing, seems not to have read my book very carefully and sometimes misunderstands me—does not think that the term anti-Semitism is a proper word to use in connection with the Church fathers. "For there is nothing in Christian antiquity which springs from racial hatred or social conflict. The opposition is purely religious" (*Bulletin de Théologie Ancienne et Médiévale* 6:205). This is exactly what I was trying to prove. But this is not sufficient reason for hesitating to speak of anti-Semitism, or, if one prefers, anti-Judaism. To circumscribe the meaning of the term as Dom Botte does is purely arbitrary. Of course, St. John Chrysostom is not a racist. His invective is not an expression of class conflict. But if what is meant by anti-Semitism is an attitude fundamentally and systematically hostile to Jews, the hostility being supported, more-over, by some very bad arguments, by calumnies, by an incomplete, tendentious representation of Judaism that falsifies the truth about it, then St. John Chrysostom deserves to be set in the front rank among the anti-Semites of all time. There is a certain type of argument and a certain kind of denigration that, whatever be the roots it springs from, can be called anti-Semitic. On the other hand, the fact that the mention of Jewish "perfidy" in the Good Friday liturgy occurs, as Dom Botte recalls, "precisely in an invitation to pray for the conversion of the Jews" does nothing to diminish its damaging nature or significance. The same liturgy embodies prayers, identical in content, for heretics, schismatics, and pagans, but it does not add any pejorative description to them. And although each is accompanied by an invitation to bow the knee (*flectamus genua*), this invitation is omitted from the prayer for the Jews, and from it alone. It is clear that this twofold oddity, addition of an epithet and omission of a gesture, is meant to be deliberately offensive. If the prayer in question is as harmless as Dom Botte alleges it to be, it is difficult to see why Pope John XXIII thought the word *perfidi* ought to be omitted from the liturgy, prompted as he was not only by many Jews but by interconfessional groups such as the *Amitiés Judéo-Chrétiennes*. On the subject of the prayer for the Jews one might consult, in addition to Peterson's article, referred to in the book (p. 471) that of J. M. Oesterreicher, "Pro Perfidis Judaeis" (*Cahiers Sioniens*, 1947, pp. 85–101); more particularly, J. Isaac, *Jésus et Israël* (Paris, 1948, pp. 264 ff); and most important of all, the same author's *Genèse de l'Antisémitisme* (Paris, 1956, pp. 296–305).

J. Isaac allows that the Good Friday liturgy, and more generally the Church's teaching about Israel and Judaism, are of great importance for the origins of modern anti-Semitism. See also his, *L'antisémitisme a-t-il des racines chrétiennes? (Paris, 1960)*, and *L'enseignement du mépris* (Paris, 1962). A more general study covering a more extensive period is Leon Poliakov's *Histoire de l'Antisémitisme, I: Du Christ aux Juifs de cour* (Paris, 1955). The polemic that Isaac's views have stimulated is well known. I stated, in my reviews of his first two books, what reservations they seemed to me to call for. It seems to me difficult to regard the Catholic liturgy as the essential vehicle of this "teaching of contempt," when it hardly ever mentions the question of the Jews outside the particular context of Good Friday. Such a suggestion assumes that the mass of believers was highly conscious of a few texts, a prayer and proper preface, which were used at one particular point in the liturgical year, and recited, moreover, in Latin, a language incomprehensible to the majority of worshipers. Their damaging influence can only have been effective at firsthand upon the clergy and on the few laymen able to follow and understand the liturgy. The rest must have been obliged to arrive at the interpretation through a translation. Now, the practice of putting bilingual texts of the liturgy at the disposal of the congregation is a relatively recent one, and as far as the less commonly used rituals are concerned, such as the one for Good Friday, there are few places in which it is done even now.

Alternatively, they may have been influenced through a sermon or explanatory commentary, drawing the hearers' attention particularly to these "anti-Semitic" passages. There is nothing to suggest that this was a very widespread practice either. Furthermore, it ought not to be forgotten that ecclesiastically inspired anti-Semitism has appeared in its most virulent forms in recent centuries not in the Catholic West, but in the orthodox lands of eastern Europe, in Tsarist Russia particularly. This fact alone suggests that the specific influence of the Roman liturgy should not be overrated.

The more general influence of the teaching of the various Christian churches and the part it played in spreading anti-Semitic ideas cannot of course be disputed, and Isaac has had no trouble in supporting his case with texts as numerous as they are convincing. It is all too evident that much remains to be done before the Christianity of our own day is rid of this miasma. But to argue from this that the Church must bear the essential responsibility, even though it be an indirect responsibility, for the Nazi atrocities, or to see the gas chambers of Auschwitz as the natural result of the Church's teaching—this is to take a step that the historian will hesitate to regard as legitimate. It seems hardly likely, on a priori grounds, that in an age as secularized as ours, and even more so, under a regime as utterly hostile to Christian ideas as that of the Nazis, it should be the theological components of anti-Semitism that are the determining factors in it. This "teaching of contempt" and this "organized disparagement" which Isaac so forcefully denounces were the product of a society, namely, mediaeval Christianity, which was built on religious foundations. They could hardly have outlived that society, except in those confessional circles which remain attached to that structural ideal we may call theocracy, and which are more or less impregnated with its fundamental concepts.

If Hitler's Germany execrated and massacred Jews, it was, first, because Nazism saw in them, by means of gross generalizations and simplifications, the principal subscribers to contemptible ideologies, democracy, political and economic liberalism, cosmopolitanism, and Marxism. Second, it was because they were categorized by a pseudoscientific racism as representatives of a biological stock that was distinct and unassimilable. It must not be forgotten, when the attempt is made to connect the Nazis' anti-Jewish persecutions too closely with Christian teaching, that the Jewish massacre was not the only example of genocide engaged in by the Third Reich. Other "inferior" races and malefactors were hunted down by the Nazis in the name of the same biological principle; the Gypsies, for example. And the Slavs would doubtless not have been in a much more enviable situation if the Nazis had won the war. From the Church's point of view, at any period, a Jew was characterized by his religion. If he was converted, he ceased to be a Jew, and the ultimate aim was just that, the conversion of Israel. The anti-Semitism of the Church was, if one may so express it, provisional and conditional. For Hitler's anti-Semites, a Jew turned Christian was still a Jew, because a Jew was characterized by his race, and it was neither desirable nor possible to change his ethnic characteristics. Total extermination was the only solution. This, in my opinion, marks a fundamental difference that forbids us to establish any very definite or close connecting link or continuity between the two.

J. Isaac is also sometimes led to depict the non-Jewish world's reactions to Israel as uniformly and continuously hostile after the intervention of Christianity. Of the polemic of Agobard, for example, he writes, "It is only one link in the unbroken chain of Christian anti-Judaism" (*Genèse de l'Antisémitisme*, p. 286). Blumenkranz, among others, has shown that even in the Middle Ages the real state of affairs was much less straightforward than that, and that the circumstances of the Jews varied perceptibly from period to period and from place to place. Conversely, Isaac has a tendency to minimize the pre-Christian anti-Semitism of the Greco-Roman world. The texts he does gather on this subject seem to him "mere trifles, the sum total of them a drop in the ocean of a vast amount of literature." The correction these opinions cry out for will be found, for example, in the weighty chapter devoted to pagan anti-Semitism by F. Lovsky, *Antisémitisme et mystère d'Israël* (Paris, 1955). This appeared before *Genèse de l'Antisémitisme*, but takes account of various articles in which Isaac expounds his views, the views that were later collected into his book. Even from the point of view of later centuries the role of pagan anti-Semitism ought not to be dismissed as negligible. For as Lovsky points out judiciously, "It will be seen that a scholarly text is never negligible; after all, Tacitus or Martial were read by more people, and over a longer period, than the fathers of the Church, whose writings were quite early confined to a few narrow circles of readers" (p. 7, n. 1).

Recent works have attempted to determine the origins, chronological and geographical, of pagan anti-Semitism. J. Yoyotte, in his "L'Egypt ancienne et les origines de l'anti-judaïsme" (*Bulletin de la Société Ernest Renan*, 1962, pp. 133 ff.) reckons that it is necessary to go back beyond Alexander, to the late Pharaonic period, in order to find the earliest manifestations in Egypt of anti-Jewish thinking. Comparative study of the various versions of the *History of the Impure*, which was given its classic form by Manetho but derives from much older sources, leads Yoyotte to locate the first appearance of the phenomenon in the fifth century, under the Achaemenid rulers. Anti-Judaism is centered at this time on the Jewish garrisons established at a number of sites in Egypt by the Great King. They were distinguished from the majority of the other foreign military colonies by an unshakable loyalty to the Persians. The Jewish nationalism that inspired Nehemiah seems to have been subscribed to by them also, and this placed them in even sharper opposition to their surroundings. Thus "the first known 'anti-Semitism' would have complained of the Jews, not that they were the insidious merchants which modern anti-Semitism pictures them to be, but that they were soldiers, and what is more, the servants of Persian power—an Aryan power" (p. 143). At this stage anti-Semitism expresses as yet only the clash of two kinds of nationalism; it is one form of xenophobia. It only takes on its characteristic features in the Ptolemaic period. But it is interesting to note that Alexandrian anti-Semitism, and by derivation that of the Romans, takes up some of its themes from the earlier centuries. In particular, "the idea that the Jews worship an ass indubitably results from the late identification of Seth with that animal" (Yoyotte, p. 142). Mme. R. Neher-Bernstein arrives independently of Yoyotte and by means of quite different arguments at the same conclusion ("The Libel of Jewish Ass-worship," in Hebrew, with a résumé in English, in *Zion, Quarterly for Research in Jewish History* 27, nos. 1–2:106–16). Yoyotte says again, "It would be amusing to compare come recurrent epithets from the Pharaonic period with a selection of expressions applied to the Jews in the Roman world: 'impious ones,' 'enemies of the gods,' 'enemies of the human race (misanthropia).' In Egypt the word 'enemy' was applied wherever it could be made to stick. It was used by the Egyptians of the Persians, then of the Greeks; it was used by the Greek kings and later by the Lagides of indigenous rebels; it was applied by the nationalists to foreign military colonies and to 'collaborators'; it was applied to the Seleucids by the priesthood, which took the part of the Ptolemies. But it seems, when the account is settled, that it was the unhappy people of Israel who were saddled eventually, by the beginning of the Christian era, with this polyvalent label" (p. 141).

The reason for this exceptional treatment is clear. It is an expression of the Hellenistic and Roman reaction to this element which, alone among those of which the world was composed, totally refused to be assimilated. And this is before the intervention of Christianity. Since these anti-Jewish activities were undertaken in the name of religion, in a society whose foundations were themselves religious, it was in a religious guise that anti-Semitism showed itself. In this respect, and at least insofar as it represents a spontaneous movement, the anti-

Semitism of mediaeval or modern Christianity is an offshoot of that of Alexandria and Rome. The anti-Semitism of Hitler was much less directly so, for it fastened even on to assimilated Jews and Jews who made no practice of their religion, and owes nothing to the anti-Semitism of Alexandria or Rome. Isaac rightly denounces "the myth of eternal anti-Semitism," but has nevertheless rather lost sight of the fact that certain factors that give rise to anti-Semitism are as old as Judaism itself. They derive from the tendency to self-segregation (at least a *relative* tendency) inherent in Judaism. It is a tendency that is the very condition of survival.

Furthermore, he has not always marked insistently enough the distinction between anti-Semitism properly so called, that is to say, hatred of Jews, which was too often encouraged by Christian teaching, and theological argument *adversus Judaeos*, which attempted to expose the error of Judaism and the rightness of Christianity. F. Lovsky proposes to designate this as anti-Judaism, to distinguish it from anti-Semitism. The choice of term is not perhaps a very fortunate one. For my own part I would more readily treat *anti-Judaism* as a synonym, a more accurate and better-fitting synonym, for *anti-Semitism*. And what Lovsky calls *anti-Judaism* I should call *anti-Jewish apologetic*. But whatever be the term preferred, the distinction so made is a vital one. It is true that anti-Jewish apologetic could sometimes be, in form and in its line of argument, anti-Semitic in the ordinary sense of that word, but it was not so in principle or in essence. The procedures by which the Church refuted the theological system of the Synagogue are of the same kind as those by which the different Christian confessions came to grips with each other and defined their own positions in terms of orthodoxy or heresy. Not only are they of the same kind, but in the eyes of even the most conscientiously impartial historian they are just as legitimate.

This confusion between two distinct domains appears more than once in the otherwise estimable and useful work of J. E. Seaver, *Persecution of the Jews in the Roman Empire (300–434)* (Lawrence, Kan., 1952). The title itself could be better chosen, for during the period under review there was no persecution of Jews in the proper sense of the word. There was nothing to compare, for example, with Diocletian's persecution of the Christians. The few instances of personal violence the author brings to light were the result of popular pressure and devoid of any legal basis. Even the imperial measures that modified the traditional status of the Jews cannot all be described as anti-Semitic. This is the case, for example, concerning Gratian's decree imposing the decurionate charges on Jews, for the legislative text that Seaver cites in this connection extends to Christian clergy, who had previously been exempt, the same financial obligation as they bore before their ordination. Likewise, the sanctions imposed on converts to Judaism are also, when seen against the background of that period, religious defensive measures rather than genuine persecution, and at the same time they militated against the missionary efforts of pagans, heretics, and Manichees. Even taken out of their context, they do not amount to an alteration in the Jews' traditional status, for though they were guaranteed the freedom to practice their religion, they had never been given an explicit right to proselytize. To assert that there is no proof at all that "the Jews as a class hated and persecuted the Christians as a class" (p. 7) betrays a curious failure to understand the mentality of the period. The Jews did not, to be sure, persecute the Christians. Had they wished to do so, they would not have been able. But the maledictions made in the Synagogues against the Nazarenes prove well enough that the hatred was by no means one-sided.

The author describes Aphraates as "violently anti-Semitic" (p. 38). This singular statement is supported only by a brief analysis of one or two homilies in which Aphraates asks his readers to abstain from Jewish observances, declares that happy is the man whose circumcision is of the heart, and tries to show that, according to the law's own terms, the Passover cannot be celebrated anywhere but in Jerusalem. These, adds the author, are examples typical of Aphraates' way of thinking. So they are; but where then is this violent anti-Semitism that is supposed to inspire him? For my part, all I can see there is a concern for the defense of his religion and a preoccupation with the prevention of Jewish-Christian syncretism. Seaver himself seems to make the same evaluation when he concludes by saying that Aphraates "seems to have feared lest some of his flock would be exposed to the danger of being led astray by Jewish practices and arguments." It is by a similar confusion and abuse of terminology that he is able to speak of Eusebius's theological and apologetic treatises as anti-Semitic works (p. 25). Neither theological controversy, even the kind that is founded on the Old Testament, nor the decrees of the councils, can properly be described as manifestations of anti-Semitism. Both one and the other have Judaizing Christians just as much in mind, and perhaps even more in mind, than the Jews themselves. Ecclesiastical authorities could not be expected to encourage or even to tolerate practices that called in question the autonomy and integrity of Christianity. The rabbinic authorities were just as hostile to Christianizing tendencies as the Church was to its Judaizers. The fence erected around the law was a vital necessity for the Synagogue. If I thus argue, it is certainly not in order to exculpate those Christians, whether fathers of the Church, bishops or emperors, who bear a heavy responsibility for elaborating the "system of denigration" and for the creation of the ghetto. I do so merely in order to draw attention to another aspect of a singularly complex phenomenon, an aspect whose importance has sometimes been misunderstood.

IV

It is fairly generally conceded that, leaving aside the periods of acute conflict corresponding to the two Jewish wars and one or two crises of shorter duration and lesser scope, Rome's attitude to Judaism and the Jews was tolerant and relatively benevolent. I have tried to show how the Jews, enjoying at first their protected status, actually saw an improvement in their standing with the authorities and with public opinion when Christianity entered on the scene. At least some emperors and some representatives of pagan religious thought dreamed of integrating Israel into a common front against the new religion. I thought I had been able at the same time to gather together and to set down very briefly (following Parkes, in particular) the facts relating to the Jews' part in the origin and development of the persecutions of the Christians. Entirely different views of the relations between Rome and the Jews have been propounded in a recent work by Y. F. Baer, "Israel, the Christian Church and the Roman Empire, from the time of Septimius Severus to the Edict of Toleration of A.D. 313," published in *Scripta Hierosolymitana*. vol. 7 (Jerusalem, 1961), pp. 79–145. The author reckons that, all the while fighting with each other, both Church and Synagogue carried on a fierce ideological struggle against paganism and the forces of evil (represented by Rome) and that Judaism as well as Christianity suffered persecution during the period in question.

I am personally quite inclined to follow Baer as far as his first point is concerned. It is clear that Judaism could not, and in fact did not, come to any understanding with polytheism and idolatry. Even when in daily life Jews and pagans were on polite, even cordial terms, and when the crises that distorted their good relations had passed, the antagonism that remained in the sphere of belief was not reduced. It was as persistent as the conflict between Christian belief and paganism, and given a practical focus, in the Jews' case, by the web of observances that isolated them. Granted that we are very badly informed about Jewish reactions to Julian's proposed reconstruction of the temple, I still consider it unlikely that the initiative came from the Jews. The opposite view is expressed by Andreotti in the review mentioned above (p. 395). I am confirmed in my opinion by the arguments of S. Lieberman, "The Martyrs of Caesarea," *Annuaire de l'Institut de Philologie et d'Histoire Orientales et Slaves* 7 (1939–44:416). Commenting on an obscure passage in the *Midrash Qoheleth Rabbah*, (X,10), which thanks God for having "taken away the disgrace of Lulianus and Pappus," the author argues, on good grounds, that the name of Pappus did not appear in the original text. It has been added because the two names generally appear together in the rabbinic texts (they were brothers who were martyred during Hadrian's reign) and the addition has seduced commentators into erroneous interpretations. They have deduced that the "disgrace" was the martyrdom of the two brothers and that it was "taken away" by the punishment of the persecutor. Lieberman has shown what difficulties the interpretation raises. On the contrary, all becomes clear if it be conceded that originally the name Lulianus stood alone and that it designated Julian. In *j. Nedar.* III, 3, 37d, the name occurs again in the same form, and the context there indicates that it can only refer to the Apostate. The "disgrace of Lulianus" in the midrash consequently refers to the disgrace it represents for Israel that the initiative for rebuilding the temple should be taken by a pagan prince; for the rebuilding of the temple was an undertaking reserved for the Messiah.

Baer further shows convincingly that the tradition of antipagan polemic was common to both religions, that the same themes often crop up in the Jewish and Christian literatures, and that even the authors of anti-Jewish treatises, such as Tertullian, would borrow Jewish arguments when they attacked the pagans.

However, when it comes to the anti-Jewish persecutions that allegedly took place during the period, Baer's attempt at proof seems to me scarcely convincing. The Talmud has preserved the memory of persecutions under Trajan, and especially under Hadrian. The former are evidently to be connected with the troubles in Egypt and Cyrenaica and the latter with Bar Cochba's revolt. It turns out that it was also under Trajan that the Roman authorities, in the person of Pliny, were moved for the first time to apply sanctions against the Christians. (The persecution under Nero is a special case.) Doubtless this coincidence in the dates is no more than fortuitous. The execution of R. Akiba is certainly very reminiscent in its form and circumstances of some of the Christian martyrdoms. As Baer emphasizes, it is not a purely political persecution, but has a well-marked religious character (p. 81). But it is equally clear that had there been no Messianic insurrection under Bar Cochba, of whom R. Akiba was one of the most ardent supporters, the rabbi would probably have ended his days in peace. The persecution may have manifested itself in religious ways, but its causes were nonetheless political. It was a consequence of the war, or, if one wishes, one of the manifestations of the war, and it ended when the war ended.

In fact all the allusions to the ill-treatment of Jews, whether they appear in rabbinic, pagan, or Christian sources, refer to the period of Hadrian's war. This is precisely the setting of Justin's *Dialogue with Trypho.* Trypho has been driven to leave Palestine by the hostilities, but even so he appears to have nothing to fear from the Roman authorities outside his own country. Baer tries to prove that the Decian persecution attacked Jews as well as Christians. But he is obliged to recognize that the words of R. Johanan on which he bases his case merely repeat identical ones attributed to R. Akiba (p. 116). Certain Christian authors do speak of the distress of the Jews, and interpret it as a manifestation of the divine wrath, under which they also stand. But insofar as this is not merely a standard literary and apologetic theme, going back to the memory of the Temple's destruction and that of the holy city, this distress seems to be no more than the lack of a national home.

Baer says again: "Whenever Origen and the other Christian scholars accuse Israel of the sin of idolatry, they are forced to seek witnesses from the sacred writings and from the distant past alone. It would not occur to them to afflict the Jews with the transgression of idolatry in their own time, with the allegation that they were traitors and weaklings in the holy war against paganism" (pp. 102 ff.). But this proves not that the Jews, being called on to apostatize, remained unshakable in their faith, but simply that, unlike the Christians, they were sheltered from persecution and other pressures. In fact, when required to cite the names of the victims of his alleged third-century persecutions of the Jews, Baer has great difficulty in finding any to add to the list of Akiba and his immediate contemporaries. He is obliged to recognize the legendary nature of the episode in which two rabbis are miraculously saved from being put to death by Diocletian. To all appearances the story is a retelling of that of the three young men in the fiery furnace (Daniel 3:19 ff.) influenced, furthermore, by the Christian *Acta Martyrum.* At the same time he has to recognize that "the Talmudic tradition actually knows only one martyrological period," namely, that of R. Akiba (p. 128). In order to account for this silence, Baer resorts to a surprising explanation: "Those who were put to death as martyrs subsequently were not, it seems, thought worthy of the crown, or, alternatively, the tradition of such things was cut down in the interests of peace and humility and from a psychological repugnance from dwelling at length on such horrors" (p. 128).

I doubt whether such an argument will convince many of his readers. Why should the Jews have been more discreet in this respect than the Christians, or more concerned than the Christians to bestow the title of martyr only where it was deserved? And why did they manage to overcome their psychological repugnance only in the case of Akiba and his companions? The argument from silence seems to me to be a weighty one. If rabbinic tradition is aware of no other martyrs than the aforementioned, the reason, it would appear, is that none existed.

As far as our evidence at present goes, the only repressive step taken against the Synagogue later than Hadrian's War is the edict of Septimius Severus forbidding all conversions to Judaism as well as to Christianity (see p. 105). Whatever the practical consequences of this (and in my own view the edict cannot have been applied very rigorously or for very long), it does not amount to a prohibition of Judaism. It aims to do no more than prevent its propagation among gentiles, and leaves intact the privileges and legal status enjoyed by those who were Jews from birth. For the official recognition of Judaism never had implied any explicit right to indulge in religious propaganda. In its consequences for Israel's religious life, therefore, it was far less serious than Hadrian's edict forbidding circumcision. Hadrian's edict was not enacted with the Jews explicitly or exclusively in mind. Its object was to put an end to the practice of circumcision, by whomsoever it was carried out, for to the Roman mind circumcision was a degrading kind of multilation, on the same footing as castration. However, Hadrian's edict did in effect forbid Israel to practice her religion and ought no doubt to be counted as one of the causes of the revolt. Baer recalls that it was again during the reign of Septimius Severus that there took place the last rebellious upsurge in Palestine that our sources mention. But it is not certain that this was a consequence of the edict, nor even that there was any connection whatever between the two events.

The gratuitous hypotheses of Baer may be contrasted with Lieberman's firm statement (and Baer quotes Lieberman with praise): "There were apparently no Jewish martyr in Palestine during the persecutions of Diocletian and Galerius" (*The Martyrs of Caesarea*, p. 416). According to a passage of the Talmud (*j. Ab. Zarah* V, 4, 44) that Lieberman quotes (p. 403), "When Diocletian came here [to Palestine] he issued an edict decreeing: All nations except the Jews must offer libations." The stipulated exception in favor of the Jews follows logically from their legal status. It does no more than confirm one of the most important of the *privilegia Judaica.* The emperors of the period were always careful to maintain the Jews' official status. In all probability this was true in the diaspora even while the war in Palestine was going on. This fact constitutes the major objection to Baer's views. Baer is well aware of this, for in a somewhat embarrassed note (p. 86) he seems inclined to think, without going so far as to affirm it clearly, that the status of Judaism as a *religio licita* was no more than a fiction. He tries to minimize the importance of Tertullian's celebrated passage in which he mentioned that the Christians, when troubled by the Roman authorities, sometimes sought refuge *sub umbraculo insignissimae religionis, certe licitae (Apol.* 21,1). It refers, says Baer without any proof whatever, to a purely temporary or local state of affairs. He recalls that it is the only text Juster cites in order to establish that Judaism was a *religio licita* in the eyes of the Roman law. He adds that the generally accepted views concerning the legal position of the Jews in the Roman Empire rest on the opinion of Mommsen, whose ideas concerning Christianity were rejected long ago.

We have here another singular argument, and one that does not require a long refutation. It does not matter for our purposes whether the Jews obtained their special status in their capacity as *religio*, as *collegium*, or as nation. Its existence cannot in any case be seriously doubted. If an emperor no more susceptible to pro-Israelite sympathies than Theodosius felt obliged to recall (as Baer notes) that *Judaeorum sectam nulla lege prohibitam satis constat (Theod. Code*, XIV, 8,2) it was because the situation was a well-established one, in law as well as in fact. To emphasize that Judaism is not forbidden amounts, to all appearances, to a recognition that it is authorized. One too often gets the impression when reading Baer's work that he has given way to a subtle and perhaps unconscious apologetic desire, and is really concerned to show that Christians were not the only ones to fight the good fight against pagan Rome. Judaism has provided enough martyrs down the centuries. It has no need to look for extra ones in a period in which the laws assured its peace.

V

My suggested interpretation of the word *minim*, which seems to me to refer in very many cases to the Christians, has not to my knowledge aroused objections. K. G. Kuhn, who seems not to know my book, and who at all events does not refer to it, arrives at conclusions identical in all respects with mine, though apparently by an independent route ("Giljonim und sifre minim," in *Judentum, Urchristentum, Kirche: Festschrift für Joachim Jeremias* [Berlin, 1960], pp. 24–61). He shows first of all that the term *gilyonim*, which appears several times in the rabbinic writings and in which some have wished to see a reference to the gospels, means nothing more than the edges or margins of a written scroll. He then analyzes various passages in which the term *siphre minim* appears and asserts that its meaning developed in a very interesting way. It was originally applied to the biblical scrolls used by communities that the Pharisaic Synagogue held to be heretical, e.g., the Essenes. From the third century it came to designate the sacred texts of other religions, of Christianity especially, i.e., it referred to books not found in the Old Testament.

This change corresponds to a parallel development in the meaning of the word *minim* itself. "In the oldest rabbinic literature, viz., that emanating from the end of the first century A.D. and the first half of the second, when the struggle to impose rabbinic orthodoxy and eliminate other tendencies in Judaism was going on, the word served to describe the 'heretics' who embodied these tendencies" (p. 36). At this stage it always refers to Jews who regard themselves as belonging to Judaism, but whose claims to do so are disputed by the rabbis. "By about the year 200 rabbinic orthodoxy has succeeded in imposing itself almost exclusively. There are now no longer any *minim* within Judaism.... In the later rabbinic texts, i.e., those written from about A.D. 180–200 onwards, and especially in those of the third-century Amoraim, *minim* no longer designates the heretics within, but the heterodox outside; most often it designates the Christians. And from henceforth these are not the Jewish Christians, who still regarded themselves as attached to Judaism, but gentile Christians, and very particularly the Catholic Church. In addition, the word *minim* can also be applied to gnostics and similar groups (p. 39). This is exactly the view to which I myself came (supra pp. 197 ff.). Kuhn reinforces it with fresh arguments. I can only rejoice in such a perfect agreement of opinions.

We are fully and unambiguously informed about what the rabbis felt concerning the *minim*. Their feelings were anything but benevolent and friendly. It could be, however, that there were exceptions to this. S. Lieberman, in his *Martyrs of Caesarea*, p. 398, recalls that R. Abbahu and R. Saphra, at the beginning of the fourth century, seem to have been on good terms with the *minim*, who engaged the latter of the two scholars as a teacher of holy scripture (*b. Ab. Zarah*, 4a). Contrary to the opinion of Travers Herford, he reckons that it is here not a matter of Jewish Christians, whom the Jews thought of as execrable apostates, but of gentile Christians, thus supporting the view of Kuhn and myself. Further on he notes: "In the beginning of the fourth century Christianity was no longer the creed of Jewish heretics, for it had long become the faith of the gentiles" (p. 409). Consequently, in Jewish eyes it no longer represented an apostasy from Judaism, but rather a first step toward a monotheistic faith.

It would no doubt be wise to treat with caution such an optimistic view of Jewish-Christian relations in the first few centuries of our era. The attitude that Lieberman ascribes to the rabbis of the period was assuredly the exception rather than the rule. It is the attitude of many liberal Jews today, but it is contradicted by too many texts to allow us to think of it as common or characteristic in the Judaism of fifteen centuries ago. The author further alleges that the Jews saw the Christians martyred under Diocletian as "God-fearers," worthy of all their admiration and sympathy. And for proof of these sentiments he appeals to a passage in Eusebius's *Martyrs of Palestine*, 8,1, where it is said that the Jews' hearts were torn as they watched the Egyptian Christians confess their faith in God in spite of torture. It would seem to me wise not to allow too much weight to a text whose apologetic purpose is so evident, and which presents in parallel the intrepid faith of the Christians (the true Israel) and the infidelity of the Jews. The martyrs in question all bear Old Testament names. Nothing forbids us to believe that the Jews sometimes did sympathize with the victims of persecution, either because of their feelings for them as fellow monotheists, or out of mere human compassion. The latter is perhaps more likely, for were the Christians who confessed faith in "another God" thought of by Israel as genuine monotheists at all? I can only repeat here what I wrote earlier in the same connection (above, p. 125). I would refer also to the fact that the early Church in general observed the Noahic commandments, this observance continuing in some sections of the Church up to a relatively late date. According to rabbinic standards, such observance virtually constituted the Christians as "God fearers" (pp. 334 ff.).

As for Lieberman's assertion that Jewish Christians were always more worthy of hatred in Jewish eyes than gentile Christians, this too perhaps goes a little far. Just as there were different grades and shades of Jewish Christians, so there were differences in the reactions they met with from the rabbis. It is best not to present too closely ordered a view of these matters. If, as I still believe, the term *posh'e Yisrael* was sometimes applied to the Jewish Christians (see pp. 256 ff.), then the use made of the term in rabbinic literature indicates that the rabbis did not necessarily always regard them as execrable apostates, but sometimes as sheep temporarily gone astray and still capable of being eventually gathered into the fold.

VI

It is on the problems relating to Jewish Christianity that recent research has produced most new ideas. With regard to this subject, the picture has changed considerably since the publication of my book. Not that it has been clarified. Quite the reverse! But this is not surprising, since the chief result of these new investigations has been exactly this, to enable us to grasp better than before the extreme complexity of the phenomenon. As I noted earlier (pp. 237–40), it is a phenomenon that is simple only on the surface. In fact, it is evident that the name *Jewish-Christian* is applied in different authors to some very diverse phenomena. Indeed, quite different writers are clearly using quite different sets of terminology. To my mind the clarification of this problem of terminology is an urgent one, for it threatens to become a barrier impeding the progress of further research in this field. It is, I hardly need say, a task I shall not myself undertake, for it seems to me exactly the kind of task that ought to be undertaken collectively. It calls for the cooperation of an entire team of specialists. Their points of view are at the moment remote from each other, or contradictory, but they are perhaps not altogether irreconcilable. To bring them face to face with each other could enable research in this subject to get out of the impasse in which it seems for the time being to be held.

For my own part, all I shall try to do is to state the position, keeping within the chronological and geographical limits I set myself, and within the limits of my subject. In particular, I thought I ought to leave out of account (p. 239) proliferation of syncretizing sects that it is in most respects legitimate to describe as Jewish Christian, but that are outside the Catholic Church and constitute a world of their own. I did not touch at all on the problem of the connection between gnosticism and Judaism or Jewish-Christianity, about which so much has been written during the last few years. I also left outside my enquiry (with the sole exception of Aphraates) eastern Christianity beyond the Roman Empire. And I omitted too the entire phenomenon of Syriac-speaking Christianity, whatever its geographical location or ecclesiastical persuasion, i.e., orthodox or sectarian. This was the Christianity that centered on Edessa and claimed to originate from St. Thomas. The efforts of quite a number of scholars have been concentrated on this sector in recent years, and they believe that this Semitic Christianity represents not only a kind of Jewish Christianity, but the direct heir of the Jewish Christianity of the apostolic period. In spite of the interesting nature of this suggestion, I can do no more than merely draw attention to it. A brief account of the problem and bibliographical references will be found in J. Daniélou and H. Marrou, *Nouvelle Histoire de l'Eglise, vol 1, Des Origines à Grégoire le Grand* (Paris, 1963, pp. 179 ff.).

To abide by the limits I have set myself, two works especially ought to be mentioned. Their titles are almost identical, but they deal with totally different subjects. This itself is a striking example of the variety of meanings the term *Jewish Christian* can at the moment take on. The works in question are H.-J. Schoeps, *Theologie und Geschichte des Judenchristentums* (Tübingen 1949) and J. Daniélou, *Théologie du Judéo-Christianisme* (Tournai 1958). Schoeps's study deals with that very special brand of Jewish Christianity which is represented by the pseudo-Clementine writings, and whose lineaments are still discernible there, beneath all the orthodox reediting to which these works have been subjected. This type of Jewish Christianity was non-conformist not only by the standards of Catholic Christianity but by those of the Synagogue too. Schoeps is dealing therefore with a highly distinctive sectarian phenomenon, and as such, it is foreign to my subject. However, by a curious twist it turns out to be relevant after all. Schoeps in fact presents the religion of the pseudo-Clementine literature as the culmination of a tradition of dissident Jewish thought. This tradition was several centuries old and included within primitive Jerusalemite Christianity. The latter thus represents a link between the pre-Christian antecedents of the movement and the Jewish Christianity of the pseudo-Clementines. It is by virtue of this connection with the apostolic community that the author believes himself justified in speaking of pseudo-Clementine Judaism not merely as a particular type of Jewish Christianity, but as Jewish Christianity par excellence.

It is evident at the outset what the difference is between Schoeps and those who have dealt with the subject before him. He is in agreement with them in acknowledging a continuity between Jewish Christianity and the initial form of Christian faith and practice. But for his predecessors, for Hort and Noennicke, for example, and more generally, for the majority of those who have written histories of early Christianity, Jewish Christianity only gradually came to be revealed as a heresy in response to the development of Catholic Christianity. For when the latter became the Church of the gentiles, Jewish Christianity clung to ritual practices and doctrinal conceptions that were outmoded. For Schoeps, by contrast, Jewish Christianity was heretical from the start, not only by comparison with the standards of later Christian orthodoxy, but by the standards that official Judaism, Sadducean or Pharisaic, observed before A.D. 70. Apostolic Christianity itself, from which Jewish Christianity was directly derived, was the product of a marginal, esoteric Judaism. In this connection Schoeps takes up and develops more systematically the views propounded by O. Cullmann in his book on the pseudo-Clementines.

Schoeps's achievement, to my mind, is that he has established that a particular stream of "heretical" Jewish thought combined, at a very early date, apparently, in the history of the Church, with Christianity. Having recognized Jesus as the one who was to restore the purity of the Jewish religion, it then preached its own doctrines under a Christian label. But I do not think—and here I part company from Schoeps—that these same doctrines were the ones taught by the apostolic community at Jerusalem. We are not, it is true, well informed about what the apostolic community did teach, but there is nothing to suggest that on the subject of the Temple, for example, they subscribed to the negative views of the pseudo-Clementine literature. According to Acts 2:46 the first Christians frequented the Temple for prayer. It is especially on this point that Schoeps has been criticized and he has attempted to reply in his *Urgemeinde, Judenchristentum, Gnosis* (Tübingen, 1956). Among the primitive Christians only Stephen and his group appear to have categorically rejected the Temple and its worship. Now Schoeps does not believe in the historicity of the figure of Stephen. He regards him as an *Ersatz-figur*, invented by the author of Acts, and thinks that this author has shifted onto his shoulders views that in reality were held by James. The author himself dislikes these views and consequently cannot admit that they could have been preached by someone as venerated as Jesus' brother. I doubt whether this hypothesis has attracted many supporters. I continue to think that at no time were the teachings now enshrined in the pseudo-Clementine literature those of an important branch of early Christianity. There is not even any evidence that they were ever subscribed to even by the majority of Jewish Christians.

Daniélou's book is to some extent a rejoinder to that of Schoeps. He sets out "to do for orthodox Jewish Christianity what Schoeps has done for heterodox Jewish Christianity" (p. 20). This implies that he does not accept Schoeps's views concerning the direct connections between the pseudo-Clementines and Jerusalemite Christianity. In fact, he allows three possible definitions of Jewish Christianity. The term "can refer, in the first place, to the Jews who saw Christ either as prophet or as Messiah, but not as the Son of God." The Ebionites of the pseudo-Clementine literature, among others, belong to this category. It includes, "alongside groups committed to strict Jewish observance...those syncretizing Jewish Christians among whom, it appears, gnostic dualism first began." The term *Jewish Christian* may also be used to describe "the Christian community at Jerusalem, dominated by James, and the tendencies which it betrayed." Here we have an element that was "perfectly orthodox," but that "remained attached to certain forms of Jewish life." At a later stage these are sometimes designated by the name *Nazarenes*. Their theology is of an archaic kind but "implies the divinity of Christ." Finally, the name *Jewish Christianity* may also be attached to "a form of Christian thought which has no necessary connection with the Jewish community, but which expresses itself in forms borrowed from Judaism." It naturally includes the two preceding categories of Jewish Christians, but extends well beyond their confines. Paul himself, for example, could on this definition be described as a Jewish Christian.

In fact, the term *Jewish Christian*, extended in this way, was at one time synonymous with Christian. There was "an original Christian theology which expressed itself in Jewish, i.e., Semitic ways" (p. 20) and one might thus speak of a Jewish Christian period "which extends from the beginning of Christianity up to about the middle of the second century" (p. 21).

But Judaism at the beginning of the Christian era was far from being a monolithic religion. Among the various guises in which it appears, therefore, how are we to pick out the one we characterize as Jewish Christianity? Its characteristics, replies Daniélou (p. 19) are those of *Spätjudentum*, though he notes that this *Spätjudentum* itself appears in numerous guises, corresponding to the principal sects or types of Judaism of the period, Pharisaic, Essene, or Zealot. He leaves out of account "the influence of Philo, who presents us with a Judaism which is expressed in the categories of Greek philosophy" (p. 20). One can only admit that he is right, for it would be risky to attempt to characterize Jewish Christianity as an original and specifically Semitic phenomenon and yet allow that it took its rise from what was most Hellenized in the Jewish thought of its time. What is most arguable is to eliminate "rabbinic, legalistic Judaism, after the fall of Jerusalem," at the same time as contrasting it, in a most unexpected fashion, with Pharisaism, which is recognized as one of the major constituents of *Spätjudentum*, and which is universally regarded as rabbinic Judaism's true ancestor. Though he acknowledges that all the varieties of *Spätjudentum*, Pharisaism included, have left their mark on Jewish Christianity, and notes "a rabbinic influence even in the eastern Syriac (Aramaic speaking) churches" (p. 20), the author in practice hardly refers at all to the Talmud in order to analyze the object of his study and it is the Talmudic writings that are incontestably those of Pharisaic Judaism. So he is left with, as the only point of reference, the Judaism of the marginal bodies, Essenes and others. He is left more precisely with apocalyptic. The author warns us in the opening lines of his book: "What is peculiar to this theology is that it expresses itself in the categories of the Jewish thought of its time, that is to say, in apocalyptic terms. It is a visionary theology" (p. 2). "In this sense," he says again, "it may be said that all Jewish-Christian literature is apocalyptic, since apocalyptic constitutes its theological method" (p. 34). He describes this apocalyptic more exactly. It "was a *gnosis*. It was made up of teachings concerning the hidden things of the heavenly world and the mysteries of the future" (p. 35).

It will be appreciated both how original such an exposition is and how open to dispute. It may be thought that the definition of Jewish Christianity with which it works is at the same time too narrow and too broad. It is too narrow in that it concentrates too closely on apocalyptic thought alone, to the exclusion of other forms, which are given no more than passing mention; too broad in that Jewish Christianity thus defined is in danger of being confused, during the period in question, with ordinary Christianity, and of including within itself all Christianity's ramificatons and manifestations. It is curious that in the critical account Daniélou gives us of Jewish-Christian sources, and of sources from which information about Jewish Christianity may be recovered, he never mentions the New Testament. Are we to assume, then, that the Jewish Christian period as he envisages it did not begin until after the apostolic period? If this is true, how does he explain this massive eruption of Jewish Christian thought during a period in which already, to judge by the evidence, the immense majority of the Church's members were gentiles, whereas the preceding generation, when the leaders of the Church were themselves converts from Judaism, is not characterized as Jewish Christian? Moreover, to consider Jewish Christianity and apocalyptic as synonyms is to carry simplification to the extreme. The two terms are not coextensive. There could be apocalyptic without Jewish Christianity, and at all events there could be a Jewish Christianity that was not apocalyptist. In particular, certain characteristics which Daniélou labels as Jewish Christian could equally well be called gnostic. When we are told that apocalyptic Jewish Christianity was a kind of *gnosis*, the question implicitly raised is the formidable one of defining the origins of gnosticism.

On a more general level, it may be asked whether it really is possible to define Jewish Christianity by reference to its categories of thought alone. Judaism itself, and not only that of Alexandria, suffered in varying degrees the impress of Hellenistic thought, and that in spite of its doctrinal intransigence. It is true, and Daniélou has very effectively proved the point, that there are in the theological repertoire of the early Church expressions and themes that have affinities with one or other document of esoteric or fringe Judaism, with Qumran texts or Old Testament apocrypha or such like things, and that these affinities are close enough to prompt us to think of them as Jewish Christian. But the criterion is a difficult one to apply, to the extent that the terms referred to themselves sometimes betray evidence of influence not exclusively Jewish. For example, the theme of the two ways seems to me too ordinary, and, in different guises, of too common occurrence in ancient literature for us to draw any very precise conclusions from it. And besides, are we to consider even an author of such indubitably Jewish origin as the writer of the *Epistle of Barnabas* as a Jewish Christian, when he devotes all his efforts to distracting his readers from Synagogue observances and, pushing allegorical exegesis to its limits, goes so far as to assert that the commandments of the law never had anything other than a symbolic value, even before the time of Christ? If one follows Daniélou in answering 'yes' to this question, one will find oneself committed to the idea of a nonlegalistic Jewish Christianity, *Judenchristentum ohne gesetzliche Bindung* (see below, p. 481 n. 107) an idea I, for my part, find paradoxical and productive of confusion. One could eventually find oneself, as Daniélou virtually does (*Nouvelle Histoire de l'Eglise*, 1:162) assigning even the Marcionites to the Jewish-Christian camp.

In fact the safest criterion, if not absolutely the only one, that we have at our disposal for characterizing and defining Jewish Christianity, remains that of observance. Jewish Christianity, just like Judaism itself, was first and foremost an orthopraxy. It was distinguished by its fundamentally legalistic attitude and by its attachment to a mode of observance not merely connected with that of Judaism but quite identical with it, and which Jewish Christians retained in whole or in part. It is true that this position could be (and logically ought always to have been) accompanied by doctrinal peculiarities, such as an Adoptionist Christology, for example. It could also express itself in original categories of thought. But neither one nor the other is always or necessarily present. When they *are* present, but without the Jewish observance, they perhaps ought not without further ado to be labeled Jewish Christian. Rejection of the doctrine of the Trinity is not enough to characterize a Jewish Christian, unless we are to rank the Socinians and Unitarians as such. Or take the Puritans: neither their use of biblical language, "the language of Cansan," and the turn of mind that such usage presupposes, nor even their conception of Sunday, assimilating it to the Sabbath, is enough to make them Jewish Christians, for they had neither identity of observance nor historical connection with the Synagogue. In this connection, the question raised by Jewish Christianity as Daniélou understands it is to know whether, and if so to what extent, it has connections with the Jewish Christianity of the apostolic community. It is difficult to decide this in the absence of precise and reliable information, first, about the theological thinking of the Jerusalemites, and second, about the mission that James and the twelve were able to inspire. For the rest, all the problems relating to Jewish Christianity thus defined are outside the chronological limits of my study, since the Jewish-Christian period in the history of the early Church is essentially that of the apostolic fathers, and closes with the first apologists.

On the other hand, the problem of the continuity of Jewish Christianity between the apostolic period and the centuries following interests us directly. The question of this continuity was resolved, negatively, by J. Munck in an article I have already mentioned and discussed (p. 390). Primitive Jewish Christianity, says Munck, did not survive the destruction of Jerusalem, because the apostolic community's migration to Pella is unhistorical. The Jewish Christianity that later appears in Palestine and Syria is a new phenomenon, having no precedent and no connection with the past. This is true in particular of the community that produced the pseudo-Clementine literature (contrary to what is said by Schoeps) and for the so-called Jewish-Christian apocryphal gospels. Consequently, we may look for the origin of postapostolic Jewish Christianity in two different directions: We may look toward the Synagogue; but Munck, as we have seen, does not believe in a missionary Judaism. Or we may seek it "in a development within the Church." This, thinks Munck, is the most profitable place to search. It was gentile believers who first began to Judaize, prompted by the simple fact that the Old Testament was for them inspired scripture and by meditation on the sacred book alone. This is already true of the Galatians, who, "more zealous for the law than their Jewish-Christian apostles," were ready to accept circumcision and the observance of the entire ritual law. The same thing happened to Christians in the following generations. It is now no longer a question of the Jewish law, but of the "works" of the new law, of Christian nomism, conceived in the image of Old Testament religion. In comparison with the New Testament the Jewish Bible possessed in the eyes of second-century Christians an authority it derived from its antiquity. And the institutions of the developing

Church were naturally modeled on the ritual institutions of Israel. The new covenant was placed on the same footing as the old.

Munck, having praised Daniélou's effort, nevertheless rejects his conception of Jewish Christianity as one that, in the last resort, makes everyone a Jewish Christian just as, all too often, inquiries into gnosticism, lacking a precise definition and well-defined boundaries to their subject, include everything under the label of *gnostic*. The Church of the gentiles in the postapostolic period was Jewish Christian in the sense that its founders were Jewish-Christian apostles such as St. Paul, and that in consequence of this, it possessed a tradition that included Jewish elements, which the Church had adopted and adapted. It is indeed possible that heretical Jewish Christianity, originating in the gentile Church in the postapostolic period, could have been based not only on developments within the Church but on intercourse with the Jewish community. But in this case the contact must have been established by Christian initiative, not that of the Jews, for Judaism was never a missionary religion, whereas the Church did continue to interest itself in Judaism. But in any event the decisive factor in the genesis of postapostolic Jewish Christianity was the debate that went on within the Church about the law and the gospel.

I have said earlier what I think of Munck's ideas concerning missionary Judaism. It seems to me difficult to believe that the Synagogue played no role in the many Judaizing movements that mark the history of the early Church except a strictly passive one, like a magnet. Even if the initiative came from Christians, the Jews, or Christians of Jewish birth, would at least have encouraged Judaizing tendencies. The texts relating to Jewish proselytism quoted and analyzed in my book (if we consider none but the homilies of Chrysostom alone) suggest that conversion to Judaism was often provoked. On the other hand, I do not see (and I shall return to this subject at length) any decisive reason for denying the historicity of the migration of the first disciples to Pella, or, by the same token, of the continuity between their Jewish Christianity and that of later periods. I would on the contrary be tempted to argue that one of the consequences of this migration was precisely that a dissident Jewish sect, already existing in the region of Pella, accepted the Christian message and, amalgamating their own beliefs with the belief that Christ was Moses *redivivus*, they elaborated the peculiar body of teaching that is revealed to us in the pseudo-Clementine literature. To deny the historicity of the episode raises more problems than it solves.

But besides, even if the evidence were to show that the migration was a myth, this would still not prove that the first Jewish Christianity became extinct in A.D. 70. For we have every reason to believe that this primitive Jewish Christianity was spread outside Palestine within the apostolic period, and that in numerous ways it pushed down roots strong enough to survive the crisis. To try to explain the Galatian situation without postulating any intervention by Jewish or Jewish-Christian missionaries, to ascribe it to a spontaneous Judaizing tendency among gentile converts, is to attempt the hazardous. It is equally foolhardy to ascribe the origins of all the various forms of Jewish Christianity and all the Judaizing tendencies of the postapostolic period simply to the reading of the Old Testament. It is necessary to draw a careful distinction between two things that Munck seems sometimes to confuse: on the one hand, Judaizing movements, in the proper sense, and on the other, the tendency from which originated what is commonly called "early catholicism" (*Frükatholismus*). The latter introduced into the Church practices of a legalistic kind and ritual institutions quite similar to those of Judaism or the religion of Israel. Although a living influence from Judaism doubtless played its part in this, the movement arose essentially, as Munck says, from reflection on the Bible, from the debate about the law and the gospel, and from the conviction of the Church that it was the new Israel, in line with the old one (see above pp. 76 ff., and p. 476, n. 4). But one cannot speak here of Jewish Christianity unless it be metaphorically. True Jewish Christianity is that which held fast to ritual and legal observances in their Jewish form, and did not merely make the odd concession to legalism here and there (circumcision itself is sometimes repudiated: see E. Molland, "La circoncision, le baptême et l'autorité du décret apostolique dans les milieux judéo-chrétiens des Pseudo-Clémentines," in *Studia Theologica*, 1955, pp. 1–39). And this presupposes either contact with contemporary Jews or a historical continuity with the first generation of Christians.

Bibliography

A. ABBREVIATIONS (collections, dictionaries, periodicals)

ARW: *Archiv für Religionswissenschaft*
CIJ: *Corpus Inscriptionum Judaicarum*
CRAI: *Comptes-rendus de l'Académie des Inscriptions et Belles-Lettres*
CSEL: *Corpus Scriptorum Ecclesiasticorum Latinorum*
DA: *Dictionnaire des Antiquités grecques et romaines* (DAREMBERG-SAGLIO POTTIER)
DAC: *Dictionnaire d'Archéologie chrétienne et de liturgie*
EJ: *Encyclopaedia Judaica* (Berlin, 1928–34)
ERE: *Encyclopaedia of Religion and Ethics*
GCS: *Die griechischen christlichen Schriftsteller der ersten drei Jahrhunderte*
HTR: *Harvard Theological Review*
HUCA: *Hebrew Union College Annual*
JBL: *Journal of Biblical Literature*
JE: *Jewish Encyclopaedia*
JQR: *Jewish Quarterly Review*
JTS: *Journal of Theological Studies*
MGWJ: *Monatsschrift für Geschichte und Wissenschaft des Judentums*
NTS: *New Testament Studies*
PEFQ: *Palestine Exploration Fund Quarterly*
PG: *Patrologia, Series Graeca* (MIGNE)
PL: *Patrologia, Series Latina* (MIGNE)
PO: *Patrologia Orientalis*
PS: *Patrologia Syriaca*
RA: *Revue archéologique*
RB: *Revue biblique*
RE: *Real-Encyclopädie der klassischen Altertumswissenschaft* (PAULY-WISSOWA)
REG: *Revue des études grecques*
REJ: *Revue des études juives*
RH: *Revue historique*
RHPR: *Revue d'Histoire et de Philosophie religieuses*
RHR: *Revue de l'Histoire des Religions*
RQ: *Römische Quartalschrift*
TU: *Texte und Untersuchungen zur Geschichte der altchristlichen Literatur* (GEBHARDT-HARNACK)
ZNTW: *Zeitschrift für die neutestamentliche Wissenschaft*

B. Sources

I. *General*

1. *Scriptural*

a) Canonical

OLD TESTAMENT. *Biblia Hebraica,* ed. KITTEL, R. Stuttgart, 1937. *Septuaginta,* Ed. RAHLFS, A. 2 vols. Stuttgart, n.d.

NEW TESTAMENT. Ed. NESTLE. Stuttgart, n.d. English translation: The New English Bible. Cambridge, 1961.

b) Apocrypha and Pseudepigrapha:

CHARLES, R. H. *The Apocrypha and Pseudepigrapha of the Old Testament.* 2 vols. Oxford, 1913.

KAUTZSCH, E. *Die Apokryphen und Pseudepigraphen des Alten Testaments.* Tübingen, 1900.

HENNECKE, E. *Neutestamentliche Apokryphen*². Tübingen, 1924.

───── *Handbuch zu den N. T. Apokryphen.* Tübingen, 1904.

2. *Patristic*

The whole documentation is assembled in *PG* and *PL,* which I cite, with exceptions noted, in preference to *GCS* and *CSEL* (still in course of publication), as being more complete and more accessible.

Analytic inventory of the anti-Jewish literature: LUKYN WILLIAMS, A., *Adversus Judaeos,* (see below, under the heading *Modern Works*).

3. *Rabbinic*

MISHNAH. Ed. BEER HOLTZMANN. Giessen, 1912 and seq. English translation: DANBY, H. *The Mishnah.* Oxford, 1933.

JERUSALEM (PALESTINIAN) TALMUD. Ed. Petrokow, 1900–02. French translation: SCHWAB, M. *Le Talmud de Jérusalem.* 11 vols. Paris, 1878–90.

BABYLONIAN TALMUD. Ed. ROMM. Vilna, 1896. English translation: Ed. EPSTEIN, I. *The Talmud.* 37 vols. London, 1935–65. German translation: GOLDSCHMIDT, L. *Der babylonische Talmud.* 12 vols. Berlin, 1930–36.

TOSEPHTA. Ed. ZUCKERMANDEL. Pasewalk, 1880.

MIDRASHIM. Detailed bibliographical information in STRACK, H. *Einleitung*², pp. 195–266 and BONSIRVEN, J. *Judaïsme Palestinien,* 1 : xxix–xxx. English translation of *Midrash Rabbah:* FREEDMAN, H. and SIMON, M. 10 vols. London, 1951.

The main texts of anti-Christian polemic are collected in the works of STRACK and TRAVERS HERFORD (see below, under the heading *Modern Works*).

4. *Conciliar texts*

MANSI. *Conciliorum omnium amplissima Collectio.* 31 vols. Florence and Venice, 1795 and seq.

5. *Hagiographic literature*

Acta Sanctorum

Analecta Bollandiana

6. *Juridical texts*

Codex Theodosianus, Ed. MOMMSEN and MEYER. 2 vols. Berlin, 1903–05.

7. *Epigraphic texts*

The Christian inscriptions are here of little interest.
Jewish inscriptions: *Corpus Inscriptionum Judaicarum*, Ed. FREY, J. B. vol 1 (Europe). Rome–Paris, 1936; see the works of MONCEAUX and KLEIN, cited below.

8. *Papyrological texts*

The essential relevant documents are collected in PREISENDANZ, K., *Papyri Graecae Magicae*. 2 vols. Leipzig, 1928–31.

9. *Archaeological documents*

A comprehensive treatment of Jewish religious art and in particular of the synagogues with images in the article "Art" *JE*, and in the works of SUKENIK, ROSTOVTZEFF, WATZING and DU MESNIL DU BUISSON, cited below.

II. *Specific*

1. *Pagan texts*

The main texts relating to Judaism are collected in REINACH, T., *Textes d'auteurs grecs et romains relatifs au judaïsme*. Paris, 1895. See also FISCHER, E. and KITTEL, G., *Das antike Weltjudentum, Tatsachen, Texte, Bilder (Forschungen zur Judenfrage, 7)*. Hamburg, 1943—tendentious, to be used with caution.
JULIAN. *Contra Christianos*. Ed. NEUMANN. Leipzig, 1880; other works, ed. BIDEZ. 2 vols. Paris, 1924–32.

2. *Jewish texts*

PHILO. *Works*, with English translation by COLSON, F. H. and others. London 1929–41 (Loeb Classical Library).
JOSEPHUS. *Works*. Ed. NIESE. 7 vols. Berlin, 1896–1930. English translations: eds. H. ST. J. THACKERAY, R. MARCUS and L. H. FELDMAN. Loeb Classical Library, 1–9. London, 1926–65. WHISTON, WILLIAM. London, 1737. French translation: ed. REINACH, T. 7 vols. Paris, 1900–32.
Oracula Sibyllina. Ed. GEFFCKEN. *GCS*. Leipzig, 1912.
4 Maccabees. CHARLES, *Apocrypha*, 2, p. 653–85. French translation with introduction and notes by DUPONT-SOMMER, A. *IVᵉ Livre des Machabées*. Paris, 1939.

3. *Christian texts*

APHRAATES. *Homilies*. Syriac text and Latin translation. Ed. PARISOT, *PS*, 1 : 1–2. English translation: NEUSNER, J., *Aphrahat and Judaism*. Leiden, 1971.
Didascalia. Syriac text and English translation by GIBSON, M. D. London, 1903. Ed. FUNK, F. X. *Didascalia et Constitutiones Apostolorum* (Latin translation of the *Didascalia* in the light of the Greek text of the *Constitutiones*). 2 vols. Paderborn, 1905. German translation by ACHELIS, H. and FLEMMING, J., *TU, New Series*, 10 : 2. Leipzig, 1904.

Epistle of the Apostles. English translation: JAMES, M. R. *The Apocryphal N.T.* London, 1924, pp. 485–503.

Epistle of Barnabas. English translation: KLEIST, J. A. in Ed. QUASTEN, J. and PLUMPE, J. C. *Ancient Christian Writers.* 1948, vol. 6. Also, HEMMER, H., OGER, G. and LAURENT, A. *Doctrine des Apôtres* and *Epître de Barnabé.* Text, French translation and notes, in *Textes et documents pour l'étude historique du christianisme.* 2nd edn. Paris, 1927.

JUSTIN MARTYR. *Dialogue with Trypho.* Text, French translation and notes by ARCHAMBAULT, G. (same collection). Paris, 1909. English translation: REITH, G., in *Ante-Nicene Christian Library.* Vol., 2. Edinburgh, 1867.

IGNATIUS OF ANTIOCH and POLYCARP OF SMYRNA. *Letters.* Text, French translation and notes by LELONG, A. (same collection). 2nd edn. Paris, 1927. English translation: in *Ante-Nicene Christian Library.* Vol. 1.

EUSEBIUS. *Ecclesiastical History.* Text, French translation and notes by GRAPPIN, E. (same collection). Paris, 1905–13. English translation: LAKE, K. and OULTON, J. E. L. Loeb Classicial Library. 2 vols.

Dialogue of Athanasius and Zacchaeus and Timothy and Aquila. Ed. CONYBEARE, F. C. (*Anecdota Oxoniensia.*) London/Oxford, 1898.

HIPPOLYTUS OF ROME. *Philosophumena.* French translation with introduction and notes by SIOUVILLE, A. (*Les textes du christianisme*) Paris, 1930. English translation: MACMAHON, J. H., in *Anti-Nicene Christian Library.* Vol. 6.

Clementine Homilies. French translation, with introduction and notes by SIOUVILLE, A. (same collection). Paris, 1933. English translation: in *Ante-Nicene Christian Library.* Vol. 17.

COMMODIANUS. *Carmina.* Ed. Dombart. *CSEL* 15. Vienna, 1887.

C. MODERN WORKS

This bibliography is confined to works—books or articles—directly relevant to the subject, or which I have used constantly: in the notes, they are cited in an abridged form. Works cited only occasionally are given in the notes under their complete title (unless they are very well-known standard works); this absolves me from including them in this list.

Further bibliography will be found in STRACK, *Einleitung*[5], pp. 150–94 (Judaism at the beginning of the Christian era), BONSIRVEN, *Judaïsme Palastinien,* 1 : xxxiv–xxxviii (do.), and PARKES, *Conflict,* end of each chapter (Jewish-Christian relations).

ADLER, M. "The Emperor Julian and the Jews", *JQR,* 1983. pp. 591–651.

ALLARD, P. *Histoire des persécutions pendant les deux premiers siècles*[3], Paris, 1903.

———. *Histoire des persécutions pendant la première moitié du IIIe siècle*[3]. Paris, 1905.

———. *Les dernières persécutions du IIIe siècle*[3]. Paris, 1907.

———. *La persécution de Dioclétien*[3]. 2 vols. Paris, 1908.

BACHER, W. *Die Agada der Tannaïten.* 2 vols. Strasbourg, 1884 and 1890.

———. *Die Agada der babylonischen Amoräer.* Strasbourg, 1878.

BACHER, W. *Die Agada der palestinensischen Amoräer.* 3 vols. Strasbourg, 1892–99.

———. *Die Agada der Tannaïten und Amoräer, Bibelstellenregister.* Strasbourg, 1902.

———. "Le mot Minim dans le Talmud désigne-t-il quelquefois des chrétiens?" *REJ,* 38, 1899 : 38–46.

BATIFFOL, P. *L'Eglise naissante et le catholicisne[12].* Paris, 1927.

———. "Le judaïsme de la dispersion tendait-il à devenir une Eglise?" *RB,* 1906, pp. 197–205.

BAUER, W. *Das Leben Jesu im Zeitalter der neutestamentlichen Apokryphen.* Tübingen, 1909.

———. *Rechtgläubigkeit und Ketzerei im ältesten Christentum.* Tübingen, 1934.

BAUMSTARK, A. *Geschichte der syrischen Literatur.* Bonn, 1922.

BELL, H. IDRIS. *Jews and Christians in Egypt.* London, 1924.

BÉHARD, P. *Saint Augustin et les Juifs.* Lyon, 1913.

BERGMANN, J. *Jüdische Apologetik im neutestamentlichen Zeitalter.* Berlin, 1908.

BERTHOLET, A. *Das religionsgeschichtliche Problem des Spätjundentums.* Tübingen, 1909.

———. *Der Untergang des jüdischen Staatswesens.* Tübingen, 1910.

———. *Die Stellung der Israëliten und Juden zu den Fremden.* Berlin, 1896.

BEYER, H. W. and LIETZMANN, H. *Die jüdische Katakombe der Villa Torlonia in Rom.* (*Studien zur spätant. Kunstgesch.,* 4). Berlin, 1930.

BIALOBLOCKI, S. *Die Beziehungen des Judentums zu Proselyten und Proselytismus.* Berlin, 1930.

BIDEZ, J. *Vie de l'Empereur Julien.* Paris, 1930.

LE BLANT, E. *La controverse des chrétiens et des Juifs aux premiers siècles de l'Eglise* (*Mémoires de la Société nationale des Antiquaires de France* 6 : 7). Paris, 1898.

BLAU, L. *Das altjüdische Zauberwesen[2].* Berlin, 1914.

———. "Early Christian Archaeology from a Jewish Point of View." *HUCA,* 1926, pp. 187 ff.

BLUDAU, A. *Juden und Judenverfolgungen im alten Alexandreia.* Munster, 1906.

BLUMENKRANZ, B. *Die Judenpredigt Augustins,* Basle, 1946.

BONSIRVEN, J. *Exégèse rabbinique et exégèse paulinienne.* Paris, 1939.

———. *Le judaïsme palestinien au temps de Jésus-Christ.* 2 vols. Paris, 1934–35.

———. *Sur les ruines du Temple.* Paris, 1928.

BONWETSCH, N. *Die Schriftbeweise für die Kirche aus den Heiden als das wahre Israël bis auf Hippolyt* (*Festschrift Th. Zahn*). Leipzig, 1908.

BOUCHÉ-LECLERCQ, A. *L'intolérance religieuse et la politique.* Paris, 1911.

BOUSSET, W. *Eine jüdische Gebetssammlung im 7. Buch der apostolischen Konstitutionen.* (*Nachrichten der wissenschaftl. Akademie zu Göttingen, phil. hist. Klasse*), 1915, pp. 435–89.

———. *Jüdisch-christlicher Schulbetrieb in Alexandria und Rom.* Göttingen, 1915.

BOUSSET, W. revised by GRESSMANN, H. *Die Religion des Judentums in späthellenistischen Zeitalter[3].* Tübingen, 1926.

BRÉHIER, E. *Les idées philosophiques et religieuses de Philon d'Alexandrie[2].* Paris, 1925.

BRIERRE-NARBONNE, J.-J. *Exégèse rabbinique des prophéties messianiques.* 5 vols., Paris, 1934–36.

BRIERRE-NARBONNE, J.-J. *Le Messie souffrant dans la littérature rabbinique.* Paris, 1940.

———. *Les prophéties messianiques de l'Ancien Testament dans la littérature juive.* Paris, 1933.

BÜCHLER, A. *Die Priester und der Kultus im letzten Jahrzehnt des jerusalemischen Tempels.* Vienna, 1895.

CAUSSE, A. *Les dispersés d'Israël. Les origines de la Diaspora et son rôle dans la formation du judaïsme.* Paris, 1929.

———. *Du groupe ethnique à la communauté religieuse.* Paris, 1937.

———. "Le mythe de la nouvelle Jérusalem, du Deutéro-Esaïe à la IIIe Sibylle." *RHPR,* 1938, pp. 377–414.

COHN-WIENER, E. *Die jüdische Kunst, ihre Geschichte von den Anfängen bis zur Gegenwart.* Berlin, 1929.

COLLON, S. *Remarques sur les quartiers juifs de la Rome antique. Mélanges de l'Ecole française de Rome.* 1940, pp. 72–94.

CULLMANN, P. *Le problème littéraire et historique du roman pseudo-clémentin.* Paris, 1930.

CUMONT, F. "Essénisme et pythagorisme d'après un passage de Josèphe." *CRAI,* 1930, pp. 90 ff.

———. "Les mystères de Sabazios et le judaïsme". *CRAI,* 1906, pp. 63 ff.

———. *Religions orientales dans le paganisme romain.* 4th edn., Paris, 1906. English translation reprinted New York and London, 1956.

———. *Recherches sur le symbolisme funéraire des Romains.* Paris, 1942.

DEISMANN, A. *Bibelstudien.* Marburg, 1895.

DELATTRE, J. *Gamart ou la nécropole juive de Carthage.* Lyon, 1895.

DERENBOURG, J. *Essai sur l'histoire et la géographie de la Palestine d'après les Talmuds et les autres sources rabbiniques.* Paris, 1867.

DIETERICH, D. *Abraxas. Studien zur Religionsgeschichte des späteren Altertums.* Leipzig, 1891.

DODD, C. H. *The Bible and the Greeks.* London, 1935.

DÖLGER, F. *Sol Salutis, Gebet und Gesang im christlichen Altertum².* Münster, 1925.

DOUAIS, Ch. "Saint Augustin et le judaïsme" in *l'Université catholique,* 1896, pp. 1–25.

DUBNOW, S. M. *Weltgeschichte des jüdischen Volkes.* Vol. 3. *Vom Untergang Judäas bis zum Verfall der autonomen Zentren im Morgenlande,* German translation, Berlin, 1926; English translation, *History of the Jews,* 5 vols., South Brunswick/London, 1968–73.

DUCHESNE, L. *Histoire ancienne de l'Eglise.* 3 vols. Paris, 1906–10 (many reeditions by separate volumes).

———. "La question de la Pâque au concile de Nicée," in *Revue des questions historiques,* 1880, pp. 1–42.

DUGMORE, C. W. *The Influence of the Synagogue upon the Divine Office.* Oxford, 1944.

ELBOGEN, I. *Der jüdische Gottesdienst in seiner geschichtlichen Entwicklung²*. Frankfurt, 1924.

FLICHE, A. and MARTIN, V. *Histoire de l'Eglise* (published under the direction of):
I. LEBRETON, J. and ZEILLER, J. *L'Eglise Primitive*. Paris, 1934.
II. LEBRETON, J. and ZEILLER, J. *De la fin du IIᵉ siècle à la paix constantinienne*. Paris, 1935.
III. DE LABRIOLLE, P., BARDY, G. and PALANQUE, J.-R. *De la paix constantinienne à la mort de Théodose*. Paris, 1936.

FREIMANN, M. "Die Wortführer des Judentums in den ältesten Kontroversen zwischen Juden und Christen", *MGWJ*, 1911, pp. 555–85; 1912, pp. 49–64, 164–80.

FREY, J. B. "Les communautés juives à Rome aux premiers temps de l'Eglise", in *Recherches de Science religieuse*, 1930, pp. 289 ff.

———. "Le judaïsme à Rome aux premiers temps de l'Eglise", in *Biblica*, 1931, pp. 135 ff.

———. "La question des images chez les Juifs à la lumière des récentes découvertes," in *Biblica*, 1934, pp. 265–300.

FRIEDLÄNDER, M. *Geschichte der jüdischen Apologetik als Vorgeschichte des Christentums*. Zurich, 1903.

———. *Die religiösen Bewegungen innerhalb des Judentums im Zeitalter Jesu*. Berlin, 1905.

———. *Synagoge und Kirche in ihren Anfängen*. Berlin, 1908.

———. *Der vorchristliche jüdische Gnostizismus*. Göttingen, 1898.

FUCHS, H. *Der geistige Widerstand gegen Rom in der antiken Welt*. Berlin, 1938.

GAVIN, F. *The Jewish Antecedents of the Christian Sacraments*. London, 1928.

———. *Aphraates and the Jews*. London, 1925.

GINZBERG, L. *Die Haggada bei den Kirchenvätern*. 5 vols. 1899–1933.

GOGUEL, M. "L'Apôtre Pierre a-t-il joué un rôle personnel dans les crises de Grèce et de Galatie?" *RHPR*, 1934, pp. 461–500.

———. "Unité et diversité du christianisme primitif". *RHPR*, 1939, pp. 1–54.

———. *La Naissance du Christianisme*. Paris, 1946.

———. *La Vie de Jésus*. Paris, 1932. English translation, *The Life of Jesus*. London, 1933.

GOLDFAHN, A. "Justinus Martyr und die Agada." *MGWJ*, 1873, pp. 51 ff.

GOODENOUGH, E. R. *By Light, Light. The Mystic Gospel of Hellenistic Judaism*. New Haven: Yale University, 1935.

GRABAR, A. "Le thème religieux des fresques de la synagogue de Doura." *RHR*, 1941, 123 : 143–92; 124 : 1–35.

GRAETZ, H. *Geschichte der Juden*. Vol. 4. *Vom Untergang des jüdischen Staates bis zum Abschluss des Talmud³*. Leipzig, 1893.

GSELL, S. *Histoire ancienne de l'Afrique du Nord*. 8 vols. Paris, 1913–28.

———. *Essai sur le règne de l'empereur Domitien*. Paris, 1894.

GUIGNEBERT, Ch. *Le Christ (Bibliothèque de synthèse historique)*. Paris, 1943.

———. *Jésus* (do.). Paris, 1933. English translation, *Jesus*. London, 1935.

———. *Le Monde juif vers le temps de Jésus* (do.). Paris, 1935. English translation, *The Jewish World in the Time of Jesus*. London, 1939.

GUIGNEBERT, Ch. "Les demi-chrétiens et leur place dans l'Eglise antique."
RHR, 1923, 88 : 65–102.

HALLER, M. "La question juive pendant le premier millénaire chrétien."
RHPR, 1935, pp. 293–334.

HARRIS, Rendel. *Testimonies*, 2 vols. Cambridge, 1916–20.

HARNACK. A. v. "Die Altercatio Simonis Judaei et Theophili Christiani,
nebst Untersuchungen über die antijüdische Polemik in der alten Kirche."
TU, 1, 3, 1883.

————. *Geschichte der altchristlichen Literatur bis Eusebius:*
I. *Die Uberlieferung und der Bestand.* Leipzig, 1893.
II. *Die Chronologie.* 2 vols. Leipzig, 1897–1904.

————. "Judentum und Judenchristentum in Justins Dialog." *TU*. 39.

————. *Lehrbuch der Dogmengeschichte*⁵. 3 vols. Tübingen, 1931.

————. *Die Mission und Ausbreitung des Christentums in den ersten drei
Jahrhunderten*⁵. 2 vols. Leipzig, 1924.

HEFELE, K. J. von. *Conciliengeschichte.* 6 vols. Freiburg, 1873–90². English
translation, *A History of Christian Councils.* 5 vols. Edinburgh, 1876–96.

HEINEMANN. F. *Alljüdische Altegoristik.* Breslau, 1936.

————. "Antisemitismus." *RE, Suppl.* 5 : 3–43.

HEINISCH, P. *Der Einfluss Philos auf die älteste Exegese.* Münster, 1908.

HERFORD, P. Travers. *Christianity in Talmud and Midrash.* London, 1903.

————. *Judaism in the New Testament Period.* London, 1928.

————. *Pharisaism.* London, 1903.

————. *The Pharisees.* London, 1924.

HERING, J. "Dieu, Moïse et les Anciens." *RHPR*, 1941, pp. 192–206.

HILGENFELD, A. *Judentum und Judenchristentum.* Leipzig, 1886.

————. *Ketzergeschichte des Urchristentums.* Leipzig, 1884.

HOENNICKE, G. *Das Judenchristentum im ersten und zweiten Jahrhundert.* Berlin,
1908.

HÖLSCHER, G. *Die Geschichte der Juden in Palästina seit dem Jahre 70 n. Chr.*
Leipzig, 1909.

HOMMES, N.I. *Het Testimoniaboek, Studien over O.T. Citaten in het N. T. en bij de
Patres.* Amsterdam, 1935.

HORT, F. J. A. *Judaistic Christianity.* London, 1894.

HOPFNER. *Griechisch ägyptischer Offenbarungszauber.* Leipzig, 1921.

HULEN, A. B. "The Dialogues with the Jews as Sources for the Early Jewish
Arguments against Christianity." *JBL* 51 (1932) : 55 ff.

JOËL, M. *Blicke in die Religionsgeschichte zu Anfang des zweiten christlichen
Jahrhunderts.* 2 vols. Breslau, 1880–82.
Judaism and Christianity. Edited by W. O. E. OESTERLEY. 3 vols. London, 1937.
JUSTER, J. *Les Juifs dans l'Empire romain. Leur condition juridique, économique et
sociale.* Paris, 1914.

KAUFMANN. *Etudes d'archéologie juive. REJ*, 1886, pp. 52 ff.

KLAUSNER, J. *Der jüdische Messias und der christliche Messias.* German translation, Zürich, 1943.

———. *Jesus of Nazareth.* English translation, London, 1925.

———. *Die messianischen Vorstellungen des jüdischen Volkes im Zeitalter der Tannaim.* Berlin, 1904. English translation, *The Messianic Idea in Israel.* London, 1956.

KLEIN, G. *Der älteste christliche Katechismus und die jüdische Propagandaliteratur.* Berlin, 1909.

———. *Jüdisch-Palästinisches Corpus Inscriptionum.* Vienna-Berlin, 1920.

KNOPF, R. *Das nachapostolische Zeitalter.* Tübingen, 1905.

KOHL, H. and WATZINGER, C. *Antike Synagogen in Galiläa.* Leipzig, 1916.

KOHLER, K. *The Origins of the Synagogue and the Church.* New York, 1929.

KRAELING, C. H. "The Jewish Community at Antioch up to A.D. 600." *JBL* 51, (1932).

KRAUSS, S. "The Jews in the Works of the Church Fathers." *JQR* 5 (1893) : 122 ff., 6 : 82 ff., 225 ff.

———. "Die jüdischen Apostel." *JQR*, 1905, pp. 370–83.

———. *Das Leben Jesu nach jüdischen Quellen.* Berlin, 1902.

LABOURT, M. J. *Le christianisme dans l'Empire perse sous la dynastie sassanide.* Paris, 1904.

LABRIOLLE, P. de. *Histoire de la Littérature latine chrétienne.* Paris, 1924.

———. *La Réaction païenne. Etude sur la polémique antichrétienne du Iᵉʳ au VIᶜ siècle.* Paris, 1934.

LADEUZE, P. *L'Epître de Barnabé.* Louvain, 1900.

LAGRANGE, M. J. *Le Judaïsme avant Jésus-Christ.* Paris, 1931.

———. *Le messianisme chez les Juifs.* Paris, 1909.

LAIBLE, H. *Jesus Christus im Talmud².* Leipzig, 1900.

———. "Judaïsme." *DAC* 8 : 1 ff.

Die Lehren des Judentums nach den Quellen. Under the direction of S. Bernfeld and I. Bamberger. 3 vols. Leipzig, 1², 1928; 2² 1930; 3, 1929.

LÉVI, Isr. "Les minim dams le Talmud." *REJ* 38 (1899) : 204–10.

———. "Le prosélytisme juif." *REF* 50 (1905) : 1 ff.; 51 (1906) : 1 ff.

LÉVY, Isid. *La Légende de Pythagore de Grèce en Palestine.* Paris, 1927.

LIEBERMAN, S. *Greek in Jewish Palestine. Studies in the Life and Manners of Jewish Palestine in the II–IV Centuries C. E.* New York, 1942.

LIETZMANN, H. *Geschichte der alten Kirche.* 4 vols. Berlin-Leipzig, 1935–41; English translation, *A History of the Early Church.* London, 1950–56.

———. *Zwei Notizen zu Paulus, Sitzungsber. der Preuss. Akad.* Berlin, 1930, pp. 153–56.

LODS, A. *La religion d'Israël.* Paris, 1938.

———. *Des prophètes à Jésus. Les prophètes d'Israël et les débuts du Judaïsme.* Paris, 1935.

LODS, M. "Etudes sur les sources juives de la polémique de Celse contre les chrétiens." *RHPR*, 1941, pp. 1–31.

LOISY, A. *La Naissance du Christianisme.* Paris, 1933.

———. *La Religion d'Israël³.* Paris, 1933.

LUCAS, L. *Zur Geschichte der Juden im vierten Jahrhundert.* Berlin, 1910.
LUCIUS, E. *Die Anfänge des Heiligenkults in der christlichen Kirche.* Tübingen, 1904; French translation, *Les Origines du culte des Saints dans l'Eglise chrétienne.* Paris, 1908.

MARMORSTEIN, A. "Judaism and Christianity in the Middle of the Third Century. *HUCA,* 1935, pp. 225 ff.
———. *Juden und Judentum in der Altercatio Simonis. Theol. Tijdschrift,* 49 : 360–83.
———. *Religionsgeschichtliche Studien, I. Die Bezeichnungen für Christen und Gnostiker in Talmud und Midrasch.* Skotschau, 1910.
DU MESNIL DU BUISSON. *Les peintures de la Synagogue de Doura-Europos.* Rome, 1939.
MICHAELIS, W. "Judaistische Heidenchristen."*ZNTW,* 1931, pp. 83–89.
MIESES, M. "Les Juifs et les établissements puniques en Afrique du Nord." *REJ,* 92 : (1932) 113–35; 93 : 53–72, 135–56; 94 (1933) : 73–89.
MOLLAND, E. *The Conception of the Gospel in Alexandrian Theology.* Oslo, 1938.
MONCEAUX, P. "Les colonies juives dans l'Afrique romaine." *REJ,* 44 (1902) : 1–28.
———. "Enquête sur l'épigraphie chrétienne d'Afrique." *RA* 2 (1903) : 59–90, 240–56; 1 : (1904) 354–79.
———. *Histoire littéraire de l'Afrique chrétienne, depuis les origines jusqu'à l'invasion arabe.* 7 vols. Paris, 1901–23.
MONTEFIORE, C. *Rabbinic Literature and Gospel Teachings.* London, 1930.
———. *The Synoptic Gospels².* 2 vols. London, 1927.
MOORE, G. F. "Christian Writers on Judaism." *HTR,* 1921, pp. 198 ff.
———. *Judaism in the First Centuries of the Christian era. The Age of the Tannaim.* 3 vols. Cambridge, Mass: Harvard University, 1927–30.
MULLER, N. and BEES, N. *Die Inschriften der jüdischen Katakombe am Monteverde zu Rom.* Leipzig, 1919.
MURAWSKI, F. *Die Juden bei den Kirchenvätern und Skolastikern.* Berlin, 1925.

OESTERLEY, W. O. E. *The Jews and Judaism during the Greek Period, The Background of Christianity.* London, 1941.
———. *The Jewish Background of the Christian Liturgy.* Oxford, 1925.
OORT, H. *Der Ursprung der Blutbeschuldigung gegen die Juden.* Leipzig, 1883.
ORPHALI, G. *Capharnaüm et ses ruines.* Paris, 1922.

PALANQUE, J. R. *Saint Ambroise et l'Empire romain.* Paris, 1933.
PARKES, J. *The Conflict of the Church and the Synagogue. A Study in the Origins of Antisemitism.* London, 1934.
PERDRIZET, P. *Negotium perambulans in tenebris. Etudes de Démonologie orientale.* Strasbourg, 1923.
PETERSON, E. ΕΙΣ ΘΕΟΣ, *Epigraphische, formgeschichtliche und religionsgeschichtliche Untersuchungen.* Göttingen, 1936.
———. "Perfidia Judaica," in *Ephemerides Liturgicae,* 1936, pp. 296–311.
PUECH, A. *Histoire de la littérature grecque chrétienne.* Paris, 1928–30.

PUECH, H. Ch. *Numénius d'Apamée et les théologies orientales au second siècle.* *Mélanges Bidez,* II. Bruxelles, 1934, pp. 745–78.

REIFENBERG, A. *Denkmäler der jüdischen Antike.* Berlin, 1937.

REINACH, T. "Judaei." *DA* 3, no. 1 : 619–32.

RENAN, E. *Histoire des origines du christianisme.* 8 vols. inc. index. Paris, 1861–83 : 5 : Evangiles; 6: Eglise chrétienne; 7: Marc Aurèle.

———. *Identité originelle et séparation graduelle du judaïsme et du christianisme* (*Discours et conférences.* Paris, 1887, pp. 311–40); *Le judaïsme comme race et comme religion,* (ibid., pp. 341–74).

RICHTER G. "Uber die älteste Auseinandersetzung der syrischen Christen mit den Juden." *ZNTW,* 1936, pp. 101–14.

ROSEN, G. *Juden und Phoenizier.* Tübingen, 1929.

ROWLEY, H. G. *Israel's Mission to the World.* London, 1939.

ROSTOVTZEFF, M. *Dura Europos and Its Art.* Oxford, 1938.

SCHLATTER, D. A. *Die Tage Trajans und Hadrians.* Gütersloh, 1897.

———. *Die Theologie des Judentums nach dem Berichte des Josefus.* Gütersloh, 1932.

SCHOEPS, H. J. I. *Die Tempelzerstörung des Jahres 70 in der jüdischen Religionsgeschichte.* II. *Agadisches zur Auserwählung Israels.* III. *Symmachusstudien* (*Conjectanea Neotestamentica* by A. Fridrichsen, VI). Uppsala, 1942.

———. *Jüdisch-christliche Religionsgespräche in neunzehn Jahrhunderten.* Berlin, 1937.

SCHÜRER, E. *Geschichte des jüdischen Volkes im Zeitalter Jesu-Christi*[4]. 3 vols. Leipzig, 1901–9. English translation, *A History of the Jewish People in the Time of Jesus Christ.* 5 vols. Edinburgh, 1890–97; rev. ed., 1973–85.

SCHWARTZ, E. *Osterbetrachtungen,* ZNTW, 1906, pp. 1–33.

———. *Christliche und jüdische Ostertafeln* (*Abhandl. der königl. Gesellsch. der Wissensch. zu Göttingen. Phil. Hist. Klasse, N. Serie,* 8 : 6). Berlin, 1905.

SCHWEN, P. *Afrahat, seine Person und sein Verständnis des Christentums.* (*N. Stud. zur Gesch. der Theol.u. der Kirche.*[2]). Berlin, 1907.

SIMON, N. "Alexandre le Grand, Juif et chrétien." *RHPR,* 1941, pp. 177–91.

———. "Sur deux hérésies juives mentionnées par Justin Martyr." *RHPR,* 1938, pp. 54–56.

———. "Le judaïsme berbère dans l'Afrique ancienne." *RHPR,* 1946, pp. 1–31 and 105–45.

———. "A propos de la lettre de Claude aux Alexandrins." *Bull. de la Fac. des Lettres de Strasbourg,* 1943, pp. 175–83.

———. "Melchisédech dans la polémique entre Juifs et chrétiens et dans la légende." *RHPR,* 1937, pp. 58–93.

———. "La polémique anti-juive de S. Jean-Chrysostome et le mouvement judaïsant d'Antioche." *Mélanges Cumond.* (*Annuaire de l'Institut de Philologie et d'Histoire orientales,* 4). Bruxelles, 1936, pp. 403–29.

STAHELIN, F. *Der Antisemitismus des Altertums in seiner Entstehung und Entwicklung.* Leipzig, 1905.

STEIN, E. *Die allegorische Exegese des Philo aus Alexandreia.* Giessen, 1929.

———. *Philo und der Midrasch.* Giessen, 1931.

STRACK, H. *Einleitung in Talmud und Midrasch* (5th edn. augmented, of *Einleitung in den Talmud*). Munich, 1921. English translation, *Introduction to the Talmud and Midrash.* Philadelphia, 1931.

———. *Jesus, die Häretiker und die Christen nach den ältesten jüdischen Angaben.* Leipzig, 1910.

STRACK, H. and BILLERBECK, P. *Kommentar zum neuen Testament aus Talmud und Midrasch.* 5 vols. Munich, 1922–28.

SUKENIK, E. L. *The Ancient Synagogue of Beth Alpha.* Jerusalem, 1932.

———. *Ancient Synagogues in Palestine and Greece.* London, 1934.

———. *The Ancient Synagogue of El Hammeh.* Jerusalem, 1935.

THIEME, K. *Kirche und Synagoge.* Olten, 1945.

USENER, H. *Das Weihnachtsfest²*. Bonn, 1911.

VERNET, J. "Juifs (Controverses avec les)." *Dictionnaire de Théol. Cathol.* 8, no. 2 : 1870 ff.

VOGELSTEIN, H. and RIEGER, P. *Geschichte der Juden in Rom.* Leipzig, 1896.

VOGT, J. *Kaiser Julian und das Judentum (Morgenland,* Heft 30). Leipzig, 1939.

VOLZ, P. *Die jüdische Eschatologie von Daniel bis Akiba.* Tübingen-Leipzig, 1903; new edition revised, under the title *Die Eschatologie der jüdischen Gemeinde im neutestamentlichen Zeitalter.* Tübingen, 1934.

WATZINGER, C. *Denkmäler Palästinas.* 2 vols. Leipzig, 1933–35.

WEBER, F. *System der altsynagogalen palästinischen Theologie.* Leipzig, 1880; 2nd edition, revised under the title *Jüdische Theologie auf Grund des Talmud und verwandter Schriften.* Leipzig, 1897.

WEBER, M. *Das antike Judentum (Ges. Aufsätze sur Religionssoziologie,* 3. Leipzig, 1921.

WEBER, W. *Josephus und Vespasian. Untersuchungen zu dem jüdischen Krieg des Flavius Josephus.* Berlin-Leipzig, 1921.

WERNER, K. *Geschichte der apologetischen und polemischen Literatur in der christlichen Theologie²*. Ratisbon, 1899.

WILCKEN, U. *Zum alexandrinischen Antisemitismus. Abhandl. der Phil. Hist. Klasse der Kgl. Sächs. Ges. der Wissenschaften* 27 (1909) : pp. 781–839.

WILLIAMS. A. Lukyn. *Adversus Judaeos. A Bird's Eye View of Christian Apologiae until the Renaissance.* Cambridge, 1935.

———. *Talmudic Judaism and Christianity.* London, 1923.

WINDISCH, S. *Der Untergang Jerusalems im Urteil der Christen und Juden.* Leiden, 1914.

ZIEGLER, I. *Der Kampf zwischen Judentum und Christentum in den ersten drei christlichen Jahrhunderten.* Berlin, 1907.

ZUCKER, H. *Untersuchungen zur Organisation der Juden vom babylonischen Exil bis zum Ende des Patriarchats.* Leipzig, 1936.

SUPPLEMENTARY BIBLIOGRAPHY

This section lists books and articles mentioned in the Postscript.

ANDREOTTI, L. Review of *Verus Israel* in *Rivista di Filologia e di Istruzione Classica*, 1949.

BAER, Y. F. "Israel, the Christian Church and the Roman Empire, from the time of Septimus Severus to the Edict of Toleration of A.D. 313," in *Scripta Hierosolymitana*. Jerusalem, 1961, 7 : 79–145.

BELL, H. I. "Anti-Semitism in Alexandria." *Journal of Roman Studies*, 1941, pp. 1 ff.

BLUMENKRANZ, B. *Juifs et Chrétiens dans le Monde Occidental*. Paris-La Haye, 1960.

BOTTE, DOM BERNARD. Review of *Verus Israel*. *Bulletin de Théologie Ancienne et Médiévale*. 6 : 205.

BRANDON, S. G. F. *The Fall of Jerusalem and the Christian Church*. London, 1951; 2nd edn., 1957.

BRAUDE, W. A. *Jewish Proselytism in the First Five Centuries of the Common Era*. Providence, 1940.

BURCHARD, C. *Bibliographie zu den Handschriften vom Toten Meer*. Berlin, 1957.

CASSIN, E. *San Nicandro*. Paris, 1957; London, 1959.

DALBERT, P. *Die Theologie der hellenistisch-jüdischen Missionliteratur*. Hamburg, 1954.

DANIÉLOU, J. *Théologie du judéo-Christianisme*. Tournai, 1958.

———. and MARROU, H. *Nouvelle Histoire de l'Eglise, 1: Des Origines à Grégoire le Grand*. Paris, 1963.

DUPONT-SOMMER, A. *Les Ecrits esséniens découverts près de la Mer Morte*. Paris, 1959. English translation, *The Essene Writings from Qumran*, trans. G. Vermès. Oxford, 1961.

FERRUA, A. *Le Plitture della nuova Catacomba di Via Latina* (*Monumenti di Antichità Cristiana*, second series, 8). Vatican City, 1960.

GOODENOUGH, E. *Jewish Symbols in the Greco-Roman Period*, 13 vols. New York, 1953–68.

GOPPELT, L. *Christentum und Judentum im ersten und zweiten Jahrhundert*. Guterslöh, 1954.

GRABAR, A. "Recherches sur les sources juives de l'art paléochrétien," in *Cahiers Archeologique* 11 (1960) : 41 ff., and 12 (1962) : 115 ff.

ISAAC, J. *Jésus et Israël*. Paris, 1948.

———. *Genèse de l'Antisémitisme*. Paris, 1956.

———. *L'antisémitisme a-t-il des racines chrétiennes?* Paris, 1960.

———. *L'enseignement du mépris*. Paris, 1962.

JAUBERT, A. *La Notion d'Alliance dans le Judaïsme aux abords de l'ère chrétienne.* Paris, 1963.
JEREMIAS, J. *Jesu Verheissung für die Völker.* Stuttgart, 1956.

KITTEL, G. "Die Ausbreitung des Judentums bis zum Beginn des Mittelalters," in *Forschungen zur Judenfrage*, 5 (1941).
KUHN, K. G. "Giljonim und sifre minim," in *Judentum, Urchristentum Kirche: Festschrift für Joachim Jeremias.* Berlin, 1960.
KRAELING, C. H. *The Excavations at Dura-Europos. Final Report*, VIII, Part I, *The Synagogue.* New Haven, Conn., 1956.

LERLE, E. *Proselytenwerbung und Urchistentum.* Berlin, 1961.
LIBER, M. "L'amandier fleuri." *Cahiers de Pensée et de Vie Juives* 1, (October–November, 1949).
LIEBERMAN, S. "The Martyrs of Caesarea." *Annuaire de l'Institut de Philogie et d'Histoire Orientales et Slaves* 7 (1939–44).
LOVSKY, F. *Antisémitisme et mystère d'Israël.* Paris, 1955.

MUNCK, J. *Paulus und die Heilsgeschichte.* Copenhagen, 1954.
———. "Jewish Christianity in Post-Apostolic Times." *NTS* 6, no. 2 (1960).

NEHER-BERNSTEIN, R. "The Libel of Jewish Ass-worship." (Hebrew, with résumé in English), in *Zion, Quarterly for Research in Jewish History* 27, nos. 1–2 : 106–16.

OESTERREICHER, J. M. "Pro Perfidis Judaeis." *Cahiers Sioniens*, 1947, pp. 85–101.

POLIAKOV, L. *Histoire de l'Antisémitisme.* 3 vols. Paris, 1955–62; English translation, *The History of Anti-Semitism.* 3 vols. London, 1974–75.

SCHOEPS, H. J. *Theologie und Geschichte des Judenchristentums.* Tübingen, 1949.
———. *Urgemeinde, Judenchristentum, Gnosis.* Tübingen, 1956.
SEAVER, J. E. *Persecution of the Jews in the Roman Empire* (300–434). Lawrence, Kan., 1952.
SIMON, M. *Les Premiers Chrétiens.* Paris, 1952 (2nd edn. 1960).
———. *Les Sectes juives au temps de Jésus.* Paris, 1960.
———. Review of *Juifs et Chrétiens dans le Monde Occidental*, by B. Blumenkranz, in *Revue des Etudes Juives*, January–June 1961, pp. 167 ff.
———. *Saint Stephen and the Hellenists in the Primitive Church.* London, 1958.
———. "Remarques sur les synagogues à images de Doura et de Palestine." in *Recherches d'Histoire Judéo-Chrétienne.* Paris–La Haye, 1962, pp. 188 ff.
STERN, H. "Quelques problèmes d'iconographie paléochrétienne" in *Cahiers Archéologique*, 11 (1962) : 99 ff.

WOLFSON, H. A. *Philo, II.* Cambridge, Mass., 1947.

YOYOTTE, J. "L'Egypte ancienne et les origines de l'anti-judaïsme" *Bulletin de la Société Ernest Renan*, 1962, pp. 133 ff.

Notes

Introduction

1. For these works and all those mentioned below, see Bibliography.

2. Thus, e.g., Fliche and Martin, *Histoire de l'Eglise*, vol. 1, mention the relations of Judaism with Christianity only in a brief chapter (1:392–95) concerned with Judaeo-Christianity. It is still Renan who gives most space to the matter: *Evangiles*, pp. 64–75, 513–36; *Eglise chrétienne*, pp. 259–89.

3. Thus Lagrange, *Messianisme*, p. 298: "Judaism then adopted a radical solution as far as the Church was concerned. It simply ignored her."

4. Harnack, *Mission*, I[4], p. 18, n. 1.

5. Harnack, *Altercatio*, p. 53.

6. Duchesne, *Histoire ancienne*, I[6]: 137–38, 568.

7. So, e.g., Graetz and Dubnow in their works on the history of the Jewish people, and in the works of Ziegler and Lucas mentioned on p. ix.

8. So, recently, Blumenkranz, *Judenpredigt Augustins*.

9. Schwartz, *Ostertafeln*, p. 117, n. 1, p. 170.

10. Bousset, *Jüd. Gebetssammlung*, p. 489.

11. See, e.g., the observations by Blau, *HUCA* 1 (1924):237, and 3 (1926):169, which he summarizes thus: "Not only did there exist a pre-Talmudic Judaism, but there was also an extra-Talmudic Judaism."

12. Bousset, *Jüd. Gebetssammlung*, p. 489.

13. See especially Hoennicke, *Judenchristentum*; Oesterley, *Jewish Background*; and the summary given in *Lehren des Judentums*, 3:399–429.

14. I have not gone beyond these geographical limits. Jewish-Christian relations in the Persian empire would need a study of their own. I have availed myself, nevertheless, of the testimony of Aphraates, although he comes from beyond these boundaries. His evidence is of the first importance, and of a kind that well illuminates the religious situation in the Semitic provinces of the Roman empire.

15. The question was raised by Harnack; see p. 378.

16. For sundry attempts to date the separation, and the reservations to which they give rise, see Schoeps, *Tempelzerstörung*, p. 3, n. 6.

17. Most of the general works (e.g. Schürer) dealing with Judaism at the beginning of the Christian era agree in carrying out their inquiry up to Hadrian's war and make the break at that point.

18. See *Homélies Clémentines*, ed. Siouville, Introd. pp. 21–28. On the date of *Contra Apionem*, see ed. Budé (Reinach-Blum), Introd. p. xv.

19. This thesis of Joël, *Blicke in die Religionsgeschichte*, who asserts that there were constant connections between Judaism and the whole Church up to the end of the first century, does not stand up to scrutiny. See review in *Theol. Lit. Zeitung*, 1883, pp. 409 ff.

20. Graetz, *Geschichte* IV[3], p. 169, dates the complete break between the two religions from the time of Hadrian's war. "They were henceforth no longer rival members of one and the same family, but two separate organisms."

Chapter 1

1. Talmudic references in Renan, *Eglise chrétienne*, pp. 214–19.

2. For detail concerning the course of the two wars, see Schürer, *Geschichte*, I[4] 600–42, 670–704.

3. *Translator's note*: Not only the author's comment here, but his subsequent observation in the addenda to the second French edition have been overtaken by events. At the time of writing, the Wailing Wall is in Israeli-controlled territory.

4. Windisch, *Der Untergang Jerusalems*, p. 19. On the consequences of this event see H. J. Schoeps, *Tempelzerstörung*.

5. Syriac Apocalypse of Baruch, 3:5 ff. Kautzsch, *Apokryphen und Pseudepigraphen des A.T.*, 2:404–46. Charles, *The Apocrypha and Pseudepigrapha of the O.T.*, 2:481-526.

6. Syriac Apocalypse of Baruch 14:9.

7. 4 Ezra, 5:27-29; Kautzsch, 2:331-401; Charles, 2:561-624.

8. 4 Ezra, 6:59. On the Syriac Apocalypse of Baruch and 4 Ezra, see P. Volz, *Eschatologie*, pp. 35-48.

9. *b. Ber.*, 3a.

10. See in particular the speech he makes to the besieged: Josephus, *De Bello Judaico*, 9, 4 and 6, 2, 1. See also Agrippa's speech in 2, 16, 4.

11. *B.J.* 5, 13, 6; 7, 8, 1; 4, 3, 12.

12. *B.J.* 4, 6, 3. The prophecy referred to is one that predicts the burning of the temple "at a time when rebellion will break out and the hands of the citizens will defile the sanctuary of God." It is not clear which prophecy is meant, but Mic. 3:9-13 and Ezek. 24:9-13 are possibilities.

13. Josephus (*B.J.* 3, 8, 9) gives himself the credit for having predicted Vespasian's rise to the throne. See Dio Cassius, *Romaika*, 66, 1, 4. Jewish tradition ascribes the prophecy to Johanan ben Zakkai. It is apparent in the secular historians that Jewish Messianic ideas have been transferred to Vespasian: Suetonius, *Vesp.* 4; Tacitus, *Hist.* 5, 13. See Weber, *Josephus und Vespasian*, pp. 34 ff.

14. For example, *b. Taan.*, 29a, *b. Yoma*, 9a, *b. Bab. Mez.*, 30b, and especially *b. Shabb.*, 119b.

15. Syriac Apocalypse of Baruch 67:3ff.

16. Baruch 1:11. On the date of this work, Schürer, *Geschichte*, III[4], p. 462, and P. Volz, *Eschatologie*, p. 48.

17. Baruch 1:12.

18. Baruch 1:19-20, 21-23.

19. Baruch 4:25.

20. Baruch 4:31-33.

21. Syriac Apocalypse of Baruch 10:18.

22. See Ps. 2, in particular. Kautzsch, 2:131, Charles, pp. 631 ff.

23. Ps. Sol. 1:8. The violent diatribe of Assump. Mos. 7 fairly certainly has in mind, amongst others, the priestly caste. See the rabbinic attacks on certain priestly families; *b. Pesach.*, 57a, *T. Menach.*, 13b, Bacher, *Ag. Tann.* I[2], p. 46; see Bousset/Gressmann, *Religion des Judentums*, pp. 115 ff.

24. For some sections of the Jews at this period the separation of the highest priesthood from the monarchy, i.e., the separation of the spiritual and the temporal power, was a cardinal principle. The concentration of both powers in the hands of one man during the period of the Hasmonaeans was, to all appearances, one of the main reasons that the Hasmonaeans were opposed by the Pharisees and Essenes. This is what seems to lie behind the two Messiahs whom we find in the Qumran scrolls. The scrolls expect an eschatological priest, of the tribe of Levi, sometimes called the Messiah ben Aaron, and also a lay political leader, the Messiah of Israel.

25. A. Lods, *La Religion d'Israël*, p. 225.

26. See A. Lods, *Prophètes d'Israël*, pp. 265 ff. The message of Ezekiel, who was "one of the leaders of the priestly and ritualist movements," centres upon the restoration of the nation and its religion, and upon the restored temple. Deutero-Isaiah, without ever repudiating the

traditional institutions, expands Yahwism into a universal religion. The task of Israel, a "light to the nations" (42:1-6), is to convert the world's peoples. Both the dispersion and the suffering inflicted on "the servant of the Lord" ought to contribute to this end. Though the Jews after A.D. 70 thought especially of Ezekiel, the spirit of Deutero-Isaiah, we would argue, was by no means dead.

27. A. Causse, *Le Mythe de la nouvelle Jérusalem*, p. 397.

28. And also the people, on whom Jewish preoccupations centered. See Klausner, *Jüd. Messias*, pp. 10, 20.

29. 4 Ezra:29, 12:34, Syriac Apocalypse of Baruch 40:3. See Volz, *Eschatologie*, p. 226. Not only the reign of Messiah but his own life will come to an end within the present era.

30. Syriac Apocalypse of Baruch, 32:4, 4 Ezra, 10:25-28. Volz, *Eschatologie*, pp. 371 ff.

31. *Shemoneh 'Esre*, Vers. Palest., 14. See Bonsirven. *Jud. Palest.*, 2:145 ff. The text of the third benediction at meals is almost identical, ibid. p. 148.

32. Baruch 4:21-23.

33. Baruch 5:1-4.

34. Syriac Apocalypse of Baruch 4:2-5.

35. Syriac Apocalypse of Baruch 32:4.

36. Baruch 5:5.

37. The comparison is briefly made by Lods, *Religion d'Israël*, p. 232.

38. Syriac Apocalypse of Baruch 85:3.

39. On the simultaneous decline in priestly authority and the prestige of the temple, see Bousset/Gressmann, pp. 113-18, and Lods, *Religion d'Israël*, pp. 212-15. As Bonsirven remarks (*Jud. Palest.*, 2:110, n. 1) lack of respect for the priests did not necessarily involve lack of appreciation of the cult. Nevertheless, it is still a fact that the more individualistic form of piety that developed in the Synagogue did, in the long run, become less sympathetic to the sacrificial cult. Such conflict as there was between the two was all the sharper in that it corresponded to the rivalry between priests and scholars.

40. Guignebert, *Monde juif*, p. 79.

41. *Shemoneh 'Esre*, 16. On the restoration of the temple and its worship in the Messianic age, see Bonsirven, *Jud. Palest.*, 1:454 ff.

42. *Ant. Jud.*, 13, 5, 9; 18, 1, 2 ff. *De Bello Judaico*, 2, 8, 2-14.

43. In the Talmudic literature the Sadducees appear as the heretics par excellence. They and the hated Samaritans are spoken of in much the same terms. See Lagrange, *Judaïsme*, pp. 304-6.

44. Guignebert, *Monde juif*, p. 218.

45. On the rabbinic opposition to Bar Cochba, see Lagrange, *Messianisme*, pp. 316 ff. On their political attitudes, *Judaïsme*, p. 272.

46. Justin, *Dialogue*, 1. 3. On the identity of Trypho, see p. 173, n. 120.

47. *b. Gittin*, 56a-b.

48. *b. Hagig.*, 27a, *b. Ber.*, 55a.

49. This applies to Israel after the destruction of the temple, as it does for the gentiles all the time. *b. Bab. Bath.*, 10b.

50. *b. Sukkah*, 49b, *b. Ber.*, 32b. See *Midr, Deut. R.* (on 16:18), Wünsche, *Biblioteca rabbinica* p. 65, which very clearly subordinates sacrifices to the practice of righteousness. Sacrifices are offered only in this world; righteousness, by contrast, is practised both in this world and the next.

51. *Mishnah, Peah* I, 1.

52. *b. Menach.*, 110a.

53. *b. Shabb.*, 119b. In the same passage the destruction of Jerusalem is ascribed by a rabbi to the contempt in which the doctors of the law were held. Other texts, in particular those of Johanan bar Nappacha and his school, are cited by Schoeps, *Tempelzerstörung*, pp. 33-5.

54. This is true even allowing for the apologetic tendencies that color some modern works, reacting against the traditional discreditable picture, e.g., those of Travers Herford, Bibliog. in Schürer, *Geschichte*, II[4], p. 447. For more recent literature, Bonsirven, *Jud. Palest.*, 1:45, n. 1.

55. See Klausner's judicious comments, *Jésus de Nazareth*, pp. 312-19 (French ed.). See a curious classification of the Pharisees, partly true and partly false, in *j. Ber.* 9:6. See *Lehren des Judentums*, 5:61 ff.

56. Guignebert, *Monde juif*, p. 210.

57. Josephus, *Ant. Jud.*, 13, 10, 6: νόμιμα πολλά τινα παρέδοσαν τῷ δήμῳ οἱ Φαρισαῖοι ἐκ πατέρων διαδοχῆς ἅπερ οὐκ ἀναγέγραπται ἐν τοῖς Μωυσέως νόμοις. The rabbinic tractate *Pirqe Aboth* has exactly this aim, to demonstrate the continuity and the antiquity of the Pharisaic tradition and its right to interpret, explain and complete scripture.

58. M. Levy, *Légende de Pythagore*, p. 342.

59. For a brief account of the arguments see Guignebert, *Monde juif*, p. 226.

60. Josephus, *Ant. Jud.*, 15, 10, 4: γένος δὲ τοῦτ᾽ ἐστί διαίτῃ χρώμενον τῇ παρ᾽ Ἕλλησι ὑπὸ Πυθαγόρου καταδεδειγμένη. Amongst recent works on this question see Cumont, "Essénisme et Pythagorisme, d'après un passage de Josèphe." in *CRAI*, 1930, p. 99.

61. Josephus, *B.J.*, 2, 8, 2-13, *Ant. Jud.*, 18, 1, 5. Philo, *Quod omnis probus*, 12. See Eusebius, *Praep. Ev.*, 8, 11. The texts are cited, in French, in Lagrange, *Judaïsme*, pp. 308-17.

62. Even in the Talmudic period, when particularism was victorious, outside influences still shine through in the speculations that gave rise to the Kabbala.

63. See especially Du Mesnil du Buisson, *Les peintures de la synagogue de Doura-Europos*, and above all, Grabar, "Le thème religieux des fresques de la synagogue de Doura." *RHR*, 1941, pp. 143-92. The penetrating exegesis of the latter work, in the light of the Talmudic texts, seems to me to have provided a definitive interpretation of the frescoes.

64. The argument of Frey in *Biblica*, 1934, pp. 265-300, is not at all convincing. For a brief account and bibliography on the subject of plastic art among the Jews, see "Art", *JE*, 2:141 ff.

65. See in this connection the remarks of G. Wodtke, *ZNTW*, 1935, pp. 51-62.

66. Du Mesnil du Buisson, *Les peintures de la synagogue*, and *RB* 43 (1934):549. See *CRAI*, 1935, pp. 175 ff.

67. Josephus, *Contra Apionem*, 2, 75; see *Ant. Jud.*, 17, 6, 2; 15, 8, 1; 18, 3, 1; and *B.J.*, 1, 33, 2.

68. Beyer and Lietzmann, *Katakombe der Villa Torlonia*.

69. On these mosaics see Franklin M. Biebel, "The Mosaics of Hammam-Lif," in *Art Bulletin* 18 (1936): 541-51.

70. 4 Macc. 17:7, Dupont-Sommer edition, p. 149. Charles, 2:683.

71. Dupont-Sommer, *Quatrième Livre des Machabées*, p. 76.

72. See Orphali, *Capharnaüm et ses ruines*; Kohl and Watzinger, *Antike Synagogen*; Sukenik, *Ancient Synagogues*; Watzinger, *Denkmäler Palästinas*, 2:107-15.

73. Account by Clermont-Ganneau in *CRAI*, 1919, pp. 87-120, 298-300, and 1921, pp. 144 ff. See also Vincent in *RB*, 1919 and 1921, pp. 581 ff.

74. See Sukenik, *Ancient Synagogues*, pp. 31-35, and *Ancient Synagogue of Beth Alpha*.

75. J. W. Crowfoot, "The Discovery of a Synagogue at Jerash," *PEFQ*, 1929, pp. 211-19. See *RB*, 1930, pp. 257-65.

76. Recent studies of Jewish iconography and its symbolism have established that the sacrifice of Isaac may have been credited with expiatory and almost redemptive value, corresponding fairly closely to that which Christian thinking saw in the sacrifice on the cross. The problem is to find out whether this interpretation antedated Christianity, or whether it developed in reaction against it and under its influence. See my own study, referred to above, "Remarques sur les synagogues à images," and more recently, G. Kraetschmar, "Ein Beitrag

zur Frage nach dem Verhältnis zwischen jüdischer und christlicher Kunst in der Antike", in *Abraham, Unser Vater* (Festschrift Otto Michel) (Leyde-Cologne, 1963), pp. 317 ff. Kraetsch-mar is cautiously inclined to allow a pre-Christian origin to this interpretation of the scene as a symbol of salvation.

77. The same three episodes (Daniel, Isaac, the Flood) also appear in the Synagogue liturgy. See Sukenik, *Ancient Synagogues*, p. 65.

78. See, for example, Sarcophagus 119 from Latran (Wilpert, *I Sarcofagi Christiani antichi* (Rome, 1929), pl. IX, 3. For other representations of Noah in paintings and sculpture see the references in F. Gerke, *Die christlichen Sarkophage der vorkonstantinischen Zeit* (Berlin, 1940), p. 188, n. 1.

79. On the Noahic precepts see Bonsirven, *Jud. Palest.*, 1:251. On the idea that the obser-vance of these commands was not enough to make pagans one with the chosen people, but represented a religious charter for all humanity, outside Israel, see E. L. Dietrich, "Die 'Religion Noahs,' ihre Herkunft und ihre Bedeutung," *Zeitschrift für Religions- und Geistesgeschichte*, 1948, pp. 301-15.

80. Gen. 9:25.

81. Gen. 9:27. This verse is applied by the rabbis to the Greek translation of the Bible. "Since the words of Shem may be spoken in all the languages of Japhet, it is permissible to write the holy books in Greek." *Midr. Deut. r.*, 1:1. See p. 300.

82. Published by Sukenik, *The Ancient Synagogue of El Hammeh*.

83. This inscription provided Sukenik with a *terminus ante quem* for the date of the building, for a *novella* of A.D. 438 (*Nov. Theod.*, 3:2) excludes the Jews from all public offices, whether real or honorary. And the *Altercatio Ecclesiae et Synagogae* (*PL*, 42:1133) on the basis of this legal text says, *Judaeum esse comitem non licet.* See Juster, *Les Juifs*, 2:245, n. 4, and 249, n. 1.

84. See Rostovtzeff, *Dura-Europos and its Art*, pp. 108 ff.

85. Goodenough, *By Light, Light*, pp. 199-234.

86. Grabar has explained this iconography on the basis of rabbinic texts. If his promised proof turns out to be convincing this will be one more reason for reducing to more moderate proportions the contrast between rabbinic Judaism and the Judaism of Philo.

87. Grabar, "Le thème religieux," p. 171, n. 1, and p. 27, n. 1, suggests the identification of this picture as the Psalmist David, but does not rule out the possibility that it is a represen-tation of Orpheus himself, who "revealed the superiority of the one God of the Hebrews." Grabar gives interesting references to Hellenistic Jewish texts. Looked at in this way, Orpheus could be the symbol of proselytism. For other representations of Orpheus in Jewish art see R. Eisler, *Orphisch-Dionysische Mysteriengedanken in der christlichen Antike* (Leipzig, 1925), pp. 3-11. Eisler sees in Orpheus the mystagogue of the proselytes.

88. Sukenik, *Ancient Synagogues*, pp. 85 ff.

89. Exod. 20:4.

90. The reason for the prohibition appears more clearly in Lev. 26:1.

91. L. Blau, "Early Christian Archaeology," *HUCA*, 1926, p. 187.

92. The principle is clearly formulated in *j. Ab. Zara*, 3:8. "An object fabricated with idolatrous use specifically in mind is forbidden outright", even if it no longer serves such a purpose.

93. The infection was especially active at certain times, hence the prohibition against visit-ing pagans at their feast times. Proximity to idols and idolaters was at such times particularly dangerous. See especially, *j. Ab. Zara*, 1:1-4.

94. Sukenik, *Ancient Synagogues*, pp. 61 ff.

95. And conversely, *b. Ab. Zara*, 43b; see *j. Ab. Zara*, 3:1.

96. *j. Ab. Zara*, 3:1. This proves clearly that pictures, etc., already existed among the Jews, in secular use.

97. *j. Ab. Zara*, 3:3; *b. Ab. Zara*, 42b.

98. *j. Ab. Zara*, 3:3.

99. Ibid. R. Johanan's attitude with regard to vessels ornamented with the figures of deities is part of a substantial body of opinion among Jewish and Christian polemists. Idols and the utensils of ordinary life were seen as related, and, give or take a few little differences, interchangeable, since they were all made by human hands and of the same materials, whether common or precious. See, for example, the *Epistle to Diognetus*, 2:2-3, and also my study, "Les dieux antiques dans la pensée chrétienne," *Zeitschrift für Religions- und Geistegeschichte*, 1948, pp. 301-15.

100. *j. Ab. Zara*, 3:3.

101. *j. Ab. Zara*, 41d. This passage, quoted by Sukenik, *Ancient Synagogues*, p. 27, does not appear in the current recensions of the Talmud, from which it has been lost by homoioteleuton. It is found in a fragment from Leningrad, published by Epstein in *Tarbiz*, 3:19, p. 19. The two texts are completed by a third, from the Targum Jonathan of the Psalms, concerning Lev. 26:1. It adds to the biblical prohibition this restriction: "Pavements decorated with figures are allowed, provided that one does not bow down before these images." Quoted by Grabar, "Le thème religieux," p. 34, n. 2.

102. The rabbi in question was the initiator of the Jerusalem Talmud, and regarded as the supreme authority, even in Babylonia. See *EJ* 9:203.

103. See p. 19.

104. Jewish shopkeepers sometimes decorated their shops with pictures, etc., in order to attract customers. Strack and Billerbeck, *Kommentar*, 4, 1:387.

105. Meanwhile, there was in the synagogue at Nehardea, in Babylonia, a bust, whose precise nature is not made clear: *b. Ab. Zara*, 43b.

106. Philo (in connection with the twelve jewels on the breastpiece of the high priest) *De Spec. Leg.*, 1:5; *De Vita Mos.*, 2:9 and 2:12; *De Opif. Mundi* 38, etc.; Josephus *B.J.*, 5, 5, 5 (in connection with the candlestick, a symbol of the seven planets, and the seven loaves of the shewbread, a symbol of the signs of the Zodiac).

107. Epiphanius. *Adv. Haer.*, 16.2: εἱμαρμένη καὶ ἀστρονομία παρ' αὐτοῖς σφόδρα ἐχρημάτιξεν .... τοῖς Ἕλλησι μάτην ἀκολουθήσαντες.

108. Bousset and Gressmann, *Religion des Judentums*, pp. 321-25.

109. Sukenik, *Ancient Synagogues*, p. 63.

110. It should also be noted that in later times strict orthodoxy was not invariably characterized by hostility to images. Some mediaeval synagogues in Poland and Bohemia contain sophisticated mural paintings (Blau, "Early Christian archaeology", pp. 177 ff.). On the other hand, contemporary liberal Judaism has as far as I know remained faithful to the biblical prohibition and has not created a religious art, though the motives for this are quite different from the ones that moved the ancient lawgiver.

111. Bickermann, in *Syria*, 18 (1937):221.

112. We need not jump to the conclusion that Christian art was dependent on that of the Jews. As far as our information goes at present, they developed on parallel lines, and it is not impossible that images found acceptance in the Synagogue because of the example of Christians and in reaction against it, being prompted in part by a preoccupation with countermissionary work among the gentiles.

113. *Evangiles*, pp. 3 ff.

114. Hippolytus, *Philosophumena*, 9:26.

115. See p. 283.

116. The Pharisaic point of view is expressed by Josephus, *Contra Apionem*, 28: "The lawgiver took the most appropriate steps to prevent us either from corrupting our national customs or repulsing those who would like to follow them. Whoever desires to live under the same laws as ourselves the lawgiver receives with goodwill, for he thinks that it is not merely

race which enables men to draw near, but conformity to principles of conduct." See, on this point, H. H. Rowley, *Israel's Mission to the World* (London, 1939), and the suggestive review by Th. Preiss, *RHPR*, 1939, pp. 328 ff.

117. In spite of their feelings of superiority and a certain degree of contempt they, as holy and wise men, felt for the '*am ha-arez* they did gain the sympathy of the mass of the populace (Josephus, *Ant. Jud.*, 18, 1, 8). They felt a similar responsibility toward the *goyim*.

118. *Pirqe Aboth*, 1. 12.

119. Renan, *Evangiles*, p. 5.

120. Ibid., pp. 11–16.

121. *Shemoneh 'Esre*, 12th benediction. Text in Bonsirven, *Jud. Palest.* 2:146.

122. See H. Zucker, *Untersuchungen*, p. 143.

123. Ibid., p. 150. In Roman usage the primitive title of *nasi* appears as "ethnarch." The title "patriarch" does not appear until the fourth century.

124. See p. 453, n. 21.

125. *b. Ber.*, 17a.

126. Renan, *Evangiles*, pp. 12 ff. See *j. Gittin*, 5:9; *b. Gittin*, 61a.

127. They will be found in Strack and Billerbeck, 4, 1:384 ff.

128. *j. Ab. Zara*. 3:4.

129. *b. Sota*, 49b; *Bab. Qam.*, 82b, 83a.

130. See Vogt, *Kaiser Julian*, p. 8.

131. Certain rites of family worship, e.g., the sacrifice of the Passover lamb, which the Mosaic legislation restricts to Jerusalem, could not be carried out in the diaspora except by modifying some of the prescriptions. See p. 494, n. 76.

132. See Acts 2:5–13; Philo, *De Spec. Leg.*, 1:69; Josephus, *B.J.*, 6, 9, 3. Josephus speaks of a census at Jerusalem at the time of a pilgrimage feast which counted nearly three million people inside the city!

133. The Jews of the diaspora sometimes tried to make up for the disparity at least after they were dead, by having themselves buried in Palestine. Thus Izates of Adiabene and his mother Helen. Josephus, *Ant. Jud.*, 20, 4, 3.

134. Acts 6:1 ff.

135. Ariston of Pella, cited by Eusebius, *HE*, 4, 6, 3. See Justin, *Apol.*, 47, *Dial.*, 16, 2.

136. The prohibition seems to have fallen into desuetude after the Severides and came back with full force under Constantine, who nevertheless permitted the Jews to enter the city once a year, on condition of paying a tax. See Juster, *Les Juifs*, 2:173 ff. The situation is still attested by Jerome at the end of the fourth century (in *Soph.*, 2).

137. Vespasian's closing of the schismatic temple of Onias in Egypt had much the same effect. Josephus, *B.J.*, 7, 10, 3. It is true that the sanctuary was hardly used.

138. *Mission*, I⁴: 16.

Chapter 2

1. *Oracula Sibyllina*, 3:271.

2. *Leg. ad Gaium*, 31. See *De Vita Mos.*, 2:27.

3. *De Bello Judaico.*, 2, 16, 4. See 7, 3, 3.

4. *Ant. Jud.*, 14, 7, 2. See Reinach, *Textes*, nn. 51, 145 (Seneca, cited by Augustine, *Civ. Dei.*, 7. 11).

5. Juster, *Les Juifs*, 1:180–209.

6. A million according to Philo, *in Flacc.*, 6.

7. Juster, *Les Juifs*, 1:209. See Guignebert, *Monde juif*, p. 278.

8. Lietzmann, *Geschichte der alten Kirche*, 1:70; Beloch, *Die Bevölkerung der griech. römisch. Welt* (Leipzig, 1886), p. 246.

9. Bonsirven, *Jud. Palest.*, 1:7.

10. Leitzmann, *Geschichte der alten Kirche*, 1:70.

11. Eusebius, *HE*, 4, 2, 4, speaks of several tens of thousands of Jews massacred by Marcius Turbo.

12. According to Josephus, *B.J.*, 6, 9, 3, the Jewish War of A.D. 70 claimed over a million victims in Jerusalem. The number is doubtless exaggerated, but it must nevertheless have been considerable. Concerning 135 A.D. Dio Cassius (69, 13, 2) speaks of 580,000 dead. .

13. See Eberlin, *Les Juifs d'aujourd'hui* (Paris, 1927), pp. 208 ff. He puts the Jewish population of Palestine at eleven and a half million, as compared with fifteen to sixteen million in the world as a whole.

14. It is possible that the Jewish diaspora eventually absorbed the Phoenicians. See Rosen, *Juden und Phoenizier*.

15. Josephus *B.J.*, 7, 10, 1-2; 11, 1.

16. There was no disturbance in the diaspora in A.D. 70. When ancient authors speak of the revolt under Trajan (Orosius, 7, 27, 6) or of Hadrian's war (Dio Cassius, 69, 13, 1-2) as a worldwide conflagration, they are guilty of manifest exaggeration. In fact, though the scale of the trouble under Trajan cannot be denied, it was nevertheless confined to the east. Under Hadrian, although the anti-Jewish measures had caused tremors throughout the diaspora, the revolt itself seems to have been confined, with a few unimportant exceptions, to Palestine. Juster, 2:192 n. 2, rightly draws attention to the silence of Christian authors on the subject of rebellions in the diaspora.

17. On the date of this measure, see p. 452, n. 5.

18. *Intolérance religieuse*, p. 189.

19. Boussett/Gressmann, *Religion des Judentums*, pp. 170-72, regards the Synagogue as a product of the diaspora. This probably goes too far. The Synagogue is in the first instance a "complement" (Guignebert, *Monde juif*, p. 99) and a successor to the temple. It met a need of the Palestinian provinces also.

20. Josephus *B.J.*, 7, 6, 6; Dio Cassius, *Romaika*, 66, 7, 2.

21. See especially the *Letter of Aristeas*. While displaying his admiration for the cult at Jerusalem, the author declares that true worship consists in honoring God "not with gifts and sacrifices, but by purity of life and with pious faith" (234).

22. Lagrange, *Judaïsme*, pp. 331-37. We now know, since the Damascus Document has been discovered among the Dead Sea Scrolls, that the Community of the New Covenant was none other than the Essene sect at a particular point in its development. See Dupont-Sommer, *Les Ecrits esséniens*, pp. 129 ff.

23. See Cullmann, *Roman pseudo-clémentin*, pp. 170 ff.

24. Philo, *Quod omnis probus liber*, 75.

25. Acts 7: 46-53.

26. See, in particular, *De migr. Abrah.*, 86-105.

27. On the chronology of the Sibylline writings, see Geffcken, *Komposition und Entstehungzeit der Oracula Sibyllina* (Leipzig, 1902), and more recently, "Sibyllinische Orakel" (Rzach) *RE*, 2nd series, 2, no. 2:2103 ff.

28. *Oracula Sibyllina*, 4. 115-16.

29. Ibid., 4. 117-18.

30. Ibid., 4. 8-12.

31. Is. 66:1; see Acts 7:49 ff.

32. *Oracula Sibyllina*, 2. 82.

33. Ibid., 4. 30-34.

34. Ibid., 2. 82.

35. *Dial.*, 117:2. The discussion concerns the text of Mal. 1:10-12, in which later Christian apologetic saw a prophecy of the Eucharistic sacrifice, and which Trypho applies to the service of *proseuchai* current in the diaspora.

36. See pp. 66 ff.

37. Juvenal, *Sat.*, 14. 97; Tacitus, *Hist.*, 5. 5; for other texts of similar import (in particular, of Strabo, Hecataeus of Abdera, Celsus) see the collection by Reinach.

38. Tacitus, *Hist.*, 5. 8-9, *nulla intus deum effigies*. Tacitus forgets that he has earlier (5. 4) recounted the tale of the ass, the sacred animal whose image stands in the sanctuary at Jerusalem.

39. See p. 112.

40. *Contra Apionem*, 2. 24.

41. See p. 5.

42. Josephus (*B.J.*, 7, 5, 2) recounts a characteristic incident: when Titus, the conqueror of the Jews, passed through Antioch, the inhabitants of that city demanded that the Jews be expelled, or at least deprived of their special status. Titus refused, saying: "The homeland of the Jews, where they would have to be sent back, is in ruins, and there is no place to receive them."

43. Tacitus, *Hist.*, 2. 2; Dio Cassius, 66. 15; Suetonius, *Titus*, 7.

44. *Réaction païenne*, p. 458. The change in enlightened pagan opinion with regard to Judaism is carefully noted by Heinemann, "Antisemitismus," *RE*, Suppl. V, 36, who places it rightly in the middle of the second century. Anti-Semitism, however, survived somewhat longer in the region of Alexandria, which was the ground that most favored it. It finds expression especially in what are called the pagan *Acts of the Martyrs*, commented on by Wilcken, *Alex. Antisemitismus*. See also p. 453, n. 26.

45. Origen, *Contra Celsum*, 1. 14-17, 23, 26; 3. 1; 4. 23, 36, 41 ff.; 6. 80.

46. *Contra Celsum*, 5. 25.

47. See, on these matters, Labriolle, *Réaction païenne*, pp. 233 ff., and especially Vogt, *Kaiser Julian*, pp. 15-18, who gives texts and references; H. C. Puech, "Numénius d'Apamée."

48. See pp. 102 ff.

49. The Jews continued to live according to pagan custom. Their persistent taste for spectacle, which is attested for the first century and which survived the catastrophe, will be particularly noted. See, for example, *The Martyrdom of Polycarp*, 12. 2; Chrysostom, *Homily against the Jews*, 1. 2 (*PG*, 48. 847). St. Augustine criticizes them for it: for references see Blumenkranz, *Judenpredigt*, pp. 64 ff. Yet Herod, by constructing theatres in Palestine, caused a scandal. Josephus, *Ant. Jud.*, 15, 8, 1.

50. *Oracula Sibyllina*, 4. 80, 108, 110, 140, 143.

51. Ibid., 5. 115 ff.

52. Ibid., 4. 49-102.

53. On these anti-Roman sentiments, Fuchs, *Der geistige Widerstand*, pp. 7 ff., 30-36, 66-68.

54. *Oracula Sibyllina*, 5, 180 ff.

55. Ibid., 5. 160 ff.

56. Ibid., 5. 165 ff.

57. Ibid., 4. 136.

58. Ibid., 5. 172-74, 177 ff.

οὐκ ἔγνως, τί θεὸς δύναται τί δὲ μηχανάαται;
ἀλλ' ἔλεγες · μόνη εἰμὶ καὶ οὐδείς μ' ἐξαλαπάξει
νῦν δέ σε καὶ σοὺς πάντας ὀλεῖ θεὸς αἰὲν ὑπάρχων.
μεῖνον, ἄθεσμε, μόνη, πυρὶ δὲ φλεγέθοντι μιγεῖσα
Ταρτάρεον οἴκησον ἐς Ἅιδου χῶρον ἄθεσμον.

59. On anti-Roman reactions in Greece and in the east, Fuchs, *Der geistige Widerstand*, especially pp. 2-8, 28-36.
60. *Oracula Sibyllina*, 5. 192.
61. Ibid., 5. 65 ff. ὥστε νοῆσαι αὐτὴν ἀίδιον θεὸν ἄμβροτον ἐν νεφέεσσιν.
62. Ibid., 5. 249.
63. Ibid., 5. 260-68.
64. Ibid., 5. 426 ff.
65. Ibid., 5. 493 ff.
66. On this point Blass, in Kautzsch, *Pseudepigraphen des A.T.*., p. 183, and Schürer, *Geschichte* III⁴, p. 582, n. 174.
67. *Oracula Sibyllina*, 4. 161-67.
68. Ibid., 4. 178-90.
69. See p. 279.
70. *Oracula Sibyllina*, 5. 497-500:
θεὸν ἄφθιτον ἐξυμνοῦντες
αὐτὸν τὸν γενετῆρα, τὸν ἀίδιον γεγαῶτα,
τὸν πρύτανιν πάντων, τὸν ἀληθέα, τὸν βασιλῆα,
ψυχοτρόφον γενετῆρα, θεὸν μέγαν αἰὲν ἐόντα.
71. Dupont-Sommer, *Quatrième Livre des Machabées*, pp. 75 ff.
72. Ibid., pp. 20-25 and 67-75.
73. 4 Macc. 1:1.
74. Ibid., 1:16.
75. Ibid., 1:1, 7:16, 13:1, 15, 20, 16:1, 18:2.
76. Dupont-Sommer, *Quatrième Livre des Machabées*, p. 35.
77. 4 Macc. 1:17.
78. Dupont-Sommer, *Quatrième Livre des Machabées*, p. 38.
79. 4. Macc. 2:23. On the Jewish interpretation of the idea of law, see Guignebert, *Monde juif*, pp. 83 ff.
80. 4 Macc. 5:25, Dupont-Sommer, *Quatrième Livre des Machabées*, p. 39. On this agreement between revealed law and natural law in ancient Christian and Jewish thought, Molland, *Conception of the Gospel in Alexandrian Theology*, pp. 16-19.
81. Dupont-Sommer, *Quatrième Livre des Machabées*, p. 40.
82. Ibid., pp. 45-46.
83. 4 Macc. 17:5.
84. 4 Macc. 14:7 ff. Dupont-Sommer, *Quatrième Livre des Machabées*, p. 47, n. 29.
85. 4 Macc. 2:22.
86. Ibid., 2:13 ff. For this analysis of virtue, Dupont-Sommer, *Quatrième Livre des Machabées*, pp. 48-56.
87. 4 Macc. 5:26. This is a rationalizing interpretation of the dietary laws, on the basis of the rules of health. It is found among certain Christian authors; thus Augustine, *Contra Faust.*, 32. 13. See p. 335.
88. On these similarities and peculiarities, Dupont-Sommer, *Quatrième Livre des Machabées*, Index, s.v. Philon. See also his *Philon d'Alexandrie*, p. 186.
89. *Hom.*, 4-6.
90. This is what we should infer from the part played by Apion and Annubion, who are both Egyptians. Cullmann, *Roman pseudo-Clémentin*, p. 130.
91. *Hom.*, 5. 28.
92. *Hom.*, 4. 13.
93. *Hom.*, 5. 26.
94. *Hom.*, 5. 23.
95. *Hom.*, 5. 25.

96. *Hom.*, 4. 22.

97. See p. xv.

98. Bousset, in *Theol. Lit. Zeitung*, 1915, p. 296.

99. C. Schmidt, *Studien zu den Ps. Klem.*, 1929, p. 112; Cullman, *Roman pseudo-Clémentin*, p. 131.

100. One might even guess that the writing appeared during or immediately after Hadrian's war, as an answer to the upsurge of anti-Semitism to which it may have given rise in the region of Alexandria. Apion was perhaps at that time enjoying a renewed popularity, and the writing sets out to show that there was no necessary connection between Judaism and the Palestinian nationalist revolt. See also the analyses by Goodenough. *Jewish Symbols*, 2:26 ff., and H.-J. Leon, *The Jews of Ancient Rome* (Philadelphia, 1960), pp. 211 ff. Leon also gives good descriptions of the various Jewish catacombs in Rome, and, in an appendix, a list of the Jewish inscriptions in the city, an improvement and expansion of that of Frey.

101. "Un fragment de sarcophage judéo-païen," *RA* 2 (1916): 1-6. The work is reproduced, "with necessary additions and corrections," in *Recherches sur le symbolisme funéraire des Romains* (Paris, 1942), pp. 484-96. References to other works on the sarcophagus on p. 484, n. 2.

102. Philo, *De Vita Mos.*, 2:9. See Josephus *B.J.*, 5, 5, 5, and Bousset, *Schulbetreib*, pp. 30 ff.

103. What makes this sarcophagus exceptional from the point of view of Jewish art "is that the figures are carved in relief" (Cumont, *Symbolisme*, p. 486, n. 2).

104. F. Cumont, *Symbolisme funéraire*, p. 496, n. 2.

105. See p. 354.

106. Cumont, *Symbolisme*, p. 495. Frey, *CIJ*, 1:306.

107. Cumont, *Symbolisme*, pp. 496-98. The cover in question could alternatively (ibid., p. 498) be one from a pagan sarcophagus that has found its way into the catacomb.

108. Ibid., p. 494, n. 1.

109. Ibid., p. 492. See N. Müller, *Katakombe am Monteverde*, and "Katakomben" in *EJ* 9:1041.

110. The same may be said of the interesting epitaph of Regina (Frey, *CIJ* 1:476) which also comes from Monteverde and which dates either from the beginning of the second century (Frey) or, with perhaps more probability, from the first (Cumont, p. 492, n. 5). See also Leon, *The Jews of Ancient Rome*, p. 134 ff, and especially pp. 248 ff.

111. Except that it seems to have extinguished the Messianic hope. The vein of apocalyptic was worked out and Messianism ceased actively to manifest itself.

112. Texts in *PG* 1:1024-35. Funk, *Didascalia et Const. Ap.*, 1: pp. 425-39.

113. W. Bousset, "Jüd. Gebetssammlung", *Götting. Nachr.*, 1915, pp. 435-89.

114. On these two prayers and their origin, Elbogen, *Jüd. Gottesdienst*, pp. 17, 27 ff., 248.

115. On the origin of the *Qedushah*, ibid., pp. 61 ff.

116. *Const. Ap.*, 7, 36, 1.

117. Bousset, "Jüd. Gebetssamlung," p. 447.

118. *De Spec. Leg.*, 2, 39 ff.

119. *Const. Ap.*, 7, 36, 4: διὰ τοῦτο ἑβδομὰς μία καὶ ἑβδομάδες ἑπτὰ καὶ μὴν ἕβδομος καὶ ἐνιαυτὸς ἕβδομος καὶ τούτου κατὰ ἀνακύκλησιν ἔτος πεντηκοστὸν εἰς ἄφεσιν.

120. Ibid., 7, 37, 1: καὶ ἐλεήσας τὴν Σιὼν καὶ οἰκτειρήσας τὴν Ἰερουσαλήμ τῷ τὸν θρόνον Δαυὶδ τοῦ παιδός σου ἀνυψ ῶσαι ἐν μέσῳ αὐτῆς.

121. *Const. Ap.*, 8, 12, 6 ff.

122. Ibid., 7, 33, 2.

123. *Const. Ap.*, 7, 33, 7. The expression "king of Gods" seems to be borrowed from an apocryphal addition to Esther (14:12 in the Vulgate) that is doubtless of Hellenistic origin, being absent from the Hebrew text. It was known already to Josephus. Schürer *Geschichte*, III[4], p. 449.

124. *Const. Ap.*, 7, 39. The beginning of the book (2-21) reproduces in expanded form the *Didache*, whose first part, the doctrine of the two ways, is also of Jewish origin.

125. See Schürer, *Geschichte*, III⁴, pp. 435-39.

126. *Const. Ap.*, 7, 33, 4.

127. Ibid., 7, 35, 4.

128. Ibid., 7, 34, 7: Παρακούσαντα δὲ τὸν ἄνθρωπον οὐκ εἰς τὸ παντελὲς ἀφανίσας ἀλλὰ χρόνῳ πρὸς ὀλίγον αὐτὸν κοιμίσας ὅρκῳ εἰς παλιγγενεσίαν ἐκάλεσας.

129. *Const. Ap.*, 7, 34, 6: καὶ τέλος τῆς δημιουργίας τὸ λογικὸν ζῷον, τὸν κοσμοπολίτην.

130. Ἑαυτοῦ πατρίδα εἶναι νομίζων. Philo, *De Spec. Leg.*, 1. 97; see 1. 210.

131. *Const. Ap.*, 7, 37.

132. Ibid., 7, 33, 2.

133. Ibid., 7, 36, 1.

134. Ibid., 8, 12, 17: τὴν λογικὴν διάγνωσιν, εὐσεβείας καὶ ἀσεβείας διάκρισιν καὶ ἀδίκου παρατήρησιν.

135. *Const. Ap.*, 7, 33, 3: ὑποδείξας δὲ ἑκάστῳ τῶν ἀνθρώπων, διὰ τῆς ἐμφύτου γνώσεως καὶ φυσικῆς κρίσεως καὶ ἐκ τῆς τοῦ νόμου ὑποφωνήσεως.

136. *Const. Ap.*, 7, 39, 2.

137. Ibid., 7, 35, 10.

138. Ibid., 7, 35, 9.

139. Ibid., 7, 33, 4.

140. Bousset, "Jüd. Gebetssammlung," p. 487.

141. There are still closer affinities, perhaps, with Christian Alexandrian thought, particularly with that of Clement, who has the same basic approach, and stands within the Jewish speculative tradition represented by Philo. See on this subject, Bousset, *Jüdisch-christlicher Schulbetrieb*, especially pp. 248 ff.

142. Bousset, "Jüd.Gebessammlung," p. 487.

143. On these ideas, Bousset/Gressmann, *Religion*, pp. 315 ff., 346 ff.; Bonsirven, *Jud. Palest.*, 1:212 ff. The law itself, which is identified with Wisdom in some of the wisdom literature (e.g., Ben Sira 24:7 ff.) tends in some rabbinic speculative writings to take on the character of a hypostasis. Bonsirven. *Jud. Palest.*, 1:165, 213 ff., 249 ff.

144. See p. 345.

145. *Const. Ap.*, 7, 36.

146. See *j. Meg.* I. 11, *j. Kidd.*, I. 1.

147. See p. 299.

148. Philo, *De Vita Mos.*, 2. 7.

149. Schürer, *Geschichte*, III⁴, p. 424.

150. Already in Origen's time Aquila enjoyed the preference of the Jews (*Ep. ad Afric.* 2): φιλοτιμότερον πεπιστευμένος παρὰ Ἰουδαίοις ἡρμηνευκέναι τὴν γραφὴν · ᾧ μάλιστα εἰώθασιν οἱ ἀγνοοῦντες τὴν Ἑβραίων διάλεκτον χρῆσθαι ὡς πάντων μᾶλλον ἐπιτετευγμένῳ.

151. *Const. Ap.*, 7, 33, 4.

152. In the review of my book printed in *Revue des Etudes Grecques* (1949), pp. 482-4, Festugière refers to a number of Hellenistic religious texts, from the Hermetic literature in particular, which offer striking parallels wth the Jewish texts I have quoted. They seem to him to confirm my opinion of the "largely open character of Hellenistic Judaism" even after A.D. 70.

153. See p. 17.

154. See Juster *Les Juifs* 1:391-99, and especially the more recent work of Zucker, *Untersuchungen*, pp. 142-66.

155. Zucker, *Untersuchungen*, p. 151, expresses the contrary view. Frey, by contrast (*CIJ*, pp. CIX ff.) is too anxious to minimize the Patriarch's authority in the diaspora, describing it as "more nominal than actual," and "being primarily liturgical in character" perhaps. The

fact remains that as far as Rome was concerned the Patriarch represented Judaism. There is nothing surprising in the fact that he is not mentioned in the epigraphical texts, which are nearly all funerary inscriptions. Catholics do not often mention the Pope on their tombstones.

156. Juster, *Les Juifs dans l'Empire romain*, 1 : 393.

157. This underlies once more the essentially religious nature of the Jewish community in Roman eyes. The principle goes back as far as the edict of Lenticulus, which absolves Jews who are Roman citizens from military service, provided that they are practising Jews: πολίτας ῾Ρωμαίων ᾽Ιουδαίους ἱερὰ ἰουδαϊκὰ ἔχοντας καὶ ποιοῦντας. Josephus, *Ant. Jud.*, 14, 10, 13. A proselyte was able to take advantage of this provision, but not an Israelite known to be nonpracticing, or excommunicated.

158. Zucker, *Untersuchungen*, pp. 120–41.

159. Juster, *Les Juifs*, 1 : 388–90. The institution continued as long as the patriarchate. Eusebius, *in Is.*, 18, 1 (*PG*, 24, 213) and Epiphanius, *Haer.*, 1, 30, 3 (*PG*, 41, 409).

160. For approval of the term, Bousset/Gressman, *Religion*; in particular pp. 3, 56–60, and especially 76 ff. and 95 ff. Similarly, Causse, *Du groupe ethnique à la communauté religieuse*, especially last chapter, pp. 318 ff. For disapproval, Batiffol, "Le judaisme de la dispersion tendait-il à devenir une église?", *RB*, 1906, pp. 197–205, and, by the same author, *L'église naissante et la catholicisme*, pp. 1–20. Similarly, Lagrange, *Judaïsme*, pp. 239 ff. Finally, on this question, see Lods, "Les antécédents de la notion d'Eglise en Israël et dans le judaïsme", *Origine et nature de l'Eglise* (conférences à la faculté libre de théologie protestante de Paris) (Paris, 1939), pp. 9–50.

161. References in Bonsirven, *Jud. Palest.*, 1 : 31. See p. 277.

162. Preiss, review of H. H. Rowley, *Israel's Mission in the World*, in RHPR, 1939, pp. 330 ff. On the reservations this judgment calls for, see p. 380.

Chapter 3

1. Sulpicius Severus. *Chron.*, 2, 3, 6 (*PL*, 20. 146). That the passage is borrowed from Tacitus is not very likely. See Schürer, *Geschichte*, 1 : 631, n. 115. That Titus is credited with a declaration of war on Christianity is due to apologetic interests: it is to show that Christianity was proof against all trials. See, already, Origen, *Hom. in Jos.*, 19. 10: *Convenerunt enim reges terrae, senatus populusque et principes Romani, ut expugnarent nomen Jesu et Israël simul. Decreverunt enim legibus suis, ut non sint Christiani. Sed sicut tunc omnes illi reges convenientes contra Jesum nihil facere potuerunt, ita . . . ut non Christianorum genus latius ac profusius propagetur, obtinere non valebunt.*

2. To say as Batiffol does (*Eglise naissante*, p. 184) that "the destruction of the temple in A.D. 70 did not affect the gentile Christian communities because Jerusalem had nothing to do with their faith," is to look at the question in too narrow a way, for the existence of Jerusalem was a concrete witness to the continued survival of the chosen people.

3. The Jewish-Christian gospels do not help us here.

4. Eusebius, *HE*, 3, 5, 3. Doubt has been cast on the historicity of the flight to Pella, but the arguments used do not seem to me to be convincing (S. G. F. Brandon, *Fall of Jerusalem*, pp. 168 ff.). Brandon says: "It would appear on *a priori* grounds very improbable that pious Jews, such as we have every reason for believing the Jerusalem Christians to have been, should have chosen so thoroughly Gentile a centre for refuge." He thus assumes that the Christian community was in agreement on all points with its fellow Jews, and with the nationalists in particular. But this is far from being proved. If, on the contrary, we concede that there was for the first disciples some danger in remaining at Jerusalem the migration becomes not at

all improbable. And in such circumstances what better place to migrate to than a gentile city? The Essenes did just the same when they sought refuge in Damascus. The existence in after years of strict Jewish-Christian communities in Pella and the surrounding region is an attested fact. And if we allow, as seems likely, that at least some elements in these communities originated in Palestine proper, then the period of the war provides the most probable date for their migration, unless (and this is an equally probable theory) they left Jerusalem before the opening of hostilities, after the execution of James the brother of Jesus and under threat of eventual persecution.

5. See Hennecke, *N.T. Apokryphen*, p. 29.

6. Hoennicke, *Judenchristentum*, p. 242.

7. Mark 13:14, 26. The parallel verses in Matt. 24:15 and Luke 21:20 provide interesting differences in the description of the disaster.

8. Justin, *Apol.*, 1. 31.

9. See p. 263.

10. Justin, *Apol.*, 1. 47. Other references in Renan, *Eglise chrétienne*, p. 221, n. 1.

11. Eusebius, *HE*, 4, 6, 4; see 5, 12, 1.

12. See in this connection, Schoeps, *Tempelzerstörung*, pp. 2-8.

13. More commonplace considerations may also have played their part. The Christians stood to gain by distinguishing themselves clearly from the Jews at a time when Israel was the object of animosity, and also subject to the *fiscus judaicus*. Joël, *Blicke*, 2:86.

14. *HE*, 2, 23, 19.

15. *HE*, 1, 1, 2; 2, 6, 8; 3, 6, 28.

16. *Adv. Jud.*, 13 (*PL*, 2. 678).

17. *Contra Celsum*, 1, 47.

18. Ibid., 4, 22 (*PG*, 11. 1060).

19. It is expressed strikingly by Sulpicius Severus. *Quotidie mundo testimonio sunt (Judaei) non ob aliud eos quam ob illatas Christo impias manus fuisse punitos* (*Chron.*, 2. 30, *PL*, 20. 146).

20. On the thorny problem of its date it seems to be impossible to reach certainty. To me it seems most probable that it should be placed in Hadrian's reign, and more likely after 135 than before. See H. Windisch, *Barnabasbrief* (*HNT*) (1980), p. 412, Leitzmann, *Geschichte*, 1:232.

21. Justin, *Apol.*, 1. 53 and 54.

22. *Comm. in Joh.*, 1. 2 (*PG*, 14. 24).

23. The Epistle of Barnabas is typical. It bears clear testimony (Windisch, *Barnabasbrief*, p. 232) to an already effective split, rather than helping to produce one. But if in this sense it marks the end of a period, the postapostolic period, it at the same time inaugurates the age of anti-Jewish controversy. As has already happened in the Epistle to the Hebrews, Judaism no longer poses a problem *inside* the Church: it continues to pose one *for* the Church, from outside.

24. Leitzmann, *Geschichte*, 1:234.

25. The Christians seem to have borrowed from the clientele of the Synagogue the title θεοσεβεῖς, which they sometimes gave themselves: ἡμᾶς, τοὺς θεοσεβεῖς καὶ χριστιανοὺς καλουμένους (Theophilus of Antioch, *Ad Autol.*, 3. 4 (*PG*, 7. 1125).

26. On this point, see J. H. Koole, *De Overname van het Oude Testament door de christelijke Kerk* (Hilversum, 1938).

27. Quoted by Irenaeus, 4, 6, 2; see Eusebius, *HE*, 4, 18, 9.

28. In Augustine, for example, anti-Jewish polemic and anti-gnostic polemic are conditioned by each other. See Blumenkranz, *Judenpredigt*, pp. 137 ff.

29. Thus for example, Origen (*Contra Celsum*, 4. 8). Replying to Celsus's criticisms he subscribes unreservedly to the statement in Deut. 32:9, "For the Lord's portion is his people."

30. Legal observances have a meaning that is primarily, though not exclusively, pre-figurative. They have only become void since the coming of Christ. Taking them as a whole, the fathers seem to subscribe, as far as Israel's past is concerned, to Philo's point of view. Though he allegorizes the ritual law, Philo condemns those who, in the name of allegorizing, rid themselves of its practice (*De Migr. Abrah.*, 88-95). Thus Tertullian, *De Idol.*, 14 (*PL*, 1, 682): *Nobis, quibus sabbata extranea sunt et neomeniae et feriae a Deo aliquando dilectae.*

31. Epiphanius, *Haer.*, 33. 3-7 (*PG*, 41. 557-68). See J. Héring, "Dieu, Moïse et les anciens", *RHPR*, 1941, pp. 192-206, and Harnack, in *Sitzungsber. des Preuss. Ak.*, 1901, pp. 507-45.

32. Even with this category the author establishes a hierarchy among the commandments.

33. Justin, *Dial.*, 30. 1. See Epiphanius's refutation of Ptolemy's thesis (*Haer.*, 33. 9—*PG*, 41. 572 ff.): ὅ δε ἔγραψε Μωυσῆς, οὐκ ἐκτὸς βουλήσεως θεοῦ ἔγραψεν · ἀλλὰ ἐκ Πνεύματος ἀγίου ἐνομοθέτησε, καὶ ὅτι μὲν νομοθεσία ἐστι, τοῦτο δῆλον.

34. *Barnabas*, 4. 6; see Justin, *Dial.*, 19. 2.

35. Augustine, *Enarr. in Ps.*, 56. 9 (*PL*, 36. 666).

36. Some authors see scripture as the common patrimony of Israel and the Church. Thus Origen, *Contra Celsum*, 2. 58. (*PG*, 11. 889): τὰ δὲ τῶν κοινῶν ὑμῶν πρὸς ἡμᾶς γραφῶν ἐν αἷς οὐκ ὑμεῖς μόνον, καὶ ἡμεῖς σεμνυνόμεθα. The contrast with Barnabas is thus more formal than real, for the Jews read without understanding. *Contra Celsum*, 2. 76 (*PG*, 11. 913): see *Hom. in Jer.*, 14. 12 (*PG*, 13. 417): ἔχουσι γὰρ τὰ βιβλία . . . ὁ νοῦς τῶν γραφῶν ἤρθη ἀπ' αὐτῶν.

37. See Augustine, *Contra adv. Leg. et Proph.*, 1, 17, 35 (*PL*, 42, 623): *Quia et Novum in Vetere est figuratum, et Vetus in Novo est revelatum.* Other references in Blumenkranz, *Judenpredigt*, p. 123, n. 3.

38. And the Jews posed the question, *Aliquid se dicere existimant, cum requirunt a nobis quomodo accipiamus auctoritatem legis et prophetarum, cum sacramenta non observemus quae ibi praecepta sunt* (Augustine, *Adv. Jud.*, 5. 6; *PL*, 42, 54).

39. It is not so much a matter of tracing an evolution in time as a logical progression. In fact, the different viewpoints are often found interwoven in the same author. Harnack has well remarked (*Mission*, I⁴, p. 259). *Das Evangelium wurde als das vollendete Judentum, als eine neue Religion und als die wiederhergestellte und auf einem abschliessenden Ausdruck gebrachte Urreligion zugleich verkündigt, und zwar war es nicht nur ein einzelner, dialektisch veranlagter Missionar, der es in dieser dreifachen Gestalt predigte, sondern diese Darstellung trat in allen ausführlicheren Missionspredigten mehr oder minder deutlich hervor.*

40. On the Jerusalemite community, see, alternatively, Guignebert, *Le Christ*, Part I.

41. Acts 6-7.

42. Gal. 3:24.

43. Rom. 10:4.

44. *Homily against the Jews*, 2:2 (*PG*, 48, 860).

45. Ibid.. loc. cit. On the metaphor of the Law as a tutor, see also Clement of Alexandria, *Strom.*, 1, 28, 3; 2, 35, 2; 7, 86, 3; *Praed.*, 1, 59, 1; 93, 3.

46. Rom. 7:6.

47. Gal. 3:25 ff.

48. John 1:17.

49. Heb. 7:19.

50. *Magn.*, 9:1.

51. It is "spiritual" (πνευματικός), Rom. 7:14. See Boussett/Gressmann, *Religion*, p. 121.

52. Rom. 7:12.

53. Rom. 7:7.

54. Rom. 6-7. "Sin will no longer dominate your life, since you are living by grace and not by law" (6:14).

55. Gal. 3:19 ff.

56. This point of view is explained in Rom. 6:15 ff.: "Does the fact that we are living by grace and not by law mean that we are free of sin? Of course not. . . . You may have been freed from the slavery of sin, but only to become 'slaves' of righteousness."

57. Rom. 2. See v. 14, "When gentiles who have not the law do by nature what the law requires, they are a law to themselves, even though they do not have the law. They show that what the law requires is written on their hearts."

58. James 2:26.

59. Nevertheless, however deeply it may be soaked in Jewish ideas, the epistle is not a Jewish Christian document. See Leitzmann, *Geschichte*, 1:212.

60. It finds its classical expression in Clement of Rome, for whom the message of Christ comes to crown the moral teaching of the Jewish law. Clement is here drawing heavily on the moral teaching of the Hellenistic Synagogue. See, for example, *I Clem.* 33 ff. on the necessity of good works.

61. Matt. 5:39.

62. Matt. 5:27 ff.

63. This way of looking at the matter is well brought out by Clement of Alexandria. See Molland, *The Gospel in Alexandrian Theology*, p. 26. Similarly Irenaeus, 4, 13, 1: *Dominus naturalia legis, per quae homo justificatur, non dissolvit sed extendit et implevit.*

64. Christ is sometimes described as a lawgiver. ὁ καινὸς νομοθέτης (Justin, *Dial.*, 18). See, already, St Paul, Gal. 6:2: νόμος τοῦ χριστοῦ.

65. Thus, for Clement of Alexandria, the unity of the old law and the new proceeds from the fact that both are given by the Logos, the former through the intermediary Moses (ὑπὸ μὲν τοῦ Λόγου, διὰ Μωυσέως δὲ τοῦ θεράποντος αὐτοῦ. *Paed.*, 1, 60, 1), the latter directly, by the incarnate Christ. Clement can thus go so far as to identify the law with the Christ-Logos (*Paed.*, 1, 9, 4; *Strom.*, 1, 182, 3; 2, 68, 2). In this optimistic interpretation of the law, the opposition between law and grace disappears. The law is χάρις παλαιά (*Paed.*, 1, 60, 1). For detailed account see Molland, *Alexandrian Theology*, pp. 18 ff.

66. See Justin, *Dial.*, 11. 2. "For I have read that there shall be a final law, the chiefest of all, which is now incumbent on all men to observe. . . . Now law placed against law has abrogated that which is before it, and a covenant which comes after in like manner has put an end to the previous one."

67. Aphraates, *Hom.*, 11. 11.

68. James 1:25.

69. Barnabas 2:6.

70. It is in the name of the law of Christ that Jewish ritual law is forbidden to Christians. Thus Socrates, *HE*, 5, 22 (*PG*, 67, 625). Ἰουδαΐζειν γὰρ χριστιανοῖς οὐδὲ εἷς τοῦ χριστοῦ νόμος ἐπέτρεψεν.

71. Heb. 7:11 ff.

72. Is. 2:3. Tertullian, *Adv. Jud.*, 3 (*PL*, 2. 642).

73. Tertullian, *Adv. Jud.*, (*PL*, 2. 643).

74. Tertullian, *Adv. Jud.*, 3 (*PL*, 2. 643 ff.).

75. Gen. 25:3.

76. Tertullian, *Adv. Jud.*, (*PL*, 2. 636).

77. Ibid.

78. Rom. 11:25–32.

79. See, for example, Theophilus of Antioch, *Ad Autol.*, 3. 4 (*PG*, 6. 1125): ἀλλὰ καὶ ὡς προσφάτου ὁδεύνοντος τοῦ καθ᾽ ἡμᾶς λόγου. Eusebius, *Praep. Ev.*, 1. 2, referring to an opponent who is doubtless to be identified as Porphyry: καὶ μηδ᾽ αὐτῷ τῷ παρὰ Ἰουδαίοις τιμωμένῳ θεῷ κατὰ τὰ παρ᾽ αὐτοῖς προσανέχειν νόμιμα καινὴν δὲ τινὰ καὶ ἐρήμην ἀνοδίαν ἑαυτοῖς συντεμεῖν μήτε τὰ Ἑλλήνων μήτε τὰ Ἰουδαίων φυλάττουσαν. Other texts referred to by Harnack in *Mission*, I⁴, pp. 280–89.

80. See p. 110.

81. Julian was shocked at such pretensions (*Contra Christianos*, Neumann's edn., p. 210): πρὸς μὲν νυνὶ Ἰουδαίους διαφέρεσθαί φασιν, εἶναι δὲ ἀκριβῶς Ἰσραηλῖται τοὺς προφήτας αὐτῶν καὶ τῷ Μωησῇ μάλιστα πείθεσθαι.

82. John 1:3, 1 Cor. 8:6, Col. 1:15, 18.

83. *Dial.*, 56, 1 ff., 59. 1 ff.

84. *Didascalia* (ed. Funck) 1. 4.

85. *Didascalia*, 2, 26, 2.

86. Theophilus of Antioch contrasts the false knowledge of the Egyptians and Chaldeans with the true knowledge granted to the Christians in the biblical past (*Ad Autol.*, 2. 33; *PG*, 6. 1105): διὸ δείκνυται πάντας τοὺς λοιποὺς πεπλανῆσθαι, μόνους δὲ Χριστιανοὺς τὴν ἀλήθειάν κεχωρηκέναι οἵτινες ὑπὸ Πνεύματος ἁγίου διδασκόμεθα, τοῦ λαλήσαντος ἐν τοῖς ἁγίοις προφήταις καὶ τὰ πάντα προκαταγγέλλοντος.

87. True Judaism has nothing in common with that of the Synagogue. Thus some authors refuse to allow the surviving remnant of Israel even the name of "Jews." See, already, Rev. 2:9, 3:9. οἱ λέγοντες Ἰουδαίους εἶναι ἑαυτοὺς καὶ οὐκ εἰσίν ἀλλὰ συναγωγὴ τοῦ Σατανᾶ. See Ignatius, *Trall.*, ψευδοιουδαῖοι; *Const. Ap.* (and *Didascalia*) 2, 60, 3: οἱ μάτην λεγόμενοι Ἰουδαῖοι. They have no right to the name, the text goes on, because "Jews" implies "confession." But they do not confess that they killed the Christ. Other texts, see Juster, *Les Juifs*, 1:260 n. The true Jews are the Christians. On the dangers inherent in this attitude see above, p. 332.

88. This argument is often appealed to against the gnostics. See Irenaeus, 4, 12, 3 (*PG*, 7. 1005). *In lege et in Evangelio cum sit primum et maximum praeceptum diligere Dominum Deum ex toto corde. . . . unus et idem ostenditur legis et Evangelii conditor.*

89. *Didascalia*, 2, 26, 2 ff.

90. Tertullian, *Apol.*, 5. 2, 7. 3, 21. 1.

91. Gal. 3:6 and 9.

92. Gal. 3:29.

93. Rom. 4:9 and 10.

94. Gal. 3:17.

95. Tertullian, *Adv. Jud.*, 3 (*PL*, 2. 640).

96. See p. 165.

97. ὁ Ἰουδαϊσμὸς οὐκ ἦν πώποτε ἀλλ' Ἑβραῖοι μὲν ὑπῆρχον. Ἰουδαῖοι δὲ οὔτ' ἦσάν πω, οὔτ' ἐχρηματίζον. *Praep. Ev.*, 7. 6 (*PG*, 21, 516). See Parkes, *Conflict*, pp. 161 ff. The idea is already there in Aristides, *Apol.*, 2. 5. "The Jews trace their origin to Abraham. . . . In Egypt they were called by their lawgiver the people of the Hebrews. Later they were given the name 'Jews.'"

98. *Praep. Ev.*, 8. 1: ὡς γὰρ μόνοις Ἰουδαίοις, οὐκ ἔτι δὲ καὶ τοῖς κατὰ τὴν οἰκουμένην ἔθνεσιν ἦν ἁρμόδια τὰ διὰ Μωυσέως, οὐδὲ δυνατὰ πᾶσιν ἀνθρώποις λέγω δὲ τοῖς πόρρω που τῆς Ἰουδαίας γῆς ἀκούσιν Ἕλλησί τε καὶ βαρβάροις φυλάττεσθαι.

99. *Dem. Ev.*, 1:2: οὐκ ἦν ἡ κατὰ Μωϋσέα πολιτεία κατάλληλος τοῖς ἔθνεσιν ἀλλ' ἢ μόνοις Ἰουδαίοις καὶ τούτοις οὐχὶ τοῖς πᾶσιν ἀλλὰ τοῖς ἐπὶ τῆς ἰουδαϊκῆς γῆς τὰς διατριβὰς ποιουμένοις.

100. *Dem. Ev.*, 1. 3.

101. *Praep. Ev.*, 7. 6. (*PG*, 21. 516). See *Dem. Ev.*, 1. 2 (*PG*, 22. 88): ἕτερον ἐχρῆν ἐξ ἅπαντος ὑποστῆναι τρόπον παρὰ τὸν Μωϋσέως νόμον, καθ' ὃν ἔμελλον βιοῦντα ὁμοίως τῷ Ἀβραὰμ τὰ καθ' ὅλης οἰκουμένης ἔθνη, τῆς ἴσης αὐτῷ κοινωνήσειν εὐλογίας.

102. Eusebius, *HE*, 1, 4, 6: ἔργῳ Χριστιανούς, εἰ καὶ μὴ ὀνόματι. The same idea is found in Lactantius, *Inst. Div.*, 4. 10. (*PL*, 6. 470), *Majores nostri, qui erant principes Hebraeorum.*

103. It goes back to the origins of humanity. *Namque in principio mundi ipsi Adae et Evae legem dedit. . . . Quae lex sufficeret, si esset custodita. . . . Igitur in hac generali et primordiali*

Dei lege. . . . omnia praecepta legis posterioris specialiter indita fuisse cognoscimus, quae suis temporibus edita germinaverunt . . . . Denique ante legem Moysi scriptam in tabulis lapideis legem fuisse contendo non scriptam, quae naturaliter intelligebatur, et a patribus custodiebatur. Tert., *Adv. Jud.*, 2 (*PL*, 2. 637 ff.). The written law is no more than a complement. *Sed quo plenius et impressius tam ipsum quam dispositiones ejus et voluntates adiremus, adjecit instrumentum litteraturae.* Tertullian, *Apol.*, 18. 1.

104. Tertullian, *Apol.*, 17. 6. *O testimonium animae naturaliter Christianae.*

105. For example, Eusebius, *HE*, 1. 4: "The Christian, thanks to the knowledge and teaching of Christ, is distinguished by modesty, fairness, force of character, manliness of conduct, and the confession and worship of the one, only sovereign God."

106. Tertullian, *Apol.*, 18. 2 and 5. The continuity between the prophets and the Christians is illustrated by the similarities between their sufferings. *Nobis igitur qui successimus in loco prophetarum, ea sustinentibus hodie in saeculo, quae semper passi sunt prophetae propter divinam religionem* (*Adv. Jud.*, 13; *PL*, 2. 676).

107. For example Wilfred Monod, *Du protestantisme* (Paris, 1928), pp. 47 ff., speaks of the prophets' Hebrew "protestantism."

108. See, for example, Clement of Rome, *1. Cor.*, 40–44; *Didascalia* 2, 26, 2–3.

109. See my essay, "Melchisédech dans la polémique et la légende," *RHPR*, 1937, pp. 58–93.

110. See Heb. 7:4, 7:11; Tertullian, *Adv. Jud.*, 2. 3; Justin, *Dial.*, 19 and 33; Aphraates, *Hom.*, 11. 4; Chrysostom, *De Melchis.*, (*PG*, 56. 262). Other references in G. Bardy, "Melchisédech dans la tradition patristique," *RB*, 1926, pp. 496 ff, and 1927, pp. 25 ff.

111. The connection between the two sacrifices is formulated for the first time by Clement of Alexandria, *Strom.*, 4, 25, 161.

112. English translation by Sir E. Wallis Budge, *The Book of the Cave of Treasures* (London, 1927).

113. Budge, pp. 19 ff.

114. See Simon, *Melchisédech*, pp. 87–89. The main object of the book is to reveal alongside the history of the patriarchs, whose importance in the last resort is quite secondary, "the succession of priests" (p. 189) and, from this sacerdotal point of view, the true history of humanity.

115. "Eden is the holy Church, and Adam officiates in it. Thus it is written (Ps. 74:2) 'Remember thy Church, which thou hast gotten of old'." (Budge, p. 53; see p. 62).

116. Ambrosiaster, *Comm. in Ep. ad Rom.*, 9. 17, 9. 27, 11. 28 (*PL*, 17, 144, 146, 161).

117. Heb. 10:1; see Col. 2:17. This view is often taken up elsewhere. E.g., Chrysostom, *in Ep. ad Heb.*; 7. *Hom.*, 13 (*PG*, 64. 105). πάντα τύποι ἦσαν, πάντα σκιά, περιτομή, θυσία, σάββατον, ἃ οὐκ ἴσχυσεν διαβῆναι εἰς τὴν ψυχὴν καὶ διὰ τοῦτο παραχωρεῖ καὶ ὑπεξίσταται.

118. Certain commands of rites are prefigurative (7–9); others are symbolic of moral truth, as, for example, the food laws (10:2): ἄρα οὐχ ἐστὶν ἐντολὴ θεοῦ τὸ μὴ τρώγειν, Μωσῆς δὲ ἐν πνεύματι ἐλάλησε.

119. The first sacrifices Israel offered were for the golden calf (Acts, 7:41). Those of the temple remained tainted by this original fault (Acts 7:46–50). On Stephen's speech and its value as evidence, see alternatively Goguel's remarks in, "Unité et diversité du christianisme primitif," *RHPR*, 1939, pp. 18 ff.

120. *Ep. Diognetus*, 3–4.

121. Aristides, *Apol.*, 14. 4 (Syriac text); cf. *Kerygma Petri*, quoted by Clement of Alexandria, *Strom.*, 6, 5, 41. See E. V. Dobschütz, *Das Kerygma Petri* (*TU*, 11. 1), pp. 35–45.

122. Exod. 32:15–19.

123. *Barnabas*, 14. 1–4.

124. *Barnabas*, 4. 8. The same interpretation (that the breaking of the tablets means the repudiation of the carnal law) is found in Origen, *in Rom.*, 2, 14 (*PG*, 14. 917).

125. Exod. 34:1–4. Barnabas, though his views are not entirely clear, seems to see in this

passage, in spite of its contents, a symbolic prefiguration of the Christian faith. It is "the testament of the beloved Jesus."

126. *Didascalia,* 6, 16, 1 ff.

127. *Didascalia,* 6, 16, 3-4.

128. *Didascalia,* 6, 17, 1.

129. *Didascalia,* 6, 15, 2 and 4. The interpretation here is reinforced by allegory. The ten commandments suggest the *iota,* which is the initial letter of the name Jesus. When Jesus says that not one *iota* will pass away from the law he is indicating that the ten commandments will remain in force (1-10).

130. Lietzmann, *Geschichte,* 1:85, and Juster, *Les Juifs,* 1:372, n. 6.

131. *C. adv. Leg. et Proph.,* 2, 1, 2 (*PL,* 42. 637).

132. Jerome, *in Matth.,* 22. 23 (*PL,* 26, 170). Other references in Juster, 1:372, n. 6.

133. E.g. Jerome, *in Is.,* 10:1 (*PL,* 24. 136). See *in Habac.,* 2. 9 (*PL,* 25. 1297).

134. *Nov.,* 146, 1, 2. Juster, *Les Juifs,* 1:374, n. 1.

135. The proof is given by the fact that even in Latin authors the term is used to the exclusion of any Latin equivalent. It is therefore a technical term used by Greek-speaking rabbis.

136. See pp. 189 ff.

137. See p. 165.

138. *Didascalia,* 1. 7.

139. *Timothy-Aquila,* ed. by Conybeare, 77a. Lukyn Williams, *Adv. Jud.,* p. 72, n. 3, professes himself embarrassed by this "extraordinary statement," for which he can find no parallel. He concludes that the identity in meaning of the terms *deuterosis* and *mishnah* has given rise to some confusion. He is well aware of the *Didascalia* and its idea of *deuterosis,* but declares that this is something quite different. On the contrary, the two are manifestly connected. The Dialogue simply goes a step further than the *Didascalia* in attributing the initiation of the second covenant code to Moses and not to God. It makes the second code into a merely human work, on the same level as the Mishnah, and emphasizes, more forcefully than does the *Didascalia,* its secondary character. It falls into place, in fact, between the *Didascalia,* and the letter of Ptolemy to Flora.

140. Jerome, *In Is.,* 59. 12 (*PL,* 24. 603). See *Ep.* 121 *ad Algasiam,* 10. The scriptural support quoted is Matt. 15:6, quoting Isa. 29:13.

141. One may imagine the pagans making this objection. It would be even more natural in the mouth of Jews and must have been particularly powerful at the time when Christians were being persecuted. The argument that Christians based on the afflictions of the Jews thus rebounded on their own heads. See Aphraates, *Hom.* 21. 1, who was asked ironically by a Jew, during a period of persecution, "Is there not a single man among you whose prayers are acceptable to God, that he may make your afflictions cease?" Tertullian (see n. 106 above) in the same chapter in which he demonstrates that the afflictions of the Jews are the results of their crime, makes reference to the sufferings of the Christians. They are inflicted, he says, on the witnesses of truth by the evil powers who tormented the prophets before them. The Christian argument rediscovered its force after the triumph of the Church. See Chrysostom, *Homily against the Jews,* 6, 3 (*PG,* 48. 908). διὰ τοῦτο οἱ μὲν εἰς αὐτὸν ἀσεβήσαντες ὑμεῖς ἐν ὕβρει καὶ ἀτιμία, οἱ δὲ προσκυνοῦντες αὐτὸν ἡμεῖς ἀτιμότεροι πάντων ὑμῶν ἔμπροσθεν ὄντες, διὰ τὴν τοῦ θεοῦ χάριν καὶ σεμνότεροι πάντων ὑμῶν ἐσμεν νῦν, καὶ ἐν μείζονι τιμῇ καθεστήκαμεν.

142. Nevertheless, there is no unanimity about this. Jerome raises the question: Are all saved? or all damned? or saved in part? and he hesitates to come down on either side. References in Parkes, *Conflict,* p. 152. Chrysostom is tempted to conclude that they are rejected for good, because they killed the Christ: *Hom.,* 6. 2 (*PG,* 48, 907). διὰ τοῦτο οὐκ ἔστιν ὑμῖν διόρθωσις οὐδὲ συγγνώμη λοιπόν, οὐδὲ ἀπολογία.

143. *Testes iniquitatis suae et veritatis nostrae. Enarr. in Ps.*, 58, 1, 22 (*PL*, 36. 705). See Juster, *Les Juifs*, 1:227, n. 6.

144. Gen. 4:15.

145. *Enarr. in Ps.*, 58, 1, 22 (*PL*, 36. 705).

146. *Serm.*, 201. 3.

147. *Adv. Jud.*, 2. 3 (*PL*, 42. 52).

148. Gal. 5:2, 4.

149. Jerome to Augustine, *Ep.*, 75. 13-14 (*CSEL*, 34. 304 ff.). The debate concerns the attitude of Peter and Paul, who, out of fear or respect for others' feelings, sometimes complied with the observances they condemn. Gal. 2:12, Acts 16:3, 18:18, 21:20-26.

150. *Ep.*, 82. 18 (*CSEL*, 34. 369).

151. *Haec ergo summa est quaestionis, immo sententiae tuae, ne post evangelium Christi bene faciant credentes Judaei si legis mandata custodiant; si hoc verum est, in Cerinthi et Hebionis haeresin delabimur* (*Ep.*, 75. 13).

152. See pp. 306 ff.

153. See Friedländer, *Jüd. Gnostizismus*; Cullmann, *Roman pseudo-clémentin*, and Siouville, *Homélies clémentines, Introd.*, pp. 45-48.

154. The Judaism of the diaspora, in its efforts to make proselytes, sometimes put the emphasis on the moral law to the extent of passing over the ritual obligations in silence. The formula that Christianity offered its members recalled that which Judaism offered its semi-proselytes. This is the case with the Didache, where it raises the question of observances with regard to food (6. 3). See p. 335, and Lietzmann, *Geschichte*, 1:209.

155. It is not impossible that the *Didascalia*'s idea of *deuterosis* has its antecedents in some Jewish group that was liberal enough to throw overboard the detail of ritual observances. The suggestion is made by Bousset, *Jüd. Gebetssammlung*, p. 488.

156. Chrysostom, *Exp. in Ps.*, 109. 1 (*PG*, 55. 167). εἰ δὲ ἔτερος ἡμῖν Ἰουδαίοις ἀνακύπτει πάλιν πρόσωπον Χριστιανοῦ περιφέρων, Παῦλος ὁ Σαμοσατεύς. . . . Similarly the Anomoeans: *Homily against the Jews*, 1. 1 (*PG*, 48. 845). ἐπειδὴ γὰρ συγγενῆ τὰ τῆς ἀσεβείας Ἀνομοίοις καὶ Ἰουδαίοις; the Sabellians and the Arians: *De Sacerdote*, 4. 4 (*PG*, 48. 667). See Juster, *Les Juifs*, 1:284, n. 1.

157. Augustine, *Ep., 196, ad Asellicum*, 7 (*PL*, 33. 893 ff). *Judaeis autem similes sunt qui, cum profiteantur se esse Christianos, ipsi gratiae Christi sic adversantur ut se humanis viribus divina existiment implere mandata, ac si etiam ipsi ignorantes Dei justitiam, et suam volentes constituere, justitiae Dei non sunt subjecti et non quidem nomine sed tamen errore judaïzant. Hoc genus hominum capita sibi invenerat Pelagium et Celestium.*

Chapter 4

1. On this point see Juster's classic study, *Les Juifs dans l'Empire romain*.

2. Ibid., 1:246.

3. Suetonius, *Domitian*, 12. See S. Gsell, *Essai sur Domitien*, (1894), pp. 287 ff.

4. Dio Cassius, 68. 1-2: οὔτ ἀσεβείας, οὔτ Ἰουδαϊκοῦ βίου καταιτιᾶσθαί τινας συνεχώρησε. See the coins with the inscription, *Fisci judaici calumnia sublata*. Cohen, *Médailles*, 1:478, no. 83-86, and A. Merlin, *Les revers monétaires de l'empereur Nerva*, (Paris, 1906).

5. *Hist. Aug., Hadrian*, 14; Dio Cassius, 69, 12, 1. It has sometimes been suggested that the edict concerning circumcision is later than the war. But this seems to be an error. See Juster, *Les Juifs*, 1:267, and 2:191.

6. See the article, "Hadrian," in *JE*.

7. *Hist. Aug. Antonius*, 5:4.

8. See p. 104.

9. Dio Cassius, 67. 15. See Śuetonius, *Domitian*, 15.

10. Pliny, *Letters*, X, 97–98.

11. *HE*, 4, 3, 1-2.

12. *Geschichte der Juden*, IV³, p. 169. Graetz takes Eusebius's comment in *HE*, 4, 3, 1, to refer to the Jews: "Evil-doers who try to make mischief for us."

13. *Intolérance religieuse*, p. 228.

14. Eusebius, *HE*, 4, 6, 4.

15. Ibid., 4, 9, 1-3.

16. Ibid., 4, 2, 1.

17. *Meditations*, 11. 3.

18. Ammianus Marcellinus, 22. 5.

19. *Apol.*, 5.

20. *In Dan.*, 11. 34 (*PL*, 25. 570). This means that the revolt that took place in Palestine in connection with the events that brought Septimus Severus to power (*Hist. Aug. Sept. Sev.*, 16. 7) neither was of great importance nor entailed lasting consequences.

21. On the question of the identity of "Antoninus," the friend of Rabbi, and who was undoubtedly Caracalla, see M. Mieses, "Etablissements puniques," *REJ* 93:148 ff.

22. Eusebius, *HE*, 6, 21, 3.

23. *Hist. Aug., Sept. Sev.*, 17. As far as the Christians were concerned, orthodox historians themselves state that the edict was enforced only for a short while and not rigorously, "for the drive to make converts does not seem to have suffered from any serious impediments" (Fliche and Martin, *Histoire de l'Eglise*, 2:115).

24. *Hist. Aug., Elagabal*, 3. 3-5, 7. 2; Dio Cassius, 79, 11, 1 ff.

25. *Hist. Aug., Alex. Sev.*, 22; 29. 2; see 28.

26. *Oxyrhynchus pap.*, X, 1242, which dates from the beginning of the third century and deals with events that took place under Trajan, emphasizes the pro-Jewish sentiments of the Empress Plotina and her influence on the emperor, and gives us to understand that his council was at the Jews' service. Whatever may be said about the date, and even the genuineness of these events, the text gives an accurate picture of the impression made by the Jewish policies of the second- and third-century emperors on the anti-Semites of Alexandria. See on this subject W. Weber, "Eine Gerichtsverhandlung vor Kaiser Trajan," *Hermes* 50 (1915): 47–92; and Fischer and Kittel, *Weltjudentum*, p. 69.

27. *Dig.*, 48, 8, 11 (Modestinus).

28. It has sometimes been maintained that the measure was not directed against the Jews, and that it only affected them indirectly. Mommsen, *Röm. Geschichte*, 5:551.

29. Paulus, *Sent.*, 5, 22, 3. And if Celsus is to be believed (Origen, *Contra Celsum*, 2. 13), the one who suffered himself to be circumcised was also to be put to death. See Juster, *Les Juifs*, 1:267, n. 2.

30. When Izates, the prince of Adiabene, was converted to Judaism, the Jew who converted him was quite prepared to let him dispense with circumcision, the essential thing being that he should observe the other rites. It was only upon the intervention of another Jew that the prince decided to have himself circumcised. Josephus, *Ant. Jud.*, 20, 2, 3-4.

31. See *Oracula Sibyllina*, 4. 24 ff., 164 ff. For R. Joshua (first century) a proselyte who has done no more than receive ritual baptism is nevertheless a true proselyte: *b. Yebam.*, 46a.

32. Juster, *Les Juifs*, 1:258.

33. *Hist. Aug., Sept. Sev.*, 17.

34. Eusebius, *HE*, 6, 12, 1; see Jerome, *De Vir. illustr.*, 41.

35. *Apol.*, 21, 1.

36. *Comm. Serm. in Matth.*, 114 (*PG*, 13. 1764). Apologetic directed simultaneously at the pagans, *in Matth.*, 16 (*PG*, 13. 1621).

37. *Passio Pionii*, 13.

38. *j. Ab. Zara*, V, 4; see Juster, *Les Juifs*, 1 : 247, n. 1.

39. Quoted by Clement of Alexandria, *Strom.*, 6, 5, 41.

40. *Diognetus*, 1.

41. Ibid., 5.

42. Aristides, *Apol.*, 2.

43. Ibid., 14. 1, 15. 1.

44. On this conflict of ideas, Harnack, *Mission*, 1⁴, pp. 259–89, who gives numerous references.

45. Tertullian, *Scorp.*, 10. The weapon forged by the apologists backfired so effectively that Tertullian takes it on himself to prove its falsity. Conversely, Eusebius, who goes back to the tripartite scheme, tries to prove the legitimacy of Christianity by showing that it is older than the other two religions. See p. 82, and F. J. Foakes Jackson, *Eusebius Pamphylii*, (Cambridge, 1933), pp. 120-8.

46. On the idea of the Jews as barbarians, see *Hom. Ps. Clem.*, 4. 7: "He let himself be led by a barbarian called Peter to behave and speak like a Jew." Ibid., 4. 8.

47. Josephus, *Contra Apionem*, 1. 1.

48. Tacitus, *Hist.*, 5. 5.

49. *Contra Celsum*, 2. 1.

50. It ought, however, to be noted with Parkes, *Conflict of Church and Synagogue*, p. 60, that Jewish privileges were in fact restricted to practicing Jews, and that an excommunicant could be deprived of them. See Josephus, *Ant. Jud.*, 14. 10. 13 ff.

51. Ps. Augustine, *Altercatio Ecclesiae et Synagogae*, PL., 42. 1131.

52. On Julian and the Jews see also, besides the articles in *JE* and *EJ*, M. Adler, "The Emperor Julian and the Jews," *JQR*, 1893, pp. 591, 651. More recently, Bidez, *Vie de l'empereur Julien*, pp. 306 ff.; Labriolle, *Réaction païenne*, pp. 401-10; and especially J. Vogt, *Kaiser Julian und das Judentum* (Leipzig, n.d.) (C. R. de Piganiol, *Bulletin d'histoire ancienne de la RH*, October-December 1941, pp. 293 ff.). Of the large work Julian wrote against the Christians, important fragments are preserved by Cyril of Alexandria in his treatise, *For the Holy Religion of the Christians against the work of Julian the Atheist* (PG, 503-1064), a work that is itself mutilated. The ten books of it that have come down to us in their entirety correspond only to the first three of Julian's.

53. *Contra Christianos*, ed. by Neumann, pp. 187 ff. See Origen, *Contra Celsum*, 5 : 15 ff.

54. Neumann, p. 177.

55. Ibid., pp. 230 ff.

56. Ibid., pp. 207, 198, 210, 219.

57. Ibid., p. 164; see p. 207.

58. Ibid., p. 219.

59. Ibid., p. 207.

60. A like attachment to tradition was not enough to give the Jewish-pagan conservative front any genuine cohesion. For the Jews, who were ordinarily so anxious to establish the antiquity of their religious and national traditions, in order to support their privileged status, could also, when it suited them, and when it suited their apologetic interests, emphasize what they had to contribute that was original. The proselyte was gathered into a καινῇ καὶ φιλοθεῷ πολιτείᾳ (Philo, *de Monarchia*, 7 : 51). They did not value tradition for its own sake, but, in agreement with both the Christians (see Origen, *Contra Celsum*, 5. 27 ff.) and the pagan philosophers (Cicero, *De Leg.*, 1. 15. 42; Porphyry, *Letter to Marcella*, 25; see Labriolle, *Réaction païenne*, p. 134), they made a distinction between good tradition and bad. In the Jewish writing in the pseudo-Clementine literature Apion picks out as the greatest impiety,

"to abandon the customs of one's ancestors and to embrace those of barbarians" (*Hom.*, 4. 7). Clement, showing himself a true Jew, replies that one ought not "to retain at all costs the usages of one's ancestors, but to preserve them when they are agreeable with piety and to reject them when they are not" (4. 8). There follows a keen criticism of the idea of custom, considered as a criterion by which to judge the good life, and which Clement contrasts with the idea of truth (4. 11).

61. Chrysostom, *Homily against the Jews*, 5. 11 (*PG*, 48. 900 ff.). On the circumstances surrounding this attempt at restoration and the texts bearing on it, see Bidez, *Vie de Julien*, pp. 306 ff.

62. Perhaps, with Vogt, we ought to take account of Julian's recognition by the Jews of Antioch, who would have taken his part very quickly.

63. Apart from his large work against the Christians, his feelings toward the Jews are expressed in some passages in his other works. See especially the edition by Bidez and Cumont (Coll. Budé) (Paris, 1922), pp. 126, 135, and 193, and the letter to the Jews, whose authenticity is disputed, ibid., pp. 280 ff.

64. *Histoire des persécutions*, 1 : 308; 2 : 353, 374; see Dom Leclerq, *Les Martyrs*, vol. 4.

65. Harnack, *Mission*, I[4], pp. 66 ff.; see Knopf, *Nachapostolisches Zeitalter*, pp. 138 ff.

66. Parkes, *Conflict of Church and Synagogue*, pp. 125 ff.

67. *Dial.*, 16. 4; see *Apol.*, 31. 5.

68. *Dial.*, 131. 2.

69. Ibid., 17. 1, 3.

70. *Ad Nat.*, 1. 14. see *Adv. Jud.*, 13; *Adv. Marc.*, 3. 23.

71. I cannot clearly see why Knopf (*Nachapost. Zeit.*, p. 145), who is so anxious to stress the anti-Christian activities of the Jews, refuses to recognize the existence of their emissaries, and fails to see in them a literary parallel to the Christian apostles. The existence of Jewish apostles, as a regular institution, is well attested, as also is their role as defenders of orthodoxy. See Zucker, *Untersuchungen zur Organisation der Juden*, p. 153.

72. Origen, *Contra Celsum*, 6. 27, attributes to the Jews the well-known accusations of anthropophagy and indulgence in orgies.

73. There was more to this, however, than the merely calculated and clever scoring of points in debate. Reasons of sentiment were also involved. There was still a feeling of solidarity, perhaps partly unconscious, between the pagan world and those Christians who were of pagan background. The Church saw itself accordingly, and by contrast with the chastised Jews, as the redeemed gentile world. These ex-pagan Christians, moreover, sometimes retained attitudes toward the Jews that they derived from their background, and tended to see the Jews as responsible for the hatred that Christianity encountered. Jewish-Christian writings would doubtless represent a quite different approach in this regard.

74. *Scorp.*, 10; see Irenaeus, 4, 21, 3; 28, 3.

75. E.g., Acts 13 : 50; 14 : 2, 18; 17 : 5; 18 : 12; 24 : 5.

76. See J. Gagé, *Mél. d'Archéol. et d'Hist.*, 44 (1927): 103-18; "Membra Christi," *DAC* 11, no. 1:290-95.

77. *Apol.*, 7. 3.

78. These were, however, somewhat exceptional measures, which did not, in any case, prohibit more normal relations. See pp. 262 ff.

79. See Justin, *Dial.*, 110. 5: "So far as you and all other men have it in your power, each Christian is to be driven out."

80. Parkes, *Conflict of Church and Synagogue*, p. 130, notes that the series of martyrs in whose deaths Jews are said to be seriously involved ends almost completely after the second century.

81. Ibid., p. 141.

82. *Martyrs of Palestine*, 8 (*PG*, 20. 1489).

83. *Martyrium Polycarpi*, 12. 2.
84. Ibid., 13. 1.
85. Ibid., 17. 2, 18. 1.
86. Ibid., 1. 1.
87. Ibid., 19. 1.
88. Ibid., 1. 2.
89. Ibid., 6. 2.
90. Ibid., 12. 2 ff.
91. Ibid., 16. 1.
92. Ibid., 17. 2.
93. *Acta Sanctorum*, 3 May.
94. *Analecta Bolland.* 31.
95. Allard, *Persécutions*, 2:373 ff.
96. Zeiller, in Fliche and Martin, *Histoire de l'Eglise*, 2:149.
97. Parkes, *Conflict of Church and Synagogue*, p. 148.
98. It is not necessary to invoke it, nevertheless, as Parkes does in connection with the persecution of Nero, for the influence of the Jews was in this case only exercised within the entourage of the emperor, and neither Christian nor pagan opinion could have known anything about it.
99. Parkes, *Conflict of Church and Synagogue*, p. 145. The martyrs referred to are Agricola and Vital, Hermes, Aggaeus and Caius, Vincentius and Orantius. See Ambrose, *Exhort. virg.*, 7 (*PL*, 16. 338) and Paulinus of Milan, *Vita Ambrosii*, 15 (*PL*, 14. 32) *Acta sanctorum*, 4 November, 4 January, and 22 January; see Harnack, *Mission*, II⁴, p. 872.
100. This is to be compared with the Jewish attempts to convert Christians in times of persecution (see p. 106) and it bears witness to the willingness of the Roman authorities to class the Christians, albeit after their death, in the ranks of Judaism.
101. See Leclerq, *Afrique chrétienne*, 1:39 ff.; Monceaux, *Histoire Littéraire*, 1:5 ff.; Delattre, *Gamart*.
102. Parkes, *Conflict of Church and Synagogue*, p. 150.
103. On the legislative texts, which is to say, for all practical purposes, on the Theodosian Code, 16:8, see Juster, *Les Juifs*, 1:160 ff. On the development of Christian policy see Juster, passim, Lucas, *Geschichte der Juden*, and Parkes, *Conflict of Church and Synagogue*, particularly pp. 150-245.
104. The rescript of Licinius, though it does not mention the Jews, does appear to include them, and to confirm the standing they already had, for it grants "to Christians *and to everyone else*" religious liberty: Lactantius, *de mort. pers.*, 48. 2-8. Later texts invoke *vetus mos et consuetudo* (*C. Th.*, 16, 8, 3) and *delata privilegia* (*C. Th.*, 16, 8, 20).
105. *C. Th.*, 16, 8, 9 (393).
106. *C. Th.*, 2, 8, 26 (409); 16, 8, 20 (412).
107. *C. Th.*, 16, 8, 8 (392); see 16, 8, 11 (396); 16, 8, 13 (397).
108. The privilege was at first reserved to two or three officers for each community, *C. Th.*, 16, 8, 3 (321), but was later extended to the whole of the Synagogue personnel *C. Th.*, 16, 8, 2 (330). Juster, *Les Juifs*, 1:407 ff.
109. Under the pagan empire, Jews who were citizens possessed in theory the *jus honorum*, but in practice were unable to exercise it until after the Severides, when a law (*Dig.*, 50, 2, 3) allowed them to dispense with the religious acts that the carrying out of public duties normally involved. This was the origin of the statute that was still in force in the fourth century. See Juster, *Les Juifs*, 2:243 ff.
110. See p. 291.
111. *C. Th.*, 16, 8, 1 (315). The death penalty is decreed for Jews who try to stone an apostate; *poenas meritas* for the proselyte and the Jew who converts him.

112. These are the *privilegia odiosa* considered by Juster, *Les Juifs*, 1 : 230 ff.

113. *C. Th.*, 16, 8, 16 (404). What are in mind here are functions of state. Municipal functions (until 438) and all the onerous charges they involved were still open to the Jews. The development of this legislation, restricting more and more the number of offices open to Jews, recalls the anti-Semitic legislation of the Nazis between 1933 and 1939.

114. Between a Jew and a Christian woman, *C. Th.*, 16, 8, 6 (339), then between a Christian man and a Jewish woman, *C. Th.*, 3, 7, 2 (388). Both offenses are punishable with death.

115. *Contra Just.*, 1 : 9, 7, which forbids polygamy at the same time. The levirate had already been forbidden by a law passed in 355; *C. Th.*, 3, 12, 2.

116. *C. Th.*, 2, 1, 10. Jewish autonomy in religious matters remained untouched. On the exclusion of Jews from the office of judge, see St. Basil, *Comm. in Is.*, 3 (*PG*, 30. 281) and Jerome, *Comm. in Is.*, 2 (*PL*, 24. 58).

117. On the nature of this contribution, the *aurum coronarium*, and the methods by which it was collected, see Juster, *Les Juifs*, 1 : 385 ff.

118. *Homily against the Jews*, 6. 5 (*PG*, 48. 911).

119. *C. Th.*, 16, 8, 14. It may be supposed that the state took it upon itself to reimburse the Jewish cult.

120. *C. Th.*, 16, 8, 17 (404).

121. This is the theory of Godefroy, (*C. Th., ad loc.*), followed by S. de Tillemont, *Histoire des Empereurs*, (Paris, 1690), 5 : 310, and Lucas, *Geschichte der Juden*.

122. *C. Th.*, 16, 8, 19 (429).

123. *C. Th.*, 9, 45, 2 (397).

124. *C. Th.*, 16, 8, 23 (416).

125. There were disturbances, for which evidence is scanty, under Constantine, and revolt under Constantius. This latter was centered on Diocaesarea, which was destroyed in the events that followed: Juster, *Les Juifs*, 2 : 197, refers to the relevant sources (nn. 1 and 2); Graetz, *Geschichte*, IV[3], pp. 315 ff., 456 n. 30; Dubnow, *Weltgeschichte*, 3 : 216–22.

126. See Parkes, *Conflict of Church and Synagogue*, pp. 257 ff., and Labourt, *Christianisme dans l'Empire perse*, p. 58, n. 2.

127. It would appear that the system was sometimes open to abuse. *C. Th.*, 16, 8, 24 calls the Patriarch *depopulator Judaeorum*; see John Chrysostom, *Contra Jud. et Gent.*, 16 (*PG*, 48. 835) φόρους συνάγων ὁ πατριάρχης ἀπείρους κέκτηται θησαυρούς: *j. Ab. Zara*, 2 : 10; *b. Shabb.*, 113b. Simony was also a factor in the nominations of officers of the local communities. Juster, *Les Juifs*, 1 : 398.

128. *C. Th.*, 16, 8, 18.

129. Under the episcopate of Cyril. Socrates, *HE*, 7, 13 (*PG*, 67, 760). See p. 224.

130. *C. Th.*, 16, 8, 21.

131. Socrates, *HE*, 7. 16 (*PG*, 67, 769).

132. *C. Th.*, 16, 8, 22. Parkes, *Conflict of Church and Synagogue*, p. 230.

133. Juster, *Les Juifs*, 1 : 397 and n. 6. The disappearance of the Patriarchate was officially recognized by the law of 429 (*C. Th.*, 16, 8, 29) referred to on p. 129.

134. It is possible, as Dubnow suggests (*Weltgeschichte*, 3 : 250) that the conflict was aggravated by the action of Palestinian bishops, in particular by the bishop of Jerusalem, who claimed for himself the title of Patriarch and was effectively granted it by the Council of Chalcedon.

135. See pp. 224 ff.

Chapter 5

1. On the various aspects of this conflict see the commentaries on the books of the New Testament, and especially on Acts. Also, Harnack, *Mission*, I⁴, in particular, Book 1 and pp. 259-300.

2. See pp. 53 ff.

3. Or in the later writings (which are for this very reason less useful) such as the *Toledoth Jeshu* and *Yosippon*. The passages referring to Jesus in the Slavonic Josephus are in all probability of Jewish origin and are examples of the Synagogue's anti-Christian polemic. But their date and place of origin are too uncertain for us to be able to make use of them here. See Goguel, *Vie de Jésus*, pp. 61-69.

4. Juster, *Les Juifs*, 1:53-76.

5. *Adversus Judaeos* (Cambridge, 1935). See, in connection with the Latin literature, Blumenkranz, *Judenpredigt*.

6. Introd., p. xvii.

7. Ibid., p. xvi.

8. *Altercatio* (*TU*, 1. 1-3). The arguments advanced by Corssen (*Die Altercatio Simonis Judaei et Theophili Christiani auf ihre Quellen geprüft* (Berlin, 1890) against the identification with *Jason-Papiscus* won over Harnack himself.

9. *Altercatio* (*TU*, 1, 2, 75 ff.).

10. Harnack professes the same scepticism about Jewish-Christian relations in connection with the Epistle of Barnabas, which he refuses to believe has anything to do with a real Jewish danger (*Altchristliche Literatur*, 2:58). For a refutation, see Veil, in Hennecke, *Handbuch zu den N.T. Apokryphen*, p. 208. Harnack's authority has sometimes ensured that his views have been accepted without discussion. Thus G. Krüger, *Geschichte des altchristlichen Literatur* (Fribourg, 1895), p. 69, sees in the Jewish literature *eine blosse Ergänzung der an die heidnische Adresse gerichteten Literatur*, and refuses to see it as serious polemic, for which, he says, there was no occasion. The introduction of a Jew to defend his religion (generally in very inadequate fashion) is simply a literary device. The same point is expressed by H. Jordan, *Geschichte der altchristlichen Literatur* (Leipzig, 1911), p. 240. And insofar as Barnabas is concerned, see also P. Ladeuze, *L'Epître de Barnabé* (Louvain, 1900), p. 4.

11. Origen, *Contra Celsum*, 1. 28-29. On the entry of a Jew into this polemic, see M. Lods, "Etude sur les sources juives de la polémique de Celse contre les chrétiens," *RHPR*, 1945, pp. 1-31.

12. On the controversy concerning the last chapters of *Adv. Jud.* and their use in the *Against Marcion*, or vice versa, see Monceaux, *Histoire littéraire de l'Afrique chrétienne*, 1:293-301; Labriolle, *Littérature latine chrétienne*, p. 107; Lukyn Williams, *Adv. Jud.*, pp. 43 ff. A similar type of work is John Chrysostom's *Demonstration to the Jews and the Greeks that Christ is God* (*PG*, 48, 813-38) and also Ps. Chrysostom, *Against the Jews, the Greeks and the Heretics* (*PG*, 48, 1075-80). Lukyn Williams, *Adversus Judaeos*, pp. 135-39.

13. The principal themes of the argument, it is well to recall, go back to St. Paul, principally to Gal. and Rom. In that context they are incontestably dealing with real problems.

14. Lukyn Williams, *Adv. Jud.*, pp. 206-92; see "Spain" in *JE*.

15. *Adv. Jud.*, pp. 206-92.

16. Ibid., pp. 132-39.

17. Ibid., pp. 95-102.

18. Hulen, "The Dialogues with the Jews," *JBL* (1932), 1:55 ff.

19. Cyprian's *Testimonia*, for example, are composed with both these objects in mind. If we leave out of account Book 3, which was probably added later by the author, for it shows no interest at all in the controversy and is only loosely connected with the rest of the work, the collection divides itself very clearly into two parts, a critique of Judaism and a Christological

proof. Book 1 deals with the call of the gentiles, who are called to supplant Israel. Book 2 demonstrates how the prophecies were fulfilled in the person of Jesus. This layout by itself entitles us to describe the work as one of anti-Jewish polemic, even though the title and prologue make no mention of the Jews. Lukyn Williams, *Adversus Judaeos*, p. 57.

20. Celsus's Jew is from this point of view typical. Because it is he who is on the attack, he makes the person of Jesus and the dogma of Christology the issue. He says nothing of Jewish observances, and indeed there is nothing he can say. It will readily be conceded that in their detail the arguments with which he is credited are not always perfectly adapted to the person addressed. Furthermore, they are only there to give added weight to the argument of Celsus himself, to which they are subordinated. Nevertheless, in their fundamental themes it may well be that these arguments are just what might be expected in the mouth of a Jewish critic of Christianity.

21. I would offer as a typical writing of this category the account in the *Acta Silvestri* (Boninus Mombritius, *Sanctuarium seu vitae Sanctorum*, reed. (Paris, 1910), 2:508-29). It tells of a public debate organized by Constantine between a team of rabbis and a team of Christian scholars led by Pope Silvester, which resulted in the total discomfiture of the Jews (see Juster, *Les Juifs*, 86 ff. and Lukyn Williams, *Adversus Judaeos*, pp. 339 ff.). The text is an interesting one in many respects, but for our present purposes it does not seem possible to make use of it. The setting is utterly fantastic. The part played by Helena rests, doubtless, on a confusion with Helena of Adiabene, who became a convert to Judaism during the first century (Josephus, *Ant. Jud.*, 20. 2-4). The author's knowledge of Jewish institutions is vague and inaccurate. The discussion resolves itself into a long Christological controversy that would not be out of place in any treatise *de fide christiana*. The main interest of the text is in the final episode. The chief of the rabbis kills a bull by means of the name of Yahweh. Silvester recalls it to life pronouncing the name of Christ. This competition in magic throws light on an important aspect of Jewish Christian relations, but it is a long way from scholarly polemic.

22. ἐκ τῶν κοινῇ ἡμῖν πεπιστευμένων. Origen, *Contra Celsum*, 1. 44.

23. Justin, *Dial.*, 9. 1.

24. Ibid., 28. 2. The same argument was taken up frequently in Christian apologetic: e.g., Ps. Cyprian, *Adv. Jud.*, 10; Lactantius, *Div. Inst.*, 7. 1; Augustine, *Adv. Jud.*, 1. 2, 5. 6, 7. 9, etc.

25. Justin, *Dial.*, 29. 2. See *Barnabas*, 4. 6-7.

26. Justin, *Dial.*, 12. 3, 14. 2. According to *Barnabas* 9. 4, it was at the instigation of an evil angel that they understood the law in its literal sense.

27. Justin, *Dial.*, 90. 2.

28. On the use of allegory by the Jews, Heinemann, *Altjüdische Allegoristik*.

29. Or even several meanings. The rabbinic principle, "Scripture must not be torn away from its ordinary meaning" (*b. Yebam.*, 11b, 24a), was far from universally observed. Bonsirven, *Exégèse rabbinique*, p. 36.

30. For a good summary of these different conceptions and the different kinds of rabbinic allegory, Bonsirven, *Exégèse*, pp. 208 ff.

31. Twenty-sixth rule of Eliezer, quoted by Bonsirven, *Exégèse*, p. 207, who gives a bibliography on the question.

32. "The words of scripture cannot lose their primary meaning." M. Guttmann, *Judentum und seine Umwelt* (Berlin, 1927), p. 250.

33. Augustine, *Ep.*, 196, 3, 13. The origin is to be sought in Paul, Gal. 4:22 ff.

34. See p. 188.

35. See p. 88.

36. Origen, *Comm. in Ep. and Rom.*, 2. 14 (*PG*, 14. 917).

37. *Barnabas*, 4. 8. See p. 87.

38. *Instr.*, 1. 38.
39. On this text, which appears in *PL*, 57, 793-806, see D. Capelle, *Revue bénédictine*, 1922, pp. 81-108; critical edn. by C. H. Turner, *JTS*, 1919, pp. 289-310; see Lukyn Williams, *Adversus Judaeos*, pp. 306 ff.
40. *Adv. Jud.*, 1.
41. See p. 90.
42. Bonsirven, *Exégèse rabbinique*, p. 215.
43. P. Heinisch, *Der Einfluss Philos auf die älteste Exegese* (Munich, 1908).
44. On Philo's exegesis, see Bréhier, *Idées de Philon*, especially pp. 42 ff., and more especially Stein, *Allegorische Exegese des Philo* and *Philo und der Midrasch*.
45. See p. 86.
46. On typology as an exegetical method, see J. Daniélou, *Sacramentum Futuri, Etude sur les origines de la typologie biblique* (Paris, 1950).
47. *Barnabas*, 7. 7-11; Justin, *Dial.*, 40. 4; see Tertullian, *Adv. Jud.*, 14. Barnabas is moreover not well informed about the details of the ritual *Kippur* and invents freely at this point, as at others.
48. Justin, *Dial.*, 42. 1. Exod. 28:33 mentions the bells, but without specifying their number. Perhaps the figure arrived at by Justin is the result of confusion with the twelve stones of the pectoral in Exod. 28:17-21 (Archambault, *Dialogue*, 1, p. 186). Tertullian sees these twelve stones as symbols of the apostles.
49. *Barnabas*, 9. 8 ff.; Clement of Alexandria, *Strom.*, 6, 11, 84, and Ps. Cyprian, *De Pascha Computus.*, 18, 20, 22.
50. Justin, *Dial.*, 14. 2.
51. *Barnabas*, 10. 3.
52. Ibid., 10. 6. See Clement of Alexandria, *Paed.*, II, 10. 81-83; Novatian, *De Cibis Judaicis*, 13.
53. Kautzsch, *Apokryphen und Pseudepigraphen des A.T..*, II, pp. 17-19. See Bonsirven, *Exégèse rabbinique*, pp. 211 ff. The same interpretation of the dietary prohibitions is found in Lactantius, *Div. Instit.*, 4, 17, 18-21, and *Altercatio Simonis et Theophili*, 7. 28.
54. There is reason to believe that the differences between the schools of Alexandria and Antioch in respect of exegesis go back also to Jewish roots, broadly repeating the contrast between the exegesis of Philo and that of the Palestinian rabbis.
55. Justin, *Dial.*, 71. 1. See 68. 7 and 72-74. On the errors of translation of which the Jews accused the LXX, see Strack and Billerbeck, *Kommentar*, 4:414.
56. Ed. Conybeare, Fol. 76, 117-99; Lukyn Williams, *Adversus Judaeos*, p. 71.
57. C. J. Elliot, "Hebrew Learning among the Fathers," *Dict. of Christ. Biog.*, 4:859 ff.; S. Krauss, "Church Fathers," *JE*, 4:80.
58. *HE*, 6, 16, 1.
59. Justin, *Dial.*, 71. 2.
60. Archambault, *Dialogue*, 1:345, n.
61. *Testimonies*, 1. Summary by Lukyn Williams, *Adversus Judaeos*, pp. 3 ff. See also Daniélou, *Théologie du Judéo-Christianisme*, pp. 102 ff., and *Message évangélique et culture hellénistique* (Tournai, 1961), pp. 195 ff.; P. Prigent, *Les Testimonia dans le christianisme primitif. L'Epître de Barnabé I-XVI et ses sources* (Paris, 1961).
62. Hatch, *Essays in Biblical Greek* (Oxford, 1889), p. 203.
63. Ed. Hartel, *CSEL*, 1:35-148.
64. Lukyn Williams, *Adversus Judaeos*, pp. 124 ff., 215 ff.
65. Ibid., p. 7 ff.
66. Jer. 7:22 ff., Isa. 1:11; see Harris, *Testimonies*, 1:35, and Lukyn Williams, *Adversus Judaeos*, p. 128, n. 6.
67. *Barnabas*, 2. 5 ff. Similarly, Baruch, 3. 36 ff. is attributed to Jeremiah by Tertullian; *Contra Gnost.*, 8; Irenaeus, *Haer.*, 4, 34, 4, and *Altercatio Simonis et Theophili*, 1. 6.

68. Justin, *Dial.*, 76. 7; Ps. Gregory, *Test.*, 1 (*PG*, 46. 196).

69. *Barnabas*, 12. 10 ff.; Ps. Gregory, 16 (*PG*, 46. 228). Both of them read Κυρίω instead of Κύρω (Cyrus) the LXX reading. The same error reappears in Tertullian, *Adv. Jud.*, 7; Cyprian, *Test*, 1. 21, etc., and this too presupposes a florilegium, from which the error has been introduced and found its way into the Latin. It is very difficult to explain otherwise this agreement between authors writing in two different languages, short of supposing that the Latins had before them a version of the Bible that was itself wrong. The Vulgate reads: *Christo meo Cyro.*

Chapter 6

1. Tertullian, *Adv. Jud.*, 1-5.

2. Ibid., 6-14.

3. *Simonis et Theophili*, 1-26.

4. Ibid., 27-30. For the composition of Justin's Dialogue and the part played in it by the three principal lines of argument, see Archambault's edition, Introd., pp. lxxxviii ff.

5. *Hom.*, 11-13, and 15.

6. Ibid., 16-19.

7. Ibid., 17.

8. Strack, *Jesus*, pp. 26-37. See Travers Herford, *Christianity*, pp. 35-95. The Talmudic tradition concerning Jesus tells us nothing we do not know from other sources. It is, in the main, dependent on the facts given in the gospels. See Goguel, *Vie de Jésus*, pp. 50-54.

9. Origen, *Contra Celsum*, 1, 28, 32-33, 69.

10. See Strack and Billerbeck, *Kommentar*. If we are to believe Justin, *Dialogue*, 10:2, Trypho is struck most by the fact that the gospel is impossible to put into practice.

11. E.g., Klausner and Montefiore. See the literary work of Fleg.

12. Acts 2:46, 3:1, 5:42.

13. Deut. 21:23, see Gal. 3:13; Justin, *Dial.*, 32. 1, 89. 2, 96. 1; *Jason-Papiscus*, 29; see Lukyn Williams, *Adversus Judaeos*, p. 29; *Timothy-Aquila*, 100.

14. *Dial.*, 10. 3, 32. 1.

15. *Dial.*, 39. 7, 90. 1, 32. 1.

16. *Dial.*, 97. 106. Jewish exegesis often saw in the same texts the sufferings of Israel herself. On the late idea of a suffering Messiah see Strack and Billerbeck, *Kommentar*, 2:237 ff., Bonsirven, *Jud. Palest.*, 1:380 ff., Brierre-Narbonne, *Messie souffrant*. The question of the suffering Messiah in Judaism would take on quite a different color if it could be firmly established that the Teacher of Righteousness in the Qumran scrolls was (a) martyred and (b) identified by his disciples with the Messiah (or one of the Messiahs they expected).

17. Justin, *Dial.*, 73. 1; Tertullian, *Adv. Marc.*, 3. 15; *Adv. Jud.*, 10 and 13, and a number of the Latin fathers.

18. Justin, *Dial.*, 91. 4, 94, 5, 112. 2.

19. Ibid., 91. 3; see 90. 4 ff. 111. 1, 112. 2.

20. Deut. 33:17.

21. *Dial.*, 91. 2; see Tertullian, *Adv. Jud.*, 13, *Adv. Marc.*, 3. 18.

22. *Dial.*, 138. 2.

23. *Dial.*, 86.'

24. Dan. 9:20-27.

25. Justin, *Dial.*, 32. 3, 4; Tertullian, *Adv. Jud.*, 8; Irenaeus, 5, 25, 3.

26. *Barnabas*, 12. 10; Justin, *Dial.*, 32. 6-33, 2, and 83.

27. Justin, *Dial.*, 34:2-6, 64:6.

28. Ibid., 33:1, 67:1, 68:7, etc.

29. Ibid., 34, 64. 5 ff., etc.

30. However, *b. Sanh.*, 94a says that Hezekiah had been chosen to be the Messiah, but that he proved unworthy. This is perhaps the origin of the interpretation advanced by Justin. On rabbinic interpretation of Ps. 110, see Strack and Billerbeck, *Kommentar*, 4:1, pp. 453 ff. On Hezekiah, Bonsirven, *Jud. Palest.*, 1:367 ff. and 377 ff.

31. Isa. 7:14; Justin, *Dial.*, 43. 8. 67. 1; see Irenaeus, 3, 21, 1.

32. *Dial.*, 49, 1 and 48. 1; see Origen, *Contra Celsum*, 1. 49, 4. 2.

33. *Hom.*, 17. 1. The anti-Jewish nature of the homily is clearly brought out by its very title: "Concerning the Messiah, in order to prove that he is the Son of God, in answer to the Jews, who insult God's people." It is the very prototype of the defensive apologetic that I described above.

34. Exod. 4:22 ff.

35. 2 Sam. 7:14.

36. Exod. 7:1.

37. On the theology of Aphraates, F. C. Burkitt, *Early Eastern Christianity*, pp. 90 ff.; Schwen, *Afrahat*. On his relations with Jews, Richter, "Uber die älteste Auseinandersetzung der syrischen Christen mit den Juden," and Gavin, *Aphraates and the Jews*, pp. 96-166. See Lukyn Williams, *Adversus Judaeos*, pp. 95 ff.

38. *Dial.*, 56. 4, see 56. 10, 60. 1-5. On Justin's theology see, in particular, *Dial.*, 58. 9, 61. 1, and the notes in Archambault's edition, 1:273, 284. See 1 *Apol.*, 10. 6: ὁ λόγος θεῖος ὤν. The same terminology is found in Philo, *De Somniis*, 1. 39, and Origen. See Harnack, *Dogmengeschichte*, 3:623.

39. Justin, *Dial.*, passim, and especially 54-63.

40. Ibid., 56. 1; see *Simon-Theophilus*, 6.

41. Gen. 18:1-15.

42. Philo, *De Abrah.*, 24.

43. *Dial.*, 56. 5. See Josephus, *Ant. Jud.*, 1:12, and for other rabbinic texts, Goldfahn, *Justinus Martyr*, pp. 111 ff. Justin's interpretation is taken up by the majority of the fathers of the Church. For references see Archambault, *Dialogue*, p. 245.

44. Justin, *Dial.*, 56. 22.

45. Gen. 32:22-30; *Dial.*, 58. 6.

46. Gen. 35:6-10; *Dial.*, 58. 8.

47. Exod. 3:2, *Dial.*, 60. 2.

48. Exod. 13:21, *Simon-Theophilus*, 11, see Justin, *Dial.*, 37. 4.

49. Jerome, *Quaest. Heb. in Gen.*, 1. 1. See Harnack, *Altercatio Simonis et Theophili*, pp. 130-34.

50. *Timothy-Aquila*, 78; see Tertullian, *Contra Prax.*, 5, *Consult. Zach. et Apol.*, 2. 3.

51. Gen. 1:26; see Chrysostom, *Homily against the Jews*, 7. 3 (*PG*, 48:919).

52. Gen. 3:22. *Dial.*, 62. 2; see *Athanasius-Zacchaeus*, 3, *Simon-Theophilus* 8.

53. *Dial.*, 61. 1.

54. *Athanasius-Zacchaeus*, 22. See Lukyn Williams, *Adversus Judaeos*, p. 121.

55. The line of argument is significantly different when the subject of legal observances arises in controversy with antinomian heretics of the Marcionite variety. In such circumstances the need is to defend the unity of the divine revelation, and it therefore has to be shown that Jewish rites were in the past indispensable media of sanctification and salvation for Israel.

56. Justin, *Dial.*, 44. 2.

57. *Dial.*, 93. 1 and 11. 2.

58. Irenaeus, 4, 13, 1 (*PG*, 7. 1006 ff.).

59. Ibid., 4, 16, 5 (*PG*, 7. 1018).

60. Schoeps, *Tempelzerstörung*, p. 21.

61. Lev. 18:1.

62. Bonsirven, *Jud. Palest.*, 1:27, 251.

63. *Hom.*, 11, 1, 3, 7. A brief summary of all the arguments Christians had worked out against circumcision of the flesh (against which they set circumcision of the heart) is given by Zeno of Verona in his *Tract.* 13 (*PL*, 11, 2, 345 ff.). This is a sermon devoted entirely to this one question.

64. *Dial.*, 16. 2-3. On Hadrian's command that no Jews should enter Jerusalem, Justin, 1 *Apol.*, 47. 5, *Dial.*, 40. 2, 92. 2, Eusebius, *HE*, 4, 6, 3, Tertullian, *Apol.*, 21. See Schürer, *Geschichte*, 1⁴:69, n. 146.

65. Tertullian, *Adv. Jud.*, 3; see Irenaeus, 4, 16, 1.

66. Jer. 9:25 ff.

67. *Dial.*, 28. 4.

68. *Barnabas*, 9. 6, *Simon-Theophilus*, 18. See Origen, *Contra Celsum*, 1. 22, 5. 41, Aphraates, *Hom.*, 11. 10, Ambrose, *Letters*, 71. 5-6 (*PL*, 16. 1243-50). Ambrose's argument is directed against antinomian heretics. It presents circumcision as a kind of sacrament and makes excuses for the Christians' having abandoned it. The same point of view is found in Jerome, *Ep.*, 19 (*PL*, 30. 188 ff.).

69. Justin, *Dial.*, 23. 5. See Zeno of Verona, op. cit., 4-5.

70. Justin, *Dial.*, 23. 4, 92. 3.

71. Ibid., 33. 2, 19. 4, 46. 3, 92. 2, Tertullian, *Adv. Jud.*, 14, Aphraates, *Homily*, 11. 4, Chrysostom, *Hom.*, 7. 4 (*PG*, 48. 922).

72. Justin, *Dial.*, 18. 2. The argument reappears several times elsewhere, e.g., Ambrosiaster, *Quaestiones Veteris et Novi Testamenti*, 44. 9, Irenaeus, 4, 15, 2 (*PG*, 7. 1013).

73. Justin, *Dial.*, 20. 3, 21. 1, 22.

74. Ibid., 46. 5; see 90. 4.

75. Ibid., 19. 6.

76. Ibid., 20. 1.

77. Ibid., 20. 1.

78. Tertullian, *Adv. Jud.*, 4, Aphraates, *Hom.*, 13. 4.

79. Joshua, 6:4, 1 Macc. 2:41. See Tertullian, *Adv. Jud.*, 4, *Simon-Theophilus*, 28. Aphraates, *Hom.*, 13. 7 also insists on the fact that in the temple worship the priests, in order to fulfil their sacrificial functions, violate the Sabbath rest in a number of ways, and have the sanction of a divine precept for doing so. Now, God cannot command some to do what He commands others not to do. He cannot hold the layman guilty for doing what the priests do in their service of God. In other instances, he remarks, infringement of the commands is a matter of opportunism, neither more nor less. If the Maccabees decided to fight on the Sabbath and thus gained a victory, it was only because Sabbath observance had earlier cost them a resounding defeat (1 Macc. 2:32).

80. Ezek, 20:25, Justin, *Dial.*, 21. 4.

81. Justin, *Dial.*, 11. 2.

82. Gal. 5:3.

83. Sometimes Christian apologists condemn the law because some parts of it contradict others. Thus Zeno of Verona (*Tract.*, 15:3) points out that a child must be circumcised on the eighth day. When the eighth day falls on a Sabbath, it is necessary either to break the Sabbath rule or to break the eight-day rule.

84. *Dial.*, 22. 2-6.

85. Jer. 7:22; see *Barnabas*, 2. 6.

86. Amos 5:25 ff.; see Acts 7:42 ff.

87. Justin, *Dial.*, 19. 6; see Irenaeus, 4:15, Tertullian, *Adv. Marc.*, 2:18, Jerome, *in Is.*, 1. 2, *in Jer.*, 7:21. This explanation is sometimes combined with an allegorical interpretation of sacrifice. It is held to prefigure either the death of Christ or the spiritual sacrifices of the new covenant. Thus St. Augustine, *Adv. Jud.*, 6. 8, 9. 12.

88. *Adv. Jud.*, 5; see Justin, *Dial.*, 28. 5, 41. 2, Augustine, *Adv. Jud.*, 9. 13.

89. *Homily against the Jews*, 4. 6 (*PG*, 48. 880).

90. *Hom.*, 6. 5 (*PG*, 48. 911): οὗτοι οἱ νῦν πατριάρχαι παρ' ὑμῖν λεγόμενοι οὐχ ἱερεῖς εἰσιν, ἀλλὰ ἱερεῖς ὑποκρίνονται.

91. *Hom.*, 7. 1-2 (*PG*, 48. 916-18). The same argument is found in Tertullian, *Adv. Marc.*, 3. 23, and Augustine, *Adv. Jud.*, 9. 12 ff.

92. *Hom.*, 4. 4 (*PG*, 48. 476). καὶ γὰρ ἐτὶ τῶν ἑορτῶν τῶν Ἰουδαϊκῶν οὐ καιρὸν μόνον, ἀλλὰ καὶ τόπον παρατηρεῖν ἐκέλευσεν ὁ νόμος.

93. Deut., 16:5 ff.

94. Ps. 137, Dan. 3, 38.

95. Dan. 10:2.

96. Chrysostom, *Hom.*, 4. 4 (*PG*, 48. 877). ἡ τοῦ τόπου παρατήρησις τῆς τοῦ καιροῦ παρατηρήσεώς ἐστιν ἀναγκαιότερα.

97. See Cyprian, *Test.*, *praefatio*; Augustine, *Adv. Jud.*, 1. 1; Commodian, *Carmina Apol.*, 262 ff. On this question see Bonwetsch, *Schriftbeweise*.

98. *Hom.*, 19. 4.

99. Isa. 11:11.

100. *Homily against the Jews*, 5. 5 (*PG*, 48. 890 ff.).

101. The text of Dan. 9:20-27 is used by Tertullian to demonstrate both the fact that the Christ is the Messiah and also that Israel has been rejected. *Adv. Jud.*, 8; see Lukyn Williams, *Adversus Judaeos*, p. 47, n. 7. On this matter of the rebuilding of the temple and its place in Jewish Christian polemic, see Schoeps, *Tempelzerstörung*, pp. 35-45.

102. See p. 188. For Cain and Abel, see Maximus the Arian, *Contra Jud.*, 1.

103. *Barnabas*, 13 (*PL*, 57. 793). See Lukyn Williams, *Adversus Judaeos*, p. 307.

104. On these allegories see Blumenkranz, *Judenpredigt* pp. 168 ff. and n. 26.

105. *Homily against the Jews*, 7. 5 (*PG*, 48. 923).

106. Aphraates, *Hom.*, 16. 1, appeals to Gen. 17:5 to show that the gentiles were called before the election of Israel. See *Barnabas*, 13:7. It should be observed that Abraham, who came from polytheism to monotheism, is sometimes seen by Jewish tradition itself as the ancestor and prototype of the proselytes. Bousset/Gressmann, *Judentum*, p. 196.

107. E.g., Justin, *Dial.*, 135-36. See Bonwetsch, *Schriftbeweise*.

108. Commodian, *Instr.*, 1, 38, 2: *Sic exheredes eritis*. See *Barnabas*, 13; Origen, *Contra Celsum*, 2. 78; Cyprian, *Test.*, 1.

109. Aphraates, *Hom.*, 16. 4.

110. *Dial.*, 123. 7.

111. Ibid., 122. 1-4, 123. 1 ff.

112. Ibid., 11-15.

113. Cyprian, *Test.*, 1. 14-17.

114. Chrysostom, *Homily against the Jews*, 7. 4 (*PG*, 48. 922) and *On Melchizedek* (*PG*, 56. 268). See Simon, *Melchisédech*, pp. 64, 86 ff.

115. Justin, *Dial.*, 52. 4, 82. 1, for argument relating to the transfer of the gift of prophecy. See Irenaeus, 2, 32, 4; 5, 6, 1; Clement of Alexandria, *Strom.*, 1, 21, 135 ff.; 4, 13, 93; Tertullian, *Adv. Jud.*, 8, 11, 13; Eusebius, *HE*, 4, 18, 8. All these texts are connected with Matt. 11:13, "For all the prophets and the law prophesied until John."

116. Justin, *Dial.*, 11. 5.

117. See Moore, *Christian Writers*, pp. 197-200. In the apologies directed toward the pagans this aspect of the argument is reduced to a bare outline.

118. *Adv. Jud.*, 1. *Nam occasio quidem defendendi etiam gentibus divinam gratiam habuit hinc praerogativam, quod sibi vindicare Dei legem instituerit homo ex gentibus nec de prosapia Israelitum Judaeus.*

119. E.g., *Contra Celsum.*, 1. 45 and 49; *Selecta in Ps.*, (*PG*, 2. 1056).

120. On the identification of Trypho with the R. Tarphon mentioned in the Talmud, and on the authenticity of some of the elements of the dialogue, see Archambault, *Dialogue 1*, Introd., pp. xcii ff. For bibliography on this question, ibid., p. xciii, no. 5.

121. Freimann, "Wortführer," *MGWJ*, 1911, pp. 556 ff.

122. Celsus's Jew is within the Alexandrian Jewish tradition. He has a theory of the logos close to that of Philo (2. 31). Trypho's Hellenism is less obvious, especially as far as hypostases are concerned. As I have pointed out, he explains the vision at Mamre by referring it to angels. But for the most part, both Trypho and Celsus's Jew are literary artifacts. They are doubtless modelled on real figures, but both Justin and Celsus have been able to adapt them to their own needs.

123. *Contra Celsum*, 1. 24, 1. 67, 2. 34, 2. 55.

124. See p. 282.

125. See pp. 189 ff.

126. See p. 137.

127. See Justin, *Dial.*, 61; Cyprian, *Test.*, 2. 1; *Athanasius-Zacchaeus*, 3-20.

128. *Dem. Ev.*, 4. 16.

129. *Dem. Ev.*, 1. 1, 6. 11.

130. *In Ep. ad Tit.*, 3. 9 (*PL*, 26. 595).

131. Justin, *Dial.*, 38. 1. See Archambault's note ad loc., 1:168. It was sometimes the Christians who were aggressive. Jerome gives them advice in his commentary on Titus, loc. cit.

132. *In Is.*, 7. 14.

133. *In locis difficillimis liberae disputationis excursu nascentes fugiunt quaestiones; in Is.*, 44. 6.

134. *Ep.*, 42 *ad Principiam*, 1. 236.

135. See p. 185.

136. *Praef. in Ps.* (*PL*, 28. 1186).

137. Οἱ Ἰουδαῖοι οἱ πάντοτε εἰς ἀντίρρησιν ἕτοιμοι (*Catech.*, 13. 7).

138. Aphraates, passim, especially 12, 11, 12. 7, 17. 1, 10, 21. 1-7. See Lukyn Williams, *Adversus Judaeos*, p. 86. Other witnesses to this controversy are Isidore of Pelusium, *Ep.*, 1. 141, 3. 93, 4. 17 (*PG*, 78, 176, 797, 1064) and St. Nilus, *Ep.*, 57 (*PG*, 69, 108). Similarly Theodoret of Cyrrhus speaks of his numerous discussions with pagans and Jews. For other references to these discussions between Jews and Christians, Juster, *Les Juifs*, 1:53, n. 4.

139. See especially, besides the exegetical works of Jerome, such interesting and controversial documents as Ambrosiaster and the *Quaestiones Veteris et Novi Testamenti*. Apart from the fact that they betray an accurate knowledge of Jewish matters, and employ an exegetical method whose sobriety contrasts favorably with the allegorism frequently resorted to by the majority of ancient writers, they are not relevant to my present subject. The one exception is *Quaestio 44* (*Adv. Jud.*), which I referred to above. Because of these very peculiarities of theirs they deserve a special study to themselves. For these texts and the problem of their authorship, see Labriolle, *Littérature latine chrétienne*, pp. 384 ff.

Chapter 7

1. Bibliography in Bonsirven, *Jud. Palest.*, 1:69.

2. See also *Bewegungen*, pp. 169-234; *REJ* 38 (1899): 37, 194-203.

3. Review by Bacher, *JQR*, 1905, pp. 171-83.

4. For the same opinion, Marmorstein, *REJ* 92 (1932): 48; Büchler, "Ueber die Minim von

Sepphoris und Tiberias im 2 und 3 Jahrhundert," *Cohen Festschrift*, 1912, pp. 271–95, refuses to see in them either Jewish Christians or even heretical Jews, but regards them as non-Jewish gnostics.

5. Criticism in general at first seemed disposed to side with Travers Herford, at least to the extent of rejecting Friedländer's theory, see Fiebig, review of *Christianity...*, in *Theol. Lit. Zeitung* 21 (1904): 588 ff., and Bousset, review of Friedländer, *Der Antichrist*, ibid., pp. 633. More recent works sometimes tend to revert to Friedländer's views, e.g., Bonsirven, *Jud. Palest.*, 1:69. A middle point of view is taken by Strack, *Jesus*, p. 47.

6. The question of the origin of the Epistle to the Hebrews has been taken up again recently by Kosmala, *Hebräer-Essener-Christen* (Leyden, 1959). The author reckons that the super-scription, *To the Hebrews*, should be taken in its most exact sense. The recipients for whom it was intended were Hebrews, i.e., Jews, and more precisely, Essenes. They had not yet been converted to Christianity, but one of them, who had been won over to faith in Christ, is here trying to win over the rest. His proof is founded basically on parallels, not all equally close or equally penetrating, between the epistle and the Qumran documents. I am surprised that the author is able to pass in silence over the theory of an Alexandrian origin for this document, and over the affinities it displays with the thought of Philo, and that he does not even mention the recent work of Spicq. In the commentary Spicq has written in the series *Etudes Bibliques* (Paris, 1954), and in his article, "Le philonisme de l'Epître aux Hébreux," *RB*, 1949, pp. 542 ff., and 1950, pp. 218 ff., he has attributed the letter to "a follower of Philo who had been converted to Christianity." Apart from this, it is best not to draw too firm a line between Qumran and the Hellenistic diaspora. See, by the same author, "L'Epître aux Hébreux, Apollos, Jean-Baptiste, les Hellénistes et Qumran," *Revue de Qumran*, 1959, pp. 365–91. There is no great help to be derived, one way or the other, from the term *Hebrews*, since it was in use also in the diaspora, where it quite often served to designate Jewish communities. On this point, most recently, H.-J. Léon, *The Jews of ancient Rome*, pp. 148 ff.

7. There is a tendency nowadays to recognize this Greek transcription in the *Genistae* of whom Justin Martyr speaks, *Dial.*, 80:4; Hennecke, *N. T. Apokryphen* [2], p. 24, n. 5; Bonsirven, *Jud. Palest.*, 1:70, n. 1; Simon, "Sur deux hérésies juives," *RHPR*, 1937, pp. 54 ff.

8. *j. Sanh.*, X, 6. On the pre-Christian Jewish Gnostics, see, in addition to Friedländer's *Gnostizismus*, Bergmann, *Jüd. Apologetik*, pp. 8, 38.

9. *Quid dicam de Hebionitis, qui Christianos esse se simulant? Usque hodie per totas Orientis synagogas inter Judaeos haeresis est quae dicitur Minaeorum et a Pharisaeis huc usque damnatur, quos vulgo Nazaraeos nuncupant.* (*Ep. ad. Aug.*, 112. 13).

10. Lévi, "Minim dans le Talmud," suggests a pattern of development exactly the reverse of this. At first there existed Jewish Christians or gnostic Christians, and only later were there antinomian gnostic Jews. On historical grounds this seems to me impossible to sustain, because, among other reasons, it ignores the existence of those pre-Christian Jewish gnostics whose presence Friedländer has recognized and who were already classed as *minim*.

11. This is also Bacher's opinion. *REJ* 38 (1899): 38–46.

12. See Cullmann, *Roman pseudo-clémentin*, pp. 220 ff.

13. Strack has collected a number of them; *Jesus*, pp. 50–56.

14. *T. Hull.*, II, 22 ff.

15. *j. Shabb.*, XIV, 4; see *j. Ab. Zara*, II, 2.

16. *b. Ab. Zara*, 27b. On these various texts, see Travers Herford, *Christianity*, pp. 103–8, and Strack, *Jesus*, pp. 21 ff.

17. Strack, *Jesus*, p. 23. The same episode, with some more detail concerning the conversation of R. Eliezer and the *min*, *b. ab. Zara*, 16b–17a; *Midr. Eccles.*, 1. 8.

18. Prov., 5:8.

19. *HE*, 3, 32.

20. *b. Ab. Zara*, 4a: see *b. Ber.*, 7a, where it is said that a *min* who was a neighbor of R. Joshua b. Levi, nearly drove him mad by quoting verses of scripture at him.

21. *Praef. in Job.*, 1. See *Ep.*, 1810, 125, 12: *Comm. ad Habac.*, 2. 15: *Am.*, 3. 10. Bardy, "St. Jerome et ses maîtres hébreux," *Revue bénédictine* 46 (1934):145 ff. It is probable that Origen and Eusebius both derived their knowledge of Hebrew from Jewish teachers. C. J. Elliot, "Hebrew Learning among the Fathers," *Dict. of Christ. Biog.*, 5:859 ff.

22. Correspondence between Augustine and Jerome, *Ep.*, 71. 5 and 75. 22.

23. It may be recalled (see Renan, *Eglise chrétienne*, p. 287) that some Christian Bible translators, Symmachus and Theodotion, had connections of one sort or another with Judaism, and also that the Syriac Peshitta, which was translated direct from the Hebrew and provides remarkable parallels with the Targums, would appear to presuppose collaboration with Jews. See Baumstark, *Geschichte der syrischen Literatur*, p. 18.

24. Other texts bear witness to the same uncertainty among the Babylonians concerning *minuth*. They do not clearly distinguish between *minim* and pagans (*b. Hull.*, 13b) and sometimes tend to confuse *minuth* with sexual immorality (*b. Ab. Zara*, 17a).

25. *M. Sota*, IX, 15.

26. *b. Sanh.*, 97b; *Midr. Cant. R.*, II, 13.

27. *b. Ab. Zara*. 17a.

28. *j. Nedar.*, III, 10.

29. Gal. 3:7.

30. Gen. 25:23. See Rom. 9:10 ff.

31. *Adv. Jud.*, 1.

32. Gen. 36:1.

33. *Ep.*, 196, 3, 13.

34. The argument between Tertullian and Augustine is gone over again and again. Cyprian, *Test.*, 1. 19; Irenaeus, *Adv. Haer.*, 4, 21, 2; Commodian, *Carmina Apol.*, 189, 251 etc.; Augustine, *Adv. Jud.*, 7. 9; *Civ. Dei*, 16. 35; *in Ps.*, 46. 6; 77. 9; 118, 5, 3; *Serm.*, 5. 4, 122. 4.

35. E.g., *b. Yoma*, 56b, *b. Ab. Zara*, 4a, *b. Pes.*, 85b, *b. Taan.*, 3b, 20a, *b. Sot.*, 38b, *b. Yebam.*, 102b. See Bacher, *Tannaiten*, 1:82; Marmorstein, "Judaism," *HUCA*, 1935, pp. 223 ff. On the eternal call of Israel, Schoeps, *Agadisches zur Auserwählung Israëls*.

36. *b. Menach.*, 53b.

37. Isa. 54:1.

38. *b. Ber.*, 10a.

39. It will be noted that the text is quoted by Justin, *Dial.*, 13. 8, and already by St. Paul, Gal. 4:27. It became part of the repertoire of anti-Jewish controversy.

40. *Tanh. B. Gen.*, 44b, *Pesiq. R.*, 14b, *b. Ber.*, 5a; see *Ex. R.*, 47, *j. Peah*, II, 6. Marmorstein, *Religionsgeschichte Studien*, 1; Ziegler, *Kampf*, p. 70.

41. See p. 165.

42. *Pesiq. R.*, 116b, 117a, *Gen. R.*, 11. 46, *Num. R.*, 14. 9; Marmorstein, *REJ*, 1914, pp. 161 ff.

43. *Ex. R.*, 30. 5; see *T. Ab. Zara*, 6. 7, *b. Ab. Zara*, 3b, *j. Rosh hash*, I, 3.

44. Aphraates, *Hom.*, 13.

45. Ziegler, *Kampf*, p. 60.

46. *j. Ber.* 3c. It is furthermore established that the decalogue originally figured in the daily Synagogue liturgy and that it was suppressed in reaction against Christianity. *b. Ber.*, 12a, see Elbogen, *Gottesdienst*, p. 242, Marmorstein, *REJ*, 1929, Bacher, *Amoräer*, 1:499.

47. *Midr. Ex. R.*, 46, on 34:1.

48. *Ab. R. Nath.*, 141; M*Makk*, III, 16; *Sifre Deut.*, 36. 75b, *b. Menach.*, 43b; *T. Ber.*, 1; *b. Shabb.*, 130a.

49. *Pesiq. R.*, 220b; *Midr. Lev. R.*, 27. 6.

50. See p. 76. The rabbis were quite prepared to admit that the covenant had been broken because of Israel's sins, but not in irrevocable fashion. *Tanh.*, 5. 49) They distinguished three successive covenants: one at the time of the flight from Egypt; one at Sinai before the sin of the golden calf; and a reentry into grace immediately following that sin.

51. *Midr. Cant. R.*, on 1;14; see Bacher, *Amoräer*, 1:469.

52. *Midr. Lam. R.*, 1. 1.

53. Schoeps, *Tempelzerstörung*, p. 9.

54. *Judenchristentum*, p. 398.

55. They are gathered together in Strack's collection, *Einleitung*, pp. 18-46, which is more complete on this point than that of Travers Herford, pp. 35-95.

56. *j. Shabb.*, VI, 10; *Midr. Ex. R.*, on 20:2, *Deut. R.*, on 6:4; Strack, *Einleitung*, p. 76; see Origen, *Contra Celsum*, 1. 29.

57. For texts see Bergmann, *Apologetik*, p. 83. See Tertullian, *Adv. Jud.*, 10, *Adv. Marc.*, 3. 18; Schoeps, *Religionsgespräch*, p. 29.

58. Travers Herford, *Christianity*, p. 263.

59. Ziegler is suffering from the same error of perspective when he writes (*Kampf*, p. 59) in connection with God's failure to observe the Sabbath, the two powers, and the nondivine origin of the ritual law: "These are without doubt questions which no Christian would ever have asked." Such a viewpoint is based on information too narrowly confined to the Talmud, and on a regrettable ignorance of Christian texts.

60. 2 Cor. 3:17.

61. *b. Sanh.*, 38b.

62. *Dial.*, 56. 22 ff.

63. Labbe, 3:258, n. 16, cited by Lagrange, *Messianisme*, p. 296, n. 3. See Eusebius, *Dem. Ev.*, 5. 8; Ps. Augustine, *Adversus quinque haereses*, 4 (*PL*, 42. 199).

64. *Athanasius-Zaccaeus*, 17, ἡ σοφία κύριος καὶ θεὸς οὖσα ἔβρεξε παρὰ κυρίου τοῦ θεοῦ πῦρ καὶ θεῖον.

65. See p. 162.

66. *Gen. R.*, on 1:26 (R. Samuel b. Nachman).

67. *j. Ber.*, IX, 1 (R. Simlai).

68. *b. Sanh.*, 38b.

69. *Sifre*, on Deut. 32:39; *b. Pes.*, 56a; *Midr. Deut. R.* on 6:4.

70. *j. Ber.*, IX, 1. Other texts, against this, assert that if man was created by himself (*M. Sanh.*, IV, 5) and last of creation (*T. Sanh.*, VIII, 7) it was in order to prevent the *minim* from saying that there were several powers in heaven or that God had a companion in his work of creation.

71. *Dial.*, 62. 2.

72. *Simon-Theophilus*, 1; *Athanasius-Zaccaeus*, 6.

73. Bonsirven, *Jud. Palest.*, 1:232.

74. Exod. 23:21.

75. *b. Sahn.*, 38b, see Bonsirven, *Jud. Palest.*, 1:236.

76. Friedländer, *Gnostizismus*, p. 103.

77. Travers Herford, *Christianity*, p. 286.

78. Deut. 5:2, *Pesiq. R.*, 100b, 101a.

79. *Midr. Ps. ad loc.*, Buber's edition, p. 188. The rabbis similarly refuted the objection raised by their adversaries to the plural form of the divine name *elohim*. The plurality of names by which God was known, El, Elohim, Yahweh, Adonai, etc., they explained on the analogy of imperial titles. These diverse titles all describe the one prince: Caesar, Augustus, Basileus, etc. See Dubnow, *Weltgeschichte*, 3:165.

80. See p. 161.

81. The connection between the two terms is illuminated by Travers Herford, *Christianity*, pp. 305, 362 ff.

82. Dubnow, *Weltgeschichte*, 3:164 ff.

83. See p. 199.

84. On these rabbis and those referred to below, and on some of the texts studied in the

course of this chapter, see Strack's index and catalogue, *Einleitung*[5], pp. 117 ff. and 230 ff.; Bacher, *Tannaiten, Amoräer* passim; Derenbourg, *Histoire et géographie de la Palestine*, and the articles in *JE* and *EJ*.

85. Ziegler, *Kampf*, p. 61.

86. Harnack, *Mission*, II[4], pp. 647–48.

87. See Bacher, "The Church Father Origen and the Rabbi Hoshaya," *JQR*, 3 (1891): 357-63.

88. *Selecta in Ps.*, (*PG*, 2. 1056). Ἰουλλῷ τῷ πατριάρχῃ must be corrected to τοῦ πατριάρχου, following the suggestion of Graetz, "Hillel der Patriarchensohn," *MGWJ* 30 (1881): 437-48. See *JE* 6:401; Moore, 1:165, proposes to read Ἰούδας i.e., Judah II.

89. *b. Ber.*, 28b, 29a.

90. Twelfth Benediction. The ancient text, which mentions the Christians, was published by S. Schechter, *JQR*, 1898, pp. 654 ff., from fragments of manuscripts discovered at Cairo. For bibliography on the question, Bonsirven, *Jud. Palest.*, 2:145, n. 1; see Elbogen, *Gottesdienst*, pp. 27 ff.

91. Graetz, *Geschichte*, 4:105.

92. *b. Ber.*, 28b-29a. See *T. Ber.*, III, 25, *j. Ber.*, V, 3.

93. M. Meg., IV, 8-9.

94. *j. Ber.*, V, 3.

95. *T. Hull.*, II, 20-21; see *b. Hull.*, 13ab. In the *Dialogue of Simon and Theophilus*, 28, the two disputants discuss the wine of the Christians and the wine of the Jews.

96. *b. Gitt.*, 45b.

97. *T. Shabb.*, XIII, 5.

98. *T. Bab. Mez.*, II, 33; *b. Ab. Zara*, 26ab (R. Abbahu).

99. *T. Shabb.*, XIII, 5. See Origen, *Hom., 1 in Ps.* (cited by Harnack, *Mission*, 1:66, n.) *Etiam nunc Judaei non moventur adversus Gentiles, adversus eos qui idola colunt et Deum blasphamant, et illos non oderunt nec indignantur adversus eos; adversus Christianos vero insatiabili odio feruntur.*

100. *Dial.*, 16. 4. See pp. 255, 116.

101. Lagrange, *Messianisme*, p. 298.

102. St. Jerome, as we have seen, tells us that *minim* is synonymous with "Nazarenes": which is to say, in his mind, it means "Jewish Christians." But this proves nothing against my interpretation. The fact must not be lost sight of that originally, when all Christians were of Palestinian derivation, "Nazarene" was synonymous with "Christian" in general. Thus it remained in Jewish usage, and Jerome either does not know or has forgotten this fact. Being a gentile Christian himself, it was hard for him to think of his own Christianity as a Jewish heresy.

Chapter 8

1. Mommsen, *Röm. Geschichte*, 5:519.

2. For a recent exposition of the subject and bibliographical notes, see Pauly-Wissowa, "Antisemitismus," *RE, Supplement*, 5:3-43. The essential texts are brought together in Reinach's collection. See the work of Fischer and Kittel, *Das antike Weltjudentum*, which is anti-semitic in tone.

3. Ovid, *Ars Amat.*, 1. 415, Reinach, *Textes*, p. 248. Other examples may be found in Juster, *Les Juifs*, 1:172, n. 4. The terra cotta caricatures found frequently in the Rhineland which date from the third and fourth centuries (see Fischer and Kittel, *Weltjudentum*, pp. 167-219) are not necessarily modeled exclusively on Jews. They may be intended to ridicule Semites in general, especially Syrians, who were very widespread in the empire.

4. *Hist. Aug., Alex. Sev.*, 28.

5. Josephus, *Contra Apionem*, 2, 4, 33, Reinach, *Textes*, p. 128.

6. This is what Juvenal's *graeculus esuriens* refers to (*Sat.*, 3. 78). For the Greeks, it was the Egyptians and Phoenicians who were famed for their money and their trading: Plato, *Republic*, 4. 436, *Laws*, 5. 316. For Polybius (6. 46) it was the Cretans and Carthaginians (6. 56) who were distinguished by their unbridled love of gain. On Carthaginian greed, see the Latin authors cited by Gsell, *Histoire Ancienne*, 4 : 217. Peoples subject to Rome often attributed the Roman conquests to the lure of material profit as well as to the desire for domination and the love of glory. See, for example, the discourses of Jugurtha, *Romanos injustos, profunda avaritia* (Sallust, *Jug.*, 81. 1) and of Calgacus: *Raptores orbis. . . . si locuples hostis est, avari, si pauper, ambitiosi* (Tacitus, *Agric.*, 30). Texts cited by Fuchs, *Geistige Widerstand*, p. 17, and nn. 52, 53. See Jerome, *in Is.*, 2. 8 (*PL*, 24. 48): *Nihil Judaeorum et Romanorum gente esse avarius*. The aiming of this charge at the Jews is not earlier than Christianity. See p. 213.

7. *Jam pridem Syrus in Tiberim defluxit Orontes* (Juvenal, *Sat.*, 3. 60). The reference is to the entire East, Greece included. For Egypt, see Tacitus, *Hist.*, 1. 11: *Superstitione ac lascivia discordem et mobilem, insciam legum, ignaram magistratuum*.

8. Vopiscus, *Vita Saturnini*, 8. On the question of authenticity, Labriolle, *Réaction païenne*, pp. 51 ff.

9. Juster, *Les Juifs*, 2 : 251-322.

10. See texts relating to the diverse professions taken up by Jews in Fischer and Kittel, *Weltjudentum*, pp. 53-58, and notes p. 222. Agriculture would take first place, especially in Egypt and Asia Minor. See Leitzmann, *Geschichte der alten Kirche*, 1 : 73.

11. Martial, 12, 57, 13; Juvenal, 3. 12 ff., 6. 542 ff. Reinach, *Textes d'auteurs grecs et romains*, pp. 289 ff.

12. Josephus, *Contra Apionem*, 1 : 12, brings out the contrast between trading people and the Jews: οὔτ ἐμπορίαις χαίρομεν οὐδὲ ταῖς πρὸς ἄλλους διὰ τούτων ἐπιμιξίαις.

13. The Western diaspora was hardly affected by it. The troubles provoked among the Jews of Rome by the first Christian preaching (Suetonius, *Claudius*, 25, Acts 18 : 2) were not concerned with the traditional kind of Messianism. What Heinemann calls political anti-Semitism arose out of fear that the Jews were becoming too powerful, and was really only found at Alexandria.

14. In this belief the place of the Messianic hope seems to have been quite modest, as far as the Jews of the dispersion were concerned. The wider Judaism had little time for this strictly national side of the religion. On the other hand, the place of "Messianic" aspirations in pagan spirituality in that era is well known. The Sibylline Oracles show that this expanded Messianism provided some common ground.

15. *Quanta concordia*. Cicero, *pro Flacco*, 28:66; see Josephus, *Contra Apionem*, 2. 39, Tacitus, *Hist.*, 5. 5, Reinach, pp. 238, 306. On Jewish xenophobia, see Reinach, especially pp. 56 (Posidonius of Apamea), 63 ff. (Apollonius Molon), 133 (Apion), 176 (Philostratus), and 255 (Trogus Pompeius).

16. Tacitus accuses both Jews (*Hist.*, 5:5) and Christians (*Annals*, 15:44) of hatred of the human race, in exactly the same terms. See Minucius Felix, *Octavius*, 8-9, who sums up the principal complaints made by the pagan masses against the Christians after having brought exactly the same ones against the Jews. On Jewish ritual murder, see Apion, Reinach, *Textes*, p. 132. On Christian ritual murders, Eusebius, *HE*, 5, 1, 26.

17. They are analyzed by Heinemann, "Antisemitismus" pp. 22 ff. The author remarks (p. 37) that Greek scholarship was not very interested in Judaism. When the Greeks did exhibit interest, as in the case of Hecataeus of Abdera and Posidonius of Apamea, it was with a certain sympathy for Jewish monotheism. This stream of thought, albeit soon contaminated with anti-Semitic criticisms, is continued, however, by Celsus, who praises the Jews for their sense of tradition (*Contra Celsum*, 5. 35) and by Porphyry (Eusebius, *Praep. Ev.*, 9. 10). See Labriolle, *Réaction païenne*, p. 458.

18. The development is clearly perceptible in the second century. Tacitus is equally hard on both religions (see above, n. 16). The anti-Jewish strand of thinking loses its virulence after Juvenal, and meanwhile the "first uneasiness" about Christianity is becoming more clearly apparent (Labriolle, *Réaction païenne*, chapter 2) working up to the great offensive by Celsus, who takes the Jews as his allies. The development of public opinion is a step ahead of the attitude of the authorities (see pp. 41 ff.).

19. Acts shows clearly this halo of sympathy which Judaism had acquired and from which Christianity benefited.

20. See especially Rom. 10:1, 11:1-32.

21. On John's anti-Judaism, see M. Goguel, *Introd. au N.T.*, pp. 537 ff.

22. See p. 70.

23. John, 19:12, 15.

24. E.g., Eusebius, *Vita Const.*, 3. 24; Gregory of Nyssa, *Or.*, 5 (*PG*, 46. 685); Asterius of Amasa, *Hom. in Ps.*, 5. 16 (*PG*, 40. 424) and especially John Chrysostom; see p. 219.

25. Thus Origen, *Contra Celsum*. 4. 32.

26. John 12:37-40.

27. Most frequently, however, outside the works that are properly anti-Jewish polemical ones, where the proof ran a serious risk of missing the mark.

28. Acts 7:51 ff.

29. Juster, *Les Juifs*, 1:45, n. 1.

30. Josephus, *Contra Apionem*, 2. 5; Origen, *Contra Celsum*, 3. 5. Reinach, pp. 130, 166.

31. *Contra Jud. et Gent.*, 16 (*PG*, 48. 835). As a good subject of Rome, Chrysostom regards the Jewish rebellions against Rome as criminal: *In Matt. Hom.*, 43. 3 (*PG*, 57. 461). Juster, *Les Juifs*, 2:184.

32. Juster, *Les Juifs*, 1:47, nn. 1, 10.

33. *Hom. 1 in Ps.*, 36 (*PG*, 12. 1321). See p. 469, n. 99.

34. Origen, *Contra Celsum*, 1. 26, 5. 6; *Kerygma Petri*, in Clement of Alexandria, *Strom.*, 6, 5, 41; Aristides, *Apol.*, 14. On the reality of this worship, references in Bousset/Gressmann, *Religion des Judentums*, p. 330. See pp. 345 ff.

35. E.g., Tacitus, *Hist.*, 5. 5, Reinach, p. 308; see Reinach's index, under "idolâtrie."

36. *Apol.*, 18. 4.

37. Except for out-and-out allegorizers, such as Barnabas.

38. Josephus, *Contra Apionem*, 2. 7; Tacitus, *Hist.*, 5. 3-4, etc; Reinach, *Textes*, pp. 50, 58, 121, 131, 139, 304, 334.

39. *Ad Nat.*, 1. 14. See Minucius Felix, *Octavius*, 19, and the famous Palatine graffito, *DAC*, 1:2, 2024, whose interpretation is otherwise controversial.

40. *Apol.*, 16. 3.

41. Juster, *Les Juifs*, 2:204, and Oort, *Ursprung der Blutbeschuldigung*.

42. *Hom.*, 1 (*PG*, 48. S52) ὡς κοινὴν λύμην καὶ νόσον τῆς οἰκουμένης ἁπάσης. Claudius: καθάπερ κοινήν τινα τῆς οἰκουμένης νόσον ἐξεγείροντας. See Simon, "A propos de la lettre de Claude aux Alexandrins," *Bull. Fac. Lettres Strasb.*, 1943, pp. 175-83.

43. *Diognetus*, 3. See *C. Th.*, 16, 8, 7: *sacrilegi coetus*; other texts in Juster, *Les Juifs*, 1:45, n. 1.

44. Reinach, *Textes*, p. 57.

45. See p. 169.

46. *Hist.*, 5. 5, Reinach, *Textes*, p. 307.

47. Jerome, *Comm. in Ezek.*, 1, 4, 13; *in Is.*, 44:6; *Ep. ad Gelas.*, 121 (*PL*, 25, 49; 24. 438; 22. 1034). Augustine, *Tract. 3 in Joh.*, (*PL*, 34-35. 1404). Ambrose, *Ep.*, 74. 3 (*PL*, 16. 1255). Asterius of Amasa, *in Ps. 5 Hom.*, 17 (*PL*, 20. 351) and especially the invective of Chrysostom; see pp. 217 ff.

48. *Hist.*, 5. 5.

49. *Hom.*, 18. 1 and 9. Lucas, *Geschichte*, pp. 38 ff., rightly sees the question of asceticism as one of the essential points of conflict between Jews and Christians.

50. On the part played by monasticism, see Parkes, *Conflict of Church and Synagogue*, pp. 225 ff.

51. E.g., Jerome, *in Is.*, 2. 8; *Praef. ad Os.*; *Ep.*, 121 (*PL*, 24, 45, 25. 855, 22. 1006). It is likely that the Patriarchs' way of life and their privileged financial position, which often made them excessively rich, helped to give rise to this complaint, which was then extended to their flock.

52. *Praef. in Job.*, 1.

53. *Ep.*, 52.

54. See p. 470, n. 6.

55. *In Ez.*, 27. 16 (*PL*, 25. 266).

56. Parkes, *Conflict of Church and Synagogue*, p. 192.

57. On this antagonism and the differences with regard to sexual morality, see *Lehren des Judentums*, 3:135-200, especially 181 ff., and 1:206 ff.

58. The roles were sometimes reversed. Certain Christian authors see ascetic preoccupations in the dietary prohibitions and condemn them for that very reason: *Deus ventre non colitur nec cibis*. See Lukyn Williams, *Adversus Judaeos*, pp. 303 ff. See Novatian, *de Cibis Judaicis*, 5 (*PL*, 3. 96).

59. The leitmotif of the entire argument is already present in Stephen's speech: "As your fathers did, so do you" (Acts 7:51). See Ps. Ambrose, *Serm.*, 7. 4 (*PL*, 17. 639): *Hoc autem non recens in ipsis sed inveteratum et originarium malum est.*

60. Lucas, *Geschichte*, p. 37.

61. For references to liturgical sources see Juster, *Les Juifs*, 1:334, n. 4. To L. Canet's study, mentioned on p. 335, n. 1, add E. Peterson, "Perfidia judaica," in *Ephemerides liturgicae*, 1936, pp. 296-311. The word *perfidia* in theological parlance does not precisely correspond to our word *perfidy*. It refers rather to an offense against the faith. But it still has an injurious meaning, and it is easy to slip from one meaning to the other.

62. Especially Exod. 33:3, 34:9; Baruch, 2:30, 33.

63. Augustine, *Adv. Jud.*, 9 (*PL*, 42. 57); Ambrose, *Ep.*, 74. 3 (*PL*, 16. 1255); Julian, *Contra Gal.*, Neumann's edition, p. 201.

64. *Carmen Apol.*, passim, e.g., 261: *Gens cervicosa nimis*. See *Instr.*, 1. 38, 1. 40.

65. *Ex. R.*, on 32:7. Wünsche's edition, p. 300.

66. *Ep.*, 74. 3 (*PL*, 16. 1255). See Ps. Augustine, *de Epiphania serm.*, *132* (*PL*, 38-39, 2008): *Caeci ad intelligendum, duri ad credendum*; Maximus of Turin, *de Epiphania, Hom.*, 25 (*PL*, 57. 279): *Quousque, Judaee durissime, obtusa aure, clausis oculis et perfido corde persistis?* See Commodian, *Inst.*, 1. 37.

67. *In Amos*, 5. 23 (*PL*, 25. 1054).

68. *In Christi resurr. orat.*, 5 (*PG*, 46. 685). When the author accuses the Jews of repudiating the faith of their fathers, he is taking up the idea of an original Christianity and identifying it with the true religion of Israel. The accusation is an odd one, if one remembers the commoner complaint that the Jews have an unseasonable attachment to defunct customs.

69. The chronology of these sermons was established first by Usener (*Weihnachtsfest*[2], pp. 233-47) and corrected by Schwartz, *Ostertafeln*, pp. 169-84. Advancing strong arguments, he places sermons 1 and 2 in the autumn of A.D. 386, sermon 3 in January 387, and nos. 4-8 in the autumn of 387. What we have, then, is a double cycle connected with the Jewish New Year festival in two successive years (the third sermon, against the protopaschites, being in some respects outside the series).

70. *Hom.*, 1. 2 (*PG*, 48. 846). The complaint is founded on Hos. 4:16.

71. *Ibid.*, 846.

72. Deut. 32:15. The quotation is from the LXX, which at this point is not very literal.

73. *Hom.*, 1. 4 (*PG*, 48. 848).

74. Ibid., 847. The orator, though he does not actually quote the texts, evidently has in mind the ideas developed in Ezek. 16 and Hos. 1-2.

75. Jer. 3:3.

76. *Hom.*, 1 (847) ἔνθα δὲ πόρνη ἕστηκεν, πορνεῖόν ἐστιν ὁ τόπος. Jerome, similarly, commenting on the imprecations in Hos. 2:4-7, calls the Synagogue a harlot, *fornicaria* and *adultera*: *Comm. in Os.* 1. 2 (*PL*, 25. 830). But Chrysostom goes further. For Jerome there is hardly any question of its being anything but a metaphor. The Synagogue signifies an abstraction, viz., Judaism. Chrysostom is speaking of the Synagogue as an actual place of worship, and sees it as genuinely a place of abomination. It is interesting to note that according to rabbinic tradition, amongst the calamities that will herald the coming of the Messiah is the woe that "the Synagogue will be used for prostitution." References in Bonsirven, *Jud. Pal.*, 1:401.

77. Jer. 7:11, 12:7.

78. *Hom.*, 1. 4, (*PG*, 48. 848).

79. See p. 211.

80. Ps. 106:37.

81. θηρίων ἁπάντων γεγόνασιν ἀγριώτεροι. *Hom.*, 1:6 (*PG*, 48:852).

82. Jer. 5:8 (LXX text).

83. Ἀλλὰ ἀσελγείας ἕνεκεν οὐχὶ καὶ τὰ λαγνότατα τῶν ἀλόγων ἀπέκρυψαν. (*PG*, 48. 853).

84. Τὰς ἁρπαγὰς τὰς πλεονεξίας, τὰς τῶν πενήτων προδοσίας, τὰς κλοπάς, τὰς καπηλείας. *Hom.*, 1. 7 (*PG*, 48. 853).

85. Τοὺς καπήλους, τοὺς ἐμπόρους, τοὺς πάσης παρανομίας γέμοντας. *Hom.*, 6. 5 (*PG*, 48. 9111).

86. Νυνὶ δὲ παίγνια τὰ παρὰ Ἰουδαίοις πάντα καὶ γέλως καὶ αἰσχύνη. . . . (Ibid., 913).

87. Νῦν κἂν πορνεῖον, κἂν παρανομίας χωρίον, κἂν δαιμόνιον καταγώγιον, κἂν διαβόλου φρούριον, κἂν ψυχῶν ὄλεθρον, κἂν ἁπάσης κρημνὸν καὶ βάραθρον, κἂν ὁτιοῦν τις προσείπη ἔλαττον τῆς ἀξίας ἐρεῖ. (Ibid., 915).

88. This is an idea dear to Chrysostom. The Jews are an abomination in the sight of all men. See *Exp. in Ps.*, 8. 3. (*PG*, 55. 110).

89. *Hom.*, 8. 1 (*PG*, 48. 927). For the same equation of fasting and drunkenness, see *Hom.*, 1. 2 (ibid., 846).

90. Μέθη γὰρ οὐδὲν ἕτερον ἐστιν, ἀλλ' ἡ ἔκστασις τῶν ὀρθῶν λογισμῶν, καὶ παραφροσύνη, καὶ τῆς κατὰ ψυχὴν ὑγιείας ἀναίρεσις.

91. Isa. 29:9.

92. Once Chrysostom's procedure has been analyzed, the accusations he formulates against the Synagogue of his own day can be evaluated with proper scepticism. When he speaks of the Synagogue as a theater, and describes it as a resort of evil-livers, what he actually means is simply that Synagogue worship provided a solemn performance that attracted the pagan society of Antioch. It is no more than a translation into polemical language of the statement made earlier by Josephus, concerning the taste that the people of Antioch, and those of Damascus too (*B.J.*, 2, 20, 2), had for things Jewish. There may well have been among this pagan public some who went because it was the fashionable thing to do. But can this be laid to the charge of the Jews themselves? And could not the same sort of people be found in contemporary Christianity? The use of the word *theater* may also be explained by the liking that Jews of the period displayed for spectacle of all sorts (texts in Juster, *Les Juifs*, 2:240, n. 6). There seems, moreover, to be some play on words, with σκηνή (scene) and σκηναί (Tabernacles). See the beginning of *Hom.* 7.

93. See p. 205.

94. Oort, *Ursprung der Blutbeschuldigung*; see above p. 471, n. 41.

95. *PL*, 20. 1165-82. See Lukyn Williams, *Adversus Judaeos*, pp. 298-305.

96. *Altercatio Simonis et Theophili*, 28.

97. Isa. 1:15, 59:7, Deut, 32:32.

98. On the interest in the unleavened bread among the mass of Christians, and its connection with magic, see p. 355.

99. Juster, *Les Juifs*, 1:322-37.

100. Ibid., p. 335.

101. It is going too far to think of the diatribes that some of the homilies contain as elements that are properly a part of the liturgy. The tenor and the tone of the homily are essentially variable, affected by the time, the place, and the speaker. There is no immutable law of homilies that directs that they be always anti-Semitic. They were so only on occasion.

102. Juster, *Les Juifs*, 1:335 ff. Juster tends, perhaps unconsciously, to treat this purely literary anti-Semitism as if it were something artificial. By doing so, he exonerates pagan opinion and throws the entire responsibility on the Church. The same tendency is apparent in Parkes's work.

103. See Athanasius, *Ep. Encycl.*, 3 (*PG*, 25. 228); Theodoret, *HE*, 4. 18 ff. (*PG*, 82:1163 and 1175); H. M. Gwatkin, *Studies of Arianism* (Cambridge, 1882), pp. 57-9; Duchesne, *Histoire ancienne*, 2³:200, 263. Doctrinal sympathies may have made such collusion easier. But it was only relatively speaking that the Arians were more tolerant of Jews than the orthodox; the legislation of Constantius, for example, does not show any signs of it. At Alexandria religion does not seem to have been the deciding factor. See Parkes, *Conflict of Church and Synagogue*, pp. 182 ff.

104. Socrates, *HE*, 7. 13 (*PG*, 67. 760). See Juster, *Les Juifs*, 2:176.

105. Philo, *Leg. ad Gaium*, ch. 20; *in Flacc.*, 8.

106. *Passio St. Salsae* (French translation in Monceaux, *La vraie légende dorée* (Paris, 1929), pp. 299-326). See *REJ* 44:8 ff.; *DAC*, 1:346.

107. *Acta Sanctorum*, II, 483.

108. See Simon, *Polémique anti-juive de S. Jean Chrysostome*, pp. 413 ff.

109. *Edessa Chronicle*, 51. Other refs. in Juster, *Les Juifs*, 1:464, n. 3.

110. Ambrose, *Ep.*, 40. 23 (*PL*, 16. 1109).

111. St. Severus, *Ep.* (*PL*, 20. 731 ff.).

112. See Nau, in *REJ* 83:184 ff.; Parkes, *Conflict of Church and Synagogue*, p. 232.

113. Evagrius, *HE*, 1, 13 (*PG*, 86. 2456); Metaphrastes, *Life of St. Symeon Stylites* (*PG*, 114. 381).

114. It is from him that we have our information about the affair. *Ep.*, 40 (*PL*, 16. 1101). For detailed analysis of the letter, see Juster, *Les Juifs*, 1:462, n. 3. See Palanque, *Saint Ambroise et l'Empire Romain*, pp. 205-7.

115. *Ep.*, 41 (*PL*, 16. 1120). Palanque, *Saint Ambrose et l'Empire Romain*, pp. 214-17.

116. Ambrose expresses the same attitude to paganism in connection with the affair of the altar of victory: *Christianus imperator aram solius Christi didicit honorare. . . . Vox imperatoris nostri Christum resultet, et illum solum quem sentit, loquatur. Quia cor regis in manum Dei (Ep.*, 18. 31).

117. In his view, legislation concerning synagogues was naturally the province of the ecclesiastical authorities. *Ep.*, 40. 7.

118. See *C. Th.*, 2, 1, 10; 12, 1, 165, which contain laws made following Chrysostom's arrival in the capital. By contrast, after his departure, *C. Th.*, 16, 8, 15 (404). Juster, *Les Juifs*, 1:231, n. 7.

119. *Feralis secta, nefaria secta: C. Th.*, 16, 8, 1 (315); *nefanda superstitio*: 16, 9, 4 (417); *abominandi Judaei*: 16, 8, 26 (423); *sacrilegi coetus*; 16, 8, 7 (357); *foedum taetrumque Judaeorum nomen*: 16, 8, 19 (401).

120. Juster, *Les Juifs*, 1:227, n. 5.

121. Ibid., 1 : 230-2 and 2 : 178-82.

122. Ibid., 1 : 462.

123. Ambrose, *Ep.*, 40, 6, 18.

124. *C. Th.*, 16, 8, 9 (493).

125. *C. Th.*, 16, 8, 2: . . . . *eorumque synagogas in quiete solita permanere.* 16, 8, 20: *quae Judaeorum frequentari conventiculis constat quaeque synagogarum vocabulis nuncupantur, nullus audeat violare.* 16, 8, 21: *non passim eorum synagogae concrementur.*

126. February, April, and June. *C. Th.*, 16, 8, 25, 26 and 27.

127. *C. Th.*, 16, 8, 25; *Pro his loca eis, in quibus possint extruere, ad mensuram videlicet sublatarum, praeberi.*

128. The law forbidding new buildings is of uncertain date. For discussion see Juster, *Les Juifs*, 1 : 469, n. 2. The prohibition of the restoration of buildings is recalled in *Nov. Theod.*, 3 : 3.

129. *C. Th.*, 16, 8, 22 (415).

130. *Nov. Theod.*, 3. 3.

131. Lucas, *Geschichte*, p. 19.

132. Ambrose, *Ep.*, 41. 27 (*PL*, 16. 1120). See the measures taken by Arcadius to forbid them access to the towns. *C. Th.*, 16, 3, 1-2; 9, 40, 16; 11, 30, 57.

133. Augustine, *in Ps. Enarr.*, 1 : 21 ff. (*PL*, 36-37, 765). See p. 92.

134. Juster, *Les Juifs*, 1 : 227.

135. *In Ps.* 108 (*PL*, 26. 1224).

136. See *In Is.*, 11. 6 and 58 (*PL*, 24. 150 and 582); *Ep.*, 121 (22, 1006); *Contra Ruf.*, 3. 25 (22. 493); *In Ezek.*, 38 (25. 370).

137. See p. 185.

138. Rom. 11 : 17 ff.

139. *In Ps.*, 77 (*Anecd. Maredsol.*, 3, 2, 196).

140. *Tract. Adv. Jud.*, 15 (*PL*, 42. 63).

141. Rom. 10 : 2.

142. *Contra Faust.*, 12. 13 (*PL*, 42. 261). This retrospective praise, which is transformed in the present into blame for hanging on to an outmoded law, reappears in Gregory of Nazianzus in his panegyric on the Maccabees, *Or.*, 15 (*PG*, 35. 912).

143. *Enarr. in Ps.*, 1 (*PL*, 15. 1032). Chrysostom himself has to recognize certain moral qualities in the Jews. *Hom.*, 6. 2 (*PG*, 48. 906 ff.).

144. E.g., Eusebius in *Praep. Ev.*, and *Dem. Ev.* See A. Puech, *Littérature grecque chrétienne*, 3 : 195. Similarly St. Augustine, but less clearly. See, however, Blumenkranz, *Judenpredigt*, pp. 186 ff.

145. In general, the writers anterior to the fourth century preserve a far more courteous tone than those who follow. For example, Aristides (*Apol.*, 14 : 2 ff.) pays homage to Jewish monotheism and Jewish charity. "They practice love for men, and pity towards the poor; they redeem prisoners and bury the dead." Political opportunism may have played its part here, at a time when Judaism was recognized and protected whereas Christianity possessed no legal status. So also may propagandist considerations; not having yet lost all hope of converting the Jews, the Christians could be generous. Taking it all in all, the attitude of the early Church toward the Jews is quite comparable, in all its aspects, to that of Islam toward the revealed religions, Judaism and Christianity, which it claims to supersede as well as to surpass.

146. Parkes, *Conflict of Church and Synagogue*, p. 193.

147. *Hom.*, 1. 3 (*PG*, 48. 847).

148. Οἱ τὰ ἰουδαϊκὰ νοσοῦντες. *Hom.*, 1. 1 (*PG*, 48. 845). See *Hom.*, 2 (859). On the two conceptions, pagan and Christian, of the Jewish evil, see Simon, *A propos de la lettre de Claude*, pp. 177-78.

Chapter 9

1. "Judéo-chrétien," *Dict. de Théologie catholique*, 8 : 2, 1681.

2. On the difficulties of defining Jewish Christianity, see Harnack, *Dogmengeschichte*, 1⁴, 310 ff.

3. *Separatio legis et evangelii proprium et principale opus est Marcionis* (Tertullian, *Adv. Marc.*, 1. 19).

4. Christianity quickly ceased to be a religion of salvation exclusively by redeeming grace, as Paul had preached it. It followed the example of Judaism in allowing once more an important place to personal effort in the observance of the "new law" (see p. 76). This is the "moralism" already apparent among the second-century Christian writers, especially *Hermas* and I *Clem.*, see Harnack, *Dogmengeschichte*, 1⁴: 190–92, 316 n. 1.

5. Leitzmann, *Geschichte der alten Kirche*, 1 : 54, 191.

6. Matt. 5 : 3, Luke 6 : 20, James 2 : 10, Rom. 15 : 26.

7. Eusebius, *HE*, 3, 27, 1: Ἐβιωναίους ... πτωχῶς καὶ ταπεινῶς τὰ τοῦ Χριστοῦ δοξάζοντας.

8. See the works of Hort, *Judaistic Christianity*, and Hoennicke, *Judenchristentum*.

9. See p. 321.

10. See in this connection Harnack's remarks, *Dogmengeschichte* 1⁴:314. He tends to minimize the phenomenon. I have tried to establish that this Judaizing tendency was inspired directly by Jews, and not by Ebionites, but it may nevertheless still be designated as Jewish Christian.

11. See especially the recent studies of the pseudo-Clementine literature, of the baptist sects, and the Elkasaïtes. Bibliography in Cullmann, *Roman pseudo-clémentin*, pp. 170–83. nn.

12. *Dogmengeschichte* 1⁴:312.

13. So Irenaeus, 1, 26, 2 (*PG*, 7. 686); Tertullian, *De Praescr. Haer.*, 48 (*PL*, 2. 82 ff.); Philaster, *Haer.*, 37.

14. *Qui autem dicuntur Ebionaei, consentiunt quidem mundum a Deo factum; ea autem quae sunt erga Dominum, similiter ut Cerinthus et Carpocrates opinantur* (1, 26, 2). The *non* which some editions insert before *similiter* completely falsifies the sense. It must be omitted, as is shown by comparison with Hippolytus, 7. 34, where the phrase is reproduced exactly, without the negation.

15. Duchesne, *Histoire ancienne*, 1⁶:p. 124. English translation (London, 1910) (from fourth French edition), 1 : 91.

16. So Tertullian (loc. cit., 48): *Hujus successor Hebion fuit, Cerintho non in omni parte consentiens, quod a Deo dicat mundum, non ab angelis factum.*

17. Eusebius, *HE*, 4, 22, 4. This was the universal opinion in the early Church, and there are still those who hold it today. See the reflections of Bauer, *Rechtgläubigkeit*, pp. 3 ff.

18. *Hebion, discipulus ejus Cerinthi, in multis ei similiter errans salvatorem nostrum hominem de Joseph natum carnaliter aestimabat, nihilque divinitatis in eo fuisse docebat.* (*Haer.*, 37.)

19. Justin, *Dial.*, 47. 1–3. It is almost exactly the same as the formula worked out at the meeting at Jerusalem. Acts 15 : 1–34.

20. Justin, *Dial.*, 47. 4. It emerges clearly from this passage that Jewish Christianity did indulge in evangelism and did not confine itself to those of Israelite birth.

21. Justin, *Dial.*, 47. 4 ff.

22. If Justin is tolerant of Judaizing, it is because he has traveled a long way from Pauline soteriology. True Christianity, which makes legal observance superfluous, consists in "hoping in Christ, and observing the everlasting practice of righteousness and natural religion" (47. 2). Paul's intransigent attitude is left far behind. "If you receive circumcision, Christ will be of no advantage to you" (Gal. 5 : 2).

23. According to this evidence, five principal tendencies may be distinguished in ecclesiastical Christianity. At the two extremes are the intransigent Judaizers and anti-Judaizers, who refuse to enter into communion with each other. In the center are liberals such as Justin, who treat the Judaizers with a leniency that hardly disapproves of them at all. A little off-center on both sides are Christians of pagan extraction who Judaize out of weakness, and those Jewish Christians who allow that Christians are not obliged to Judaize.

24. It is true that Justin speaks a little later (48. 4) of a class of people who, though recognizing Jesus as the Christ, see in him "a man among men," who became Messiah by divine election (49. 1). But although this passage is fairly close to the one dealing with legal observances, there is no connection between them, and there is no certainty that the categories of men spoken of in the two passages are coterminous. Even if we ought to read ἀπὸ ὑμετέρου γένους rather than ἡμετέρου, the fact remains that Christians of Jewish origin were not the only ones to deny the divinity of Christ. The word *genos* does not necessarily designate race; it is freely applied to the society of Christians (see pp. 107 ff.) and it does not therefore by any means exclude the reading ἡμετέρου. See Goguel, *Naissance*, p. 161 and n. 2; Archambault, *Dialogue* 1:215 n. 4. In any case, the way Justin looks at it, these people who reject the divinity of Christ, whoever they may be, are not outside the Church. "I am not of their opinion, and there are a great many who think as I do, who would not be willing to say so." (48. 4).

25. The interconnections, sometimes close ones, between the two, were made easier by common legal observances and perhaps by a certain doctrinal laxity, carried over from Judaism.

26. Origen, *Contra Celsum*, 2. 1 ff. (*PG*, 11. 793). See 5. 61 (*PG*, 11, 1278).

27. *Panarion, Haer.*, 29 and 36 (*PG*, 41. 388 ff. and 406 ff.).

28. *Ep.* 89 *ad Aug.*

29. It is curious that, if the word was explained as referring to doctrinal poverty (which is the explanation given by both Origen and Eusebius), Epiphanius could apply it to systems as developed as those which he postulates of his Ebionites. The word cannot have referred exclusively to such groups. On the contrary, since the term *Nazarenes* is attested in Jewish usage as referring to Christians, we may conceive that both names were in use, the one by the Jews, the other by the Christians, for designating the Jewish-Christian community.

30. *Panarion, Haer.*, 29. 1 (*PG*, 41. 389) καὶ πάντες δὲ Χριστιανοὶ Ναζωραῖοι ποτε ὡσαύτως ἐκαλοῦντο; ibid., 29. 6 (*PG*, 41. 400).

31. Ibid., 29. 7 (*PG*, 41. 401).

32. Ibid.

33. Ibid., 29. 6 (*PG*, 41. 400).

34. Ibid., 29. 7 (*PG*, 41. 401).

35. Eusebius says more exactly that they add Jewish observances to Christian ones. Sabbath to Sunday (*HE*, 3, 27, 5): καὶ τὸ μὲν σάββατον καὶ τὴν ἄλλην Ἰουδαϊκὴν ἀγωγὴν ὁμοίως ἐκείνοις παρεφύλαττον, ταῖς δ' αὖ κυριακαῖς ἡμέραις ἡμῖν τὰ παραπλήσια εἰς μνήμην τῆς τοῦ κυρίου ἀναστάσεως ἐπετέλου.

36. *Perseverant in his consuetudinibus, quae sunt secundum legem, et Judaico charactere vitae, ut et Hierosolymam adorent, quasi domus sit Dei* (1, 26, 2). Epiphanius says the same thing of the Elkasaïtes (*Haer.*, 19, 3, 5 ff.). We know that the rite is continued in Islam, though in Islam the holy city towards which the worshiper turns is Mecca. It is generally recognized that this feature of Islamic piety is of Jewish-Christian derivation. It is borrowed from the Synagogue. On the other hand, the orientation of Christian churches, far from copying that of the synagogues, is exactly the opposite (this appears as early as the *Apost. Const.*, 2, 57, 3). It is more like that of the ritual of the Essenes of En Gedi (a ritual itself influenced by pagan practices), who prayed with their faces toward the rising sun and their backs toward Jerusalem. The early Christians did not turn toward Jerusalem when they prayed. Wherever they happened to be they turned east. See Dölger, *Sol Salutis²*, pp. 185-98.

When Bonsirven, *Jud. Palest.*, 2:154, writes, "still *less* well attested is the practice of turning towards Jerusalem," he means to say, "still *better* attested . . . " as the context and the references he gives in the notes indicate.

37. Epiphanius, *Haer.*, 29. 7 (*PG*, 41. 401).

38. The book of the Preaching of Peter is not to be "made available to all and sundry, but only to one who is good, pious, devoted to the teaching, a circumcised believer." (*Hom. Clem.*, Diamarturia, 1).

39. Irenaeus, loc. cit., see 3. 15 and Eusebius, *HE*, 3, 17, 4. Epiphanius tells us us (30. 16) that according to the Jewish Christians, Paul was born a gentile, but had himself made a proselyte in order to solicit the hand of the daughter of the High Priest in marriage. When he was refused, out of spite he set himself to write against circumcision, the Sabbath, and the law.

40. *Quae autem sunt prophetica, curiosius exponere nituntur.* (1, 26, 2).

41. *Contra Celsum*, 5, 65 (*PG*, 11. 1288).

42. *Solo autem eo, quod est secundum Matthaeum, Evangelio utuntur* (loc. cit.).

43. Eusebius, *HE*, 3, 17, 4.

44. The problem is set out and the discussions summarized in Goguel, *Introd. au N.T.*, 1:380-94. See Waitz, in Hennecke's *N.T. Apokryphen*, pp. 17-29, who argues for an original Greek text, later translated into Aramaic. Waitz, "Neue Untersuchungen über die sogenannten judenchristlichen Evangelien," *ZNTW*, 1938, pp. 60-81.

45. Clement, *Strom.*, 2, 45, 5; Origen, *Comm. in Joh.*, 2, 12, 87. See Waitz in Hennecke, *Neutestamentliche Apokryphen*, pp. 48-55.

46. Bauer, *Rechtgläubigkeit*, pp. 55 ff., sees it, however, and doubtless correctly, as the gospel belonging to a Jewish Christian group that was Greek-speaking. Opposing it in Egypt was an equally sectarian body of indigenous Christians who read the gospel called the Gospel of the Egyptians. According to the usage of the period, the term *Hebrew* was applied only to Hebrew-speaking Jews living in Palestine, thus distinguishing them from Hellenists (Acts 6:1). In the diaspora, where the use of Hebrew was exceptional, the word lost its linguistic reference and reverted to its ethnic sense, designating Israelites, as opposed to gentiles (Eusebius, *HE*, 2, 4, 2). It is not, however, precisely synonymous with "Jew," for it could not with strictness be applied to proselytes.

47. Epiphanius, *Haer.*, 29. 7.

48. Or the Jewish Gospel, τὸ Ἰουδαϊκόν; see Waitz in Hennecke, *NTA*, p. 14. The appellation Ἰουδαϊκόν appears in the marginal notes to certain MSS of the gospels that appear to go back to a lost commentary on St. Matthew by Apollinarius of Laodicaea.

49. *Chaldaico quidem Syroque sermone, sed hebraicis litteris* (*Dial. Adv. Pelasg.*, 3. 2; see *de Vir. illustr.*, 2. 3).

50. Irenaeus, loc. cit.

51. Tertullian, *de Praescr. Haer.*, 48 (*PL*, 2. 82). See p. 242 and n. 16. According to Irenaeus (1, 26, 1), Cerinthus attributed the creation to a Power, who was inferior to God and did not know about God. *Non a primo Deo factum esse mundum docuit, sed a virtute quadam valde separata.* Carpocrates, on the other hand, credited it to the angels; 1, 25, 1 (*PG*, 7. 680).

52. Irenaeus, 1, 26, 1.

53. *Philosophumena*, 7. 34.

54. The term *Christ* ("anointed") was originally an adjective that could be used in a variety of contexts (it was applied, for example, to the kings in Israel), but by the period of which we are speaking it had acquired a much narrower and more exact sense, even in the usage of the Jews themselves. It had almost become a proper noun, signifying in particular "*the* anointed," viz., the Messiah.

55. This is just the objection Irenaeus seems to be making when he asks of the Ebionites:

Quomodo possunt salvari, nisi Deus est qui salutem illorum super terram operatus est? Et quomodo homo transiet in Deum, si non Deus in hominem? (4, 33, 4; *PG*, 7. 1074).

56. Hippolytus, *Philosophumena*, 7. 33.

57. Philaster, *Haer.*, 37.

58. *Nudum hominem . . . plane prophetis aliquo gloriosiorem, ut ita in illo angelus fuisse dicatur,* (Tertullian, *de Carne Christi*, 14; *PL*, 2. 823).

59. Irenaeus, 5, 1, 3 (*PG*, 7. 1122).

60. Irenaeus, 3, 21, 1 (*PG*, 7, 946).

61. *Contra Celsum*, 5. 65 (*PG*, 11. 1288).

62. Ibid., 5. 61 (*PG*, 11. 1277): οὗτοι δ᾽ εἰσὶν οἱ διττοὶ Ἐβιωναῖοι, ἤτοι ἐκ παρθένου ὁμολογοῦντες ὁμοίως ἡμῖν τὸν Ἰησοῦν, ἢ οὐχ οὕτω γεγεννῆσθαι ἀλλ᾽ ὡς τοὺς λοιποὺς ἀνθρώπους.

63. Eusebius, *HE*, 3, 27, 3. The identity of the names, to which Eusebius draws attention, shows plainly that in this sphere the labels were not applied with great exactness, and that Epiphanius is wrong in reserving the name *Ebionites* for a single category. It is a category, moreover, that does not correspond to either of the ones Origen and Eusebius single out, which are connected with Ebionism of the common sort.

64. *Haer.*, 29. 7 (*PG*, 41. 401).

65. *Ep. ad Aug.*, 89. 13 (*PL*, 22. 924).

66. *Christianos esse se simulant* (Jerome. loc. cit.).

67. *Haer.*, 29. 9 (*PG*, 41. 403): τρὶς τῆς ἡμέρας, ὅτε εὐχὰς ἐπιτελοῦσιν ἐν ταῖς αὐτῶν συναγωγαῖς, ἐπαρῶνται αὐτοῖς, καὶ ἀναθεματίζουσιν φάσκοντες ὅτι Ἐπικαταράσαι ὁ θεὸς τοὺς Ναζωραίους.

68. *In Is.*, 5. 18 ff. (*PL*, 24. 87); see *In Is.*, 49. 7, 52. 4.

69. Justin, *Dial.*, 16. 4. See Archambault *Dialogue*, ad loc.

70. It is then combined with the hatred for "Edom," i.e., the empire, and was strengthened thereby. See pp. 29, 188.

71. See p. 182.

72. Marmorstein, "Judaism and Christianity," *HUCA*, 1935, pp. 233 ff. See *Religionsgeschichtliche Studien*, vol. 1.

73. Pss. 37:38, 51:15, Isa. 1:28, Hos. 14:10.

74. References in Marmorstein, "Judaism and Christianity."

75. Thus *b. Erub.*, 19a.

76. It has sometimes been translated "apostate." This, it seems to me, is to force the sense somewhat (thus, for example, Marmorstein, *Religionsgeschichtliche Studien*, "Die Abtrünnigen Israëls").

77. There is a prima facie assumption that it was so applied. The appellation appears in a text of the Talmud in connection with Jesus. It is told of a certain Onkelos (*b. Gitt.*, 56b–57a) that he was tempted to become a proselyte. Desiring, however, to make his decision with his eyes open, he conjured up, one after the other, the spirits of those who at first sight appeared to him to be Judaism's bitterest opponents: Titus, Balaam, and Jesus. The first two of these strongly encouraged him in hostility to the Jews. Jesus, on the contrary, encouraged him to pay them honor. The passage ends by drawing out the difference between the *poshʿe yisrael* and the prophets of the gentiles. If Jesus could be regarded as a *poshea‘*, so could his disciples.

78. *b. Kerit.*, 5b.

79. *b. Hull.*, 5a; *b. Erub.*, 69a; *Midr. Lev. R.*, on 1:2.

80. See p. 184.

81. References in Marmorstein, "Judaism and Christianity," pp. 225 ff.

82. *b. Hagig.*, 27a; *b. Erub.*, 19a.

83. *Midr. Ps.*, on 31, Buber's edition, p. 240.

84. 1. Cor. 15:20.

85. According to another Talmudic passage, certain *poshʿim* did not acknowledge the

prophets and writings as revealed scripture (*M. Tanh.*, Buber edition, cited by Marmorstein, "Judaism and Christianity" p. 230). Marmorstein suggests that this refers to the Jewish-Christian circles that produced the pseudo-Clementine literature. The theory is a tempting one. It should nevertheless be noted that the beliefs of these circles tend in their audacity toward those characterized as *minuth*.

86. Even in Palestine the Catholic Church was numerically much more important than the Jewish Christian communities (Harnack, *Mission*, II⁴, p. 635 and n. 2). In the eyes of the Jews, therefore, it was the Catholic Church that represented Christianity.

87. Acts 2:46.

88. On his attitude to Bar Cochba, see Schürer, *Geschichte*, I⁴, p. 683, n. 99; Graetz, *Geschichte*, 4³:pp. 137 ff. On his prestige in Israel, "Akiba," *JE*, 2:7 ff.

89. The low opinions the rabbis professed concerning Christ most certainly embarrassed relations between Jewish Christianity and the Synagogue. But it is not certain that they were subscribed to everywhere. They are explicit mainly in late texts. It will also be noted that even Bar Cochba himself, greeted by Akiba as "Son of the Star," became later, by a play on words, "the Son of the Lie" (*kozba*). Schürer, *Geschichte*, 1:683.

90. Eusebius, *HE*, 2, 23, 2.

91. Ibid., 2, 23, 1.

92. Ibid., 3, 5, 3.

93. It was nevertheless not this act which provoked the hostility in the first place. It rather presupposes the existence of such hostility. That this already existed is shown by the martyrdom of James, and it was probably in order to avoid fresh acts of cruelty that the community left the city.

94. Justin, *Apol.*, 1:31. On the other hand, it does not appear that the execution of Simeon during Trajan's reign can be laid to the charge of the Jews. Eusebius, quoting Hegesippus (*HE*, 3, 32, 2 ff.), attributes it to a denunciation by "heretics." The Jews have no part in the matter, and it is the Roman authorities who agitate against this descendant of David, in connection, probably, with a fresh upsurge of political Messianism in preparation for the Eastern rebellion in A.D. 117.

95. When Akiba had greeted Bar Cochba with the title of Messiah, R. Johanan b. Torta replied to him: "Akiba, the grass will grow out of your cheeks a long time, and the son of David not yet be come" (j. Taan., IV, 8). The theory that there was some collusion between Christians and Zealots during the first war in Judaea has been taken up by S. G. F. Brandon. In a review of this work in *The Modern Churchman* (March 1952, pp. 49 ff.), I have set out the objections the theory seems to me to raise. To my mind there is no evidence to suggest that the Christian community in Palestine took part on any large scale in the insurrection. There could have been individual exceptions. And it is certain that Jesus, who lived in an environment in which the Zealots and their ideas were very prominent, and who was executed by the Romans for being himself a Zealot, must repeatedly have taken his stand against this activist wing of Jewish nationalism. See O. Cullmann, *Dieu et César* (Paris, 1956).

96. It seems certain that at least a portion of the refugees of Pella came back to Jerusalem shortly after the war: Hoennicke, *Judenchristentum*, pp. 105 ff. Eusebius gives us to understand this, without saying it explicitly (*HE*, 3, 11; 4, 5). This is a sign of their attachment to Judaism, and doubtless also of their expectation of the imminent coming of the kingdom, which would be realized at Jerusalem. In this respect the return is similar to the gathering of the first disciples in Galilee after the death of Christ.

97. The dispersion that followed the martyrdom of Stephen only affected the Hellenists. The group of apostles remained in Jerusalem (Acts 8:1). The execution of James, the brother of John (Acts 12:2) was carried out on the initiative of Agrippa. Both motives and circumstances remain obscure. It should be noted that Josephus (*Ant. Jud.*, 20, 9, 1) imputes the death of James, "the brother of Christ" (the phrase may be an interpolation), and of

several others whose religious affiliation is not specified, to the high priest Ananos. He incurred the criticism even of the legalists and was consequently deprived of his office by Agrippa at their request.

98. The same doubtless goes for the various gnosticizing sorts of Jewish Christians. This is contrary to the opinion of Marmorstein, who sees them as the *posh'im*, and regards them as the circles that produced the pseudo-Clementine literature. See pp. 285 f.

99. The movement began with those believers among the apostolic group who, leaving the country after A.D. 70, established themselves outside Palestine in gentile Christian communities. This seems to have happened at Ephesus. Bauer, *Rechtgläubigkeit*, pp. 89 ff.

100. Epiphanius, *Haer.*, 29. 7 (*PG*, 41. 401).

101. Eusebius, *HE*, 4, 5, 3; 4, 6, 4.

102. On this Palestinian Jewish Christianity, see Harnack, *Mission*, II⁴, p. 97.

103. Epiphanius, *Haer.*, 29. 7.

104. Ibid., 30. 2.

105. Ibid., 30, 18, 8.

106. Bauer, *Rechtgläubigkeit*, pp. 55-57.

107. To speak as Bauer does (*Rechtgläubigkeit*, p. 91) of a nonlegalistic Jewish Christianity (*Judenchristentum ohne gesetzliche Bindung*) is to bring out the complexity of the problem but also to obscure the facts. On this basis St. Paul himself could be described as a Jewish Christian, because he was born of the tribe of Benjamin. We really need two different terms, one to designate Jewish birth, the other to indicate observance of Jewish religion. It is in the latter sense that Hoennicke uses the word *Judaismus*.

108. This was where the first gentile converts came from. In the team of Hellenists grouped around Stephen appears "Nicholas, a proselyte from Antioch" (Acts 6:5). The queen of Ethiopia's eunuch (Acts 8:27) and the centurion Cornelius (Acts 10:1) were also "Judaized" before passing over into Christianity.

109. Thus, for example, in the pseudo-Clementine circles. The letter of Peter to James and the Solemn Warning with which the collection of homilies opens, without absolutely thrusting aside those Christians who were of pagan origin, explicitly reserves initiation for those who are circumcised, and whose attitudes are approved of (i.e., who faithfully observe the Jewish law). μηδενὶ τῶν ἀπὸ τῶν ἐθνῶν μεταδοῦναι μήτε ὁμοφύλῳ πρὸ πείρας (*Peter's letter*, 1, *PG*, 2. 25). βίβλους μηδενὶ μεταδοῦναι . . . πρὸ πείρας (ibid., 3, 2, 28). ἐμπεριτόμῳ τε ὄντι πιστῷ (*Warning*, 1, *PG*, 2. 29).

110. This is the category Justin has in mind, *Dial.*, 47 (see p. 243), who allow themselves to be seduced by the Christians of Jewish origin into Judaizing. There were some of them too among the Galatian Judaizers, if not among those who were persuading them to Judaize. E. Hirsch has attempted to establish this in his essay, "Zwei Fragen zu Galater," *ZNTW* 6 (1930): 192 ff.

111. Acts 15.

112. Leitzmann, "Zwei Notizen zu Paulus," *Sitzungsber, der Preuss. Ak.* (Berlin, 1930), pp. 153-56, II. *Die Reisen des Petrus*; see *Geschichte der alten Kirche*, 1:108 ff.

113. See especially Goguel, "L'Apôtre Pierre a-t-il joué un rôle personnel dans les crises de Grèce et de Galatie?," *RHPR*, 1934, pp. 461-500.

114. Goguel, "L'Apôtre Pierre," pp. 488, 500.

115. Eusebius, *HE*, 5, 10, 3. The gospel in question is probably not our Matthew, but the gospel called the Gospel of the Hebrews, which the Nazarenes used. This distribution of Jewish Christianity in Arabia takes on particular importance from the fact that it exercised some influence on the origins of Islam. See Renan's remarks in *Evangiles*, pp. 460 ff., and *Eglise chrétienne*, pp. 284 ff.

116. *Magn.*, 8. 1.

117. *Magn.*, 9. 1.

118. *Magn.*, 10. 1.

119. *Philad.*, 4.

120. *Philad.*, 6:1: ἄμεινον γάρ ἐστιν παρὰ ἀνδρὸς περιτομὴν ἔχοντος Χριστιανισμὸν ἀκούειν ἢ παρὰ ἀκροβύστου Ἰουδαϊσμόν.

121. Eusebius, *HE*, 6. 17. According to Epiphanius, whose authority is somewhat doubtful, he was a Samaritan converted to Judaism (*De Mens. et Pond.*, 16, *PG*, 43. 264).

122. Philaster, *Haer.*, 63 (*PL*, 12. 1177) is no use to us. He is speaking of dualistic gnostics who, out of contempt for the flesh, give themselves over to every vice.

123. *Comm. in Ep. and Gal.*, Prol. (*PL*, 17. 357).

124. *Contra Cresc.*, 1. 31 (*PL*, 43. 445).

125. Ibid.

126. *Contra Faust. Man.*, 19. 4 (*PL*, 42. 349).

127. *Ut et gentes cogerent judaizare. Ii sunt quos Faustus Symmachianorum . . . nomine commemoravit.* (*Contra Faust.*, 19. 17).

128. See p. 296.

129. *Hoc si mihi Nazaraeorum objiceret quisquam, quos alii Symmachianos appellant* (*Contra Faust.*, 19. 4, *PL*, 42. 349).

130. Ibid., 19. 17.

131. On the reasons for the defeat of Ebionism in the face of Hellenistic Christianity, see the noteworthy remarks of Goguel, *Naissance*, p. 167: "It did not possess, as Paulinism did, the feeling of Christ's presence and activity. . . . Once the conviction of the imminent end of the world had disappeared it was no longer possible to see him as anything more than a teacher of wisdom. Even this type of role was perceptibly diminished by the absolute authority which continued to be accorded to the Jewish law. Under these conditions there was a danger that Christianity would become no more than a theory of cosmological speculation."

Chapter 10

1. See Bertholet, *Stellung der Israeliten und Juden zu den Fremden*, whose conclusions are discussed by I. Lévi (*REJ*, 1905, pp. 1 ff., and 1906, pp. 1 ff.). Bertholet's work is by now old, however, and a more recent discussion is Bialoblocki, *Die Beziehungen des Judentums zu Proselyten und Proselytismus*. See also the fine study by Moore in his *Judaism*, 1:323-53. Numerous Talmudic references are given by Strack and Billerbeck, *Kommentar*, 1:102 ff., 354 ff., 927 ff., and 4:358 ff.

2. Duchesne, *Histoire ancienne* I[6], p. 568 (English translation, p. 412).

3. Schwartz, *Christliche und jüdische Ostertafeln*, especially pp. 117, n. 1, and 170.

4. Harnack, *Mission*, I[4], p. 18, n. 1.

5. As far as Israel is concerned, religion and politics seem to us to be closely connected. It is not quite certain whether this was so for Roman opinion, since Roman authority refused to extend to the diaspora the responsibility for the insurrections in Palestine. The memory of these rebellions did not, outside Palestine, persist very long. Judaizers and proselytes, in yielding to the attractions of a conquered people's way of worship, were merely demonstrating a tendency that was common among the Romans: *Graecia capta ferum victorem capit*, said Horace. Seneca, quoted by Augustine (*Civ. Dei*, 6:11) denounces the Jewish danger in the same terms: *Cum interim usque eo sceleratissimae gentis consuetudo convaluit, ut per omnes jam terras recepta sit, victi victoribus leges dederunt.* And St. Ambrose, replying in the affair of the altar of Victory to the defenders of Roman tradition, asks ironically: *Quid . . . captarum simulacra urbium, victosque deos et peregrinos ritus sacrorum alienae superstitionis aemuli receperunt?* (*Ep.*, 18. 30).

6. See pp. 44 ff.

7. *b. Kidd.*, 70b, *b. Yebam.*, 47b and 109b; see *b. Nidd.*, 13b, which adds that the proselytes hold back the coming of the Messiah.

8. E.g., *b. Yebam.*, 48b, *Midr. Eccl. R.*, 1, on 8:8; *Midr. Gen. R.*, 70, on 28:20. Evils increase for those who make proselytes. The "enemy" of Exod. 23:4 is the proselyte, for his nature is evil through and through: *Mechilta*, ad loc., 99a. R. Eliezer, b. Hyrcanus, who suggested this interpretation, was particularly hard on proselytes.

9. See Derenbourg, *Palestine*, p. 228.

10. The rabbis paid careful attention to the motives for conversion, and often refused to consider as true proselytes those who had become so for purely worldly considerations. Thus (*b. Yebam.*, 24b, see *j. Kidd.*, IV, 1) a man who became a proselyte because of a woman, or a woman who became one because of a man, are not true proselytes; neither are those who become proselytes in order to gain access to the royal table, or those of the time of Mordecai and Esther, or those of the time of David and Solomon. See *Midr. Eccl. R.*, on 8:10.

11. *Midr. Gen. R.*, on 8:10.

12. *j. Ber.*, IV, 5.

13. *Midr. Gen. R.*, 28, on 6:7.

14. *Midr. Ruth. R.*, on 1:18.

15. *Midr. Lev. R.*, 1, on 1:1. See *Midr. Num. R.*, 8, on 5:6.

16. *Sifra, Ahare Moth*, 13; see *b. Sanh.*, 59b; *b. Ab. Zara*, 3a.

17. *Tanhuma*, Buber edn., 1:63 (R. Simon b. Laqish).

18. *Mechilta* on Exod. 22:20. Friedmann's edition p. 95a.

19. *j. Sanh.*, X, 2 (see 2 Kings, 5:27 and Job, 31:32). *Midr. Lev. R.*, 2, on 1:2 is even more positive: "The wise taught in the Mishnah, if a pagan wished to be converted, one must take him by the hand and lead him under the wings of the Shekhinah." According to certain rabbis, Abraham was punished in the person of his descendants exiled in Egypt, because he had prevented men from being converted (*b. Nedar.*, 32a).

20. *b. Pes.*, 87b. The opinion was doubtless widespread, since Chrysostom quotes it too: *in Ps.*, 8. 34 (*PG*, 55. 112).

21. *Midr. Eccl. R.*, on 5:11.

22. *b. Ab. Zara*, 3b and 24a. For certain rabbis these conversions out of self-interest are unacceptable.

23. It is depicted picturesquely in *b. Shabb.*, 31a, where an account is given of the different receptions proselytes met with from the two scholars: "The irascible Shammai would banish us from the world, but the gentleness of Hillel has brought us under the wings of the Shekhinah." The rabbis comment on this praise (ibid.): "Let a man be always gentle like Hillel, and not irritable like Shammai."

24. *b. Yebam.*, 47a.

25. *b. Bekhor.*, 30b.

26. Rabbinic references in Moore, *Judaism*, pp. 343-5.

27. See *b. Yebam.*, 47a, *j. Kidd.*, IV, 1. One ought to respect every proselyte, and assume that he is a sincere convert. See *Midr. Ex. R.*, 19, on 12:43. "'I welcomed the Gibeonites,' says God, 'who were Amorites, and who came through fear. And I watched over their interests. And shall I not welcome those proselytes who come through love, and bestow prosperity on their children?'"

28. *M. Yadaim*, 4:4. See Deut. 33:4. According to R. Johanan, the daughter of a proselyte from Ammon may marry a priest; according to R. Abbahu, she may marry the High Priest himself (*j. Yebam.*, VIII, 3).

29. *j. Yebam.*, I, 5.

30. *b. Yebam.*, 46a. Useful material concerning the catechetical instruction given to proselytes on baptism is given by D. Daube. "A Baptismal Catechism," in his volume of essays, *The New Testament and Rabbinic Judaism* (London, 1956), pp. 106-40. On the

baptism of proselytes in general, there is a good summary treatment in "Jewish Proselyte Baptism and the Baptism of John," in *From Moses to Qumran* (London, 1963), pp. 211-35.

31. See Strack and Billerbeck, *Kommentar*, 1 : 105.

32. They had earlier been in conflict at the time of the conversion of Izates, who was the king of Adiabene. The Jew who converted him initially absolved him from the necessity of circumcision, but he complied with the rite at the insistence of another Jew. Josephus, *Ant. Jud.*, 20, 2, 5.

33. See Acts 10 : 1ff. Cornelius is described as εὐσεβὴς καὶ φοβούμενος, and "well spoken of by the whole Jewish nation" (10:22). Peter was nevertheless scandalized at the thought of eating at table with him (11 : 3).

34. See *Midr. Gen. R.*, 53, on 21 : 7. The "children" Sarah was to suckle, though she had only one son, are the gentiles of good will, the "God-fearers." See *Pesiq. R.*, 180a, *Midr. Ps. R.*, 22. 29. R. Joshua b. Levi regards Ps. 22 : 24 as a reference to the traditional God-fearers (*Midr. Lev. R.*, 3, on 2 : 1).

35. *b. Hull.*, 5a.

36. Harnack, *Mission* I⁴, p. 18, n. 1. I. Lévi, *REJ*, 1905, p. 9.

37. *Homily against the Jews*, 8. 4 (*PG*, 48. 933).

38. *b. Kerit.*, 9a. Graetz, *Geschichte*, IV⁴, p. 100.

39. E.g., that of a Roman lady, Veturia or Valeria, who discussed scriptural exegesis with R. Gamaliel (*b. Rosh hash.*, 17b).

40. *b. Gittin*, 57b, *b. Sanh.*, 96b. The two scholars are reckoned as descendants of Sennacherib.

41. Irenaeus, 3, 21, 1 (*PG*, 7. 946). *Midr. Gen. R.*, 70, on 28 : 20, etc.

42. Meir passes for a descendant of Nero (*b. Gittin*, 56a) who is said to have become a proselyte himself. As is the case with the descendants of Sennacherib, the fact emphasizes the grace of God, who accepts into the covenant even those who are of the line of miscreants. It equally demonstrates Israel's revenge on her enemies. The prestige of Akiba, scholar and martyr, was such that it rivalled even that of Moses. Moses, admitted to sit with the eighth rank of Akiba's disciples, is unable to comprehend the master's teaching (*b. Menach.*, 29b).

43. *Midr. Ex. R.*, 19, on 12:43.

44. *T. Kidd.*, 5.

45. *b. Ber.*, 17b.

46. *Sat.*, 1, 9, 67 ff.

47. *Sat..*, 14. 96 ff. (Reinach, *Textes*, p. 292). See J. Bernays, "Die Gottesfürchtigen bei Juvenal," *Ges. Abhandl.*, 2, (Berlin, 1885): 71-80. Also Schürer, *Geschichte*, III⁴, pp. 167 ff.

48. *Adversus omnes alios hostile odium . . . . Transgressi in morem eorum idem usurpant; nec quidquam prius imbuuntur quam contemnere deos, exuere patriam, parentes, liberos, fratres vilia habere.* (*Hist.*, 5. 5; Reinach, *Textes*, pp. 306 ff.).

49. Dion Cassius, 37. 16 ff. This is exactly the point of view of the Jews themselves: ἐὰν ὁ ἀλλόφυλλος τὸν νόμον πράξῃ Ἰουδαῖός ἐστιν, μὴ πράξας δέ Ἕλλην. (*Hom. Ps. Clem.*, 11. 16, *PG*, 2. 288).

50. Justin, *Dial.*, 123. 1: προσήλυτος ὁ περιτεμνόμενος ἐν τῷ λαῷ προσκεχωρηκέναι ἐστιν ὡς αὐτόχθων.

51. *Dial.*, 17. 1.

52. Ibid., 23. 3.

53. Ibid., 122. 2.

54. Tertullian, *Adv. Jud.*, 1 (*PL*, 2. 635).

55. *In Matth. Comm. Ser.*, 16 (*PG*, 13. 621).

56. Matt. 23 : 15; see Strack and Billerbeck, *Kommentar*, ad loc.

57. *Die religiösen Bewegungen*, p. 32.

58. Ibid., p. 34.

59. The same impression is given by the verse of Horace:

> *. . . Ac veluti te*
> *Judaei cogemus in hanc concedere turbam,*

which Reinach juxtaposes against the gospel verse as an "allusion to the passion for proselytizing which at that time characterized the Jews" (*Textes*, p. 244). We have here a clear illustration of the affinities between the Pharisees and the diaspora Jews. The conjunction of the two texts demonstrates too that A.D. 70 did not mark any sudden break as far as proselytism was concerned. The missionary journeys of the Pharisees were continued by those of the Jewish apostles (see Krauss, "Jüdischen Apostel," *JQR*, 1905, pp. 370–83) whose activities in part fulfilled the needs of spreading the faith.

60. The verse is clarified by a comparison with Matt. 23 : 13: "Woe to you, scribes and Pharisees, hypocrites! because you shut the kingdom of heaven against men." We are to understand "by turning them away from the Christian message."

61. Proselytes: nos. 21, 68, 72, 202, 222, 256, 462, 523, 576. *Metuentes*: nos. 5, 285, 529, 642. On the two categories see Frey, "Inscriptions inédites des catacombes juives de Rome," *Riv. Arch. Crist.*, 1930, pp. 251 ff. On Frey's corpus, see the review by L. Robert, *REJ*, 101 (1937): 73–86, repeated in *Hellenica*, 3 (1946): 90–108.

62. Frey, *CIJ*, p. ix, n. 5.

63. In addition to the epigraphical and archaeological evidence, we have the fact that the biblical quotations are sometimes made according to Aquila's text. Frey, *CIJ*, p. lxvi.

64. Of the eight Roman inscriptions relating to proselytes, six refer to women, against whom the law could do nothing. Frey, *CIJ*, p. lxiii.

65. Frey, *CIJ*, pp. lxvi ff. and "Inscriptions inédites," pp. 255 ff.; Juster, *Les Juifs*, 2 : 229. The description "Jew" in the inscription does not necessarily apply only to Jews by birth, as opposed to converts. It is sometimes used of proselytes (*CIJ*, n. 68: Crescus Sinicerius Judaeus proselytus), which invites us to understand it in a religious rather than an ethnic sense even when it appears alone (no. 778: D. N. Septimae Mariae Judaeae). There is nothing to tell us, therefore, whether an individual who is called a Jew is an Israelite or a convert, though a convert might be expected to draw attention to his Jewishness more than a native-born Israelite would, since it was this which gave him full rights of membership among the chosen people. This neophyte's pride sometimes induced proselytes to apply to themselves, by an extension of meaning, even the name "Israelite." No. 21: Εἰρήνη Θρεσπτὴ προσήλυτος πατρὸς καὶ μητρὸς Ἐιουδέα Ἰσδραηλίτης.

66. Frey, "Inscriptions inédites," p. 253; *CIJ*, p. lxiv.

67. It is by the joint action of these three factors that we may explain the initial formation, on the edge of orthodox Judaism, of the Jewish-pagan sects; e.g., the Sabaziastes (see Cumont, "Les Mystères de Sabazios et le judaïsme," *CRAI*, 1906, pp. 63 ff., and *Religions orientales*[4], pp. 60 ff.) and the Hypsistarians (see Cumont, *Religions orientales*, pp. 59 ff., and also "Hypsistos," *RE*) and eventually the Jewish-pagan-Christian, such as the Caelicoles of Africa (see Simon, "Judaïsme berbère," *RHPR*, 1946, pp. 108 ff.)

68. Tertullian, *Ad Nat.*, 1.13. The text seems to be inspired by Josephus, *Contra Apionem*, 2. 39, who, having observed that "the Greek philosophers followed Moses in their conduct and philosophy," goes on, "The populace also has for a long time shown great enthusiasm for our pious practices, and there is not a city among the Greeks nor a people among the barbarians where our custom of a seventh day rest has not spread, and where the fasts, the lighting of lamps and many of our laws concerning foods are not observed." This perhaps exaggerates the extent to which the Jews were imitated; nevertheless, the importance of such imitation is attested by a number of writers. See Reinach, *Textes*, especially pp. 246 ff. (Horace), 247 (Tibullus), 248 (Ovid), and 264 (Persius).

69. See Schürer, *Geschichte*, III[4], 181 ff.

70. Description from Strack and Billerbeck, *Kommentar*, 1:110. Especially necessary was the presence of witnesses (*b. Yebam.*, 46b). These were a kind of godparents. It is not certain, however, whether we ought to identify them, as Schürer has suggested (p. 185) with the *patroni* sometimes mentioned in the epitaphs of proselytes (Frey, *CIJ*, nos. 256, 462, 53). The *patroni* could equally well be "patrons" in the Roman sense, of slaves who were freed at the time of their conversion. These patrons would themselves be Jews.

71. See p. 278. It seems assured that certain groups in the diaspora regarded baptism as sufficient in itself. See *Oracula Sibyllina*, 4. 164.

72. Thus Theodoret, *in Hebr.*, 6. 4 (*PG*, 82. 717): μὴ νομίζειν τό πανάγιον βάπτισμα τοῖς Ἰουδαϊκοῖς ἐοικέναι βαπτίσμασιν . . . καὶ πολλὰ καὶ συνεχῶς προσεφέρετο.

73. Thus, for example, Cyprian, *Ep.*, 75. 13; Optatus of Milevi, *de schism. Donat.*, 5. 3.

74. The Apostolic Constitutions (7, 44, 3) insist on the necessity of prayer for the Holy Spirit, for lack of which baptism, like that of the Jews, has no effect except on the body.

75. *Catech. ad Illum.*, 1. 2 (*PG*, 49. 225 ff.).

76. *Ep.*, 4. 24, to Paulinus of Antioch (*PL*, 13. 364).

77. See pp. 346 ff.

78. *Hom. de Magis.*, cited p. 356.

79. The prohibition of proselytism is reasserted in Spain as late as 1092. M. Hallier, "La question juive pendant le premier millénaire chrétien," *RHPR*, 1935, p. 318.

80. *Quaestiones*, 115. 14 (*PL*, 35. 2390): . . . *cum videamus ex paganis, licet raro, fieri Judaeos.*

81. Chrysostom, when he begins his cycle of homilies against the Jews, is engaged in a controversy with the Anomoeans, and he notes that they are clearly similar to the Jews in their denial of the divinity of Christ (*Hom.*, 1. 1, *PG*, 48. 845). Chrysostom also treats as a Jew Paul of Samosata, who does seem to have been heavily under Jewish influence (*Exp. in Ps.*, 110. 2, *PG*, 55. 267).

82. See pp. 111 ff.

83. *C. Th.*, 16, 5, 44 (408). *Judaeorum nova atque inusitata detexit audacia, quod catholicae fidei velint sacramenta turbare.*

84. *B.J.*, 7, 3, 3: ἀεί τε προσαγόμενοι ταῖς θρησκείαις πολὺ πλῆθος Ἑλλήνων, κἀκείνους τρόπῳ τινὶ μοῖραν αὐτῶν πεποίηντο. These are the semiproselytes, who attach themselves to the Synagogue without entirely becoming part of it.

85. Josephus, loc. cit., notes as one of the attractions the beauty and the rich ornamentation of the synagogues of Antioch.

86. This is what Chrysostom means when he compares the Synagogue with a theater (*Hom.*, 1. 2, *PG*, 48. 847; see pp. 217, 220).

87. Χοροὺς μαλάκων . . . . γυμνοῖς τοῖς ποσὶν ἐπὶ τῆς ἀγορᾶς ὀρχούμενοι. *Hom.*, 1. 2 (*PG*, 48. 846). The celebration of worship out of doors is prescribed on fast days by the Mishnah. *Taan.*, II, 1. See *Altercatio Simonis et Theophili*, 28.

88. *Hom.*, 1. 1.

89. *Hom.*, 4. 1 (*PG*, 48. 871).

90. *Ep.*, 93 (*PL*, 22. 669).

91. Strack and Billerbeck, *Kommentar*, 1:925.

92. See pp. 301 ff.

93. *C. Th.*, 16. 8. The law prescribes the death penalty for Jews who were prepared to stone those of their community who were converted to Christianity. It then goes on to speak of proselytes in terms that are not altogether clear: *Si quis vero ex populo ad eorum nefariam sectam accesserit . . . . cum ipsis poenas meritas substinebit. Ipsis* doubtless refers to the Jews, previously mentioned, who rage against the apostates, and *poenas meritas* consequently means death. It could apply also to those who were the agents of conversion.

94. *C. Th.*, 16, 8, 7: *Si quis . . . . ex Christiano Judaeus effectus sacrilegis coetibus*

adgregetur, cum accusatio fuerit conprobata, facultates ejus dominio fisci jussimus vindicari. The basis of the accusation is perhaps that the proselyte is known to be circumcised.

95. *C. Th.*, 16, 7, 3 (383) a law against conversions to paganism, to Judaism, and to Manichaeism. *Auctores vero persuasionis hujus, qui lubricas mentes in proprium deflexerant consortium, eademque reos erroris hujusmodi poena comitetur, quive etiam graviora plerumque pro motibus judicum et qualitate commissi extra ordinem promi in nefarios sceleris hujus artifices supplicia censemus.*

96. *C. Th.*, 16, 8, 19: *Si quis ex Christiana fide incredulitate Judaica polluatur....* *Si quisquam hanc legem venire temptaverit, sciat se ad majestatis crimen esse retinendem.* The law has in mind at the same time the propaganda of the Judaizing Caelicoles and that of the Jews.

97. *Nov. Theod.*, 3: *Quicumque servum seu ingenuum, invitum vel suasione plectenda, ex cultu Christianae religionis in nefandam sectam ritumve transduxerit, cum dispendio fortunarum capite puniendum.* At the same time the transition for Jews into Christianity is made easier. A law of A.D. 428 (*C. Th.*, 16, 8, 28) forbids Jewish parents to disinherit their children who are converted to Christianity.

98. *C. Th.*, 16, 8, 6 (339): *Ne Christianas mulieres suis jungant flagitiis vel, si hoc fecerint, capitali periculo subjugentur.*

99. *C. Th.*, 3, 7, 3, and 9, 67, 5: *Ne quis Christianam mulierem in matrimonio Judaeus accipiat, neque Judaeae Christianus conjugium sortiatur.* Canons 17 and 78 of the Council of Elvira enact the same prohibitions.

100. The Talmud firmly forbids the marriage of Jews with non-Jews (*b. Ab. Zara*, 36b; see *b. Kidd.*, 66b, 68b; *b. Yebam.*, 23a; similarly Josephus, *Ant. Jud.*, 8, 7, 5; Philo, *De Spec. Leg.*, 3, 5, 29; Tacitus, *Hist.*, 5. 5). It condemns, moreover, extraconjugal relations between Jewish women and pagan men, for such occasions might lead to idolatry. A liaison between a Jewish man and a pagan woman is looked on more leniently.

101. *C. Th.*, 16, 9, 1 (335): *Si quis Judaeorum Christianum mancipium vel cujuslibet alterius sectae mercatus circumciderit, minime in servitute retineat circumcisum, sed libertatis privilegiis, qui hoc sustinuerit, potiatur.*

102. *C. Th.*, 16, 9, 2 (33).

103. *C. Th.*, 16, 9, 3 (415).

104. *C. Th.*, 16, 9, 4 (417): *Ut eos nec invitos nec volentes caeno propriae sectae confundat.* In rabbinic law, and from as early as pre-Talmudic times, the circumcision of slaves of non-Jewish origin was the normal rule. Gen. 17:12 ff.; *b. Shabb.*, 135ab. The prohibition against possessing such slaves doubtless largely contributed to the withdrawal of Jews from agriculture and their concentration in trade and in the petty artisan class. The development is apparent by the end of antiquity. See Haller, "La question juive," p. 318.

105. See pp. 227 ff.

106. See p. 130.

107. *C. Th.*, 16, 8, 22 (415): *Ac deinceps nullas condi faciat synagogas .... Si Christianum vel cujuslibet sectae hominem ingenuum servumve judaica nota foedare temptaverit vel ipse vel quisquam Judaeorum, legum severitati subdatur.* This prohibition for the future implies that the Patriarch is regarded as guilty of this abuse in the past.

108. *b. Sota*, 49b; *b. Bab. Qam.*, 83a.

109. See p. 42. It is still more interesting to observe the same attitude among the Palestinian rabbis. R. Huna (middle of fourth century) asserts that the Greeks in three respects surpass the wicked empire (Rome), in laws, in books, and in language (*Midr. Gen. R.*, 16, on 2:14).

110. Jos. 1:8, *T. Ab. Zara.*, I, 20; *b. Menach.*, 99b.

111. *b. Bab. Qam.*, 82b: "Cursed be he who praises pigs. Cursed be he who teaches his son Greek wisdom." See *b. Sota*, 49b, *b. Menach.*, 64b.

112. *b. Hagig.*, 15b.

113. Bousset/Gressmann, *Religion*, p. 95.

114. Out of 554 Roman inscriptions "only one is written exclusively in Aramaic (no. 290) one other is half Greek, half Aramaic (no. 291)," Frey, *CIJ*, p. lxv. The position is typical. The Jewish inscriptions from the rest of Europe and from Africa exhibit the same paucity of Hebrew. See Monceaux, "Enquête sur l'épigraphie chrétienne," *RA*, 1904, pp. 354 ff. There are three inscriptions in Hebrew, two of which are no more than the ritual *shalom*.

115. A dozen examples at Rome. Frey, *CIJ*, p. lxv.

116. Inscriptions from southern Italy (Frey, *CIJ*, pp. 420 ff.). They seem to be connected with the arrival in the eighth century of African Jews fleeing from the Arab invasion, i.e., Jews who were already familiar with semitic idiom. See M. Mieses, "Les Juifs et les établissements puniques," *REJ*, 1933, pp. 83-86. Africa is the place where our one Hebrew epitaph of the period was found — at Volubilis (Monceaux, "Enquête," p. 372).

117. See Juster, *Les Juifs*, 1:365, and Lietzmann, *Geschichte der alten Kirche*, 1:83 ff.

118. Especially at Rome, and up to the fourth century, according to Frey. He notes 74 percent inscriptions in Greek, only 24 percent in Latin. The chronology is not easy to clarify. The study of brick stamps has allowed Frey to establish that the great catacomb of Monteverde, for example, was in use from the beginning of the Christian era at least up to Diocletian's reign. Frey, *CIJ*, pp. liv and nos. 212-27.

119. See Strack and Billerbeck, *Kommentar*, 4:1, pp. 171-88; Elbogen, *Gottesdienst*, pp. 194, 196. Tertullian, equally with Chrysostom, observes the public nature of synagogue worship: *Sed et Judaei palam lectitant: vectigalis libertas; vulgo aditur sabbatis omnibus* (*Apol.*, 18. 8). Similarly, *Quaest. Vet. et Novi Test., Quaest.* 44. 1: *Sed forte dicant Judaei: Domus Dei, id est synagoga, omnibus patet. Nec renitimur.*

120. In the synagogue at Caesarea, for example. *j. Sota.*, VII, 1; Schürer, *Geschichte*, III[4], p. 141.

121. *T. Meg.*, II.

122. E. Albertini, "Fouilles d'Elche," *Bulletin Hispanique*, 1907, pp. 120 ff. Frey, *CIJ*, nos. 662-64.

123. Frey, *CIJ*, n. 661.

124. Frey, *CIJ*, pp. 420 ff. (nos. 569-619).

125. The use of Greek was quite common in Oriental religions. See, for example, Firmicus Maternus, *De Errore*, 22. 1; Cumont, *Religions orientales*[4], p. 71. *Mystères de Mithra* (Brussels, 1894-1901), p. 25 (English translation, Chicago, 1903).

126. It is possible that among the Jews there were political reasons for fidelity to Greek, and that they did not wish to use as a sacred language the language of Rome. It will be observed, however, that Greek is completely absent from North African Jewish epigraphy. According to Monceaux, there are thirty Latin inscriptions as opposed to three in Hebrew. Here again there is a striking similarity with Christianity, for Christianity in Africa, however far back we trace it, was always Latin-speaking. However, it does not appear that here or anywhere else there was ever a Latin translation of the Bible in use among the Jews. Tertullian manifestly knows of none. He mentions the Septuagint as being destined to make the revelation accessible to all, *ne notitia vacaret*. And it is from the Septuagint that he goes on to say, *Judaei palam lectitant*.

127. *Fouilles*, op. cit., p. 125.

128. The vitality of Spanish Judaism persisted right through the Middle Ages and stimulated quite a tradition of Christian anti-Jewish polemic. See "Spain," *JE*, and Lukyn Williams's *Adversus Judaeos*, pp. 207-92.

129. See p. 21. Lieberman's recent work, *Greek in Jewish Palestine*, has brought clearly to light the diffusion of Greek in Jewish circles (see review by Abel, *RB*, 1946, p. 275). Perhaps this had been increased by the colonization to which Palestine was subjected after the wars in Judaea. But if any considerable number of Jews had thus taken over the language of the

goyim, this in itself testifies that the retrenchment was far from being accomplished.

130. The discovery was noted in the newspapers on the eve of World War II, and I have not yet seen a scholarly account.

131. *M. Sota.*, VII, 1-2.

132. *j. Sota.*, VII, 1.

133. *Ep. 121, ad Algasiam*, 10.

134. *M. Sota*, IX, 14: "From the time of the War of Quietus it was forbidden to teach one's son Greek."

135. See p. 30.

136. *j. Ab. Zara*, II, 2. R. Gamaliel's son, R. Simon, affirms that Greek is authorized for the translation of the Bible, and considers that, alone among foreign languages, it lends itself perfectly to the task. *M. Meg.*, I, 8; *j. Meg.*, 1. 7; *b. Meg.*, 9b.

137. Bacher, *Tannaiten*, 2:454. Watzinger, *Antike Synagogen in Galilaea* 1916, p. 212.

138. *b. Sota*, 49b, *b. Bab. Qam.*, 82b.

139. *b. Bab. Qam.*, 82b; "The Greek language is one thing, Greek wisdom is another."

140. *b. Sota*, 49b, *b. Bab. Qam.*, 83a.

141. *j. Sota*, IX, 13.

142. *j. Sanh.*, X, 14.

143. Jerome, *Praef, in Dan.* (*PL*, 28. 135 ff.).

144. See p. 59. Concerning Theodotion, the evidence is confused. Ancient authors reckon him sometimes as a Jew, sometimes as a Jewish Christian. Schürer, *Geschichte*, 3:439-42.

145. The LXX was at that time judged rather severely. "Long ago five elders translated the Torah into Greek for King Ptolemy, and the day of its translation was as grievous for Israel as the day when the golden calf was made, for the Torah could not be translated adequately." (Tr. *Soferim*, I, 7). See *Sepher Torah*, I, 8. When the translation was finished darkness covered the earth for thirty days, as a punishment (*Meg. Taan.*, 13).

146. Graetz, *Geschichte*, 4³:103-5, 405-7.

147. Ps. 45:3, *j. Meg.*, I, 11; see *j. Kidd.*, I, 1.

148. Gen. 9:27; *yapht elohim le-yephet*.

149. *yapht* from the root *patah* is similar to *yaphah*.

150. *b. Meg.*, 9b.

151. See Juster, *Les Juifs*, 1:369-77.

152. Juster, *Les Juifs*, p. 370, regards the Hellenists' claim as an innovation. The traditional usage was to read exclusively in Hebrew. It seems to me impossible to accept such a view, which goes against all that we know of the development of Judaism and of the part played by the Septuagint in the worship of the diaspora. The accompanying prohibition of the Mishnah (δευτέρωσις) by the same *novella* plainly shows that Justinian wished to impede the development of rabbinic and Hebraic Judaism. The text of the Mishnah that Juster appeals to (*Meg.*, IV, 5) and that prescribes reading in Hebrew followed by an oral translation, verse by verse, is codifying Palestinian usage. It was the encroachment of this usage that the Hellenists wished to resist.

153. There is some contradiction in the actions of the legislators here, in prohibiting proselytism yet favoring the use of Greek, which might be proselytism's instrument. It is explained either by a desire gratuitously to make things difficult for the Jews, or by a wish not to let Israel become too isolated, so that the possibility of converting her might remain open.

154. There were nevertheless some survivals of the older attitudes and practices. In the Middle Ages the Jews of Crete used to read, on the Day of Atonement, in common Greek (transcribed into Hebrew letters) the Book of Jonah. See "Jüdisch-griechisch," *EJ*, 9:553. Similarly in the West, the profane languages the Jews habitually spoke did sometimes figure in the cult. They were used for the sermon almost always, but not for the liturgy. At Lyon,

quite early during the Middle Ages, Jews went to the synagogue to hear sermons. See I. Loeb, "La controverse religieuse entre les Juifs et les chrétiens au moyen âge." *RHR*, 1888, pp. 324 ff.

155. Simon, "Judaïsme berbère," *RHPR*, 1946.

156. Josephus, *Ant. Jud.*, 20. 2. This conversion itself was preceded, under the Hasmoneans, by the forcible Judaization of Idumaea and by part of Ituraea. Josephus, *Ant. Jud.*, 13, 9, 1 and 13, 11, 3. Jewish influence was prolonged by, amongst other things, the existence of Jews among Zenobia's entourage at the court of Palmyra.

157. On the connections between Phoenician/Punic and Hebrew, see Renan, *Histoire générale des langues sémitiques* (Paris, 1870–8), p. 198, and Gsell, *Histoire ancienne*, 4:179.

158. On this legend see "Judaïsme berbère," pp. 7 ff.

159. *Histoire des Berbères*, trans. by Slane, 1:208.

160. See Josephus, *De Bello Judaico*, 7. 11; Dio Cassius, 68. 32; Eusebius, *HE*, 4. 2. According to a Jewish tradition, and a fairly late one at that, Titus settled 30,000 Jewish prisoners of war in Punic territory. See Rachmuth, "Die Juden in Nord Afrika," *MGWJ*, 1906, pp. 22 ff.

161. See "Judaïsme berbère," p. 124 and n. 150.

162. Gautier, *Genséric, roi des Vandales* (Paris, 1932), p. 296, and *Le passé de l'Afrique du Nord* (Paris, 1937), pp. 225 ff., 271.

163. See "Judaïsme berbère," pp. 125 ff.

164. Ibid., pp. 132 ff.

165. Ibid., p. 143 and nn. 206, 207. On the parallel expansion of Jewish Christianity, see p. 264 above.

166. The majority of these Eastern peoples practiced circumcision. The main obstacle Jewish missionary work met with in the West did not therefore appear in the East. See Jerome, *in Jerem.*, 10. 25 ff. (*PL*, 24. 746): *Multarum ex quadam parte gentium, et maxime quae Judaeae Palestinaeque confines sunt, usque hodie populi circumciduntur, et praecipue Aegypti, et Idumaei, Ammonitae et Moabitae, et omnis regio Sarracenorum.*

167. On this rehabilitation of peoples who were previously accursed, such as Ammonites and Moabites, see "Judaïsme berbère," p. 143, and also p. 277 above.

168. Its last noteworthy success was the conversion, in the eighth century, of the Khazars of southern Russia, and even this was only a partial conversion.

Chapter 11

1. See p. 352.

2. Peterson, ΕΙΣ ΘΕΟΣ (Göttingen, 1936), and especially, "Jüdisches und christliches Morgengebet in Syrien," *Zeitschr. für kath. Theol.*, 1934, pp. 110–13. It is likely that the additions represent a precaution taken by the Church authorities in view of the Jewish character of the formula, and that they are intended to give it an unmistakably Christian coloring. Epiphanius has preserved for us an even more characteristic variant, which appears in a long digression in the middle of his account of the Ebionites. The digression concerns a converted Jew called Joseph (on which character see Graetz, *Geschichte* 4³:310–13). Joseph on one occasion foiled some Jewish black magic by the virtue of the name of Jesus and the sign of the cross, whereupon the spectators cried out, εἷς θεός, ὁ βοηθῶν τοῖς Χριστιανοῖς (*Haer.*, 1, 30, 12). In this form the acclamation illustrates the conflict that existed between the two religions, especially on the subject of the efficacy of rites. It is not impossible that Jews and Christians hurled this formula at each other, the former in its primitive form and the latter in its longer, reworked version, much as the orthodox and the Donatists of Africa used *Deo gratias* and *Deo laudes* as war cries or rallying cries of their respective parties.

3. Edited in the series *Analecta Bolland.* 50 (1932) 241 ff.

4. "ΕΙΣ ΘΕΟΣ in der sepulkralen Epigraphik," *Zeitschr. für kath. Theol.*, 1934, pp. 400-402.

5. Swarensky, *Die Begräbnis- und Trauerliturgie der Samaritaner* (Berlin, 1930), p. 21. Cited by Peterson, op. cit., p. 400.

6. *Didascalia*, 2, 22, 12-16. See 2 Chron. 33:12, 18 ff.; trans. and comm. in Kautzsch, *Apokryphen und Pseudepigraphen des A.T..*, pp. 165-71. The Christian origin of the work has sometimes been maintained, wrongly, it seems. The most recent supporter of this view is Nau. See *Revue de l'Orient chrétien*, 1908, p. 137.

7. This use can be explained by the fact that the work is found in certain MSS of the Septuagint. But like the plagiarizing of the *Didascalia* by the Apostolic Constitutions, this is the only evidence for its use in Christian liturgy. A direct borrowing from the liturgy of the Synagogue seems more likely. See Bousset, *Jüd. Gebetssammlung*, p. 487.

8. See pp. 53 ff.

9. See Oesterley, *Jewish Background*, p. 6.

10. These themselves are in some respects dependent on synagogue rites. Gavin, *The Jewish Antecedents of the Christian Sacraments* (1928).

11. See Lietzmann, *Geschichte*, 1:215, and *Messe und Herrenmahl*, pp. 230 ff. The document bears the marks of Hellenistic Judaism, and of a fairly enlightened sort, at that. From this source it appears to have borrowed not only its catechetical instruction on the two ways, but also the arrangement and inspiration of its liturgy, and its attitude to the dietary laws. The latter are halfway between strict Jewish rigorism and the position that Christianity finally adopted. Observance of them is recommended, but not insisted on (6:3). Other observances are either tacitly condemned, or are taken over (as, for example, fasting). The Jews are regarded as hypocrites (8:1).

12. There is a good summary of the whole discussion in "Dimanche," *DAC*, 4:858-994, and "Pâques," *DAC*, 3:1521-74. These articles contain a full bibliography. But add, on the subject of Sunday, P. Cotton, *From Sabbath to Sunday* (Oxford, 1933). On the question of Sabbath and Sunday in the early Church, see H. Riesenfeld, "Sabbat et jour du Seigneur," in *New Testament Essays*, published in memory of T. W. Manson (Manchester, 1959), pp. 210-17. Also W. Rordorf, *Der Sonntag* (Zurich, 1962).

13. See Ignatius of Antioch, *Magn.*, 9. 1.

14. Pliny, *Letters*, 10. 97: *Quod essent soliti stato die ante lucem convenire carmenque Christo quasi Deo dicere secum invicem.* Justin, *Apol.*, 1. 67: καὶ τῇ τοῦ ἡλίου λεγομένῃ ἡμέρᾳ πάντων κατὰ πόλεις ἢ ἀγροὺς μενόντων ἐπὶ τὸ αὐτὸ συνέλευσις γίνεται. See *Dial.*, 24. 1, 41, 4, 138. 1, and *Didache*, 14. 1.

15. Σαββατίζειν is practically a synonym for Ἰουδαΐζειν. When Athanasius was speaking on the occasion of a feast that fell on a Saturday, he felt obliged to make excuses for the co-incidence. *Hom. de Semente* (*PG*, 28. 144) ἐν ἡμέρᾳ σαββάτου συνήχθημεν, οὐ νοσοῦντες Ἰουδαϊσμόν.

16. To follow Jewish usage is to 'limp': Athanasius, *de Synod.* (*PG*, 26. 688).

17. That is, whether one celebrates Easter at the same time as the Passover, on 14 Nisan (this was the Quartodeciman use) or, still following Jewish calculations, on the Sunday after Passover: Socrates, *HE*, 5. 22 (*PG*, 67. 629). See *Dict. de Théologie Catholique*, "Pâques" (11. 2, 1955).

18. *Didascalia*, 5, 14, 1-14.

19. Ibid., 5, 14, 15; see 5, 13 and 5, 15, 21.

20. Ibid., 5, 14, 22.

21. This was also the meaning of the feast according to the Quartodecimans of Asia Minor. But the aspect of propitiation for the Jews seems to have been missing.

22. *Didache*, 8.

23. *Didascalia*, 5, 14, 8 and 21.

24. Ibid., 5, 14, 17.
25. Ibid., 5, 19, 9.
26. Ibid., 5, 20.
27. Texts cited by Juster, *Les Juifs*, 1:280, n. 2.
28. Deut. 16:3. Etymology was appealed to. The Passover prefigured the sacrifice of Christ: *Immolatio pecudis ab iis ipsis qui faciunt pascha nominatur ἀπὸ πάσχειν, quia passionis figura est.* (Lactantius, *Inst. Div.*, 4. 26, *PL*, 6. 531).
29. Epiphanius, *Haer.*, 70. 11 (*PG*, 42. 360 ff.). See Schwartz, *Ostertafeln*, pp. 104 ff.
30. See Juster, *Les Juifs*, 1:307 ff.
31. Didascalia, 5, 17, 1. The same order is given in the *Diataxis:* ἀλλὰ ποιεῖτε ὅταν οἱ ἀδελφοὶ ὑμῶν οἱ ἐκ περιτομῆς· μετ' αὐτῶν ἅμα ποιεῖτε. (Epiphanius, *Haer.*, 70. 10, *PG*, 42. 356). Epiphanius, drawing attention to the fact that the text says ἐκ περιτομῆς and not ἐν περιτομῇ mistakenly thinks that it refers to converted Jews. In fact it is suggesting that actual synagogue usage should be the norm. "When the people celebrate the Passover, you, for your part, fast and zealously keep vigil in the midst of their unleavened bread," *Didascalia*, 5, 20, 10.
32. See pp. 90, 325.
33. Isa. 66:57.
34. *Didascalia*, 5, 14, 23.
35. This example shows how inadequate the accepted terminology is. The traditional classification just does not apply here. We are concerned here, as Schwartz puts it in his *Ostertafeln*, p. 115, with a "conglomerate" in which Jews and gentile converts live together in the same communities.
36. *Didascalia*, 6, 18, 11; see 6, 15, 1.
37. Ibid., 6, 18, 11.
38. Ps. Cyprian, *De Pascha Computus*, 1 (*PL*, 3. 943). These are the provinces of Syria, Mesopotamia, and Cilicia, where, in contradiction with the Western usage, the Jewish calculation was followed. Athanasius, *Ep. ad Afros episcopos*, 2 (*PG*, 26. 1036 ff.).
39. *Haer.*, 70. 9 (*PG*, 42. 354): μετὰ Ἰουδαίων βούλονται τὸ πάσχα ἐπιτελεῖν.
40. *Haer.*, 70. 10 (*PG*, 42. 356 ff.): κἂν πλανηθῶσιν, μηδὲν ὑμῖν μελέτω.
41. See *Chronicon Paschale* (*PG*, 92. 72). These errors which the Jews make with regard to the Passover are also a consequence of their crime against Christ. See the imperial letter to the Council of Nicaea, Eusebius, *Vita Const.*, 3. 18 (*PG*, 20. 1073). The Church accused the Jews in particular of paying no attention to the equinox, which ought always to fall before the feast.
42. *Homily against the Jews*, 3. 3 (*PG*, 48. 864): προετιμήσαμεν τὴν συμφωνίαν τῆς τῶν χρόνων παρατηρήσεως.
43. Ibid., 3 (*PG*, 48. 866).
44. 1 Cor. 5:7; *Hom.*, 3. 4 (*PG*, 48. 866).
45. *Hom.* 3. 4 (*PG*, 48. 867): πάσχα γὰρ οὐ νηστεία ἐστίν, ἀλλ' ἡ προσφορὰ καὶ ἡ θυσία ἡ καθ' ἐκάστην γινομένη σύναξιν.
46. Ibid., 4 (867): οὐ γὰρ διὰ τὸ πάσχα νηστεύομεν, οὐδὲ διὰ τὸν σταυρὸν ἀλλὰ διὰ τὰ ἁμαρτήματα τὰ ἡμέτερα, ἐπειδὴ μέλλομεν μυστηρίοις προσιέναι.
47. Ibid., 5 (870).
48. Ibid., 5 (869). What is in question is a whole week fast, (πᾶσαν τὴν ἑβδομάδα), including the Sunday following.
49. See p. 160.
50. *Hom.*, 12, on the Passover (ed. by Bert, *TU*, 3:3-4, pp. 179-95).
51. *Hom.*, 12. 8.
52. *Hom.*, 12. 4.
53. "Because he who gives his flesh to eat and his blood to drink is reckoned among the dead." *Hom.*, 12. 8.

54. *Hom.*, 12. 4, 12. 6: "The Jews' Passover is the 14th Nisan, its night and its day." 12. 8: "It was on the margin of the fourteenth that our Lord celebrated the Passover." This chronology is neither that of the Synoptics, who place the Last Supper on the evening of the fourteenth and the crucifixion on the fifteenth, nor of John, who puts the trial before the Passover feast of the Jews, and therefore during the day of the fourteenth. On these divergences see Guignebert, *Jésus*, pp. 514-22, and also Goguel, *Vie de Jésus*, pp. 414-22. It is probable that in Aphraates' area the Jews celebrated the Passover on the night of the thirteenth-fourteenth Nisan, and not on the following night, as they do nowadays. The relevant biblical texts (Exod. 12 : 3-6, Deut. 16 : 6) are sufficiently imprecise to allow for such differences. In particular, the expression "between the two evenings" (Exod. 12 : 6) could have increased confusion, as did the doubts about the "seven days of unleavened bread" (see Strack and Billerbeck, *Kommentar*, 2 : 812 ff.). The rabbis disagreed as to whether these seven days included the fourteenth or not.

On the date of the Last Supper and the possible connexions between the ancient Christian calendar and a Jewish one that was made use of by dissident groups, in particular the Qumran sect, see now A. Jaubert, *La Date de la Cène. Calendrier biblique et liturgique chrétienne* (Paris, 1957).

55. *Hom.*, 12. 8.

56. Ibid.

57. Ibid.

58. He is not concerned with the stages of Holy Week, which is the week of Christ's passion, and on which Chrysostom, for example, insists. *Hom.*, 3. 5 (*PG*, 48. 869).

59. *Hom.*, 12. 6.

60. Ibid.

61. *Hom.*, 12, 1 ff.

62. Ibid., 8. Chrysostom, conversely: οὐδὲ γὰρ ἡ ἐκκλησία χρόνων ἀκρίβειαν οἶδεν (*Hom.*, 3. 6, *PG*, 48. 871).

63. The paschal fast itself had an antecedent in the Jewish Passover. *M. Pes.*, X, 1 lays it down that one must not eat on the eve of the feast "from about the time of the evening offering . . . until nightfall." We have here a simple interchange of rites. The Eucharist, which corresponds to the Passover meal, precedes, in Aphraates' scheme, a seven-day fast, which takes the place of the seven days of unleavened bread.

64. See Epiphanius, *Haer.* 70, and Sozomen, *HE*, 6. 24 and 7. 18 (*PG*, 67. 1353-57, and 1468-73). For a list of the sects that follow a Judaizing practice in the matter of Easter, see Ps. Chrysostom, *in Pascha*, 7. 1 (*PG*, 59. 747).

65. On the subject of syncretizing and Judaizing tendencies, see Augustine, *Serm.*, 9. 3 (*PL*, 38. 76). *Tu vis dimisso uno Deo tanquam legitimo viro animae fornicari per multa daemonia; et quod est gravius, non quasi aperte deserens et repudians sicut apostatae faciunt, sed tanquam manens in domo viri tui admittis adulteros; id est tanquam Christianus non dimittis Ecclesiam, consulis mathematicos. . . . . Dicitur tibi ut spiritualiter observes sabbatum: non quomodo Judaei observant sabbatum carnali otio.*

66. Chrysostom, when trying to persuade the Protopaschites to give up their practice (*Hom.*, 3. 1, *PG*, 48. 863) states that it really is in the proper sense heretical.

67. Duchesne, *La question de la Pâque au Concile de Nicée*, p. 14.

68. *Const. Ap.*, 8, 33, 1-2. They ought to rest ἐν τῇ ἐκκλησίᾳ διὰ τὴν διδασκαλίαν τῆς εὐσεβείας. Saturday is thus characterized by services of worship, which are designed to keep the faithful away from the synagogue. Saturday is consecrated "because of the creation," and Sunday "because of the resurrection."

69. *Canon*, 29, Mansi, 2 : 570: ὅτι οὐ δεῖ Χριστιανοὺς Ἰουδαΐζειν καὶ ἐν τῷ σαββάτῳ σχολάζειν, ἀλλὰ ἐργάζεσθαι αὐτοὺς ἐν τῇ ἡμέρᾳ. This conflict over the subject of the Sabbath rest is paralleled by a similar one over the Sabbath fast, which gave rise to a wealth

of controversy (see "Jeûne," *DAC*, 7:2490). In Roman usage it was obligatory to fast on the Sabbath, and a fairly widespread practice throughout the rest of the West. But throughout most of the East it was held that fasting was as incompatible with the sanctity of the Sabbath as it was with the sanctity of Sunday. When the *Didascalia* insists on the fast, but appeals to Moses as its authority for doing so, it differs from the Eastern usage of its day. Nevertheless, though it does it in a different way, it agrees with the common Eastern usage in expressing respect for Jewish institutions.

70. *Hom.*, 13, on the Sabbath.

71. *Hom.*, 13. 2.

72. *Hom.*, 13. 4.

73. *Hom.*, 13. 2. Draft animals, since they had to work all week, had no time to commit sin. But the Sabbath rest provided them with an opportunity for it. On that day they relaxed and practiced incest. But God does not impute sin to them, for the law of rest applies to them just as it does to men, and for them the idea of good or evil does not exist.

74. *Hom.*, 13. 7.

75. Deut. 16:5 ff.

76. E.g., Justin, *Dial.*, 40. 2 and 46. 2; Aphraates, *Hom.*, 12. 2. But it was established custom among the Jews to eat the lamb in whatever place they held the festival. This is firmly attested in the Talmud itself, though it condemns the custom (*b. Pes.*, 53ab). The aim of the Talmud is most likely to translate the rite from being part of the official, public cult into a family ritual. The emphasis should thus fall on the meal, not on the sacrifice. See Mishnah, *Pesachim*, Beer's edition, pp. 76-78.

77. Thus Aphraates, *Hom.*, 12. 4.

78. *Chronicon Paschale*, 6 and 7 (*PG*, 92. 80-81). The text appeals for support in this assertion to the facts reported by the fourth Gospel. According to John 18:8, the Jews did not go into the praetorium of Pilate's residence along with Jesus "that they might not be defiled, and might eat the Passover." The Last Supper therefore could not have had the character of a Passover meal.

79. Ibid., 6, quoting Hippolytus of Rome, against an adversary who said: ἐποίησε τὸ πάσχα ὁ Χριστὸς τότε τῇ ἡμέρᾳ καὶ ἔπαθεν · διὸ κἀμὲ δεῖ ὃν τρόπον ὁ κύριος ἐποίησεν, οὕτω ποιεῖν.

80. *Hymni Azym.*, 19. 11 ff. and 16, ed. by Lamy, Malines, 1882, pp. 624 ff. See Juster, *Les Juifs*, 1:325, n. 4.

81. *Canon* 38, Mansi, *Conciliorum*, etc., 2:570.

82. Elvira, *Canon* 50, Mansi, 2:14. Laodicaea, *Canon*, 37, Mansi, *Conciliorum*, etc., 2:570.

83. *Ep. ad August.*, 112. 15 (*PL*, 22. 926). *Suscipe aliquem Judaeorum, qui factus Christianus natum sibi filium circumcidet, qui observet sabbata, qui abstineat se a cibis quas Deus creavit ad utendum cum gratiarum actione, qui quarta decima die mensis primi agnum mactet ad vesperam.* Animal sacrifice seems to have been widespread among the Christians of the East (see Conybeare, "Les sacrifices d'animaux dans les anciennes églises chrétiennes," *RHR* 44 (1901):108-14) and especially in Armenia. But the practice is too common for us to be able to conclude with certainty that it developed under Jewish influence, insofar as the practice of sacrifice in Judaism outside Jerusalem is by no means established. Sacrifice in the Church could therefore be a survival from paganism, Christianized with the help of pentateuchal texts. The sacrifice of the paschal lamb, on the contrary, which is equally well attested among the Byzantine and Armenian churches, is very likely to be derived from Jewish practice, as an imitation of current synagogue usage.

84. See Juster, *Les Juifs*, 1:270, n. 5.

85. See, however, Aphraates' instruction regarding circumcision (*Hom.*, 11, Bert's edition, pp. 166-78). Similarly Chrysostom, *Homily against the Jews*, 2 (*PG*, 48. 857).

86. See p. 90.

87. Acceptance of the term *deuterosis* itself is, however, hesitant, sometimes disconcertingly so. The book of Leviticus, whose ritual prescriptions seem to be included in the term *deuterosis*, is sometimes quoted as if it were authoritative for Christians. Thus, for example, the freedom from physical abnormality that, according to Lev. 21:17 (see 13:15) is required in a worshiper, appears among the requisite qualities of a bishop, who must suffer from no deformity. Jerome, in the name of true Christianity, repudiates such considerations: *Si tantum litteram sequimur ... quamvis bonae mentis sit qui cicatricem habuerit et deformis est, privetur sacerdotio (Ep. 42 ad Nepot.,* 10). It will be seen from this how complex and how difficult to hold was the position adopted by the *Didascalia.* Its warning concerning the *deuterosis* is addressed initially to all believers (1. 6) but then, at the end, more especially to converted Jews (6, 21, 6).

88. *Didascalia,* 6, 21, 8.

89. *Didascalia,* 6, 22, 8 ff. See the development in 6, 21, 1-9 of Lev. 15. The rites thus disapproved of reappear in what the fathers freely refer to as "Jewish baptism" (see p. 287).

90. *Didascalia,* 6, 22, 1 ff.

91. *Hom.,* 15, on the distinguishing of foods (Bert, pp. 259-69).

92. *Homily against the Jews,* 6. 7 (*PG*, 48. 916).

93. *Hom.,* 1, 1 (*PG*, 48. 845), 1. 4 (849), 2. 2 (859).

94. *Hom.,* 1. 1 (48. 844).

95. *Hom.,* 2. 3 (860 ff.), 4. 7 (881).

96. *De Bello Judaico,* 2, 20, 2.

97. *Hom.,* 8. 4 (*PG*, 48. 933): κἂν πολλοὶ ὦσιν οἱ νηστεύσαντες, σὺ μὴ ἐκπομπεύσῃς, μηδὲ παραδειγματίσῃς τῆς Ἐκκλησίας τὴν συμφοράν, ἀλλὰ θεράπευσον.

98. See p. 355.

99. *Est Judaeorum vere de resurrectione talis opinio, quod resurgunt quidem, sed ut carnalibus deliciis et luxuriis caeterisque voluptatibus corporis perfruantur ... Judaei autem et nostri judaizantes ... hostiarum sanguinem, cunctarumque gentium servitutem et uxorum pulchritudinem desiderantes.... (Jerome, in Is., 36, PL, 24:378.) Amatores tantum occidentis litterae, et in mille annis exquisitos cibos gulae ac luxuriae praeparantes.... Qui post secundum in gloria Salvatoris adventum sperant nuptias et parvulos centum annorum et circumcisionis injuriam et victimarum sanguinem et perpetuum sabbatum.* And Jerome, having thus characterized the movement, invites his readers not to join it. *Nec judaica deliramenta sectari. (in Is.,* 44, *PL,* 24:522).

100. *In Is.,* 49. 14 (*PL,* 24. 488).

101. *Si quis ergo Christianorum, et maxime novorum prudentium, quorum nomina taceo, ne quemquam laedere videar, existimat necdum prophetiam esse completam, sciat falso Christi portare se nomen et judaicam animam, circumcisionem tantum corporis non habere.* (*Comm. in Soph.,* 3. 14, *PL,* 25. 1382.)

102. *Videntur igitur observationes, judaicae apud imperitos et vilem plebeculam imaginem habere rationis humanaeque sapientiae.* (*Ep.* 121, *ad Algasiam.*)

103. *De Bello Judaico,* 7, 3, 3. These are not outright conversions, but more likely Judaizing tendencies: ἀεί τε προσαγόμενοι ταῖς θρησκείαις πολὺ πλῆθος Ἑλλήνων, κἀκείνους τρόπῳ τινὶ μοῖραν αὐτῶν πεποίηντο.

104. *Canon* 7 (Judaizing sects: Novatians, Photinians, Quartodecimans); *Canon* 16 (liturgical readings on Saturdays); *Canon* 29 (prohibition of Judaizing and of refraining from work on the Sabbath); *Canon* 35 (worship of angels); *Canon* 36 (magic, phylacteries); *Canon* 37 (gifts and feasts of the Jews); *Canon* 38 (unleavened bread and participation in Jewish rites).

105. *Canon* 16.

106. *Canon* 49.

107. Hefele-Leclerq, *Histoire des Conciles,* I, 2, pp. 1009.

108. Novatian, *De Cibis Judaicis* (*PL*, 3. 953-963). Other works by the same author on Passover, circumcision, and the Sabbath, all mentioned by Jerome (*De Vir. Ill.*, 70, *PL*, 23. 681) are no longer extant. See also Zeno of Verona, *Tract.*, 15, on circumcision (*PL*, 11. 345-54); Ambrose, *Ep.* 72, on circumcision (*PL*, 10. 1243-50); *Ep.*, 73, 74, and 78 on the law (*PL*, 16. 1251 ff.): Ps. Jerome, *Ep.* 149 and 19 (*PL*, 22. 1220-24, and 30. 188-210). See Blumenkranz, *Judenpredigt*, pp. 17, 28, 37, 47.

109. On the controversy about Ambrosiaster, Labriolle, *Littérature latine chrétienne*, pp. 384-88, where a bibliography is provided.

110. See Lukyn Williams, *Adversus Judaeos*, pp. 206-92.

111. *Canons*, 16, 26, 49, 50 and 78. See A. W. Winterslow Dale, *The Synod of Elvira and Christian Life in the Fourth Century* (London, 1882), pp. 254 ff.

112. See Monceaux, *Histoire Littéraire*, 3:451-67; Labriolle, *Littérature latine chrétienne*, pp. 234-51; and more recently, Blumenkranz, *Die Judenpredigt Augustins*, p. 19.

113. *Histoire Littéraire*, 3:462.

114. *Carmina Apol.*, 791 ad fin.

115. *Carmina Apol.*, 11; see *Instr.*, 1, 41, 4: *Nil ego composite dixi, sed de lege legendo.*

116. *Instr.*, 1, 37, 1.

> *Quid in synagoga decurris saepe bifarius?*
> *Ut tibi misericors fiat quem denegas ultro?*
> *Exis inde foris, iterum tu fana requiris;*
> *Vis inter utrumque vivere, sed deinde peribis.*

Carmina Apol., 695:

> *Ac idolis servit, iterum tricesima quaerit;*
> *Nunc azyma sequitur qui castum sederat ante.*

117. *Hom.*, 4. 3 (*PG*, 48. 875).

118. *Instr.*, 1, 24, 11 ff.

119. Tertullian, *ad Nat.*, 1. 13; see p. 286.

120. Simon, *Judaïsme berbère*, pp. 105 ff., 132 ff.

121. *PL*, 42. 51-64; see Lukyn Williams, *Adversus Judaeos*, pp. 312 ff.

122. Collected and collated by Blumenkranz, *Die Judenpredigt Augustins*, vol. 2.

123. *Ep.*, 196 (*PL*, 33. 891-99).

124. This is a much less extreme point of view than that defended by Augustine in his correspondence with Jerome. See p. 93. It is somewhat theoretical. The change is due to the intervention of Judaizing tendencies.

125. *Adversus Judaeos*, 3. 10 (33. 894).

126. 3. 9 (ibid.): *Verum tamen cum quisque isto modo fuerit verus germanusque Christianus, utrum etiam Judaeus vel Israelita dicendus sit merito quaeritur.*

127. Ibid. *Quod quidem si non carne sed spiritu hoc esse intellegitur, non debet ipsum nomen sibi in consuetudine sermonis imponere, sed spirituali intellegentia retinere ne propter ambiguitatem vocabuli, quam non discernit cotidiana locutio, illud profiteri videatur, quod est inimicum nomini Christiano.* See 4:14 (897).

128. 16 (898). *Denique Aptus iste nescio quis, de quo scripsisti quod doceat judaizare Christianos, eo modo se. . . . Judaeum et Israelitam vocat ut ab eis escis prohibeat, quas pro temporis illius congruentia lex . . . prohibebat, et ceteras illius temporis observationes jam nunc apud Christianos abolitas remotasque persuadeat.*

129. See "Asellicus," *Dict. d'Histoire et de Géographie ecclésiastique*, 4:914.

130. Ibid., "Aptus," 3, 3:1091.

131. See Gsell, *Histoire ancienne*, 4:496.

132. *Apol.*, 9. 13 ff.

133. *Octavius*, 30. 6: *Nobis homicidium ne in theatro quidem nec videre fas nec audire, tantumque ab omni omnino sanguine cavemus ut nec edulium pecorum in cibis sanguinem noverimus.*

134. Eusebius, *HE*, 5, 1, 26.

135. Acts 15:20 and 15:29.

136. Lev. 17:10-14. The reason for the prohibition is that "the life of the flesh is in the blood."

137. The prohibition appears in Gen. 9:4, which is a list of the commandments given to Noah. The terms are very close to those of Leviticus.

138. Gal. 2:7. On the contradictions between this text and that of Acts, and the possible solutions (the letter drafted in Paul's absence, after his departure) see Lietzmann, *Geschichte*, 1:105, 107.

139. I Cor. 10:27 ff.

140. I Cor. 8:4.

141. On this question see, K. Böckenhoff, *Das apostelische Speisegesetz in den ersten fünf Jahrhunderten*, 1903.

142. *Didache*, 6. 3.

143. *Contra Faust.*, 32. 13 (*PL*, 42. 504) *Morticinum autem puto quod ad escam usus hominum non admisit, eo quod non occisorum sed mortuorum animalium morbida caro est, nec apta ad salutem corporis, cujus causa sumimus alimentum.*

144. Eph. 2:11-22.

145. *Contra Faust.*, ibid., *Quia et si hoc tunc apostoli praeceperunt ut ab animalium sanguine abstinerent Christiani, ne praefocatis carnibus vescerentur, eligisse mihi videntur pro tempore rem facilem, et nequaquam observantibus onerosam in qua cum Israelitis etiam gentes, propter angularem illum lapidem duos in se contendentem, aliquid communiter observarent.... Transacto vero illo tempore ... ubi Ecclesia genitum talis effecta est ut in ea nullus Israelita carnalis appareat, quis jam hoc Christianus observat? Et qui forte pauci adhuc tangere ista formidant, a caeteris irridentur.*

146. Matt. 15:11.

147. Even in the West there were some hints of a return to this observance. In the eighth century Gregory III imposed forty days of penitence on anyone who contravened it. (Reference from Hefele-Leclerq, *Histoire des Conciles*, I, 2, 1933).

148. Ibid.: εἴ τις ἐσθίοντα κρέα (χωρὶς αἵματος, καὶ εἰδωλοθύτου καὶ πνικτοῦ) μετ᾽ εὐλαβείας καὶ πίστεως κατακρίνοι, ὡς ἂν διὰ τὸ μεταλαμβάνειν ἐλπίδα μὴ ἔχοντα, ἀνάθεμα ἔστω. (*Canon 2.*)

149. *Canon 67.*

150. *Canon 65.*

151. *M., Rosh hash*, II, 3-4.

152. *Canon 11.*

153. Juster, *Les Juifs*, 1:277 ff.

154. See, for example, Josephus, *De Bello Judaico*, 2, 18, 2; Gal. 2:14; Commodian, *Instr.*, 1. 37. All these texts refer to pagans.

155. Commodian roundly accuses them of being easygoing in this respect. *Instr.*, 1. 37 (*CSEL*, 15:50).

> *Dicant illi tibi si jussum est deos adorare.*

Carmina Apol., 685-88:

> *Si Deus praecepit ab idolis valde caveri*
> *Quid illi decipiunt gentes puros esse lavacris?*

Immo cum recipiunt tales, docere deberent
Servire non aliis, nisi tantum Summo placere.

156. Eusebius of Alexandria, *Serm.*, 7, (*PG*, 86. 353 ff.): περὶ νεομηνίας καὶ σαββάτων καὶ περὶ τοῦ μὴ φυλάττειν φωνὰς ὀρνέων.

Chapter 12

1. For a full treatment see "Mageia," *RE*, 14. 1, 301–993. More recent is the work of Prümm, *Religionsgeschichtliches Handbuch für den Raum der altchristlichen Umwelt* (Freiburg im Breisgau, 1943), pp. 366–462, which contains a complete bibliography. See also Cumont, *Religions orientales*[4], p. 292, n. 74. On Roman magic, E. Massoneau, *La magie dans l'antiquité romaine* (Paris, 1934). The basic documents are brought together in Preisendanz's collection, *Papyri graecae magicae*, vols. 1 and 2.

2. Tertullian, *Apol.*, 5; *ad Scap.*, 4; Eusebius, *HE*, 5, 5, 1-6. The miracle is attributed to the prayers of the emperor in *Hist. Aug.*, *Marc. Aurel.*, 24. Dio Cassius (71:8) credits it to the activities of the Egyptian magician Arnuphis.

3. *Dig.*, 48, 19, 30.

4. Labriolle, *Réaction païenne*, pp. 78 ff.

5. J. Réville, *La religion à Rome sous les Sévères* (Paris, 1886), p. 142.

6. *Sat.*, 6. 546 ff., Reinach, *Textes*, p. 292. On the Jews' reputation as magicians, Juster, *Les Juifs*, 2:209 ff.

7. Lucian, *Tragodopodagra*, Reinach, *Textes*, p. 159.

8. Lucian, *Alexander*, 32:13, Reinach, *Textes*, p. 160, n. 1.

9. Origen, *Contra Celsum*, 1. 26, Reinach, *Textes*, p. 165. The origin of this statement is to be sought in the Bible itself, and particularly in the story of the ten plagues of Egypt, Exod. 7-11.

10. Pompeius Trogus, reported in Justinus, 36. 2, Reinach, *Textes*, p. 253.

11. Quoted by Eusebius, *Praep. Ev.*, 9:8, Reinach, *Textes*, p. 175. The allusion is to Exod. 7:11, 22 and 8:14, where the Egyptian magicians rival the skill of Moses and Aaron. Reinach is wrong when he translates Numenius's νεανικωτάτας as "cruel" or "odious," seeing it as expressing feelings hostile to the Jews. In fact, as Puech has shown (*Numénius d'Apamée*, pp. 749-54), Numenius was a confirmed admirer of Judaism and probably a Semite, if not actually a Jew. That he was actually a Jew seems to me unlikely.

12. Leitzmann, *Geschichte der alten Kirche*, 3:38 ff.

13. Schwartz, *Christliche und jüdische Ostertafeln*, p. 117.

14. See pp. 356 ff.

15. E.g., Chrysostom, *Homily against the Jews*, especially 8. 6 (*PG*, 48. 930).

16. See especially the *Toledoth Jeshu*, which transfers to Jesus some of the characteristics ascribed by Christian legend to Simon Magus. "Jesus," *EJ*, 9:77-79.

17. Origen, *Contra Celsum*, 1, 6, 69 etc. Origen agrees with Celsus in acknowledging the efficacy and, within certain limits, the legitimacy of magic. See 1, 24; 2, 51. The Jews considered that it was as a magician that Christ had been put to death: κἂν ἐρωτήσῃς αὐτοὺς διὰ τί ἐσταυρώσατε τὸν Χριστόν; λέγουσιν ὡς πλάνον καὶ γόητα ὄντα, Chrysostom, *in Ps.*, 8:3 (*PG*, 55:110). The Jews themselves sometimes used the name of Jesus in exorcisms. See Acts 19:13, and "Beschwörung," *EJ* 4:362-6.

18. Magic was bound up with idolatry. References in Bonsirven, *Jud. Palest.*, 2:187-90, and "Aberglaube," *EJ* 1:229 ff. See *Ps. Clement. Hom.*, 5. 4-7: magic is peculiarly pagan, often ineffective, and always immoral.

19. Josephus thinks of magic as one of Judaism's prerogatives and advantages. God revealed

it to Solomon for its general usefulness and its capacity to heal. *Ant. Jud.*, 8, 2, 5. Throughout both Jewish and Christian tradition Solomon remained the father of good magic. Though forbidden by some texts (*b. Sanh.*, 65b-66a), magic is permitted by others. *b. Sanh.*, 17a requires that members of the Sanhedrin should have some knowledge of it. R. Johanan ben Zakkai understood the language both of angels and of demons and also the murmurs of the palm trees (*b. Sukkah*, 28a).

20. On this question see L. Blau, *Das altjüdische Zauberwesen.* See "Magic (Jewish)," *ERE.*

21. Blau, pp. v-vi.

22. The various Eastern nations all accused each other of being magicians. Blau, p. 36. The Chaldaeans and the Egyptians especially attracted this reputation. Of ten measures of magic that descended on the earth nine fell on Egypt (*b. Kidd.* 49b).

23. Cumont, *Religions orientales*[4], p. 175.

24. See W. Davies, *Magic, Divination and Demonology among the Hebrews* (1897).

25. ἐξορκίζω σε κατὰ τῆς ἐβραϊκῆς φωνῆς: Preisendanz, *Papyri Graecae Magicae*, 1:38, 119. This feature was not peculiar to Hebrew. In the Mithraic liturgy, which is in Greek, "barbarian words, incomprehensible to the uninstructed, were mixed in the sacred text and increased the awe for this ancient formula as well as confidence in its potency" (Cumont, *Mystères de Mithra*[3], p. 154; see Dietrich, *Mithrasliturgie*, p. 36). Hebrew only possessed this power insofar as it was incomprehensible. Conversely, in Hebrew texts another language becomes the language of magic. The Aramaic verse inserted into Jer. 10:11 is doubtless borrowed from an exorcism formula. It will be noted that according to rabbinic rules the texts written on the *tephillin* and the *mezuzah* may only be written in the square Hebrew script. Now, the *tephillin* had a great reputation among non-Jews as magical charms (see p. 354).

26. Blau, *Das altjüdische Zauberwesen*, pp. 97 ff.

27. 2 Sam. 7:27, Isa. 21:10, etc.

28. In the West the same power was sometimes attributed to Greek words or letters. This explains the occasional formulae that are in Greek but written in the Latin alphabet (Frey, *CIJ*, no. 229: EN IRENE QUIMESIS SU, i.e., ἐν εἰρήνῃ ἡ κοίμησίς σου) and at least some of the Latin inscriptions in Greek characters. These are probably not merely epitaphs of Roman Jews (Frey, *CIJ*, nos. 215, 235, 248, 257) produced by mixed Greco-Roman and therefore bilingual communities. They are more likely to be exorcism formulae (e.g., Frey, *CIJ*, no. 674). In a similar way magical formulae in Latin were current in the East, sometimes transliterated into the local alphabet and sometimes not. The well-known *Sator Arepo* exists in both Greek and Coptic characters. "Amulettes," *DAC*, 1:2, 1812-15. For a Greek inscription in Hebrew letters, Frey, *CIJ*, no. 595. For Coptic in a Greek text, Preisendanz, 1:114.

29. When Moses whispered the divine name into Pharaoh's ear, he fell to the ground stupefied, according to Artapanos, quoted by Eusebius, *Praep. Ev.*, 9, 27, 24. It was enough simply to recall the name without even pronouncing it: ὁρκίζω σε τὸ ἅγιον ὄνομα ὃ οὐ λέγεται; tablet from Adremetum, Blau, *Das altjüdische Zauberwesen*, pp. 97 ff. and Deissmann, *Bibelstudien*, pp. 29, 41.

30. References from Bonsirven, *Jud. Palest.*, 1: 118-21.

31. On the pronunciation of the name, see Deissmann, op. cit., pp. 1-29.

32. See Preisendanz, passim, especially 1:38, 149; 112, 1200; 112, 1209; 114, 1220; 2:135, 9.

33. Preisendanz, 2:194; see pp. 180-91.

34. Origen, *Contra Celsum*, 1:22; see 4:33. The magicians use the formula "God of Abraham" without knowing who Abraham is, διὰ τὸ ὄνομα καὶ τὴν πρὸς τὸν δίκαιον τοῦ θεοῦ οἰκειότητα. The same remark applies to the names of Isaac, Jacob, and Israel. Justin, *Dial.*, 85, 2, 3, disputes the fact that the names of the patriarchs have any power at all, but he says

that demons exorcised in the name of the God of Abraham, Isaac, and Jacob, even by a Jew, would no doubt obey.

35. Some magical documents are attributed to biblical characters. The great Leyden papyrus (Preisendanz, 2:87 ff.) calls itself the eighth book of Moses. Another papyrus records a prayer of Jacob (ibid., 2:148 ff.). Yet another brings Adam into the picture (ibid., 1:38, 146).

36. Origen, *Contra Celsum*, 5, 6.

37. Ibid., 1. 26. See p. 340.

38. See Guignebert, *Monde juif*, pp. 133 ff.; Bonsirven, *Jud. Palest.*, 1:222 ff. It is to the angels that St. Paul attributes the promulgation of the law (Gal. 3:19).

39. Col. 2:18.

40. Aristides, *Apol.*, 14. 4; see Justin, *Apol.*, 1. 48.

41. Quoted by Clement of Alexandria, *Strom.*, 6, 5, 41.

42. The secret books of the Essenes, who were experts in magic, contain among others the names of the angels. Josephus, *B.J.*, 2. 8. Angelology is especially prominent in the apocryphal literature, particularly in the books of Enoch. See Bousset/Gressmann, *Religion*, pp. 320–31.

43. Preisendanz, passim, e.g., 1:128, 1815: Thuriel, Michael, Gabriel, Uriel, Misael, Israel, Istrael. There is a curious example of the taking over of Jewish angelology into ancient magic in the formula from a gemstone reproduced in the article "Anges," *DAC*, 1:2138.

44. On the relations between angelology and demonology, see Bousset/Gressmann, *Die Religion des Judentums*, pp. 331 ff. See A. Lods, "La chute des anges," *RHPR*, 1927, pp. 295–315.

45. Michael is especially the repository of the divine name: Enoch 69:14–23.

46. On this point see Lucken, *Michael*.

47. Origen, *Contra Celsum*, 5. 6.

48. Similarly the name "watchers," which the Jewish tradition bestows on the angels (especially the fallen ones) betrays this connection clearly. Dan. 4, Enoch 10:9, 15; 12:4; 13:10, etc. Jub. 4:22, 7:21, 8:3, 10:5.

49. See *b. Erub.*, 43a, *b. Pes.*, 110a, *b. Gittin*, 66a, *b. Yebam.*, 122a.

50. See p. 22.

51. On the relations between astrology and ancient magic, see Cumont, *Religions orientales*[4], pp. 168–79. Jerome gives a theological explanation to Jewish angelology. He sees it as a sign of divine disfavor, consequent upon the murder of Christ. When God withdrew from Israel, he gave them over, as he did after the sin of the golden calf, "to the worship of the host of heaven" (Acts 7:42), which does not mean to the worship of celestial spirits, but to that of the fallen angels. Even when it is ostensibly addressed to God, Jewish worship is exclusively directed toward *angelis refugis et spiritibus immundis. . . . Militia autem caeli non tantum sol appellatur et luna et astra rutilantia, sed omnis angelica multitudo eorumque exercitus, qui Hebraice appellantur* Sabaoth, *id est virtutum sive exercituum* (*Ep.* 121 *ad Algasiam*, 10). This clearly underlines the connexions between angelolatry and astrology, and between angelology and demonology.

52. In *Revue des Etudes Grecques*, 1903, p. 59, following Renan, *Marc Aurèle*, p. 143.

53. See Guignebert, *Monde juif*, pp. 310, 315 ff.

54. *RHR*, 1923, pp. 65–102.

55. Some documents go back to the first centuries A.D., but the majority are later than Constantine, fourth and fifth centuries principally.

56. Deissmann, *Bibelstudien*, pp. 21 ff. English translation, *Bible Studies*[2], 1903, pp. 271 ff.

57. Blau, *Das altjüdische Zauberwesen*, pp. 97 ff.

58. Morning Prayer, in the introduction to the *shema*, Elbogen, *Jüd. Gottesdienst*, p. 114.

59. Gen. 1:17.

60. *Shemoneh 'Esre*, 1. Text from Lagrange, *Judaïsme*, p. 466.

61, Borrowings noted by Blau, p. 130.

62. Line 23.

63. *Abraxas*, pp. 138-41. The text, which appears in the great magical papyrus from Paris, has been republished by Preisendanz, *Papyri Graecae Magicae*, 1:170-72.

64. Lines 36-38.

65. Lines 31 ff.

66. Lines 28 ff.

67. Lines 53 ff.

68. Line 62.

69. Line 51.

70. Line 44.

71. *Praep. Ev.*, 9, 17, 18.

72. See Dieterich, *Abraxas*, p. 143.

73. For other references to Jesus in syncretistic magical texts, see Preisendanz, 1:50, 420; 114, 1233. It is useless to seek a rational explanation for the formula. For the Hebrew Christians, i.e., the anti-Trinitarian Ebionites, Jesus was not God. This is a very clear case of syncretism, in which the differences between religious groups and divinities disappear. In the same manner the angels were sometimes in Judaism equated with Yahweh, being treated as manifestations of him. See Perdrizet, *REG*, 1928, p. 76. "Hebrew" here means either "translated from Hebrew" or, perhaps more likely, "of Jewish origin." In the diaspora the term does not necessarily have a linguistic reference, (see above, p. 477, n. 46).

74. Line 67.

75. Dieterich, *Abraxas*, pp. 143 ff.

76. There are other examples of Jewish-pagan materials: a magic stud ("Amulettes," *DAC*, 1:1792) with the inscriptions *Ter dico, ter incanto, in signo Dei et signo Salomonis et signo de nostra Artemix*. Also numerous gems: see, e.g., Haas, *Bilderatlas, die Religion in der Umwelt des Christentums* (Leipzig, 1926), no. 73. There is also a gem from Berlin, on one face of which is pictured the dog-headed Anubis, and on the other an archangel with the inscription ΓΑΒΡΙΗΛΣΑΒΑΩ.

77. *Bull. de Corresp. hell.*, 1901, pp. 430-56.

78. Homolle's suggestion of connections with Christian liturgical texts is very convincing.

79. B, Lines 15-18.

80. A, Lines 2-12.

81. B, Lines 1-4.

82. A, Lines 30 ff., B, Lines 7-9.

83. It is connected with Rev. 21:23: "And the city has no need of sun or moon to shine upon it, for the glory of God is its light, and its lamp is the Lamb." But there is also a reminiscence of the blessings in the Jewish order of morning prayer: "O cause a new light to shine upon Zion." What we are faced with is perhaps a Jewish-Christian adaptation of a Synagogue ritual. See Dölger, *Sol Salutis*[2], p. 121.

84. It is equally significant that no saint's name is mentioned.

85. See Peterson, ΕΙΣ ΘΕΟΣ, especially pp. 82-109.

86. *Negotium perambulans in tenebris*, p. 32. The same inscription appears on an amulet published by Perdrizet, *REG*, 1903, p. 49. See Peterson, op. cit., p. 103.

87. On Solomon's role in magic, see Perdrizet, *Negotium* and "Sphragis Solomonos," *REG*, pp. 42-61. Origen, *Comm. in Matth.*, 100 (*PG*, 13.1757) notes the use some Christians made of the name and the writings of Solomon for magical purposes.

88. For a sizable bibliography and all essential references, see Dornseif, "Das Rotas Opera Quadrat," *ZNTW*, 1938, pp. 222 ff. The oldest form is *Rotas opera tenet arepo sator*.

89. See *CRAI*, 1937, pp. 84 ff. See *Recherches de Sc. Relig.*, 1935, pp. 196 ff., and 1937,

pp. 326 ff. For a similar view, see A. Omodeo, "La croce d'Ercolano e il culto preconstantiniano della croce," *La Critica*, 1940, p. 4, n. 3.

90. Quoted by Jerphanion, *Recherches*, 1937, p. 331. Ezekiel's influence is equally admitted by Dornseif, who brings some new arguments to bear on the problem.

Several scholars have criticized me for assigning a Jewish origin for the magic square. J. Carcopino published an article in *Museum Helveticum*, 1948, pp. 16-59, too late for me to take proper account of it in my first edition. See by the same author, "Le christianisme secret du 'carré magique,'" *Etudes d'histoire chrétienne*, 2nd edn. (Paris, 1963), pp. 11-102. In the notes to this latter article will be found a complete bibliography (and it is quite an abundant one) on the question since 1935. I would be much less dogmatic on this matter than I was fifteen years ago. The arguments advanced by Carcopino and certain others in favor of a Christian origin are impressive. If, as everything suggests, the mysterious *arepo* is a Celtic term meaning "a plough," we should be justified in looking for the origin of the square in Gaul. Carcopino connects it with the milieu of St. Irenaeus, which, as Daniélou has shown (*Les Symboles chrétiens primitifs* [*Paris, 1961*], pp. 95-107), saw the plough as a symbol of the cross. The presumption in favor of a Christian origin is today stronger, though it is still not possible to speak with absolute certainty. The Jewish hypothesis has been revived, though with arguments more ingenious than convincing, by D. Daube, *The New Testament and rabbinic Judaism*, pp. 403-5. According to Daube, *arepo* can be broken down into *arep-o*, which represents a transliteration into Hebrew or Aramaic of *alpha-omega*. *Arep* takes the place of *aleph* because an *R* was needed here and because in the Semitic languages the two consonants are very close.

91. Ezek. 1:15 ff., 9:4 ff.

92. They are those of the divine chariot, the *merkabhah*, which plays a sizable role in Jewish esoteric speculations. Dornseif, "Das Rotas Opera Quadrat", p. 228. Rabbinic references, Strack and Billerbeck, *Kommentar*, 1:974-79.

93. To this should be added the word *opera* itself, if we start from the Vulgate. Ezek. 1:15: *Aspectus rotarum et* opus *earum . . . et aspectus earum et* opera *quasi sit rota in medio rotae*. The rebus is distinctly older than the Vulgate, but LXX reads ἔργον in the same passage. Jerphanion, *Recherches*, p. 332; Dornseif, p. 230.

94. It will be observed that on the *tephillin* that the Jews wore on their foreheads appeared the letter *shin*, the initial letter of Shaddai (the Almighty) and of *shem* (the Name). The object of this was to guard against the evil powers.

95. See Klausner, *Jésus de Nazareth*, p. 544. The reference to God as Father is particularly common with a plural possessive pronoun, "our." Rabbinic references in Strack and Billerbeck, *Kommentar*, 1:392-94, 410. See also Guignebert, "Le Pater," *Mélanges Glotz* (Paris, 1932), 1:417-30.

96. Rev. 1:8, 22:13.

97. Strack and Billerbeck, *Kommentar*, 3:789. The origin of this idea is in Isa. 44:6, "I am the first and the last." *Aleph* and *tav* together make up the particle *et*, which in Hebrew is the sign of the direct object. It appears in the first verse of Genesis (*bereshith bara elohim et hashshamayim*) and Jewish speculation, isolating it from its context, sometimes translated the verse as follows: "In the beginning God created *et*." Looked at in this way, the word became a kind of epitome, in which the entire creation was condensed. Dornseif, p. 223.

98. See R. P. Allo, *L'Apocalypse* (*Etudes Bibliques*), (Paris, 1921), p. 8; Reitzenstein, *Poimandres*, p. 286.

99. Dornseif connects it, in very debatable fashion, with *arripere*, "that which tears up." Jerphanion (*Recherches*, 1937, p. 233) sees it as a "stopgap," a proper name invented for the purposes of making up the square. It might also be thought of as a magical term of the *abraxas* variety.

100. Ezek. 10:2, see 10:6.

101. One might also, by leaving *arepo* out of account and taking *opera* as an ablative with adverbial sense, understand *sator* as referring to God and translate: "The sower directs his wheels with care," meaning perhaps, "The creator watches over the universe." This would be an assertion about the divine providence, which orders the world. *Sator* is used in the sense of "creator" in a panegyric of Constantine from the year 313: *Summe rerum sator*, quoted by Piganiol, *L'empereur Constantin* (Paris, 1932), p. 69. For connections with the phrase *Logos spermaticos*, which was so widespread in Hellenistic speculation, see Jeanmaire, "Pneuma et Sperma," *Annales d'Hist. du Christ.* (Congrès Loisy) (Paris, 1928), 2:138 ff.

102. For this opinion, see Jerphanion, *Recherches*, 1937, p. 334, who compares the movement of the wheels as Ezekiel describes it with "that of a reversible formula which, by going straight forward and never turning back on itself, ends at the point where it began."

103. *Comm. in Matth.*, 33. 6 (*PL*, 26. 175): *Hoc apud nos superstitiosae mulierculae in parvulis evangeliis et in crucis ligno et istius modi rebus (quae habent quidem zelum Dei, sed non juxta scientiam) usque hodie factitant.*

104. *Ep.*, 75. 3 (*PL*, 22. 687): *Ad imperitorum et muliercularum animos concitandos, quasi de hebraicis fontibus hausta barbaro simplices quosque terrent sono.*

105. Clement of Alexandria, *Strom.*, 5. 6 (*PG*, 9. 60).

106. References in Martigny, *Dictionnaire des antiquités chrétiennes* (Paris, 1865), p. 113.

107. E.g., Toutain, "Lucerna," *Dict. des Antiquités*, 3:1329. Other references in "Chandelier," *DAC*, 3:216 ff., where a summary of the discussion is provided.

108. Kaufmann, "Etudes d'archéologie juive," *REJ*, 1886, pp. 52–55.

109. As in certain catacombs at Syracuse: Orsi, *RQ*, 1900, pp. 187 ff. Other examples in *DAC*, 3:218. On the apotropaic nature of the candlestick see Peterson, ΕΙΣ ΘΕΟΣ, pp. 279–81.

110. Delattre, *Lampes chrétiennes de Carthage* (Lyon, 1880), p. 38, and *Revue de l'art chrétien*, 1892 p. 136, n. 694. See Le Blant, *Controverse des chrétiens et des juifs*, p. 249. Monceaux, "Colonies juives'," *REJ*, 1902, pp. 17 ff.; lamp reproduced in *DAC*, 1:737.

111. This interpretation is strengthened by the fact that in ancient Christian art Christ is commonly represented as treading under foot and transfixing with his cross all sorts of noxious animals, serpents, basilisks, and lions. Such pictures are especially common on lamps, and the animals are the very ones the magic studs are intended to combat. See, for example, *DAC*, 1:1138; 2:511–14; 3:2101; 8:1169–71 and pl. 1173–74. This is an illustration of Ps. 91:13: "You will tread on the lion and the adder." It militates against Reinach's explanation (*RA*, 1889, 1:412 ff.), which sees the picture of Christ standing above the candlestick as an image of "the new law founded upon the old."

112. Oort, *Ursprung der Blutbeschuldigung*.

113. On modern survivals of this practice, "Jüde," *Handwörterbuch des deutschen Aberglaubens*, 4:81.

114. See p. 221.

115. The connection with astrology is clear as far as observance of the festivals is concerned. Their dates were determined astronomically. See Guignebert, *Monde juif*, p. 316.

116. *Hom.*, 1. 6 (*PG*, 48. 852).

117. *Hom.*, 1. 3 (*PG*, 48. 848): φοβερωτέρους τοὺς ἐκεῖ γινομένους ὅρκους εἶναι.

118. They laid claim to this reputation themselves, on occasion. Josephus (*Ant. Jud.*, 18, 2, 5) tells of a healing he witnessed in the presence of Vespasian, when a Jew cured a possessed man by means of Solomonic magic. Magical powers were attributed to some of the rabbis. Thus, for example, R. Eliezer b. Hyrcanus (*b. Sanh.*, 68a) was able to make plants grow, and R. Jushua b. Hananya could change plants into animals (*j. Sanh.*, 7). R. Hanina and R. Hoshaya, studying texts relating to the creation on a Sabbath eve, were able to create a calf, alive, which they afterwards reared (*b. Sanh.*, 65b). Rabba even managed to create a man (ibid.). This is the primary origin of mediaeval traditions about the Golem.

119. See the texts cited on pp. 339-40.

120. For a Jewish sorcerer in Africa, see Augustine, *Civ. Dei*, 22, 8, 21 (*PL*, 41. 769). Another example is in Sozomen's *History*, 5:15: Ἰουδαῖοι, ἐπῳδαῖς καὶ περιεργίαις τισι χρησάμενοι, οὐδὲν ἤνυον. Against this powerless magic the author sets Christian exorcism in the name of Christ. See, similarly, Chrysostom, *Homily against the Jews*, 1. 2 (*PG*, 48. 935): εἰ καὶ θεραπεύουσιν ἀληθῶς ... τὰς ἐπῳδάς, τὰ περιάμματα, τὰς φαρμακείας ... φαρμακοὺς καὶ γοήτας.

121. *De magis, incantoribus et divinis, et de fine et consummatione*. The text has come down to us under the name of St. Ephraem. Lamy edition, Malines, 1886, pp. 393-426. On the author, Baumstark, *Geschichte der syrischen Literatur*, pp. 63 ff.

122. Ruphael is doubtless identical with Raphael. Raphuphael, even if he is not a mere double of Raphael, is much less frequently met with.

123. These are the Egyptian magicians who according to tradition opposed Moses (Reinach, *Textes*, pp. 174, 282, 338) but who here are lumped with the Jews under the same condemnation.

124. See pp. 90, 325.

125. Reinach, *Textes*, p. 401.

126. *Hom.*, 1, 3 (*PG*, 48. 847).

127. *Hom.*, 2. 3 (*PG*, 48. 861), 6. 2 (907).

128. *Hom.*, 1. 3 (*PG*, 48. 847): τῶν δαιμόνων καταγώγιον. 2. 1 (857), 4. 1 (873).

129. *Hom.*, 8. 6 (*PG*, 48. 935 ff.).

130. Ibid., (936) and *Hom.*, 8. 7 (938).

131. See especially *C. Th.*, 16, 10, 4 ff., 9 ff.; 9, 16, 3-5, 7-9.

132. F. Martroye, "Les mesures de Constantin contre la superstition," *Bull. de la Soc. Nat. des Antiq.*, 1915, pp. 280-92, and "La répression de la magie et le culte des Gentils au IVᵉ siècle," *Revue Historique du Droit français et étranger*, 1930, pp. 673 ff. But a measure such as that of Constantius (*Cesset superstitio, sacrificiorum aboleatur insania*), *C. Th.*, 16, 10, 2, in condemning paganism's fundamental practices equated the whole pagan system with *superstitio*.

133. *Paganae superstitionis* (*C. Th.*, 16, 10, 20), *idolorum superstitionem* (16, 7, 6).

134. As early as Cicero (see Labriolle, *Réaction païenne*, p. 44) a contrast could be drawn between *religio* and *superstitio*, *superstitio* being a malformation of *religio*. *Non philosophi solum, verum majores nostri superstitionem a religione separaverunt. ... Falsas opiniones erroresque turbulentos et superstitiones paene aniles* (*De Nat. Deor.*, 2, 28, 70 ff.). The word *superstitio* could alternatively be employed to designate beliefs and practices foreign to the national religion. Thus Virgil *Aen.*, 8. 187-89. On the relations between the two terms, W. Otto, "Religio und Superstitio," *ARW*, 1909, pp. 533-54.

135. *Haereticae superstitionis turba*: *C. Th.*, 16, 5, 10; see 16, 5, 34; 16, 5, 39.

136. On the designation of the Jewish cult in official terminology, see Juster, *Les Juifs*, 1:252.

137. Ibid., pp. 159-67.

138. *C. Th.*, 9, 16, 6; 16, 10, 4 ff. The law makes a distinction between good magic and malign.

139. Maurice, "La terreur de la magie au IVᵉ siècle," *CRAI*, 1924, 182 ff. On the amnesties, *C. Th.*, 9, 38, 3 ff.

140. *Nov. Theod.*, 3. 7.

141. *Canons* 29, 35, 37, Mansi, II, 370.

142. *Canon 36*: ὅτι οὐ δεῖ ἱερατικοὺς ἢ κληρικοὺς ... ποιεῖν τὰ λεγόμενα φυλακτήρια ἅτινα ἐστι δεσμωτήρια τῶν ψυχῶν αὐτων.

143. E.g., Plutarch, *Mor.*, 378b; Dioscorides, 5. 159. A. Festugière, in his review above (p. 444, n. 152), regards it as "erroneous to connect every mention of magical phylacteries with the

specifically Jewish sort," because the word *phylacteries* means no more than "amulets." I agree with him in this, but I think, nevertheless, that for Christians who, particularly in the East, lived side by side with Jews and knew their ways, and who, moreover, read their gospels in Greek and found there the word *phylakterion* used precisely of the Jewish ritual phylacteries (Matth. 23:5), the word must always have recalled the Jewish phylacteries primarily. It might also be asked why the word for *tephillin* (Biblical Hebrew *totaphoth*) should have been translated into Greek by a term that lent itself to ambiguity and never appears in the LXX (in which *totaphoth* is rendered by *asaleuton*: Exod. 13:16, Deut. 6:8, 11:18). Two possible explanations come to mind. Either the objects concerned did in fact fulfil the role of talismans, and the name *phylacteries* was given to them by superstitious Jews or by pagans, or else the Septuagint, in which the word *phylacteries* does not appear, nevertheless provides it indirectly. The first allusion to phylacteries in the Bible is Exod. 13:9, and in the LXX text of the verse immediately following there appears the word *phylassein*. It is not impossible that this suggested a name from the same root for those objects which recalled and symbolized the observance of divine law. As for the word *desmoteria*, applied to the phylacteries (see above n. 142), Festugière rightly observes that it too could be used to designate any kind of amulet. Nevertheless, here again the word is peculiarly appropriate to the *tephillin*, which were attached to the arms and forehead and which therefore, from the Christian angle, could be viewed as bonds imprisoning the soul. But it is quite certain that the magic of the period was syncretistic and that the element of Jewish ritual it contained was no more than one component of it.

144. Matt. 23:5. On Jewish phylacteries, see G. Langer, *Die jüdischen Gebetsriemen* (Vienna, 1931).

145. *b. Sukkah*, 41b. The rabbis were preoccupied with the distinction between true and false *tephillin*. False *tephillin* were amulets that the devotees of magic fabricated in imitation of the Jewish ritual objects (*b. Erub.*, 96b). I am inclined to identify as phylacteries the κατάδεσμοι of whose use Justin accuses the Jewish magicians (*Dial.*, 85. 1).

146. See pp. 90, 354. Similarly, Chrysostom, *in Ep. ad Col. Hom.*, 8. 5 (*PG*, 62. 385).

147. *Auguriis vel incantationibus servientem a conventu separandum, similiter et superstitionibus judaicis vel feriis inhaerentum* (*PL*, 56. 887).

148. *Canon 50: Si vero quis clericus vel fidelis cum Judaeis cibum sumpserit, placuit eum a communione abstinere, ut debeat emendari. Canon 49: Admonere placuit possessores ut non patiantur fructus suos, quos a Deo percipiunt, a Judaeis benedici; ne nostram irritam et infirmam faciant benedictionem. Si quis post interdictum facere usurpaverit, penitus ab ecclesia abjiciatur* (Mansi, 2:14).

149. Juster, *Les Juifs*, 1:293.

150. *C. Th.*, 9, 16, 3.

151. *Homily against the Jews*, 1. 7 (*PG*, 48. 853 ff.).

152. Ibid., 1. 7 (*PG*, 48. 855); see 8. 5 (48. 935).

153. *Hom.*, 8. 7 (*PG*, 48. 939) ἀλλὰ χαλεπὸς ὁ πυρετός; Ἀλλα' ἀντίστησον τῷ πυρετῷ τὸ τῆς γεέννης πῦρ·

154. See "Exorcisme," *DAC*, 5:964 ff., which cites some interesting texts. F. Dölger, *Der Exorcismus im altchristlichen Taufritual* (1909), and *Die Sonne der Gerechtigkeit* (1918).

155. Socrates, *HE*, 7. 4 (*PG*, 67. 745). See *Acta Silvestri*, passage quoted above, p. 458, n. 21.

156. See Harnack, "Medizinisches aus der ältesten Kirchengeschichte," *TU*, 8. 4. (1892), pp. 125–47, and *Mission*, I⁴, 129–70. See Ignatius of Antioch, *Eph.* 7. 1: εἷς ἰατρός.... Ἰησοῦς Χριστός.

157. Carcopino, "L'invocation de Timgad au Christ médecin," *Rendic. della Pont. Accad. Rom. di Arch.*, 1927, pp. 79–87. Gsell, *Revue africaine*, 1928, p. 20.

158. Christian authors sometimes interpret Jesus' name by connecting it with ἰάσασθαι,

and take it to mean "physician." Thus Cyril of Jerusalem, *Catech.*, 10:13 (*PG*, 33. 677): Ἰησοῦς τοίνυν ἐστὶ κατὰ μὲν Ἑβραίους σωτήρ, κατὰ δὲ τὴν Ἑλλάδα γλῶσσαν ὁ ἰώμενος, ἐπειδὴ ἰατρός ἐστι ψυχῶν καὶ σωμάτων, καὶ θεραπευτὴς πνευμάτων. See the baptismal exorcism formula cited by Homolle, *BCH*, 1901, p. 439, n. 1: ὁ ἰώμενος πᾶσαν νόσον καὶ πᾶσαν μαλακίαν.

159. *Comm. in Matth.*, 23. 110 (*PG*, 13. 1757). It is curious to note that just as the Jews had a reputation as healers in the eyes of Christians, so had the Christians in the eyes of Moslems. The Lord's Prayer, transposed into Arabic, was used as a prophylactic prayer among Muhammad's first disciples. Massignon, " Le 'Hadith al ruqya' musulman, première version arabe du 'Pater,'" *RHR*, 1941, pp. 57-62.

160. See "Signe de la croix," *DAC*, 3:3139 ff.

161. *In Ep. ad Col. Hom.*, 8. 5 (*PG*, 62. 358): πιστὴ εἶ; σφραγῖσον. To make such a sign on entering a Synagogue was to baffle the demoniacal powers who lived there. *Homily against the Jews*, 8:8 (*PG*, 48:940).

162. See "Amulettes," *DAC*, 1:1784 ff., and more recently, "Amulett," *Reallexikon für Antike und Christentum*, pp. 407 ff., with numerous references.

163. See p. 354. Chrysostom also mentions this usage, which he disapproves of, and compares with the Pharisaic use of *tephillin*: ἃ φυλακτήρια ἐκάλουν ὡς πολλαὶ νῦν τῶν γυναικῶν εὐαγγέλια τῶν τραχήλων ἐξαρτῶσαι ἔχουσι (*in Matth. Hom.*, 72. 2 (*PG*, 58. 669). Other references in "Amulett," *Reallexikon*, p. 410.

164. See J. Gagé, "Eglise et reliquaire d'Afrique," *Mélanges de l'Ecole française de Rome*, 1927, pp. 108 ff.

165. See Harnack, "Märtyrer und Heilungsakten," *Sitzungsber. der Preuss. Ak.*, 1910, pp. 106 ff.

166. *Civ. Dei*, 22, 8, 20 (*PL*, 41:768 ff.).

167. *Epistola Severi* (*PL*, 41:821 ff.).

168. See *Scriptura de translatione sancti Stephani* (*PL*, 41:822), which recounts the miraculous conversion of a Jew at the time of the *inventio* of the saint's relics.

169. *Civ. Dei*, 22, 8, 21 (*PL*, 41. 768).

170. Harnack, p. 110.

171. Lucius, *Origines* (French translation, p. 216).

172. Simon, *Polémique anti-juive de S. Jean-Chrysostome*, pp. 413 ff.

173. John Chrysostom, *Hom. in Macc.*, 3 (*PG*, 35. 627).

174. *Serm.*, 300. 5 (*PL*, 38. 1377).

175. *Homily against the Jews*, 8. 6 (*PG*, 48. 938).

176. Ibid., 8. 6 (*PG*, 48. 937): μὴ πρὸς τοὺς ἐχθροὺς αὐτοῦ καταφύγῃς τοὺς Ἰουδαίους ... ἀλλὰ πρὸς τοὺς φίλους αὐτοῦ, τοὺς μάρτυρας, τοὺς ἁγίους ... πολλὴν ἔχοντας πρὸς αὐτὸν παρρησίαν.

177. *In Ep. II ad Cor. Hom.*, 26. 5 (*PG*, 61. 582 ff.) see *PG*, 50. 640 and 664.

178. Lucius, *Origines*, pp. 166-67.

179. See Epiphanius, *Haer.*, 79. 5 (*PG*, 42. 748); Augustine, *Civ. Dei*, 10. 19 (*PL*, 41. 298); Turmel, "Histoire de l'angélologie," *Rev. Hist. et Litt. Relig.*, 1898, pp. 537 ff.

180. See Lukyn Williams, "The Cult of the Angels at Colossae," *JTS*, 1909, pp. 412-38.

181. Lucius, *Origines*, p. 358.

182. Ibid., p. 359.

183. Christian hagiolatry poses another problem, of which the absorption of the cult of St. Michael into orthodox worship is only one example. The problem is that of the Jewish saints of the old covenant, who were felt to merit worship by Christian believers. This is another aspect of Jewish-Christian relations. I shall not broach the subject further here. I have touched on it in my study "Alexandre le Grand, Juif et chrétien," *RHPR*, 1941, pp. 185 ff., in connection with the cult in Alexandria centered on the prophet Jeremiah.

Conclusion

1. Hefele and Leclerq, *Histoire des Conciles*, 3:564.

2. *Ob hier nur die äussere Zertrümmerung und innere Versteifung des Judentums in Betracht kommt—warum aber versteifen sie sich in ihrem Gesetz?—oder ob auch andere Gründe, z. B. die wachsende Rivalität des Christentums, darüber wage ich kein Urteil* (Mission, I⁴:18, n. 1).

3. See p. 59.

4. See p. 489, n. 145.

5. Bonsirven, *Jud. Palest.*, 1:214.

6. *Mission*, I⁴:20, quoted by Bertholet, *Das religionsgeschichtliche Problem des Spätjudentums*.

7. References to this tradition in Schoeps, *Agadisches zur Auserwählung Israëls*, p. 46, n. 1.

8. Guignebert, *Monde juif*, p. 206.

9. *M. Bikkurim*, I, 4.

10. *Hist.*, 5. 5.

11. *Apol.*, 18. 4.

12. These sentiments are expressed by Chrysostom precisely in the middle of a diatribe against the Jews (*Hom.*, 4. 3, *PG*, 48. 875). It is as irregular for a Christian to Judaize as it would be for a Roman citizen to live like a barbarian or to be a supporter of the Persians. "Whoever lives within the Empire lives under *our* laws." The same Christian speaker condemns the revolt of A.D. 66 as a crime against Roman order (see p. 470, n. 31).

13. Tertullian, *Adv. Jud.*, 3 (*PL*, 2. 643).

14. Chrysostom, *Hom.*, 1. 2 (*PG*, 48. 845).

15. Grabar, "Thème religieux des fresques de Doura," *RHR* 124:25.

16. Ibid., p. 27.

17. Ibid., p. 26, n. 1.

18. Justin Martyr, *Dial.*, 123. 5.

Translations from Greek, Latin and German

p. 17
There are three kinds of people in this world: the worshipers of those called by you "gods", the Jews, and the Christians.

p. 33
and in every region of the earth the incense of prayer and supplication is sent up to Thee.

p. 38
Not a sacrifice; God wants mercy instead of sacrifice.

p. 40
They worship nothing except the clouds and the divinity of the sky.

The Jews acknowledge only one divinity, and with the mind alone. They regard as profane those who portray the gods in human likeness and in perishable materials. They regard the Highest as eternal, inimitable and immortal. Therefore they set up no images in their cities or even in their temples.

p. 44
because of unlawful acts

p. 54
begotten, not created

p. 55
Abraham, defender of your people, blessed forever.

p. 56
Israel, Thy church on earth, taken from the gentiles

p. 57 (top)
[see above, p. 33.]

p. 57 (bottom)
the knowledge of the unbegotten God

p. 65
All those to whom righteous witness has been borne, going back from Abraham himself to the first man, (we may call) Christians in fact, if not in name.

ibid.
Indeed, these two religions (he argued), though opposed to each other, had come from the same origin; the Christians had arisen from the Jews; if the root were destroyed, the shoot would soon perish.

p. 71
The Jew carries the book from which the Christian takes his faith. They have become our librarians, like slaves who carry books behind their masters; the slaves gain no profit by their carrying, but their masters profit by their reading.

ibid.
The New Testament lies hidden in the Old, the Old Testament becomes plain in the New.

p. 76
The Lord gives the law.

p. 77
Isaiah announces that a new law too will proceed out of this "house of the God of Jacob."

ibid.
For the old law used to avenge itself by the vengeance of the sword, and to destroy "eye for eye" and inflict retaliatory revenge for injury; but the way of the new law is to point to mercy, and to change the old fierceness of swords and spears into peacefulness.

p. 78
Accordingly, we, who were not the people of God previously, have been made His people, by accepting the new law above mentioned, and the new circumcision before foretold.

ibid.
of course, the people of the Jews, that is, of Israel, and the people of the gentiles, that is, ours.

ibid.
anterior in time, and "greater" through the grace of primary favor in the Law

ibid.
Beyond doubt, through the edict of the divine utterance, the older and greater people—that is, the Jewish—must necessarily serve the lesser; and the lesser people—that is, the Christian—overcome the greater.

p. 82
for a sign of that time, not for a prerogative title to salvation.

p. 85
The Jews of old, through their hope of a future Christ Savior, were Christians. Therefore they should now necessarily be regarded as apostates, since as long as they do not accept Christ they are guilty of violating the law. . . . Although the Jews have sinned gravely by rejecting the house of God and are worthy of death, nevertheless . . . if they return to the faith, they will be received with joy.

p. 89
But he does not know that the Jews have, besides the genuine prophetical Scriptures, their own traditions, which they do not have in writing, but retain in memory and have handed down, one to another, by word of mouth. These they call *deuterosis*.

ibid.
The Pharisees upheld the justice of traditions and comments, which they call *deuterosis*.

ibid.
The *deuterosis*, as it is called among you, we forbid entirely.

p. 91
Despising the law of God, and following the traditions of men, which they call *deuteroseis*.

p. 93
They are necessary to the believing Gentiles.

ibid.
in order that they may receive judgment for themselves and provide testimony for us.

ibid.
Why do you retain the Old Testament, the commandments of which you do not keep? . . . What good is your reading of the Law and the Prophets, if you are not willing to keep their commandments?

ibid.
They will not become Christians, but they will make us Jews. . . . The ceremonies of the Jews are pernicious and deadly; and whoever observes them, whether Jew or Gentile, has fallen into the pit of the Devil. For Christ is the end of the Law, for the justification of every believer, that is, both Jew and gentile.

p. 94
I entirely confirm this pronouncement of yours.

p. 96
Jews and those of us who are Judaizers.

p. 98
Judaism is at war with Hellenism, and both with Christianity.

p. 104
It is permitted by the decree of the divine Pius to Jews only to circumcise their sons; anyone not of that religion who does so is liable to the penalty for castration.

ibid.
to mutilate the genitals

ibid.
Jews are born, not made.

ibid.
Roman citizens who allow themselves or their slaves to be circumcised by the Jewish rite are deprived of their goods and banished to an island for life; the doctors (who perform the operation) suffer capital punishment.

p. 106
He forbade people to become Jews on pain of a severe penalty.

ibid.
He forbade the same thing in relation to Christians.

p. 107
under the protection of a most distinguished and undoubtedly legal religion

p. 109
How far the "third kind"? (i.e., "Are there no limits . . . ?")

p. 110
"On the Antiquity of the Jews"

ibid.
These rites, however they may have originated, are defended by their antiquity.

p. 111
propped up by the scepter and the legions.

p. 113
This too is equally Hellenic.

p. 117
depraved superstition

ibid.
crimes

ibid.
the seedbed of our disgrace

p. 119
The Jewish synagogues were the origins of the persecutions.

p. 119f.
It has as many foes as there are strangers to it; the Jews, as was to be expected, *from a spirit of rivalry*; the soldiers, out of a desire to extort money; our very domestics, by their nature.

p. 126
It is sufficiently established that the Jewish sect is prohibited by no law.

p. 131
let the Jewish nation remain

ibid.
Behold, the Jew is the slave of the Christian.

p. 135
Not denying the prophecy of Moses, but proving from that very source the truth of the statements regarding Jesus.

p. 143
They are opposed by the Jews as aliens

p. 146
from the Scriptures and from the facts themselves

p. 148
Indeed, this apostolic and catholic doctrine shows sufficiently plainly to us that according to the origin of the flesh, the Jews belong to Sarah and the Ishmaelites to Hagar; but according to the mystery of the spirit, the Christians belong to Sarah and the Jews to Hagar.

p. 149
You see the law which Moses dashed down in his anger,
And the same God gave him a second Law.
He placed his hope in it, but you proudly mock it,
And therefore you will not be worthy of the kingdom of heaven.

p. 156
Therefore there was a legal argument.

p. 162
In the Son, God made the heaven and the earth.

p. 164
the natural (precepts) of the law, by which man is justified, and which those who were justified by faith and pleased God also observed before the giving of the Law

ibid.
particular laws, precepts of slavery

p. 165
for a sign, not for salvation . . . a sign whereby Israel might be distinguished in later time, recently past, when because of their deserts they were prohibited from entering the Holy City.

p. 177
with loose lips and twisted tongue, and with spittle spluttering from their shaven, grinning jaws.

ibid.
to give some reply to the calumnies of the Jews, one by one.

p. 179
They curse and anathematize them in the synagogues, saying three times a day, "May God curse the Nazarenes."

p. 185
I remember that I paid a certain man of Lydda no small sum.

ibid.
gourd-sellers

p. 188
The earlier and greater people, that is the Jewish, must necessarily serve the lesser, and the lesser people, that is the Christian, overcome the greater.

ibid.
who is Edom

ibid.
According to the origin of the flesh, the nation of the Idumaeans belongs to Esau, who is also called Edom, and the nation of the Jews belongs to Jacob, who is also called Israel. But according to the mystery of the spirit, the Jews belong to Esau and the Christians belong to Israel. So indeed what Scripture says is fulfilled: "the greater will serve the lesser", that is, the Jewish people, which was born first, will serve the Christian people, which was born afterwards.

p. 194
If anyone does not accept that the text, ""The Lord rained fire from the Lord", refers to the
Father and the Son, but says that the Lord Himself rained from Himself—he is anathema. For
the Lord the Son rained from the Lord the Father.

p. 202
the common ruin and disease of the entire world.

p. 209
a war-making race

p. 210
Once these things were with us, too, the theme of ridicule.

ibid.
We are of your stock.

p. 211
And as Christianity is nearly allied to Judaism, from this, I suppose, it was taken for granted that
we too are devoted to the worship of the same image.

p. 212
hated by the gods

ibid.
a nation abandonded to lust

p. 213
a love of propagating

p. 216
He knew that the Jewish people were stiff-necked, fickle, low, inclined to treachery, a people who
heard with the ear and did not hear, saw with the eyes and did not see, superficial with the
unreliability of an infant and unmindful of commandments.

ibid.
the grunting of a pig and the braying of an ass

p. 229
The monks commit many crimes.

ibid.
witnesses of their own iniquity and of our truth

p. 231
We are connected with the same root; we are the branches, and they are the root. We should not
curse our roots, but pray for our roots.

ibid.
Let us not boast proudly against the broken branches. Let us rather reflect by whose grace, and
by what great mercy, and to what root we are connected.

ibid.
Jews possess chastity.

p. 237
As long as they wish to be Jews and Christians, they are neither Jews nor Christians.

p. 246
What shall I say about the Ebionites? These are commonly called Nazarenes.

p. 248
They accuse the Apostle Paul of being an apostate from the Law.

p. 249
Those who are called Ebionites agree that the world was made by God; but their opinions with
respect to the Lord are similar to those of Cerinthus and Carpocrates.

p. 252
He asserted that he (Jesus) had the grace of God in the same way as all the prophets.

ibid.
not wishing to understand that the Holy Spirit came upon Mary, and the power of the Most High overshadowed her.

ibid.
Behold, a young woman will conceive and bear a son.

p. 253
They believe in Christ the son of God, born of the virgin Mary, and they say that he was the one who suffered under Pontius Pilate and rose again, in whom we too believe.

p. 255
Three times every day in the synagogues they anathematize the appellation "Christian" under the name of "Nazarenes."

p. 268
Certain heretics, who call themselves Nazarenes, are called by some "Symmachians."

ibid.
because Jesus said that he had not come to dissolve the Law.

ibid.
Even until our own times they persist, in tiny numbers indeed, yet still maintaining those numbers.

p. 271
We were cast out in order that we might become the teachers of the world.

p. 279
so that the report should not become conspicuous.

p. 281
Certain men, having happened to have a father who feared the Sabbath, worship nothing except the clouds and the divinity of the sky, and think that pork is not much different from human flesh, their father having abstained from it; soon they even circumcise themselves.

ibid.
Having become accustomed to despise the Roman laws, they learn, keep, and fear the Jewish law, whatever Moses handed down in his mysterious volume: not to show the roads to anyone who does not worship the same rites, and to guide only circumcised men to a sought-for spring of water.

p. 282
hatred of the human race

ibid.
godless and lawless heresy

p. 283
It happened very recently that a dispute was held between a Christian and a Jewish proselyte.... For the opportunity, indeed, of claiming Divine grace even for the gentiles derived a preeminent fitness from this fact, that the man who set up to claim God's law for himself was of the gentiles, and not a Jew of the stock of the Israelites.

p. 286
It is you, at all events, who have even admitted the sun into the calendar of the week; and you have selected its day, in preference to the previous day, as the most suitable in the week for either an entire abstinence from the bath, or for its postponement until the evening, or for taking rest and for banqueting. By resorting to these customs, you deliberately deviate from your own religious rites to those of strangers. For the Jewish feasts are the Sabbath and the meal of purity, and Jewish also are the ceremonies of the lamps, and the fasts of unleavened bread, and the open-air prayers, all of which are, of course, foreign to your gods.

p. 287
We are baptised only in the name of the Father, the Son, and the Holy Spirit, and not in that of the archangels or angels, as the heretics or the Jews or even the gentiles do in their madness.

p. 289
And would to God that the Jewish serpents did not disturb us by their speeches. . . . The crowd of them, in the likeness of wolves, circle round the flock of Christ, and cause us no little sleeplessness and toil, when we wish to guard the sheep of the Lord and protect them from being torn to pieces.

p. 297
Whenever, on certain days, they expound their traditions, they are accustomed to say to their disciples (in Greek), "The sages are teaching *deuterosis*."

p. 306
Not indeed in name, but by their error, they are Judaizers.

p. 307
One God

ibid.
and His Christ

p. 308
alone

p. 316
It should never be possible for Christians to stray from the way of truth and to trail like ignorant people after the blind and stupid Jews as to the correct day for Easter.

p. 328
The Jews and our Judaizers think that a golden and bejeweled Jerusalem will be deposited from the heavens.

p. 331
Why do you mix things that cannot be mixed?

ibid.
What? Is it moderate to be a Jew? Is it the quality of moderation to be impious?

p. 332
The Apostle Paul teaches that it is especially wrong for gentile Christians to Judaize.

ibid.
If, then, we are Jews not carnally but spiritually, how are we the seed of Abraham? Not according to the flesh, but according to the spirit of faith.

p. 339
Celsus says that they worship angels and are addicted to sorcery, which Moses first expounded to them.

p. 340
For a tiny amount of money, the Jews sell whatever kind of dreams you want.

ibid.
Whoever may arise from the Hebrews or the Phoenicians. (Possible translation, but the phrase is obscure.)

p. 343
Iao Aoth Abaoth god of Israma

ibid.
(Heb.) The Lord of hosts, God of Israel

p. 344
the hidden and ineffable Name
barbaradonai kentabaoth iabezebuth
or or phor Eloei Adonai Iao Zabaoth Michael Iesou Christe

p. 349
the glorious, awesome and great Name

ibid.
the god of Abraham and of Iaw and of Jacos, Iaw Aoth Abaoth, god of Israma.

p. 350
the sacred eons

ibid.
for the word is Hebrew

ibid.
pure men

p. 352
One God who conquers evil things

p. 362
as he ought to be corrected

ibid.
Their science should be punished and deservedly afflicted with the severest penalties, who, equipped with magic arts, are detected in working against people's health or in having perverted innocent minds into depravity. However, no charges apply to remedies intended for the good of human bodies; or, in country regions, for the prevention of showers or damage by hailstones to the ripe crops; innocently applied aids by which no one's health or reputation is damaged, but the influence of which is to prevent the frustration of divine gifts and the toils of men.

p. 363
after the deicide

p. 364
The only physician for saints and penitents, the hands and feet of God, to love.

ibid.
He who observes Jesus giving orders to the demons, and also giving power to his disciples over all demons, and to cure sicknesses, will say that it is not in accordance with the power given by the Savior to conjure demons; it is rather a Jewish thing. Even though something like this is done sometimes by our people, it is similar to the practice of Solomon who used to conjure demons by written conjurations. But those who use those conjurations often use books that are not suitably composed: they conjure demons even with books obtained from a Hebrew.

p. 366
the first martyr of ancient times

p. 380
We are of your stock.

ibid.
Christians are made, not born.

p. 381
third kind

ibid.
We who were not the people of God formerly . . . have become his people.

p. 436, n. 57
The Pharisees have delivered to the people many observances by succession from their fathers that are not written in the laws of Moses.

ibid., n. 60
These men live the kind of life that was taught among the Greeks by Pythagoras.

p. 438, n. 107
Fate and astrology had very great influence on them ... vainly following the Greeks.

p. 443, n. 119
On this account were appointed one week, and seven weeks, and the seventh month, and the seventh year, and the revolution of these, the jubilee, which is the fiftieth year for remission.

ibid., n. 120
and hast had mercy on Zion, and compassion on Jerusalem, by exalting the throne of David thy servant in the midst of her.

p. 444, n. 150
who has obtained credit among the Jews of having interpreted the Scriptures with no ordinary care, and whose version is most commonly used by those who do not know Hebrew, as the one that has been most successful.

p. 445, n. 157
Jews who are Roman citizens who hold and practice the Jewish rites.

ibid., n. 1
For the kings of the earth assembled, the Roman senate and people and leaders, in order to overcome the name of Jesus and Israel together. For they decreed by their laws that Christians should not exist. But just as then all those assembled kings could do nothing against Jesus, so ... they were not able to bring it about that the race of Christians should not be propagated more widely and more profusely.

p. 446, n. 19
The Jews are a continual testimony to the world that they were punished for no other reason than that they raised impious hands against Christ.

ibid., n. 25
us, called God-fearers and Christians

p. 447, n. 30
By us, to whom Sabbaths are strange, and the new moons and festivals formerly beloved by God

ibid., n. 33
What Moses wrote, he wrote not without the counsel of God. But he legislated from the Holy Spirit, and it is plain that it is the legislation of God.

ibid., n. 36
the statements of the Scriptures that are common to us both, in which not you only, but we also, take pride

ibid.
they have the Bible ... the meaning of the Scriptures has been removed from them.

ibid., n. 37
Because both the New is figured in the Old, and the Old is revealed in the New.

ibid., n. 38
They think they are saying something of weight, when they ask us how we accept the authority of the Law and the Prophets when we do not observe the rites that are commanded there.

ibid., n. 39
The Gospel was proclaimed at the same time as a fulfilled Judaism, as a new religion, and as a restored original religion brought to a definitive form, and indeed it was not just a single, well-distinguished missionary who preached it in these three forms, but this representation appeared in all introductory missionary preaching, more or less plainly.

p. 448, n. 63
The Lord did not dissolve the natural law, through which man is justified, but extended and completed it.

ibid., n. 64
the new lawgiver

the law of Christ

ibid., n. 65
by the Logos, through Moses his servant

ancient grace

ibid., n. 70
not one law of Christ inclined towards allowing Christians to Judaize.

ibid., n. 79
but our Logos, as a new arrival . . .
that they do not adhere to the God worshiped by the Jews according to their laws, but cut across for themselves a new and lonely road, which is no road, keeping neither the rites of the Greeks nor the rites of the Jews.

p. 449, n. 81
They say that they are different from the present-day Jews, and that they are the true Israelites according to their prophets, and that they show the true obedience to Moses.

ibid., n. 86
Therefore it is plain that all the rest have erred, and only the Christians have spread the truth, since we are taught by the Holy Spirit, which spoke in the holy Prophets and foretold all things.

ibid., n. 87
Those who call themselves Jews but are not, but the synagogue of Satan.

pseudo-Jews

those who are wrongly called Jews

ibid., n. 88
As in the law, therefore, and in the gospel, the first and greatest commandment is to love the Lord God with the whole heart. . . . The author of the law and the gospel is shown to be one and the same.

ibid., n. 97
Judaism did not exist, but there were Hebrews at first. There were no Jews, and they had not yet begun.

ibid., n. 98
only for the Jews; but the laws of Moses could not be suitable for the nations of the world, nor could they possibly be observed by all men; I mean by those outside Judaea called Greeks and barbarians.

ibid., n. 99
The polity of Moses did not apply to the rest of the nations but only to the Jews, and not even to all of them, but only to those dwelling in the land of Judaea.

ibid., n. 101
I wished to set up an entirely different way from the Mosaic law, according to which I intended that all the nations of the world would live like Abraham and share in equal blessing with him.

ibid., n. 102
Christians in fact, if not in name

Our ancestors, who were the leaders of the Hebrews.

ibid., n. 103
For in the beginning of the world, he gave a law to Adam himself and Eve. . . . This law would have been enough, if it had been observed. . . . For in this general and primal law of God . . . we

recognize all the commandments that were detailed in the later Law, and that were given out in their own time and sprouted forth. . . . So I argue that before the Law of Moses written on the tablets of stone, there was an unwritten law, which was understood by nature, and was observed by the Fathers.

But, that we might attain a fuller and more authoritative knowledge both of Himself, and of His counsels and will, He added a written revelation.

p. 450, n. 104
O testimony of a soul naturally Christian!

ibid., n. 106
We, then, who have succeeded to the place of the prophets, at the present day sustain in the world that treatment which the prophets always suffered on account of divine religion.

ibid., n. 117
All were types, all a shadow: circumcision, sacrifices, the Sabbath, things that were not strong enough to penetrate the soul and therefore yield and give way.

ibid., n. 118
It is surely not the command of God not to eat; but Moses spoke in a spiritual sense.

p. 451, n. 141
Therefore, you, who treated him with impiety are treated with insolence and dishonour, while we, who worship him, being formerly less honored than all of you, are now by the grace of God more respected than all of you, and stand in greater honor.

ibid., n. 142
Therefore you no longer have any remedy, or forgiveness, or defense.

p. 452, n. 143
Witnesses of their own iniquity and of our truth.

ibid., n. 151
This, then, is the nub of your question, or rather of your opinion, whether Jews who believe in Christianity do well if they observe the commandments of the law; if this is true, we fall into the heresy of Cerinthus and Ebion

ibid., n. 156
the other rises out of the Jews again for us, though he wears the face of a Christian, Paul of Samosata.

since the impious views of the Anomoeans and the Jews are related

ibid., n. 157
Those people are similar to the Jews who, though they profess to be Christians, are so opposed to the grace of Christ that they regard themselves as fulfilling the divine commandments by human powers, and since they are ignorant of the justice of God, and wish to set up their own, they are not subject to the justice of God, and Judaize, not indeed in name, but by their error. This sect had found for its leaders Pelagius and Celestius.

p. 454, n. 60
a new and God-loving community

p. 457, n. 127
ravager of the Jews

the Patriarch, by levying tributes, has acquired limitless treasures

p. 459, n. 22
on the footing of our common beliefs

p. 462, n. 38
the Logos, being divine

p. 464, n. 90
These who are now called patriarchs by you are not priests, but play the part of priests.

ibid., n. 92
For the law commanded, in regard to the feasts of the Jews, not only the time of the observance, but also the place.

ibid., n. 96
The observance of the place is more necessary than the observance of the time.

ibid., n. 118
For the occasion, indeed, of claiming Divine grace even for the gentiles derived a preeminent fitness from this fact, that the man who set up to vindicate God's Law as his own was of the gentiles, and not a Jew of the stock of the Israelites.

p. 465, n. 133
In the most difficult passages, they avoid questions as they arise by digressing into undisciplined disputation.

ibid., n. 137
the Jews, who are always ready for altercation

p. 466, n. 9
What shall I say about the Ebionites, who pretend that they are Christians? Even today it is a heresy through all the synagogues of the East among the Jews, and is called that of the "Minaeans" and is completely condemned by the Pharisees; the common name for them is the "Nazarenes."

p. 468, n. 64
Wisdom, being Lord and God, steeped us with Divine fire from the Lord God.

p. 469, n.99
Even now the Jews are not moved against the gentiles, against those who worship idols and blaspheme God, nor do they hate them or grow angry against them; but against Christians they are borne by an insatiable hatred.

p. 470, n. 6
greedy little Greek

the Romans were unjust, their greed was profound

The plunderers of the world . . . if the enemy is rich, they are greedy for riches, if he is poor, they are greedy for power.

There is nothing greedier than the nation of the Jews and of the Romans.

ibid., n. 7
For a long time already the Syrian Orontes has flowed into the Tiber.

Contrary and changeable by reason of superstition and lecherousness, with no knowledge of laws or of magistrates.

ibid., n. 12
We do not delight in trade, nor in such mingling with other men as arises from it.

p. 471, n. 42
as the common ruin and disease of the whole world

as if stirring up a common disease of the world

p. 472, n. 58
God is not worshiped with the belly or with foods

ibid., n. 59
This is not a recent thing with them, but an inveterate and inborn evil.

ibid., n. 64
A people with too much neck.

ibid., n. 66
Blind to understand, obstinate to believe.

How long, most obstinate Jew, will you persist with deaf ears, closed eyes, and treacherous heart?

p. 474, n. 116
A Christian emperor has learned to honor only the altar of Christ.... Let the voice of our emperor echo Christ, and speak only that which he knows to be true. For the heart of a king is in the hand of God.

ibid., n. 119
Deadly sect, wicked sect.

abominable superstition

abominable Jews

sacrilegious assemblies

the filthy, hideous name of the Jews

p. 475, n. 125
their synagogues to remain in their accustomed peace.

which, by established usage, are frequented by assemblages of Jews and are called "synagogues," no one may date to violate.

their synagogues may not be burned down indiscriminately.

ibid., n. 127
In compensation for these, ground is to be provided for them, in which they may build, up to the measure of the buildings that were removed.

p. 476, n. 3
The separation of the Law and the Gospel is the characteristic and principal work of Marcion.

ibid., n. 7
The Ebionites ... thinking about Christ in a beggarly and mean manner

ibid., n. 14
Those who are called Ebionites, however, agree indeed that the world was made by God; but in matters relating to the Lord, they have opinions similar to those of Cerinthus and Carpocrates.

ibid., n. 16
His successor was Ebion, who did not entirely agree with Cerinthus, since he says that the world was made by God, not by angels.

p. 477, n. 35
And they observed the Sabbath and the rest of the Jewish manner of life, but also they observed equally our Lord's Days, in memory of the resurrection of the Lord.

ibid., n. 36
They continue in the customs that are according to the Law, and in the Jewish type of life, so that they even worship Jerusalem, as if it were the house of God.

p. 478, n. 40
As to the prophetic writings, they endeavor to expound them in a rather singular manner.

ibid., n. 42
But they use only the Gospel according to Matthew.

ibid., n. 49
In Chaldaic and Syrian speech, but in Hebrew letters.

ibid., n. 51
He taught that the world was not made by the First God, but by a certain power that was very much removed from Him.

ibid., n. 55
How can they be saved, unless it is God who has worked their salvation on earth? And how can a man pass into God, unless God has passed into man?

p. 479, n. 58
Just a man ... yet somehow more glorious than the prophets, so that an angel is said to have been in him.

ibid., n. 62
These are the twofold sect of Ebionites, who either acknowledge with us that Jesus was born of a virgin, or deny this, and maintain that he was begotten like other human beings.

ibid., n. 67
Three times a day, when they perform their prayers in their synagogues, they curse them, and anathematize them, saying, "May God curse the Nazarenes."

p. 481, n. 109
... not to communicate to anyone of the gentiles, nor to one of our own tribe before trial.

to communicate books to no one before trial.

and to a circumcised person who is trustworthy.

p. 482, n. 120
For it is better to hear Christianity from a circumcised man than Judaism from an uncircumcised man.

ibid., n. 127
... so that they might compel even gentiles to Judaize. These are those whom Faustus mentioned under the name of "Symmachians."

ibid., n. 129
If any of the Nazarenes (whom some call Symmachians) should make this objection to me ...

ibid., n. 5
Captured Greece captured its cruel conqueror.

Meanwhile the way of life of the most wicked nation has prevailed to such an extent that through the whole world it has been accepted, and the conquered have given laws to their conquerors.

What ... have they received with eagerness the images of captured cities and foreign rites of an alien superstition?

p. 484, n. 48
Against all others they have implacable hatred.... Those who adopt their religion observe the same customs; and the first instruction they receive is to despise the gods, abjure their country, and disregard their parents, children, and brothers.

ibid., n. 49
If a gentile practices the Law, he is a Jew; if he does not practice it, he is a Hellene.

ibid., n. 50
A circumcised proselyte is accepted among the people exactly like one born in it.

p. 485, n. 59
Like Jews, we will force you to join our camp.

ibid., n. 65
Irene, a minor-proselyte, through her father and mother, a Jewess and an Israelite.

p. 486, n. 72
Do not think that the Holy Baptism is similar to the baptisms of the Jews ... they are practiced frequently and continually.

ibid., n. 80
... since we see that pagans, though rarely, become Jews.

ibid., n. 83
He discovered new and unaccustomed audacity on the part of the Jews, because they wish to disturb the sacred rites of the catholic faith.

ibid., n. 84
They always drew a great many of the Greeks to their religion, and made them in a way part of themselves.

ibid., n. 87
Dances of wanton people . . . with bare feet they dance in the open.

ibid., n. 93
If anyone of the people joins their wicket sect, he will undergo deserved punishment with them.

ibid., n. 94
If anyone . . . having become a Jew from being a Christian joins their sacrilegious assemblies, when the charge has been proved, we order his property to be delivered to the treasury.

p. 487, n. 95
Let those responsible for this persuasion, who perverted fickle minds into joining their own community, suffer the same penalty, being guilty of such an error; though we consider that even graver penalties should often be applied against the abominable practicers of this crime, according to the feelings of the judges and the unusual character of the offense.

ibid., n. 96
If anyone of the Christian faith is polluted by Jewish unfaith . . . If anyone has tried to go against this law, let him know that he liable to a capital charge.

ibid., n. 97
Anyone who has transferred a slave or a freedman from the practice of the Christian religion into an abominable sect or cult, either against his will or by entrapping him by persuasion, is subject to capital punishment together with the loss of his possessions.

ibid., n. 98
They shall not join Christian women to their sins, or, if they have done this, they will be put on trial for a capital offense.

ibid., n. 99
No Jew shall receive a Christian woman in marriage, nor shall a Christian man choose marriage to a Jewish woman.

ibid., n. 101
If any Jew has bought a slave who is a Christian or of any other sect and then circumcises him, he may not keep the circumcised man in slavery, but he who has suffered this gains the privileges of freedom.

ibid., n. 104
That he should not disturb others, whether willing or unwilling, with the filth of his own sect.

ibid., n. 107
and let him not cause any synagogues to be built subsequently. . . . If he tries to soil any Christian or a person of any other sect, whether free or slave, with the Jewish brand, he is subject to the severity of the law.

p. 488, n. 119
The Jews too read them publicly; under a tribute-liberty, they are in the habit of going to hear them every Sabbath.

But perhaps the Jews may say, "The house of God, that is the synagogue, is open to all. Nor do we deny this."

ibid., n. 126
lest knowledge of them should be lacking

the Jews read it openly

p. 490, n. 166
The peoples of some part of many nations, and especially those which border on Judaea and Palestine, even today practice circumcision, notably the Egyptians, the Idumaeans, Ammonites, Moabites, and the whole region of the Saracens.

ibid., n. 2
One God, the Savior of the Christians.

p. 491, n. 14
because they were accustomed to assemble on the appointed day before dawn and recite a psalm to Christ as God, taking turns.

And on the day called Sunday, all who live in cities or in the country gather together in one place.

ibid., n. 15
We met together on the Sabbath day, not that we were suffering from the disease of Judaism.

p. 492, n. 28
The sacrifice of a lamb is called by those themselves who make it, *pascha*, from the Greek *paschein*, "to suffer," because it is a symbol of the Passion.

ibid., n. 31
But make it when your brothers of the circumcision do so; do it with them at the same time.

ibid., n. 39
For they wish to observe Easter together with the Jews.

ibid., n. 42
We preferred harmony in our observance of times.

ibid., n. 45
For the Pasch is not a fast, but an offering and a sacrifice that takes place at every synaxis (Holy Communion).

ibid., n. 46
We do not fast because of Easter, nor because of the Cross, but because of our sins, since we intend to approach the mysteries.

p. 493, n. 62
For the Church does not know the times precisely.

ibid., n. 65
You wish to send away the one God, who is, so to speak, the legitimate husband of the soul, and to fornicate with many demons; and what is still worse, not deserting and rejecting Him more or less openly as the apostates do, but, so to speak, while still in your husband's house you let in adulterers; it is as if you do not reject the Church as a Christian, yet consult astrologers.... You are told to observe the Sabbath in a spiritual manner; not in the way the Jews observe the Sabbath, with carnal rest

ibid., n. 68
in the church for the teaching of piety.

ibid., n. 69
that Christians ought not to Judaize and rest on the Sabbath, but to exert themselves on the day.

p. 494, n. 79
Christ performed the Paschal offering on that very day when he suffered it. Therefore I too should perform it in the same way that the Lord performed it.

ibid., n. 83
Take, for example, a Jew who, having become a Christian, circumcises his son, observes the Sabbath, abstains from foods that God created so that we might use them with thanksgiving, and sacrifices a lamb on the evening of the fourteenth day of the first month.

p. 495, n. 87
If we follow only the letter . . . someone who has a scar and is disfigured would be barred from the priesthood, however excellent in character he may be.

ibid., n. 99
The opinion of the Jews, indeed, about the resurrection is as follows: that they rise again, to be sure, but in order to enjoy carnal delights and luxuries and the rest of the pleasures of the body . . . but the Jews and our Judaizers . . . desiring the blood of sacrifices and the enslavement of all nations and the beauty of women

Lovers only of the letter that kills, and preparing exquisite food for gluttony and luxury for a thousand years. . . . Who after the second coming of the Savior in glory expect marriages and a few palty centuries, and the injury of circumcision, and the blood of sacrifices, and a perpetual Sabbath

Not to chase after Jewish lunacies.

ibid., n. 101
If any Christian, especially of the new wise, whose names I forbear to mention, lest I should seem to harm anyone, thinks that prophecy is not yet complete, let him know that he bears the name of Christian falsely, and has a Jewish soul, lacking only the circumcision of the body.

ibid., n. 102
Jewish observances, then, seem to unskilled people and the common people, to have an appearance of reason and human wisdom.

p. 496, n. 116
Why do you run to the synagogue often, playing a double part? So that he should have mercy on you, whom you also deny? You go out of the doors, again you seek the shrine; you want to live between them both, but therefrom you perish.

And he serves idols, again he seeks them on the thirtieth day; and now he follows unleavened bread, who had sat before the chaste one.

ibid., n. 126
But he asks whether, since in that way a man has been a true German and a Christian, he may correctly be called a Jew or an Israelite.

ibid., n. 127
Because indeed, if this ought to be understood not carnally but spiritually, he ought not to apply the name to himself in ordinary speech, but keep it for a spiritual meaning, lest because of ambiguity, which everyday speech does not distinguish, he should seem to be expressing that he is hostile to the Christian name.

ibid., n. 128
Lastly, Aptus (I don't know who he is), about whom you wrote that he is teaching Christians to Judaize, calls himself a Jew and an Israelite to such an extent that he forbids those foods which the Law, suitably for that time, forbade, and he urges the rest of the observances of that time now abolished and removed among Christians.

p. 497, n. 133
Homicide is forbidden to us even to see or hear it in the theater, and we are on our guard so much from all blood that we are not acquainted even with edible blood of cattle in our food.

ibid., n. 143
But I regard as deadly what the use of men has not allowed for food, for the reason that the flesh of animals that have died, and not been killed, is diseased and not suitable for the health of the body, for the sake of which we take nourishment.

ibid., n. 145
Because although the apostles then commanded that Christians should abstain from the blood of animals, and that they should not eat the meat of strangled animals, they seem to me to have chosen something easy, for the time, and in no way burdensome to observe, in which gentiles together with Israelites, might find a common observance of something, because of that

cornerstone which made them both meet in Himself.... But when that time had gone by ... when the Church has become so composed of Gentiles that no carnal Israelite appears in her, what Christian now keeps this observance? And those few, perhaps, who still fear to touch those things are laughed at by the rest.

ibid., n. 148
If anyone condemns, deliberately and as a matter of faith, one who eats meat (apart from blood, meat sacrificed to idols and meat of a strangled animal), as one who has no hope of salvation through taking part in it, let him be anathema.

ibid., n. 155
Let them tell you whether it has been commanded to worship gods.

If God has commanded us to guard ourselves strongly from idols, why do they deceive the nations into thinking that they have washed clean? Nay, when they receive such people, they ought to teach them not to serve other gods, but to please the Highest alone.

ibid., n. 156
about the New Moon and the Sabbaths, and about not attending to the sounds of birds.

p. 498, n. 17
And if you ask them, "Why did you crucify Christ?," they say, "Because he was a vagabond and a sorcerer."

p. 499, n. 25
I exorcise you by the Hebrew word

ibid., n. 28
May your sleep be in peace.

ibid., n. 29
I adjure you in the holy name which is not spoken.

ibid., n. 34
through the name and the friendship of God to the righteous.

p. 500, n. 51
the fallen angels and the impure spirits.... But the host of the heavens do not take their name from the sun alone, and the moon and the shining stars, but the whole angelic multitude and army of those who are called in Hebrew Sabaoth, that is of powers and armies.

p. 501, n. 88
The Sower Arepo holds with care the wheels.

p. 503, n. 103
Among us even today, superstitious little women do this, with small gospels, and wood of the Cross, and such things (they have indeed zeal for God, but not combined with knowledge).

ibid., n. 104
to stir up the minds of ignorant people and little women, since, being drawn from Hebrew sources, they frighten all simple people by their barbaric sound.

ibid., n. 117
that the oaths that take place there are more dreadful.

p. 504, n. 120
Jews, having used charms and jugglery, accomplished nothing.

Even if they cure truly ... the charms, the amulets, the medicines ... sorcerers and enchanters.

ibid., n. 132
Let superstition cease, let the madness of sacrifices be abolished.

ibid., n. 134
Not only philosophers, but also our ancestors distinguished between superstition and religion ... false opinions and confused errors and superstitions almost for old women.

ibid., n. 135
the crowd of heretical superstitions.

p. 505, n. 147
One who reverences auguries or incantations is to be separated from the community, and similarly one who adheres to the superstitions or feasts of the Jews.

ibid., n. 148
If any cleric or believer has taken food with Jews, it was decided that he should refrain from communion, as one who ought to be corrected.

It was decided to warn landowners that they should not allow their crops, which they receive from God, to be blessed by Jews, lest they should render our blessing vain and ineffectual. If anyone dares to do this after this ban, let him be excluded entirely from the Church.

ibid., n. 153
Grievous is the fever, but put against the fever the fire of Gehenna

ibid., n. 156
one physician . . . Jesus Christ.

ibid., n. 158
Jesus, then, is according to the Hebrews, "savior," but according to the Greek tongue the "healer," since he is the physician of souls and bodies, and the healer of spirits.

The healer of every illness and every disease.

p. 506, n. 161
Are you a believer? Make the sign of the cross.

ibid., n. 163
What they called phylacteries, as many women now have gospels hanging from their necks.

p. 507, n.2
Whether here only the outward destruction and inner rigidification of Judaism come into consideration—but why did it rigidify in its Law?—or other causes too, for example, the growing rivalry of Christianity, I offer no judgment.

Index

Aalen, 392
Abbahu, R., 184–5, 198, 298, 407
Abel, 54, 170
Abodah Zarah, 24
Abraham, 9, 57, 77, 79, 81–2, 112–13, 152,
   161, 164–6, 171, 190–1, 193–4
Abtalyon, 279
Abun, R., 25, 216
Acts (of the Apostles), 37, 119, 260, 266, 411
Acts of the Martyrs, 120–5, 404
Adam, 9, 77, 85, 160, 195
Adiabene, 302
Adrametum, magical tablet from, 343, 348
Africa, 268, 289, 331–4; *see also* Berbers,
   Egypt, etc.
Agrippa II, 41
Aha, R., 187–8, 191
Ain Duq, synagogue of, 19–23, 27, 297
Akiba, R., 12, 184, 190, 260, 262, 280, 282,
   300, 403–5
Alexander Severus, 103, 203
Albertini, 296
Alexander of Abonoteichos, 339–40
Alexandria: Jews of, 35, 59, 329, 372–3; anti-
   Semitism in, 130, 206, 224–5; Hadrian's
   comments on, 203–4
Allard, P., 116, 123
Ambrose, St., 216, 226–7, 231
Ambrosiaster, 268, 288, 330
Amoraim, 27, 197–8
Amorgos, lamella from, 351–2
Amos, 167, 184
Andreotti, L., 395, 403
angelology, 27, 345–7
Antioch: Jews of, 35; anti-Semitism in, 206,
   225–6; Judaizing in Christian community
   at, 289, 326–8, 331, 355, 373
Antiochus Epiphanes, 7
anti-Semitism, 202–33, 395–402: pagan,
   202–7, 398–400; in early Church, 207–11;
   Christian accusations of immorality and
   impiety, 212–16; invective of St. John
   Chrysostom, 217–23; Christian actions
   against and imperial legislation on
   synagogues, 224–30; Christian sympathy
   for Jews, 230–2; in Nazi Germany, 397–8,
   400
Antoninus, 100, 102, 104, 281
Aphraates, 77, 94, 140–1, 145, 156, 160–1,
   165, 170–1, 177, 190–1, 213, 318–21,
   323–6, 373, 401

Apion, xv, 203, 207, 209
Apocalypse, 353
'apostles' (appointed by the Patriarch), 62,
   117, 128
Apostolic Constitutions, xi, 53–9, 308, 310,
   316, 323–4, 372–3
apostolic decree (from Jerusalem), 334–7
Aptus, 332–3
Aquila, translation of the Bible, 55–6, 59–60,
   160, 267, 280, 299–300, 308, 349
Arcadius, 129, 227, 229
Arians, Arianism, 96, 224
Aristides, 86, 108, 345
Ariston of Pella, dialogue of, 68, 137
art, Jewish, 17–27; *see also* Ain Duq, Dura
   Europos, etc.
Ashi, R., xvii, 280
Asellicus, 332–3
astrology, 26–7, 346–7
Athanasius and Zacchaeus, dialogue of, 140,
   162, 194
Audians, 313, 316, 321–2
Augustine, St., 71, 89, 92–4, 96, 188, 216,
   231, 268, 332, 335–6, 365–6

Babylon, Babylonia, 185–6, 350; exile in,
   169–70
Bacher, W., 298
Baer, Y.F., 402–6
Bamberger, B., 392
baptism of proselytes, 278, 286–7
Bar Cochba revolt, xiv–xv, 11, 53, 67, 99,
   101, 116, 260–2, 403–4
Bar Hanina, R., 185
Bar Kappara, 197
Barnabas, epistle of, 68, 70, 71, 140, 149,
   152, 155, 165, 188, 216, 414
Barsauma, 225
Bartholomew, 267
Baruch, apocalyptic writings of, xiv,
   6–9
Bell, H.I., 395
Beloch, 34
Ben Azzai, 192
Ben Sira, 373
Berbers, 302–3
Berenice, 41
Beroea, 264
Beruria, 189
Beth Alpha, synagogue of, 19–23, 27,
   297

Bible: in Christian theology, 71–2, in anti-Jewish polemic, 146–55; anti-Semitism in, 207–8
Biblis, 334
Billerbeck, P., 289
Blau, L., 342, 348
Blumenkranz, B., 393–5, 398
Bonsirven, Father, ix, 34
Botte, Dom Bernard, 395–6
Bouché-Leclerq, A., 35, 101
Bousset, W., ix, xi, 50, 53–6, 295
Brandon, G.F., 386
Braude, W.A., 392
Burchard, C., 387

Caesarea, 177, 198
Caesarius of Arles, St., 361
Cain, 93, 170
Caligula, 225
Callinicum, 226–9
candlestick: as Jewish symbol, 51–2; in magic, 354–5
Capernaum, sculptures in synagogue of, 19, 23, 27
Caracalla, 29, 102, 105
Carpocrates, 241–2
Carthage, 302, 304, 333; Jews of, 35, 211; burials at, 124; candlestick from, 354–5
Cassin, E., 394
Causse, A., 8
Cave of Treasures, 85
Celsus, 41, 110, 138, 157, 173–4, 209, 245, 340–1, 344–6, 373
Cerinthus, 241–2, 250
Chaeretopa, 368
Christ, *see* Jesus
Christianity: and Israel, 65–97; Roman policy towards, 100–7; Jewish involvement in Roman persecution of, 115–25; *see also* Christianity, Jewish; Judaism and Christianity; Talmud, Christians in
Christianity, Jewish, 237–70, 409–17: definition of the term, 237–40; Ebionites and Nazarenes, 240–7; the nature of Ebionism, 247–54; Jewish attitudes towards, 254–64; Jewish Christians outside Palestine, 264–70
Christology: in anti-Jewish polemic, 159–63, 192–6, Ebionite, 249–50
Chrysostom, St. John, 73, 94, 114, 128, 140–2, 144–5, 153, 168–71, 188, 209, 211, 217–23, 227, 229, 232, 279, 286–7, 289, 293, 314, 316–18, 320–1, 323, 326–8, 331, 337, 356, 358, 363, 366–7, 373, 381, 395
circumcision, 63, 99–100, 104–5, 112, 164–5, 247, 292–3, 417
Claudius, 211, 218, 232

Clement of Alexandria, 248
Colossians, epistle to the, 345, 367–8
Commodian, 149, 216, 331
Commodus, 102
Constantine, 99, 126–7, 229, 291–2, 358, 362
Constantius, 291–3
Constantius II, 360
Cullmann, O., 50, 411
Cumont, F., 51–2, 284, 352
Cyprian, *Testomonia* of St., 140, 142, 154
Cyprus, 34, 264
Cyrene, xiv, 34–5, 303
Cyril of Jerusalem, 177
Cyril, Patriarch of Alexandria, 224

Dalbert, P., 391
Damascus, 327
Damasus, Pope, 287
Daniel: 159, 169–70; in mosaic at Ain Duq, 20; book of, 404
Daphne, synagogue of, 355
Dead Sea Scrolls, 387
Deissmann, A., 348
Dertona, 225
Deuteronomy, 90, 150, 195, 220
deuterosis, 88–91, 150, 314, 325, 357
Diataxis, 313, 316
Didache, 309, 312, 335
Didascalia, 79–80, 88–90, 94, 149–50, 308, 310–18, 321, 324–5, 357
Dietrich, D., 349–50
Dio Cassius, 282
Diocletian's persecution, 107, 404–5, 408
Diognetus, epistle to, 86, 108
Domitian, 99–100, 117
Domnus, 105
Donatian, Primate of Byzacena, 333
Dornseif, 353
Dubnow, S.M., 197
Duchesne, L., x, 271, 322
Dupont-Sommer, A., 387
Dupont-Sommer, M., 47
Dura Europos, synagogue frescoes of, 17–23, 26–7, 297, 382, 388–9

Easter and the Passover, controversy over, 310–21: in the *Didascalia*, 311–16; in St. John Chrysostom, 316–18; in Aphraates, 318–21
Ebionism, 247–54
Ebionites, 66–7, 237–47, 255–70 *passim*, 411–12
Edessa, 186, 225
Egypt, xiv, 33–4, 165, 170, 203–4, 248, 329; in sibylline oracles, 43, 45
Egyptians, Gospel of the, 264
Elagabalus, 103

Elche, synagogue of, 296
Eleazar, 13, 366
Eleazar ben Azariah, 190
Eleazar ben Damah, R., 183–4
Eleazar ben Pedath, 275–6
Eleazar of Modein, 197
Eliezer, R., 184, 187, 300
Eliezer ben Hyrcanus, 197
El Hammeh, synagogue of, 21, 297
Elisha ben Abuya, R., 295
Elvira, council of, 296, 330–1, 361–2
Ephraem, St., 140, 142, 324
Ephraim, 171
Epiphanius, 26–7, 240–1, 245–9, 253–4, 264, 269, 313, 316
Esau, 148, 171, 188
Esphia, synagogue of, 22
Essenes, 11–12, 15–16, 36, 350, 387–8
Eupolemus, 350
Eusebius, 67–8, 82–3, 101–2, 106, 121, 142, 154, 177, 184, 197–8, 241–2, 248, 252–3, 261, 267, 350, 402
Exodus, 249
exorcism, 363–4
Ezekiel, 219, 352–3
Ezra, xiv, 170; 4 Ezra, 4, 8

Ferrua, A., 389
Festus, 261
food laws, 152, 166, 210, 326, 334–6
Freimann, M., 173–5, 177
Frey, R.P., *Corpus Inscriptionum Judaicarum*, 284
Fridrichsen, 393
Friedländer, M., 180, 182, 196, 283

Gabriel, archangel, 346, 351, 356, 368
Galatia, 329
Galatians, letter to the, 93, 266–7
Galerius' persecution, 405
Gamaliel II, R., 29, 190, 197–8, 277, 294, 298
Gamaliel VI, Patriarch, 130, 229, 293
Gangra, council of, 336
Gaul, Christians of, 334
Gautier, E.F., 303
Genesis, 194, 349
Gerasa, synagogue of, 21
gnosticism: Jewish, 94–5, 180–3; gnostic crisis, xvi, 69–70; Judaizing gnostic sects, 244–5
Gobaeans, 280
Goodenough, E., 22, 388
Goppelt, L, 385–6
Grabar, A., 382, 388–9
Graetz, H., 101, 279
Gratian, 291, 400

Greek language, its persistence in Jewish religion, 21, 293–301
Gregory of Nyssa, 216
Gressman, H., ix
Guignebert, C., 12, 347

Hadrian: war of, xvi, 34, 197; persecution of Jews under, 3, 102, 403; made pagan sanctuary in Jerusalem, 7, 99; edict prohibiting circumcision, 35, 67, 99–100, 281, 405; treatment of Christians, 101–2; letter to Servianus, 203–4
Hagar, 148
Hammam-Lif, synagogue of, 19
Hanina, R., 275
Harnack, A., x, 32–3, 116, 137–41, 143–5, 173, 175, 240, 366, 370–1, 374, 378
Harris, Rendel, 154
Hatch, 154
Headlam, 154
Hebrew language: used by Ebionites, 247–9; use of in proselytism, 302–3; use of in magic, 343
Hebrews, epistle to the, 77
Hebrews, Gospel of the, 248–9, 264
Hefele-Leclerq, 330
Hegesippus, 67, 242
Helbo, R., 274–5
Herod, 7, 10
Hezekiah, 159
Hillel, 29, 61, 198
Hippolytus, 241, 250–2
Hoennicke, G., ix, 192
Hololle, 351
Honorius, 126, 128–9, 293
Horace, 280
Hulen, B., 142–4

Iamblichus, 42, 373
Ibn Khaldun, 303
iconoclasm, 18–19, 23–7
Idi, R., 195
Ignatius of Antioch, 73, 267
Irenaeus, 164, 241–2, 247–8, 250, 252
Isaac, 20, 171, 193
Isaac, J., 396–8, 400
Isaac, R., 187
Isaac of Antioch, 287, 356–7
Isaac the Jew, 330
Ishmael, R., 183–4, 294
Ishmael ben José of Sepphoris, R., 194
Isaiah, 155, 158, 170, 209, 252, 280, 314
Isidore of Seville, 141, 154
Islam, 302, 304–5
Israel, Church's claim to be the true, 79–80, 169–73, 333

Jabneh, academy at, 13, 29, 262
Jacob, 148–9, 161, 171, 188
Jacob of Kephar Sekanya, 183–4
Jacob of Kephar Siknin, 184
Jambres, 340
James, brother of Jesus, 67, 120, 261, 263, 267, 411
James, epistle of, 75
Jannes, 340
Jason and Papiscus, dialogue of, xvi, 137, 162
Jaubert, A., 392
Jerash, synagogue of, 19–21, 27, 297
Jeremiah, 165, 167, 170
Jeremias, J., 392
Jerome, St., 91, 93–4, 102, 153, 177, 182–3, 185, 197–8, 214, 216, 230–1, 240–1, 245–6, 249, 253–6, 289, 297, 299, 325, 328, 354
Jerphanion, 352–3
Jerusalem, its destruction: as a starting-point for study, xiv–xvi; reaction of Jews, 3–11; effect on Essenes, Zealots and Pharisees, 11–17; decisive influence on Jewish religious history, 28–32; reaction of diaspora Jews, 33–53; reaction of Jewish Christians, 65–7; reaction of Christians, 67–8
Jesus: and the law, 72–80; in anti-Jewish polemic, 157–63; viewed as magician by Jews, 157, 341; Ebionites' views of, 250–3; as healer, 364–5
Job, 214
Johanan, R., 25, 195, 404
Johanan ben Zakkai, 13, 29, 30, 262
John XXIII, Pope, 396
John, St., 79; anti-Semitism in his gospel, xv, 207–9
John Chrysostom, St., *see* Chrysostom
José ben Halafta, R., 276
Joseph, 171, 340–2
Joseph of Pumbeditha, R., 280
Josephus, 5–6, 18, 26, 33, 40–1, 68, 110, 262, 289, 327–8; his picture of Judaism, 11–17
Joshua, 158–9, 166, 323
Joshua, R., 277–8, 294, 300
Joshua ben Hananiah, 197
Joshua ben Levi, 197, 280
Joullos, *see* Hillel
Judah I, R., 29, 30, 187, 298
Judah II, R., 30, 280
Judah ben Ilai, 277–8
Judaism and Christianity, 306–38; Jewish ritual incorporated into Christianity, 306–10; controversy over Easter and Passover, 310–21; persistence of Judaizing within the Church, 321–8; widespread

extent of Judaizing Christianity, 328–33; abstinence from meat 333–8
Judas, 230
Judas the Ammonite, 280
Julia Mammaea, 102
Julian the Apostate, xvii, 40, 111–15, 216, 229, 289, 402–3
Juster, J., xi, 33–4, 61, 99, 105, 136, 209, 222–3, 227, 230, 362
Justin Martyr, xvi, 38–9, 68–71, 79, 116–19, 139–40, 142–3, 147, 151–6, 158–9, 161–3, 165–7, 171–5, 177, 194, 200, 241, 243–4, 253, 255, 267, 282–3, 310; *see also* Trypho
Justinian, *Novella 146*, 89, 300–1
Juvenal, 40, 204, 207, 280–2, 285, 340, 375

Kerygma Petri, 108, 345
Kittel, G., 392
Kokhaba, 264,
Kraeling, C.H., 388–9
Kuhn, K.G., 406–8

Labriolle, P. de, 41
Laodicaea, council of, 323–5, 329–30, 361, 367
law (Torah): in Jewish religion, 9, 12, 30–1; natural, 47; and reason, 48–9; St. Paul's anti-legalism, 71–5; new law of Christianity, 76–85, 149–50; ritual, 85–91; arguments for Jewish law's relativity, 163–73; as safeguard of Judaism, 374
Le Blant, E., 20
Lerle, E., 393
Levy, Isidore, 15
Liber, Maurice, 388, 390
Lieberman, S., 403, 405, 407–8
Lietzmann, H., 33–4, 266
liturgy of the synagogue: in the Apostolic Constitutions, 53–5, 373; in magic, 348–9
Lods, Adolphe, 7
Logos, 161–2, 176, 193, 195–6, 372
Lovsky, F., 398, 400
Lucas, L., ix
Lucian of Samosata, 340
Lucius, E., 367–8
Luke, St., 391
Lukyn Williams, A., ix, 136–8, 141–2, 155
Lydda, 198
Lyon, letter from Church at, 334

Maccabees, 54, 166, 225, 323, 366
Maccabees, Fourth Book of, 19, 46–9, 52, 372
Maghreb, 303, 331
magic, 339–68: Jewish reputation for, 339–43; basic elements of Jewish magic, 343–8; Judaism within magic formulae,

348–54; magical powers ascribed to Jewish symbols and persons, 354–6; suppression of magic, 356–58

Magona, 225

Malachi, 168

Manasseh, Prayer of, 308

Manetho, 398

Marcion, xvi, 69–71, 74, 82, 238

Marcus Aurelius, 102, 339,

Marcus, bishop, 67

Mark, Christian leader in Jerusalem, 101

Marmorstein, A., 263

marriages, legislation on mixed, 128, 293

Marron, H., 410

Martial, 204, 398

Maspero, 348

Mata-Mechasya, 280

Mattathias, 54

Matthew, St., 154, 248–9, 283, 361, 391–2

Maurice, 360

Maximinus, 225

Maximus, bishop of Hippone, 150

Maximus of Turin, 150

Meir, R., 280, 296

Melchizedek, 84–5, 165, 171

Menyamin, 280

Mesopotamia, 185–6, 318

Messianism, 8, 204, 298, 303

Metatron, 195

Michael, archangel, 346, 351, 356, 368

Milan, Edict of, 126

minim: its meaning, 179–201, 406–8; equated with *Nazarenes*, 255–6; and *posh'im*, 259, 263, 337

Minorca, 365

Minucius Felix, 334

Mishnah, 25, 58, 199, 297–8, 336; and *deuterosis*, 89–91; as part of Sinai revelation, 189–91

Mithraic cult, 273

Molland, E., 417

Mommsen, T., 406

Monceaux, P., 331

Monteverde catacomb, 52

Moore, G.F., ix

Moses, 21–2, 42, 77, 79, 82, 87, 89, 149–50, 158–61, 164, 170, 189–91, 194, 312, 340–2, 344–5

Mousaios, 340

Munck, J., 390–4, 415–17

Nahum, R., 24–5

Nazarenes, 240, 245–7, 260, 262–3, 268, 271, 401, 412; as term denoting Christians generally, 198, 254–6

Nehemiah, R., 187

Neher-Bernstein, Mme, R., 399

Nero, 117, 403

Nerva, 99

Nicaea, council of, 310, 316–18

Nisibis, 186

Noah, 20–1, 77, 159, 166; Noahic precepts, 164, 334, 337

Novatian, *De cibis judaicis*, 330

Novatians, 321–2

Numenius of Apamea, 340, 373

Oea, 185

Oesterreicher, J.M., 396

Oort, H., 221, 355

Origen, 68, 102, 107, 110, 149, 153–4, 173–5, 198, 210, 241, 245, 248, 252–4, 283–4, 364, 404

Orpheus, in fresco at Dura Europos, 22, 26

Ovid, 203

Palmyra, 277

Pantaenus, 267

Papias, 249

Parkes, J., ix, 116, 120–1, 124–5, 214, 227, 231, 402

Parousia, xv, 9–10, 67, 158, 327–8

Passion of St. Romanos, 307, 310

Passio Pionii, 107, 123

Passover, *see* Easter

Patriarch: authority of, xv, 61–2; privileges granted to by Romans, 126–7; restrictions and attacks on, 128–31

Paul, St., xii, 69, 72–5, 79, 81, 93, 119, 121, 135, 157, 167, 188, 192, 207, 231, 237, 248, 251, 260–1, 266–7, 269, 334–5, 367

Pauline letters, 57–8; *see also* Colossians, Galatians, Hebrews, Romans

Paul of Samosata, 96

Pella, 246–7, 251, 263–4, 415–6

Perdrizet, P., 347, 352

Peter, 245, 266–7

Peterson, E., 307–8, 396

Petronia of Carthage, 365–6

Pharisees, Pharisaism: adaptability of, 12–14, 35–6, 58; misrepresentation of, 14–15, 27–9, 174; and the Essenes, 15–17; interest in astrology and angelology, 26–7, 345; proselytism of, 283–4, 390–1; Pharisaic Judaism, 412–13

Philaster, 242–3, 252

Philo, 16, 26, 33, 37, 46, 48, 51, 56, 59, 150–1, 161, 176, 195, 372, 392, 412

Phrygia, 329, 367–8

phylacteries, 354, 361; *see also* relics

Pionius, 123; *see also Passio Pionii*

Plato, 140, 381

Pliny, xvi, 101, 310

polemic, anti-Jewish, 135-78: its purpose, 135-46; its recourse to the Bible, 146-55; Christology in, 156-63; arguments for the Jewish law's relativity, 163-73; literature as a reflection of real controversies, 173-8
Poliakov, Leon, 396
Polycarp of Smyrna, *Martyrium Polycarpi*, 121-3
Pompey, 7
Pontius, *Acts of Pontius*, 122-3
Poppaea, 117
population, size of Jewish, 33-4
Porphyry, 42, 373
Poseidonius of Apamea, 212
posh'e yisrael, 256-8, 337, 408-9
posh'im, 257-63, 328
proselytism, Jewish, 271-305, 390-5: effect of catastrophes in Palestine on it, 271-8; extent, 278-88; decline in the classical world, 288-301; in the Semite world, 301-5
Psalms, 158-9, 196, 216, 218, 258, 349
pseudo-Aristeas, 176
pseudo-Barnabas, 86-8, 151
pseudo-Baruch, 9
pseudo-Clementine writings, xv, 36, 49-50, 248, 274, 372, 410-11, 416
pseudo-Cyprian, 316
pseudo-Gregory of Nyssa, *Testimonia* of, 140, 154-5
pseudo-Josephus, *see* Maccabees, Fourth Book of
pseudo-Tertullian, 241
Ptolemy, letter to Flora, 70-1
Punic language, 302
Pythagoreanism, 16

Quadratus, 101
Quietus, war of, 197
Qumran, community and texts, 387-8

Rab, 257
Rabbula, bishop of Edessa, 225
Rahlfs, 55
Raphael, archangel, 346, 368
Rebecca, 78, 171, 188
relics, their use in healing, 364-7
Renan, E., 28-9
Revelation, book of, xv
Réville, J., 339
ritual murder, Jews accused of, 211, 221-2, 333-4
Romanos, Passion of St., 307, 310
Roman, epistle to the, 266
Rome, her attitude to Judaism and Christianity, 98-132, 402-6: Roman policy towards Jews, 98-100, 102-7;

Roman policy towards Christians, 100-7; the categories of gentile, Jew and Christian, 107-11; Julian's attitude, 111-15; Jewish involvement in Roman persecution of Christians, 115-20; *Acts of the Martyrs*, 120-5; repressive Roman policy towards Jews from Constantine onwards, 125-32; Baer's views discussed, 402-6

Sabbath and Sunday, 310-13, 315, 323-4, 329-30
Sabina, mosaics of St., 78
Sadducees, 12, 28, 182, 199; their view of Pharisees, 14-15
Samuel ben Nahman, R., 190, 197-8
Sanday, 154
Sanhedrin, 30, 62
Saphra, R., 184-5, 407
Sarah, 148
sarcophagi, 51-2
Schmidt, C., 50
Schoeps, H.J., 192, 410-11
Schürer, E., ix, 59-60, 390-1
Schwartz, E., xi, 271, 316, 341
Seaver, J.E., 400-1
Septimius Severus, 102, 106, 405
Septuagint, 55-6, 59-60, 69, 153-4, 159-60, 267, 299-300, 349, 373
Serapion of Antioch, 106
Sheik Abrek, 297
Shemaiah, 279
Shemoneh 'Esre, 198, 200, 349
Sibylline books, 33, 37-8, 42-6, 274, 294, 371-2
Sicarii, 28
Simeon ben Johai, R., 275
Simeon, bishop of Jerusalem, 184
Simlai, R., 195, 197-8
Simon, R., 199
Simon and Theophilus, dialogue of, 137, 156, 162, 165, 221
Simon ben Gamaliel, R., 25
Simon ben Laqish, R., 189, 191, 258
Simon the Pious, R., 257
Sirmium, council of, 194
slaves of Jews, legislation concerning, 128, 292-3
Smyrna, 123
Socrates, 363
Solomon, 159-60; in magic, 342, 350, 352
Spain, 296, 330-1; Spanish authors, 141
Spartianus, 107
Stephen, 37, 86, 120, 209, 411; relics of, 365-6
Stern, H., 389
Strabo, 33

Strack, H., ix, 289
Sulpicius Severus, 65
superstitio, meaning of, 359–60
Symmachians, 268
Symmachus, 160, 267–8
Symeon Stylites, St., 226
synagogues: art of the, 17–27, 297; Christian
    actions against, 224–7; legislation against,
    227–30, 297
Syria, Jewish influences in, 307–8

Tacitus, 40, 65, 110, 210–13, 282, 380, 398
Talmud, xii, 4, 14, 23, 58, 63, 95, 159, 263,
    274, 279, 294, 373, 403, 405, 407, 412–13
Talmud, Christians in, 179–201: meaning of
    minim, 179–83; *minim* referring to
    Christianity, 183–6; Talmudic texts
    answering Christian polemic, 186–96;
    development of anti-Christian polemic,
    197–201
Tarphon, 197, 200
Tatian, 101
tephillin, 361, 364
Tertullian, 68, 70, 77–8, 83, 102, 107, 117,
    119–20, 124, 139–40, 165, 168, 173, 188,
    210–11, 252, 283, 286, 331, 333–4, 380–1,
    406
Theodosian Code, xvii, 127, 226–30, 291–3,
    358–9
Theodosius, 126, 292, 406
Theodosius II, 120, 225–9, 293
Theodotion, 160
Therapeutae, 350
Tiberius, 198,
Timgad, inscription from, 364

Timothy and Aquila, dialogue of, 90, 140,
    150, 153, 162
Tipasa, 225
Titus, 6–7, 34, 65, 100
Toledoth Jeshu, 157
Tortosa, 296
Tozeur, 333
Trajan, xiv, 29, 34, 99, 101, 303; persecution
    under, 184, 403
Travers Herford, R., ix, 180–1, 184, 186–8,
    193, 407
Tripolitania, 303
Trullan Synod, 336, 369–70
Trypho, 12–13, 38–9, 57, 147, 154, 158–61,
    163, 171, 174, 404; *see also* Justin Martyr

Valens, 360
Valentinian I, 360
Valentinus, 243, 291
Venosa, catacomb of, 296
Vespasian, 5–6, 13, 99, 303
virgin birth, 159–60, 252–3
Vopiscus, 203

Watzinger, C., 298
Windisch, S., 3
Wisdom, 57–8, 162, 176, 193–5, 372–3
Wolfson, H.A., 392

Yoyotte, J., 398–9

Zealots, 5–6, 12, 28, 35, 101
Zeiller, 123
Ziegler, I., ix, 190, 197